KOREA

The First War We Lost

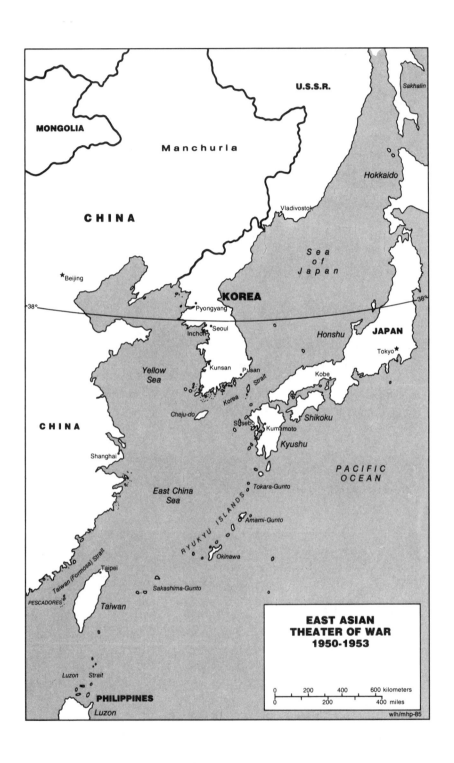

MONGOLIA

U.S.S.R.

Sakhalin

Manchuria

Hokkaido

CHINA

Vladivostok

Sea
of
Japan

★Beijing

38°

KOREA

Pyongyang

38°

Inchon Seoul

Honshu

JAPAN

Tokyo★

Kunsan

Yellow
Sea

Pusan

Korea Strait

Kobe

Cheju-do

Shikoku

Sasebo

Kumamoto

CHINA

Kyushu

Shanghai

PACIFIC
OCEAN

East China
Sea

Tokara-Gunto

RYUKYU ISLANDS

Amami-Gunto

Okinawa

Taiwan (Formosa) Strait

Taipei

**EAST ASIAN
THEATER OF WAR
1950-1953**

PESCADORES

Sakashima-Gunto

Taiwan

| 0 | 200 | 400 | 600 kilometers |
| 0 | | 200 | 400 miles |

Luzon Strait

PHILIPPINES

Luzon

wlh/mhp-85

KOREA
The First War We Lost

Bevin Alexander

HIPPOCRENE BOOKS

NEW YORK

In loving memory of my father, John McAuley Alexander (1896-1951),
who believed in reality.

Hippocrene Books Revised Illustrated Paperback Edition, 2000
Hippocrene Books Paperback Edition, 1993
Copyright© 1986 by Bevin Alexander

For information, address:
Hippocrene Books, Inc.
171 Madison Avenue
New York, NY 10016

ISBN 0-7818-0808-1

Printed in the United States of America.

Contents

LIST OF MAPS

PREFACE

The Korean War endured for three years, June 25, 1950, to July 27, 1953, as an official, international act of violence. It ended only after one and a half million men, women and children had died and two and a half million persons had been wounded or injured. It was one of the most devastating wars in history, and its consequences of hate, distrust and division abide with us today. This book is an attempt to show that the war need not have been protracted for so long, nor to have demanded so much in lives and treasure, nor to have left behind such hostility between nations that had much to lose and little to gain by enmity.

This book is an effort to demonstrate that Western leaders, especially those from the United States, received ample signals that, had the leaders responded to them, could have prevented the entry of Red China into the war and, even after Communist China did enter, could have ended the war much sooner and at much less cost.

This book attempts to show that the United States — with the aid of South Korea and the support of some United Nations members — won one war against the North Koreans and lost another war against the Red Chinese. The causes of these two wars were essentially and totally different: the North Koreans were bent on overt aggression and were thwarted; the Red Chinese were trying to protect their homeland from the potential threat of invasion and were successful.

Finally, this book tries to show the Korean War as it actually was fought and as the tactical and strategic decisions, good and bad, were made. In this, the dedication and devotion of men on both sides to what they believed to be their nations' needs were demonstrated in such full measure as to suggest the awesome powers of human sacrifice and endeavor that leaders everywhere hold in their hands, and what immense responsibility for the exercise of those powers they assume.

In the Korean War many men on both sides exhibited great heroism. Coming as Korea did so soon after the universal trauma of world war, this heroism was and has been little appreciated. Some men in the war showed cowardice, others displayed great cruelty and inhumanity, and nearly all showed fear of the dangers they faced.

The Korean War became the arena for fateful clashes of national wills, in which leaders at all levels made decisions ranging from remarkable sagacity to desolating error. Korea is thus a human story of mortals in high and low places acting in crisis as their individual lights directed them.

ACKNOWLEDGMENTS

I have the happy privilege rare among writers to be able to cite as sources of much of the material on the Korean War works produced by personal friends and former comrades in arms. Without the outstanding work done by these and other researchers this book would have been impossible. This volume is a product of the immense amount of work done by dedicated historians over a long period. The conclusions in this book I lay on no other shoulders but my own; the facts contained in it are drawn from the rich mines of material uncovered by the historians and the basic researchers of the war. If this book is accepted as a fair representation of the immensely involved and complicated story of the war, it should be seen as a monument to them.

I specifically wish to thank the following army historians, most of whom I served with in Korea and most of whom, like myself, commanded Historical Detachments: Roy E. Appleman, Martin Blumenson, Pierce W. Briscoe, A. Stuart Daley, Edgar Denton, Robert F. Fechtman, William J. Fox, Russell A. Gugeler, Hunter Haines, William D. Magnes, John Mewha, Harry Joe Middleton, Billy C. Mossman, James F. Schnabel, and Edward C. Williamson.

I want to single out especially Roy Appleman, Bill Mossman and Jim Schnabel. Roy Appleman's official history of the first five months of the war is one of the three seminal works on the conflict and is stunning in its thoroughness and objectivity. Jim Schnabel's official history on the policy and direction of the first year of the war and his history with Robert J. Watson of the Joint Chiefs of Staff in the war are the other two seminal works and constitute magnificent historical records which have vastly improved the understanding of the war. Bill Mossman, who is working on the official history of the war from November, 1950, to July, 1951, has been extremely helpful to me with advice and assistance.

I have not had the pleasure of meeting the authors of the official histories of the other services, but I wish to take this opportunity to acknowledge the essential contributions they have made in their painstaking and accurate studies: Robert Frank Futrell for the air force, Lynn Montross and Captain Nicholas A. Canzona for the marines, and Malcolm W. Cagle and Frank A. Manson for the navy.

Without the ready assistance and encyclopedic memory of John E. Taylor, archivist in the Modern Military History Headquarters Branch of the National Archives, my research work would have been well nigh impossible. All of the staff at the Headquarters Branch and at the Field Branch at Suitland, Maryland, were helpful, and I wish to thank especially Victoria S. Washington at the Field Branch for her industrious search for documents and for her patience with me.

William S. Simpson, Jr., reference librarian at the Richmond (Virginia) Public Library, treated my demands for obscure documents and volumes as entirely reasonable and always produced them, and I thank him for that and for his enthusiastic help in many ways. I thank William R. Chamberlain, assistant director of the Virginia State Library, for accepting my outrageous requests for specialized volumes and other esoterica, and Teresa Puckett, with the State Library's Interlibrary Loan, for industriously finding this material at depositories far and near.

I thank my three sons for their great help and support: Bevin, Jr., for insisting I write the book in the first place and for performing all the legal work; Troy and his wife, Mary, for searching the vast commercial sources in New York for pictures of the war, and David, for helping with the harvest at Arvon Grove, since crops wait for no scribbler.

I thank Robert Pigeon, managing editor of Hippocrene Books, for his sound advice and great assistance, and for leading me to Sidney Shapiro of Beijing, author of *Jews in Old China*, who was extremely helpful in directing me to sources on the war in Communist China.

To no one am I obligated more than to my editor, Donald J. Davidson. He asked relentlessly (and sometimes ruthlessly) intelligent questions, searched out and destroyed manifold errors, and always guided my airy flights firmly back to solid facts.

Cartographers William L. Hezlep and Michelle Picard spent much time and effort in producing accurate maps for this volume.

Finally, I thank my wife, Peggy Tyndall Alexander, for her astute counsel on the content of the book and research sources, for ready help and extreme patience, and for undertaking the stupendous task of searching through thousands of pictures in the official archives to find representative photographs of the war.

BEVIN ALEXANDER

ARVON GROVE,
VIRGINIA

List of Abbreviations

AAA	Antiaircraft Artillery	CJCS	Chairman of the Joint Chiefs of Staff
AC/S	Assistant Chief of Staff		
AMS	Army Map Service	CNO	Chief of Naval Operations
AP	Armor-piercing		
Arty	Artillery	CO	Commanding Officer
Asst	Assistant	Co	Company
ATIS	Allied Translator and Intelligence Section	CofS	Chief of Staff
		Col	Colonel
BAR	Browning Automatic Rifle	Comdr	Commander
		CP	Command Post
Bn	Battalion	C/S	Chief of Staff
Brig	Brigade	CSA	Chief of Staff, United States Army
Btry	Battery		
Capt	Captain	CSUSA	Chief of Staff, United States Army
Cav	Cavalry		
CCF	Chinese Communist Forces	DA	Department of the Army
CCS	Combined Chiefs of Staff	DIS	Daily Intelligence Summary
CG	Commanding General	Div	Division
CIA	Central Intelligence Agency	DOW	Died of wounds
		DUKW	Amphibious truck
CINCFE	Commander in Chief, Far East	Eng	Engineer
		EUSAK	Eighth United States Army in Korea
CINC-UNC	Commander in Chief, United Nations Command	FA	Field Artillery
		FEAF	Far East Air Forces

FEC	Far East Command	LSD	Landing ship, dock
FECOM	Far East Command	LSMR	Landing ship, medium (rocket)
G-1	Personnel section of divisional or higher staff	LST	Landing ship, tank
		LSV	Landing ship, vehicle
G-2	Intelligence section of divisional or higher staff	Lt	Lieutenant
		Lt Col	Lieutenant Colonel
		LVT	Landing vehicle, tracked
G-3	Operations and training section of divisional or higher staff	Maj	Major
		MATS	Military Air Transport Service
G-4	Logistics section of divisional or higher staff	Memo	Memorandum
		MG	Machine gun
		MIA	Missing in action
GADEL	United Nations General Assembly delegation of United States	MIN	Minutes
		MIS	Military Intelligence Service
		MLR	Main line of resistance
Gen	General		
GHQ	General head-quarters	Mort	Mortar
		MS	Manuscript
GO	General order	Msg	Message
HE	High Explosive	MSR	Main Supply Route
HEAT	High explosive antitank	NK	North Korean
		NSC	National Security Council
Hist Sec	Historical Section		
How	Howitzer	OCJCS	Office of the Chairman of the Joint Chiefs of Staff
Hq	Headquarters		
Inf	Infantry		
JCS	Joint Chiefs of Staff	OCMH	Office of the Chief of Military History, U.S. Army
JLC	Japan Logistical Command		
JSSC	Joint Chiefs of Staff Joint Strategic Survey Committee	OP	Observation Post
		Opn	Operation
		Opn Dir	Operation Directive
KIA	Killed in action	Opns	Operations
KMAG	Korean Military Advisory Group, U.S. Army	PIR	Periodic Intelligence Report
		PLA	People's Liberation Army, People's Republic of China
LCVP	Landing craft, vehicle, personnel		

Plat	Platoon	SCR	Set complete radio
PLR	Periodic Logistical Report	Sec	Secretary, section
		SecDef	Secretary of Defense
POL	Petroleum, oil, and lubricants	SecState	Secretary of State
POW	Prisoner of war	Sitrep	Situation Report
POR	Periodic Operations Report	SP	Self-propelled
		TACP	Tactical air control party
PW	Prisoner of War	Telecon	Teletypewriter conference
QM	Quartermaster Corps		
RCT	Regimental Combat Team	TF	Task Force
		T/O	Table of Organization
Recon	Reconnaissance	TO&E	Table of Organization and Equipment
Regt	Regiment		
ROK	Republic of Korea (South Korea)		
		UN	United Nations
ROKs	South Korean soldiers	UNC	United Nations Command
Rpt	Report		
S-1	Adjutant (personnel)	USA	United States Army
S-2	Intelligence officer	USAF	United States Air Force
S-3	Operations and training officer		
		USMC	United States Marine Corps
S-4	Supply officer		
SAR	Special Action Report	USN	United States Navy
		VHF	Very high frequency
SCAP	Supreme Commander for the Allied Powers	VT	Variable time fuse
		WD	War Diary
		WIA	Wounded in action

CHAPTER 1

June 25, 1950

O N THE EARLY MORNING of June 25, 1950, the army of communist North Korea invaded South Korea, and the world has never been the same since. The attack made real the fear of direct communist aggression against the West, raised in the Russian blockade of Berlin two years before. It appeared to validate the existence of a world-wide communist conspiracy of conquest. This specter of a far-reaching plot, actual or not, insured that the McCarthy-era witch hunt for Red agents and sympathizers would be supported by many. The panic precipitated Europe to subdue its fear of the German army and allow West Germany to rearm as a Western ally. American response to the attack crystallized the practice of confrontation diplomacy with the communist world in the Truman and Eisenhower administrations, and that affected American policy all the way through the Vietnam War years. Korea provided the opportunity for the spectacular zenith and caused the dizzying sudden nadir of General of the Army Douglas MacArthur, one of the most brilliant but contradictory leaders in American military history. Korea motivated the American people to undergo a weeks-long examination in Senate committee hearings of what the country should do about the war and communism. Yet by the end of the Korean War, it had become manifest to many Americans, though by no means to all, that the simple verities about total victory and the conflict between good and evil that had guided American policy for many years were inadequate in the dismaying world that arose from World War II.

* * * * * * * *

The North Korean army's prime assault troops, 89,000 men in seven divisions and three independent units, attacked south from the 38th parallel boundary in six closely packed columns. They achieved total

1

tactical and strategic surprise. Facing them were four understrength Republic of Korea (ROK) divisions and one regiment, totaling 38,000 men, and not all of them were on the line. Some ROK units were in reserve at various distances below the 38th.[1] Since no one had predicted the attack, large numbers of South Korean soldiers were away on weekend passes. South Korea's other four divisions were spread out in various places in the south.

The North Korean numerical superiority was something on the order of five or six to one at the crucial points on the battle line where the North Koreans concentrated their effort. The North Koreans possessed three times as much artillery as the ROKs and nearly all of it outranged the South Korean guns.[2] The North Koreans could shell ROK positions at will while standing well out of range of retaliatory fire.[3]

But superior numbers and guns were not the decisive factors for the North Koreans, because they possessed an ultimate weapon: the tank. It is a bizarre fact, but five years after a world war which proved beyond all doubt the blitzkrieg capability of the tank to break great gaps in enemy defenses, the American-equipped South Koreans possessed nothing to stop a tank—neither a single tank of their own, nor armor-piercing artillery shells, nor combat aircraft, nor antitank land mines.

The North Koreans themselves had only 150 tanks, a ludicrous number compared to the thousands employed by both sides in World War II. But with little to stop them, they formed an omnipotent juggernaut that nullified whatever courage, devotion or tenacity the South Korean troops exhibited. The tanks themselves were Russian-built T34s, big thirty two-ton, heavily armored-plated, low-silhouette monsters that carried high-velocity 85mm guns.[4] It was this tank, then equipped only with a 76mm gun, that was credited by German panzer leader Heinz Guderian with stopping the 1941 drive on Moscow.[5]

The only weapons the South Koreans had which possessed even remote potential for stopping the T34s were American 57 mm flat-trajectory antitank guns and 2.36-inch rocket launchers (bazookas). The 57mm guns were obsolescent relics of World War II and could halt the heavily armored T34s only with occasional lucky shots. One of the few partially vulnerable spots was the grating above the engine at the rear. The bazooka shells blew up harmlessly against the sides of the North Korean tanks or bounced off.[6] Only the newly developed and still-untested 3.5-inch super bazookas, hurriedly flown to Korea in the early weeks, were effective in some cases, but not all.

The North Koreans obviously knew the ROKs had no effective antitank weapons, because they adopted tactics that under normal conditions of warfare would have invited annihilation: they lined up their armor in columns, one tank behind the other, on the narrow eighteen-foot-wide Korean dirt roads and headed south, their infantry strung out behind them.

Even a few antitank mines well placed in roadbeds could have stopped entire columns. Armor-piercing shells from some of the ROKs' eighty-nine field pieces (short-range 105mm light howitzers M3, used in U.S. infantry cannon companies in World War II) could have destroyed a stalled column of tanks in minutes, as could have jellied gasoline napalm bombs from attack aircraft. But as the ROKs at first had none of these weapons, the North Koreans brazenly drove down the roads in daylight, destroying South Korean emplacements and any troops with the temerity to fire upon them, and opened virtually unopposed paths for the infantry to follow.

The North Koreans adopted their tactics not only because the South Koreans could not counter them, but because Korean terrain encouraged tanks to remain on roads. About three-fourths of Korea consists of mountains which are difficult or deadly for tanks. Most of the relatively flat land in the summer of 1950 was covered with tiny, wet rice paddies divided by narrow raised walkways and embankments. In many of these paddies armor would have mired, and in nearly all it would have had difficult going. It was this appraisal of Korea's terrain, plus a judgment (largely erroneous, it turned out) that Korea's one-lane bridges over small streams were too weak to support tanks, that United States military advisors cited in 1949 in denying a South Korean request for tanks.[8] Perhaps the advisors reasoned the Russians and North Koreans would draw the same conclusion and omit tanks from the North Korean arsenal. More likely, Americans used the terrain as an excuse to turn down the request for tanks because they feared South Korea's pugnacious president, Syngman Rhee, would use them to attack the North, as he had threatened to do.[9] Though the United States deliberately provided only defensive weapons to South Korea, it is a comment on the peculiarity of American thinking that the advisors failed to include any adequate means of defense against the tank.[10] The first antitank mines were flown into Korea from Japan on June 30, the sixth day of the invasion.[11] By that time the disarray of the ROK army was such that training in mine use and distribution of them took much time. Meanwhile the T34s rolled on.

The North Koreans were very like their South Korean brethren in many ways. The soldiers of both states were largely of peasant origin, used to hard work, endurance and privation, stoic both in success and in failure, tenacious in what they believed, and largely obedient to their superiors. Koreans on both sides were able to march long and hard on short rations and still fight at the end. They could climb ridgelines and mountains without dropping from exhaustion and overexertion. In this, they were unlike most American soldiers, who were largely garrison troops, used to being carried in motor vehicles, with little physical conditioning and little experience in long marches and climbing mountains.

Although Koreans north and south of the 38th were much alike, their armies were quite dissimilar, for each army reflected the military doctrines of the respective armies which had created them: the Soviet Army and the U.S. Army.

The North Korean army's overwhelming strength (89,000 men) lay in its seven assault infantry divisions, a tank brigade and two independent infantry regiments. In addition, the army had 23,000 men in three reserve divisions, and about 18,000 were in the Border Constabulary. Only 5,000 men were assigned to command and service units. In comparison, the South Koreans had only 65,000 men in their eight understrength combat divisions, while they had 33,000 in headquarters and service troops.[12] The South Korean army reflected the American military establishment: large numbers of support personnel as compared to fighting men. The North Koreans, on the other hand, exhibited perfectly the lean doctrine of the Soviet Army: every man possible was pushed to the front and given a weapon to fire.

The North Koreans had one additional manpower advantage in the short run: about one-third of their army was made up of Koreans who had served in the Chinese Communist forces in China and had been demobilized and returned to Korea about the time the Nationalists fled to Taiwan.[11] These men gave the North Korean army a degree of battle experience and combat hardiness which the South Korean army at the outset largely did not enjoy.

Tactically, the North Koreans repeated time after time one technique which was marvelously effective: they engaged fixed enemy positions with direct frontal attacks or fire, then sent forces around both flanks, if possible, in an envelopment movement designed either to surround the enemy and then squeeze him into a small perimeter to destroy him or force him to surrender, or, if this failed, to cut off his retreat or reinforcements by means of roadblocks in his rear.[14]

This system worked well in the fluid situation which existed during the summer of 1950, when there were no fully manned main lines of resistance extending over many miles which could not be flanked easily. It was especially successful in tactical situations in which the T34 tanks could move directly against enemy positions on the roads, pinning the enemy in place with fire, while North Korean infantry slipped around both sides of the positions to the rear. Even if one of the envelopments did not work, the other often did.

Double-envelopment tactics were natural to North Koreans. Flank envelopments have been basic techniques of war for thousands of years, but some soldiers have more success in carrying them out than others. When they could, the North Koreans followed the model of the greatest of all armies at envelopment, the Mongols of the thirteenth century under Genghis Khan and his successors. The Mongol method of attack was based upon their method of hunting, and Genghis Khan trained his armies by means of a great hunt each winter in peacetime.[15] An army would begin by pressing the game backward, then the flanks of the army would advance ahead of the center, around the game and to the rear, encircling the increasingly terrified animals, then pressing them together from all points of the compass. The training for the Mongol soldiers consisted primarily in teaching them to prevent the escape of even a hare or a deer as the trap was closing. This required an incredible degree of control of all encircling elements. When it worked, practically no animals broke free on their own. For soldiers adept in corralling animals in a great hunt, hunting men became easy.

When envelopment worked for the North Koreans, and it often did, practically no organized units, and often few men, escaped the traps. Fortunately for South Korea, the North Koreans possessed no military genius like Genghis Khan who could expand this limited tactical concept into a far-reaching strategic plan to conquer the South in a single great coordinated campaign.

CHAPTER 2

How Did It Happen?

WHEN THE ATTACK STRUCK, the shock in Seoul was stunning. It was scarcely less so in Washington and in General MacArthur's Far East Command headquarters in Tokyo. Questions instantly began to be asked how, with the immense, sophisticated and ultrasecret means the United States intelligence services had at their disposal, a huge communist army could have assembled directly opposite a friendly state's border with all the equipment, ammunition, supplies and turmoil this entailed, and nobody have suspected it until the first shells began landing on ROK positions.

The director of the Central Intelligence Agency, Rear Admiral Roscoe H. Hillenkoetter, moved only a day after the attack to clear the CIA's skirts. He implied to the Senate Appropriations Committee that the CIA had provided ample clues that the attack was coming. This ploy set off an immediate, intense undercover hunt in Washington and Tokyo for a scapegoat to blame for the breakdown in intelligence. None was found. Every responsible agency finally proved it had predicted a North Korean attack could come, but none, including the CIA, had predicted it *would* come.[1]

The South Koreans doubtless would have been grateful if the United States had been able to predict the attack, if for no other reason than to cancel weekend passes. But in the United States the failure of the intelligence services was only of academic interest: the United States had no plans whatsoever to counter any invasion of Korea, whatever the date.[2]

The intelligence agencies were of little more help in explaining who had instigated the attack.[3] Though most fingers were pointed at Russia and some at Red China, there was really no clear evidence. Still, the

6

bewildering speed of the advance into South Korea made many officers suspect that such success could be accomplished only with the massive support of the Soviet Union, if not the Red Army itself. In the panic that ensued no one recognized the disarming simplicity of the reason: the North Koreans had tanks. No active involvement by any other forces was needed; the North Koreans were invincible until something to stop tanks was introduced into the Korean peninsula.

* * * * * * * *

The origin of the war goes back to the enforced division of Korea into two competing and antagonistic states after World War II, a situation hardly anyone in Korea wanted, but which was imposed on the Koreans by the postwar geopolitical pressures of the Soviet Union and the United States. Russia, acting in 1945 as it had acted for centuries, tried to keep control of every bit of territory its troops occupied. The Russians refused to accept an all-Korea government that presented a possibility that the Soviet-occupied north could be incorporated into a unified Korea which might then vote out communist control.[4] It was the same policy the Russians adopted in Germany and which led to division of that land into two competing states.

American antagonism to the Russians was not directed entirely at their land-grasping urges. Another anger had smoldered ever since the end of World War II, and it burst into flame when the North Koreans, construed as being clients of the Soviet Union, crossed the 38th parallel and embarked on overt aggression. The anger was based on the belated recognition that the United States could have kept the Soviet Union entirely out of the Pacific war if it had recognized clear signals that the Japanese were beaten while the Russians were still locked in combat with the Germans.

North Korea was one of the spoils the Russians gained in their intervention in the war against Japan. Another was Manchuria, where Japanese forces, upon surrendering to the Russians, provided abundant war equipment that the Russians gave to the Chinese Communists. This equipment and the secure base that Manchuria provided assured the Chinese Communists the strength they needed in the Chinese civil war. By October, 1949, the Chinese Reds had driven the Chinese Nationalists off mainland China and forced them to flee to the island province of Taiwan, one hundred miles offshore.

The Russians, who had done practically nothing in the war against Japan, became the major beneficiary of the defeat of the Japanese. The United States, which had provided 95 per cent of the men, material and brains, lost most of the fruits of victory and opened the way for communist expansion.

The great American error was, as late as the Potsdam conference of the Allies in July, 1945, to insist upon Russian entry into the Pacific war, although by the fall of 1944 the United States had destroyed the Japanese navy and had won the war. The Japanese would have been unable to counter a strangling blockade of their home islands. Because they were dependent upon imports for raw materials, but most of all for food, the Japanese could have been brought to their knees by a blockade.[5] However, the Americans were afraid the Japanese would resist to the end, whatever their condition, and moreover were locked into a position demanding unconditional surrender. This doctrine, adopted by President Franklin D. Roosevelt and British Prime Minister Winston Churchill, arose out of the American idea of the war as a giant contest between good and evil. Thus war was aimed at total victory and complete subjugation of the enemy.

This idea was at odds with the concept of war as an extension of state policy, as the great nineteenth-century Prussian military theorist, Karl von Clausewitz, preached in his major treatise, *On War*. Clausewitz defined the critical need to connect political aims with the prosecution of war in this statement: "The political design is the object, while war is the means, and the means can never be thought of apart from the object."[6] Clausewitz's view is far closer to describing the proper purpose of war than is a doctrine of total victory.

Not only was American prosecution of the Pacific war hopelessly distorted by the doctrine of unconditional surrender, but its apparent success led many Americans to believe total victory had been demonstrated as the only purpose in war. This American propensity to think of war as a pursuit to complete victory was to cloud American thinking intensely in the Korean War. Clausewitz, the most profound of Western military thinkers, however, rejects the idea that crushing one's opponent under one's heel is a valid purpose of war. "War," Clausewitz says, "is nothing but a continuation of political intercourse with an admixture of other means....Does the cessation of diplomatic notes stop the political relations between different nations and governments? Is not war merely another kind of writing and language for their thought? It has, to be sure, its own grammar, but not its own logic."[7]

The Japanese would have surrendered much earlier, possibly by late 1944 and certainly by the spring of 1945, except for the unconditional-surrender rule.[8] The reason for the hesitation was that unconditional surrender would have exposed their Emperor to the danger of being shot as a war criminal. The Japanese could not accept this; the Emperor was a divinity to the people and the focus of authority for the armed forces. The Japanese were willing to concede everything else, but not the loss of their Emperor, upon whom their own concept of themselves as a people depended. The greatest irony of all, therefore, was that President Harry S. Truman finally conceded this point to the Japanese and modified the unconditional surrender to exclude the Emperor—but only *after* the Americans had dropped the atomic bomb on Hiroshima on August 6, 1945, and *after* the Russians entered the war on August 8.

Thus the Russians were given a free and cordial invitation to enter the war against Japan. Americans found afterward they had been fooled by the Russians, most especially by Russian expressions of solidarity with the West. Americans, who had fought the war to destroy evildoers and bring about friendship between nations, found they had not only eliminated Germany and Japan as counters to the power of the Soviet Union, but also succored and advanced the Soviet Union, a totalitarian state with a drive toward territorial expansion and domination of neighboring states equal to that shown by the Third Reich.

It is no wonder, then, that Americans, in their frustration, came to despise the Russians, and to suspect a Russian communist conspiracy everywhere.

It was this situation which prevailed when North Korean gunfire broke the summer stillness. Americans readily believed that the war had been instigated by Russia and that North Korea and Red China, also construed to be a Russian client state, were joint conspirators. It was this suspicion of all communists everywhere which impaired the ability of American leaders to deal with the communist powers as ordinary states with interests, limitations and needs; the communist states were seen as Principalities of Darkness which could be given no quarter. Thus the Korean War—though none of the conditions of a holy war were present—was viewed from the first (and almost to the last by many) as some sort of Mithraic-Manichean contest between the forces of light and the diabolical powers of darkness. It was this which produced the feeling among many military leaders, most especially General MacArthur, that the war should be pursued to total victory, no matter what the cost.

CHAPTER 3

Partition

IT IS STRANGE, but the partition of Korea along the 38th parallel, from which so much else was to follow, came about quite casually and without a great deal of calculation on anybody's part. Its original purpose was only to mark a line between United States and Soviet forces which were moving into Korea to accept the surrender of Japanese troops. Although the Allies had promised Korea ultimate independence, the peninsula at war's end was still considered enemy territory, since it had been annexed by Japan in 1910 after nearly two thousand years of more or less independent history, most of it under the suzerainty and protection of Imperial China.

The question of a boundary between Russians and Americans did not arise at the Potsdam conference. If it had, American officers were prepared to suggest a line quite near the one ultimately selected. Lieutenant General John C. Hull, then chief of the army operations division (G-3), and present at Potsdam, decided with his staff that the United States needed at least two major ports in its zone. They selected Inchon, the port city of Seoul, the capital, and Pusan, Korea's major deepwater port at the southeastern tip of the country.[1]

The army G-3 officers doubtless had no inkling of the fateful importance these two ports would hold five years later for the Korean people and the United States. The war was to show their instincts had been right, for the outcome of the critical first phase of the war hinged upon possession of Inchon and Pusan.

The actual move was made on August 11, 1945, by an American army officer, Colonel C. H. Bonesteel, III. He was helping to draw up a draft for General Order No. 1 to instruct General Douglas MacArthur, then Allied supreme commander, on the surrender and occupation of Japan. As an easy-to-determine line, Colonel Bonesteel settled on the 38th parallel, running about twenty-five air miles north of Seoul and Inchon. Bonesteel's proposal remained in the final draft, was approved by the Russians,[3] and became, with the developing Cold War, the frontier between the two Koreas. As an administrative, much less a political boundary, the 38th had nothing to commend it. It crossed Korea at its widest point and had no connection with any geographical features. Moreover, it cut off the Ongjin peninsula in the west from the remainder of South Korea. The selection of the 38th as a boundary immediately angered Koreans,[4] and its unnatural division of the country played a strong role in the vehemence of Koreans on both sides in their desire to eliminate it and reunite the country.

The Soviets set about quickly to consolidate their control of North Korea in 1945 and to destroy any possibility of a unified country, except one dominated by the communists. They undercut an all-Korea trusteeship government under a four-power Joint Commission (Russia, United States, Britain, China) approved in late 1945.[5] Russia insisted the commission work only with those Korean political groups supporting a trusteeship—in effect, only minority communist groups and communist-sympathizer groups, since all other Korean political factions opposed trusteeship and wanted quick independence. The Russians also sealed off the border at the 38th and severely restricted traffic into and out of North Korea. This effectively created two Korean states. Unable to overcome Soviet intransigence, the United States in 1947 laid the issue before the United Nations. The UN General Assembly voted on November 14, 1947, for an all-Korea election, and named a nine-nation UN Temporary Commission on Korea (UNTCOK) to supervise it.

The commission, less one of its members (the Ukrainian Soviet Socialist Republic refused to participate), met January 8, 1948, at Duksoo Palace in Seoul, but Russia banned the election in the north and refused to allow the commission to enter North Korea. This failure raised doubts within the commission about its legal status, and the chairman asked for a further UN resolution. On February 26, 1948, the UN Interim Committee resolved that the commission proceed with the election in as much of Korea as was accessible to it.[6] This meant, of course, only the part of Korea south of the 38th parallel, which came under U.S. military government. In this situation, just two extreme right-wing parties in South Korea endorsed the UN election: Syngman Rhee's National Society for the Rapid Realization of Korean Independence and the Korean Democratic Party.[7]

Few Koreans believed setting up a separate government in the south, even if endorsed by the United Nations and labeled an all-Korean government, would result ultimately in a unified Korea. Instead, most

Koreans feared such an election would perpetuate the division of Korea, because the Russians would quickly set up a rival communist state in the north. Extremely unhappy at the prospect, the moderate and leftist parties urged a boycott of the UN election, set for May 9, 1948.

In the interim (April 22–23, 1948), the North Korean communist-run People's Committee invited Korean groups on both sides of the 38th to a huge conference on unification in Pyongyang, North Korea's future capital. It was attended by 545 delegates, 360 of them from the South. The only rightist Korean of stature to attend was Kim Koo, former chairman of the Korean provisional government in exile (established in 1919 at Shanghai), but many moderate and leftist organizations in the South participated.[8] The U.S. military commander in Korea, Lieutenant General John R. Hodge, denounced the conference as a communist political plot.[9] At about this time, Russia proposed the withdrawal of all foreign troops from Korea and leaving Korean affairs in the hands of the Korean people, a proposal which paralleled the main points contained in the Pyongyang conference communiqué.[10]

The Pyongyang conference was a last-ditch effort by the Soviet Union and the North Korean communists to block the UN election, and it had the effect of polarizing the political situation in Korea to an astonishing degree. As all moderate leaders in South Korea opposed the UN election, Syngman Rhee, who had spent forty years in exile outside Korea, was left with no powerful challengers in the South. Thus, a UN election meant a right-wing government would be established in the South; and it would be countered in the North by Russia with a communist government. The moderates, who doubtless represented a majority on both sides of the 38th, were thereby finessed completely, and Korea at a stroke was divided into two extreme political camps, which, moreover, were cut into two territories by the 38th parallel. Thus, Korea found itself in May, 1948, split with an ideological and geographical clarity that was as stark as the division of North and South in the United States in 1860. The conditions were consequently ripe for civil war. The great casualty was what little hope the moderates in Korea had before the UN election of bringing about peacefully a unified, democratic country in the face of Russian intransigence and American suspicion of communist motives. Now, in a house divided, the only means of achieving unity would be war.

If the world in 1948 had not been separated into two opposing sides, and if Korea had not been located between these two sides, the conflict in the Land of the Morning Calm might have been sad and perhaps bitter, but it ultimately would have been resolved within the parameters of a Korean solution. But Korea was to become, by the accident of history and geography, a pawn in a great power play between the United States and the Soviet Union. Korea was manipulated by both sides for purposes wholly extraneous to the peninsula, and the Koreans themselves became expendable.

Had the United States and the Soviet Union been willing to take a chance on a truly democratic all-Korea election by all parties, then neither a right-wing South Korea nor a communist North Korea would have developed. A moderate government, inimical both to communists and to right-wing landlords, would have been elected. But the United States, with the evidence of communist subversion in eastern Europe fresh in memory, did not trust Russia. And the Soviets, paranoid about Western antipathy, did not trust the United States.

Perhaps more than anything else, the Russians, who long had coveted control of Korea, were not willingly going to withdraw from a position they held merely to satisfy the national aspirations of the Korean people.

Korea consequently found itself following doubly a policy it had adopted a millenium before: *sadae-sasang,* reliance upon a big power as a safeguard of its independence.[11] This policy had enabled Korea to maintain a separate existence from China for centuries, thereby benefiting both countries: Korea by its near independence and China by keeping (and protecting) Korea as a buffer against the Japanese and other possible invaders from the east.

The policy of *sadae-sasang* reached its fullest flowering under the Korean Yi dynasty. The dynasty's founder, King Yi Sung-gai, in accepting the status of "civilized tributary state" from China, said in 1392: "Our little kingdom may well serve as fence and wall and still do grace to the wide and limitless favor of the Emperor."[12]

In 1948, however, Korea found itself forced to play *sadae-sasang* with two opposing powers, not one. In the South a U.S.-supported and UN-endorsed Republic of Korea emerged, with Syngman Rhee, seventy-three years old, as the autocratic president. In the North the Soviet Union created the People's Republic of Korea, and selected as premier Kim Il Sung, a thirty year-old communist and former officer in the Soviet Army.

There has been much dispute as to the degree to which Syngman Rhee relied upon *sadae-sasang,* that is, whether he expected the United States to come to his aid in the event he triggered an open conflict with North Korea. The United States, for its part, had no clear idea, when it supported the UN election, that it was acquiring a "civilized tributary state" in the form of South Korea and that it, like the Chinese Empire of yore, was assuming an "older brother" relationship with a "younger brother" South Korea. Yet Rhee regularly advocated using force to bring about Korean unification, and it was clear to all informed military men that Rhee did not have this force. Rhee treated views on peaceful unification as heresy, and as late as March 1, 1950, he was quoted as saying: "Despite advice given by friends from across the seas not to attack the foreign puppet in North Korea, the cries of our brothers in distress in the North cannot be ignored. To this call we shall respond."[13]

It also is not clear that the Soviet Union knowingly stepped into the role of an older brother with North Korea. Russia's strategic view extended beyond Korea and was directed at the United States. Nevertheless, Kim Il Sung in the North adopted aggressive postures hardly different from those of Rhee. By the end of 1948, therefore, two hostile Korean governments faced each other across the 38th parallel, each claiming to represent all of Korea and each dedicated to the other's destruction. Both sides initiated border raids, some of them quite bloody. North Korean guerrillas also infiltrated into mountainous areas of the South and from there staged terrorist raids. These acts of violence on the parallel and internally in the south continued intermittently right up to the start of the war.[14]

North Korea, though larger in area (48,000 square miles, slightly smaller than England or New York State) and possessing most of the relatively few industrial plants, built by the Japanese, is mostly mountainous and less productive and, in 1950, had only 9 million people. South Korea (37,000 square miles, slightly larger than Portugal and a little smaller than Virginia) had 21 million people, the best agricultural land, most of the light industry, and most of the big cities.

In both states the majority of the people (62 per cent in the North, 70 per cent in the South) were peasant farmers who tilled tiny rice paddies or upland fields largely by hand or with the help of oxen or water buffalo.[15] The peasants clustered together in small villages of thatched-roof cottages and went out every day to work their fields nearby. In a country of astonishing natural beauty, the villages, built wholly of local materials and seeming to grow naturally out of the earth, were often the most lovely sights of all. In the lowlands and low uplands, where practically all of the agriculture was carried on, villages usually were only a mile or so apart. Like unpolished jewels, they studded the landscape of green and manicured small fields and formed a human-scale contrast to the high, stark and underbrush- or forest-covered mountains. Soldiers on both sides used the villages as convenient and easily recognizable targets and objectives and as assembly and defense points. Though the villages thereby often shared in the general destruction of the war, it was a rare person who was not moved by their homely beauty, or by the surpassing serenity of the Korean landscape.

The focus of the country people's lives was the village. They seldom voluntarily strayed far from it. As the Korean writer Younghill Kang says of his native village, Song-Dune-Chi, or Village of the Pine Trees, "The people had been happy in the same costumes, dwellings, food and manners for over a thousand years," and the water that flowed down from the mountains, through their fields, into a river and then to the sea, "was the only far wanderer among them."[16]

Aside from the war itself, there were two aspects of Korea, both olfactory, which kept the country from seeming to be an Eden, at least to Americans and Europeans. One was the ubiquitous buffalo-pulled "honey wagon," in which the frugal peasants collected their own excrement for spreading on their fields, and which possessed a smell so deep, pungent and penetrating that it could literally stupefy a Westerner. The other was the national vegetable dish of the Koreans, a fermented collection of cabbage, garlic, peppers, turnips and other matter known as *kimchi*, which when encountered, for example, on the breath of a lovely Korean girl, generally had so devastating an effect on a Western soldier that his interest in her vanished and his libido sank without a trace. Korean mothers doubtless could thank *kimchi* for preserving the virtue of many of their daughters in a land overrun by foreign soldiers.

CHAPTER 4

Hands Off Taiwan and Korea

OVER TIME, superiority in population would have given South Korea preponderance on the peninsula. In the short run, however, North Korea possessed military superiority in the form of a Russian-built army and air force that was much stronger than South Korea's. Kim Il Sung and other North Korean leaders evidently reasoned they had to strike soon if they were to strike at all.

Yet the conditions for aggressive adventures in the Far East could hardly have been less opportune for the communist cause as a whole. In late 1949, the Communist Chinese had finally won their civil war on the mainland against the Chinese Nationalists and formally established the People's Republic of China with its capital at Beijing (Peking). Only the leadership and remnants of the Nationalist army had withdrawn to the Chinese island province of Taiwan. In early 1950 the Red Chinese were actively preparing for an invasion of Taiwan,[1] a move that would complete the reunification of all China under one government and finally end the long civil war. Red China needed to be left alone, not harassed, by the United States. Yet the disaster that had overcome Chiang Kai-shek and the Nationalists set in motion an urgent call by the "China Lobby" and conservative Republicans in the United States to come to Chiang's aid and prevent Red takeover of Taiwan.

The Chinese Communists themselves precipitated a crisis on the matter. On January 8, 1950, Beijing's premier and foreign minister, Zhou Enlai, cabled the United Nations Secretary-General Trygve Lie to insist on the admission of Red China and the ouster of Nationalist China. The Soviet Union's Security Council representative Yakov (Jacob) Malik introduced a resolution to expel Nationalist China.[2]

In the debate that followed, the United States argued against the Soviet resolution, but announced it would accept an affirmative vote of

16

seven Security Council members and would not exercise a veto. Malik failed: the vote on January 13 was 6—3, with Britain and Norway abstaining. Although he was only one vote short, Malik immediately walked out of the Security Council chamber, announcing that the Soviet Union would boycott the United Nations so long as the Nationalist delegate remained.

This was an unbelievably extreme move, because twenty-six nations already had recognized the People's Republic of China (fifteen of them UN members), and had the Soviet Union been more patient and conciliatory, the question might have been settled quickly. The Truman administration, despite much conservative support in the United States for Chiang Kai-shek, was determined not to press the issue to a showdown. Malik's move angered other UN members and increased their opposition to admitting Red China.[3]

The suspicion was quickly raised by Sir Alexander Cadogan, British delegate to the United Nations, that the Soviet Union's real motive in causing this crisis was not to assist Red China in admission to the world body, but to discourage recognition of the People's Republic of China in order to keep Beijing "more effectively in isolation from the West and under Russian domination."[4] In the byzantine thinking of the Kremlin, such a policy would have made good sense because the Soviet Union had little incentive to share the major world arena and its pre-eminent position as the communist world's leader with another communist state possessing the potential power and influence of Red China.

For alert Westerners, Malik's move should have been a tip-off that there existed the possibility of cracking communist solidarity and at least beginning a process of separating Red China from Russia. Unfortunately, Western leaders, especially American leaders, did not see this, and continued to believe communism represented a monolithic, indivisible threat. As late as Senate committee hearings in the spring of 1951, then Secretary of Defense George C. Marshall stated as fact that China was under the control of the Soviet Union.[5] This belief was generally accepted in the United States, and few heeded voices like Edgar Snow, an acquaintance of Red Chinese leader Mao Zedong and author of *Red Star Over China,* who wrote in the April 9, 1949, *Saturday Evening Post* that "China will become the first communist-run major country independent of Moscow's dictation."[6]

It was about the time of the Soviet walkout that two pronouncements were made in Washington. One probably fixed the North Koreans' resolve on aggression, while the other eased Red Chinese anxieties about the United States. The fact that the leaders of both communist states accepted these statements at face value and then were dead wrong in their appraisal of subsequent U.S. actions makes all the more tragic their misreading of the changeable American political scene.[7]

The first statement was produced on January 5 by President Truman.[8] Truman said the United States did not want to establish bases on Taiwan and did not "have any intention of utilizing its armed forces to interfere in the present situation [in Taiwan]. The United States government will not pursue a course which will lead to involvement in the civil conflict in China. Similarly the United States will not provide military aid or advice to Chinese forces on Formosa [Taiwan]."

The second statement was made by Secretary of State Dean Acheson on January 12 before the National Press Club.[9] Acheson said the American "defensive perimeter" ran along the Aleutians to Japan, thence to the Ryukyus [Okinawa] and the Philippine islands, and these positions would be defended militarily by the United States if necessary. Neither Korea nor Taiwan was included by Acheson in this defensive perimeter. Elsewhere in his speech, he spoke of "other areas" in the Pacific, and "it must be clear that no person can guarantee these areas against military attack....Should such an attack occur...the initial reliance must be on the people attacked to resist it and then upon the commitments of the entire civilized world under the charter of the United Nations."[10]

The statements reflected anxiety about the commitment of American troops to a land war in Asia and the severe disillusionment of Americans with China in general and the Nationalist Chinese in particular. As early as 1947, the Joint Chiefs of Staff had decided, with Truman administration acquiescence, that the United States had little strategic interest in keeping ground troops in Korea and could deal with any communist aggression there by air strikes.[11] The American attitude toward China was more complicated, but by 1950 American leaders had come to the conclusion that American military forces should not be committed to bolstering Chiang Kai-shek.[12] This decision came after agonizing soul-searching over a long period.

Immediately after World War II the United States made a remarkable, sincere effort to prevent civil war in China between the Nationalists and the Communists. President Truman sent General of the Army George Marshall, the wartime army chief of staff, as special presidential envoy to China to undertake the virtually impossible task, in the words of China expert A. Doak Barnett, "to mediate between the leaders of a friendly government and the leaders of a revolutionary movement committed to that government's overthrow."[13] The effort to overcome irreconcilable differences and more than two decades of struggle between the two sides was foredoomed to failure.[14] Marshall returned home in January,

1947, blaming both sides for their intransigence. By 1948, the Truman administration had begun a gradual disengagement from China after it became clear that the Nationalists, despite strong U.S. aid, were losing the war. The disengagement was slowed because Republicans in Congress urged more aid and effort in China, not less, and the political pressure of the China Lobby was intense. But on August 5, 1949, the Truman administration committed itself firmly to cutting its losses in China and withdrawing.[15]

This occurred in the form of a State Department White Paper issued by Dean Acheson, which had the distinction of being roundly condemned by both the right wing in the United States and by Chinese Communist Chairman Mao Zedong himself.

The White Paper was designed to clarify the Truman administration position and to win more support for it. It related the course of events in China over the past five years, and tried to explain why the United States no longer could aid the Nationalist Chinese militarily and had no choice but to stand on the sidelines.[16]

The Nationalists, the White Paper said, had allowed much of the U.S. military equipment furnished them to fall into communist hands, and even more American military aid would not have saved the Chiang Kai-shek regime. Full-scale U.S. military intervention, Acheson said, would have been resented by the Chinese people and would have reversed historic U.S. policy.

"The unfortunate but inescapable fact is that the ominous result of the civil war in China was beyond the control of the government of the United States," Acheson concluded. "Nothing that this country did or could have done within the reasonable limit of its capabilities could have changed that result; nothing that was left undone by this country has contributed to it. It was the product of internal Chinese forces, forces which this country tried to influence but could not."

Critics in the United States quickly accused Acheson of producing a self-serving justification of American policy that tried to gloss over mistakes on the part of the the State Department. The columnist Walter Lippmann, however, took the position that the information revealed in the White Paper raised the question as to why the United States had gone as far as it had.

In Congress, the White Paper enraged Republicans. Senator H. Styles Bridges of New Hampshire said it more than ever convinced him "that the Chinese war was lost in Washington, not in China." And Senators William F. Knowland of California, Kenneth S. Wherry of Nebraska, and Patrick McCarran of Nevada (a Democrat closely associated with conservative Republicans) joined Senator Bridges in declaring the White

Paper was "a 1,052-page whitewash of a wishful, do-nothing policy which has succeeded only in placing Asia in danger of Soviet conquest."

It's curious, but Mao Zedong also in effect called the White Paper a whitewash, but he said it was a cover-up to evade responsibility for the failure of the administration "to turn China into a U.S. colony." In August, 1949, Mao wrote four commentaries on the White Paper for the Red Chinese Hsinhua News Agency.[17] In one of these he said the White Paper disclosed "the United States refrained from dispatching large forces to attack China, not because the U.S. government didn't want to, but because it had worries. First worry: the Chinese people would oppose it, and the U.S. government was afraid of getting hopelessly bogged down in a quagmire. Second worry: the American people would oppose it, and so the U.S. government dared not order mobilization. Third worry: the people of the Soviet Union, of Europe and of the rest of the world would oppose it, and the U.S. government would face universal condemnation."

Mao may have been more correct than Truman or Acheson wanted to admit. But, despite Republican condemnation, there is every reason to believe the United States would have honored its nonintervention pledge in regard to Taiwan if the Korean War had not broken out. Despite some extreme Republican opposition, the basic American hands-off-Asia mood was not transformed until after the North Koreans crossed the 38th parallel and the idea of a holy war against communism gained ascendance.

Although Acheson was much criticized later for his Press Club statement on the "abandonment" of South Korea, he was only articulating an established U.S. policy decision which other nations might have known by careful attention.[18] Especially pertinent was a 1949 study by the National Security Council which outlined the identical American "defense line" in the Far East—Japan, Ryukyus and the Philippines.[19] And nearly a year before Acheson spoke to the Press Club, MacArthur had laid out the same line of defense in an interview with a British journalist.[20]

The North Koreans doubtless had no problem understanding these American statements. The mistake they made was to believe them.

On the face of it, North Korea's reliance on the chance the United States would ignore aggression in Korea can only be viewed as in the same realm of prophecy as a throw of the dice. Even in controlled conditions, human response is seldom predictable. At the time, American attitudes toward the communists were almost totally hostile and subject to sudden emotional and subjective reactions, whatever the cool strategic calculations and policies the leaders in the Pentagon formulated.

The standard American view was that the Russians egged on the North Koreans to attack, and that the Russians miscalculated the American response. Although this theory grew out of the general theory that all communist states were jointly conspiring against the West, it contained an element of logic. It was senseless for the North Koreans alone to risk such a hazardous play with no stronger hole card than an expressed American policy of nonintervention. This was the reason for much of the anxiety and uncertainty in Washington and other Western capitals: Western leaders couldn't believe the North Koreans would have attacked unless they had assurances that Russia or Red China or both would come to their aid if the Americans did intervene. To leaders in the West it was as if the Korean attack in 1950 paralleled Sarajevo in 1914. The North Koreans were emboldened to defy the United States, as Serbia in 1914 was emboldened to defy Austria-Hungary, given the assurance that Russia would come to its aid if confrontation failed.

Indeed, if North Korea had such an assurance, it was never honored. Far more likely is that North Korean leaders believed, if they got into trouble, the Soviet Union or Red China would feel compelled to move to their aid. In fact, the Soviet Union never made the slightest effort to do so, ignoring even a U.S. Air Force attack on a Siberian airfield, mistakenly thought by the pilots to be within North Korea. And Red China's motivations were unrelated to saving the North Korean leaders' necks, but rather to protecting China from possible American aggression.

There is no evidence the Soviet government actually instigated the invasion.[21] Rather, the evidence seems preponderant that the North Koreans planned it, and that the Russians, when informed, went along, hoping with the North Koreans that the Americans would stay out.

In the memoirs of Nikita Khrushchev, later Soviet prime minister,[22] Kim Il Sung is reported to have discussed North Korean attack plans with Joseph Stalin at the end of 1949 and afterward. According to Krushchev's account, "The North Koreans wanted to prod South Korea with the point of a bayonet. Kim Il Sung said the first poke would touch off an internal explosion in South Korea" that would lead to the overthrow of Syngman Rhee. The idea appealed to Stalin, Khrushchev says, but Stalin told Kim to think it over and come back with a concrete plan. On Kim's return, some time later, Stalin was doubtful, because of possible U.S. intervention. Stalin, the memoir states, consulted Mao Zedong, who answered affirmatively and gave the opinion that the United States would not intervene in an internal Korean matter.

Khrushchev's memories of the course of the war itself contain factual errors. Whether his memories of Stalin–Kim and Stalin–Mao talks are more accurate is impossible to determine. If Stalin was indeed a co-

conspirator with Kim Il Sung, he was guilty of gross failure to understand the world-wide implications of the attack. At the time, the Soviet Union was still boycotting the United Nations Security Council in protest against the refusal to seat the Chinese Communists. This made it possible for the United States to rush a condemnation of North Korea through the Security Council and to call for military action by member nations against North Korea. As a result, the American action in Korea was vested with the sanction of orthodoxy while the North Koreans were anathematized as aggressors.

In the propaganda war, the United States won a major, and uncontested, victory. If the Russians knew in advance of the North Korean attack, they should have returned beforehand to the Security Council to veto any punitive action against their ally and client state. Perhaps the failure to return was due to the Russians' glacial slowness in making changes of policy, whatever the events. Even so, the Soviet Union never made this mistake again. From August 1, 1950, its agent was in place to veto any Security Council proposals it did not like.

Nevertheless, there are indications of significant Russian involvement, or at least acquiescence. One pointer is the presence of Russian advisors with the North Korean army. These officers should have detected preparations for war and alerted their Russian superiors, even if the Soviet Union was not itself a party to the preparations. The extreme position in this connection is taken by James F. Schnabel and Robert J. Watson in their history of the Joint Chiefs of Staff in the Korean War. They maintain that Soviet control of the North Korean army was so great the attack required approval from Premier Stalin himself.[23] Another pointer toward Soviet participation is the discovery, in October 1950, by U.S. forces in Seoul of two attack orders in *Russian*, dated June 22, 1950, three days before the assault, and issued by North Korean military officials to the chief of staff of the 4th North Korean Division.[24] A third pointer is the large shipments from the Soviet Union of heavy artillery, automatic weapons and new propeller-driven aircraft that arrived in North Korea in the spring of 1950,[25] material unlikely to have been shipped without the Soviets' asking what the North Koreans planned to do with it.

The case for Chinese Communist involvement in the attack rests entirely on Khrushchev's statement that Stalin consulted with Mao before the attack. In fact, the Red Chinese could have had no reason whatsoever to encourage adventures in the Far East until they completed the conquest of Taiwan. The Reds probably would have launched their attack on the island in the summer of 1950 if the Korean War had not intervened. Therefore, Chinese advice, if asked for, almost certainly would have been negative.

There is one other argument in regard to the origins of the war. It points the finger, not at the communists, but at South Korea's president Syngman Rhee. The case was made in 1952 by I. F. Stone.[26] Stone argues Rhee possibly started the war himself or possibly deliberately provoked a massive attack as the only way to save his regime by bringing in American forces to shore it up.

The May 30, 1950, elections to the South Korean National Assembly had been devastating to Rhee. The moderates and independents, who had boycotted the 1948 election, came out strong in 1950. Aided by anger at Rhee's high-handed methods of operations (he tried but failed to postpone the elections until November), they captured a large majority of the seats. This meant Rhee became a lame-duck president, retained in office only because he had been elected for four years. It was clear, in the changed national assembly, that Rhee would not be re-elected.[27]

Stone asks whether the attack began from the North or was deliberately provoked by minor forays from the South, as the North Koreans claimed.[28] Stone recounts the North Korean version that the South attacked first, that the North repelled the invaders and then went over to the offensive. This North Korean attempt to heap culpability on the South Koreans does not stand the test of inquiry. An army defending a long border spreads out to absorb attacks at all vulnerable points, because a corridor that is undefended can provide a route for an invading army to break through into the rear. The North Korean army was not spread out in defensive positions along the 38th parallel. Quite the contrary, it was concentrated in depth along one minor and three major corridors of approach, and along each of the major approaches two North Korean divisions were echeloned in classic offensive dispositions. On the other hand, only four of South Korea's eight divisions were near the 38th parallel when the attack occurred, indicating South Korea had no offensive intentions (see page 2).

The argument that Rhee counted on the United States coming to his aid in the event of a North Korean attack likewise is suspect. The argument presumes Rhee had a better knowledge of American attitudes and feelings than members of Congress and most American executive officials themselves—because no ground swell occurred in the United States to aid South Korea. Had Truman not decided to move decisively, chances are the United States would not have intervened. For example, General Omar N. Bradley, chairman of the Joint Chiefs of Staff, at first had little or no thought that the United States might reverse its policy of nonintervention and fight to save South Korea.[29]

Syngman Rhee had another cause for caution regarding American intentions toward South Korea: despite South Korean requests, the United States had refused to provide offensive arms to the ROK army. Rhee's logical and probable belief was, not that the United States would help in case of attack, but that it would *abandon* him. The United States not only had announced publicly that South Korea was beyond the U.S. defense perimeter, but had deliberately scaled down South Korean military requests because U.S. leaders feared Rhee would use a strong, offensive force to invade North Korea. The United States was more fearful of an aggressive move by the South against the North than vice versa. Rhee was palpably aware of this and also aware that the United States was attempting to disengage from Korea, not commit to Korea.[30]

For Rhee to have extrapolated from these realities a sophisticated conspiracy of either feigned attack on the North or deliberate invitation of a North Korean attack in order to draw in the United States presumes a capability to predict American attitudes, reactions and responses that Rhee never demonstrated before or after and that no American leader exhibited, including the person who abruptly reversed American policy, President Truman himself. Evidence is overwhelming that Truman, and no other person, committed the United States to intervene in Korea, and that he made this decision suddenly and without reflection.[31] Although Acheson developed the plan and provided the leadership, the decision was Truman's. The reason was not to save the Rhee regime, but to strike at a suddenly suspected Soviet conspiracy of conquest, with the same sort of blind instinct and fury that a cowboy strikes at a rattlesnake unexpectedly found coiled at his feet.

CHAPTER 5

Attack Across the 38th

THE NORTH KOREANS heavily weighted their western wing in a
a move to reach Seoul quickly. (See Map 1.) Of his seven assault
divisions, the North Korean commander, General Chai Ung Jun[1]
committed four to two western corridors of approach, plus 120 of his 150
tanks. He sent two more divisions into the central sector, one driving
from Hwachon to the important crossroads of Chunchon barely below
the 38th, and the other (with the remaining 30 tanks) pressing from Inje
toward Hongchon, about twenty miles south of Chunchon. Beyond the
Taebaek mountain range, which forms a high, formidable spine down
the east coast, the North Koreans committed their last division (the 5th)
and a separate regimental-sized independent infantry unit (the 766th) to
drive down the narrow east-coast road and attempt to get behind the
South Korean army. The final attack was a brigade-sized assault against a
ROK regiment on the isolated and indefensible Ongjin peninsula. The
ROKs evacuated by sea after losing a battalion.

The immediate outcome was stunning North Korean success everywhere but at Chunchon. There the North Korean (NK) 2nd Division of
11,000 men, with no tanks to help it, ran into the ROK 6th Division's 7th
Regiment with 2,400 men (none of whom had been given weekend
passes). The ROKs, emplaced in concrete pillboxes on a ridge just north
of town, stopped the North Koreans' two assault regiments cold. By late
afternoon, the NK division commander committed his third and last
regiment, but by that time the ROK division's reserve regiment had
arrived from Wonju, and the North Koreans got nowhere.[2] Chunchon
offered convincing testimony to the effectiveness of the ROKs against
ordinary attacks of infantry unsupported by armor.

The North Koreans captured Chunchon only by ordering the tanks
and the 7th NK Division heading toward Hongchon to turn back and

close on Chunchon. They and the 2nd NK Division secured the city on June 28 when the ROKs withdrew southward.

The two-pronged western attack was entirely different. Against the four North Korean assault divisions and the 120 tanks of the 105th North Korean Armored Brigade, the South Koreans had one division (the 1st) in the vicinity of the ancient Korean capital of Kaesong, two miles below the parallel, and another (the 7th) guarding the northern approaches to the Uijongbu (pronounced wee-jong-boo) corridor, the historic invasion route from the north for thousands of years.

The ROK 1st Division around Kaesong was badly placed for the attack it received from the 1st and 6th NK Divisions, plus forty tanks. It came straight down the main Pyongyang-Seoul highway and railway. American advisors and Korean officers had decided before the attack that the only possible defense line the 1st Division could hold was the Imjin river, south and east of Kaesong. However, on the morning of the attack, two regiments of the division (the 12th and 13th) were spread from Yonan, fifteen air miles west of Kaesong, to Korangpo-ri, fifteen air miles east of Kaesong, while the third (the 11th) was in reserve north of Seoul.

The North Korean tank-led thrust down the road and railway to Kaesong shattered the 12th Regiment, whose survivors fled south-eastward toward Munsan-ni at the Imjin river. The 1st Division commander, Colonel Paik Sun Yup, quickly sent the reserve 11th Regiment to Munsan-ni as left-flank guard for the 13th at Korangpo-ri and to protect the Imjin road bridge until the 12th Regiment's survivors could escape across it, and then to destroy it. The North Koreans pursued the 12th's remnants so closely, however, that the bridge fell intact to the North Koreans, and only two companies of the 12th Regiment escaped.

Some of the South Koreans of the 13th Regiment, realizing the NK tanks were the decisive weapon, tried to hurl high explosives, or satchel or pole charges under them. They destroyed or damaged a few tanks, but most of the ROK volunteers were killed in the process, and such kamikaze attacks soon ceased. Even so, the 1st Division held its positions for three days, until the debacle soon to take place on the Uijongbu corridor forced it to retreat to avoid encirclement.

The Uijongbu corridor is a gap in the Korean hills running almost due north-south between Chorwon and Seoul (the so-called Tongduchon-ni road). Another lowland corridor running northeast-southwest joins the corridor at Uijongbu (the so-called Pochon road). The North Koreans sent a full 11,000-man division supported by forty tanks down each of these corridors. Blocking the two North Korean divisions (the 3rd and

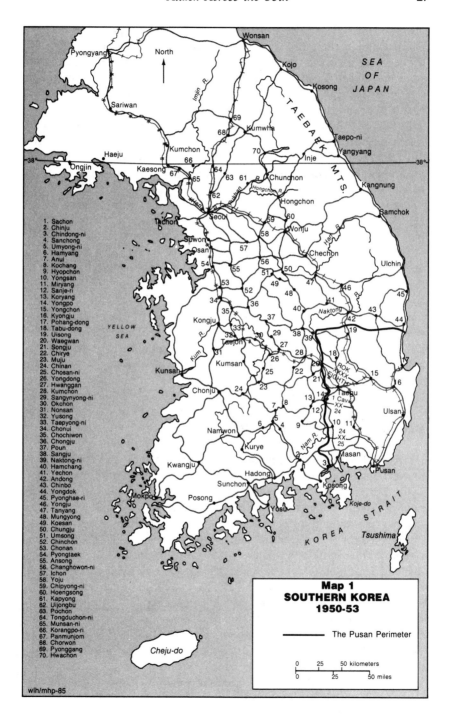

1. Sachon
2. Chinju
3. Chindong-ni
4. Sanchong
5. Umyong-ni
6. Hamyang
7. Anui
8. Kochang
9. Hyopchon
10. Yongsan
11. Miryang
12. Sanje-ri
13. Koryang
14. Yongpo
15. Yongchon
16. Kyongju
17. Pohang-dong
18. Tabu-dong
19. Uisong
20. Waegwan
21. Songju
22. Chirye
23. Muju
24. Chinan
25. Chosan-ni
26. Yongdong
27. Hwanggan
28. Kumchon
29. Sangyryong-ni
30. Okchon
31. Nonsan
32. Yusong
33. Taepyong-ni
34. Chonui
35. Chochiwon
36. Chongju
37. Poun
38. Sangju
39. Naktong-ni
40. Hamchang
41. Yechon
42. Andong
43. Chinbo
44. Yongdok
45. Pyonghae-ri
46. Yongju
47. Tanyang
48. Mungyong
49. Koesan
50. Chungju
51. Umsong
52. Chinchon
53. Chonan
54. Pyongtaek
55. Ansong
56. Changhowon-ni
57. Ichon
58. Yoju
59. Chipyong-ni
60. Hoengsong
61. Kapyong
62. Uijongbu
63. Pochon
64. Tongduchon-ni
65. Munsan-ni
66. Korangpo-ri
67. Panmunjom
68. Chorwon
69. Pyonggang
70. Hwachon

Map 1
SOUTHERN KOREA
1950-53

—————— The Pusan Perimeter

0   25   50 kilometers
0   25   50 miles

wlh/mhp-85

4th) was the ROK 7th Division with 9,700 men, one regiment on the 38th parallel and a regiment deployed on each of the corridors. The 7th Division suffered the hardest blows of all South Korean units, not only from the eighty T34 tanks but from twenty-four SU-76 Russian-made self-propelled guns firing flat-trajectory high-velocity 76mm shells. The North Koreans made steady gains down both corridors.

By 9:30 a.m. June 25, the ROK high command at Seoul had decided the North Korean attack was not a familiar "rice raid," but a real offensive. The Uijongbu corridor had to be protected or Seoul would be wide open to capture. The ROK high command immediately ordered the divisions spread out over South Korea's interior to move toward the battlefront. The 2nd Division (8,000 men) at Taejon, about 140 rail miles south of Uijongbu, was the first under way, elements of it leaving by train at 2:30 p.m.

The ROK chief of staff, Major General Chae ("Fat Boy") Byong Duk, wanted the 7th Division to counterattack the next morning (June 26) up the left-hand Tongduchon-ni road and the still-arriving 2nd Division to counterattack up the right-hand Pochon road. This would require the 7th Division to disengage its heavily committed troops on the Pochon road and concentrate them on the Tongduchon-ni road, while the 2nd Division, still only gathering at Uijongbu during the night, would have to assemble and deploy up the Pochon road by break of day. It clearly was an impossible task, and the 2nd Division's commander, Brigadier General Lee Hyung Koon, and General Chae's American advisor, Captain James W. Hausman, told him so. General Chae overruled them, and ordered the attack to proceed.

Elements of the 7th Division withdrew from the Pochon road about midnight. The division the next morning assembled on the Tongduchon-ni road just north of Uijongbu and launched its counterattack. For a while it made progress, greatly encouraging officials, who flashed the news to Seoul, Tokyo and Washington. But it was an illusion, because a disaster was taking place on the right-hand Pochon road. The 2nd Division commander, General Lee, with only division headquarters and two infantry battalions in place by the morning of June 26, apparently decided a counterattack would be futile—and he never launched it. By 8 a.m. a tank-led column of North Koreans appeared on the road, moving south. ROK artillery fired on the tanks, scoring some direct hits, but doing no damage. The North Korean tanks stopped briefly, then rolled through the 2nd Division positions and into Uijongbu. The following North Korean infantry engaged the ROKs, who, fearing encirclement, evaporated into the surrounding hills.

With its right flank now wide open, the 7th Division had to abort its counterattack and fall back below Uijongbu. Effective coordinated defense now ceased around Uijongbu, and the 1st Division, still holding around Korangpo-ri, found itself flanked and had to withdraw.

The debacle on the front was mirrored by panic in Seoul. The next morning (June 27) the ROK army headquarters abandoned Seoul and moved to Sihung-ni, about seven miles below the Han river south of the capital, without notifying Colonel William H. S. Wright, commander of the Korean Military Advisory Group (KMAG), or KMAG headquarters. Colonel Wright, following after the ROK command, received a direct flash from Tokyo over the KMAG truck-mounted radio: "Personal MacArthur to Wright: Repair to your former location. Momentous decisions are in the offing. Be of good cheer." With this in hand, Wright was able to persuade Chae to return ROK headquarters to Seoul that evening. Doubtless it was events like this, in which KMAG officers felt they were often left holding the bag in highly dangerous situations, that led Americans to joke that KMAG really stood for "Kiss My Ass Goodbye."

The South Korean government decided on June 27 to move to Taejon. Before going, the National Assembly formally asked the United States and the United Nations for "effective and timely aid" against North Korean aggression.[3]

The United States ambassador, John J. Muccio, and his staff moved to Suwon, about twenty miles south of Seoul. Muccio had already initiated the evacuation of American and other foreign women, children and nonmilitary men from Korea, and the process was still in full swing as Muccio and the U.S. Embassy evacuated to Suwon. Following an operational plan developed almost a year before to provide for such an emergency, Muccio set the civilian departure in motion at about 10 p.m. June 25. By 1 a.m. June 26 American families were moving from their housing compound in Seoul to a hurriedly commandeered Norwegian fertilizer ship in Inchon harbor, and by 6 p.m. 682 women and children were aboard as the ship stood out to sea for Japan. The same day another ship at Pusan loaded American dependents from southern Korea, and the next day (June 27) air evacuation of U.S. and other foreign nationals continued at an accelerated pace from Kimpo airfield, a few miles southwest of Seoul, and from Suwon airfield.

U.S. fighter planes from Japan flew numerous escort and surveillance missions to protect the evacuation movement, while the U.S. Navy took the two dependent-filled ships under escort. It was during this evacuation that the first clash occurred between Americans and North Koreans: on the morning of June 27 three NK Yak-3 piston-driven fighters had the audacity to fire on four U.S. jet fighters covering the air evacuation from Kimpo and Suwon. The Americans promptly shot down all three Yaks, and later in the day shot down four more. Thus in one day American jets destroyed one-sixth of the entire NK fighter force.

The evacuation went off without a hitch and without casualties. In four days, the United States moved 2,001 persons from Korea to Japan—1,527 of them U.S. nationals.[4] The British minister to South Korea, members of his staff, and some British nationals decided to stay in Seoul and claim diplomatic immunity. They got almost three years in North Korean prisons instead.[5]

At about midnight on June 27, KMAG officers learned the South Koreans were about to blow the previously mined bridges over the Han river at Seoul, a move that would be disastrous for the thousands of ROK troops still north of the river, not to speak of the many refugees trying to get south and the immense amounts of equipment and supplies clogging the streets of Seoul that would have to be abandoned.

KMAG earlier had extracted a promise from General Chae that the bridges would not be blown until North Korean tanks reached the street on which ROK army headquarters were located. KMAG officers hurried to ROK headquarters. There they learned from General Kim Paik Il, ROK deputy chief of staff, that General Chae had previously departed across the Han by jeep and that the South Korean vice minister of defense had ordered the blowing of the bridges at 1:30 a.m. June 28, and they had therefore to be blown at once. General Kim was the senior officer remaining at ROK headquarters. Another officer pleading to keep the bridges intact was General Lee, 2nd Division commander, who wanted a delay at least until his troops and equipment could get across. General Kim, under great pressure, turned to Major General Chang Chang Kuk, ROK G-3, and told him to drive to the river and stop the blowing of the bridges. Frantically plowing through people and vehicles overflowing the streets, General Chang tried to reach a police telephone box near the north end of the highway bridge, the closest point at which he could talk with the demolition party on the south side of the river. General Chang had reached a point about 150 yards from the bridge when huge orange flames illuminated the sky and immense roars signaled the simultaneous blowing of the highway and three railway bridges.

The time was 2:15 a.m. June 28. The gigantic explosions dropped two spans of the highway bridge into the Han river far below. All three lanes of the bridge were crowded with closely packed soldiers, civilians and vehicles. There was no warning. Best-informed American officers in Seoul at the time estimated that 500 to 800 persons were killed or drowned when the two spans fell. Probably double this number were on sections of the bridge over the water which did not go down. The broad eight-lane highway on the north side of the river leading up to the bridge was packed with civilians, marching soldiers, and bumper-to-bumper vehicular traffic, including army trucks and artillery pieces.

It was an incredible, unnecessary catastrophe, not only because of the innocent people slaughtered, but because, as Roy Appleman states in his official army history of the early part of the war, of "the utter disregard for the tactical situation, with the ROK army still holding the enemy at the outskirts of the city, and the certain loss of thousands of soldiers and practically all the transport and heavy weapons if the bridges were destroyed."[6]

The South Koreans had at least six to eight hours until the North Koreans approached the bridges. In this time, many of the soldiers of the three ROK divisions north of the river and much of their equipment could have got across. The KMAG party crossed the Han at 6 a.m. by commandeered ferry (a ROK officer with KMAG put a bullet through a ferryman's shirt to encourage him to dock). The KMAG officers reported fighting still was some distance from the river. North Korean sources state their troops did not reach the center of the city until noon.

As it was, the blowing of the bridges was a military disaster. The troops had to abandon nearly all their transport, most of their supplies and most of their heavy weapons. The majority of the troops who escaped waded the river or crossed in small boats and rafts. The destruction of the bridges commenced the disintegration of the ROK army. Of the 98,000 men in the army on June 25, only 54,000 could be accounted for a week later, many of them disorganized stragglers. The figures are even more dismal because a third of the ROK army consisted of headquarters and service troops, and the combat units suffered by far the bulk of the losses. General Chang estimated only 40,000 troops were under organized ROK command on July 1. General MacArthur was even more pessimistic: his estimate on June 29 showed only 25,000 effectives. Whatever the number, the battle potential of the divisions engaged north of Seoul had become pitiful: less than a third of their weapons remained.

CHAPTER 6

Decision in Washington

THIS WAS THE SITUATION that faced American leaders in Washington and Tokyo: the imminent dissolution of the South Korean army and government, and therefore the imminent swallowing up of all Korea into a communist state.

It was John Foster Dulles, later to be President Dwight Eisenhower's secretary of state and notorious for his "brinkmanship" with the communists, who pointed the way toward the initial course the United States was to follow.[1] In the interest of a bipartisan foreign policy, Republican Dulles had recently been appointed a special advisor to Secretary of State Acheson. Dulles was in Tokyo when the North Koreans struck, and he quickly flashed a message to Acheson that, if the South Koreans were unable to hold, U.S. forces should be used "even though this risks Russian counter moves. To sit by while Korea is overrun by unprovoked armed attack would start disastrous chain of events leading most probably to world war." When he got back to Washington, Dulles said he had meant sending in U.S. air and naval forces only, not troops.[2]

Dulles's belief that nonintervention by the United States would lead to world war was not exactly logical. But it was hair-raising all the same, particularly since anything Dulles said about communist threats would likely raise affirmative echoes among Republicans in Congress. General Omar Bradley, chairman of the Joint Chiefs of Staff, initially didn't have any such fears, though. He told his JCS colleagues, "If Korea falls, we may want to recommend even stronger action in the case of Formosa in order to offset the effect of the fall of South Korea on the rest of east Asia."[3] But events were to rush quickly past the nonintervention views of Bradley and the air-sea intervention views of Dulles.

Almost immediately after getting word of the invasion, Acheson decided tentatively that the United States should put the matter before the United Nations. He called President Truman, spending the weekend at his home in Independence, Missouri, and got his approval. The UN secretary-general, Trygve Lie of Norway, called an emergency Security Council meeting for Sunday afternoon, and Dean Rusk, assistant secretary of state, and his colleagues spent the rest of Saturday night drawing up a proposed resolution for the council.[4]

On Sunday morning, fourteen hours after Washington first got a flash on the attack (Washington time is 14 hours earlier than Seoul and Tokyo time), state department and army officials held a conference, attended by Acheson and General J. Lawton Collins, army chief of staff. The conferees agreed, subject to President Truman's approval, to establish a protective air zone over Seoul, Kimpo airfield, and Inchon to assure safe evacuation of American dependents, to send arms and equipment to the ROK army, and, if the UN Security Council asked for direct action in Korea, to authorize General MacArthur to use his forces and the U.S. Seventh Fleet "to stabilize the combat situation."[5]

President Truman flew back to Washington Sunday afternoon and called a dinner conference that evening at Blair House, his residence while the White House was undergoing renovation. Attending were the President's military and diplomatic policy advisors.

Truman's thoughts already were turning toward intervention while en route to Washington. He later wrote: "If the communists were permitted to force their way into the Republic of Korea without opposition from the free world, no small nation would have the courage to resist threats and aggression by stronger communist neighbors."[6]

Acheson also was moving abruptly away from his January 12 statement before the Washington Press Club that put Korea outside the line of American strategic interests. In his memoirs, he writes: "Plainly, this attack did not amount to a *casus belli* against the Soviet Union. Equally plainly, it was an open, undisguised challenge to our internationally accepted position as the protector of South Korea, an area of great importance to the security of American-occupied Japan....It looked as though we must steel ourselves for the use of force."[7]

While Truman was flying toward Washington, the Security Council was in emergency session at Lake Success, New York.[8] The Soviet representative, Jacob Malik, was still boycotting the body because it had not admitted Red China, and the United States was free of a Soviet veto. After several hours of debate, the Security Council, with a few changes, approved the U.S. resolution by a vote of 9–0 (the Yugoslavs abstained because, they said, their principal delegate was on vacation and couldn't be reached). The resolution called for the "immediate cessation of hostilities" and the withdrawal of North Korean forces to the 38th parallel.[9] But few informed persons seriously thought the North Koreans would heed the resolution.[10]

Truman's Blair House conference lasted nearly all evening, and it was fraught with consequences. Present were Acheson and his principal assistants; Louis Johnson, secretary of defense; all three service secretaries—Frank Pace, Jr. army; Francis P. Matthews, navy, and Thomas K. Finletter, air force; JCS Chairman Bradley, and the other three JCS members—General J. Lawton Collins, army; Admiral Forrest P. Sherman, navy, and General Hoyt S. Vandenberg, air force. After dinner, Truman asked Acheson to give his views on the Korean crisis. Acheson presented the major recommendations drawn up earlier in the day by the state-army conference, though, since the Security Council had not called upon UN members to take direct military action, Acheson did not propose that General MacArthur be authorized to use U.S. forces to stabilize the situation.

Truman approved immediate dispatch to South Korea of arms and equipment from stocks in Japan and use of American forces to protect evacuation of U.S. nationals.[11]

Then Secretary Acheson exploded a bomb that had been lying around all evening: he proposed that the U.S. Seventh Fleet be ordered northward from the Philippines and be given the mission of preventing any attack from mainland China against Taiwan or vice versa.[12] Defense Secretary Johnson had already broached the subject of Taiwan, which, he said later, "entered into our security more than Korea."[13] Before dinner, Johnson had asked Bradley to read a memorandum given him by General McArthur during a recent visit by Johnson and Bradley to Tokyo. The memo urged that MacArthur be authorized to send a survey party to Taiwan to determine the amount of aid Nationalist leader Chiang Kai-shek needed to keep the island out of communist hands.[14]

After Acheson spoke, Truman authorized the Seventh Fleet to proceed to Sasebo on the Japanese southern island of Kyushu, but stipulated the fleet's mission would be subject to review. He evidently had not finally made up his mind. Upon reminder by General Collins, Truman also authorized MacArthur to send a survey team to Taiwan.[15] Nobody expected that MacArthur *himself* would go to Taiwan, or that he would do so with a great blare of publicity that would severely embarrass the United States—and arouse the deepest suspicions of the Red Chinese government.

Although the Blair House conference on June 25 did not make irrevocable decisions, it set in motion a process that led to American military intervention in Korea. More significantly for the long run, the conference also equated the preservation of Taiwan as a Nationalist Chinese stronghold with the stopping of North Korean aggression. The two were unrelated. Not only did the meeting foreshadow an abrupt change of national policy by the abandonment of Truman's January 5 statement that the United States would not interfere in the domestic affairs of China, but it also implied that the Red Chinese somehow were involved in the North Korean invasion and that interposing the Seventh Fleet between mainland China and Taiwan somehow would counter this involvement and help to protect South Korea. It is true that the men meeting that night in Blair House were under incredible pressure, and it also is true that they construed the North Korean attack as being part of a general communist conspiracy aimed at conquest, and the Red Chinese, being communist, were therefore somehow guilty.

The next day (June 26, Monday, in Washington; June 27, the day of panic in Seoul) it became clear the North Koreans would ignore the Security Council resolution and shortly would occupy Seoul. About 7:30 p.m. Acheson telephoned Truman and persuaded him to call another meeting at Blair House later that evening.[16] Most of the men who had taken part in the conference the night before assembled in Blair House about 9 p.m.[17] This time, Truman approved decisive steps.

Truman accepted an Acheson recommendation that restrictions on U.S. air and naval forces be lifted and that they attack North Korean troops, armor and artillery at will. Truman stipulated, for the time being at least, that the attacks be limited to points below the 38th parallel.[18] Truman also approved Acheson's proposal that the United States present a resolution to the Security Council, meeting the next day, to seek international sanction for this open military intervention.[19] Truman also approved a third Acheson proposal that the Seventh Fleet be charged with preventing hostilities between Taiwan and the Chinese Communists.[20]

CHAPTER 7

War and the Quarantine of Taiwan

T HE RESOLVE to neutralize Taiwan was taken at exactly the same time the decision was made to intervene militarily in Korea. The instructions of the Joint Chiefs of Staff on both matters were contained in the same teleconference with MacArthur, and these instructions were sent to MacArthur before the Security Council met—although council assent was certain so long as the Soviet Union continued to boycott it.[1]

The next morning, June 27, President Truman announced his decisions to the nation.[2] The commitment of U.S. military forces he covered in a brief, single sentence: "I have ordered United States air and sea forces to give the Korean government troops cover and support," citing as reason that the North Koreans had ignored the original Security Council resolution. On Taiwan, he was more detailed, and his statement provides an instructive commentary on the thinking in Washington at the time:

"The attack upon Korea makes it plain beyond all doubt that Communism has passed beyond the use of subversion to conquer independent nations and will now use armed invasion and war. It has defied the orders of the Security Council of the United Nations issued to preserve international peace and security. In these circumstances the occupation of Formosa [Taiwan] by Communist forces would be a direct threat to the security of the Pacific area and to United States forces performing their lawful and necessary functions in that area.

"Accordingly I have ordered the Seventh Fleet to prevent any attack on Formosa. As a corollary of this action I am calling upon the Chinese government on Formosa to cease all air and sea operations against the mainland. The Seventh Fleet will see that this is done. The determination of the future status of Formosa must await the restoration of security in the Pacific, a peace settlement with Japan, or consideration by the United Nations."[3]

As the statement demonstrates, Truman had a hard time making a logical connection between Taiwan and Korea, but he gave it a solid try. The fact his argument doesn't make sense was less important than its effectiveness as a smoke screen.

Even assuming the Red Chinese were co-conspirators with the North Koreans and were bent on aggression themselves, which they almost certainly were not, Taiwan would have made a poor offensive base for them. If the Seventh Fleet could prevent the Red Chinese from attacking Taiwan, this same fleet could keep them from using it "to conquer independent nations." An island in a sea controlled by the world's greatest navy is worse off as an offensive base than a mainland that cannot be encircled by ships and cut off.

But Truman's description of Taiwan as a security threat to the United States was designed to throw pursuers off the real track he was on. An indication of this is that, before he released his statement, he discussed the whole matter of Korea and Taiwan with key leaders of Congress in both parties and got their backing.[4] Truman had resolved to help South Korea. But he did not want to leave his rear open to attacks by Republicans and members of the China Lobby who had criticized his January 5 hands-off-Taiwan policy and who vehemently wanted to aid Chiang Kai-shek. Politically, Truman could not have withstood such attacks if the Chinese Communists—while American forces were engaged in Korea—had moved to occupy Taiwan, and the United States had done nothing to stop them. Truman's interposition of the Seventh Fleet in the Taiwan Strait was a pre-emptive move to eliminate any possible effort by Red China and thus to prevent political catastrophe at home.[5]

Another precipitating factor in the abrupt reversal of policy on Taiwan was the persuasive voice of MacArthur, who had altered his previous views on the strategic importance of the island. On May 29, 1950, he had sent a long message to the JCS maintaining that communist occupation of Taiwan would threaten U.S. positions in the Far East and urged that it not be allowed to happen. Taiwan under communist control, he said, would be "the equivalent of an unsinkable aircraft carrier and submarine tender." These same views were contained in a memorandum MacArthur prepared on June 14, 1950, and gave to Bradley and Secretary of Defense Johnson when they were on a trip to the Far East, June 11–24. According to Bradley in his autobiography, the memorandum fired up Secretary Johnson, who started an all-out campaign to reverse U.S. policy and produced a Bradley-drafted memo to this effect for the President.[6]

It is no surprise Truman made the decision he did on Taiwan. Popular opinion in the United States would have opposed Americans fighting communist aggression in Korea and ignoring a communist assault on Taiwan—despite the fact the two issues were not related. The argument that Korea represented aggression of one state against another whereas Taiwan represented an internal domestic Chinese dispute was a fine distinction for many Americans. This was especially true because the idea of North Korea as a separate state rubbed a lot of Americans the wrong way; many held that it was an illegal trumped-up Russian puppet. At the same time, many Americans could not accept the idea of communists forming the legal government of China; to them, it still rested with the Nationalists. Thus many Americans—refusing to look at the reality of affairs in the Far East—could not see a lot of conceptual difference between an (illegal) North Korea and an (illegal) Communist China. If the United States was going to oppose one, it should oppose the other.

Truman was a master politician, and he doubtless sensed American thinking. Neither he nor any other major American leader was willing to risk political suicide by trying to distinguish clearly in the public mind the fundamental differences between the Chinese and Korean situations. In this Truman was following an obligatory course laid down long before. Alexis de Tocqueville in his classic study of the United States in the 1830s focused on an American reality when he wrote: "The men who are entrusted with the direction of public affairs in the United States...may frequently be faithless and frequently mistaken, but they will never systematically adopt a line of conduct hostile to the majority."[7]

De Tocqueville also observed there is a propensity in the United States "to obey impulse rather than prudence, and to abandon a mature design for the gratification of a momentary passion."[8] De Tocqueville noted that only George Washington's inflexible stand and his immense popularity kept Americans from allying themselves with France and going to war against Britain at the time of the French Revolution. Truman, in the summer of 1950, had neither Washington's inflexible conviction nor his popularity—and the neutralization of Taiwan was the outcome.

More specifically to the point, de Tocqueville also spotted another American propensity—to cloak whatever we do, however harsh or unfair or inconsistent, with a mantle of legality.[9] Truman's statement on Taiwan, probably written by Acheson,[10] is a masterwork in this genre. To begin with, the first paragraph immediately transforms the North Korean assault from a one-state act of aggression into an abstract general *communist* attack, drawing by implication all communists everywhere into a common conspiratorial effort at "armed invasion and war," but not naming any specific state, since the United States did not want to confront Russia directly. The statement then says "it"—the antecedent is this abstract, all-encompassing but unspecific communism—has "defied the orders of the Security Council" to bring about peace and security. This two-sentence trial and conviction of all communists thereupon establishes the legal rationale in the third sentence to strike at Red China—while, at the same time, neatly passing right by the assumed real culprit, the Soviet Union, considered to be too dangerous to challenge directly. Not only was Red China weaker, but it was the object of specific antagonism of those domestic U.S. forces that wanted to aid the Nationalist Chinese. Thus Truman created the legalistic excuse to neutralize Taiwan, while simultaneously neutralizing the potential opposition of Republicans and the China Lobby. In its last sentence, the statement pulls off another marvelous bit of legalistic legerdemain. Having, in the first paragraph, convicted the Chinese Communists of defiance of the Security Council and thus implied Red China was a lawless and irresponsible power, the statement goes on tacitly to renounce Truman's January 5 statement declaring Taiwan to be an internal Chinese matter and throws its legal status back into the international arena for disposition. The statement makes Taiwan subject to "restoration of security in the Pacific," a Japanese peace treaty, or consideration by the United Nations (of which Red China was not even a member).

The Red Chinese were not able to penetrate, as was de Tocqueville, into the inscrutable American mind, and thus were not able to comprehend how Americans *need* to create legal excuses for harming other people. Is it any wonder, then, that Communist China's leaders must have felt they were confronted with a faithless and unreliable nation? Not a single Red Chinese soldier had marched, not a single Red Chinese government threat had been uttered. Yet Red China had been labeled an aggressor and the U.S. Seventh Fleet had been placed between the Chinese mainland and the Chinese province of Taiwan. Far from seeing this move as a necessary political action to avert domestic difficulties for the Truman administration, the Red Chinese saw it as a direct challenge to their sovereignty and feared it was only the first move of an *American* conspiracy to help the Nationalists reconquer the mainland.

Within twenty-four hours of Truman's announcement, Zhou Enlai, Communist China's foreign minister, gave the first signal in a campaign to alert the U.S. government to the Chinese government's position. A few days later, Mao Zedong added another signal. Both were blunt and clear, and had Washington been listening, they would have shown long in advance the position the Red Chinese would take to preserve what they considered to be their vital national interests. Minister Zhou denounced Truman's move as "armed aggression against Chinese territory and a total violation of the United Nations Charter."[11] Mao said the United States had broken its promises not to interfere in China's internal affairs and called on the Chinese to "defeat every provocation of American imperialism."[12]

Acheson, rather than pondering how to reduce the ill effects on Red China of the abrupt reversal of U.S. policy, chose to interpret Zhou Enlai's statement as tantamount to a declaration of war.[13] Of course, it *was*, if the United States intended to continue to confront Red China. Although Red China became an enemy when the United States denied it Taiwan, the matter might have rested there bloodlessly if the United States had been content to restore both Koreas at the 38th parallel and not threaten Red China directly by advancing to the Yalu, the boundary between Korea and Manchuria. The American domestic political situation which coupled Taiwan with Korea was temporary and could have been clarified to the electorate after peace had been restored to Korea. Instead of working wholly within this framework, however, the United States itself decided on aggression in Korea—by attempting to destroy North Korea and create a unified Korea under Syngman Rhee that would place American troops on the Yalu. When this action was added to the neutralization of Taiwan, the Red Chinese were thoroughly convinced the United States was bent on direct aggression against mainland China.

In fact, the United States might have avoided the Korean War entirely if the administration had worked out a strategy to disengage from Taiwan and Korea *before* it issued the January 5 and January 12 statements. This is where the mistake came. Quite obviously the North Koreans would see these announcements, plus the denial of substantial arms to South Korea, as an opportunity to pick off the South.

However, Truman's hands-off-Taiwan pronouncement was a major American effort in favor of detente with China — made at great political sacrifice at home because it guaranteed a powerful Republican issue to use against the administration. The situation argued eloquently for an effort to work out a quid pro quo with the Chinese Communist government. In exchange for the United States' backing away from Taiwan, the Red Chinese would exercise every effort within the communist camp to maintain peace in Korea. By emphasizing to the Chinese Communist leaders that, in American domestic politics, the issues of Taiwan and Korea were joined, the Red Chinese would have had every incentive to dissuade the North Koreans from any contemplated attack (certainly until after Red China had safely secured Taiwan), and to urge the Russians to keep offensive weapons out of North Korean hands.

CHAPTER 8

The Army of
the United Nations

ALTHOUGH TRUMAN had committed only air and sea forces, his action changed the American attitude toward Korea (and Taiwan) fundamentally. It was only a step thereafter to sending in the ground forces. There is no question but that Truman's decision reflected the will of the American people. Despite confusion over the nation's goals in the Far East, Americans overwhelmingly approved the idea of stopping communist aggression.

The same day Truman announced intervention, June 27, Congress discussed the crisis and the President's response, and the vast majority of members supported him. The House of Representatives voted 315–4 to approve a one-year extension of the draft, a measure which also authorized the President to call up reservists of all the services. On the next day, the Senate approved the bill 70–0.[1] Truman had congressional support for his actions, but he did not want to go to Congress, as the Constitution calls for, and ask it to declare the Korean conflict a war. He was loath to assume the heavy political burden of leading the nation into war. He preferred to view the conflict as a "police action." Thus was born an unfortunate presidential precedent to try to sanitize and minimize American military actions by avoiding formal congressional declarations of war. This course has been followed by every American President since Truman.

The UN Security Council met again on June 27. The stage was set for a crushing propaganda defeat for the Russians. Truman's morning announcement made clear to the world what was in the offing. But council members already knew beforehand. Neutral India and Egypt, in a panic, secured postponement of the session until the afternoon so their representatives could consult their governments. The only way the U.S. resolution could be stopped was for the Soviet Union, one of the five major powers, to exercise its veto. One wonders what messages flowed that day between the Kremlin and the Soviet delegate, Jacob Malik! A hurried return to the Security Council and a veto would bring down condemnation on the Soviet Union for cynical misuse of its power, and would instantly label the Soviet Union as a co-conspirator with North Korea. But failure to do so would brand North Korea as an aggressor, and give democratic countries a chance to exercise their anger with communist intransigence and aggrandizement. There could be no doubt that a vote against North Korea would be construed in Western circles as a vote against the Soviet Union. Still, condemning North Korea was a step removed from directly challenging the Soviet Union. Besides, the Soviet Union had already signaled by its silence that it was treating the crisis as a Korean internal affair. It shortly took this position officially, thereby prompting Secretary of State Acheson—recognizing this as another of the Kremlin's deliberately obscure Delphic oracles—to conclude on June 29 that the Soviets really meant they did not intend to commit their own military forces to Korea.[2]

Thus the Soviet Union faced two dismal choices. One was to use its veto and bring down world vilification and brand the North Korean invasion as Russian-inspired, with all the implications this had for drawing the Russians more directly and heavily into the peninsula. The other was to treat the whole affair as a little intramural squabble between factions (however much one faction was aided by big Russian-built tanks) and to brazen the whole thing out. The Russians took the latter course, and Malik's chair remained empty that day in the Security Council.

In the council the United States achieved a great victory. The United States called the Russian hand, and the Soviet Union, rather than commit itself publicly to supporting overt communist invasion, folded. Despite a lot of alarms and excursions thereafter, mainly on the part of nervous American leaders, there was never a serious threat that the Soviet Union would intervene in Korea.

The U.S. resolution urged UN members to "furnish such assistance to the Republic of Korea as may be necessary to repel the armed attack and to restore international peace and security to the area." Despite knowing it was coming, some council members recoiled before the resolution's harsh implication—it meant that the United Nations declared war on North Korea and that all members were obligated, at least morally, to become belligerents. Debate lasted all the rest of the day, and it was just before midnight when the council approved the resolution. Of course, the United States knew it would: the American delegation had polled the members beforehand and had the necessary seven votes in the bag. Only Yugoslavia (with no veto) disapproved, and India and Egypt abstained.[3] The United States had secured official world approval for the action it was about to take.

It also got essential control of the United Nations effort on July 7 when the Security Council recommended that all forces offered by UN members be placed under the command of the United States and asked the United States to designate a UN commander. Truman promptly named MacArthur. The United Nations made no provision for overseeing the conduct of the war and requested only that the United States report "as appropriate" on actions taken under the unified command. On July 12 MacArthur set up a United Nations Command headquarters in Tokyo (coextensive with his Far East Command headquarters), and on July 14 South Korea's President Rhee placed ROK troops under this command.[4]

* * * * * * * *

General MacArthur's advance commander in Korea, Brigadier General John H. Church, arrived at Suwon airfield at 7 p.m. June 27, the evening before the South Koreans blew the Han river bridges. General Church quickly realized the ROK army was in a state of impending dissolution, and the next day he radioed MacArthur that U.S. ground troops would have to be committed for there to be any hope of driving the NK troops back to the 38th.[5]

Church's message galvanized MacArthur into action. The next morning MacArthur himself flew into Suwon in his personal four-engine C-54 transport (the *Bataan*), escorted by four jet fighters. MacArthur's pilot set down on a runway shortened by a burning C-54, strafed earlier in the day by a North Korean fighter. President Rhee, U.S. Ambassador Muccio and General Church met MacArthur, who was accompanied by seven high-ranking officers of his staff, plus news reporters. MacArthur's pilot immediately took off and flew to Kyushu to refuel and await MacArthur's call to return. It was a good move: that afternoon North Korean planes bombed the airfield and destroyed a recently arrived two-engine C-47 transport.[6]

MacArthur insisted on driving up through streams of refugees and disordered soldiers to the Han river, still a barrier before the North Koreans. It was this trip which evidently convinced MacArthur that Church had been right: ships and aircraft alone could not retrieve the situation, although the U.S. Navy was uncontested at sea and the 350 combat-ready planes of the Far East Air Force, many of them top-of-the-line jet fighters, immediately wrested air supremacy from the 110 piston-driven combat aircraft the North Koreans had at the start of hostilities.[7]

That night, back in Tokyo, MacArthur drafted a message for Washington, which, oddly, given its urgent recommendations, he did not dispatch for almost twelve hours.[8] It was a pessimistic appraisal. "The Korean army is entirely incapable of counteraction and there is grave danger of a further breakthrough," he said. "If the enemy advance continues much further it will seriously threaten the fall of the republic."

MacArthur asked for authority to commit a U.S. regimental combat team (RCT) and later possibly to build up to two full divisions, sent over from Japan. President Truman, when he got the request at 5 a.m. June 30 (he was already up), approved sending the RCT, but delayed a decision on the buildup to two divisions.[9] That decision awaited the outcome of a conference of 9:30 a.m. the same day in the White House.

Truman called in Acheson, Johnson, the service secretaries, and the JCS. The President had an incredible proposal he wanted them to consider: an offer from Chiang Kai-shek of 33,000 Chinese Nationalist troops, and he, Truman, was inclined to accept it.[10] Perhaps no better example could be found of Truman's indifference to or misunderstanding of the situation in China at the time; his decision to interpose the Seventh Fleet between the mainland and Taiwan had been made on the basis of domestic U.S. problems, not its effect upon the Chinese. But his proposal to send Chiang's troops to Korea could only have been construed by the Red Chinese as proof that the United States planned to support a Nationalist counterinvasion of the mainland.

Fortunately, Secretary Acheson understood the implications, and he protested that sending Nationalists might stimulate the Red Chinese to intervene in Korea.[11] The Joint Chiefs also joined in, pointing out that the Nationalists, then more or less military refugees on Taiwan, were no better equipped than the South Koreans, and transport facilities needed to take them to Korea could be used more productively to send U.S. troops and supplies.[12]

Truman gave in, agreed to turn down Chiang's offer, and then made a stunning decision: he would give General MacArthur, not just two divisions, but full authority to use whatever ground forces he had under his command in the Far East, without limit. He also approved a recommendation by Admiral Sherman for a naval blockade of North Korea. The meeting, which definitely committed the United States to war, had lasted half an hour.[13]

CHAPTER 9

Goodbye to the Good Times

T HUS IT CAME: the abrupt and, in many cases, bloody end of the great good life of the American occupation forces in Japan. It had been a life the ordinary young soldier or officer and his dependents could only have dreamed of: constantly bowing Japanese "maid-sans" and "boy-sans" at one-twentieth of a second lieutenant's pay to do all the cleaning, shining and dirty work; generally relaxed working conditions and lots of leisure time; excellent clubs for noncommissioned officers and officers, commandeered from the Japanese and having highly professional Japanese bands and singers playing to all hours; cocktails costing so little (some of them ten cents each) there was the standard joke that one simply could not afford to stay sober; a free railway system, including the line running north from Tokyo called, officially, "the Yankee Special," and the one headed south called "the Dixie Limited."

The transition of American occupation troops to Korea was brutal, not only physically, but because, in the laid-back peacetime atmosphere of an occupation army, the difficult, tedious work of keeping units in fighting trim, with ammunition, weapons and equipment always combat-ready, simply had not been adequately done, either by the Pentagon or by the individual unit commanders.

It is almost impossible to recapture the feeling of unreality, outrage and shock that affected American troops in the first days of the war. It may have been axiomatic in the safe, clean and rarefied atmospheres of congressional appropriations committees and the war-plans rooms in the Pentagon that "high-priced soldiers" were expected always to be in top physical shape, to fight hard, to remain in their assigned positions and never to run from the enemy. But the mostly young and inexperienced soldiers thrust without warning into the Korean maelstrom had not been prepared emotionally, psychologically or

46

physically—and in many cases they didn't have the weapons—for the almost inconceivable trial by fire that they faced. Some experienced veterans of combat in World War II, including officers, buckled under the physical and emotional strains and dangers of Korea. It long had been a doctrine of the U.S. Army, as doubtless in every other army, that soldiers on duty were to be prepared at all times to leap to the defense of their country. But every officer who has ever served with troops knows this is a counsel of perfection, unattainable in real life. It was all the more visionary in the years immediately after World War II. Despite the conflicts with the Russians, most Americans trusted to their nation's atomic monopoly and could not conceive of an abrupt return to the battlefield. Korea itself was the catalyst that ended this euphoria. Ever since, the world has been on edge, always expecting some crisis somewhere to erupt into violence; and because it has been anticipated, it has occurred more often than it should. But Korea was the first crisis: a radical, unexpected shattering of what most Americans thought of as a deep peace.

In the event, American soldiers in some instances performed from the outset with bravery and tenacity; in some instances they did not. When officers started looking for the reasons afterward, they found them in the strength or weakness of two of the oldest and most commonplace precepts of military theory: leadership and training. There was little or no correlation between how well men performed and the danger or discomfort they faced. But there was a decided correlation between good performance and men who were well and confidently led, and who had learned how to service and fire their weapons, care for their persons and their equipment, and achieve a fair degree of comfort in field conditions.

The effectiveness or ineffectiveness of individual soldiers was one factor in the equation. Another was the actual combat strength of the four American divisions occupying Japan. With one exception (the 24th Regiment), the three organic regiments in each division in Japan had only two instead of the three normal infantry battalions. There were corresponding shortages in the other combat arms; for example, the artillery battalions had only two of the normal three firing batteries. Because of these shortages, the divisions averaged only about 70 percent of full war strength.[1]

Weak as these four divisions were, they represented well over a fourth of total American ground strength throughout the world.[2] Therefore, Truman's decision to allow MacArthur to use any and all of the Far East forces indicated a commitment to Korea that, in terms of total American strength, was awesome. The commitment soon became all the greater, as MacArthur demanded more and more support to meet the needs demonstrated in battle.

The United States had got itself into this posture of weakness deliberately and methodically in the years after World War II. Part of the reason was the understandable urge to "bring the boys home" after the war. Another was the false security of the atomic bomb, a security shown to be ephemeral in September, 1949, when United States sources confirmed that the Soviet Union had exploded a nuclear device. A third was the traditional isolationism of many Americans, an attitude strengthened by disillusionment with negotiations with the Soviets and an atavistic feeling that by withdrawing again behind America's two oceans the problems of the rest of the world could somehow be avoided.

These conditions were accentuated by President Truman himself. As David S. McLellan says in his astute analysis of Dean Acheson during his State Department career,[3] there was no effective coordination of military strategy and planning. Truman annually added up all expected expenditures of the civilian government and anything left over went to the military. The result was a continual battle between the services over relative shares of an arbitrary and artificial budget. As McLellan says, "Given the choice of spending money on ground forces or on air power, the American people and the Congress had given the preference to air power."[4] This was understandable, because American strategy rested almost wholly upon atomic weapons: in the event of war, primary reliance was upon air power to attack the Soviet Union with nuclear bombs.

This atomic shield seemed secure while the United States had a monopoly on nuclear bombs, and even later when mutual nuclear attack became equated with mutual destruction. Yet Korea was to demonstrate that the strategy was useful only in avoiding a cataclysmic confrontation with Russia. It was useless against smaller crises and smaller confrontations. Although there was a lot of talk about using atomic bombs in Korea, the political damage alone of such a decision would have been enough to restrain any American President from their use, leaving aside the worldwide moral revulsion that would have resulted. Korea proved nuclear weapons of mass destruction can be used only in a situation where the strategic or military position of the United States is so grave that nothing short of the bomb can restore a bearable status. This means, in effect, only situations that are viewed as threatening to the very integrity of the United States or to vital American interests. A lesser war, however dirty and however costly to individual American combat personnel, is not a reasonable candidate for nuclear weapons.

For this reason the North Koreans were able to duck, as it were, *under* the American nuclear shield and strike the United States where it was weakest: in conventional ground forces. Thus the North Korean effort, though clearly a great and dangerous gamble, was not so mad as it might appear—a nation of 9 million people against the most powerful nation on earth with enough nuclear capacity to destroy most of the people and practically everything of value in the entire country. The North Koreans did not *know* the United States would forswear the bomb, but they could be reasonably certain it would.

Dean Acheson realized when he became secretary of state in 1949 that the United States was relying too heavily on its atomic weapons and was dangerously weak in what came to be known as "conventional weapons," especially ordinary ground forces. In early 1950 he was able to engineer a decision by Truman to order a complete review of American overreliance on nuclear weapons.[5] The study was aimed at developing a more balanced military establishment. But by June, 1950, nothing had changed.

On that date, the United States had ten combat divisions, the equivalent of another division in the German occupation, and nine separate regimental combat teams.[6] Most of these units were under strength. In addition, the U.S. Marine Corps had in its Fleet Marine Force less than the equivalent of a single war-strength marine division.[7]

The great shortage of men in the divisions initially committed to action led the Pentagon to begin a frenetic process of reassignments and transfers of officers and enlisted men from units not alerted for action to units scheduled for fighting. At the same time, numerous reserve and National Guard units and thousands of individual reservists not assigned to reserve units were called up and hastily sent to fill up vacancies throughout the globe, but mostly in Korea. Many officers and noncommissioned officers who had served in World War II found themselves back in uniform. They were quickly dubbed "retreads." It was obvious to everyone that it was unfair to call men who had already served to serve again, while most adult males who had never served were either safely deferred from the renewed draft or over the draft-age limit. Not so the "retreads." There were thousands of veteran officers and noncoms in their thirties, and many in their forties, who were wrenched out of their civilian careers and flung into their second war. Many of these men died. Yet as a group the retreads gave a quality of professionalism and competence that never could have been attained so quickly by training new men.

Another inequity arose out of the American practice of treating military detachments as vessels to be filled with officers and men to a certain level of numbers, skills and ranks. Not followed was a practice of semipermanent groupings of men who could, over long association, develop a sense of camaraderie, closeness and interdependence. As the traditional army phrase had it (to explain any military practice that defies logic), "the exigencies of the service" prohibited the use of any other replacement system. But this practice weakened American military organization in the Korean War. The men in their units felt little sense of permanence, and often little sense of identity and loyalty to fellow soldiers whom they did not know. The situation was especially acute in the early days of the war, because many units were cannibalized in order to fill out other units hurriedly being readied for battle. A man assigned to one unit might, within a few hours time, be sent hurrying off hundreds or thousands of miles to another unit, where he might not know a single person.

The replacement system in Korea was officially titled the Pipeline, which bespoke eloquently its insensitive and dehumanized nature. But the Pipeline was only the outward manifestation of a much deeper attitude in all the services: that the ship or the unit was the crucial factor, and not the men within it. In this, the American system was in direct contrast to the traditional British army practice of creating a home for the officer and soldier in a regiment whose individual battalions were kept intact as much as possible. In practice the American system meant a unit might remain in combat situations for weeks or months, while individual soldiers within the units might be rotated in and out. The British practice was to rotate whole battalions in and out, while the individual men in each battalion remained together.

The only virtue of the American system was the great rapidity with which units could be created (and others cannibalized). The system also permitted quick reconstitution of a unit which had suffered great losses in battle or had been rendered ineffective by cannibalization. The Pipeline could be directed to the unit until it was filled up again, then diverted to another unit needing filling. But a collection of strangers is not a cohesive and viable combat entity: to create such an organization takes time, familiarity and a common sense of purpose among members. The American system did not promote this or a sense of security for the individual soldier. There were cases in the first weeks of the war in which new replacements were assigned to a unit, thrown into battle, and killed or wounded and evacuated to hospitals before anyone in the unit even knew their names.

There is no way to calculate the impact of such a system upon the effectiveness of the individual units and the morale of the individual soldiers. So much depended upon the quality and fiber of the officers and men who happened to be assigned, to their state of training, and to the army- or marine-wide standards of performance and conduct they had acquired and had brought with them. Nevertheless, there is no question but that the individual soldier, especially the young man only recently out of basic training, often felt bewildered and insecure when flung into a hastily filled-up unit commanded by noncoms and officers who were total strangers, but who, because of their grave responsibilities, had to demand much and demand it quickly.

In war, military units exist to be used. They tend in battle to be worn down by friction. The numbers of men originally assigned to a combat unit are steadily being diminished by deaths and wounds. This requires that vacant spaces be made up by replacements. Heavily engaged units in Korea consequently began to change rapidly.

Despite it all, however, man's need for community asserted itself strongly, and officers and men, given the slightest opportunity, quickly formed tight bonds inside their units. These tended to be closest in the most heavily engaged units—the infantry, the artillery, the armor, the combat engineers. In platoons and companies a marvelous and mutually supportive system closely akin to a family sometimes developed. Highly sensitive commanders encouraged such support, not only by sympathetic understanding of their men's anxieties and fears, but by demanding hot food promptly served, opportunities for men to get back briefly for showers and clean clothes, and prompt delivery of mail from home and of the few amenities available, like cigarettes, candy, magazines and books, and beer (a dozen cans a month per man—and the prohibitionists in the States even made a big stink about that). As a consequence, there sometimes was a phenomenon rare in war: often the best food was served by infantry units right on the line where conditions were worst, while service units in the rear, where conditions were good, frequently endured indifferent food.

If the manpower problems had been the only deficiences of the U.S. military, the army and marines might quickly have overcome them simply by sheer force of traditional American military power: excellent weapons and other equipment and lots of it. It was incredible fire power and mobility which made American units so awesome in most of World War II. But Korea in the early days was another story. The greatest single weakness of the ground forces was equipment and ammunition. Because of budgetary shortages, army procurement after World War II had been limited largely to food, clothing and medical supplies.[8] The army had to operate almost exclusively with older and obsolescent equipment and stockpiles of ammunition left over from World War II. This left some strange anomalies: machine guns and towed artillery were in plentiful supply, but heavy construction equipment, newly developed radios, self-propelled artillery, new tanks, antiaircraft guns and certain types of ammunition were extremely scarce. An item as simple as radio batteries turned out to be critical: most batteries were old, and they frequently were useless or went dead after a short time, with devastating results to communication in combat situations.

The four divisions in the Japanese occupation were spread out the length of the islands. The 7th Division was in the north; the 1st Cavalry (really an infantry division, but retaining the old cavalry name out of nostalgia—some of the officers still wore crossed sabers instead of crossed rifles on their collars and blouses) was around Tokyo; the 25th was in southern Honshu; and the 24th occupied Kyushu, the southernmost island of Japan and closest to Korea.

The greatest problem of all was time: the ROK army could scarcely slow the North Koreans, and the only forces that could were American troops in Japan. Almost from the first days of the war, MacArthur had developed a plan to foil the North Koreans; but for his or anybody else's plan to work the North Koreans had to be stopped and held in place. Otherwise, the defenders would run out of South Korean real estate and lose the southern port of Pusan, upon which supply and reinforcements depended. If that happened, the ROK army and the Republic of Korea would disappear, and the United States would have the choice of accepting a *fait accompli* or mounting a massive and costly invasion. Much depended, therefore, upon the ability of the few available American units to slow and then to stop the North Koreans. They had only a few days to do it.

Although when the balloon went up American logistical officers commenced frantic, and extremely fast, loading of troops, equipment and supplies on anything that could get them across the Korea Strait, by air or sea, it was a physical impossibility to deliver many troops to the firing line in the first days.

The result was that the first-committed American units, practically all from the 24th Division, had to take the powerful initial shock and then try to stem the advance. This meant that relatively tiny units—battalions and even companies—were thrust into blocking positions against regiments and divisions of the enemy. It was an extreme crisis that only time could correct; and these first units were sent in for just that purpose: to buy time. In a few weeks the overwhelming logistical potential of the U.S. Army, Navy and Air Force would begin to assert itself, and the chance would pass that United Nations troops might be driven into the sea. But in the first weeks only the small, understrength units of the 24th Division, flung into battle almost the moment they arrived at the front, were available to prevent disaster.

The Potsdam Conference of victorious Allies in July, 1945, brought the Soviet Union's commitment to entering the war against Japan. The result was a Soviet occupation of northern Korea and Korea's partition along the 38th parallel.

At the Moscow conference in December, 1945, Ernest Bevin (left), British foreign secretary; V.M. Molotov (center), Soviet foreign minister, and James F. Byrnes, U.S. secretary of state, agreed on a four-power commission to rule Korea. But the Soviets undermined the commission and established communist rule in the north.

Task Force Smith arrives at the Taejon rail station. On July 5, 1950, near Osan, this untried force of about half a battalion, mostly teenagers, stood alone against a North Korean division and a large tank force.

These are the Joint Chiefs of Staff who served during the most crucial period of the Korean War (from left): General Omar N. Bradley, chairman; General Hoyt Vanderberg, air force; General J. Lawton Collins, army, and Admiral Forrest P. Sherman, navy.

U.S. bombs drop on railway bridges at Seoul in early July, 1950. The broken highway bridge at top was blown without warning by South Koreans themselves early on June 28, sending hundreds of fleeing South Korean soldiers and civilians to their deaths.

The Soviet Union's seat is conspicuously vacant as the UN Security Council votes on June 27, 1950, to use force to push North Korean troops out of South Korea.

CHAPTER 10

The Teenagers Stand and Fight

S OME NORTH KOREAN SOLDIERS slipped across the Han west of Seoul on June 28, the same day the capital fell, and occupied Kimpo airfield. This closed one of the two main air supply and reinforcement points available to the ROK army and the American advanced headquarters. The other field, at Suwon, about twenty miles below Seoul, was near ROK and advanced U.S. command headquarters.

It wasn't until the morning of June 30, however, that substantial numbers of North Koreans ferried over the Han a short distance upstream from the destroyed Seoul bridges. This was the same day that General "Fat Boy" Chae (he weighed nearly 250 pounds) was relieved as ROK chief of staff by Lieutenant General Chung Il Kwon, who had arrived from Tokyo.

It had become clear the ROK army would be unable to maintain a line, despite successful efforts by American logistical officers to get resupplies of ammunition and weapons to the ROKs by sea and airlift.

The time was set for intervention with American troops. But where? The farther north they could be emplaced the better, and the Han river line, though wavering, still had not been cracked. General Church, MacArthur's advance commander, decided that evening to drive down to Osan, twelve miles south of the command post (CP) at Suwon, to talk with Tokyo by a commercial telephone relay station there. He reached Major General Edward M. (Ned) Almond, MacArthur's chief of staff. Almond agreed to airlift two U.S. infantry battalions into Suwon airfield the next day (July 1), provided Church could hold the field, Church agreed and headed back to Suwon.[1]

Meanwhile, one of the inexplicible events born of uncertainty and fear that were to strike many soldiers during the early stages of the war was taking place at Church's Suwon CP: the officers and men there were caught up in a phenomenon that came to be known as "bug-out fever."[2]

First, an American airplane radioed an erroneous message that a column of enemy troops was approaching Suwon from the east. Then a red flare went up on the railroad about five hundred yards away. Someone yelled the enemy was surrounding the town. "We'd better get out of here!" In the chaos that followed, CP communications personnel started destroying their equipment with thermite grenades; these set fire to the schoolhouse CP, which thereupon burned to the ground. Within minutes the Americans drove off pell-mell to form a defensive perimeter at Suwon airfield in the best tradition of the Wild West ("Form the wagons in a circle!"). On hurried reflection, the men at the airfield decided they had better go instead on to Taejon, ninety miles south by road. The group, along with a small American antiaircraft detachment at the field and U.S. Embassy people, were ready to start when General Church came driving back from Osan. He was livid, and immediately ordered his CP group back to Suwon. When he got there, he found the smoldering schoolhouse.

Church's first impulse was to hold Suwon airfield. On consideration, however, he doubted his ability to keep the field free of enemy fire to permit landing of troops. At last, in a miserable downpour of rain, he led the dejected little caravan south to Osan. The next day (July 1) he continued on to Taejon.[3]

The North Koreans didn't break through the Han line until July 3, after taking heavy losses against ROK troops in close-in fighting without tanks at Yongdungpo, an industrial suburb south of the river. It was not until July 4 that the North Koreans, who finally had got their tanks across the Han by repairing one of the railway bridges, were able to move south in force. ROK army headquarters stayed at Suwon until that day.[4]

Tank thrusts disorganized an attempt by a ROK 2nd Division regiment to slow the North Korean advance and inflicted heavy casualties on ROK units trying to escape. The road from Suwon through Osan toward Pyongtaek was almost solid with ROK men and vehicles moving south the afternoon and evening of July 4. U.S. and Australian aircraft (the Aussies had committed an F-51 squadron) tried to slow the North Koreans, but they made mistakes that day and strafed ROK troops several times in the vicinity of Osan.[5] Debacle was setting in once more in the ROK army.

* * * * * * * *

Instead of being airlifted into Suwon and thereby giving both actual and moral support to the South Koreans still defending the Han river line, the first U.S. troops had to be sent into Pusan on July 1. From this port at the extreme southeastern end of the country, the first little group of Americans—destined to carry the name of Task Force Smith—embarked on an exhausting four-day odyssey by rail and truck to a point north of Osan. There, on July 5, only half a dozen miles south of Suwon airfield itself, Americans met the North Koreans for the first time in ground combat.[6]

In the time this little battle group took to make its arduous trek into battle, the South Korean front on the Han collapsed and the ROK army retreated south in disorder and mounting chaos.

The men in Task Force Smith occupy a special place in American military history. Not only were they the first to engage the North Koreans on land, but they fought under conditions practically opposite to what American troops had become accustomed to expect. That is, they were vastly inferior in numbers and firepower to their opponent, they were at the end of an incredibly long and tenuous supply string, and they were absolutely alone, with no troops on either side to support them. The fact that they had been wrested overnight from a comfortable garrison life in Kyushu and flung unprepared into the battle did not help their physical condition or mental attitude. Task Force Smith epitomizes the American experience in the early stages of the war. And it is a remarkable story in itself.

Lieutenant Colonel Charles B. (Brad) Smith, West Point class of 1939, was awakened at 10:30 p.m. on June 30 by his wife in their quarters near Kumamoto on Kyushu. On the telephone was his boss, Colonel Richard W. Stephens, commander of the 21st Infantry Regiment of the 24th Division. Stephens told Smith: "The lid has blown off. Get on your clothes and report to the CP."

Five and a half hours later Smith, with parts of the 1st Battalion, which he commanded, and a few other men, were on trucks en route to Itazuke airbase, seventy-five miles away. At Itazuke, Smith was met by Major General William F. Dean, commander of the 24th Division. Dean told him: "When you get to Pusan, head for Taejon. We want to stop the North Koreans as far from Pusan as we can. Contact General Church. If you can't locate him, go to Taejon and beyond if you can. Sorry I can't give you more information. That's all I've got. Good luck to you, and God bless you and your men."

One-third of Smith's officers were combat veterans of World War II, but very few of the enlisted men were; most were young, twenty years old or less. It was a tiny force: 406 officers and men. It consisted of two understrength rifle companies (B and C), a few headquarters, communications and heavy-weapons troops, two 75mm recoilless rifles, two 4.2-inch mortars, four 60mm mortars, and six 2.36-inch bazooka teams. Each man carried 120 rounds of rifle ammunition and two days supply of C rations.

Six C-54 transports were available to carry the men, but mountain-edged Pusan airfield was fogbound, and it took most of the day of July 1 to get them there. A KMAG officer had assembled Korean trucks and vehicles to transport Task Force Smith the seventeen miles into Pusan from the airstrip. Cheering crowds lined the streets, waving flags and streamers, and Korean bands were at the railway station to give them a noisy, happy—and, considering what lay ahead, a bizarre—send-off at 8 p.m.

The train arrived at Taejon twelve hours later, and Smith found General Church, who pointed to a place on the map and said, "We have a little action up here. All we need is some men up there who won't run when they see tanks. We're going to move you up to support the ROKs and give them moral support." That was not the way things worked out.

While his men bivouacked at Taejon, Smith and his principal officers got into jeeps and headed north over the bumpy, bad dirt road to Osan, eighty miles north. All along the way, ROK soldiers and civilians were clogging the road and moving south.

Three miles north of Osan, while North Korean fighters flew overhead without seeing them, Colonel Smith and his officers found what they were looking for: a highly defensible infantry position commanding both the highway and the parallel Seoul-Pusan railroad line. An irregular ridgeline crossed the road at right angles, its highest point about 300 feet above the low ground that stretched toward Suwon. From this ridge, Smith could see almost the entire distance to Suwon, eight miles north.

The night of July 2, Smith moved his men north by train to Pyongtaek, a point on the main highway and railway about fifteen miles south of Osan, and to Ansong, twenty miles southeast, to form blocking positions. July 3 was a wild day: a northbound ammunition train on its way to ROK units pulled into Pyongtaek station for instructions and was shortly attacked by four Australian F-51 Mustang fighters. They made six strafing runs over the train, firing rockets and machine guns. The train blew up, demolished the station and parts of the town, and ammunition kept exploding all night. Many civilians died or were injured. The same afternoon, friendly air also attacked Suwon, still in ROK hands (one KMAG officer said five times), and strafed a South Korean truck column near the town. ROK rifle fire forced one plane to land at Suwon airfield, where KMAG and ROK officers "captured" an embarrassed American pilot. In the afternoon, four friendly jet planes made strikes at Suwon

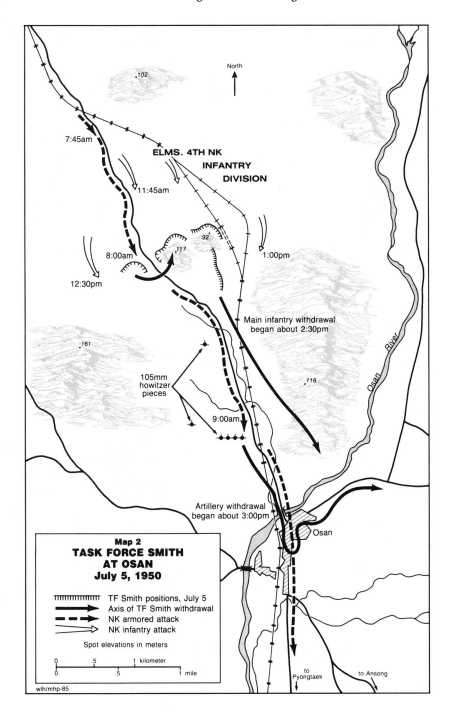

North

.102

7:45am

ELMS. 4TH NK
INFANTRY
DIVISION

11:45am

8:00am

.117

92

1:00pm

12:30pm

.161

Main infantry withdrawal
began about 2:30pm

Osan River

105mm
howitzer
pieces

.116

9:00am

Artillery withdrawal
began about 3:00pm

Osan

Map 2
TASK FORCE SMITH
AT OSAN
July 5, 1950

TF Smith positions, July 5
Axis of TF Smith withdrawal
NK armored attack
NK infantry attack

Spot elevations in meters

0   .5   1 kilometer
0   .5   1 mile

to
Pyongtaek

to Ansong

wlh/mhp-85

and along the highway south, setting fire to the railway station in Suwon and destroying buildings and injuring civilians. On the road they strafed and burned 30 ROK trucks and killed 200 South Korean soldiers. Because of the incidents, General Church sent a strong protest to Far East Air Force asking that air action be held to the Han bridges or northward.

On July 4, Smith's two separate detachments reunited at Pyongtaek, and there were joined by 134 men with six 105mm howitzers from the 52nd Field Artillery Battalion that had arrived July 2 in Pusan by LST and had immediately moved north. The artillery detachment, under Lieutenant Colonel Miller O. Perry, was attached to Task Force Smith.

A little after midnight on July 5, the combined force moved out of Pyongtaek to take up the defensive positions Smith had selected north of Osan. The infantry went in commandeered Korean vehicles, which were promptly deserted by the Korean drivers when they discovered which direction the vehicles were going.

About 3 a.m. July 5 Smith's little group got into blocking position and Colonel Perry moved five of his artillery pieces in place about a mile behind the infantry. (See Map 2.) The artillery had 1,200 rounds of 105mm ammunition, but only six rounds were high-explosive antitank (HEAT) shells. These special shaped-charge shells were extremely scarce in the Far East because the Department of the Army had given priority to Europe for the few it had.[7] The antitank shells Colonel Perry issued to a sixth 105 he emplaced as an antitank gun right off the road halfway between the infantry and the rest of his howitzers.

It was a rainy day, but Smith could see almost to Suwon. He discerned movement about 7 a.m., and a half hour later saw clearly it was a tank column, coming straight down the road. In the lead group were eight tanks. About 8 a.m. the artillery's forward observer with the infantry called in a fire mission on the openly exposed tanks, which by then were about 2,000 yards in front of the American infantry. The 105mm shells started exploding all around the T34s, but they kept coming up the road, undeterred and apparently unaffected.

Smith had instructed the two 75mm recoilless-rifle teams to hold their fire until the T34s had closed to 700 yards, a distance which made hits almost certain. The 75mm rifles immediately scored direct hits, but apparently did no damage: the T34s kept rumbling on up the road as it rose toward the ridgeline and the American emplacements. The enemy tanks could not find the weapons firing at them, and shot their 85mm high-velocity shells and machine guns aimlessly all around. The tanks were almost abreast of the infantry when Lieutenant Ollie D. Connor, in a ditch along the road, fired several rockets from a 2.36-inch bazooka at fifteen yards range into the rear of the tanks where their armor was weakest—and nothing happened.

The two lead tanks were stopped, however, just as they came over the crest of the road at the pass: there they were hit by direct fire of the single 105mm howitzer emplaced as an antitank gun and firing the antitank ammunition. The two damaged tanks pulled off to the side of the road, making way for the following tanks. One of the two caught fire and burned; two men came out of the turret with their hands up; a third jumped out with a burp gun and fired directly into a machine-gun position, killing a gunner. American fire quickly killed all three North Koreans.

By this time, the six antitank rounds had been fired, and the 105 had switched to high-explosive shells. These merely ricocheted off the tanks. The third tank through the pass knocked out the forward 105 and wounded one of the crew members.

The tanks made no effort to engage the infantry, merely firing at them as they passed through, moving past the American positions without hesitation and on down the road toward the remainder of the artillery pieces, tearing up as they went telephone wire strung along the road back to the artillery.

The artillery kept firing, though the gunners had nothing but high-explosive shells to throw at them. The counterfire by the T34s was haphazard because most of the North Koreans had not located the artillery. A few hundred yards from the American battery position, the T34s stopped behind a small hill that offered protection from direct fire, and, one tank at a time, the North Koreans rushed past, their hulls down, and clanked on south toward Osan. The 105mm howitzers fired at ranges of 150 to 300 yards as the tanks went by, but the shells only jarred the tanks or bounced off.

Bazooka teams from the artillery battery tried to stop the tanks, but their rockets, too, bounced off. A 105mm howitzer round finally hit the tracks of one tank and stopped it. Colonel Perry tried to get the tank crew to surrender, but got no response; Perry ordered the 105s to fire at it; after three rounds, two men jumped out and ran, but a squad chased them down and killed them. During the action, small-arms fire hit Colonel Perry in the right leg, but he refused to be evacuated.

About ten minutes after the first group of tanks had passed through and moved on south, a second wave of T34s came through, in ones, twos and threes, close together, with no organization or interval. With the frightening apparition of more tanks, a sudden bug-out fever seized some of the artillerymen, and they left the scene hurriedly. Officers had to drag the ammunition up and senior noncommissioned officers fired the pieces. The panic ceased soon, and the chastened men returned to their positions.

Many of the second group of tanks ignored the artillery entirely, although the 105s fired point-blank at the monsters. U.S. fire did,however, hit one T34 in its tracks, disabling it in front of the artillery position, and some of the tanks had one or two infantrymen riding on their decks; these were blown off or killed by the artillery fire. T34 fire hit a nearby ammunition dump, and about 300 rounds of 105 artillery shells began to explode.

In all, thirty-three North Korean tanks passed through the American position in the space of an hour. Colonel Perry said each of his howitzers fired several rounds at each tank, and the tanks averaged a return fire of about one round per tank. The score: the forward 105 firing antitank shells had knocked out and left burning one tank and stopped another so it could not move, while the battery had stopped two more in front of its firing position. In addition, three other T34s had been damaged but were able to continue on with the remainder of the tanks toward Osan. The T34s had destroyed the forward 105 howitzer in antitank position, had killed or wounded twenty-three men, and had destroyed all the vehicles the infantry had parked behind their positions.

When the last of the tanks had passed through and disappeared south, the American position became eerily quiet. It was still raining, but visibility remained fairly good and the Americans could see nothing coming toward them. They deepened their foxholes and waited.

An hour later, Colonel Smith saw movement near Suwon. It slowly materialized into the incredible sight of a column of trucks and foot soldiers six miles long, led by three tanks. Thousands of men: two complete regiments, as the Americans found out later. It was a sight that, aside from the tanks and the trucks, might have resembled a major troop movement in the nineteenth century, before the days of airplanes and long-range artillery. The North Koreans clearly had no idea the Americans were emplaced in front of them, and, packed together in march order, they obviously had no fear of air attacks, apparently because they figured the rain had kept UN aircraft on the ground. They need not have worried anyway, because General Church had requested, after the disasters of July 3, that UN air strikes be kept north of the Han river; and because Colonel Smith's telephone lines had been cut and his radios were wet and hardly functioning, he couldn't have called in air strikes even if they had been available.

The unsuspecting North Koreans moved forward in close formation while the Americans waited in their emplacements, knowing they were vastly outnumbered and whatever advantage they would have with surprise soon would be nullified by the crushing weight of superior forces. Still, they didn't run: four hundred Americans, most of them still boys in their teens, routed out of their soft peacetime billets only five days before, having just been overrun and cut off by one of the most terrifying weapons of war, tanks that were almost immune to their fire. The American soldiers waited for the word of their commander— to *attack* five thousand advancing enemy troops.

MacArthur later called this commitment an "arrogant display of strength" designed to fool the North Koreans into thinking the Americans had a much larger force at hand. The North Koreans were not fooled or didn't notice. But the soldiers in this tiny forward point of American "arrogance" did know theirs was a bluff and nothing was behind them. Still, they stayed and fought. In all American history, no group of soldiers has displayed greater bravery and dedication than the mostly untried young men of Task Force Smith.

Colonel Smith held the fire of his men until about 11:45 a.m., when the point of the North Korean column was a thousand yards away. Then on his order they let go with everything they had: mortars, machine guns, artillery, rifles. Trucks burst into flames, men fell. The North Korean column erupted in pandemonium, the men scattering into ditches. The three lead tanks moved within two hundred or so yards of the American positions and began firing directly at the ridgeline with cannons and machine guns. About a thousand North Korean infantry quickly began moving up a finger ridge on the east side of the road, setting up a base of fire and sending two columns to attempt to envelop the American positions. Task Force Smith stopped this advance in its tracks. But another enveloping movement was under way on the west side of the road, and in about three-quarters of an hour a strong force threatened a U.S. platoon on the dominating hill there. Smith quickly withdrew the platoon to the east side of the road.

Soon, however, North Korean mortar and artillery found the range of the task force emplacements and began to batter them. North Koreans also got machine guns firing from hills overlooking the right flank. Incredibly, Task Force Smith held its positions for almost three hours. But about 2:30 p.m., with large numbers of North Koreans on both his flanks and moving toward his rear, Colonel Smith decided the time had come to get out. Small-arms ammunition was almost gone; his communications had evaporated, even with his artillery a mile behind.

Smith quickly set up a leapfrog withdrawal plan, with each unit protecting the others as they withdrew, and then itself being protected as it withdrew. First off was Company C, then the medics, then head-quarters, and finally Company B—except its 2nd Platoon never got the withdrawal order. The platoon leader, Lieutenant Carl F. Bernard, realized his group was alone when a platoon runner came back from the company CP and reported it was empty. Second Platoon survivors could only take themselves and help the slightly wounded men: they had to leave their dead and about 25 wounded litter cases.

The task force suffered its heaviest losses in the withdrawal, when the men had to come out of their foxholes into the open. By then machine guns had been moved in close, and they extracted casualties among the exposed Americans.

The artillery gunners abandoned their weapons, but removed sights and breech blocks and took their aiming circles as they retreated to their vehicles, left on the northern outskirts of Osan and still generally undamaged. Smith and Perry hoped to take a road leading southeast to Ansong on the assumption the North Korean tanks had gone on down the main road toward Pyongtaek. But just inside Osan, they came upon three North Korean tanks stopped in the streets, with crew members standing around smoking. Stunned, the North Koreans and Americans gazed at each other for a moment, then the Americans turned back and found a small dirt road that led eastward. Not a shot was fired.

The vehicles picked up task force survivors as they found them, many who had climbed over hills or walked through rice paddies. There was no pursuit by the North Koreans. The American vehicles got back to Pyongtaek after midnight and later went on south to Chonan, about fourteen miles below Pyongtaek.

Before nightfall, about 250 of Smith's infantry had got back; about 150 were killed, wounded or missing. In addition, 31 officers and men of the artillery detachment were lost. For the next several days, the survivors straggled into American lines at Pyongtaek, Chonan and Taejon and elsewhere in southern Korea. Lieutenant Bernard and twelve men of his platoon reached Chonan two days after the fight; they had to go around five North Korean roadblocks, and they reached Chonan only a half hour before the North Koreans arrived.

CHAPTER 11

Withdrawal in Disorder

WITH OSAN GONE, the next logical defense point on the main north-south road and railway was Pyongtaek, about ten miles south. That town and the town of Ansong, twelve miles east, formed a potential defense line because, just west of Pyongtaek, a deep estuary of the Yellow Sea comes in and just east of Ansong mountains rise as a partial barrier.

General William Dean, 24th Division commander, had arrived in Taejon on July 3, and the next evening the first elements of the division's 2,000-man, two-battalion 34th Infantry Regiment started north from Pusan by rail. The 34th was the second U.S. Army infantry unit to arrive in Korea, and, like Task Force Smith, it was destined to be flung into battle without support.

General Dean hoped to use this regiment to stop the North Koreans on the Pyongtaek-Ansong line, because he had no illusions Task Force Smith could do more than delay the North Koreans. On the same day the task force was engaged (July 5), he directed the 34th's 1st Battalion to emplace two miles north of Pyongtaek and the 3rd Battalion to block any North Korean movement south at Ansong.

The main North Korean assault, however, was coming straight down the Osan-Pyongtaek road, and Dean was asking too much in expecting a single battalion to do more than slow it, much less stop it. Given its poor state of training and its lack of artillery, tanks and antitank guns, the 1st Battalion could not have held long against the thousands of North Koreans and their tanks.[1] In the event, the battalion performed even worse than anyone expected.[2]

General Dean's representative in the forward area was with the artillery of Task Force Smith when the first fire mission started to rain down shells on the advancing North Korean tanks. The officer, Brigadier

63

General George B. Barth, 24th Division artillery commander, realized immediately that the task force's infantry and artillery could not stop the T34s. He quickly drove back to Pyongtaek to alert the 34th's 1st Battalion, still digging in while a cold rain fell.

General Barth changed the battalion's mission: instead of holding in place, Barth told the commander to hold only until the enemy threatened to envelop him, then to retreat, delaying in successive rearward positions to gain time.[3]

Despite the battle raging ten miles to the north, 1st Battalion spent a quiet July 5 and only began to become apprehensive when five survivors of Task Force Smith arrived about midnight with an account of the action. Realizing that no task force vehicles would be coming down the road, the battalion commander ordered a detachment to blow up a small bridge over a stream about 600 yards north of the battalion position. This was done about 3 a.m. July 6.

At break of a rainy and fogbound day, the men of the battalion heard the sounds of engines running, and some men could see through the fog the faint outlines of several tanks halted by the blown bridge. Two columns of infantry also appeared. The battalion commander and other officers at first thought the troops were from Task Force Smith. But the presence of tanks, which Smith did not have, and the huge size of the group quickly showed the officers they were facing North Koreans. The battalion commander immediately ordered mortar fire. The North Koreans quickly spread out across the rice paddies on either side of the road after the first round landed, but continued to advance. By this time, thirteen tanks were visible, lined up bumper to bumper on the road. The crew of the lead tank, which had been out examining the blown bridge, returned, closed the turret, swung the tube until it pointed directly at Company A positions on a hill southwest of the road—and commenced firing. The exploding shells splattered dirt over the center platoon as the men sank into their water-filled foxholes.

The noncoms yelled to their men to fire, but response was slow, although the soldiers could see the North Korean infantry advancing steadily and spreading out across the flat ground in front of the hill. It took fully fifteen minutes before the two Company A platoons on the hill built up an appreciable volume of fire, and then fewer than half the men were operating their weapons; most of the fire came from squad and platoon leaders. Many of the riflemen appeared to be stunned and unable to believe that the North Koreans were firing at them. Later examination of thirty-one weapons in one platoon showed that twelve of the rifles were broken or dirty or had been assembled incorrectly, an astonishing commentary on the state of training of the individual riflemen.

The North Korean infantry began enveloping the Company A positions and also moved against Company B emplacements on a hill about 750 yards east of the road. The battalion commander watched the attack for a few minutes, then ordered Company A to withdraw and departed the hill for his CP, where he telephoned Company B to withdraw as well.

Both companies moved off the hills, but not all the members of Company A's 1st Platoon, emplaced in the low rice-paddy land west of the road, heard the shouted order to withdraw. In addition, about twenty of them, afraid to move across the flat paddies, stayed behind. The 1st Platoon leader, Lieutenant Herman L. Driskell, and a group of seventeen men emplaced between the road and the parallel railway embankment a few yards west of the road had missed the withdrawal order entirely. However, they had seen Company B men withdrawing, and Driskell sent a runner back to see if the rest of Company A was still in position. The runner returned and said the hill was empty. Driskell's group immediately started back, using the railroad embankment for protection from the North Koreans on the highway only a few yards to the east. At the edge of the paddies, Driskell started looking for the rest of his men; someone told him that several, including some wounded men, were near the base of the hill Company A had occupied, and Driskell moved off in search of them.

Meantime, the withdrawal of the rest of Company A had become disorderly. Some men left the hill without their weapons or ammunition, and when an enemy machine gun opened up on a couple of squads, the men panicked and raced to the rear; their panic infected other soldiers, and some ran all the way back to Pyongtaek. By that time, they had lost much of their initial fear, and they stood around in the muddy streets, waiting.

Company officers arrived in Pyongtaek and immediately began organizing the men for the march south. Then the observer who earlier had directed the mortar fire arrived; he had been severely shocked by a T34 round that exploded near him. His eyes showed white, he walked as if drunk, he talked incoherently and stared wildly, and he constantly kept moaning, "Rain, rain, rain." This unnerved the green troops, and they became further frightened by a report about Lieutenant Driskell and three other men. A 1st Platoon member claimed he had seen Driskell and the three men move toward some houses near the original company emplacements, searching for wounded members of Driskell's platoon. North Korean soldiers suddenly surrounded them; the Americans tried to surrender, the informant said, but the North Koreans had shot all four.

Before leaving, a battalion demolition team dynamited the bridge over a stream just north of Pyongtaek. This move to slow the NK advance was to have unheard-of consequences four days later.

The company formed up in two single-file lines and moved south rapidly. One-fourth of the 140 men of the company were dead or missing, and most of its equipment and supplies were gone. The company had no communication with any other unit because the radios had been abandoned, and no one had any plan except to go south. The other companies of 1st Battalion also moved back, and by midafternoon the battalion began arriving in Chonan, with Company A the last to get there in the early evening. Meantime, the 34th's 3rd Battalion at Ansong also had withdrawn to Chonan.

General Dean was angry at the precipitous retreat of the 34th Regiment.[4] There had been no attempt to defend the first available position south of Pyongtaek, where it might have been possible to block the T34s. Instead, the 1st Battalion had withdrawn the entire distance.[5] That evening, Dean considered ordering the regiment back north immediately, but he reconsidered for fear of a night ambuscade. Instead, he directed a company to go north the next morning to make contact with the North Koreans. A company and a reconnaissance platoon of the 3rd Battalion got about five miles north of Chonan when it was halted by small-arms and mortar fire. Meantime, General Dean had decided to send the whole battalion forward, and, in another action, he relieved the 34th Regiment's commander, Colonel Jay B. Lovless, and replaced him with Colonel Robert R. Martin, a fellow officer of Dean's in World War II whom Dean felt was an outstanding regimental commander.

The 3rd Battalion reached a good defensive position. But when Major John J. Dunn, operations officer (S-3) of the 34th, arrived on another mission, he found the battalion had begun withdrawing, and he could find neither the battalion commander nor the executive officer. Dunn, quickly getting regimental approval, headed the retreating 3rd Battalion back north. With Major Boone Seegars, the 3rd Battalion S-3, two company commanders and a few men in two jeeps, Major Dunn went on ahead. The jeeps were fired on at close range by a North Korean ambush party of thirty or forty scouts. Both majors were badly wounded and others were hit. Dunn, concealed in some roadside bushes, saw the lead rifle company of the 3rd Battalion coming up behind, but the men stopped and dropped to the ground when the North Korean firing began. They did not advance, and their officers apparently made no attempt to send a party to rescue the wounded men. Instead, after a few minutes, an officer shouted for the Americans to fall back. The main enemy body did not arrive for two hours. Dunn was captured and remained a prisoner for thirty-eight months in North Korea. Major Seegars apparently died that night.[6]

By 5 p.m. July 7 the 34th's 3rd Battalion, on orders of the new regimental commander, Colonel Martin, was in position in a defensive arc north and west of Chonan. North Koreans began to infiltrate the town shortly before midnight, and sometime before daybreak five or six T34s entered the town and opened fire on all vehicles they saw and any buildings the crews thought might house Americans. In the street fighting that followed, Colonel Martin met his death at about 8 a.m. July 8 when he fired a bazooka rocket at a tank the instant the tank fired at him. Martin posthumously became the first soldier in Korea to receive the Distinguished Service Cross.

The North Korean troops and tanks caused havoc in Chonan, and only a continuous screen of white phosphorous shells, laid down by the 63rd Field Artillery Battalion, arrived only the night before, provided a shield for some of the 3rd Battalion to escape from the town. Only 175 men got out; two-thirds of the battalion was killed or surrendered. The battalion commander, physically exhausted, was evacuated a day or two later.

CHAPTER 12

One Bonanza, Several Defeats

N OW THE ONLY LINE at which the North Koreans might be stopped
was the Kum river, a major stream running more or less west across
southwestern Korea. At its closest point it was about twenty-five miles
south of Chonan, and it formed a potential barrier before the important
communications center of Taejon, about forty airline miles southeast of
Chonan. (See Map 1.)

Defense of the Kum river line was complicated, not only because
South Korea extends to the west at Chonan, permitting a wide flanking
movement, but because two routes to Taejon cross the Kum river, and
this required the greatly outnumbered American forces to defend both
crossings.

The main road between Chonan and Taejon followed the railway
southeast through Chochiwon, while the other road branched off a few
miles below Chonan and ran almost due south to the Kum river at
Kongju, where it turned southeast to Taejon.

At this time, Lieutenant General Walton H. Walker, commander of the
Eighth Army, until then Japan's garrison command, flew into Taejon and
told General Dean he soon would have more support: Eighth Army
headquarters itself was moving to Korea, along with additional combat
forces. Meantime, General Walker emphasized, Dean had to make do
with his 24th Division, still struggling unit by unit to the front.

Dean had to divide his tiny force immediately. He ordered the 21st
Infantry Regiment, Task Force Smith's parent outfit, now coming up, to
delay the North Koreans down the southeastward (Chochiwon) road to
Taejon, and he laid on the battered and dispirited 34th Regiment the
same task on the southern (Konju) road.[1]

Fortunately, some American artillery units were arriving, including
some 155mm howitzers, greatly increasing firepower. A combat

68

engineer battalion (the 3rd) also arrived, and was immediately set to work preparing roadblocks on both roads to the Kum river. So far, the only U.S. tanks to get to the front were a few M24 light Chaffees, with 75mm guns but without the gun velocity or the armament of the T34. Fortunately, the weather cleared, permitting air force strikes against the enemy tanks and North Korean troop movements.

The air force had been smarting under severe criticism for its mistaken attacks on ROK and American forces in the first days of the war. To solve the problem it quickly set up tactical air-control parties, each having an experienced pilot, a radio operator and a radio repair man and jeep driver. These parties moved up close to the front and directed air strikes right on to the targets. The air force sent six of these tac-air parties to the 24th Division, and on July 3 it set up a joint operations center at Itazuke, on Kyushu, to control all fighter planes operating over Korea—air force, navy, marine and Australian. Finally, the air force began sending up "mosquitoes," slow T-6 trainer aircraft, to locate targets behind enemy lines and direct air strikes. These mosquitoes had radio contact both with the fighters and with frontline ground troops.[2]

The system paid off on July 9. In midafternoon men of the 1st Battalion of the 21st Regiment were at a forward blocking position they had set up on the Chochiwon road at Chonui, twelve miles south of Chonan. Observers spotted eleven tanks and several hundred infantry in front of them. They called for an air strike, and it roared in a few minutes later, setting fire to five of the tanks and several trucks. Meanwhile U.S. fighters and fighter-bombers ravaged the road between Pyongtaek and Chonui: at dusk aerial observers reported that, of 200 vehicles spotted on the road that day, 100 were destroyed or burning.

But the next day brought one of the great moments for air power in the Korean War: late in the afternoon, a flight of F-80 jet fighters dropped through an overcast at Pyongtaek and discovered a large convoy of tanks and vehicles stopped bumper to bumper on the north side of the bridge destroyed July 6 by the retreating troops of the 34th Regiment. It was an incredible bonanza. Fifth Air Force quickly launched every combat plane that would fly straight at the stalled column—B-26 light bombers, F-80s and twin-Mustang F-82s. Observers reported the strikes destroyed 38 tanks, 7 half-tracks and 117 trucks, plus a large number of soldiers. Doubtless the figures were exaggerated. But this strike, and that at Chonui the day before, probably resulted in the greatest destruction of North Korean armor in the war.

More important, the invincibility of the T34 vanished that day. American ordnance supply still had not got many antitank shells, antitank mines, tanks or big bazookas into the war, but the United States' command of the air changed the balance. Even if fast-flying aircraft, especially jets, found tanks, they could not always hit single tanks or vehicles with their five-inch rockets, 110-gallon napalm tanks, or bombs. Moreover, tanks could still move at night with impunity against air attacks. But no longer could the North Koreans line up T34s in long columns on the narrow roads and move south, with nothing to stop them. The North Koreans were smart, and they were resourceful: they quickly camouflaged their tanks and other vehicles, and they started running their convoys at night, holing up trains in tunnels and dispersing tanks and trucks under cover during the day. But a new element had been laid on the scales: the immense strength of U.S. air power. Except in extreme circumstances, the North Koreans no longer dared to move tank columns or convoys on the days planes could fly. The power and efficiency of the North Korean army suffered a startling drop.

Air power alone was not going to stop the swift enemy advance, however. Troops on the ground had to do that. Next to take on the task were the just-arrived, untried troops of the 21st Regiment. It also had only two battalions, and it was even weaker when it emplaced at Chonui because two companies of its 1st Battalion had constituted the infantry of Task Force Smith. At the moment, survivors of the task force were getting new equipment, and the units were getting replacements at Chochiwon; they would not rejoin the 21st Regiment until July 11.

At daybreak on the morning of July 10, the day after the successful air strike against tanks at Chonui, a heavy ground fog billowed up from the rice paddies toward American troops emplaced on hills on both sides of the road and railway leading south out of Chonui. Through the fog Americans heard Korean voices, and fifteen minutes later a whistle blew, followed by firing. Nervous 21st Regiment troops began shooting blindly into the fog until Colonel Richard W. Stephens, commanding the 21st, stopped them. Then enemy mortar fire began landing on the ridge, and shortly afterward Lieutenant Ray Bixler's platoon of Company A on the left of the ridge came under heavy NK attack from higher ground beyond it. U.S. 4.2.-inch mortar fire kept the North Koreans from advancing directly on the ridge. Instead, they passed around the right flank of the battalion and attacked the heavy mortars located on lower ground behind the ridge. About the same time, tanks came through Chonui on the highway and passed through the battalion's hill positions on either side and joined the attack on the mortars. The Americans could hear the tanks but couldn't see to fire because of the fog. At 8 a.m. the fog lifted, and Colonel Stephens saw four additional T34s in the village. He called for an air strike. Meantime, the mortars fell silent.

At 9 a.m. North Korean infantry coming directly out of Chonui assaulted the center of the American ridgeline positions. An artillery forward observer (FO) called down shellfire on them and drove them back. T34s in Chonui now moved out of the village and began spraying the Americans with machine-gun fire. At 11 a.m. Lieutenant Bixler's platoon on the left came under intense small-arms fire and sustained a direct assault by NK infantry. Bixler radioed Stephens he had had many casualties and needed more men and asked permission to withdraw. Stephens said relief was on the way: it came five minutes later in the form of two American jets. They rocketed the tanks without visible effect and then strafed the NK infantry moving up on Bixler's positions. Shortly afterward the jets, their ammunition expended, departed—and the North Koreans resumed the attack. Tank fire had destroyed wire communication to the artillery, and now the FO's radio stopped working. U.S. artillery shells began landing on the ridge, apparently because the artillery fire-direction center thought the forward infantry positions had been overrun and they were firing on the North Koreans. Colonel Stephens ran to the radio on his jeep behind the foxholes and sent an order to stop the artillery fire. But it kept falling heavily. Three minutes later Bixler reported that the enemy had surrounded him and most of his men were casualties. It was his last report. Most of Bixler's men died in their foxholes.

Meantime, some American troops on the right end of the ridge already had run off, and about the time Bixler's platoon was overrun others began bugging out. Colonel Stephens called to noncoms to "get those high-priced soldiers back into position," but nothing stopped the panic: only a few men remained on the right.

Shortly after noon, Stephens realized that the men still on the ridge would have to retreat if they were to escape with their lives. He gave the signal and the men ran down the ridgeline and across open ground to an orchard and rice paddies beyond. There they found that trying to get across flooded rice paddies on the narrow, slippery dikes and paths was extremely difficult, especially as two American jets swooped down and strafed them, thinking they were North Koreans. The Americans flung themselves into the paddies and were not hit, but no one came out of the experience with any kind words for the air force.

The 1st Battalion had lost one-fifth of the men engaged in the short battle: 33 killed and 35 wounded, while the Heavy Mortar Company had lost 14 men.

Colonel Stephens ordered the 3rd Battalion, in reserve behind the 1st, to counterattack the North Koreans. The attack went in hard and regained the ridge, except for Bixler's position, which the North Koreans defended fiercely. In the process, the 3rd Battalion rescued ten men who had not tried to withdraw under the shellfire.

The 3rd Battalion uncovered the first known North Korean mass atrocity against American captives. The bodies of six Americans with the Heavy Mortar Company were found with hands tied behind their backs and shot through the back of the head.

Several M24 Chaffee light tanks assisted in the 3rd Battalion's attack, the first use of U.S. armor in the war. One M24 got in a first shot against a T34 tank and disabled it. But two M24s were lost.

Just before midnight the 3rd Battalion's CO, Lieutenant Colonel Carl C. Jensen, withdrew the battalion from the captured ridgeline and moved back to the battalion's former reserve position. There the men had a surprise: North Koreans had infiltrated and were in the old foxholes. It took an hour of battle in the darkness to drive the NK troops away. Meantime the 1st Battalion had moved down the road to new blocking positions two miles north of Chochiwon.

At 6:30 a.m. next day (July 11), men in the 3rd Battalion heard, but because of the fog could not see, tanks to their front on the other side of a mine field that U.S. troops had previously laid down. Within minutes four T34s crossed the minefield and materialized in the battalion area. Either North Korean troops had lifted the mines in the night, the tanks had missed them, or the mines were improperly armed or duds.

At the same time, a heavy concentration of enemy mortar fire fell on the battalion CP, blowing up the communications center and the ammunition point and causing heavy casualties. About a thousand NK infantry quickly came around both flanks of the battalion position, while other enemy troops established blocks on the road south, preventing evacuation of the wounded or resupply of ammunition.

It was an almost perfect double envelopment. The North Koreans who had been driven from the positions the night before must have provided detailed information about the 3rd Battalion's dispositions, because the first enemy rounds destroyed communications and disorganized the battalion. The Americans fought hard, sometimes in desperate hand-to-hand encounters, before they were overrun. The toll was heavy: more than half the 667 men in the battalion were lost, including the commanding officer, Colonel Jensen, and those who survived often had to walk for days across hills and through enemy-occupied areas to get back. Some men were so tired and dispirited they refused to go on, and simply stopped and waited for the North Koreans to arrive.

The 1st Battalion of the 21st Regiment under Colonel Smith rested nervously that night in their blocking positions on both sides of the road and railway two miles north of Chochiwon: they knew the North

Koreans were coming. At dawn (July 12) a North Korean patrol approached, and Americans saw movements on their flanks. At 9:30 a.m. an estimated NK battalion attacked the 1st Battalion's left flank and quickly afterward a general attack developed by an estimated 2,000 enemy, supported by artillery fire. Colonel Stephens decided the understrength battalion, with a large percentage of replacements, would have to withdraw. Colonel Smith disengaged the battalion one company at a time, moving the men to trucks. The North Koreans did not try to pursue closely, and the retreat was orderly. By nightfall, the 21st Regiment was across the Kum river in another blocking position at Taepyong-ni. In the words of Roy Appleman, the official army historian of this part of the war, "The understrength two-battalion 21st Infantry Regiment had delayed two of the best North Korean divisions [3rd and 4th] for three days. It was the most impressive performance yet of American troops in Korea, but the regiment paid heavily for it in loss of personnel and equipment."

On the westerly Kongju road south of Chonan, the 34th Regiment with four M24 tanks and a company of engineers fought a series of minor delaying actions against leading elements of the 4th North Korean Division, which had turned away from the Chochiwon road. On July 11, enemy artillery destroyed two of the M24s and a close-in infantry ambush destroyed a third. On July 12, most of the 34th and supporting troops crossed the Kum, leaving a company to hold the bridge and north bank.

While the Americans had been retreating down the Seoul-Taejon road for a week, finally coming to rest at the Kum river, the remaining ROK army units had withdrawn across the rest of Korea to about the same distance south.[3] (Map 1.) By July 13, remnants of the Capital, 1st and 2nd Divisions faced the 2nd NK Division at Chongju, twelve miles east of Chochiwon. It had been a hard fight for the 2nd NK Division after it moved westward upon the capture of Chinchon. The ROK Capital Division and South Korean police had ambushed a battalion at Chunchon on July 9, and fought a hard three-day battle that ended only after the ROKs were outflanked by the American withdrawal from Chonan and Chonui. Tired and drained by casualties, the 2nd NK Division was forced on to Chongju by its commander. North of the town, on July 11, ROK artillery caught the division in the open and inflicted several hundred casualties. The ROKs only evacuated Chongju after the Americans lost Chochiwon.

Eastward, the 7th NK Division moved down the central Korean corridor after the Chunchon battle to Hongchon and on to Wonju, with the ROK 6th Division retiring slowly in front of it. After the fall of Wonju on July 5, the North Korean high command relieved the division commander because he was behind schedule on the advance. It redesignated the 7th as the 12th Division, and activated a new 7th Division.

The 15th NK Division, which got most of its troops only after the war had started, followed the 7th NK Division to Wonju and, veering southwest, by July 13 was at Koesan, twenty airline miles northeast of Chongju and on a road leading to Mungyong, twenty miles southeast. Behind this division also came the 13th NK Division, the last North Korean unit mobilized for the invasion and only just getting troops as the war opened.

The 1st NK Division, which had participated in the battle for Seoul, moved southeastward to aid the 7th NK Division in trying to displace ROKs from the central corridor. At Chungju, this NK division, supported by a tank regiment, turned south and pressed the ROK 6th Division to Mungyong. This was an important point, because it is one of two passes over a high spur range of mountains running southwest for sixty miles from the north-south Taebaek along the east coast of Korea. The other pass over this range is approached at Tanyang, about twenty airline miles northeast of Mungyong. At Tanyang, the 12th NK Division, moving south from Wonju, was blocked by the ROK 8th Division, which had climbed over the Taebaek range from the east coast. The previously unengaged 8th NK Division also moved up to support the 12th NK Division. The spur range of mountains separates the valley of the Han river (running past Seoul) and the valley of the Naktong river (emptying into the Korea Strait at Pusan). Thus blocking the North Koreans along this range was extremely important; otherwise, North Korean troops could debouch into the Naktong valley and drive to Taegu, sixty-five airline miles southeast of Mungyong, in the rear of the ROK and American forces. Taegu was a critical rail and road center. To lose it meant to lose the only reasonable place around which a perimeter defense could be built to protect the port of Pusan, sixty airline miles south of Taegu. Holding the spur range also was important for a second reason: a pass at Andong on the far side of the upper Naktong valley opened a path to the east coast port of Yongdok and a route from there south by way of Pohang-dong to Pusan.

The 5th NK Division and the brigade-sized 766th Independent Unit meanwhile were pressing almost unopposed down the highway on the narrow mountain-edged east coast. On July 13 they had reached Pyonghae-ri, twenty-five miles north of Yongdok.

Although American attention naturally was concentrated on the Kum river line against two NK divisions (the 3rd and 4th), the bulk of the NK forces (six divisions) were poised to the east for a potentially massive attack across the upper Naktong valley, aimed either at Taegu or, by a long sweeping end run, directly at Pusan. A seventh NK division (the 2nd) was at Chongju, where it could participate in a converging attack, either on the Americans defending the Kum river or toward Taegu to support an attack in that direction.

Fortunately for the South Koreans and Americans, the NK strategy on the central front was extremely direct. Although the North Koreans initially had great superiority of strength and weapons, they continued to press their foes in a great, general movement on all central corridors available, a strategy that locked the Americans and ROKs in a tight combat grip, but drove them steadily back on their supply points and concentrated the resistance they could give.

CHAPTER 13

The Kum River

HOWEVER PREDICTABLE, the North Korean blow against the Americans on the Kum river was devastating. When the assault began on July 14, American forces had been in Korea only two weeks, and in ground combat for only ten days. In that period Americans' attitudes had changed from easy overconfidence to thorough alarm. But the Kum river attack created a new anxiety: that the few U.S. forces so far landed just might not be able to contain the North Koreans and that they might overrun the peninsula. At the Kum river, the race against time by both sides was a dead heat.

Meantime, MacArthur and the Joint Chiefs of Staff had made a major commitment to Korea: on July 12 Eighth Army formally moved its headquarters from Japan to a large school compound (formerly a Japanese army station) in Taegu, and the next day Lieutenant General Walton H. Walker, Eighth Army commander, arrived at Taegu to assume command. The day after (July 14), South Korean President Rhee placed the ROK army under MacArthur as United Nations commander, and MacArthur deputized Walker as field commander of all UN forces in Korea.[1]

Korea no longer was a sideshow: it became the main event, both in the Far East Command and for the United States military as a whole. An emergency airlift of critically needed equipment and men began between the United States and the Far East. The Military Air Transport Service (MATS) quadrupled, with the help of a Canadian squadron of six transports and several from Belgium, from 60 four-engine carriers to 250. West coast ports began to be stacked up with equipment of all kinds hastily requisitioned for Korea, and every available ship was thrown into service. MacArthur and the Joint Chiefs got into detailed and sometimes heated discussions via intercontinental teletype over the amount and

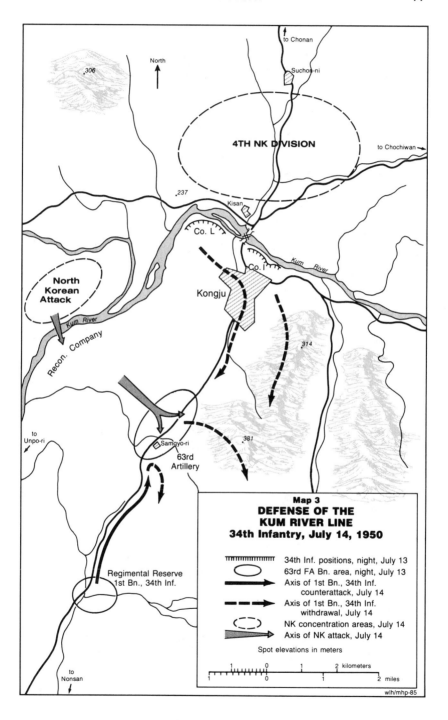

to Chonan

North

Suchon-ni

.306

4TH NK DIVISION

to Chochiwan →

.237

Kisan

Co. L

Kum River

Co. I

North Korean Attack

Kongju

Kum River

Recon. Company

314

to Unpo-ri

Samgyo-ri

.381

63rd Artillery

Regimental Reserve 1st Bn., 34th Inf.

Map 3
DEFENSE OF THE
KUM RIVER LINE
34th Infantry, July 14, 1950

⊤⊤⊤⊤⊤⊤⊤⊤⊤⊤⊤⊤⊤⊤⊤ 34th Inf. positions, night, July 13

◯ 63rd FA Bn. area, night, July 13

➤ Axis of 1st Bn., 34th Inf. counterattack, July 14

➤ Axis of 1st Bn., 34th Inf. withdrawal, July 14

NK concentration areas, July 14

➤ Axis of NK attack, July 14

Spot elevations in meters

1   0   1   2 kilometers

1   0   1   2 miles

to Nonsan

wlh/mhp-85

kinds of reinforcements needed in light of the astonishing North Korean successes. The great U.S. buildup was under way.

But along the Kum river, the United States on July 13 had been able to assemble just one understrength division to oppose the NK advance. On this battered 24th Division and its 11,400 men hung the hope that the UN line would not be blown open.[2] It was a slender reed, because the division's three infantry regiments were all, in differing ways, debilitated. The 19th Regiment had the most men (2,276), but it had to be flung immediately into direct defense of the river line with no time for adaptation. The 34th Regiment had 2,000 men, but it had been badly handled north of the Kum the week before and was shaky. The 21st Regiment had performed relatively well in its attempts to block the North Korean advance, but its very success had eroded its strength terribly. The regiment was down to 1,100 men (the 3rd Battalion, overrun by NK forces, had only 132 men and was reformed into two understrength companies).

Against the 24th Division, the North Koreans had committed their 3rd and 4th Divisions, which also were greatly worn down by three weeks of combat to about 70 percent of their strength (about 6,000 men each). They had about fifty tanks left by the time they reached the Kum, twenty with the 4th NK Division and about thirty with the 3rd. But the North Koreans had the initiative and, in case of need, they could also call on the 2nd NK Division at Chongju a few miles east.

The 24th Division's commander, General Dean, had emplaced the 34th Regiment at Kongju on one of the two roads leading to Taejon, and the 19th Regiment at Taepyong-ni (-ni and -ri mean "village" in Korean), eight air miles east of Kongju and upstream on the Kum. But the 19th was forced to be responsible for the entire river front on up to the Seoul-Pusan railroad bridge nine air miles farther eastward upstream at Sinchon. Moreover, in moving to the river, the 19th Regiment passed the troops of the 21st Regiment retreating from Chochiwon. To the green and impressionable men of the 19th, the 21st troops seemed in bad shape and this caused confidence to plummet.

Dean had placed the 21st Regiment in reserve blocking position at Okchon, on the main Seoul-Pusan highway six miles east of Taejon (twelve air miles southeast of Taepyong-ni). The 21st's mission was to keep open the vital highway and rail line and also to stand in the way if the North Koreans decided to commit the 2nd NK Division in an attempt to break through the ROKs in the east and sweep behind American lines.

On the night and morning of July 12–13, engineers dynamited sections in the highway bridges over the Kum river at Kongju and at Taepyong-ni and the railway bridge at Sinchon. Reconnaissance troops burned all the ferryboats they could find along the river.

At Kongju, the 34th Regiment's newly appointed commander, Lieutenant Colonel Robert L. Wadlington, had emplaced two 3rd Battalion companies (L and I) at the river on high ground on the left and right sides of the road, with some mortars behind. (See Map 3.) The regiment's Company K, a composite group of forty men, originally had been placed in line, but their mental and physical condition made them liabilities, and the company was withdrawn and sent to Taejon for medical disposition. About the same time the regiment's S-2 (intelligence) and S-3 (operations) officers were evacuated because of combat fatigue.[3]

Supporting the two infantry companies was the 63rd Field Artillery Battalion (105mm howitzers), emplaced at a hamlet (Samgyo-ri) about two and a half miles south of the river. And three miles farther south down the same dirt-track road was the regiment's reserve, the 1st Battalion.

Within the front-line 3rd Battalion units at Kongju communications were virtually nonexistent, primarily because live batteries for the battalion's SCR-300 and SCR-536 radios were not available and telephone wire could not be found. Equally astonishing, the 63rd Artillery had communication with the regimental CP at Nonsan, eighteen miles south of Kongju, but none with the infantry units or the artillery forward observers with them on the river line. This effectively eliminated the possibility of directed artillery fire on any North Koreans assaulting the infantry positions.

The action started shortly after daybreak on July 13. Soldiers of the 4th NK Division walked to the north side of the blown Kum river bridge, seven hundred yards opposite the American positions, and set up machine guns and moved tanks. That afternoon, NK guns began shelling Kongju and vicinity. Early the next morning the U.S. troops heard tanks in the village across the river from Kongju, and soon thereafter flat-trajectory weapons, presumably the T34 guns, started firing into Company I's area. At the same time, airbursts (probably from enemy howitzers farther back) exploded over Company L, but were too high to do damage.

Then Company L lookouts sent word back to the company commander, Lieutenant Archie L. Stith, that North Korean soldiers were crossing the river about two miles downstream on two barges, each holding about 30 men. The lookouts estimated about 500 North Koreans crossed in this way in the hour and a half before 9:30 a.m. With no communication with the 63rd Artillery, the infantry could not call for artillery concentrations. However, during the morning the artillery battalion sent aloft a liaison plane for aerial observation, and the observer spotted the North Korean crossings. But the artillery battalion S-3 decided not to fire on the barges but to wait for larger targets. One section of 155mm howitzers with the 11th Field Artillery Battalion, emplaced farther east, did respond to the liaison's plane's call, but Yak fighter planes soon drove the liaison craft away, and the artillery fire ceased.

Company L's commander, Lieutenant Stith, had been unable to find the machine-gun and mortar sections supporting his company, and his men were coming under increasingly accurate enemy mortar and artillery fire. Stith decided his position was untenable, and ordered Company L to withdraw. The company vacated its positions shortly before 11 a.m. Lieutenant Stith went in search of the 3rd Battalion headquarters; when he told the battalion commander what had happened, he was immediately relieved of his command.

Meanwhile the damage had been done: the entire left flank of the 34th Regiment's position had been abandoned, opening up a huge hole for the North Koreans. They promptly drove into it.

About 1:30 p.m. an outpost guarding the artillery battalion at Samgyo-ri saw troops moving toward it. The outpost had been instructed to hold fire unless fired upon, as the men might be friendly troops. The result: the North Koreans overran the outpost and turned the captured machine gun there on the artillery headquarters. Shortly afterward, supported by accurate mortar fire which destroyed men, howitzers and equipment, North Korean troops overran the artillery headquarters and both firing batteries. The battalion lost all ten howitzers plus 11 officers and 125 men.

The 34th Regiment's CO, Colonel Wadlington, learned about the destruction of the artillery battalion between 3 and 4 p.m. and immediately ordered a counterattack by the 1st Battalion, in reserve three miles south. The 1st Battalion's CO said this was the first word he had received about the attack, although a communications officer of the artillery battalion reported he had gone to the 1st Battalion CP at about 2 p.m. and reported the attack. The 1st Battalion CO said this might have occurred while he was absent, and no one on his staff had told him.[4]

It took 1st Battalion until about 5 p.m. to move northward in a column of companies. It advanced without incident until the lead company approached the overrun artillery position. There a few bursts of enemy machine-gun and rifle fire halted the company. The regimental CO's orders had been to retire if the battalion's mission was not accomplished by dark. As dusk was at hand, the battalion CO ordered the battalion to withdraw. Back at the starting position, the battalion loaded on trucks and drove south toward Nonsan.

Meanwhile, Company I had remained all day under intermittent shelling in its positions on the Kum river, although Company L to its left long since had withdrawn. The company commander, Lieutenant Joseph E. Hicks, tried to reach Company L and battalion headquarters, but failed; he stayed in position until 9:30 p.m., when he moved back on orders through the mountains southeast of Kongju and rejoined the regiment.

CHAPTER 14

Taepyong-ni

JULY 14 HAD BEEN a disaster for American arms and an especial disaster for the 34th Regiment. In a single day the North Koreans had breached the Kum river line and dispatched the 34th Regiment, which had withdrawn completely out of the fight. The disappearance of the 34th Regiment left the 19th Regiment on the right with its flank wide open.

Everything now was up to the 19th, which faced an assault by the 3rd NK Division: an untried regiment in an untenable position.

The 19th's trial by fire started on the afternoon of July 14 when NK tanks and self-propelled guns moved in across the river from Taepyong-ni and started shelling American positions.[1] The regiment's tactical dispositions were a virtual guarantee of catastrophe. But given the almost thirty miles of river frontage the two-battalion regiment was called upon to defend, there is perhaps little that could have been done to improve them. (See Map 4.)

The regiment had one company (E) blocking the railway crossing on the east at Sinchon. Between this company and the main defense position around Taepyong-ni there was a two-mile gap that was entirely undefended. Along the river at Taepyong-ni three companies were emplaced, C on the east of the northern slopes of Hill 200, A and a platoon of B along a river dike east and west of the village, and the rest of B on some high ground west of the highway leading south out of Taepyong-ni. The 1st Battalion's headquarters were a mile south of Taepyong-ni in the hamlet of Kadong-ni, near the mortar emplacements. The regimental CP was less than a mile farther south down the road at Palsan-ni. Behind the infantry were three battalions of artillery: the 52nd at Tuman-ni, two miles south of Palsan-ni, and the 13th and 11th about two miles south of the 52nd.

West of these positions, there was little protection. A few recon-naissance and detached units manned outposts along the river. But, with the retreat of the 34th Regiment the day before, there was nothing substantial to stop a flank attack. For this reason, the regimental CO, Colonel Guy S. Meloy, Jr., dispatched as a flank guard Lieutenant Colonel Thomas M. McGrail, 2nd Battalion commander, with Company G and some machine guns, two light M24 tanks, and two quad-mount .50-caliber machine-gun antiaircraft vehicles. McGrail's group moved about six air-line miles to the west (and many more by road). These men of Task Force McGrail constituted two-thirds of Colonel Meloy's entire reserve force. All that was left was Company F, emplaced behind Company B.

The 19th Regiment's primary weakness was quickly apparent: the main American emplacements could be flanked by crossing the river both east and west of the village—where there were no defending troops. This is precisely what the North Koreans did. On the afternoon and evening of July 15, they made probing attacks that were not pressed home from the end of the blown bridge at Taepyong-ni and in front of Company C. Tanks and artillery emplaced north of the river also shelled American positions sporadically. During the afternoon U.S. B-29 bombers dropped bombs on enemy positions north of the river, and at 7:45 p.m. two U.S. fighters came over. Eight NK tanks took cover in the woods, but one tank stayed on the road and was hit by the fighter. The tank burned for hours.

All during the night North Koreans made probing attacks after rafting the river and infiltrating U.S. positions. The real attack, however, came at 3 a.m., July 16. A North Korean plane flew over the Kum and dropped a flare. It was the signal for the general assault. Tank and artillery fire opened up from the north bank with an intensity as great as the heaviest bombardments in World War II. Under cover of this fire, the North Koreans launched boats or rafts to get across, or they waded or swam. American artillery, mortar and small-arms fire met the attack.

Forward observers for the American artillery and mortars needed illumination to direct accurate fire on the North Koreans surging across the river. One 155mm howitzer of the 11th Artillery had been designated to fire flares over the river position on call. At the most critical time of the NK crossing, the observer with the infantry called down to the gun for a slight shift of the flare area. Normally this would have taken only a minute or so. But the gunners misunderstood the request and laid the howitzer on a setting (azimuth) that required moving the heavy trails of the piece. The result was that no flares were fired for a considerable period. It was a bad error, because in the ensuing darkness many North Koreans safely reached the south shore of the river.

Company C, on the forward slopes of Hill 200, was targeted now for a major assault. Just before 4 a.m. Lieutenant Henry T. McGill, commanding Company C, phoned Lieutenant Thomas A. Maher, 1st Platoon leader, and asked how he was doing. "We're doing fine," Maher replied. "We eat this stuff up." Thirty seconds later Maher was dead with a burp-gun bullet in his head. The North Koreans overran the 1st Platoon and only a dozen men got away. McGill consolidated the remainder of Company C on a finger just west of the one that had been occupied by the 1st Platoon—and waited for daylight to see what was happening. The company quickly found out: at dawn four NK machine guns opened up on the company and NK 82mm and 120mm mortars began pounding the positions.

Counterfire from big American 4.2-inch mortars was controlled by the Heavy Mortar Company CO from the regimental CP. The purpose was to direct fire only on the most lucrative targets. Lieutenant Joseph M. Ebbs, commanding a platoon of 4.2s, objected because it took too long to get the rounds off. One forward observer, waiting for shells to land on a target he had called in, observed: "If you don't get some rounds out soon, you'll have to fire to the rear because they'll be on your ass."

Enemy forces got across in strength in the gap on the right flank of the 19th's line, circling around to the east of Company C on Hill 200 and heading south, infiltrating the rear and attacking three 4.2-inch mortars emplaced a few hundred yards south of Hill 200. The mortarmen left the scene. A larger force crossed into the undefended stretch of the river to the left (west) of the Company B positions. By daybreak, men of Company B on the hill west of Taepyong-ni saw several hundred North Koreans on high ground south and west of them, already safely over the river and moving around to the rear of the American positions. At the same time other North Koreans crossed from the partially destroyed highway bridge at Taepyong-ni by swimming and wading and advanced at early light straight through the village on the heavy-mortar emplacements and the battalion headquarters south of it. On the way, North Koreans overran parts of Companies A and B, in place along the river dike, and kept right on going, screaming and firing their burp guns, in a dramatic advance that seized the high ground at the 1st Battalion command post at Kadong-ni.

The attempted coup de main not only held the 19th Regiment by the throat while North Korean units enveloped it on both flanks, but it threatened the entire 19th Regiment line: it penetrated right into the center of the regimental position. The regimental command post lay less

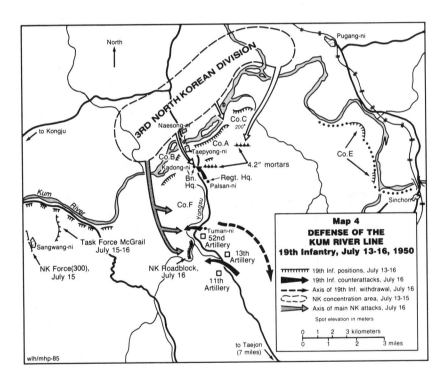

North

to Kongju

3RD NORTH KOREAN DIVISION

Pugang-ni

Naesong-ni

Co.C
200*

Co.A
Taepyong-ni

Co.B
Kadong-ni

4.2" mortars

Co.E

Bn.
Hq.

Regt. Hq.
Palsan-ni

Kum River

Yongsu

Co.F

Sinchon

Tuman-ni
52nd
Artillery

Task Force McGrail
July 15-16

Sangwang-ni

13th
Artillery

NK Force(300),
July 15

NK Roadblock,
July 16

11th
Artillery

to Taejon
(7 miles)

Map 4
DEFENSE OF THE
KUM RIVER LINE
19th Infantry, July 13-16, 1950

〰〰〰〰 19th Inf. positions, July 13-16
�▸ 19th Inf. counterattacks, July 16
▪ ▪ ▪ ▶ Axis of 19th Inf. withdrawal, July 16
⌐ ⌐ ⌐ NK concentration area, July 13-15
▷ Axis of main NK attacks, July 16

Spot elevation in meters

0   1   2   3 kilometers
0   1   2   3 miles

wlh/mhp-85

than a mile farther south.

The 19th CO, Meloy, and the 1st Battalion CO, Lieutenant Colonel Otho T. Winstead, immediately organized a counterattack, using every possible man available in the two headquarters—cooks, drivers, mechanics, clerks and the security platoon. The counterattack drove the North Koreans back around 9 a.m. and regained the high ground at Kadong-ni. Major John M. Cook, the battalion executive officer, and Captain Alan Hackett, battalion personnel officer (S-1), led the counterattack. Shortly after the Americans recovered the hill, North Koreans set up machine guns and killed Cook and Hackett.

Companies A and B had largely been dislodged by a North Korean assault all along the front at Taepyong-ni in support of the attempted coup de main. But some Americans were pinned down in their positions on the river dike. About 8 a.m. a platoon of Company B on the dike west of the village was heavily engaged by North Koreans. The platoon commander, Lieutenant William B. Hotchkiss, was killed. Seeing the disarray from Company B's other positions on the hill to the southwest, Lieutenant John H. English, Weapons Platoon leader, rushed forward, swam the small Yongsu river, and led fourteen men out of danger.

Although the counterattack from battalion and regimental head-quarters raised cheers by the Americans, it was only a temporary success, because the enemy troops that had crossed on the unguarded left had moved behind the regimental position and set up positions on high ground above the highway south of the 52nd Artillery's emplacements. From there, NK fire blocked all movement up and down the road. The roadblock was first spotted by a second lieutenant, Robert E. Nash, as he was coming up the road with a resupply of ammunition. He telephoned the news to Colonel Meloy, who gave Nash a mission, and Meloy himself started down to the roadblock with Major Edward I. Logan, regimental S-3.

Meanwhile, a force of North Koreans had assaulted a battery of the 52nd Artillery. It was halted only after the gunners turned their 105mm howitzers in direct fire on the enemy and the battalion commander hastily improvised a counterattack using any man he could find.

When Meloy and Logan arrived at the north end of the roadblock, they found conditions decidedly unsatisfactory. American soldiers were firing in the general direction of the unseen enemy roadblock, but doing little else. Colonel Meloy, while trying to organize a group to attack the North Koreans, was wounded in the calf, and he gave to 1st Battalion CO Colonel Winstead command of all troops along the Kum river.

Major Logan got through by radio to General Dean about 1 p.m. and told him the regimental situation was bad. Dean told Logan he was improvising a relief force from the south, but the 19th should withdraw at once, getting out as much equipment and as many men as possible. Shortly thereafter, enemy fire destroyed the regimental radio truck, and that ended all communication with the division.

Colonel Winstead, arriving at the roadblock, ordered Major Logan to try to reduce it and establish contact with the relief force coming up. He returned to the troops moving back from the river, and on the way he met his death.

Company C, receiving no order to withdraw, had doggedly remained all morning in its positions on a finger ridge leading north from Hill 200, sustaining heavy machine-gun and mortar fire. Now it was alone and virtually surrounded. Shortly after noon, Sergeant Chester W. Van Orman returned to Company C from Company A's position, where he had gone to try to contact battalion headquarters. He found Companies A and B were withdrawing and battalion wanted Company C "to come along if possible."

Company C started off the hill about 12:30 p.m. with the wounded moving off first with two company officers and supply personnel. Lieutenants McGill and Augustus B. Orr, a platoon leader, had difficulty getting the men out of their foxholes because they were so terrified. Enemy fire was still coming in. McGill told Orr to lead the company out while McGill remained as rear guard to make certain all men got off the hill. Lieutenant McGill did not return and was presumed dead. Orr led a hundred survivors down toward the Kum river to the dike and walked on the north side—because the men were getting small-arms fire from the *south*, not from the north across the river. Halfway to Taepyong-ni, Orr turned his men south to cross rice paddies. There Orr saw a North Korean lying in a ditch, apparently dead, a grenade in his hand. Orr's steps washed water over the Korean's face, and Orr saw bubbles on the water. Puzzled, he kicked the body in the ribs. There was no reflex. Orr passed on. The man behind said, "Say, lieutenant, this man just opened his eyes." Orr turned quickly and shot the Korean with his carbine—then shot six more suspiciously dead North Koreans in the ditch. Orr led his men to a pass that would lead over to Palsan-ni and south; there the company took mortar rounds. The men tried to circle around to the east, but caught enemy fire there as well. Orr decided the lesser of two evils was to press on through the pass to Palsan-ni. As the badgered company moved, at least six enemy machine guns opened up from hills on both sides of the pass. The company somehow got through and into the village. There machine-gun fire hit Orr in the side and arm. The lieutenant was knocked down and dazed, and the men of Company C scattered. Some medical personnel still in the village bandaged Orr, but he remained there trying to recover his wits.

As elements of the regiment came up to the roadblock, various efforts were made to organize assaults, all with no success. Men crowded the roadside ditches seeking shelter from the enemy fire. U.S. fighter planes arrived and strafed the North Korean positions, but were unable to halt the fire of three or four machine guns.

All during this period an incredible task was being undertaken by Lieutenant Nash in response to Colonel Meloy's orders. Meloy, believing the roadblock spelled the destruction of his regiment unless it was broken, had told Nash to go back, find Colonel McGrail and the tiny task force guarding the left flank and get McGrail to move up from below the roadblock to crack the road open.

Lieutenant Nash boldly drove through the roadblock heading south. He was met by a curtain of fire. He saw machine-gun bullets hitting the road ahead. Then a bullet punctured a tire and the jeep ran off the road into a rice paddy. Nash, unhurt, took cover. Looking up, he saw a U.S. M24 tank trying to run the gauntlet, its turret turning to fire at the enemy machine guns. Suddenly a round from an antitank rifle hit the tank, setting it afire. All hatches opened and the crew spilled out. The bullet came from a 14.5mm Russian-made antitank rifle, an obsolete relic from before World War II. But on this day it worked.

Nash decided to go on foot. He reached the 13th Field Artillery Battalion south of the block, borrowed a jeep and drove to McGrail's position at Sangwang-ni, about nine air miles west, but many roundabout road miles. Nash explained the situation to Colonel McGrail, who responded, "Okay, fine. Where are the trucks for transporting the troops?"

Nash drove back to the Service Company of the regiment, but was told all the trucks were in Taejon airstrip drawing ammunition. Nash drove to the airstrip but could find no 19th Regiment vehicles. He did find some empty quartermaster trucks, but the quartermaster people would not release them. Lieutenant Nash was a persistent young man: he found the 24th Division's assistant commander, Brigadier General Person Menoher, and got the general to order the QM trucks to go immediately to pick up the task force foot soldiers. Meanwhile, McGrail's two M24 tanks and two quad-mount .50s started for the south end of the roadblock accompanied by McGrail.

Major Logan, at the north end of the roadblock, was getting nowhere. M24 tank commanders refused to move out to try to silence the NK machine guns. Logan himself led a group in a circle east to try to find a bypass that vehicles could use, but he could not. Logan, however, arrived at the 13th Artillery below the block shortly before General Dean arrived with a couple of M24s and some AAA weapons and Colonel McGrail appeared with his task force armor and AAA guns.

At this time five jeeps came racing toward them, led by Lieutenant Colonel Homer B. Chandler, 19th Regiment executive officer. Chandler's convoy, loaded with wounded, had dashed through the roadblock. During the wild ride every one of the wounded men had been hit again one or more times by enemy fire.

McGrail organized the assault of the relief force from the south. He placed one light tank in the lead, followed by four AAA vehicles loaded with soldiers and a second tank bringing up the rear. About a mile north of the 13th Artillery position, just after it rounded a bend, the relief force came under fire from heavy machine guns and light antitank guns. The force had reached to within 300 yards of the point on the north where the 19th Regiment men and vehicles were piled up. The American weapons returned fire while the infantry jumped into the roadside ditches. The North Koreans destroyed all four AAA vehicles and killed or wounded nine out of ten of the AAA gunners. The two M24 tanks shot off their ammunition, turned around, and headed back down the road. Colonel McGrail and most of the infantry crawled back along the roadside ditches and eventually got out of enemy fire.

The journey of the infantry of Task Force McGrail to help break the roadblock had strange turnings—hinged on suddenly rampant rumors of a breakthrough of North Korean tanks. The infantry was led by Captain Michael Barszcz, CO of Company G. When the riflemen arrived on trucks about seven miles south of the roadblock, General Menoher intercepted them and ordered them deployed in defense along a stream because he feared T34s were approaching. They weren't.

Later, Captain Barszcz got orders to move up to the south end of the roadblock. On the way the company met a fast-moving small convoy of vehicles led by a 2½-ton truck with a military police officer riding on the front fender. The officer yelled "Tanks, tanks!" as he passed. Barszcz quickly ordered his driver to run the jeep across the road to block it and signaled for his troops to scramble off the vehicles into ditches. Barszcz and his men anxiously looked ahead for the expected armor. Nothing came. After a few minutes, Barszcz got his men up and they advanced on foot up the road. There they met General Dean, who told him to make contact with the enemy and try to break the roadblock.

Barszcz's company came under long-range enemy fire along the road slightly north of the 13th Artillery positions, though the gunners now had displaced south. He was told the North Koreans were on a dominating hill about half a mile north and west. Barszcz moved his infantry off the road and onto the hill, the men suffering several casualties in the process. At dusk, the unit got to the top of the ridge to the south of the North Koreans, and started digging in. A short while later, a runner reached Barszcz and told him to bring his men down to the road and withdraw: the effort to break the roadblock had ended.

It had been a long day for the survivors of the 19th Regiment's debacle on the Kum river, and not many had broken through the trap. Not all of the men arrived at or remained behind the roadblock; many at the block, seeing they could not get through, abandoned vehicles and heavy weapons and scattered into the hills, moving off singly or in small groups to south and east, toward Taejon. Other Americans avoided the road entirely and walked off through the hills trying to find safety. Lieutenant Orr of Company C, who had been wounded at Palsan-ni, meanwhile slowly recovered his reason and his strength. At nightfall he and a sergeant crept down to the little Yongsu river, which roughly paralleled the road south, and walked up the stream southward, picking up occasional stragglers as they went. By the time they got past the NK roadblock, walking in the stream bed, Orr had thirty men with him from various units. The group continued south and out of danger.

About 6 p.m. several staff officers at the roadblock decided they would use the last M24 tank they had to carry Colonel Meloy through to the south. It took the tank four tries before it could knock aside a pile of still-smoldering 2½-ton trucks and other equipment blocking the roadway. Then the M24 rumbled southward, followed by about twenty vehicles, including a truck towing a 105mm howitzer of the 52nd Artillery. They got through. Then the block closed again behind them.

The M24 stopped a few miles south of the block because of mechanical failure, but nobody was able to get any of the vehicles coming behind the tank to stop even long enough to pick up Colonel Meloy or go for help. They sped past the disabled tank, oblivious to it or deliberately ignoring it. It was left for Captain Barszcz and his infantry company, withdrawing on foot down the road, to discover the tank. Colonel Meloy ordered the tank destroyed with a thermite grenade, and eventually an officer returned with a commandeered truck and took Meloy and the other wounded men to safety.

About an hour after the tank had led the convoy through the block, Captain Edgar R. Fenstermacher, assistant regimental S-3, still on the north end of the block, ordered all remaining soldiers (about 500) to prepare for cross-country movement. He directed that the critically wounded and those unable to walk be placed on litters, which unwounded men were to carry as they marched to the south. Fenstermacher himself and some others then poured gasoline on the hundred vehicles at the roadblock and set them afire. During this operation Captain Fenstermacher was shot through the neck.

By 9 p.m. all of the men at the block had moved eastward into the hills. One group of about a hundred took with them about thirty wounded, including several litter cases. Forty men were detailed to serve as litter bearers, but many of these disappeared as they were making the climb up the first hill. At the top the men still remaining with the seriously wounded decided they could take them no farther. Chaplain Herman G. Felhoelter volunteered to remain behind with these wounded men. When he heard a party of North Koreans moving up on the stranded men, Felhoelter urged the medical officer, Captain Linton J. Buttrey, to escape. Through binoculars, First Sergeant James W. R. Haskins saw a group that appeared to be young North Koreans murder the wounded men and the brave chaplain as he prayed over them.

It had been a day of calamity for the 19th Regiment and the attached artillery. All night and into the next day (July 17) stragglers filtered into Yusong and Taejon. Of the 3,400 infantry and artillerymen engaged in the action, 650 were lost. The 1st Battalion was almost cut in half: 338 out of 785 men were dead, wounded or missing, and the battalion's Company C lost 134 men out of 189. The regimental headquarters suffered 57 casualties out of 191 men, and the 52nd Artillery 55 out of 393.

The collapse was caused, of course, by the North Korean roadblock. This had been made possible by a strong frontal attack that held down the U.S. troops on the river line while other troops completed a double envelopment on both flanks. The 19th had stopped all the frontal attacks, except the penetration of Company C on Hill 200 to the east. But with only a company in reserve, the regiment had failed to deal with the flank movements, especially the strong left-flank penetration into the rear that made possible the roadblock. Colonel Meloy felt the reason stemmed from the necessity of sending two-thirds of his reserve to guard the left regimental boundary after the retreat of the 34th Regiment at Kongju. Unfortunately, Meloy was unable to develop an alternate means of dealing with the emergency because he was wounded early in the day.

The remaining reserve unit, Company F, emplaced on the heights behind Company B, was positioned so it could have moved on the rear of the North Korean roadblock force. Although it was covering the Company B withdrawal, it could have attacked the roadblock later. Even if it had been unable to destroy the North Korean force, it might have interrupted the resupply of ammunition to it. In the event, no unit north of the roadblock, Company F or any other, made a sustained effort.

CHAPTER 15

Taejon

T HE KUM RIVER LINE was broken. The 3rd and 4th NK Divisions were across it, and the city of Taejon lay wide open. Taejon was an important road center, with five highways going into it. But with the Kum barrier gone, General Dean did not plan to hold it long. Then the Eighth Army commander, General Walker, flew into the Taejon airstrip on July 18 to talk with Dean, and everything changed.

Walker had a great problem: he had to find a line quickly that could be defended to stop the North Korean advance. For the previous twenty-four hours, Walker's chief of staff, Colonel Eugene M. Landrum, and his officers had been involved in a frantic appraisal of the American military position. Their recommendations led Walker to decide that the no-retreat position had to be the north-south line of the Naktong river and then east to Yongdok on the east coast. (See Map 1.) If the North Koreans penetrated over the Naktong as they had the Kum, the vital road and railway center of Taegu would be uncovered and lost and the Americans and ROKs would be forced back on Pusan—an untenable situation.

American reinforcements were just arriving in quantity, but they needed time to get into position and to set up a line on the Naktong. This meant the much-battered 24th Division, still the only force available on the battle line, had to delay the North Korean advance as long as possible.

That, effectively, is what Walker told Dean at their July 18 conference at the Taejon airstrip.[1] Hold for two days, Walker said. That would give him time to get the 1st Cavalry Division into position behind the 24th at Okchon and south of Taejon along the Kumsan road. The 1st Cav was unloading that day at the southeast coast port of Pohang-dong. With the 1st Cav in place south and east of Taejon, the Americans' retreat could be slowed. That was the plan. Dean nodded and changed his orders: Taejon would be defended.

It is rare in military history for one combat element to be thrown time after time into the breach to save a desperate situation with no relief and with virtually no time to draw a breath. Many a battle-tested force would have wilted under this sort of demand. The essentially unready and ill-equipped 24th Division, by the mere chance of its station in Japan, drew this unenviable assignment. And despite many profound failures, it did better than anyone might have expected. But by July 18, the 24th Division was very near the end of its strength. The 19th Regiment was combat ineffective after its first fight and had been withdrawn to re-equip at Yongdong, the division rear headquarters about thirty miles southeast of Taejon. The 21st Regiment was in no better condition after its battles north of the Kum river. Neither regiment could muster much more than a battalion of troops. That meant the primary defense of Taejon fell on the 34th Regiment, which Dean hastily called in from the vicinity of Nonsan to new defensive positions along the Kapchon river three miles west and northwest of Taejon. (See Map 5.) The 34th also had a new CO, Colonel Charles E. Beauchamp, just flown in from Japan for the job.

The division was extremely low on artillery, not only because each battalion had only two firing batteries, but because the 63rd Battalion had been overrun south of Kongju and the 52nd Battalion had been cut off near Taepyong-ni and had brought out only one 105mm howitzer. General Dean consolidated all of his 105mm howitzers into one composite battalion and emplaced it at the Taejon airstrip to defend the city and to back up the 34th Regiment. That composite unit, along with the 11th Battalion of 155mm howitzers, meant Dean had just two battalions of artillery to meet the assault of two NK divisions.

The 24th had no medium tanks to match the T34s. The U.S. Army's excellent M26s, mounting 90mm high-velocity guns, still were in the Pipeline on the way, as, indeed, were the old World War II standbys, the high-silhouette Sherman M4A3s, many now refitted with high-velocity 76mm guns. A number of the M4A3s had been renovated in army ordnance shops in Japan. There were pitifully few rounds of armor-piercing 105mm artillery shells (HEAT) anywhere in the Far East Command. Dean already had called for emergency deliveries. But so far few had arrived.[2]

The closest thing to an equalizer that the division had was the 3.5-inch rocket launcher which replaced the disappointing and now virtually discarded 2.36-inch bazookas.[3] The 3.5-inch "super bazooka" was something of a secret weapon. Its secret was not its increased caliber but its ammunition. The big bazooka fired a shaped charge—an explosive-filled cylinder with an inverted metal cone at the front end. Detonation drove the cone forward like a liquified-metal jet at velocities of 10,000 feet per second, greatly increasing the penetrating force. The shaped charge was designed to burn through the armor of any tank then known. The big bazooka had been under development since the end of World War II, but ordnance designers had experienced great difficulty in perfecting the ammunition. It had been standardized and in production for only fifteen days when the war started. General MacArthur asked for the new weapon on July 3 and on July 8 the first shipment, plus an instruction team, left Travis Air Force Base in California. On July 10 the team arrived at Taejon, and two days later the first weapons. The team started immediately to train selected soldiers in use of the rocket and the aluminum launcher, which closely resembled a five-foot stovepipe.[4] When the T34s attacked at Taejon, these hastily trained teams were more or less ready.

The division's tactical problem was that its entire left flank was floating in the air, with essentially no American or ROK troops on that wing. Nor were Walker and Dean sure that the ROKs on the right could defend in case the 2nd NK Division decided to move on Taejon from Chongju. The North Koreans' now-familiar double-flanking envelopment could be expected, the danger being that the enemy could get around to the rear of the American positions. As a precaution, Dean had placed the 21st Regiment about six miles east of Taejon on the vital Seoul-Pusan road and railway leading to Okchon, Yongdong and Taegu beyond. If the 24th Division was to escape in any order, this road had to be kept open. In this position the 21st also could watch for any move on the division's right flank.

To the south of Taejon on the road leading to Kumsan, Dean at first stationed the division's mobile Reconnaissance Company to protect and warn of any movement on the division's rear. Then Dean reconsidered and released the Recon Company to shore up the 34th Regiment, which in its precarious and greatly overextended positions was shielding the city on the roads from both Taepyong-ni to the northwest and Nonsan to the west. The immediate result was that the 24th Division lost all knowledge of what was happening on the southern approaches to the city.

Despite its condition, the battered 19th Regiment could not be allowed to sit out this crisis. General Dean ordered the 2nd Battalion of the 19th, which had received less damage in the Taepyong-ni battle, to move back to Taejon as the division reserve. It was a pitiful one: fewer than 700 men.

The battle for Taejon started with air strikes by both sides on July 19. In the morning, Yaks bombed the railway bridge east of Taejon, damaging it, but by noon U.S. engineers had it repaired. The Yaks also

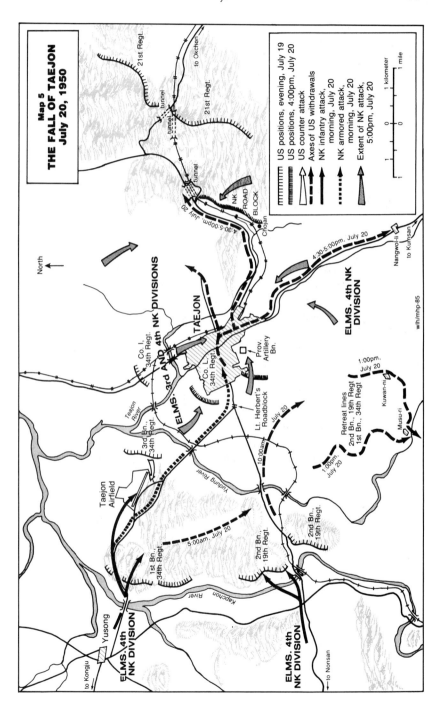

Map 5

THE FALL OF TAEJON
July 20, 1950

US positions, evening, July 19
US positions, 4:00pm, July 20
US counter attack
Axes of US withdrawals
NK infantry attack, morning, July 20
NK armored attack, morning, July 20
Extent of NK attack, 5:00pm, July 20

1 kilometer

1 mile

North

to Okchon

21st Regt.

21st Regt.

tunnel

tunnel

tunnel

4:30-5:00pm, July 20

NK
ROAD
BLOCK

Chŏan

4:30-5:00pm, July 20

Nangwol-li

to Kumsan

ELMS. 4th NK
DIVISION

TAEJON

ELMS. 3rd AND 4th NK DIVISIONS

Co. I,
34th Regt.

Co. L,
34th Regt.

Prov.
Artillery
Bn.

Taejŏn
River

3rd Bn.,
34th Regt.

Yudŭng River

Lt. Herbert's
Roadblock

10:00am, July 20

July 20

1:00pm,
July 20

Retreat lines
2nd Bn., 19th Regt
1st Bn., 34th Regt

Kuwan-ni

Musu-ri

1:00pm,
July 20

Taejon
Airfield

5:00am, July 20

2nd Bn.,
19th Regt.

2nd Bn.,
19th Regt.

Kapchŏn River

1st Bn.,
34th Regt.

Yusong

to Kongju

ELMS. 4th
NK DIVISION

ELMS. 4th
NK DIVISION

to Nonsan

wh/mhp-85

dropped propaganda leaflets and strafed the Taejon airstrip, but during the afternoon AAA guns brought down two Yaks just west of Taejon. U.S. airplanes bombed all known or suspected NK concentration areas, and also observed that the North Koreans had repaired the Kum river bridge at Taepyong-ni and were moving tanks and artillery across. The U.S. tactical planes at the time were at a disadvantage because most had to fly out of Japan due to the inadequacy of fields in Korea. This greatly shortened the time they could stay over the battlefield.

The North Koreans called upon their exhausted 2nd Division at Chongju to envelop the American right flank, but it did not come up in time and did not figure in the battle. They continued to rely on the 3rd and 4th NK Divisions. The 3rd Division was ordered to attack straight down from the north, through Taepyong-ni, while the 4th Division, which had crossed the Kum at Kongju, split into two tank-led forces— one two-regiment detachment with most of the artillery and tanks going south to Nonsan, then wheeling east toward Taejon, the other one-regiment detachment moving on a secondary road through mountains direct from Kongju to Yusong, where the road joined the main road from Taepyong-ni at a point just west of the Kapchon river emplacements of the 34th Regiment.

Although sending two regiments the roundabout way to Nonsan and then east might seem to have been sending two-thirds of the division out of the fight, the North Koreans had a plan. And it was a good one: the bulk of the force struck the Kapchon river defenses of the 34th directly from the west, where it was less expected, while the NK command ticked off some of this infantry to move still farther south and strike the Kumsan road below Taejon. This was the very road from which the Recon Company had been withdrawn, leaving the 24th Division blind to any advance from the south.

First to spot the movement on the Nonsan road was a platoon of the Recon Company, dispatched in the early afternoon by the 34th's CO, Colonel Beauchamp, to go out the Nonsan road in search of the enemy. Three miles west of the Kapchon the platoon drew fire from both sides of the road and withdrew back across the Kapchon, where it joined a Company L, 34th, roadblock. Within a short time, the North Koreans moved up and the battle at the Nonsan road crossing began. Company L began to give way.

At that moment, the division reserve, the 2nd Battalion of the 19th, under Colonel McGrail, arrived at Taejon, and division ordered it to attack immediately down the Nonsan road to restore the line on the west. When McGrail and his battalion got to the river, General Dean was already there with two light tanks, directing fire. McGrail attacked without delay with two companies abreast astride the Nonsan road and restored the situation. But the battalion remained closely engaged all day.

Farther north, near Yusong, the 34th Regiment's 1st Battalion came under heavy attack. Flanking parties cut off two platoons of Company B north of Yusong. U.S. air strikes and artillery concentrations delayed the North Korean advance, but in the afternoon Colonel Beauchamp authorized Company B to withdraw to safer positions behind the Kapchon and the company got back in the evening.

About noon, North Korean artillery began shelling the Taejon airstrip from the north and northwest, trying to destroy the American artillery by counterbattery fire. Intense NK artillery fire also pounded the main positions of the 34th Regiment.

In the early afternoon, the 1st Battalion's CO, Lieutenant Colonel Harold B. Ayres, convinced that a major NK attack was brewing, recommended to Beauchamp that the 34th withdraw that night. Beauchamp refused, believing he could hold the enemy out of Taejon another day, and so informed General Dean. Even so, after dark Beauchamp moved the regimental command post from the airfield into Taejon; the artillery also displaced to safer positions south of the city.

The evening was strangely quiet, although ominous things were going on. Troops of the 19th Regiment, protecting the Nonsan road, heard noises to their north indicating North Koreans were slipping across the Kapchon in the gap between the 19th and 34th Regiments' positions. About 10 p.m. Colonel Ayres at the battalion CP in the 34th's sector heard tanks to his north. He sent out a patrol, but it never came back. Ayres informed Beauchamp. Before midnight, a report reached the 34th CP that enemy forces were six miles *south* of Taejon on the Kumsan road. If true, this meant an envelopment of the city on three sides. Nine members of the Recon Company went down in four jeeps to investigate. Six miles below Taejon the detachment was halted at a roadblock; the patrol reported the beginning of an action by radio; then silence. About 3 a.m. a platoon of the Recon Company drove down the road—and was stopped by the same roadblock. The platoon saw the bodies of several men and their four destroyed jeeps. Meanwhile, at 2 a.m. a report came into Taejon that a jeep had been ambushed on the main Seoul-Pusan road, the division's bolt-hole.

Astonishingly, General Dean did not get word of the roadblock on the Kumsan road, and he dismissed the report of the jeep attack on the Seoul-Pusan highway because the road thereafter appeared to be clear.

Meanwhile, the North Korean assault came. At 3 a.m. on July 20, Ayres, CO of the 1st Battalion in the 34th sector, got word enemy forces had penetrated the battalion's main line of resistance along the Kapchon and were moving on both sides of the main Seoul-Pusan highway from Yusong with infantry and armor. The movement quickly rolled up the 1st Battalion's flank; within an hour NK troops were firing on the battalion CP a mile back from the river. Ayres signaled regimental headquarters in Taejon that tanks were headed toward the city. There was evidence that 34th bazooka teams abandoned their positions along the road when the attack began, and the rifle companies did not stay long in place.[5]

In the confusion, Colonel Ayres decided to evacuate the CP. The battalion executive officer, Major Leland R. Dunham, led about two-hundred men from the mortar and headquarters units, followed by Ayres and his S-3, southward away from the sound of enemy fire.[6]

At the 34th CP in Taejon, telephone communications with the 1st Battalion ended, and Colonel Beauchamp sent linemen to check the wires; they came back saying NK infantry were on the road near the airfield. The regimental S-3 did not believe this report, and Beauchamp decided to check out the situation himself. He drove to the road junction a mile west of the city where the road from Taepyong-ni and Yusong joined the road from Nonsan. There a T34 tank suddenly loomed up and fired its machine guns at Beauchamp's jeep, setting the vehicle afire and grazing the colonel. Beauchamp crawled back several hundred yards, where he found a 3.5-inch bazooka team. He guided it back to the road junction, and the team shot off the first combat-use round of the new weapon—and promptly set the tank on fire. The crew members jumped out and surrendered. The bazooka team stationed itself at the junction and with another bazooka team from the Recon Company that arrived later destroyed two more T34s coming from the direction of the airfield. It was an auspicious beginning for the super bazooka.

Although Beauchamp was not entirely clear about what was happening on the front, he was disturbed by reports of enemy penetrations in the gap along the Kapchon between the 19th and 34th positions. Accordingly, after daylight he ordered an attack into the gap by the regimental reserve, the 3rd Battalion, in place on a ridge to the east of the airfield. The attack got practically nowhere: on the road leading from the airfield the battalion was met by six T34s and an estimated battalion of NK troops, who scattered some of the 3rd Battalion, which withdrew to its just-vacated positions. There it remained undisturbed throughout the morning, except for occasional mortar and artillery rounds.

The North Koreans essentially had broken through the American defenses on the northwest with the shattering of the 34th's 1st Battalion on the Kapchon and the withdrawal of the 3rd Battalion. Most of the NK troops halted, however, and only small groups of infiltrators, mostly riding on tanks, entered the city shortly before daylight. There they did incredible damage, but the main force held up northwest of the city and waited on developments elsewhere.

The infiltrators into Taejon quickly spread out into buildings, and began sniping that continued all day. The tanks carrying the snipers went on a rampage. Two shot up a kitchen and motor pool where 34th and 19th trucks and about 150 men were located, killing several men and destroying vehicles, then rumbling away firing at various targets as they went. Not until after the tanks had gone did anyone locate a 3.5-inch bazooka. Then, using a white-phosphorous bazooka shell to drive out snipers in a nearby building, the soldiers set it afire. The flames spread rapidly to other wooden, straw-roofed structures until large parts of the city were burning from this and other causes. Bazooka teams from the Recon Company set out after the tanks, which meanwhile had killed or wounded two jeeploads of men at the Medical Company headquarters. A recon man finally got a shot at one of the T34s, hitting it in the side and bouncing the tank off the ground; nevertheless, the T34 kept on going, shooting at supplies at the railway station and starting big fires. There a track came off and the T34 stopped. Rifle fire killed the tank commander. Another 3.5-inch bazooka rocket hit the second tank and took a piece of armor three feet square off its front plate, while another bazooka shell penetrated the top turret of a third T34. By this time, even General Dean had joined in the tank hunts, but that morning he and his teams never caught any. Even so, four of five T34s that entered the city in the morning were destroyed by bazooka fire.

Around noon another tank entered the city, and a big bazooka rocket destroyed it. Soon afterward still another tank rumbled past the 34th Regiment's command post, and General Dean and bazooka teams started out in pursuit, dodging sniper fire as they went. About 2 p.m. Dean and a bazooka team climbed into a second-story window and discovered a T34 immediately below them. The team fired three rounds into the tank, destroying it and the crew.

Figures on the number of T34 kills in Taejon that day are not precise, but it appears the big bazookas destroyed ten tanks, while artillery fire stopped two more. It was an astonishing haul for the 3.5-inch bazooka in its first day in the field. The North Koreans, of course, in their overconfidence and their ignorance of the new weapon, sent their tanks singly into a closely built-up city, where tank-killing teams could approach undetected to within yards of the T34s. In open country the big bazooka was not the ultimate weapon against tanks, because teams often had to fire at much longer ranges. Besides, not all rounds were deadly: three teams with the Recon Company made seven hits at close range on three tanks and stopped only one of them.

Not every American was clear about who or where the enemy was. For example, a tank stood in a Taejon alley for several hours, ignored by nearly everyone. A Korean soldier leaned against it, then finally went over to an American and got ten gallons of diesel fuel from him. Some time during the afternoon, the tank departed, and later the Americans realized it had been a North Korean tank. Everything in Korea was new to the Americans, and it was impossible to tell a North Korean from a South Korean, or, for the inexperienced newcomers, one tank from another. Therefore, one NK tank, apparently out of fuel, got away courtesy of donated American fuel. It was a chaotic day in Taejon.

While the tank hunts were going on in the city, the troops of the 19th Regiment defending the Nonsan road were thrust into a heavy fire fight just after daylight. About this time, the refugees from the 34th's 1st Battalion debacle on the Kapchon passed behind some troops of the 19th, expecting to reach the Nonsan road and turn east into Taejon. While passing, they witnessed the fight and saw some 19th men begin to leave their hill emplacements.

Major Dunham, leading the 34th party, talked briefly with Colonel McGrail, commanding the 19th troops. Dunham was told NK tanks had cut the Nonsan road behind them leading into the city. Dunham decided to abandon the plan to go into Taejon and instead led his men south into the mountains; Ayres and his small party, coming behind, followed. Other 1st Battalion, 34th, survivors also scattered for the most part into the same mountains south of Taejon.

The report McGrail had got about tanks blocking the road behind him really was a sighting of the three T34s knocked out early in the morning at the road junction just west of Taejon by the new 3.5-inch bazooka teams. The observers thought the tanks were still intact and had not approached closely.

The incorrect information motivated McGrail to send a platoon of forty-nine men under Lieutenant Robert L. Herbert to reopen the road. Herbert's platoon reached the three burnt-out tanks and joined the two bazooka teams, but apparently did not get a message back to McGrail that the road was open.

While waiting at the roadblock, Lieutenant Herbert heard a tank coming from town. Someone shouted, "Don't fire. It's ours." Herbert had heard that four American tanks had come into Taejon the previous night. The tank halted thirty yards from the road junction. The hatch opened and someone looked at the still-smoldering T34s and several bodies on the road. The hatch slammed shut, and the tank moved on down the toward the North Korean lines. It was eighty yards away before Herbert realized it was a T34. Shortly afterward, General Dean drove up to look things over; as he left, Dean told Herbert to get the T34 if it came back. A little while later it did, rumbling toward the junction. Herbert rushed to a nearby bazooka team. "Get him, get him, for Christ's sake!" he shouted. It was an easy shot, but the man's hands were trembling. He fired, but the shell hit the ground several yards behind the tank. The tank clanked on by and the bazooka men ran along the road behind it, fired again, and this time struck the tank in the rear. But it was not damaged, and continued on into Taejon.

Meantime, McGrail's CP had lost radio contact with Beauchamp's command post, and McGrail, fearing the road into Taejon was blocked, withdrew the battalion into the mountains south of the road. By 1 p.m. the only infantry left in battle positions west of Taejon was in the small group under Lieutenant Herbert at the crossroads with the three knocked-out T34 tanks. The rest had withdrawn into the mountains southwest of Taejon—yet all could have gone straight into the city.

When General Dean and Colonel Beauchamp sat down together at lunch in Taejon to eat a cooked C ration, they were unaware both battalions supposedly blocking the NK advance from the northwest and west actually were in the hills south of Taejon. Even so, Dean directed Beauchamp not to wait until night to withdraw, as planned earlier, but to do it during the day, because transportation could move more safely. Dean designated the 21st Regiment east of Taejon to stand in place but to keep the road and railway and the several tunnels open. About 2 p.m. Beauchamp told his CP to send radio and telephone messages to the units to withdraw and also to send runners to the three infantry battalions. There was no phone or radio communication with the 1st Battalion of the 34th or the 2nd Battalion of the 19th, and the runners, naturally, did not reach the units since they already had withdrawn. But it appears that neither Dean nor Beauchamp received any word of this. The 3rd Battalion, 34th, still sitting in its reserve position east of the airfield, did receive the order, as did various units in and about Taejon. The 3rd Battalion got the job of leading the withdrawal convoy.

Some time in the afternoon, an urgent call came into the 34th CP from an artillery observer who insisted on talking with the senior commander present. Beauchamp took the call. The observer said he had seen a large column of troops approaching Taejon from the *east,* and he was positive they were the enemy. Beauchamp interpreted the "road to the east" to be the main Seoul-Pusan highway leading out to Okchon, and he believed these troops were men from the 21st Regiment. Beauchamp had misunderstood Dean's instructions and thought the 21st was going to move up to Taejon to protect the withdrawal, not remain in place.

Beauchamp therefore told the artillery observer the moving troops were American.[7]

Events proved that this body of troops was not on the Okchon road to the east, but on the Kumsan road to the *south*. Thus, an error as to the road by the artillery observer coupled with a misunderstanding by Beauchamp as to the movement of the 21st Regiment resulted in nothing being done to counter a major thrust of NK forces into the Americans' rear.[8]

Actually, some Americans did see the movement of the North Koreans up the Kumsan road. They were survivors of the 1st Battalion, 34th, in the mountains south of Taejon and west of the Kumsan road. Colonel Ayres saw the North Koreans at close hand, but, lacking a radio, could not get word to Taejon. He therefore directed Major Dunham with 150 men of the 1st Battalion to move down to the Kumsan road and establish a roadblock to keep the North Koreans from moving north. He, meanwhile, started off with a small party to make contact with other American forces.

A few hundred yards short of the Kumsan road, Ayres and his party ran into a party of North Korean soldiers on the hillside. In the frantic scramble that ensued, four men escaped, including Ayres, but the others were killed or captured. Ayres and the other three hid in the bushes, but were unable to get away until night.

Meantime, Major Dunham led his men toward the Kumsan road, getting into a fire fight in the mountains with what they took to be guerrillas. They disengaged soon thereafter, but coming into a draw were fired on by enemy troops on nearby finger ridges. Dunham was struck mortally in the neck, and other men were hit. All the remainder fled west, away from the Kumsan road, abandoning the mission to set up a roadblock.

The North Koreans now began to close in on Taejon from three sides, and there were no substantial U.S. troops to block them anywhere. Lieutenant Herbert's platoon was still in place, though, at the knocked-out T34s. Early in the afternoon, Herbert spotted a battalion-sized column of North Koreans on the high ground west of the road junction. The NK unit stopped and observed the small American blocking unit. The North Koreans created a great target. Lieutenant Herbert rushed back a short distance to an emplaced four-piece battery of 155mm howitzers. The gunners were in foxholes around their howitzers with the lanyards connected by ropes running into the holes so they could fire from there. Herbert asked that the pieces fire on the enemy in front of him. The battery commander declined without permission of the battalion operations officer; Herbert talked with this officer by field telephone, but could not get his approval. Meantime, the North Koreans had set up mortars and started shelling Herbert's position and the artillery battery. The mortar fire killed several artillerymen and also caused some casualties in Herbert's group. Herbert sent a runner into Taejon for instructions. Herbert was told to hold until the artillery could be evacuated, and a hastily assembled group of fifty men from the 34th headquarters was sent to help him.

Meantime, the 34th Regiment's CO, Colonel Beauchamp, was on a strange adventure. While reconnoitering the withdrawal route from Taejon, he had encountered in the southeastern edge of the city four light M24 tanks from the Recon Company. Beauchamp told the tankers to remain in position and defend the highway leading out of Taejon to Okchon. As he drove back into the city, Beauchamp glanced back and saw the tanks were leaving their positions. He turned around and caught up with them moving down the Okchon road. While chasing the M24s, however, Beauchamp came under small-arms fire—a disturbing occurrence, since this road was the division's only route to safety. Beauchamp climbed a nearby eminence to look around. From there he saw many North Korean troops moving cross-country south of Taejon toward the Okchon road.

Beauchamp knew convoys were going to be starting down this road momentarily. Therefore, he decided to take two of the M24s and go down to a pass four miles east of the city to organize a defense at this critical point on the evacuation route. At the pass he intercepted some AAA quad-mount .50s coming out of Taejon and emplaced them, but an attempt to flag down a retreating infantry company in trucks failed: the infantry commander simply waved in friendly greeting and kept on going.

Still thinking the 21st Regiment was moving up to Taejon to cover the withdrawal, Beauchamp decided to hurry it up. He drove to the first 21st unit he met, and from there called the 21st CP at Okchon. It happened that the 24th Division's assistant commander, General Menoher, was there, and he told Beauchamp to come on to Okchon to give a detailed report. Thus the regimental commander moved entirely out of the Taejon action. None of this was known back at Taejon.[9]

About 5 p.m., when General Dean discovered no one knew where Beauchamp was, he turned command of the 34th over to Colonel Wadlington, the executive, and told him to get the withdrawal under way at speed.

Enemy fire now was increasing greatly in Taejon itself, wounding many men and spreading panic among Americans and Koreans alike. Colonel Wadlington got the convoy together, placed General Dean in it and put himself at its head, and started off, just before 6 p.m. Left behind as perimeter guard was Company L of the 34th's 3rd Battalion; its instructions were to stay in place for forty-five minutes to give the convoy a chance to get away.

By now Taejon was in flames. Debris and walls were falling into the streets. Many buildings not ablaze had enemy snipers in them. At one intersection a military police vehicle had been destroyed. A dead MP lay behind the steering wheel. Two dead North Koreans lay in the road. At one corner, a 2½-ton truck went around a corner too fast and ran into a building, leaving barely enough room for the convoy to pass between it and a burning building opposite. Enemy small-arms fire halted the convoy momentarily from time to time. Men in the vehicles returned the fire.

As the convoy swung into a broad avenue, it encountered heavy machine-gun and small-arms fire. Colonel Wadlington and the men in the two lead jeeps stopped, got out and opened fire. The enemy fire slackened after a while, and Wadlington ordered the convoy to go ahead; he would rejoin as soon as he saw the convoy was moving. When Wadlington started out, however, he was unable to pass the trucks; he swung around a corner to go around the block—and promptly got lost in the burning, labyrinthine streets of the city. Wadlington's jeep finally dead-ended into a schoolyard. The rear now was cut off by small-arms fire. He and his companions therefore destroyed the jeep and took off up a nearby mountain.

The convoy, now leaderless, rushed through the city, drawing sniper fire all the way. Fifty vehicles of the convoy took a wrong turn and ended up in the same dead-end schoolyard as had Wadlington; men in these trucks, too, abandoned their vehicles and started off through the hills away from the sound of the firing. Some of these men got back, but many others never were heard from again.

The remainder of the convoy continued on through one street with buildings on both sides burning fiercely. General Dean's vehicle and an escort jeep mistakenly sped past the turnoff to the Okchon road. When enemy fire prevented the two vehicles from stopping and turning around, they continued on south—down the Kumsan road. Other convoy vehicles also missed the tricky turn and went down the Kumsan road behind Dean, as did the rear guard, Company L under Captain Jack E. Smith.

The rest of the convoy got on to the Okchon road, but just outside the city an enemy mortar shell hit the lead vehicle and it began to burn. A half-track pushed it out of the way. Enemy fire now struck the half-track, killed the driver and set the vehicle afire. Machine-gun fire ranged over the road. Everyone rushed for cover in the ditches, and some Americans saw North Koreans rise from rice paddies and spray the column with burp guns.

Although a sergeant set up a mortar and fired smoke shells to hide the convoy from the North Koreans, no effort was made to clear the road of the destroyed half-track; soon enemy mortars destroyed three more vehicles. The men at the head of the column then destroyed the rest of their vehicles with gasoline and moved out quickly on foot for high ground to the north. This action effectively blocked the road for all the rest of the convoy.

Enemy mortar fire walked up and down the road, destroying most of the remaining vehicles. When darkness came, Lieutenant Ralph C. Boyd, a quartermaster platoon leader, found six vehicles in operable condition, including two half-tracks, and he loaded up the seriously wounded and other soldiers and led the small group of vehicles on a narrow track northward. Enemy machine-gun fire suddenly erupted, knocking Boyd off the vehicle he was riding. As he fell, he hit his head on a rock and lost consciousness; when he came to, the vehicles were gone. He walked to the lines of the 21st Regiment.

Acts of heroism were common that night. Engineer Private Charles T. Zimmerman, though wounded by a mortar fragment and eleven bullets, killed five enemy soldiers and destroyed two machine guns. Engineer Sergeant George D. Libby twice crossed the heavily shelled road to give medical aid to wounded, and he stopped an artillery tractor going through and loaded it with wounded, "riding shotgun" for the driver, and getting wounded himself several times. The tractor got through, but Libby died from loss of blood. He received the Congressional Medal of Honor posthumously.

On orders from General Menoher, Colonel Beauchamp led a group of light tanks and infantry (Company I, 34th, which earlier had come from Taejon) back up the highway from the 21st's positions to hold the road open at the pass. Before reaching it, one of the tanks hit an enemy mine in the road, and an unseen enemy soldier detonated other mines electrically. The infantry moved forward cautiously, but never got control of the pass and retired after expending their ammunition.

All night survivors came into the 21st Regiment's lines, many of them wounded; others walked long distances through mountains and valleys before reaching U.S. lines twenty miles farther southeast at Yongdong. Among these was Colonel Wadlington: he got back to U.S. positions on July 22. The men of the 19th and 34th Regiments who had climbed the mountains south of Taejon mostly got back by various circuitous routes over several days.

The 21st was the only force now holding up the North Korean

advance, and it had to withdraw on July 21 to a position four miles northwest of Yongdong.

Company L under Captain Smith, the last unit out of Taejon, went down the Kumsan road, where the enemy had lain in wait all day. Smith found the road littered with abandoned American vehicles and equipment. At one enemy roadblock Smith organized about 150 men, including about 50 wounded, salvaged some vehicles and joined the group with his company, and then led the whole party through a series of small roadblocks, getting past the last one just before dark. And when Smith got through, he kept right on going—all the way through Kumsan to Anui to Chinju, almost at the southern tip of Korea. Smith left the wounded at Pusan, then continued with the rest back up to Taegu, where on July 23 Colonel Wadlington had assembled about 300 men of the 34th Regiment.

General Dean's story was less happy: a mile south of Taejon on the Kumsan road, Dean stopped his jeep where a wrecked truck lay with several wounded men. He loaded these men onto his two jeeps and told them to go on. He and two other soldiers got on an artillery half-track that followed behind. A mile down the road, Dean's aide, Lieutenant Arthur M. Clarke, riding in one of the jeeps, was hit in the shoulder by small-arms fire, and a mile farther on the group, with the half-track following, came to a stop where a knocked-out truck blocked the road and NK troops with rifles and machine guns were laying down fire. Dean and the rest of the group crawled down to the bank of the Taejon river, which ran beside the road, and waited until darkness. During this time, Smith's party fought its way down the road and passed on. After dark, Dean and his group crossed to the west side of the small river and started climbing a mountain.

A little after midnight, Lieutenant Clarke, leading the group, found no one behind him. He went back and found several men asleep, but not Dean. Clarke did not know what had happened to his boss. He waited two hours, then awakened the men, and all climbed to the top of the mountain, where they waited all day, hoping to see Dean. That night, Clarke led the group eastward into the mountains, then south, eventually reaching U.S. lines at Yongdong on July 23.

Dean actually had gone down for water for the wounded men. On the way he fell down a steep slope and was knocked unconscious. When he came to his senses, he had a broken shoulder, bruises and a head gash. General Dean wandered through Korea for thirty-six days, before he was betrayed to North Koreans by two South Koreans who were pretending to help him. Dean spent more than three years as a North Korean prisoner. He won the Medal of Honor.

Taejon had been another disaster for the 24th Division. Of the nearly 4,000 men engaged there on July 19–20, nearly 30 percent (1,150 men) were now dead, wounded or missing (most of them dead). At noon on July 22, the division turned over the front-line positions, now back at Yongdong, to the 1st Cavalry Division. The 24th Division's strength that day was 8,660 men. In the seventeen days since Task Force Smith had first engaged North Korean forces at Osan, two NK divisions had driven the 24th back a hundred miles and had killed, wounded or captured three out of ten of the 12,200 soldiers in the division when it was committed to Korea.[10] It had lost enough equipment to provide for a division. Its losses of officers had been high. On July 22, with General Dean still missing, Eighth Army ordered Major General John H. Church to take command of the division.

Roy Appleman, the great chronicler of the first five months of the war, offers this summary of the seventeen days when the division stood alone:

"There were many heroic actions by American soldiers of the 24th Division in these first weeks in Korea. But there were also many uncomplimentary and unsoldierly ones. Leadership among the officers had to be exceptional to get the men to fight, and several gave their lives in this effort. Others failed to meet the standard expected of American officers. There is no reason to suppose that any of the other three occupation divisions in Japan would have done better in Korea than did the U.S. 24th Division in July, 1950. When committed to action they showed the same weaknesses.

"A basic fact is that the occupation divisions were not trained, equipped, or ready for battle. The great majority of the enlisted men were young and not really interested in being soldiers. The recruiting posters that had induced most of these men to enter the army mentioned all conceivable advantages and promised many good things, but never suggested that the principal business of an army is to fight."[11]

CHAPTER 16

The Ghost Division

THE AMERICAN AND ROK FORCES were now rapidly approaching the Naktong river line west of Taegu where General Walker had determined the retreat had to stop if any foothold was going to be kept in Korea. Despite the disasters which had hit the 24th Division, that force had slowed the North Koreans just enough to permit other American reinforcements to bolster the line and give the Americans and ROKs a fighting chance at stabilizing a front.

Nevertheless, there were two extremely dangerous North Korean movements on either coast and they threatened to undo all the work of Eighth Army and the ROK forces.

It was not clear to Generals MacArthur or Walker at the time, but the North Korean command had conceived a grand and spectacular double-envelopment strategy for all South Korea—a theater-wide movement like that the NK forces used on a local, tactical scale. The left-hand envelopment, down the east-coast road along the Sea of Japan, was carried out by the 5th NK Division and the 766th Independent Unit. The right-hand envelopment, along the Yellow Sea and through southwest Korea was conducted by the 6th NK Division under Major General Pang Ho San. Both divisions were targeted at Pusan.[1]

Meantime, the rest of the North Korean army pressed fiercely against the central front in order to hold the main American and ROK forces in place while these flanking divisions closed behind them.

Unlike the famous 1905 German plan Count Alfred von Schlieffen designed to conquer France, the North Korean strategy did not call for weighting a wing with the great bulk of the troops, and thus driving to the rear of the enemy by sheer overwhelming power. Rather the reverse was the case: the North Korean strategy called for *creeping*, as it were, around their enemies, not driving around them. Therefore, both wings were relatively weak, and their efforts were characterized by inconspicuous rather than noisy drives. They sought to gain breakthroughs by moving into empty or at least lightly defended space. The North Korean strategy was to draw the main enemy forces into the central front by means of a strong offensive effort in that sector, thus leaving the flanks denuded of troops.

Consequently, the North Korean thrust meant to draw the most attention and elicit the greatest reaction was down the main highway and railway route of Korea—the Seoul-Taejon-Taegu axis—with secondary thrusts down the center of the country, roughly through Chunchon to Wonju toward Taegu. The drive down the Seoul-Taejon-Taegu road and rail line used two divisions (3rd and 4th) plus 120 of North Korea's 150 tanks. This was the attack that drew the first American troops like a magnet, because it was obviously extremely dangerous. Yet against the ROKs on the central front east of this axis the North Koreans committed six divisions plus a regiment of tanks. It was a far greater concentration of force than anywhere else. Because NK troops potentially could break into the upper Naktong valley through the passes near Mungyong and Tanyang, and thus possibly drive through to Taegu, this sector drew in not only the bulk of the ROK army but forced General Walker to commit elements of the U.S. 25th Division there when it arrived July 12.

The North Korean strategy worked like a charm: all three of the first American divisions committed, as well as practically all of the ROK army, were positioned on the central fronts against the main strength of the North Korean army.

Along the east-coast road separated from the rest of Korea by the high Taebaek mountain range, the 5th NK Division and the 766th Unit were opposed only by a regiment of the ROK 3rd Division. Against the 6th NK Division, which was moving down the west coast, there were only a few hundred disorganized survivors of the ROK 7th Division, plus various police and miscellaneous units, none of them effective fighting forces.

The stage was therefore set for a stunning North Korean victory, and nothing could have stopped it. The American and ROK forces were deeply committed against the hard-driving NK divisions in the center. All the flanking forces had to do was race hell-for-leather along the outside roads for Pusan. There was nothing substantial in their paths. Having conceived, as B. H. Liddell Hart says, that the long way around may be the quickest way home, the North Korean command relied upon their flank commanders to drive all out for Pusan.

Things might have been different if either wing had possessed a commander like George Patton, who pressed the American Third Army beyond exhaustion across France in similar circumstances in 1944, or like Erwin Rommel, whose German 7th Panzer Division moved so fast and mysteriously in the 1940 attack on France that its opponents called it the Ghost Division.

Neither North Korean division possessed a Patton or a Rommel. Rather, where boldness was called for, these divisions acted with timidity.

Along the east coast, the North Korean forces dissipated their strength and lost much time in reconnaissance probes into the wild Taebaek range, for fear of rear attacks, although the range was almost trackless and had few lateral routes through it, all of which could have been blocked easily. By July 17 the North Koreans had pressed only just below Yongdok, and the time had passed when they could have driven without further opposition on to Pohang-dong and then across the back of the American and ROK lines via Kyongju through open valleys to Pusan. In fact, with the aid of U.S. and British naval bombardment and UN air strikes, the ROKs rallied at Yongdok, threw in new troops, and, in three weeks of bitter seesaw fighting, held the North Koreans in place.

On the west coast, the situation was stranger still. The 6th NK Division on July 11 turned southwest from Chonan when the only American forces in Korea were a few hard-pressed battalions and batteries of the 24th Division. Breaking out into undefended space, the NK division passed entirely from the view of Eighth Army intelligence (G-2). It became a ghost division itself, but in another sense: American G-2 didn't even know it was there. The various light encounters it had with South Korean police and other units did not unveil its identity. Eighth Army G-2 thought it was dealing with extended elements of the 4th NK Division, then converging on the Kum river and, later, on Taejon. Eighth Army simply did not anticipate any North Korean attack would go through southwest Korea.

Yet, instead of driving all-out for Pusan, the 6th NK Division took up priceless days occupying all of the ports in southwestern Korea. This incredible and unnecessary tour of the southwest delayed the division just enough for a frantic Eighth Army, finally realizing on July 23 that there was a major force advancing on Pusan from the west, to rush the battered 24th Division southward to block it. The 24th had been in reserve for exactly one day. Even then Eighth Army still thought it was dealing with the 4th NK Division. It was July 31 before G-2 identified the 6th Division.[2]

General Walker later received intelligence reports indicating the North Koreans had wanted the ports to supply NK forces in southwest Korea by water.[3] This appears to be unlikely, given total UN command of the sea. More logically, the North Korean commander could not believe there were no defending troops in southwest Korea, and he traveled all over the southwestern countryside hunting for them and capturing the ports for fear of attack by a sea-supplied UN force.

When the North Koreans toted up their errors afterward, the failure of the 6th Division to forget its rear and strike with all speed for Pusan was the inexcusable one. Had the division moved with haste and resolution, Pusan would have fallen. Eighth Army's no-retreat position on the Naktong would have been untenable, and Americans and ROKs would have been forced to embark hastily from the small ports on the east coast.

*   *   *   *   *   *   *   *

The exhausted and understrength 19th Regiment of the 24th Division started moving before midnight on July 24 to Chinju, 55 air miles west of Pusan and 27 air miles west of Masan. (See Map 1.) On July 26 the equally battered 34th Regiment moved to Kochang, 35 miles north of Chinju and only 27 air miles west of the Naktong. Both regiments were down to little more than battalion strength: about 1,150 men each. The 24th Division's third regiment, the 21st, temporarily had been placed in a blocking position behind the ROKs engaged in their huge mutual bloodletting with the North Koreans for possession of Yongdok on the east coast.[4]

Despite their delay in getting into position, the soldiers of the 6th NK Division knew their mission exactly. In the words of their commander, General Pang, it was "the liberation of Chinju and Masan" and the final battle "to cut the windpipe of the enemy," meaning Pusan.[5]

The two weak 24th Division regiments obviously were inadequate to halt the North Korean thrust. There was, however, another two-battalion regiment that had just arrived in Pusan from Okinawa, and it was flung without ceremony into the fight. This regiment, the 29th, was in many ways a microcosm of the urgent, almost panicky, situation of the U.S. military in July, 1950. Its history epitomizes graphically the unanticipated challenges that unprepared American soldiers had to face. On July 20, the USS *Walker* docked at Okinawa with four hundred recruits who had been hastily rounded up in the United States and sent over. The recruits were driven to the 29th's battalion areas, assigned to companies, issued arms and field equipment, and immediately trucked back to the docks at Naha. The next day, the 29th's two battalions, now at full strength, sailed for Pusan. Regimental headquarters remained on Okinawa to form a new unit.

The two battalions arrived at Pusan on the morning of July 24, and, instead of having time at least to zero-in and test-fire their weapons, they were ordered immediately to proceed to Chinju. They arrived the next afternoon and were attached to the 19th Regiment. The battalions found themselves in a forward position, their rifles still not zeroed, mortars not test-fired, and new .50-caliber machine guns with the cosmoline rubbed off but not cleaned.

Immediately upon arrival, the 19th Regiment's CO, Colonel Ned D. Moore, told the 29th's 3rd Battalion to move out and seize Hadong, a road junction thirty-five miles southwest of Chinju, upon which about five hundred NK troops were reported moving. The 3rd Battalion CO, Lieutenant Colonel Harold W. Mott, alerted his troops, and a half hour after midnight on July 26 the green and totally inexperienced battalion departed with the mission, all alone, of attacking the enemy.

The battalion was accompanied by, of all people, Major General Chae ("Fat Boy") Byong Duk, the ROK army chief of staff who had been relieved immediately after the fall of Seoul. Chae had come down in the world: on this occasion he was to serve only as interpreter, guide and advisor to Colonel Mott.

Colonel Mott had hoped to arrive in Hadong before daylight, but a ford on the direct road was impassable and General Chae led the Americans along a narrow, circuitous route through Konyang which took the entire night and frequently engaged the exhausted 29th soldiers in pulling vehicles out of rice paddies.

Shortly after daylight the battalion was sobered when it encountered a truck with about 15 South Koreans who said they were the only survivors of 400 local militia at Hadong, which the North Koreans had attacked the night before. Colonel Mott sent his executive officer, Major Tony J. Raibl, back to inform Colonel Moore, since the battalion did not have radio communication with Chinju. Raibl, knowing the condition of the 3rd Battalion, recommended to Moore that it dig in west of Chinju to cover the Hadong road. Colonel Moore said no: go on and seize Hadong.

The goings and comings of Raibl took time, and it was dusk when the 3rd Battalion arrived at the village of Hoengchon, three miles east of Hadong and below the high Hadong pass. Mott stopped the battalion for the night.

At 8:45 a.m. the next day (July 27), the battalion moved out toward the pass, Company L in the lead. About a thousand yards from the top the CO of Love Company, Captain George F. Sharra, saw a patrol of North Koreans come over the pass and start toward them. He ordered two 75mm recoilless rifles to fire, but the rounds passed harmlessly overhead and the North Koreans ran back. Sharra ordered the company to rush the pass; at the top his men deployed on either side of the road and dug in, waiting for a scheduled 9:45 a.m. air strike on Hadong, a mile and a half westward. The pass was bounded on the north by a higher ridge; to the south the ground dropped away rapidly to paddy land along the Somjin river.

The command group, including Colonel Mott, most of the battalion staff and General Chae, hurried forward to the pass. Captain Sharra, thinking the group offered an unusually attractive target, moved to the left and dropped to the ground. Colonel Mott directed Major Raibl's attention to a column of enemy troops in about company strength moving up the road toward them. Sharra, who also saw the column, told his machine-gunners to withhold fire until the North Koreans were closer and he gave the word. The NK troops seemed unaware Americans were on the pass. Some wore American green fatigue uniforms and others the mustard brown of the NK army. When they were about a hundred yards away, General Chae shouted to them in Korean to identify themselves. At this they rushed to the ditches without answering, and the Company L machine guns, with a much less vulnerable target now available, opened fire.

Almost simultaneously, North Korean machine-gun, mortar and small-arms fire swept over the pass from the high ground to the north. The first burst killed General Chae and wounded Colonel Mott, Major Raibl, the S-2 and the assistant S-2. Mortar fire knocked out parked vehicles, including the radio jeep of an air force tactical air-control party which was on hand to direct air strikes. Just after the fight opened, two flights of two airplanes each flew back and forth over the area, trying vainly to contact the air-control party; the planes finally departed without making any strikes.

The 3rd Battalion had walked into a preregistered enemy ambush, as proved by the fact that the first enemy rounds landed dead on target. The battalion's staff was almost eliminated in the first minute of fire. Raibl was wounded again by mortar fragments and went down the hill seeking medical aid. Colonel Mott, wounded only slightly by a bullet crease, got out of the line of fire; he was helping to unload ammunition when a box dropped and broke his foot. A soldier dug him a foxhole.

At the pass itself, a hard fire fight flared between Company L and the North Koreans higher up the hill. The 1st Platoon, on the north side, sustained a direct attack on their foxholes, and two Americans were bayoneted. Nevertheless, the company held in place, a tribute to the leadership of company officers and noncoms and to the surprising steadiness of the soldiers, half of them young recruits.

Captain Robert M. Flynn, the S-3, had not been hit in the attack on the battalion staff. He hastened down the hill to hurry up supporting elements of the battalion. One Company I platoon moved into rice paddies on the south side of the road trying to cover its advance toward the hill mass.

About noon, a Company L lieutenant found Colonel Mott and carried him to Captain Sharra's position. Mott told Sharra to take command and get the battalion out. Sharra sent word to his three platoons to withdraw to the road at the foot of the pass, but the runner to the 1st Platoon on the north side of the pass never reached it. Captain Flynn, however, climbed up to the platoon's positions. The leader, Lieutenant J. Morrissey, and twelve men were left, along with the battalion S-2, Captain William Mitchell, who, though wounded, had fought all morning as a rifleman. The unidentified air force captain of the air-control party also had fought as a rifleman, but he was either dead or missing.

As the 1st Platoon fell back down the road, a battalion of North Korean troops started down off the hill at the pass. Mortar and machine-gun fire swept the paddy area where the platoon of Item Company was still emplaced; men there had to cross a deep, twenty-foot-wide stream to get back. Several drowned, and others discarded helmets, shoes, clothing and weapons in crossing. The largest group of survivors—97 men— escaped to the tiny port of Noryangjin, five miles south, where a fishing vessel carried them out to a South Korean patrol boat. More than half of the battalion was lost in the single engagement at Hadong pass. Only 354 officers and men, including some walking wounded, were available for duty the next day. An enemy soldier captured later said about 100 Americans were captured at the pass, and a subsequent search found 313 American bodies, most of them along the river and in the rice paddies.

The broken 3rd Battalion of the 29th moved back to Chinju to join the 19th Regiment. Meanwhile, the 1st Battalion of the 29th had been sent to blocking positions at Anui, about thirty-five airline miles north of Chinju. There troops of the 4th NK Division attacked, driving the battalion back south, first to Umyong-ni and then to Sanchong, twenty miles north of Chinju.

The 4th NK Division also turned on the 34th Regiment at Kochang on July 28, and the next day drove the 34th east fifteen miles to new blocking positions near Sanje-ri, only eighteen air miles west of the Naktong and perilously close to the river crossings leading to Taegu. With a crisis impending, General Walker moved the 2,000-man ROK 17th Regiment, one of the best South Korean outfits, to support the 34th and also sent the 1st Battalion, 21st Regiment, then behind the ROKs on the east coast at Yongdok, into positions west of Hyopchon, six air miles south of Sanje-ri.

The 6th NK Division on July 31 struck the 19th Regiment and the remnants of the 3rd Battalion, 29th, at Chinju, and the Americans withdrew ten miles eastward to Chinju pass. This blocked the retreat of the 1st Battalion, 29th, still at Sanchong, and forced the unit to retreat over a mountain trail to American positions east of Chinju.[6]

General Walker was under no illusions about the danger in the extreme south: the 6th NK Division still had a chance to break through the fragile American defense line at Chinju pass and strike for Masan and Pusan.

CHAPTER 17

Retreat to the Naktong

WHILE THE 6TH NK DIVISION poised to strike toward Masan in the extreme south, the North Korean command decided on one last try at breaking through on the east coast. The 5th NK Division and the 766th Unit were being chewed up on the killing ground at Yongdok. Because the high Taebaek mountains ran down almost to the Sea of Japan, these units were unable to carry out the typical NK flanking movement. Thus, held on the coast, they were fair game for U.S. and British warships standing offshore and for UN aircraft overhead.

The effort was a forlorn hope for the NK command, in the original sense of the term as a lost force of men. The 12th NK Division, selected for the task, already was tired and worn. The division earlier had pushed through the pass near Tanyang over the high mountain watershed dividing the Han and Naktong river valleys running sixty miles southwest from the Taebaek range. By July 21 the 12th NK Division had captured Yongju and faced the ROK 8th Division north of Andong. (See Map 1.)

With the east-coast attack stymied at Yongdok, the NK command ordered the 12th Division to attack through the ROK 8th Division behind the Yongdok front and capture the east-coast port of Pohang-dong by July 26. It was an inconceivable task: the air distance from Yongju was seventy-five miles, and the greater part of the route beyond Andong lay across high mountains which had little more than foot and oxcart trails.[1] To meet the deadline, the 12th Division bravely resumed daylight marches, giving the UN aircraft almost daily opportunities to strike at moving columns and equipment. The ROK 8th Division contested every step. It was the end of July before the 12th Division reached Andong, and the battle for this town consumed five days and large portions of the NK division, as well as the defending ROK 8th

Division and the Capital Division, which came up to help. NK prisoners reported air attacks alone killed 600 North Korean soldiers, that much of the artillery had been sent back to Tanyang because the NK supply could not get ammunition to the guns, that eleven of the division's thirty tanks had been lost, and that the division commander had been killed. The division was exhausted and had to halt.

Stopped in the east, the NK command girded for other major movements farther west. Along this sector the just-committed U.S. 25th and 1st Cavalry Divisions were about to face the harsh realities of Korea.

General Walker, trying to put some order into the battle line, on July 24 moved the ROK 1st Division to Hamchang, six air miles west of the upper Naktong, to assist the tired ROK 6th Division which was defending against the 1st NK Division. The ROK command also inactivated the shattered ROK 2nd Division and incorporated its 3,000 survivors into the 1st Division. Thus the ROK army's five remaining divisions were concentrated on the northern front: the 1st and 6th around Hamchang, the 8th and Capital around Andong, and the 3rd on the east coast at Yongdok.[2]

General Walker threw the 25th Division into blocking positions on roads west of Sangju, a town about ten miles south of Hamchang and just west of the Naktong. Farther south, at Yongdong on the main Seoul-Pusan road, the 1st Cavalry Division on July 22 had relieved the 24th Division after the battle to hold Taejon. Both American divisions, though understrength, were unbloodied. The 25th Division had 13,000 men, the 1st Cavalry 10,000.[3]

Since July 22 the 25th Division's 35th Regiment had been retreating south from the Hamchang area on division orders. By July 29 it was about three miles north of Sangju and blocking the road to Hamchang. Meanwhile, the three-battalion all-black (except for some white officers) 24th Regiment of the 25th Division was committed twenty miles northwest of Sangju to block elements of the 15th NK Division, which were moving down a secondary road. The 24th Regiment began a series of engagements in which soldiers often exhibited a tendency to panic.[4] These events, plus an underlying prejudice against black soldiers on the part of some white troops, gave the 24th Regiment a bad reputation in the Eighth Army as a bug-out unit. Quite a few white units exhibited the same sort of shakiness in combat, but these units did not suffer the lingering criticism the 24th had to endure. One fortunate thing did come out of the situation, however: by order of General Matthew B. Ridgway, the 24th was desegregated on October 1, 1951, and afterward the army wholly eliminated its abominable practice of separating soldiers by race. A fully integrated and officially race-blind U.S. Army was the outcome.[5]

The 25th Division's third regiment, the 27th, was sent in farther south on July 22 to relieve the soon-to-be-dissolved ROK 2nd Division, which was retreating down the road from Chongju and Poun toward Sangnyong-ni before the 2nd NK Division. The 27th Regiment fared better than the 24th Regiment, but by July 28 it had been forced back by the familiar North Korean double-envelopment movements to the vicinity of Hwanggan, where 1st Cavalry units were holding.

Meantime, the 3rd NK Division, worn down but victorious in its fight for Taejon, moved southeast on July 23 and closed with a battalion of the 1st Cavalry's 8th Cavalry Regiment on the main Seoul-Pusan road northwest of Yongdong. Using their double-envelopment movement to establish a roadblock in the rear, the North Koreans cut off some 8th Cavalry troops, who had to abandon equipment and flee over the mountains back to American lines. American artillery was arriving at the front in strength now, however, and the 3rd NK Division faced heavy concentrations of fire as it advanced. Although the North Koreans entered Yongdong on the night of July 25, the enemy division had suffered nearly 2,000 casualties in its attack on the 1st Cavalry, mostly from artillery fire. The division was down to 5,000 men.[6] Despite this, the 3rd NK Division maintained the initiative and the 1st Cavalry withdrew east of the town.

To the Americans, the situation looked bad. Unbroken North Korean successes, through determined envelopment movements and constant infiltration into American positions, had created an uneasy feeling among the green U.S. troops that nothing could stop the enemy. An example of the kind of anxiety this engendered occurred on the night of July 25–26, after the headquarters and 2nd Battalion of the 7th Cavalry Regiment had arrived in positions west of Kumchon, well behind American lines. The men had been delayed in landing at Pohang-dong because of a typhoon. After midnight there was a report the enemy somehow had achieved a breakthrough. Seventh Cavalry headquarters aroused all troops and ordered an immediate withdrawal. The men scattered in panic. That evening 119 men of the 2nd Battalion were still missing.[7]

On July 29, the 25th Division's 27th Regiment, under pressure, got permission to withdraw through 1st Cavalry positions. It did so before dawn and backed up to Kumchon, then moved to Waegwan on the Naktong as army reserve.

The 27th remained in army reserve for only one day, then was hurriedly dispatched to the far south to bolster the sagging American front west of Masan after the 19th Regiment had withdrawn from Chinju. This regiment now stood at the Chinju pass a few miles eastward. While the 27th Regiment took up defensive positions west of Chingdong-ni on the coast road southwest of Masan, the 19th Regiment, with attached ROKs and the weakened 29th Regiment, moved back to "the Notch," a pass on the northern Chinju-Masan road southwest of Chungam-ni.[8] (See Map 6.) On August 2, a reconnaissance in force by the 1st Battalion of the 27th reached the foot of the Chinju pass on the east under heavy pressure, but returned, successfully running a gauntlet of fire, after NK troops cut the road in several places behind the Americans. An attempted support for the reconnaissance by the 1st Battalion, 29th Regiment, on the northern road ran straight into an NK attack at the Notch, and both attacks got nowhere. Casualties on both sides were heavy. The return of the 1st Battalion, 27th Regiment, to Chindong-ni on the night of August 2 was a stroke of good fortune: North Koreans, infiltrating through the Sobuk-san mountainous area northwest of Chingdong-ni, attacked the village without warning on the morning of August 3, but were driven off by the 1st Battalion after a hard fight. The North Koreans lost about 600 men—400 killed in a single area north of town where American artillery caught an NK battalion detrucking.

* * * * * * * *

First Cavalry stood east of Yongdong in positions the division commander, Major General Hobart R. Gay, believed were increasingly dangerous. General Walker's advice had been ringing in General Gay's ears ever since he had arrived in Korea: "Protect Yongdong. Remember there are no friendly troops behind you. You must keep your own back door open. You can live without food but you cannot last long without ammunition, and unless the Yongdong-Taegu road is kept open you will soon be without ammunition."[9]

Patrols reported to General Gay's headquarters that NK troops were moving in a large flanking movement on the 1st Cavalry's rear by means of the Chosan-ni-Muju-Chirye route. Although the division was under no immediate enemy pressure, General Gay decided to withdraw to prevent its being cut off from Taegu.[10] The division began withdrawing on July 29 after the 27th Regiment had passed through. The division fell back all the way to the vicinity of Kumchon, twenty air miles east of Yongdong and only thirty air miles northwest of Taegu.

General Walker was unhappy with both the 25th and 1st Cavalry Divisions, the 25th because of its steady withdrawal, often in circumstances that seemed not to justify it, and the 1st Cavalry because of its inability to check the NK advance. He let both division commanders know his feelings.

On July 27 General MacArthur flew into Taegu with a small group of Far East Command high brass. During a closed conference with Walker and Major General Edward M. Almond, MacArthur's chief of staff, MacArthur emphasized the necessity of Eighth Army's standing its ground. Afterward, in the presence of several members of the Eighth Army staff, MacArthur said there would be no evacuation of Korea—no Korean Dunkirk.[11] MacArthur's position fitted perfectly with General Walker's bulldog tenacity. He knew as well as MacArthur the time for retreat had passed. Something, he knew, had to be done. And fast.

First, Walker conveyed his personal disappointment sharply to General Gay on the afternoon of July 29 when he visited the 1st Cavalry command post in a schoolhouse at Kumchon. Walker questioned Gay's withdrawal order. Gay replied he himself did not know whether it had been sound, but he had feared his communications would be cut. Walker told Gay the withdrawals had to stop.[12]

The same day, Walker visited the 25th Division's CP at Sangju. There he conferred with Major General William B. Kean, division commander, and afterward talked with the division staff. It was here that General Walker articulated the most famous order he gave during the Korean War. It came out in a talk to officers of the division staff. Within hours it was big news in the United States and had electrified practically every officer and man along the Eighth Army battle line. A paraphrase of Walker's talk recorded in notes taken at the time said: "We are fighting a battle against time. There will be no more retreating, withdrawal, or readjustment of the lines or any other term you choose. There is no line behind us to which we can retreat. Every unit must counterattack to keep the enemy in a state of confusion and off balance. There will be no Dunkirk, there will be no Bataan; a retreat to Pusan would be one of the greatest butcheries in history. We must fight until the end. Capture by these people is worse than death itself. We will fight as a team. If some of us must die, we will die fighting together. Any man who gives ground may be personally responsible for the death of thousands of his comrades. I want you to put this out to all men in the division. I want everybody to understand that we are going to hold this line. We are going to win."[13]

Walker's "stand-or-die" order, taken literally, did not jibe with his own plans to move the line back to the Naktong river. This caused some confusion at the time, but Walker obviously was not talking about some insane command to "stand and die where you are," as Hitler demanded of some German units in World War II. Rather, Walker wanted to change the American attitude of easy retreat in the face of North Korean envelopment movements and infiltration. Fortunately, Walker's direc-

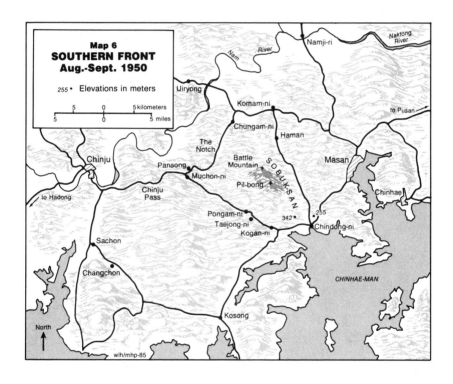

Map 6
SOUTHERN FRONT
Aug.-Sept. 1950

255 • Elevations in meters

tive coincided with the arrival of sufficient U.S. Army and U.S. Marine Corps troops to permit the ROKs and Americans to form a reasonably solid and continuous front. Such a front, protected by interlocking fields of fire from artillery, mortars and small arms, would be difficult to flank because an envelopment movement against one defending unit would uncover the attackers' own flanks to fire from other defenders. Moreover, a continuous front was the familiar, routine and safe tactical method employed by the American army wherever possible in World War II (and before), and provided the very essence of the kind of security which American troops had come to depend upon.

Americans excelled in this kind of war, in which the American preponderence in artillery, air power and heavy firepower of all kinds was employed to its maximum. Americans always have been outstanding in swapping high expenditures of ammunition and bombs for casualties. In these circumstances, they stand like rocks. Since World War I and the general American adoption of a doctrine of long main lines of resistance supplied by protected roads and railways, Americans often have been less sure and confident in situations where their flanks drop off into undefended air, where their lines of retreat and supply are cut off or threatened, or where they can call on no other units to support them in case of emergency. These latter conditions, of course, were precisely those in which the North Koreans excelled. A retreat to a fully defended line, therefore, was to return the Americans to the kind of warfare in which they were tops, while it created conditions in which the North Koreans' great advantages were reduced.

Eighth Army's withdrawal behind the Naktong took place between August 1 and 3. There was one radical shift: General Walker sent the 25th Division to the extreme south. This division, plus a just-arrived marine brigade and the army's 5th Regimental Combat Team attached to it, got the mission of stopping and driving back the 6th NK Division, still pushing for Masan and trying to break through to Pusan.

When the withdrawal order came, the 1st Cavalry Division was heavily engaged with the 3rd NK Division in the vicinity of Kumchon. But by nightfall of August 3, all 1st Cavalry units were across the Naktong except the rear guard of the 1st Battalion, 8th Cavalry Regiment, southwest of the main-line railway and highway bridges at Waegwan. These bridges were the most important on the river. General Gay, 1st Cavalry commander, gave orders that no one but himself could order detonation of the bridges.

At dusk on August 3, the 8th Cavalry rear guard stood on the west end of the highway bridge. Just behind them were thousands of refugees, pressed up against the Naktong bridge, trying to flee southward.

According to Appleman's official history of the early months of the war, this is what happened: as soon as the 1st Cavalry rear guard got across the bridge, General Gay planned to blow it up. But the Korean refugees refused to remain on the western side. Repeatedly, as the rear guard started across the bridge, a mass of refugees would follow. General Gay ordered the rear guard to return to the west side and hold back the refugees. When all was ready, the guard was to run across to the east side so the bridge could be detonated. The guard tried this plan several times; each time the refugees followed on the heels of the retreating guard. Finally, nearly at dark, General Gay felt he had no alternative but to order the bridge blown. It was a hard decision; many refugees were lost when the bridge was demolished.[14]

In moving to the Naktong, Eighth Army and the ROKs fell back to form the so-called Pusan Perimeter, a rectangle about 100 miles long north to south and about 50 miles east to west. The south-flowing Naktong formed the western boundary except for a fifteen-mile stretch from the confluence of the Nam river and the Naktong to the Korea Strait in the extreme south. Here the Naktong turns abruptly east and southeast to debouch at Pusan. This fifteen-mile-wide sector was the very front the 6th NK Division was attempting to crack through to reach Pusan. The northern flank of the perimeter ran from near Naktong-ni eastward through mountains toward Yongdok on the Sea of Japan. The entire northern flank and the northwest corner of the perimeter were defended by the ROK army's five divisions. On the west, the 1st Cavalry Division manned the line from Waegwan south for about 18 air miles (35 miles of river front). Next came the 24th Division with a front running to the confluence of the Nam and Naktong, a distance of 25 air miles (40 river miles). Southward to the Korea Strait was the 25th Division, which absorbed the battered two battalions of the 29th Regiment, thus becoming the first American division to get the normal three battalions for each regiment (the 24th Regiment already had three). In addition, the 5th Regimental Combat Team (RCT), newly arrived from Hawaii, and the 4,700-man 1st Provisional Marine Brigade (5th Marines), just arrived from the United States, were attached to the 25th, as was a regiment-sized group of South Korean survivors of the ROK 7th Division and smaller units reorganized as a task force under Colonel Min Ki Sik. The 5th RCT brought fourteen medium M26 Pershing tanks armed with high-velocity 90mm guns, and the marines brought a whole battalion of M26s. In addition, shops in Japan had repaired fifty-four World War II M4A3 Sherman medium tanks salvaged from the Pacific islands; these were assigned to the newly activated 89th Medium Tank Battalion.[15] The United States at last had tanks to counter the T34. And eighty more were on the way from the United States by ship.

Finally, two regiments of the 2nd Infantry Division (the 9th and the 23rd, plus supporting artillery battalions) arrived at Pusan from the United States to be followed in mid-August by the division's third regiment, the 38th. The great buildup in American power was under way.

The view at the time, despite American reinforcements, was that the North Korean army still vastly outnumbered the Americans and ROKs. For example, the New York *Times* reported on July 26, 1950, that North Koreans had attacked the 1st Cavalry Division at Yongdong with "wave after wave" of troops. On July 30, the *Times* reported U.S. and ROK troops were "still outnumbered at least four to one."[16]

In fact, American and ROK combat strength on August 4 was 92,000 men, while North Korean combat forces numbered only 70,000 in eleven committed divisions. In addition, NK artillery strength had declined greatly, and tank numbers were down to forty, fewer than the number of tanks in the newly arrived U.S. 89th Tank Battalion alone.[17] North Korean artillery pieces and mortars were down to about one-third the number NK forces had at the start of the war. The 4th NK Division, for example, reportedly had only twelve guns on August 5 when the division reached the Naktong, as opposed to at least forty-eight howitzers in a U.S. division in Korea at the time.[18]

Part of the reason for the great overestimation of North Korean strength was the failure of U.S. Army intelligence to realize how many casualties the ROK army had inflicted on the North Koreans. On July 29, General MacArthur's Intelligence Section set NK losses at 31,000, while the Department of the Army estimated them at 37,500. Actually, NK casualties were about 58,000, according to study of prisoner-of-war interrogations.[19] Whatever the variance, there was no reason to believe U.S. and ROK forces were still greatly inferior in numbers. Using MacArthur's own figures of NK casualties, North Korean and United Nations forces on August 4 would have been at rough parity, with firepower immensely greater in the U.S. units and also higher in the ROK units, now being supplied with more weapons from the United States.

Despite these figures, the myth has continued for decades that American and ROK troops faced almost overwhelming odds from "human waves" of attacking troops during the hot and dusty days along the Naktong. Perhaps one reason for the perpetuation of the myth is that the North Koreans had the initiative going into the Naktong battle, and they continued to attack. They were weary and battle worn, and in many cases had hardly enough food to keep going, yet the North Koreans persisted against incredible odds. The illusion of strength that aggressive, victorious and confidently led soldiers can project has never been proved more decisively than by the North Korean army in the summer of 1950.

CHAPTER 18

The First Counteroffensive

THERE WAS STILL one open front on the Pusan Perimeter, and it was in the most dangerous spot of all: just west of Masan and within thirty-three air miles of Pusan. For this reason Walker had concentrated there a formidable force of more than 20,000 men: the 25th Division, a marine brigade and the 5th RCT.[1] Two battalions of medium tanks, the marines' and the 89th, gave Americans in this sector two-thirds of the number of tanks the North Koreans had in all when they started the war. In addition, the marines had two close-support squadrons of Corsair fighter-bombers standing immediately offshore in the Korea Strait on the two escort carriers *Sicily* and *Badoeng Strait*.[2]

General Walker decided he had enough troops in the south to launch a major counterattack, the first by Americans in the war. The target was the North Koreans' ghost division, the 6th, still pressing hard toward Masan. Eighth Army intelligence estimated the division had 7,500 effectives. This was incorrect: the 6th NK Division was down to 6,000 men. However, unknown to Eighth Army, the 83rd NK Motorized Regiment had joined the 6th Division, and its 1,500 men brought NK strength to Eighth Army G-2's 7,500 figure. The North Koreans had 36 pieces of artillery and 25 tanks.[3]

American superiority in numbers was well over two to one, in tanks four to one, and in artillery more than two to one. In addition, American control of the air was complete. Besides the marine Corsairs on the baby flattops, the navy in case of need had two fast fleet carriers in Korean waters— the *Valley Forge* and the *Philippine Sea*—and the Fifth Air Force had several hundred fighters and fighter-bombers ready to provide support. By mid-July North Korean forces had virtually stopped movement by daylight because of overwhelming U.S. air power. By the end of the month, the American and ROK forces in Korea were getting more air support than General Omar Bradley's 12th Army Group in Europe in World War II.[4]

Eighth Army's plan was to attack westward to recapture Chinju between August 5 and 10, to move farther west about the middle of the month, then to wheel north toward the Kum river. It was an ambitious plan, but was based on the expected arrival of the entire 2nd Division and three more tank battalions by August 15. The first part of the attack—to recapture Chinju, twenty-seven miles by air west of Masan, forty miles by the closest road—seemed relatively easy, given the great superiority of American weapons and firepower. (See Map 6.) In addition, General Walker wanted to relieve pressure on the Taegu front, where NK forces were reported massing, by requiring the North Korean command to reinforce the 6th Division.[5]

Jump-off for the attack was August 7, and the units for the counter-offensive were named Task Force Kean after the commander of the 25th Division. The plan called for attack along three roads, with one regiment assigned to each road. On the north the 35th Regiment of the 25th Division was to move from the Notch near Chungam-ni westward to Muchon-ni, then on through Chinju pass to Chinju. The 5th RCT was to attack from Chindong-ni (southwest of Masan on the coast) along a secondary inland road past Kogan-ni to join with the 35th Regiment at Muchon-ni. The marines would follow the 5th RCT, then branch off southwestward on the coast road beginning just east of Kogan-ni and attack through Kosong, Sachon and up toward Chinju from the south.

The 25th Division's 27th Regiment was to revert to army reserve at Masan, and the division's 24th Regiment, along with the ROK Task Force Min, was assigned to clean out North Korean troops holed up in the mountainous Sobuk-san northwest of Chindong-ni.

It was to be another engagement in an extremely hot and dry Korean summer. The weather plagued soldiers on both sides, but especially the unconditioned Americans used to garrison conditions. In July and August only one-fourth the usual twenty inches of rain fell on South Korea, and temperatures on the frequently cloudless days often reached 105° Fahrenheit and sometimes higher. The heat and the exertion of climbing high hills caused more dropouts among the newly arrived marines and soldiers than did enemy fire.[6]

The 2nd Battalion of the 35th Regiment led off the counterattack on the morning of August 7, moving westward from the Notch. The 35th immediately encountered about five hundred NK troops supported by several self-propelled guns. The two forces joined in a battle that raged for five hours. But at the end, with the help of an air strike, the 35th secured the western reaches of the Notch and the high ground to the north. The NK position shattered, the 35th moved rapidly westward and reached a position just short of the Muchon-ni road fork. Here it dug in to wait for the 5th RCT, which was supposed to be moving northward up the middle road.

But the 5th RCT had not been doing well. First of all, there had been a disturbing occurrence on the night of August 6–7, just before the RCT was to attack. North Korean troops moving out of the Sobuk-san mountains dislodged a platoon of the 5th RCT's 2nd Battalion that was holding part of Hill 342 (Fox Hill), only a mile north of the coast road and a couple of miles west of Chindong-ni. The NK troops thereupon moved around a Fox Hill spur and from there could look right down on the command posts of the 5th RCT and the marine brigade's 5th Marine Regiment, on artillery emplacements, and on the main supply road at Chindong-ni.

Nevertheless, the RCT moved out on the morning of August 7, led by its 1st Battalion. It arrived without difficulty at the road junction east of Kogan-ni, but, making an incomprehensible blunder, the RCT turned *left* down the coast road that had been allotted to the marines—instead of continuing west on the road leading through Kogan-ni and toward a junction with the 35th Regiment at Muchon-ni. By noon the RCT was on a hill mass three miles south of the road junction, pointed in the wrong direction, and leaving uncaptured a hill northwest of the road junction which the battalion should have occupied to cover the advance of the rest of the RCT and the marines.

Meantime, the 2nd Battalion of the 5th Marines moved out at 11 a.m. to relieve the 2nd Battalion, 5th RCT, on a Fox Hill spur so the army unit could follow in the attack. The marines ran right into a hornet's nest of North Koreans who had come around the hill during the night. In addition, other NK soldiers had infiltrated around Chindong-ni. On the morning of August 7, they were occupying Hill 255 just northeast of town—and thus dominating the road to Masan. While the marines attacked the enemy on Fox Hill, troops of the 2nd Battalion, 24th Regiment, and the 3rd Battalion, 5th Marines, tried to break the Hill 255 roadblock on the Masan road. The attacks were made more difficult by the temperature, which had quickly risen above 100°F. The marines climbing Fox Hill suffered thirty heat-prostration cases, six times their battle casualties. The marine attack failed, and the fight developed into a general melee, with troops of the 27th Regiment, supposedly in reserve, getting involved. In addition, communications were interrupted when the treads of U.S. tanks tore up telephone lines strung along the sides of the road. Against Hill 255 the attacks were equally unsuccessful.

Artillery fired nearly 2,000 rounds at the NK forces emplaced there, but it took three days of stubborn fighting by marines and soldiers to dislodge the enemy. The marines resumed their attack against Fox Hill on the morning of August 8, and this time the 2nd Battalion succeeded.

After the 5th RCT's 2nd Battalion was relieved on Fox Hill, it moved immediately west to seize the hill northwest of the road junction near Kogan-ni that the 1st Battalion, 5th RCT, was supposed to have captured the day before. The 2nd Battalion was unable to secure the hill against NK resistance. In the late afternoon, General Kean moved up to the 2nd Battalion position and told the battalion CO, Lieutenant Colonel John L. Throckmorton: "I want that hill tonight." Throckmorton sent two companies against the hill, supported by three tanks and mortars. Although near exhaustion, the men got the hill.

What had been billed as an "easy" counterattack had degenerated into a vicious dogfight on bitterly contested ridgelines—not the anticipated great sweeping advance of American troops down the roads, led by invincible armor. The damage was being done by individual North Korean soldiers firing small arms, throwing grenades and firing mortars. Despite the presence of overwhelming American firepower, the individual enemy soldier with very little backup was stopping the U.S. advance in its tracks.

By August 9, however, the disconcerting enemy penetration into the American rear on Fox Hill and Hill 255 had been eliminated, and the 5th RCT and 5th Marines were at last ready for the advance that was supposed to have been made two days before.

On the afternoon of August 9, the 5th Marines moved rapidly down the coastal road, leapfrogging battalions as they advanced. Corsairs of the 1st Marine Air Wing, flying from the *Sicily* and the *Badoeng Strait* standing close inshore, patrolled the road ahead and the adjoining hills and were able to deliver strikes within minutes after a target appeared.

The marine assault, so close to the Korea Strait, was perfect for the marine system of attack, organized as it was around an amphibious mission. Since marines normally anticipated being put ashore by small craft, they could not expect much immediate support by organic artillery. Marine tactics called instead for close air support as a substitute for artillery in early landing stages. Thus air observers accompanied each infantry battalion, and to insure an air strike within five to ten minutes, the marine aircraft orbited on station above the marines on the ground.[7] It was an extremely effective, albeit extremely expensive, system, and was made possible in Korea not only because the marines had the fighters and wanted to use them but because North Korean air power was completely absent. Hostile fighter opposition could have prevented the baby flattops from operating so close to the target areas and also eliminated the practice of Corsairs orbiting for long periods over the battle area, waiting to be called down for strikes.[8]

The marine air demonstrated its incredible capability on August 11, as the marine infantry neared the town of Kosong. The marine supporting artillery adjusting fire on a crossroads west of town happened to drop a few shells near camouflaged NK vehicles. The North Koreans, believing their position had been discovered, quickly moved to their vehicles and started down the road toward Sachon. By pure happenstance the errant shells of the marine artillery had flushed out the major part of the 83rd Motorized Regiment, which had arrived to support the 6th NK Division.

As the long column of about two hundred vehicles, trucks, jeeps and motorcycles got on the road, a flight of four Corsairs from the *Badoeng Strait* came over on a routine reconnaissance mission of shepherding the ground marines. They spotted the NK vehicles, swung low over them, and strafed the length of the column. Trucks crashed into each other, others ran into ditches, still others attempted to drive off the road and into the hills. North Koreans sprang out of the vehicles, seeking cover. The Corsairs turned for another run over the stricken column. This time the North Koreans struck back with small arms and automatic weapons. They hit two of the marine planes, forcing one down and causing the other to crash. But the Corsair attack had left forty NK vehicles wrecked and burning. Alerted to the scene, another flight of marine Corsairs and air force F-51 Mustangs arrived and continued the destruction. When ground troops arrived later in the day, they found 31 trucks, 24 jeeps, 45 motorcycles and much ammunition and equipment destroyed or abandoned. North Korean casualties in this brief engagement totaled about two hundred. It was a heavy blow to the NK motorized regiment.

The next morning, the marines started on what they expected to be a rapid movement on Sachon, about eight miles below Chinju. The marines advanced over eleven miles unopposed, and were within about three miles of Sachon when the leathernecks drove into an NK ambush at Changchon (known to the marines as "Changallon"). Fortunately for the marines, the North Koreans gave away their ambush too early, and the marines were able to pull up quickly into a defensive alignment. A huge fire fight developed and went on through the afternoon and into the evening. Corsairs repeatedly struck at the NK positions, and marine infantry gained control of two hills on the north side and one on the south side of the road. Before daylight on August 13 a group of North Koreans infiltrated the southern hill and overran a platoon of marines. Shortly after daylight, the marines received orders to withdraw and return to Masan: overriding dangers elsewhere in the perimeter required the immediate removal of the marine force from the southern counterattack.

Meantime, on the middle road, the 5th RCT artillery suffered a devastating attack before light on August 12 at Pongam-ni. It was made possible by the familiar North Korean tactic of cutting the main supply routes and attacking targets in the rear. Two NK tanks and several antitank guns were able to approach down a valley out of the Sobuk-san to within point-blank range of two artillery battalions (the 555th and the 90th) after a U.S. section of tanks and a platoon of infantry blocking the valley had withdrawn. NK infantry also had been able to infiltrate into hills north of Pongam-ni and pour automatic-weapons fire down on the village. The 105mm howitzers of the 555th fired without effect on the enemy armor, and the 155mm howitzers of the 90th could not depress their tubes low enough to engage the NK tanks and guns. North Korean infantry finally overran the 555th positions. The men of the 90th, also attacked by enemy infantry, were able to hold their positions. After day broke, Corsairs flew in to strafe and rocket the NK forces. They had no radio communication with the ground, but they followed tracer bullets from the action and were able to locate the NK weapons.

The troops called it Bloody Gulch: the 555th lost all eight of its 105mm howitzers in two firing batteries, the 90th lost all six 155mm howitzers it had emplaced. About 80 men of the 555th were killed and another 80 wounded; the 90th lost 10 killed, 60 wounded and 30 missing.[9]

It was an anticlimax, but on August 13 a battalion of the 5th RCT drove up the road to Muchon-ni and rendezvoused with the 35th Regiment, and together the two units proceeded on to the Chinju pass and looked down on Chinju. But that was the high-water mark. Task Force Kean receded back approximately to the positions from which its units had started.[10] Even the effort to rout out the enemy from the Sobuk-san failed; the abandoned coal mines in the hills were crawling with North Korean troops, and soldiers of the 24th Regiment and Task Force Min in ten days of effort were unable to dislodge them.[11]

The first American counterattack had collapsed; not a single North Korean soldier had been diverted from other fronts. The sadly under-strength 6th NK Division and the 83rd Motorized Regiment had stopped well-equipped forces more than twice as powerful. The key, it became obvious, was the failure to clear Sobuk-san.[12] From these heights in the rear of the advancing Americans, North Koreans moved down daily on the main American supply routes and blocked or mined them. The anxieties and disruptions these caused, not to speak of the damage, as at Bloody Gulch, were incalculable. The lesson was sobering: it was not enough for American forces to possess high mobility or even vastly more powerful weapons. Mobility signified primary reliance on the roads. Immediately off the roads the high Korean mountains were easily occupied by the enemy. The conclusion which American commanders reached: to beat the North Koreans, Americans had to climb mountains and flush out the enemy directly from his positions with guns, grenades and carefully directed mortar and artillery fire.

The days of the dirty war had arrived.

Men of the 25th Division and the attached 5th RCT experienced the reality of this dirty war to the fullest throughout the last half of August as they attempted to neutralize Sobuk-san by capturing its high, steep, dominating peaks, Pil-bong and the adjoining ridge crest, named Battle Mountain by the Americans.[13]

This two-week-long battle became particularly associated with the 24th Regiment; while the 5th RCT was continuously engaged on Pil-bong in defense of that part of Sobuk-san south of Battle Mountain, the 24th took on reduction of Battle Mountain itself.

Battle Mountain changed hands so many times there was never an agreement on the exact number, but it certainly was nineteen or twenty. On some days the peak was captured or recaptured two or three times by one side or the other. The usual pattern was for the North Koreans to take the hill at night and for the 24th to recapture it the next day. The 24th always captured Battle Mountain the same way: heavy fire from artillery, mortars and tanks raked the crest; then aircraft dropped napalm; then the infantry attacked up an accessible slope while supporting mortars kept up a base of fire on the hill crest until the infantry had arrived just short of the crest; then the mortar fire lifted and the riflemen rushed up the final stretch, usually finding it deserted by the enemy.

As August ended, the Americans and North Koreans on the Masan front maintained a precarious stalemate, like two exhausted boxers hanging on and exchanging blows, but anxious to hear the bell sound the end of the round.

CHAPTER 19

The Days Along the Naktong

AFTERWARD THE SURVIVORS called the period "the days along the Naktong," those strange shared days of August and most of September when an anxious North Korean command, knowing the sand was rapidly running out on its gamble to defeat the South Koreans and their allies, flung attack after attack against an increasingly strong and resilient defensive line. Though the Americans and ROKs thought they were still outnumbered, and were not, the North Koreans knew they were both outnumbered and outgunned. Yet with great audacity, temerity and sheer desperation the North Korean army crashed valiantly time after time against well-emplaced American and ROK (and later British) positions, driving in penetrations and making some gains, especially against the less heavily armed ROKs in the north.

To most of the ROK and UN soldiers, the illusion of North Korean strength was thoroughly convincing. Ever since June 25, the North Koreans had been attacking, and generally they had been winning. They expected to advance, and the ROKs and Americans expected to defend. Though by August the NK army had been bled white by losses, yet the North Koreans continued to attack, when the odds had tilted fatally against them. By early August the United States had landed three divisions and parts of two more—the 2nd Infantry and a brigade of marines—plus numerous independent units, including the 5th RCT. Although some of these units were woefully understrength, both because they entered the peninsula that way and because they sustained casualties, the Americans' immense potential strength was growing daily as reserves and National Guard units were called up and the draft was reinstituted. These men not only filled up holes in the American defense system elsewhere, but many men and individual units were dispatched directly to Korea, often in emergency drafts sent by air.

In July, the Pipeline delivered more than 5,500 officers and men, in August 11,400, and in September 13,000.[1] By the end of August the four army divisions then in Korea had been built up to their standard wartime allotment of three battalions for each of the three regiments in each division. In addition, practically all of the four artillery battalions in each division (three firing 105mm and one firing 155mm howitzers) had received three firing batteries, while the supply of medium tanks had passed two hundred and was rising.[2]

In addition, in late August the first Allied ground reinforcements other than American arrived to create a true United Nations effort on the battle line. The UN Command already had been operating since the early days of the war at sea with British and Netherlands ships and in the air with Australian F-51s. The ground force was the British 27th Brigade, a near regimental-sized unit of nearly 1,600 men made up of a battalion of the Middlesex Regiment and a battalion of the Argyll and Sutherland Highlanders Regiment; the brigade was quickly thrown into the battle line near Taegu.[3]

In addition to delivering troops, the American logistical system was producing prodigies in the amounts of equipment and supplies it was landing. Critically needed items, such as the new 3.5-inch bazooka and a new 5-inch shaped-charge rocket for navy fighter planes, were airlifted from the United States. At Pusan, more than 300,000 tons of material were offloaded July 2–31. In the last half of July alone, 230 ships arrived in Pusan harbor.[4]

Against this kind of buildup, the North Koreans in the long run had no chance whatsoever of victory. Their leaders hoped that somehow, before the steel bands the United States was drawing around the perimeter got much tighter, they might break through to Pusan and drive the hated Yankee into the sea along with his ROK minions. It was a dream that paled with every passing day and with every additional casualty; but it was what kept the North Korean leadership going.

The North Korean attacks came all around the perimeter in early August, all more or less at the same time, the NK command hoping that, if one attack failed, another might succeed. (See Map 1.) The 6th NK Division tried to break the stalemate in the Sobuk-san west of Masan in the south. The 4th NK Division made a fierce try to ram through a bulge of the Naktong almost due west of Yongsan. The 3rd NK Division made another effort about three miles south of Waegwan. The 10th NK Division attempted to coordinate in this attack with a crossing farther south at Yongpo on the Koryang-Taegu road. North and northwest of Taegu the 1st, 13th and 15th NK Divisions launched a major offensive which rolled up ROK troops to within twelve miles of Taegu. On the east coast a concurrent attack through the Taebaek mountains by the 12th NK Division and the 766th Unit flanked the ROK 3rd Division, which was battling the 5th NK Division near Yongdok, and forced the ROK division, pressed against the shore, to be evacuated by sea. NK troops then occupied Pohang-dong, until forced out by naval gunfire, and threatened nearby Yonil airfield, causing the air force to displace two F-51 squadrons operating out of the field. Nevertheless, in desperate engagements on the important northeastern front, the ROKs held, and by August 20 had driven the North Koreans into the mountains northwest of Pohang-dong.[5]

The Pusan Perimeter shrank back fifteen to twenty miles in the north, but there it held. The Naktong river line held without cracking, despite temporary and deep penetrations; but there were anxious days when U.S. commanders feared a breakthrough. A major factor contributing to the success of the American and ROK effort was the vital Pusan-Kyongju-Taegu-Pusan railroad loop within the perimeter, run magnificently by army Transportation Corps trainmen. It carried the burden of supply with such success the troops finally began to get adequate quantities of ammunition and weapons. The rail supply system permitted the artillery to pour out thousands of rounds of fire on NK troop concentration points. It also permitted General Walker to move troops quickly in emergencies from one part of the perimeter to the other. The old doctrine that an army operating on interior lines is more flexible than one operating on exterior lines was proved in the battles of the perimeter. Whereas American and ROK troops had adequate, even abundant, supplies, NK supply was generally poor: the troops of the 12th NK Division on the mountainous northeastern front not only sent their artillery to the rear because they could not get ammunition, but for days in early August received no rations and had to forage at night in the villages for food.[6]

The Pusan Perimeter gave the Americans their first chance to establish something approaching a continuous line, with known units on the left and right and some reserves in the rear. This was the familiar way the U.S. Army fought, and its re-establishment became an almost instant security blanket for commanders and troops alike. American battle efficiency improved dramatically.

The tactical plan adopted by General Walker along the Naktong was a series of strongpoints on the highest hills along the east side of the river. These strongpoints afforded views of the river itself and the natural routes of travel from it into American-held territory. These points were lightly manned in daylight, serving as little more than observation posts (OPs). At night they were turned into listening posts and small defense perimeters. The mission of these OPs was to serve as advance listening posts, as trip wires to alert commanders of attempted penetrations. The real fight for the Naktong line was left to reserve troops, some miles back from the river, who were always on call to counterattack against any enemy penetration. It was an excellent system because it afforded the maximum concentration of force against any danger spot. Artillery and mortars emplaced back of the river were laid to fire on known ferry and other crossing points; artillery fire could be massed, within limits, and all of the avenues of approach available to the North Koreans could be raked by American small-arms fire and pounded by artillery and mortars.[7] Most important of all were the howitzers: high numbers and high efficiency of cannon had been a hallmark of the U.S. Army since the Civil War, and along the Naktong American artillery rapidly moved back to its traditional position as the arbiter of battles.

* * * * * * * *

On August 5 North Koreans made three crossings of the Naktong. Two were north of Waegwan in the ROK sector. The third was thirty miles south of Waegwan, opposite Yongsan, in the 24th Division sector. This last crossing was extremely dangerous, and threatened the entire perimeter. A breakthrough to Yongsan would have split U.S. forces north of the Naktong bend from the 25th Division around Masan; also, NK troops might have penetrated east of Yongsan to Miryang and thereby cut the main Taegu-Seoul railway and road, with disastrous effects on supply. (See Map 1.)

This attack was made by the now-famous 4th NK Division, which, with the 3rd NK Division, had pressed the Americans down the Seoul-Pusan road. The division was down to about 7,000 men, with about 1,500 men in each of the three infantry regiments.[8] The division's target was the so-called Naktong Bulge, seven miles north of where the Nam river joins the Naktong. The bulge was defended by the 34th Regiment.

North Korean troops attacked at midnight, August 5, without artillery preparation. They rafted across or stripped off their clothes and waded through shoulder-deep water. They lodged on a north-south ridgeline two and a half miles long on the eastern edge of the bulge and about three miles from the river. The ridgeline was known as Cloverleaf hill (north) and Obong-ni ridge (south). Between the two eminences was a low pass with a small road running through it back to Yongsan. Several counterattacks by battalions of the 34th and the 19th Regiments could not drive out the North Koreans. By August 11, the entire 4th NK Division had got across the river, along with artillery and heavy equipment, by means of an underwater bridge. These bridges had been much used by the Russians in World War II, and apparently the Russians had taught the North Koreans how to build them. The North Koreans employed them extensively along the Naktong. They consisted of sandbags, rocks and logs laid onto the bed of the river to a depth of about a foot below the surface. In muddy water they were extremely difficult for air observers to see and were highly useful for moving guns and heavy equipment across.

On August 11, a major U.S. attack, including two battalions of the recently arrived 9th Infantry Regiment of the 2nd Division, the 19th Regiment and a battalion of the 21st Regiment, completely failed to dislodge the North Koreans on Cloverleaf and Obong-ni ridge. Meanwhile, NK troops moved around the main battle positions within the bulge and brought Yongsan, five miles to the east, under artillery fire. NK soldiers also infiltrated east of Yongsan and built up a strong block on the road to Miryang. South of Yongsan, NK troops surprised and killed a squad of U.S. soldiers guarding the bridge over the Naktong at Namji-ri. If not driven away, these NK soldiers would isolate the 25th Division south of the Naktong bend from direct assistance in case of need.

In this crisis, General Walker ordered the 27th Regiment, in reserve at Masan, to attack north and recapture the Namji-ri bridge, and it did so, scattering about two hundred NK troops in the process. Meanwhile, Colonel John G. Hill, CO of the 9th Regiment, sent a force to break the roadblock east of Yongsan, and a scratch force from 24th Division headquarters at Miryang moved west to block any further penetrations by NK troops into the division rear. The next day three American forces converged on the enemy roadblock east of Yongsan: the 27th Regiment, the 9th Regiment, and a battalion of the newly arrived 23rd Infantry Regiment of the 2nd Division, committed from Miryang. The attack dislodged the NK roadblock force, killing some and driving the rest away.

General Walker's prompt movement of troops from several directions eliminated the dangerous North Korean penetration toward Miryang and put Eighth Army in a position to press the advancing 4th NK Division back across the Naktong.

The 9th Regiment, plus 24th Division troops organized as a task force under Colonel Hill, launched an attack against enemy troops on the Cloverleaf and Obong-ni ridgeline in the bulge. The battle went on through August 15, with high losses on both sides; in one encounter soldiers in the 34th Regiment got into a grenade and fire fight at five to ten paces. The engaged platoon lost 25 men killed or wounded of 35 who advanced on the ridge. The 4th NK Division fought Colonel Hill's task force to a standstill.[9]

General Walker was getting impatient with the failure to pinch off the Naktong Bulge salient, and on August 15 he decided to commit the marine brigade to help Task Force Hill. Walker delayed the attack until August 17 to give time for the escort carriers, *Sicily* and *Badoeng Strait*, to get in position to launch the marines' close-support Corsairs.[10] Meanwhile, NK forces counterattacked Task Force Hill on August 16 in intense and close-quarter engagements which added to the fatigue and depression of the American soldiers. However, conditions on the NK side were worse. The NK division was getting little food or resupply of ammunition because heavy American artillery fire and air attacks were isolating the North Koreans on the battlefield. Desertion among replacements was running high, and many wounded died because it was difficult to evacuate them.[11]

A now thoroughly aroused Walker was taking no chances on the new attack on the 4th NK Division. In addition to the 5th Marine Regiment, he added the army 9th, 34th and 19th Regiments, and laid in fifty-four 105mm howitzers and a battalion of 155mm howitzers. And the marines had their black Corsairs.

The attack was under the command of General Church, 24th Division commander. He planned to send the 9th Regiment against Cloverleaf while the marines attacked Obong-ni. But the 5th Marines CO, Lieutenant Colonel Raymond L. Murray, thought he could capture Obong-ni with relative ease, because both he and Church thought the North Koreans would make their major effort on a higher ridge west of Cloverleaf-Obong-ni and closer to the Naktong. General Church agreed, therefore, to let the marines go in first.

The marines started at 7:35 a.m. August 17 for the mile-and-a-half long Obong-ni, which rises 300 to 450 feet above the valley floor. There had been no artillery preparation on the ridgeline itself: instead, eighteen Corsairs zoomed in and delivered a strike at the ridge, doing so much damage that Obong-ni seemed, as General Church said, to be "floating."[12] Two 120-man companies were the lead 2nd Battalion unit, and four platoons constituted the assault force; from the ridge they received no fire, but they got a lot from the north toward Cloverleaf: machine-gun, rifle and mortar. Only twenty men, in Lieutenant Michael J. Shinka's platoon, got to the top of the narrow ridge. As the marines fell into abandoned NK foxholes, enemy machine-gun fire swept over them, and North Koreans in another row of foxholes just down the reverse slope jumped up and attacked the leathernecks with grenades, quickly wounding five men. Shinka ordered the platoon off; they moved fast, pulling their wounded back on ponchos.

The Corsairs came back, this time raking the reverse slope with a hail of explosives. The marine infantry started back up from down the slope where they had waited. At first the North Koreans responded very little; but after the Corsairs had gone, the North Koreans climbed back into their forward foxholes and fired and rolled grenades down on the climbing marines. Again Shinka's platoon was the only one to reach the top; starting with fifteen men this time, only nine got to the top, and they, too, had to withdraw, but Shinka was wounded twice. Of the 240 marines in the 2nd Battalion attack, 23 were killed and 119 wounded. Colonel Murray, seeing the punishment the battalion had taken, passed the 1st Battalion through to resume the attack.

The marine Corsairs had failed to kill North Koreans in deep foxholes on the reverse slope. And, NK fire from Cloverleaf and vicinity had caused many of the marine casualties. Colonel Murray now was convinced the 9th Regiment should attack Cloverleaf when the marines advanced on Obong-ni once more.

The combined assault got going at 4 p.m. The 9th Regiment's assault was preceded by all the fire 24th Division's artillery could lay on Cloverleaf, including time-on-target air bursts, which exploded over NK foxholes and showered down shell fragments on the enemy soldiers huddled in their holes. The 9th Infantry secured Cloverleaf without difficulty; the artillery had done its work. The NK soldiers who survived abandoned the hill and ran to the rear. On Obong-ni, however, the North Koreans again stopped the marines, but detachments, not having to endure fire from Cloverleaf, this time were able to work around the north side and secure the top, though NK fire from the south still contested possession.

The 4th NK Division now was hanging on by a thread. And it was facing a new kind of war. Six days before, the division had made a spectacular breakthrough into the American rear east of Yongsan and had set up a roadblock on the main road. In earlier weeks this would have guaranteed the collapse of American resistance, the abandonment of vehicles and equipment, and the frantic scattering of American soldiers over the mountains to safety. Instead, three powerful American forces converged on the NK soldiers and shattered them and their roadblock. Now, intense shellfire and coordinated infantry attacks were driving the remnants of the division inexorably back against the Naktong. In their desperation, the North Koreans turned to the weapon that had pulled them through so many times before: the T34 tank. This time they were to realize in full measure that the world they had known had been turned upside down.

Just before dark, marines on Obong-ni saw three T34s coming from the west, followed by a fourth tank not in view. They came steadily and confidently along the road toward the pass between Obong-ni and Cloverleaf. Three U.S. M26 Pershings rolled forward to meet them. At the pass 75mm recoilless rifles already were in position and waiting. Two 3.5-inch bazooka teams hurried toward the pass. Three F-51 Mustangs sighted the tanks and made strafing runs without visible effect, but the word was out and U.S. fighters quickly made for the point. The T34s rumbled on toward the pass. As the hull of the leading tank came into view, one bazooka team fired at a hundred yards and hit the tank in its treads. The tank came on with all guns firing. A second rocket from the other bazooka team struck the T34 at the same instant as a shell from a 75mm recoilless rifle tore a hole in the hull. The tank stopped, but its guns continued to fire. In the next moment, the leading M26 Pershing scored a direct hit on the T34, setting it on fire. The second T34 came into view: the bazooka teams knocked it out. Then two Pershings destroyed the third T34 the instant it swung into sight, and fighter planes knocked out the fourth tank before it got to the pass. *Sic transit gloria mundi.*

That night, the marines at Obong-ni beat off a fierce North Korean infantry attack that left 183 enemy bodies in front of marine positions and cost the marines scores of men. The next morning the marines drove south down the Obong-ni ridgeline against continued NK resistance, which finally ended when a Corsair pilot, carefully checking his target, dropped a 500-pound bomb directly on an NK machine-gun emplacement, killing the crew.

That was the end. The once-proud 4th NK Division's survivors were now streaming back toward the Naktong, in open view. They provided a marvelous target for U.S. artillery forward observers who quickly adjusted airburst (VT) and quick-fuse fire on the retreating enemy. Fighter planes roared over all the roads and trails, catching many enemy soldiers in the open. On the morning of August 19, army and marine troops met at the river; virtually all of the 4th Division had fled in the night. They left behind thirty-four sorely needed artillery pieces and scores of machine guns and other weapons. Prisoners captured at the end of the battle reported each of the division's three rifle regiments was down to three hundred to four hundred men each. The division had been virtually eliminated as a fighting force.

CHAPTER 20

"We Are Going to Hold This Line"

THAT THE NORTH KOREAN ARMY was facing a new kind of war was proved not only by the fate of the 4th NK Division in the Naktong Bulge, but in two other coordinated assaults in the same period aimed at a concentric movement on Taegu. They showed that General Walker's "stand-or-die" order of July 29 was being taken seriously by men all across the front.

The first enemy move on Taegu came from northwest of the city across the Naktong a short distance south of Waegwan. The second was from the southwest at Yongpo, a minuscule village where the Koryang-Taegu road crossed the Naktong. (See Map 1.)

The attack from the northwest was by the now-legendary 3rd NK Division, first to enter Seoul at the start of the war, victor (with the 4th Division) over the U.S. 24th Division on the Kum river and at Taejon, and pursuer of the 1st Cavalry Division from Yongdong. The assault from the southwest over the Koryang-Taegu road was by the recently organized and previously uncommitted 10th NK Division.

The concentric assault started in the early hours of August 9 when the 7th Regiment of the 3rd NK Division waded across at a ferry site two miles south of the destroyed bridges at Waegwan. Men of the 5th Cavalry Regiment spotted the North Koreans and quickly called in preregistered artillery concentrations.[1] Some of the North Koreans, however, got across and moved eastward away from the river. Shortly thereafter, the other two regiments of the NK division tried to cross farther south. By this time the entire opposite American lines of outposts had been alerted, and flares and star shells lighted up the two regiments at midstream. U.S. artillery and automatic-weapons fire poured down on

141

the two regiments. Most of the North Korean survivors fled to the safety of the west bank, and the attack dissolved. But about a thousand men of the 7th Regiment got on Hill 268 about two miles east of the river and only ten air miles from Taegu. Hill 268, which came to be known as Triangulation Hill, was important because the main Seoul-Pusan highway and railway ran along its base. The 1st Cavalry's commander, General Gay, immediately sent in a battalion of the 7th Cavalry to eliminate the North Koreans, and in two days of fighting the regiment, supported by heavy artillery and mortar fire and tanks, drove 300 NK survivors back beyond the river; the other 700 enemy soldiers were casualties, most of them killed by artillery and mortar fire.

American firepower was assuming once again the devastating strength it possessed in the later stages of World War II. As a result of the attacks, the proud 3rd NK Division was reduced to a disorganized force of about 2,500 men and had to be pulled entirely out of the North Korean order of battle to be rebuilt.

American response to the attack of the 10th NK Division at Yongpo was equally devastating.[2] A regiment of the 10th Division got across the river in the early hours of August 12, but was stopped by a battalion of the 7th Cavalry with the help of artillery and air strikes. The division tried again on August 14, but was driven back by a 1st Cavalry counterattack, plus air strikes and heavy artillery barrages. The 77th Field Artillery Battalion fired more than 1,800 rounds so fast it damaged its howitzer tubes. Of the 1,700 North Koreans who were able to get across the river at Yongpo, 1,500 were killed, while total division casualties were 2,500.

Despite the violence of the NK battering along the Naktong, the main thrust of the North Korean attacks was being aimed from the north and northwest toward Taegu. But MacArthur, like some others, believed the assaults were coming primarily from the west and that NK troops were massing on the west side of the Naktong just north of Waegwan.[3] Some Far East Command G-2 reports estimated there were 40,000 North Korean soldiers in the area, an extraordinary figure given that actual NK strength had declined to less than 70,000 men around the entire perimeter, and a still unbelievable number when set against the inflated figures of NK strength being used at Far East Command.[4]

Nevertheless, on August 13, General MacArthur called into his office in Tokyo Lieutenant General George E. Stratemeyer, Far East Air Force commander, and laid out one of the most astonishing missions in the history of military aviation. MacArthur said he wanted to use the air force's entire B-29 bomber force to "carpet bomb" the area where the NK troops were allegedly massing.[5]

Major General Emmett (Rosie) O'Donnell, Jr., Far East Air Force Bomber Command chief, figured he could saturate a three-square-mile area with 500-pound bombs, but found out to his dismay that the target area which MacArthur's headquarters had selected measured twenty-six square miles (3½ miles wide and 7½ miles long, running along the Naktong north of Waegwan).[6] Even with the ninety-eight B-29 Superfortresses that Bomber Command had in Japan and Okinawa, O'Donnell knew he would be unable to saturate twenty-six square miles of rough mountain terrain and its innumerable hills and valleys that could deflect or contain the heaviest explosions. But Bomber Command operations officers divided the area into twelve equal squares and assigned each of the twelve B-29 squadrons in the Far East an aiming point in the center of one of them.

The attack came on August 16, and within thirty minutes the ninety-eight B-29s had bombed their assigned aiming points, flying at altitudes from five to ten thousand feet. The Superfortresses released 3,084 bombs weighing 500 pounds each and 150 bombs weighing 1,000 pounds each. It was the biggest use of airpower in direct support of ground forces since the Normandy invasion. The bombs had a blast effect equivalent to 30,000 rounds of heavy artillery.[7]

There is no evidence this incredible outlay of bombs and aircraft killed or maimed a single North Korean soldier. General Walker reported the damage could not be evaluated because smoke and dust prevented observation from the air, and U.S. and ROK troops were too far away to tell what had happened.[8] Ground patrols sent out to reconnoiter never reached the area. Information obtained later from prisoners confirmed that the NK divisions the Far East Command thought were still west of the Naktong had already crossed to the east side.[9] General O'Donnell personally reconnoitered the area by air for two and a half hours and reported no evidence of any activity—no troops, no vehicles, no armor, no antiaircraft fire. He recommended that no more such missions should be flown unless the ground situation became extremely critical.[10] A personal intercession by General Stratemeyer with General MacArthur led to the cancellation of a second carpet bombing of an area east of the Naktong on August 19.[11] Stratemeyer told MacArthur that air force fighter-bombers or navy dive bombers could provide the best air support for Eighth Army.[12] In the rarefied ceremonial of high command, in which elaborate politeness disguises many degrees and subtleties of reproach, the supreme commander in the Far East had been informed he had used a precision instrument as a bludgeon.

* * * * * * * *

This was the time when American troops discovered a tragedy on a hill (303) above Waegwan that had been occupied by North Koreans during the general advance in August. After American troops recaptured the hill on August 17, they found the bodies of twenty-six American soldiers who had been captured earlier. Their hands had been tied in back, and they had been sprayed with burp-gun bullets. Five men had survived the massacre by burrowing under the bodies of their murdered comrades.[13]

On August 20 an incensed MacArthur broadcast a warning to the North Korean command that it would be held responsible unless the murders of prisoners stopped. But evidence was lacking that the NK command had sanctioned the shooting of prisoners. Rather, the atrocities appeared to have been caused by vicious individuals or uncontrolled small units, possibly because they themselves faced desperate situations. But the murders on Hill 303 cast a pall over the front for a long time.

* * * * * * * *

North and northwest of Taegu, where the defensive line turned eastward through the mountains toward the Sea of Japan, the North Koreans made their major effort in the August offensive. It was directed against the ROK 1st, 6th and 8th Divisions, and the North Koreans achieved their greatest success here. The forces moving against the ROKs were the 15th NK Division, which crossed the Naktong at several points north of Waegwan, using underwater bridges to get heavy equipment over; the 13th NK Division, which drove from Naktong-ni southeast straight toward Taegu; the 1st NK Division, which attacked down the north-south road from Kunwi, and the 8th NK Division, which penetrated south from Uisong into the mountains northeast of Taegu.[14] (See Map 1.)

A little over a week after the attacks got under way on August 5, the 13th, 15th and 1st NK Divisions were pressing on Tabu-dong, about fifteen miles due north of Taegu. There the ROK 1st Division blocked the way. Here was a major threat; unless stopped, and stopped quickly, the North Koreans could drive straight down the Tabu-dong corridor to Taegu, unhinging the entire perimeter defense.

By August 16 the NK penetration had already begun to jeopardize Taegu, swollen from its normal 300,000 people with 400,000 refugees. Panic ensued on August 18 when seven rounds of NK artillery landed near the Taegu railway station and killed one and wounded eight civilians. The provincial government ordered the evacuation of Taegu, and President Syngman Rhee moved his capital to Pusan. These actions frightened thousands of Koreans into trying frantically to flee southward, and this threatened to create chaos in supplying the military forces. Firm action by Eighth Army halted the evacuation, although NK gunners twice more shelled the city, the last time on August 20.[15]

General Walker also took firm action directly against the North Korean threat on the Tabu-dong corridor. On August 18, he committed the force that had become his "fire brigade": the 27th Regiment plus artillery and tank support under Lieutenant Colonel John H. (Mike) Michaelis. This 25th Division regiment only shortly before had helped to clear the North Korean penetration around Yongsan east of the Naktong Bulge. At this moment, the 5th Marines, the army 9th Regiment and 24th Division were deeply into their battle to oust the North Koreans from the Cloverleaf-Obong-ni ridge in the Naktong Bulge.

Mike Michaelis and his regiment, along with a company of M26 medium tanks and two artillery battalions (the 8th and the 37th), closed on Tabu-dong just as the North Korean command, suffering greatly from a shortage of troops, withdrew its 15th Division from the Tabu-dong sector and transferred it posthaste to the northern front, where the 8th NK Division had stalled south of Uisong. The 1st NK Division meanwhile was still in the mountains moving south and had not materialized at Tabu-dong.

Withdrawal of the 15th NK Division more than evened the odds on the Tabu-dong corridor, despite the fact that the North Korean command had received its only substantial tank reinforcement during the perimeter battles—twenty-one new T34s. The attacking 13th NK Division at Tabu-dong got fourteen of them.

It was just north of Tabu-dong that one of the most bizarre battles in the Korean War went on for seven consecutive nights. The battleground became known as the "the Bowling Alley," because it was on a mile-long straight stretch of a north-south road that was hemmed in closely by high roadless mountains ranging on either side for miles. If the NK forces here were going to break through to Taegu, they had to drive through the Bowling Alley: and the 27th Regiment barred passage at the southern end while the ROK 1st Division held the bordering hills.

Shortly after dark on the first night, August 18, NK mortars and artillery fired a heavy preparation for the attack, then two T34s and a self-propelled 76mm gun, followed by infantry on foot and in trucks, moved down the Alley. The lead tank rolled on without firing, while the tank behind fired indiscriminately in widely different directions. The 27th bazooka teams waited until the tanks were close to the American lines before they responded: a 3.5-inch rocket destroyed the second tank. Two bazooka hits on the lead tank failed to explode, but the scared crew abandoned the tank anyway. Meantime, armor-piercing shells from the

8th Artillery destroyed the self-propelled gun, two trucks and an estimated one hundred infantrymen. Three more T34 tanks started down the valley, but seeing what had happened to their comrades, they turned around and went back north.

For the next six nights this sort of engagement was played out in hours of high tension and drama. Preceded by heavy artillery, mortar and tank fire, the North Koreans would advance down the corridor while Americans waited for a favorable opportunity to fire at them. Awed GIs watched T34 tanks line up at the north end of the corridor and fire armor-piercing shells straight down the road toward American positions, hoping to knock out the M26 tanks emplaced there. The great flashes from the guns, the high-velocity shells hurtling as visible red balls through the dark night, the explosions where the shells landed, and the deafening thunder of the gun reports and detonations bouncing and rebouncing off the sides of the mountains caused some GIs to liken the road to a mile-long bowling alley; but instead of bowling balls, giants threw great projectiles of exploding fire in an attempt to knock out the tanks at the other end.

There were other twists to this strange battle: the North Koreans used flares to coordinate their actions, and the Americans quickly recognized that green flares signaled an attack on a given area. Thus, once an attack began, the Americans fired green flares over their own positions, often drawing the confused NK infantry right into the jaws of the waiting American guns. The Americans also laid down antitank mines across the narrow valley. That stopped the tanks. As the NK infantry moved in to try to lift the mines, U.S. illumination flares lighted up the scene, and preregistered artillery and mortar fire and aimed automatic-weapons fire poured down on the hapless North Koreans. Fire from both sides was intense. On the night of August 21 a single battery of the 8th Artillery fired 1,660 rounds of 105mm shells, a 4.2-inch mortar platoon fired 900 rounds, and an 81mm mortar platoon dropped 1,200 rounds— and the valley nowhere was more than a few hundred yards wide. In that night battle, the North Koreans suffered 1,300 casualties.

During the day the North Koreans got little respite. American aircraft attacked the NK positions repeatedly. On August 20, they started their strafing runs so close in front of the American infantry that spent .50-caliber machine-gun cartridges fell into the foxholes of the 27th Regiment.

The 13th NK Division was being torn to pieces in the Bowling Alley. The North Korean commanders seemed to arrive slowly at the realization that they were playing according to American rules, not their own. They had walked repeatedly into an American trap—emplaced positions having great firepower that could not possibly be penetrated with the forces the North Koreans had on hand, while their troops were subject to daily harassment by American guns and aircraft.

Something had to be done. The North Koreans returned to their old tried-and-true formula: envelopment of the flank and attempts to establish roadblocks behind the American positions. By this time, the 1st NK Division had arrived east of the Bowling Alley, and on the night of August 21–22 an NK regiment infiltrated through the mountains from the east and emerged at noon about six miles behind the 27th Regiment's position and only nine miles north of Taegu. The North Koreans rapidly brought a five-mile stretch of the main supply route under small-arms fire. The same afternoon they attacked a battalion of the 23rd Regiment of the 2nd Division, which a few days before had been sent to guard the two supporting artillery battalions emplaced eight miles north of Taegu. Shortly thereafter, an intense barrage of shells began to fall on the 8th Artillery, and a few minutes later a direct hit destroyed the battalion's fire-direction center, killing four officers and two noncoms.

But the old days of the Kum river and Taejon were not to return for the Americans. Air force, navy and Australian aircraft struck the ridge east of the road where most of the North Koreans were emplaced, one blow by B26 bombers unloading 44,000 pounds of bombs. The next morning, the 23rd Regiment commenced an all-day sweep that cleared the ridgelines of NK soldiers.

The battle of the Bowling Alley was over. The exhausted and demoralized North Korean soldiers stopped to rest. The 27th Regiment moved back to Masan and its parent 25th Division.

CHAPTER 21

Forging a Sword of Vengeance

ALTHOUGH THE MEN on both sides in the vicious battles of the Pusan Perimeter believed theirs was the center stage of a great military drama, the fact is the perimeter had become a sideshow—a vital sideshow, it is true, but not the main event. The decisive battle was shaping up, but it was going to be fought elsewhere.

General MacArthur had devised a plan to destroy the North Korean army. And though no one else in the West quite grasped the point at the moment, his plan envisioned the destruction of the North Korean state as well.

In order to make his plan work, MacArthur needed a totally committed enemy driving without thought of anything else and with all his strength against a defensive line that held, but just barely held, thus giving the North Koreans courage and enticing them to fling every last ounce of strength against it. If the North Koreans could be held in close, all consuming-combat—and Eighth Army and the ROKs in August and September made this the case—then the crucial stroke could be delivered *behind* the fully engrossed North Korean army.

MacArthur conceived the idea of the stroke only days after the war started, and he planned it from the start for where it was to fall: Inchon, the port city of Seoul, the capital.

The remarkable thing about this plan is that it was what the situation practically demanded, and yet MacArthur had to fight a dogged battle with the top American military leadership, the Joint Chiefs of Staff, to get it approved. And after it was approved and had succeeded, the inevitable fallout was to create in the minds of many persons, not least the Joint Chiefs and many of the most influential political leaders in the country, that anybody who could be so right about Inchon must be right about other things.

148

Lieutenant General Matthew B. Ridgway, army deputy chief of staff and later to replace MacArthur, said, "A more subtle result of the Inchon triumph was the development of an almost superstitious regard for General MacArthur's infallibility. Even his superiors, it seemed, began to doubt if they should question *any* of MacArthur's decisions."[1]

From this fundamental error a great deal of tragedy was to spring.

When a military historian looks at the Korean military operations in the summer of 1950, the question that flashes almost instantly is, Why did not *every* military commander see that MacArthur's plan was the obvious, logical course? Yet clearly the North Korean command did not see it, and neither did the Joint Chiefs. MacArthur, rather than getting a casual nod for asserting the self-evident, gained instead a reputation for omniscience in warfare.

Of course, all great ideas are simple. The trick is to see them before anyone else. In this case, MacArthur did see when his contemporaries did not. And perhaps this is the true test of genius. Nevertheless, the lesson which MacArthur sought to teach was over two thousand years old, and had been applied on numerous occasions down the centuries.

The origin and the execution of the Inchon landing are exceptional because the events that made it possible showed that North Korean leaders repeatedly misread a situation that should quickly have become transparent to men responsible for the lives and welfare of their people and, indeed, for the existence of their state.

The first mistake was, in many ways, the most incredible of all. This was the error North Korean leaders made in persisting in their attack after the United States entered the war. Their decision to go to war in the first place perhaps can be explained by their misreading of American attitudes regarding communist aggression, especially Secretary of State Acheson's January, 1950, statement placing Korea outside the American strategic defense line. But the North Koreans strategically were doomed to failure the longer they persisted and the more successful they were. By locking practically all of their army into a giant effort to drive the South Koreans and Americans into the sea in the extreme southern part of the country, they unwittingly created the opportunity for a Cannae writ large.

The farther the North Koreans penetrated into the south, the farther they fell into a sack which the United States could close at will anywhere behind them. The North Korean leaders looked at the *land* of Korea and saw that as their objective. They failed to understand fully the significance of the fact that the Korean peninsula is surrounded by *water* on three sides, and the United States had complete command of this water. With the greatest navy on earth, the United States could place an amphibious force anywhere it chose behind the North Korean army and be absolutely certain, by means of air and naval bombardment, that North Korea could not stop lodgment of the force on shore or its supply and protection thereafter.

Cannae, in 216 B.C., is the great example in history of the perfect battle of annihilation. The parallel of Cannae with Korea in the summer of 1950 is so close as to be uncanny. The Carthaginian general, Hannibal, posted his heavy infantry and cavalry on either flank and advanced the weak central portion of his line to form a salient *toward* the opposing Roman army. The Romans, vastly superior in numbers, gleefully attacked and drove the center back, bending Hannibal's army into the shape of a concave half-moon. Hannibal's heavy infantry on either side then struck the deeply penetrated Romans from the flanks while the Carthaginian cavalry, which had scattered the Roman horse, attacked the Romans from the rear and cut off retreat. Only about 3,000 Romans escaped the trap; 70,000 died. Fewer than 6,000 Carthaginians and allied Celts were killed.[2]

The North Korean attack into the depths of South Korea paralleled the Roman penetration into the center of the Carthaginian line, while MacArthur's rear attack at Inchon resembled Hannibal's closing of the sack on the Roman flanks and rear by his heavy infantry and cavalry. The fact that the North Korean army on the Naktong was not attacked directly made no difference in assuring that it was defeated, because the capture of Seoul meant the North Korean army's possibility of supply was destroyed—and that was enough to destroy the army.

MacArthur saw almost immediately after the war started the jeopardy in which the North Korean generals had placed their army. He began preparations in the first days of July for a landing at Inchon.[3] The JCS fought the Inchon landing because of the extremely high tides there and the narrow approach channel, which, in the JCS view, made the landing difficult and possibly dangerous. General J. Lawton Collins, the army chief of staff, and Admiral Forrest P. Sherman, chief of naval operations, urged instead a landing at Kunsan, a small port city one hundred air miles south of Inchon and only about seventy air miles west of the Naktong river line.[4] A landing at Kunsan would not have severed the North Korean lines of communication at all. Rather, it would have permitted the North Korean command to shift forces quickly from the Pusan Perimeter to form a new line across South Korea. Any U.S. attack thereafter along this line would have had to be a direct assault on defended emplacements and would merely have driven the North Koreans farther back *on* their reserves and supplies. It would not have severed the North Korean army *from* these reserves and supplies.

Ridgway called Inchon a "5,000-to-1 gamble."[5] It was no such thing. It was, in fact, almost a sure bet. Far more important, Inchon strategically could be decisive, while Kunsan could only be disturbing. Ridgway, despite his odds-making, ended up himself endorsing Inchon.[6] The great reason for selecting Inchon was its potential for total surprise and for ending the war.

Military history shows quite a few examples of the successful application of MacArthur's Inchon strategy. They have been comparatively rare because of the traditional rigidity and directness of thinking of most military commanders. Imaginative and daring commanders, on the other hand, usually have sought ways, as the great Confederate leader, Stonewall Jackson, expressed it, to "mystify, mislead and surprise" their opponents, rather than to beat out their strength in bloody frontal assaults against expectant and well-emplaced foes.

The celebrated British military writer B. H. Liddell Hart expresses the theory quite succinctly in two maxims: (1) "in the face of the overwhelming evidence of history, no general is justified in launching his troops to a direct attack upon an enemy firmly in position," and (2) "instead of seeking to upset the enemy's equilibrium by one's attack, it must be upset before a real attack is, or can be, successfully launched."[7]

MacArthur's Inchon plan was a version of the *manoeuvre sur les derrières*, which was Napoleon's constant aim and key method of operation.[8] Among others, MacArthur's plan had direct parallels with Hannibal's destruction of a Roman army at Lake Trasimene in 217 B.C., Napoleon's defeat of the Austrians at Marengo in 1800, and British Field Marshal Edmund Henry H. Allenby's shattering of the Turkish front in Palestine in 1918. In every case, the victorious general unexpectedly swept *behind* the opposing army and established a strategic barrage or block between the enemy army and its sources of supply and reinforcement—and thereby caused the enemy army to disintegrate.[9]

The parallel of Inchon with Hannibal's victory at Lake Trasimene in central Italy is almost perfect. Instead of marching directly on a Roman army at Arretium (Arezzo), Hannibal chose a terribly difficult march through the treacherous Arnus marshes of the Arno river, considered to be impassable in the spring floods, and unexpectedly debouched near Clusium (Chiusi), thus placing himself between the Roman army and Rome. Realizing too late that Hannibal now had a clear road to Rome, the Roman commander, Gaius Flaminius, gave up his strong defensive position, marched south rapidly to seek battle, and was ambushed and his army destroyed by Hannibal on the shores of the lake.

MacArthur adopted precisely the policy of Hannibal. He called for an attack on the rear both to avoid and to outflank the North Korean army emplaced along the Naktong. Therefore, he planned to operate on the line of least resistance. And in choosing the difficult and potentially treacherous site of Inchon, he also selected the line of least expectation.

What few reserves the North Koreans had were not concentrated at Inchon, because the North Korean leaders, knowing about the high tides and narrow channel, didn't expect a landing there. MacArthur's plan was strategically splendid: the unexpected movement on a vital point would not only dislocate the North Koreans psychologically by its surprise, but also reduce to a minimum the possibility of North Korean resistance by striking a target that was essentially undefended. The true purpose of strategy is to win while reducing the fighting and killing to the least possible. As the great Chinese military theorist Sun Tzu wrote in *The Art of War* in 500 B.C., "To fight and conquer in all your battles is not supreme excellence; supreme excellence consists in breaking the enemy's resistance without fighting....Thus it is that in war the victorious strategist only seeks battle after the victory has been won."[10]

MacArthur as well exemplified the ideal enunciated by Liddell Hart: "History shows that rather than resign himself to a direct approach, a Great Captain will take even the most hazardous indirect approach... Natural hazards, however formidable, are inherently less dangerous and less uncertain than fighting hazards. All conditions are more calculable, all obstacles more surmountable, than those of human resistance."[11]

MacArthur also chose Inchon as the landing site for the soundest of military reasons. The city is only about twenty miles from Seoul. As the capital of Korea, Seoul was of great symbolic importance; but it was also the hub of the Korean communications system. The only railroads and highways which could supply the North Korean army effectively ran through or near Seoul. To cut these links at Seoul meant to sever the North Korean umbilical cord. Moreover, the strategic position of Seoul was such that, from there, MacArthur could move north toward North Korea, south toward the North Korean army's rear, or east across the peninsula, cutting all secondary roads and all possibility of retreat. These alternative threats alone, not considering the key effect of shutting off all supplies and reinforcements, would have been enough to force the North Korean command to order a precipitate retreat—in hopes of saving the army, at least. The landing at Inchon, therefore, acted both against the mind of the North Korean commander, frightened that his country's military strength would be destroyed if he kept his army in place, and against the morale of the North Korean soldiers, frightened at the possibility of losing their lives unless they ran.

A successful landing at Inchon and the quick capture of Seoul consequently meant the destruction of the North Korean army on the Naktong without a shot being fired. A modern army without food or oil, but especially ammunition, cannot survive for more than a few days. More important than material loss, however, is the loss of confidence of a cutoff army. An army that has no way to retreat stops looking boldly at the enemy to its front and instead begins glancing anxiously over its shoulders toward the rear. The basic motivation of a cutoff soldier becomes, not resolute action against the enemy, but how he personally is going to get out of the trap he is in. An army made up of soldiers in this frame of mind remains an intact force only briefly before it disintegrates into a mob of refugees frantically seeking safety. That is the reason attacks on an enemy's rear and upon his lines of communication are so devastating. At Cannae, the Roman soldiers, though they had witlessly rushed into a cul-de-sac, did not succumb to panic and disintegration as a military force until they realized their means of retreat had been destroyed by the Carthaginian cavalry on their rear. The North Koreans themselves had demonstrated that principle in full in their persistent flanking movements and their determined establishment of roadblocks behind American and ROK units. What they had practiced so successfully in tactical engagements, MacArthur was about to teach them on a strategic scale.

* * * * * * * *

MacArthur's strategy for Korea closely resembled the winning strategy of the Pacific campaign in World War II. In this brilliant effort, MacArthur, in the southwest Pacific, along with Admirals Chester Nimitz and William F. Halsey, Jr., commanders in the central and south Pacific, developed the celebrated "island-hopping" strategy that by-passed islands or positions heavily garrisoned by the Japanese and struck at individual targets beyond them, leaving the isolated Japanese garrisons "to wither on the vine." These bypassed Japanese were as effectively locked up and useless for further military purposes as if they had been marched off to prisoner-of-war camps.[12]

MacArthur's plan for Inchon was a variation on the Pacific island-hopping approach, and it is remarkable that no one, not least the Joint Chiefs of Staff, quickly recognized the similarity between the situation in the Pacific, where overextended Japanese troops could be cut off by strategic amphibious landings far in their rear, and Korea, where overextended North Korean troops pressing into the south of the peninsula likewise could be cut off by a strategic amphibious landing in their rear.

The dispute MacArthur had with the Joint Chiefs constitutes one of the most fascinating cases in modern times of how one military leader sees in a situation the opportunity for great victory while other military leaders see in the same situation great dangers. It was the resolution of this dispute, since MacArthur was proved right, which reinforced MacArthur's aura of military genius while it dimmed the luster of the Joint Chiefs. Out of this grew the idea that MacArthur could do no wrong while, at the same time, it inhibited the Joint Chiefs from calling down the Far East commander when afterward he carried out operations which were the extreme of military recklessness. Many people could not believe that General MacArthur carried within himself the attributes of a military Dr. Jekyll and Mr. Hyde. A hero, in American eyes, should be a hero always. Yet the general who conceived and doggedly pushed through the Inchon landing ignored open warnings and walked into a devastating Chinese Communist ambush only weeks thereafter.

MacArthur then was revealed as a mortal man like everyone else, subject both to inspiration and to error. Surely, however, the recognition of MacArthur as a man and not a god adds to the credit he should be accorded when he looked beyond the terrible physical conditions he found at Inchon and, like Hannibal in the Arnus marshes, saw these very difficulties as a guarantee of surprise—and victory. Beyond this, it is awesome to realize the incredible vigor and persistence of this seventy-year-old warrior in talking the Joint Chiefs not only into approving the operation but also into providing the forces he felt he needed for the attack. Getting the troops was no easy task; the American military establishment was in an extremely unprepared state, and many military and political leaders were firmly convinced that the threat to the United States lay, not in a peninsula jutting out from Asia, but in Europe, where millions of Russians stood under arms ready to move on signal from the Kremlin.

The ultimate success of MacArthur's efforts was immense, despite his own view that "those people in Washington" were only concerned with Europe, while Asia was where he felt the fate of the Western world would be decided. When the Inchon landing took place, every substantial combat-ready unit in the United States, with the sole exception of the 82nd Airborne Division, had been committed to MacArthur. At the same time, the delivery of this immense force was a credit to the Joint Chiefs of Staff and to the American military establishment. They produced a miracle of training, organization and logistics only two and a half months after the Korean War started.

A marine air-observer team guides a marine Corsair in for a strike on an enemy-held hill. The "black Corsairs" were highly praised by army and marines alike for their precision strikes on targets and their extremely close support of forward units.

Marines move around North Korean T34 tanks knocked out in Pusan Perimeter battle in late summer, 1950. A dead North Korean soldier lies on the tank in the foreground.

Bagpipers of the Argyll and Sutherland Highlanders on August 29, 1950, pipe ashore at Pusan a battalion of their Scottish regiment and a battalion of the English Middlesex Regiment; the first allied ground troops to join the Americans and South Koreans.

Marines seek cover behind an M26 Pershing tank west of Masan during Pusan Perimeter engagement in late summer, 1950. A dead North Korean soldier lies on ledge at left.

Millions of Koreans were uprooted from their homes by bombing, shelling or fear and attempted to flee to safety. Pusan and other cities in the south became giant refugee camps, with people sleeping on the streets.

Republic of Korea (ROK) soldiers march in typical column formation toward the front in August, 1950, during the Pusan Perimeter battles. This is a standard narrow dirt Korean road raised above rice paddies.

Brigadier General F. W. Farrell, Korean Military Advisory Group chief, confers on August 18, 1950, with Lieutenant General Walton H. Walker (seated in jeep), Eighth Army commander, during the height of the Pusan Perimeter battle.

CHAPTER 22

MacArthur v. the Joint Chiefs

THE DISPUTES the development of the Inchon landing plan (code-named Chromite) caused within the high American military establishment emphasize the differences between a collegial institution like the Joint Chiefs and a solitary military thinker and commander like MacArthur. The Joint Chiefs had been set up to provide unified, overall guidance and direction for the military forces. They were to take in the entire spectrum of American security needs and propose solutions accordingly. The Chiefs were to think big. It was perhaps too much to hope that they would also think creatively. The biggest creative thinker in regard to Korea, not unexpectedly, was not the Joint Chiefs, but MacArthur. Committees seldom make stunning innovations.

The Joint Chiefs, in fact, found themselves responding pro or con to the initiatives of MacArthur; they proposed few ideas of their own. Part of the reason, of course, was the role the American theater commander had assumed in World War II, a role carried over to Korea: a high degree of independence of Washington and a great deal of authority to develop policies of his own.

There was one other factor as regards MacArthur: the highest ranking officer in the Joint Chiefs at war's outbreak was the chairman, Omar Bradley; at the time, he had four stars, but MacArthur had five. As the last general of the army still on active service, MacArthur actually outranked his Pentagon bosses. In the extremely hierarchical atmosphere of the military services, a general of the army was seldom second-guessed, not even by the Joint Chiefs of Staff. It was not until September that Truman decided to promote Bradley to five-star rank.[1] And the question must arise whether there was not an element in this belated but well-deserved elevation of the great World War II army group commander that also was aimed at downstaging MacArthur. There has not been another five-star general since Bradley.

MacArthur started his plans for an amphibious landing in the North Korean rear on July 2, immediately after U.S. forces had been committed to Korea. On that date he asked the Pentagon for a marine RCT plus marine air support for the RCT.[2] Although they didn't know precisely how MacArthur planned to use this marine force, the Chiefs approved his request the next day.[3] Two days later, on July 5, MacArthur asked for a lot more: the entire 2nd Infantry Division, the 2nd Engineer Special Brigade and one regiment of the 82nd Airborne Division, all to be used between July 20 and August 20.[4] These requests represented a sizable chunk of the entire American strategic reserve. Of the six American army divisions outside Japan, one was on occupation duty in Germany, and only five were in the general reserve in the United States: the 2nd and 3rd Infantry Divisions, the 11th and 82nd Airborne Divisions, and the 2nd Armored Division, which all military experts considered unsuited for use in Korea. The 11th Airborne, however, was in a poor state of readiness.

The Joint Chiefs temporized briefly, but on July 7 asked the secretary of defense, Louis Johnson, to approve the deployments MacArthur had requested. Johnson and President Truman did so several days later; meanwhile, the Chiefs alerted the units for shipment. They made only one substitution: an RCT from the 11th Airborne, because they considered the 82nd Airborne too valuable to break up.[5] This division, the only U.S. force at virtual full strength and effectiveness, could be moved at a moment's notice by air to any other crisis point that developed. The 82nd was the American hole card.

On July 9 and 10, the real blows fell on the Chiefs: on July 9 MacArthur raised his demand for troops to four additional divisions. "The situation has developed into a major operation," MacArthur radioed Washington. On July 10 he pressed the Pentagon to bring the four divisions already in the Far East to full war strength (they were at 70 percent), and he demanded that the marine RCT already alerted be built to a full division and sent to him. Within two days MacArthur had approximately doubled his estimate of forces he would need in Korea, from four to eight divisions. It was a requirement the United States could not meet at the moment.

The Joint Chiefs were faced with a dilemma: here was a highly respected theater commander demanding more troops than currently existed to fight what had started out as a rather limited police action in a country not of vital strategic interest to the United States. Admiral Sherman, chief of naval operations, said it was time "to grapple with certain basic questions in the realm of national strategy: how far the

United States should commit troops for a land war in Asia, and how much risk should be accepted in other parts of the world."[6]

The Joint Chiefs moved swiftly. First, they decided to send two JCS members to Tokyo to find out what MacArthur wanted to do with these troops, because he had been less than candid with his plans. Second, the Chiefs looked around the world for every possible military unit that could be rushed to Korea, and found two, the 29th Infantry Regiment on Okinawa and the 5th Regimental Combat Team on Hawaii, and they were promptly shipped. Third, the Chiefs commenced a massive enlargement of the American military forces.[7]

This latter decision finally was to bring home to the American people the reality of war in Asia. They had generally applauded the entry of the United States into Korea; now they began to realize what it was going to cost. The Chiefs got the immediate backing of Secretary Johnson and President Truman, and on July 19 the President went on national radio and television to announce a huge expansion of U.S. forces (200,000 more in the army alone) and the call-up of selected National Guard and reserve units and individuals. By the end of August, the army had brought in more than 93,000 men in 404 units of the Organized Reserve and 205 units of the National Guard (including four divisions), plus 10,500 individual reserve officers. By the same time the navy and marines had called in almost 104,000 reservists (including the entire marine reserve of 32,800 officers and men), and the air force had called back almost 50,000 men.[8] The total: over a quarter of a million men.

Although the money to pay for these men had not wholly been appropriated by Congress, the President approved an army of 834,000 men with eleven divisions and twelve separate regiments, a navy of 580,000 men and 911 ships, a marine corps of 138,000 men with two divisions, and an air force of 569,000 men and 62 combat wings, plus sixteen separate combat and twenty separate transport squadrons.[9]

The JCS special deputation appointed to call on MacArthur arrived in Tokyo on July 13. The leaders were General Collins, army chief of staff, and Hoyt S. Vandenberg, air force chief of staff. It was at this meeting that the Chiefs got their first substantial information concerning MacArthur's strategy.[10]

Flanked by General Walker, Eighth Army commander, and his chief of staff, General Almond, MacArthur made a big impression on the two Chiefs and Admiral Arthur Radford, commander of the Pacific fleet, who arrived during the conference. Collins describes him thus: "MacArthur was cool and poised as always. He spoke with confidence and élan as he paced back and forth in his customary fashion. He always gave the impression of addressing not just his immediate listeners but a large audience unseen."[11]

General Bradley had a somewhat less charitable view of MacArthur. In his autobiography, Bradley describes MacArthur as follows: "He was awesomely brilliant; but as a leader he had several flaws: an obsession for self-glorification, almost no consideration of other men with whom he served, and a contempt for the judgment of his superiors." He was, says Bradley, like U.S. General George Patton and British Field Marshal Bernard Montgomery, a megalomaniac.[12]

"The General," as MacArthur was frequently referred to by Chiefs and underlings, no matter how elevated their own ranks, put on an impressive show for Collins, Vandenberg and Radford. He refused to guess where or when the North Koreans would be stopped, but he exuded confidence at a time when Americans and ROKs were retreating pell-mell before the victorious NK forces. They would be stopped, he assured them, but—using the occasion to twist the vise a little tighter on the Pentagon—he cautioned that the speed and success of an American counterstroke would depend upon how quickly the Chiefs sent him the troops and equipment he needed.[13]

"The General" argued frankly that Korea should be given priority over all other areas in which the United States had a strategic interest. The outcome of the Cold War, MacArthur contended, would be decided in the Far East.[14] When Collins asked MacArthur the number of troops he would need to restore and maintain the 38th parallel border, MacArthur said his intention was to *destroy* the North Korean forces, not merely to repulse them.[15]

Here, for the first time, a silhouette of MacArthur's ultimate purpose in Korea appeared: not to restore the status quo ante bellum, which essentially is what the UN resolution called for, but to destroy the North Korean army, a task that could not possibly be completed without invading North Korea, where the command, supply and training centers lay. MacArthur told the Chiefs that a task after hostilities ended would be to "compose and unite Korea," and it might be necessary to occupy all of North Korea, though this was speculation at the moment.[16]

Thus, MacArthur's goal contained the seeds of a far more grandiose purpose than the mere turning back of an incursive force. An invasion of the North, once approved, would not likely be stopped voluntarily until not only the North Korean army was destroyed but the North Korean state as well. In the great press and anxiety of the moment, this radical MacArthur goal was not addressed. Yet it was implicit: MacArthur was proposing that the United Nations do precisely what they were punishing the North Koreans for—invade a neighboring state.

If the United States leadership in July had faced up to the implications of MacArthur's stated purpose, it might have been able to develop a policy that would have assuaged Red China's fears yet eliminated the military threat of Kim Il Sung and the North Korean command. Despite the moral issue raised, there were strong arguments for at least a limited invasion of North Korea along clearly delineated and previously announced lines, an invasion to chastise or topple the North Korean leadership and smash its military potential but not to absorb the North into South Korea under the autocratic rule of Syngman Rhee. These issues were not fully addressed; and when a policy on North Korea was needed, the United States was only in the process of creating one. A plan for a UN-ordered election for the whole country was only a late overlay on the already developing reality of a campaign of total conquest being carried forward by MacArthur.

During the conference, MacArthur gave a brief outline of his counter-offensive strategy. As soon as the North Koreans were stopped, he would attack their rear on the west coast, and he believed Inchon would be the best place to strike. General Collins, before leaving Washington, had been briefed on possible west-coast landing sites. The navy staff in Washington was skeptical of Inchon because of the narrow sea approaches and notoriously high tides (sometimes thirty-five feet high).[17] The day after the conference with MacArthur Collins questioned the feasibility of a landing at Inchon.[18] He talked with Rear Admiral James H. Doyle, assistant to Vice Admiral C. Turner Joy, commander of naval forces in the Far East, and an expert on amphibious operations. Doyle told Collins a landing at Inchon would be difficult, but could be done.[19]

MacArthur was aware his performance alone had not convinced the Joint Chiefs. Navy and marine questions about the wisdom of an Inchon landing had not been resolved.[20] However, the conference did provide MacArthur with some assurances, as well as disappointments, on the number of troops he could expect. Collins told the General privately he believed the entire 1st Marine Division would be made available to him. Otherwise MacArthur would have to get along with the divisions already in the Far East and the forces that had been earmarked for him: the 2nd Infantry Division, 5th RCT, 29th Regiment and the 187th Airborne RCT.[21]

As it turned out, Collins's private assurance regarding the full 1st Marine Division ran into a roadblock that was tied into the argument over Inchon. Immediately after the army chief of staff got back to Washington, he told the other Chiefs his doubts about Inchon. When General Bradley heard Collins's report, "I had to agree that it was the riskiest military proposal I had ever heard of," Bradley writes in his autobiography. Bradley called it a "blue-sky scheme" and said, "Inchon was probably the worst possible place ever selected for an amphibious landing."[22]

The Joint Chiefs had not definitely decided to give the marine division to MacArthur, although urged to do so by Admiral Radford and Lieutenant General Lemuel C. Shepherd, commander of the Pacific Fleet Marine Force.[23] The fat got in the fire on July 19 when MacArthur, doubtless encouraged by Collins's private assurance, renewed his request for the full marine division, plus a supporting air wing—and then added that he wanted it to arrive on September 10. Here was the first clear word from MacArthur about when he wanted to carry out his landing. To the Chiefs, it was shockingly early.[24]

Admiral Sherman asked the Chiefs to reply to MacArthur that it would be impossible to provide the 1st Marine Division before November without depleting the Atlantic Fleet Marine Force "to an unacceptable degree."[25] MacArthur recognized the entire success or failure of an Inchon landing might ride on delivery of the marine division; it was the only available major U.S. force whose mission and training was in amphibious operations. An assault landing by sea by an army unit would require it to be specially trained and equipped, and time was short. Perhaps this explains to some degree the vehemence with which MacArthur responded to the Sherman-inspired message. Regarding the marine division, MacArthur said: "There can be no demand for its potential use elsewhere that can equal the urgency of the immediate battle mission contemplated for it."[26]

Two days later, building up the pressure, MacArthur radioed the Pentagon the following message, which outlined precisely the rationale for attacking the enemy at Inchon: "I am firmly convinced that an early and strong effort behind his front will sever his main line of communications and enable us to deliver a decisive and crushing blow. Any material delay in such an operation may lose this opportunity. The alternative is a frontal attack which can only result in a protracted and expensive campaign to slowly drive the enemy north of the 38th parallel."[27]

This message arrived in Washington just after Taejon had fallen, and many American military leaders were wondering whether the army could even hold out in Korea. And here came a completely optimistic and expectant plan to destroy the enemy in September! This called for a Chiefs-MacArthur teleconference. It was set up on July 23. The JCS were cool, almost caustic: considering the increasing NK pressure and the accelerating fighting, did MacArthur really believe it wise to schedule an amphibious landing in September? MacArthur: yes. But the General added a condition: provided he received the full marine division.[28] Yet

MacArthur was still sparing of details about his Inchon plans, revealing his continued suspicion of the level of security prevailing in Washington.[29]

Meanwhile the Joint Chiefs decided to add two marine RCT's to the 1st Provisional Marine Brigade (5th Marines) already en route to the Far East. The 1st Marine RCT would be built out of men from the Atlantic Fleet Marine Force and marine security forces in the United States, while the 7th Marine RCT would be created from Atlantic Fleet Marine Force cadres, marine reservists, and dispatch of a full marine battalion from Suda Bay, Crete, in the Mediterranean, through the Suez Canal and directly to the Far East.[30] Even so, the 7th Marine RCT didn't arrive in time for Inchon,[31] though it helped shortly thereafter in the attack on Seoul.

The problem of the 187th Airborne RCT's unreadiness to ship out caused MacArthur finally to drop plans for an airborne assault on a "key communications center" shortly after D-Day, although the airborne RCT actually arrived shortly after the Inchon landing.[32]

* * * * * * * *

The dispute about Inchon was building to a climax. The issue separating MacArthur and the opposition, mainly the navy and the marines, did not concern an amphibious landing itself; it was that the navy and the marines didn't want to land at Inchon.[33]

At Inchon the tides are funneled in from the narrow Yellow Sea by the Korean peninsula on the east and the Shantung (Shandong) peninsula of China on the west. Ocean waters rushing into these narrow seas produce extremely high tides, much as they do in Canada's Bay of Fundy, closed in by New Brunswick on the north and Nova Scotia on the south. In addition, the islands offshore from Inchon inhibit the flow of waters. These cause sluggish tides that produce huge mud flats along the waterfront at Inchon and on either side of Flying Fish Channel leading to the port. These flats are so soft and deep they will not support men on foot.

Naval experts and marines believed small landing craft would need 23-foot minimum tides to operate safely over these mud flats and a 29-foot tide before Landing Ship Tanks (LSTs) could come in.[34] This put an extreme constraint on a landing force: the navy could land men and equipment only from the time an incoming tide reached 23 feet until the outgoing tide dropped to 23 feet, a period of about three hours. Troops ashore then would be stranded until the next high tide, about twelve hours later.[35]

It was the reading of the tide tables, not the relieving of the pressure on the Pusan Perimeter, which dictated MacArthur's adamant position on the timing of the invasion. Low seas are common at Inchon from May through August; September is a month of transition; high seas prevail from October through March. This left September as the earliest period when tidal conditions would be suitable for a contested amphibious invasion. The next opportunity would not come again until mid-October, and by that time bad weather would be coming to Korea, greatly limiting potential exploitation of any breakout from the beachhead. Even in September, only four days had suitable tidal conditions: September 15 to 18. On these days the average tidal surges were high enough to cover the mud flats so the landing craft could float in to shore. It had to be mid-September, or an indefinite postponement of the invasion.[36]

MacArthur's pick was September 15. Morning tide for that day was forecast at 6:50 a.m., evening tide at 7:20 p.m.[37]

That was not the only problem: the Flying Fish Channel, separating Inchon from the offshore islands, was narrow and treacherous even in daylight; it was flanked by mud flats, and was twisting and could be approached only from the south because north of Inchon it turned into a labyrinth wickedly winding between islands and flats. If the North Koreans mined this channel, any approach would be impossible until the mines were swept. In addition, the entire seaward face of Inchon was protected from high tides by a seawall immediately beyond the mud flats; the wall ranged from twelve to fourteen feet in height and would have to be broken through or scaled by the attacking marines. Directly behind the seawall was the heavily built-up city, which could offer extremely good protection to any forces defending there. Finally, there was an island with a 350-foot peak, Wolmi-do or Moon Tip Island, located immediately off Inchon, dominating the harbor and approaches. It was connected to the city by a causeway, and supposedly was heavily fortified.[38]

When the navy and marines looked at all the negative aspects of Inchon—high tides, mud flats, narrow channel and protecting island—it is no wonder they balked. Surely, they suggested, there must be a better place to land.

CHAPTER 23

MacArthur Calls on Chiang Kai-shek

IT WAS PRECISELY at this juncture that a new crisis between MacArthur and Washington developed, this time over Taiwan, and it angered Truman so greatly he seriously considered relieving the General on the spot.[1] This double play of disputes—one on an essentially political level regarding Taiwan and pitting Truman and Secretary of State Acheson against MacArthur, and the other on a military level regarding Inchon and pitting the Joint Chiefs, plus their allies in the navy and marines, against the General—greatly agitated the leadership in Washington in late July and August. The crisis proved MacArthur for the moment to be virtually a match for the entire opposition, and made him, in regard to the issue of Taiwan, which surfaced publicly, the darling of the Republicans and the China Lobby. It also, as David McLellan says in his biography of Dean Acheson, raised MacArthur's status "to that of a virtual policy maker on co-equal terms with the President and his advisors in Washington."[2] The seeds were sown for the greater crises caused by MacArthur's pursuit of his own goals, which were radically different from the administration goals.

The crisis over Taiwan emerged from a logical fallacy contained in the Truman administration's treatment of Chiang Kai-shek after it reversed the hands-off-Taiwan policy on June 27. Although officially the United States had "neutralized" the island, thus unilaterally creating a Far Eastern Switzerland, the difference between a Taiwan neutralized and a Taiwan protected by a great power was difficult to see with the naked eye, especially one looking from Beijing.

Furthermore, once Taiwan had become what greatly resembled an old nineteenth century-style imperialistic protectorate, it was difficult to

163

limit direct military aid to Chiang Kai-shek, the agreeable ruler of the protectorate. But despite the urging of the Joint Chiefs and Secretary of Defense Johnson, President Truman had not yet authorized such aid.[3]

It was obvious that the matter of military aid had to be examined, and Truman on June 25 authorized a survey team to be sent from MacArthur's headquarters for this purpose.[4] The press of events in Korea had prevented anything being done immediately, but MacArthur told Collins and Vandenberg, when they visited Tokyo in mid-July, that he himself planned to make the trip to Taiwan as soon as the situation in Korea permitted him to do so.[5]

Meantime, U.S. intelligence sources picked up indications of a major Chinese Communist troop buildup on the mainland opposite Taiwan, involving as many as 200,000 troops and 4,000 craft (doubtless most of them sampans and junks). The Chiefs on July 25 directed MacArthur to send the Seventh Fleet to make a demonstration around the waters of Taiwan, even though this meant withdrawing ships from support of troops in Korea.[6] In a message on July 27 to the State Department, the Chiefs recommended that urgently needed military supplies be sent to Chiang immediately and that the U.S. survey team be dispatched quickly to Taiwan to determine other defense needs.[7] On July 28 the Chiefs wrote Secretary of Defense Johnson that a determined Red Chinese attack against the island probably could not be wholly stopped by the Seventh Fleet and that some Red soldiers might get through to jeopardize Chiang's government and induce defections among National-ist Chinese troops; the Chiefs recommended Chiang's forces be authorized to make air strikes at amphibious concentrations on the mainland and to mine waters off the Chinese mainland opposite the island.[8]

Secretary Johnson endorsed the Chiefs' recommendation, but Secretary Acheson had grave objections. Said Acheson: mining would be acceptable, provided international shipping was warned, but bombing the mainland, even if done entirely by Chinese Nationalist airplanes, was out of the question, because the United States manifestly would be responsible, and this would anger friendly governments (notably Britain) and possibly might lead to war with Red China.[9]

The Chiefs' recommendations on aid to Taiwan and the survey mission were approved July 27 by the National Security Council,[10] but Acheson insisted that MacArthur himself not go to Taiwan.[11] However, when the Chiefs discussed the matter with MacArthur, the General said he was planning a personal "brief reconnaissance of the situation" in Taiwan on July 31. The Chiefs, though they tried to get him to send someone else, did not positively forbid MacArthur to go. MacArthur told the Chiefs he thought it advisable to go himself, in view of the "many conflicting reports" coming from the island.[12] It was the beginning of the breach between MacArthur and Truman.

Accompanied by Vice Admiral Arthur D. (Dewey) Struble, commander of the Seventh Fleet, which was protecting Taiwan,[13] MacArthur arrived in Taipei, Taiwan's capital, "like a visiting head of state, and was entertained accordingly" during his two-day stay, says Omar Bradley in his autobiography.[14] Statements by Nationalist Chinese officials in Taiwan did nothing to dispel an impression MacArthur himself created to suggest the United States was increasingly identifying its interests with those of the Nationalists. Yet when he got back to Tokyo, MacArthur denied any political significance to his visit.[15]

MacArthur's visit gave Chiang an opportunity to embarrass the United States by implying the existence of secret agreements between himself and MacArthur and announcing "the foundation for...Sino-American military cooperation has been laid."[16] It also infuriated Truman and the British, who had already recognized the Red Chinese regime. But the greatest damage was the effect upon the Red Chinese, who naturally viewed the visit of the Far East commander himself to Taipei as evidence of a new and possibly offensive alliance being forged between Chiang and the United States.

Secretary of Defense Johnson entertained the naive hope that MacArthur's walking on the edge of insubordination would be forgotten quickly, because he asked the Chiefs to draft a message giving MacArthur standing authority to permit the Nationalists to attack the Chinese mainland whenever intelligence indicated a Communist Chinese attack was imminent.[17]

Instead, Johnson's proposal drew Truman's wrath and further weakened Johnson's own deteriorating position with the President. MacArthur himself caught a full burst of Truman's determination to keep anyone else from trying to act as President of the United States. In a message on August 5, under Secretary Johnson's name but by Truman's order, MacArthur was told that Truman's Taiwan-neutralization order of June 27 remained in force, that Taiwan's status had not changed.[18] The message added: "No one other than the President as commander-in-chief has the authority to order or authorize preventive action against concentrations on the [Chinese] mainland. You should report currently and urgently intelligence regarding such concentrations and make every effort to keep reconnaissance reports current. Your recommendations are desired from time to time to the Joint Chiefs of Staff, on appropriate action which you recommend be taken to meet the facts you report. The most vital national interest requires that no action of ours precipitate general war or give excuse to others to do so. This message has the approval of the President and the Secretary of State."

MacArthur quickly ate humble pie. He responded the next day that "the President's decision of June 27 is fully understood here and this headquarters has been and is operating meticulously in accordance therewith....I understand thoroughly the limitations of my authority as theater commander and you need have no anxiety that I will in any way exceed them. I hope neither the President nor you has been misled by false or speculative reports from whatever source, official or non-official."[19]

MacArthur's careful stepping back into the role of an obedient subordinate cooled Truman's temper. In an attempt to lay the whole matter to rest, he sent W. Averell Harriman, his ambassador-at-large, to Tokyo to explain fully the administration's views on Taiwan and to come to a genuine meeting of the minds with MacArthur.[20] It was a generous gesture on Truman's part.

The JCS used the occasion of Harriman's journey to send along two deputies to try to learn from the General something more concrete about his invasion plans and troop needs. Selected were Lieutenant General Matthew B. Ridgway, deputy chief of staff for administration, and Lieutenant General Lauris A. Norstad, air force acting vice chief of staff.[21]

The visit took place on August 6–8, and the General dazzled his guests. Ridgway, who had called the Inchon plan a "5,000-to-1 shot," listened to MacArthur's two-and-a-half-hour presentation of his master plan for Inchon, and was won over to MacArthur's views. So were Harriman and Norstad.[22] They even agreed with MacArthur that the 3rd Infantry Division should be sent to him at once, although Ridgway admitted he left the Pentagon sharing the strong feeling there against sending the division to MacArthur because it was "tragically under-strength, completely unready for combat, and its removal would reduce the general reserve to a single major unit, the 82nd Airborne Division."[23] Ambassador Harriman also agreed to MacArthur's demand for more troops, and he told Ridgway that "political and personal considerations should be put to one side and our government [should] deal with General MacArthur on the lofty level of the great national asset which he is."[24]

But when Harriman got back to Washington, his views about the General regarding Taiwan betrayed a great deal of doubt. He told the President: "For reasons which are rather difficult to explain, I did not feel that we came to a full agreement on the way we believed things should be handled on Formosa and with the Generalissimo [Chiang Kai-shek]. He accepted the President's position and will act accordingly, but without full conviction."[25]

Truman, however, decided the meeting of minds had occurred,[26] and told a news conference on August 10 that "General MacArthur and I are in perfect agreement and have been ever since he has been in the job he is now....I am satisfied with what he is doing."[27] The President might not have been so sanguine. Less than two weeks later it became clear the two men were far from "perfect agreement."

* * * * * * * *

Another subject that came up in the MacArthur-Harriman talks attracted little attention at the time, but it should have been seen by Dean Acheson and President Truman as a red flag: MacArthur assumed he would drive into North Korea after Inchon, although official U.S. policy was merely to push the North Koreans back to, but not over, the 38th parallel. On July 13 MacArthur had already told Generals Collins and Vandenberg he intended to destroy, not merely defeat, the North Korean army, and that this might mean occupation of all of North Korea. (See page 158.) Harriman's report quoted MacArthur as planning all-Korea elections after the war, and showed MacArthur as saying "the North Koreans will also vote for a non-communist government when they are sure of no Russian or communist intervention."[28] In two utterances, on July 13 and sometime during the Harriman visit, MacArthur disclosed what he thought U.S. policy should be: destruction of the North Korean state and its absorption into a unified Korea produced through a UN election.

This issue should have been dealt with immediately by the Truman administration and resolved on the basis of American national interests. MacArthur's plan was as aggressive as North Korea's invasion of South Korea, and contained the danger of Russian and Red Chinese intervention. The administration, most especially the State Department, was obligated to examine the implications of a possible American commitment to a major land war in Asia. In the event, the administration did not make a final decision until September 27, and then it was based on an opportunistic and politically popular exploitation of what Washington hoped could be achieved, not upon a reasoned, careful judgment of long-term American national interests.

It is tragic that Dean Acheson did not assume a larger role in dealing with the challenge MacArthur presented to the Truman administration and to U.S. policy and interests in the Far East. It is not known whether Acheson would have come to a more realistic appraisal of the dangers the United States would face by undertaking MacArthur-style aggression instead of restricting itself to an essentially passive "police action" to restore the prewar situation. However, as Acheson's biographer, David McLellan, says, the secretary of state was the "only one in the administration with the perspicacity and willpower to have challenged MacArthur."[29] And since the Korean War was being fought for a limited and essentially political purpose, Acheson's refusal to intervene, McLellan says, "was a fatal derogation of the statesman's responsibility." The result was that the Far East commander was left in possession of a field in which no remaining American leader had the capability of meeting MacArthur head on and countering him. The General mesmerized his contemporaries; American leaders sent over to Tokyo to talk MacArthur out of positions tended to be won over to the General's views, sometimes against their wills. Thus, MacArthur's influence on political decisions was far greater than it should have been as essentially a military theater commander.

CHAPTER 24

The Decision on Inchon

ARRIVING BACK IN WASHINGTON on August 9, Ridgway described MacArthur's presentation on the Inchon plan as brilliant. And Harriman, no military man himself, but highly influential with the President, strongly endorsed it and persuaded Truman that Inchon could be the solution to the Korean War. The Chiefs spent most of the day discussing the plan with Harriman, Ridgway, Norstad and Secretary Johnson. But as Omar Bradley says in his autobiography, "We approved the concept of an amphibious assault to the rear of the North Koreans on the Korean west coast, but we still had gravest doubts about Inchon as a site."[1]

The next day the Chiefs went personally to see Truman and got his endorsement on sending the full marine division to MacArthur. They also got his approval to dispatch the 3rd Infantry Division. The United States was thereupon left with a single major force, the 82nd Airborne, for any emergency anywhere else in the world.[2] During the session with Truman, Admiral Forrest P. Sherman observed that he was "confident that General MacArthur would make good use of the forces, but that the Joint Chiefs of Staff would have to pass on his plans for amphibious landings."[3] The Chiefs were not washing their hands of responsibility so long as they had any doubts.[4]

MacArthur now had the troops committed, but practically everything sent to the Far East had to be thrown into battle almost immediately upon arrival to shore up the line in Korea. None of these units could be withdrawn except the 1st Provisional Marine Brigade (5th Marines), required as part of the invasion assault force. As a result, MacArthur was forced to designate the only unit he had left in Japan, the 7th Infantry Division, as the backup unit for the Inchon operation. This severely cannibalized division was down to half strength, about 9,000 men. It was fleshed out only by diverting most of the Pipeline to it for several weeks in August and by the inauguration of one of the most curious experiments in the history of the United States Army: the sending of South Koreans to fill out the division ranks. The program was not a success, although it was extended to other American army divisions. Difficulties with language were overwhelming, crippling training and combat operations, despite a "buddy system" whereby one Korean was teamed with one American who was supposed to teach the Korean how to be a soldier. American and Korean habits and characteristics were greatly different, leading to much misunderstanding. The program was slowly phased out over time, much to everyone's satisfaction.[5] The 7th Division got 8,600 South Koreans, many of them picked up off the streets, all of them civilians, all stunned and confused.[6] But the combination of South Koreans and Pipeline replacements filled up the division to almost 25,000 men as it embarked for the invasion.[7]

On August 21, with Joint Chiefs approval, MacArthur created a new corps headquarters (X Corps) within the Far East Command to direct the two assault divisions in the invasion. And, much to the recipient's surprise, he designated General Ned Almond, Far East Command chief of staff, as commander. But MacArthur left Almond in his job as chief of staff "in absentia," assuring the non-plussed Almond the war would be over in a few weeks and he'd soon be back in his job in Tokyo.[8]

* * * * * * * *

Although the time for D-Day was approaching rapidly, MacArthur still had not provided any further information of note to the Joint Chiefs concerning his plans. The Chiefs decided to take the matter into their own hands. On August 19 they sent General Collins and Admiral Sherman to the Far East, along with a staff of other officers, including Lieutenant General Idwal H. Edwards, air force deputy chief, to represent General Vandenberg.[9]

The group arrived in Tokyo on August 21, receiving a cordial welcome from MacArthur. The next day Collins and Sherman flew to Korea to have a talk with Walker and then back to Tokyo for the full-scale Inchon briefing on August 23 that MacArthur was preparing.[10]

In the interim, Major General Oliver P. Smith, commander of the 1st Marine Division, landed in Tokyo and reported to Rear Admiral James H. Doyle, commander of Amphibious Group One, which was to be responsible for the Inchon landing. General Smith, who had arrived ahead of his division to work out plans for the invasion, found Doyle extremely skeptical about Inchon.[11] Doyle had sent reconnaissance parties in at various places along the Korean west coast to find a better landing site. He had found one to his satisfaction: Pusong-myon about fifty miles south of Inchon and southwest of Osan.[12] This was an area containing several small towns and villages. Navy underwater teams had made trial landings at Pusong-myon and found better beach conditions and no restrictions on landings at any particular day or hour. Furthermore, the rural area was not built up and was within striking distance of the North Korean lines of communication south of Seoul.[13]

That same day, Smith called on Almond and protested the selection of the Inchon site. Almond brushed aside Smith's objections: there were no organized North Korean forces at Inchon, and the only difficulties the marines would face would be mechanical and physical. Smith thereupon was ushered into MacArthur's office. There he received a warm greeting and more assurances: Inchon would be decisive, the war would be over in a month, the North Koreans had committed all of their troops against the Pusan Perimeter, and the September 15 date, though admittedly early, was the only date that could be considered.[14] Smith was thus deflected, though not convinced.

The next day, just before the full-blown briefing, General Smith went to Almond again, this time to discuss the possibility of landing at Pusong-myon instead of Inchon. Almond told Smith in no uncertain terms he was not interested in landing at Pusong-myon. The real objective of the amphibious move, he told Smith, was to capture Seoul at the earliest possible date—and thus sever North Korean communications and supply lines. Pusong-myon was too far from Seoul, he said, and Far East Command planners did not believe Pusong-myon had the necessary road net to support heavy vehicles in any breakout.[15]

MacArthur had no illusions that the whole Inchon operation hinged on the report Collins and Sherman would take back to Washington. It had become obvious that the Joint Chiefs, as a group, were less than enthusiastic.[16] Therefore, a great deal was riding on the August 23 briefing, which was held in MacArthur's briefing room in the Dai Ichi building. All the top brass was there: MacArthur; Collins; Sherman; Almond; Vice Admiral C. Turner Joy, commander of naval forces in the Far East; Vice Admiral Arthur D. (Dewey) Struble, Seventh Fleet commander and boss of the amphibious force; Major General Edwin K. Wright, Far East Command G-3; Admiral Doyle, and various other officers.[17]

General Wright outlined the basic plan: an assault landing by the 1st Marine Division directly into the port of Inchon; rapid movement to seize Kimpo airfield, the south side of the Han and Yongdungpo directly to the east of Inchon; movement across the river to seize Seoul and the high ground to the north. The 7th Division was to land after the marines and advance to secure the marines' right flank and link up with the Eighth Army moving up from the south.[18]

Admiral Doyle's planning officers then covered the problems the navy would face. They emphasized the great difficulties and risks involved and were decidedly pessimistic.[19] Doyle's conclusions: the operation was not impossible, but he did not recommend it.[20]

General Collins's report on his comments after Doyle's presentation is as follows: "I questioned the ability of the Eighth Army to make a quick junction with the X Corps at Inchon, particularly since General Walker's forces would be weakened by the withdrawal of the First Marine Brigade. Failure to make this junction might result in disaster to the X Corps. I suggested, as an alternative to Inchon, that consideration be given to a landing at Kunsan, which had few of Inchon's physical drawbacks, was close to the enemy's main supply routes through Nonsan and Taejon, and should ensure more prompt union with the Eighth Army in the vicinity of Taejon. Admiral Sherman seconded my suggestion."[21]

No more succinct description of the fundamental difference between MacArthur's and Collins's conceptions of the war could be found than this argument by Collins. First, Collins saw X Corps as being in potential danger. Elsewhere, in his book, War in Peacetime, he says, "There was a serious strategic question whether the Eighth Army could break through the North Korean cordon along the Naktong river and drive on Inchon quickly enough before the enemy could concentrate on overwhelming force against the amphibious attackers. In many instances throughout military history the division of forces beyond supporting distances has led to disastrous defeats."[22] Second, Collins's suggestion to land at Kunsan, far to the south and directly west of the Naktong line, was not a strategic movement on the enemy rear at all, but a direct attack right into the North Korean strength. MacArthur himself answered both of these arguments with devastating counterarguments. And Collins manfully acknowledged in his book the power of MacArthur's logic.[23]

Laying down his corncob pipe, MacArthur talked for forty-five minutes. This eloquent and articulate exposition made a profound and lasting impression on the generals and admirals who witnessed it; most of their reports on the briefing described in awed terms the effect MacArthur's words had on them personally and upon their arguments. This presentation assured the acceptance of MacArthur's plan and established the basis for the legend of MacArthur's omniscience in Korea.

Using a conversational tone that was all the more effective because it lacked rhetorical bombast, MacArthur made a series of points: the enemy had neglected his rear and was hanging on a thin logistical rope; this rope could be severed quickly by the capture of Seoul and the lines of communication running through or near it; the North Koreans had committed practically all their forces against Eighth Army in the south and had no trained reserves to oppose the landing and little power to recover from a blow that would destroy those forces facing Eighth Army; Seoul was the political and psychological key to Korea, and its quick capture would seize the imagination of Asia; a landing at Kunsan, a hundred miles south of Inchon, would be too shallow and would not sever the North Korean supply lines and destroy the North Korean army; an amphibious landing was the most powerful military tool the United Nations Command possessed, and proper use of it meant to strike deep and hard into enemy-held territory, not at Kunsan, where the North Koreans quickly could create a new front facing both Eighth Army and X Corps, thus requiring a direct assault against the enemy and a bitter winter campaign.[24]

Collins admitted he was favorably impressed by MacArthur's presentation, but still had some reservations.[25] To him, the greatest unanswered question was the strength of the North Korean forces in the Inchon area and the ability of the North Koreans to concentrate there quickly.

This was a most curious reaction. Here was Collins's fear that an "overwhelming force" could be concentrated against the landing troops. Where was this "overwhelming force" going to come from? And what could the North Korean troops that could be found do against the American and Allied armada assembling to assault Inchon? It numbered nearly 70,000 men in the expeditionary troops (25,000 in the 1st Marine Division with attached troops; almost 25,000 in the 7th Division with attached Koreans; plus artillery, engineer and tank units).[26] At sea was to be a truly overwhelming force: 230 vessels, including cruisers, destroyers and minesweepers, two marine escort carriers with Corsair support aircraft, three U.S. attack carriers and a light British carrier; together these carriers provided as many support aircraft as the airspace over Inchon would permit.[27] Aircraft and supporting fire from cruisers and destroyers insured that the entire Inchon landing area could be sealed off from North Korean reinforcements. But the possibility of substantial North Korean opposition was simply absent. Intelligence estimates showed the vast bulk of the North Korean army was concentrated against the Eighth Army in the south. G-2 calculated North Korean strength at about 5,000 troops in Seoul, 500 at Kimpo airfield, about 1,800 to 2,500 in the Inchon area. G-2 considered inconsequential the NK command's ability to reinforce the Inchon-Seoul area quickly;

only small rear-area garrisons, line of communications units, and newly formed, poorly trained groups were scattered back of the Pusan Perimeter. North Korean naval elements were almost nonexistent, and the air force had only nineteen aircraft.[28]

American G-2 estimates of North Korean strength in the Pusan Perimeter battle were consistently too high, but even the highly inflated figures would not have given the North Koreans enough men to counter the Inchon landing and also defend against Eighth Army. By mid-September, 1950, United Nations strength had risen to a point where it was dominant over North Korean forces. Eighth Army G-2 in mid-September credited the NK forces facing the perimeter at 101,000 men; actually, NK strength had eroded to about 70,000 men.[29] Possibly a fourth or more of these were recruits forcibly conscripted in South Korea and rushed to the front with little or no training and often without weapons.[30] Morale was low; food was scarce; no more than 30 percent of the original men in the divisions remained, and it was common at this time for veterans to shoot anyone who showed reluctance to go forward when ordered or who tried to desert.[31]

Eighth Army's four divisions, on the other hand, had been built up to an average of 15,000 men each (plus a total of about 9,000 South Koreans attached as part of the "buddy system"); the five ROK divisions numbered about 50,000 men, and the British 27th Brigade had about 1,600 men. Total combat strength of Eighth Army, therefore, was around 120,000 men.[32] Firepower was on the order of six to one over the North Koreans.[33] The United States had more than five hundred medium tanks in the Perimeter by mid-September, more than five times what the North Koreans possessed.[34] UN forces, even using the inflated G-2 estimates of enemy troops, were far superior to the North Koreans.

G-2 estimates showed North Korea had no other substantial trained forces. How General Collins figured enough North Koreans could be found to affect the issue at Inchon-Seoul is unknown. Eighth Army G-2 estimated that only three NK divisions (about 24,000 men) could be diverted from the perimeter to attack the Inchon landing force.[35] This figure itself is an incredibly high estimate, because it would have denuded large sectors of the Naktong line. More important, the United Nations' absolute command of the air precluded movement of these forces by day, thus lengthening greatly the time it would take them to reach Inchon-Seoul.

Actually, it made little difference whether the NK forces moved toward Inchon or stayed and fought Eighth Army; the key was to deprive the North Koreans of their ammunition, oil supplies and food, and thus render them unable to fight. Cutting the communications lines insured that this would happen. There was some fear at the time that the North Koreans could use secondary roads and rail lines east of Seoul and through the eastern mountains to transport supplies to North Koreans holding the perimeter. There was no way, however, that such routes could have carried enough supplies to keep the NK army effective. Even use of the main Seoul corridor with the mainline double-tracked railway and road through it was barely keeping the North Koreans supplied along the Naktong. Any interruption of this corridor would have destructive effects.

Nevertheless, MacArthur's able presentation did not convince the naval and marine officers completely. The next morning, August 24, they assembled in a meeting which included Admirals Sherman and Joy and General Shepherd, commander of the Pacific Fleet Marine Force in Hawaii. All present felt MacArthur should give greater consideration to Pusong-myon. They selected General Shepherd, known to be influential with MacArthur, to make a personal appeal for Pusong-myon. Shepherd called on MacArthur, but got nowhere. From that moment, the navy and marine officers abandoned Pusong-myon and concentrated on Inchon.[36]

When Collins and Sherman got back to Washington, they stated their misgivings to the other Chiefs.[37] The JCS inclined toward postponing Inchon until they were sure Eighth Army could hold the Pusan Perimeter, now under renewed attack. But Truman and Secretary Johnson were convinced.[38] Truman called Inchon a daring strategic conception and was confident it would succeed.[39]

It is remarkable that civilians—Truman, Johnson and Harriman—were highly supportive of MacArthur's plan, while the top military men in the country—the Joint Chiefs—were hesitant. And Truman continued in his endorsement even while he was livid from a new MacArthur political transgression over Taiwan that erupted just as the final decisions of Inchon were being made. It is to the President's credit that, angry as he was, he did not let his anger influence his judgment of MacArthur's military strategy.

CHAPTER 25

MacArthur Alienates Truman

TRUMAN BECAME irreparably estranged from MacArthur less than a fortnight after Ambassador Harriman returned from his peace-making trip to Tokyo. The cause was a message the General sent to the annual encampment of the Veterans of Foreign Wars (VFW) to be held at the end of August in Chicago. Unable to attend as invited, MacArthur asked his message to be read on August 28.

The VFW message was largely a repeat of MacArthur's June 14 memorandum to General Bradley and Secretary Johnson stressing Taiwan's strategic importance and urging that it not be allowed to fall into communist hands (see pages 34 and 37). But there was a short addition that a quite neutral person easily could read as an attack on Truman's wary handling of the island's status: "Nothing could be more fallacious than the threadbare argument by those who advocate appeasement and defeatism in the Pacific that if we defend Formosa we alienate continental Asia. Those who speak thus do not understand the Orient. They do not grant that it is in the pattern of Oriental psychology to respect and follow aggressive, resolute and dynamic leadership—to quickly turn on a leadership characterized by timidity or vacillation—and they underestimate the Oriental mentality. Nothing in the last five years has so inspired the Far East as the American determination to preserve the bulwarks of our Pacific Ocean strategic position from future encroachment, for few of its people fail accurately to appraise the safeguard such determination brings to their free institutions."[1]

The message had been released ahead of time and had been sent out over the wire services and had been published in *U.S. News and World Report*, which went to press August 25.

Irrespective of how the American people read these sentences, the Chinese Communist leadership could hardly understand them as endorsing the neutralization of Taiwan. Rather, as General Collins later said, they implied that the United States wanted the island as a military base.[2]

The text of MacArthur's VFW address was released on August 26 by the FEC headquarters public relations office,[3] but it had come to the attention of Secretary of State Acheson the day before. He was outraged at its "effrontery and damaging effect at home and abroad."[4] The same day, Ambassador Harriman told Truman, who concluded at once that it "could only serve to confuse the world as to just what our Formosa policy was."[5]

MacArthur's deliberate attempt to force a change in American policy, or his gaucherie and insensitivity to the political situation facing the United States at the moment (which is possible), could not have been better timed or demonstrated than by his dropping of this bombshell. And he did it without any prior notification or intimation to either the Joint Chiefs or the President.[6]

Only a month before, on July 19, Truman, in a message to Congress on the Far East situation, had emphasized that the United States sought no "special position or privilege" on Taiwan. "The present military neutralization of Formosa is without prejudice to political questions affecting that island," Truman said. "Our desire is that Formosa not become embroiled in hostilities disturbing to the peace of the Pacific and that all questions affecting Formosa be settled by peaceful means as envisaged in the Charter of the United Nations."[7]

On August 25 the Chinese Communist government had sent to the UN Security Council a communication accusing the United States of "open encroachment" on Chinese territory and demanding the withdrawal of "armed invading forces from Taiwan and from other territories belonging to China,"[8] the latter presumably being the Pescadores and other small islands off the mainland still occupied by the Nationalists. Truman had immediately directed the U.S. ambassador to the United Nations, Warren R. Austin, to send a letter to Trygve Lie, the secretary-general, that reiterated Truman's July 19 message to Congress, denied any U.S. aggression against China, and assured Red China that the neutralization of Taiwan "was not inspired by any desire to acquire a special position for the United States."[9]

MacArthur's VFW message, if allowed to stand unchallenged, could be interpreted by the world, but especially Red China, as a refutation of Ambassador Austin's reassurance. It chopped at the foundations of a carefully put together administration edifice, only barely holding up, that was designed to assure world opinion the United States had no aggressive intentions against Red China even as it was denying the

Chinese Communists access to a province that everyone, including the Nationalist Chinese, agreed was an integral part of China. The Red Chinese were not the only ones who could see that this shaky edifice could be demolished easily because of its essential illogicality: after all, how was the United States-China-Taiwan situation fundamentally different from a foreign power's telling the United States to keep its hands off Hawaii, or Britain to stay off the Channel Islands, or France off Corsica?

Truman was furious. He called a meeting at 9:15 a.m. on Saturday, August 26, of Acheson, Johnson, Harriman and the Joint Chiefs, minus General Collins and Admiral Sherman, who were just returning from the Far East.[10] Truman, "lips white and compressed,"[11] read the MacArthur message, then asked everyone present whether anyone knew of it in advance. All said no. Acheson felt "this insubordination could not be tolerated";[12] Bradley said he was shocked and felt the message seemed the height of arrogance.[13] Truman directed Secretary Johnson to order MacArthur to withdraw the statement.[14]

It was quite manifest that MacArthur's message could not be taken back; it had long since been disseminated to the world's press, and the presses were rolling. A withdrawal could only be seen for what it was: a harsh and immediate disciplinary move against the General. Secretary Johnson did not relish being delegated to beard the lion, and, according to Bradley, "spent most of the day trying to weasel out of it." Finally, an exasperated Truman called Johnson and himself dictated the order to MacArthur.[15]

This was the message: "The President of the United States directs that you withdraw your message for national encampment of Veterans of Foreign Wars, because various features with respect to Formosa are in conflict with the policy of the United States and its position in the United Nations."[16]

Despite his anger, Truman did not dismiss MacArthur, although he talked about it with Johnson,[17] and seriously considered it.[18] Truman wrote later he had no desire to hurt MacArthur personally, and doubtless the impending Inchon landing, which the General was to lead, stayed his hand.

The reprimand did not have the effect on MacArthur that Truman and Acheson might have wished. MacArthur's response was remarkable, considering the clear implications that his VFW message contained. MacArthur immediately fired back a protest to Secretary Johnson, asserting his message had been prepared carefully to support the President's June 27 order neutralizing Taiwan. He added that Taiwan was being discussed freely in public and private throughout the world, and his views as expressed to the VFW were "purely my personal ones,"[19] as if the American officer charged by the U.S. government with keeping Taiwan neutral could express private views in opposition to this neutrality and not create an international flap of the first water. Either it was an example of incredible naiveté, or it was a calculated move to shift American policy as regards Red China or Taiwan. Whatever MacArthur's motives, the effect was to rally the Republican opposition to MacArthur and, as David McLellan says in his biography of Acheson, "further reinforced him in his megalomania and in his career of insubordination."[20]

MacArthur withdrew his message to the VFW, and Truman, trying to be conciliatory, wrote him directly on August 29, giving the text of Ambassador Austin's letter to Trygve Lie. He added, "I am sure that when you examine this letter ... you will understand why my action of the 26th in directing the withdrawal of your message" was necessary. Finally, Truman congratulated the General on the outcome of his conference of August 23 on the Inchon landing.[21] It was a letter that suggested bygones be bygones and the two men move on forward in concert. Unfortunately, this was not what MacArthur had in mind.

The immediate consequences of the VFW incident were to increase Red China's suspicions of American aggressive aims toward the mainland, and to provide the Russians with a propaganda victory. Andrei Vishinsky, Soviet ambassador to the United Nations, in a speech said: "None other than General MacArthur recently informed, with cynical candor, the whole world about the decision of the ruling circles in the United States at all costs to turn Taiwan into an American base in the Far East."[22]

The one soldier to fall in the VFW battle was Secretary Johnson. Truman had learned through Averell Harriman that Johnson was conniving with Republican Senator Robert Taft for Acheson's ouster, and his reluctance to carry out the President's order and reprimand MacArthur was the last straw.[23] Truman called for Johnson's resignation (it came on September 12[24]) and immediately asked General of the Army George C. Marshall to take the job. In his Senate confirmation hearings, this famous soldier (army chief of staff, 1939–45) and former secretary of state (1947–49) was approved, but he had to undergo brutal attacks by members of the China Lobby and some Republican extremists. They used the occasion to launch opening salvos for the upcoming November off-year elections in which they planned to make campaign issues of the administration's "loss of China" and "softness on communism."[25]

CHAPTER 26

The North Koreans Try Once More

THE JOINT CHIEFS, despite the highly distracting VFW affair, could not allow a decision on Inchon to hang fire. Almost seventy thousand assault troops were assembling, along with a huge naval armada and great fleets of combat aircraft. D-Day was only a little over two weeks away. Since the President continued to endorse Inchon and they as a body still harbored strong reservations, the Chiefs sent MacArthur a message on August 28 that was a masterpiece of ambiguous Washingtonese. Although they gave general approval of the operation, the Chiefs carefully did not fix any definite location and made it plain they wished the landing site to be subject to last-minute reconsideration. The message read:

"After reviewing the information brought back by General Collins and Admiral Sherman we concur in making preparations and executing a turning movement by amphibious forces on the west coast of Korea either at Inchon in the event the enemy defenses in vicinity of Inchon prove ineffective or at a favorable beach south of Inchon if one can be located. We further concur in preparation, if desired by CINCFE [Commander in Chief, Far East: MacArthur], for an envelopment by amphibious forces in the vicinity of Kunsan. We understand that alternative plans are being prepared in order best to exploit the situation as it develops. We desire such information as becomes available with respect to conditions in the possible objective areas and timely information as to your intentions and plans for offensive operations."[1]

If MacArthur suspected the Chiefs were setting up a rationale to abort the Inchon operation, he gave no indication. In fact, MacArthur went right on with his Inchon plans without even responding to the Chiefs' message.[2]

On August 30 he issued his operations order for Inchon, which set in motion the immense and extremely complicated movement of men, ships and aircraft into positions for the assault. But he did not immediately send the Joint Chiefs a copy.[3]

Just at this moment, the North Korean command, knowing its chances of breaking through to Pusan were declining with every day, unleashed a desperate general offensive all around the Pusan Perimeter.[4]

The North Koreans had assembled about 98,000 men for the September assault, about a third of them raw recruits, and most of them conscripted by force in South Korea and rushed to the front with little training and often without weapons.[5] Against these troops, the UN Command had about 120,000 combat troops, plus 60,000 support personnel.[6]

Constant UN air attacks on the long North Korean lines of communication had failed to stop rail transport, but had greatly diminished it. Ammunition and motor fuel, which took precedence over all other resupply, continued to arrive at the front, but in reduced quantities. There also was a considerable resupply of tanks, artillery and mortars, but nothing to challenge the overwhelming superiority of UN weapons. A shortage of small arms developed by mid-August and worsened with each week. New trucks were virtually impossible to obtain, and there was no resupply of clothing. The greatest deprivation for the NK troops, however, was food; with priority given to ammo and oil products, only enough rations got through for one or two meals a day. By September 1, the food situation was so bad that most of the North Koreans showed loss of stamina and impaired combat effectiveness.[7]

Nevertheless, these hungry and numerically inferior North Korean soldiers attacked. They broke through at several points, and in early September were flooding through these holes into the U.S. and ROK rear. The NK offensive came in five main thrusts: a two-division drive against the U.S. 25th Division toward Masan in the south; a two-division thrust along the middle Naktong against the U.S. 2nd Division toward Miryang and the Pusan-Taegu railway and highway; a three-division attempt to break through the U.S. 1st Cavalry and the ROK 1st Divisions at Taegu; a two-division attack through the ROK 6th and 8th Divisions toward Yongchon and the lateral corridor east of Taegu; and a two-division effort to break through the ROK Capital and 3rd Divisions on the east coast and from there to drive down the Kyongju corridor to Pusan.[8] (See Map 1.)

In the fierce battles that followed, the North Koreans made important gains. By September 3, General Walker faced five dangerous situations: an NK penetration at Pohang-dong, severance of the lateral corridor at

Yongchon between Taegu and Pohang-dong, strong NK gains in the mountains north of Taegu, a penetration of the Naktong Bulge on the lower Naktong, and a thrust behind the greater part of the 25th Division near Masan in the extreme south.

It was an incredible effort by the North Koreans, no matter that it was spawned by the NK command's realization that this was shooting the army's final bolt. The NK command also had figured out improvements in tactics that reduced to some extent the shattering effects of American air power and artillery, which was virtually ruling out all daylight front-line activities whenever UN fighters or bombers could get aloft or artillery forward observers could see. These tactical changes were explained by Major General Pang Ho San, commander of the 6th NK Division. His summary, discovered in August in prisoner-of-war interrogations, said, "From now on, use daylight hours for full combat preparation, and commence attacks soon after sunset. Concentrate your battle actions mostly at night and capture enemy base positions. From midnight on, engage enemy in close combat by approaching to within 100 to 150 meters of him. Then, even with the break of dawn, the enemy planes will not be able to distinguish friend from foe, which will enable you to prevent great losses."[9]

In the mountainous central front and along the east coast at Pohang-dong, ROKs and North Koreans for two weeks engaged in bitter and extremely costly battles which wore down both sides. With the aid of the U.S. 24th Division, several battalions of American artillery and unrelenting UN air and naval bombardment, the ROKs finally drove the Northerners back into the mountains. In this sector, the NK command's greatest failure was its inability to keep its advancing troops adequately supplied. The offensive literally died at the end of logistical arteries that petered out in the often trackless mountains into inadequate small capillaries feeding the front. These capillaries were constantly subject to being cut by air interdiction strikes.[10]

Eighth Army faced a severe challenge north and northwest of Taegu. On September 2 three NK divisions attacked the 1st Cavalry Division. Despite several U.S. counterattacks, the North Koreans pushed the Americans back toward Taegu in an arc from Waegwan on the west to the old Bowling Alley near Tabu-dong on the north.[11] On September 3 the 1st Cavalry lost Tabu-dong and the ancient "walled city" of Ka-san, whose centuries-old fortress ruins and rock wall crowned the summit of Hill 902, a couple of miles east of Tabu-dong and only ten miles north of Taegu.[12]

On the Naktong Bulge just north of the confluence of the Nam and the Naktong the danger was even greater. NK troops crossed the river on

September 1 at numerous points at the bulge and north and south of it, and struck the 2nd Division, which only recently had gone into the line.[13]

At the southern end of the bulge, 9th NK Division troops, using flares and whistles to signal, hit Company C of the 9th Regiment with unusual force. The company kept in its positions only a short while, then the men broke and attempted to escape, most of them moving all the way across the lower Naktong into the positions of the 25th Division. At the western edge of the bulge other 9th NK Division troops drove away Company B of the 9th Regiment with heavy casualties. The defection of Company C and the shattering of Company B left a wide hole through which thousands of NK troops surged, past the bitterly contested August battlefield of Cloverleaf hill and Obong-ni ridge, and straight for Yongsan.[14] Meanwhile, just north of the bulge troops of the 2nd NK Division overran Company C of the 23rd Regiment, killing most of its members; only twenty men survived. Company B of the 23rd, emplaced a little farther north, also lost heavily and withdrew to the east. By the morning of September 1 North Koreans had penetrated all the way through to the north-south Changnyong-Yongsan road and had cut the 2nd Division in two—the 23rd and 38th Regiments to the north and the 9th Regiment and division headquarters to the south.[15] The enemy had punched a hole six miles wide and eight miles deep in the middle of the 2nd Division line, and the frontline battalions of the 9th and 23rd Regiments were reeling from the blows.[16]

On the far southern front west of Masan, the 6th and 7th NK Divisions launched ferocious attacks on the night of August 31 against the 25th Division's 35th Regiment, emplaced along the Nam river, and against the 2nd Battalion of the 24th Regiment, emplaced just west of Haman and just north of Battle Mountain and Pil-bong.[17] A ROK police force of about three hundred men was in the line just south of a Nam river ferry and about two miles north of Komam-ni. NK troops struck this police detachment a half hour after midnight on September 1, and crumpled and scattered it immediately, thus creating a wide hole through which NK elements streamed, moving behind the 35th Regiment emplacements still holding along the Nam. At the same time, soldiers of the 6th NK Division struck the 2nd Battalion of the 24th Regiment, emplaced west of Haman in the Sobuk-san. Most of the battalion broke and ran. NK troops rushed through and encircled Haman. The 24th Regiment commander, Colonel Arthur S. Champney, ordered his 1st Battalion, in reserve about three miles south of Haman, to counterattack and restore the line. The 1st Battalion effort got under way about 7:30 a.m. September 1, but upon contact with the North Koreans the battalion broke and fled to the rear. Thus shortly after daybreak two battalions of the 24th Regiment effectively had ceased to exist as fighting units, and the North Koreans were streaming to the east. (See Map 6.)

The Pusan Perimeter situation was critical. Eighth Army commander Walker decided the greatest danger was at the Naktong Bulge, where the NK breakthrough was greatest and the penetration deepest. He asked the air force to attack North Korean supply columns and reinforcements west of the Naktong in the bulge area in a maximum effort to isolate the battlefield. Far East Command asked the navy to join in the effort, and the Seventh Fleet quickly turned back from stations in the Yellow Sea where it was preparing for strikes at Inchon and Seoul and sped southward at full steam to get its aircraft in range to assist the Naktong Bulge defense.[18] General Walker also alerted the marine brigade (5th Marines), already preparing to move to Pusan to embark on the Inchon landing (though of course the troops did not know this). Walker ordered the marines back into the line to bolster the 2nd Division on the Naktong Bulge.[19]

With the shattering of the 9th Regiment, the 2nd Division commander, Major General Lawrence B. Keiser, had virtually no troops to defend Yongsan. In the emergency, he called on the 2nd Engineer Combat Battalion and added the 2nd Division Reconnaissance Company and the 72nd Tank Battalion, plus a few AAA weapons. Although the North Koreans captured Yongsan, the scratch force kept them from moving on toward Miryang and severing the main railway and highway there. The engineers held positions south and east of town that commanded all the main roads into and out of Yongsan. About 3 a.m., September 2, NK troops attacked the engineers, who had neither artillery nor mortar support. Instead, they used nine new 3.5-inch and nine old 2.36-inch bazookas. The bazookas, plus machine-gun and rifle fire and grenades, inflicted heavy casualties on the North Koreans. Medium tanks of the 72nd Battalion, emplaced at the exits south and east of Yongsan, blocked the NK advance with heavy shellfire. The battle raged all morning, littering the slopes south of town with the bodies of hundreds of North Koreans, but costing the Americans highly, too. As an example, in Company D of the engineers, every officer but one was killed or wounded, along with 12 men killed and 18 wounded.

During the melee, Colonel John G. Hill, 9th Regiment CO, reorganized about eight hundred men of the regiment who had arrived near Yongsan from the overrun Naktong positions. During the afternoon, this composite unit attacked through the engineers and regained possession of the town. Air strikes and bazooka fire destroyed several NK T34 tanks, and by evening the North Koreans had been driven into the hills west of Yongsan.

The 5th Marines arrived at Yongsan and went into position to attack westward the morning of September 3 in conjunction with the 9th Regiment and the engineers—the marines to move west along either side of a road running to the Naktong, most of the 9th Infantry Regiment along with tanks and AAA weapons to the north, and the engineers and the remainder of the 9th and tanks to the south.

The first day of the counterattack, September 3, the army and marine advance reached positions two miles west of Yongsan, much of it in the face of heavy NK defensive fire. Marine armor destroyed four T34 tanks and an NK crew abandoned a fifth. Marines gained one hill position west of town when NK troops broke under air attack and fled. On another occasion, NK reinforcements were caught in rice paddies while moving forward and were shattered by air strikes, artillery concentrations and machine-gun and small-arms fire. Even so, the day was costly to the Americans: the marines alone lost 34 killed and 157 wounded.

The counterattack commenced again the morning of September 4 against little opposition. Marines quickly overran what had been the CP of the 9th NK Division; tents were still standing and two T34s in excellent condition had been abandoned. Americans found the road westward littered with North Korean bodies and destroyed or abandoned equipment. By nightfall the counterattacks had gained another three miles.

Early on September 5 North Koreans launched a strong sally against the 9th Regiment in the midst of heavy rain. The enemy troops penetrated close into the infantry positions, and the Americans stopped the assault only by hand-to-hand fighting in which U.S. soldiers had to use bayonets.

After daybreak on September 5, the American counterattack started on its third day. It was another day of rain, and it was a day of déjà vu: at mid-morning, the marines approached Obong-ni ridge and the 9th Regiment Cloverleaf hill, their old battlefield of the August offensive. The marines this time drove through the pass between the two halves of the ridge and took positions beyond; the U.S. advance was so swift the North Koreans were not able to reoccupy and refortify these two formidable positions.

In the afternoon, an NK force came out of concealed positions and struck Company B of the marines, emplaced on a small hill just south of the road at the pass. Two T34 tanks surprised and destroyed two leading marine Pershing M26 tanks. U.S. assault teams armed with 3.5-inch bazookas rushed forward, and in an action resembling the tank fight in the same pass in August, destroyed both T34s, as well as an armored personnel carrier coming behind. The North Korean attack was savage, causing twenty-five casualties in Company B; and it continued to advance until reinforcements from Company A moved up and army artillery and marine 81mm mortars brought it to a stop.

The next day, at fifteen minutes after midnight on September 6, the 5th Marines, in response to General MacArthur's order, began to move out of their positions at Obong-ni and back to Pusan to load for the Inchon invasion. Release of the marines occurred only over the vehement protests of General Walker, who earlier had told General Almond he could not be responsible for the safety of the perimeter if he lost the 5th Marines.[20] The 1st Marine Division commander, General Smith, however, insisted he could not make the Inchon landing without the 5th Marines, especially as the third marine regiment would not arrive in time for the assault. Almond proposed as a compromise that the 5th Marines remain in the perimeter and the 1st Marine Division use instead the 32nd Regiment of the 7th Infantry, a proposal Smith rejected out of hand. The issue reached a climax on September 3 when General Smith, accompanied by Admirals Joy, Struble and Doyle, went to the Dai Ichi building for a showdown with MacArthur and Almond. It must have been a stormy session. The dry reports of the meeting show only that the two sides "reached an impasse." Then Almond, in the midst of the session, asked MacArthur into a private office and told the General that Smith and the navy would not go into Inchon without the 5th Marines. MacArthur thereupon said, "Tell Walker he will have to give up the 5th Marine Regiment."[21]

On September 4 MacArthur sent General Wright, FEC G-3, to Taegu to deliver the order about the marines to Walker personally. Such gingerly handling of the Eighth Army commander was a reflection of Walker's fears about the safety of the perimeter at the moment. Wright told Walker the 5th Marines had to be released not later than the night of September 5–6; but, attempting to lessen the blow, Wright said the 17th Regiment of the 7th Division, instead of going directly by ship to Inchon to participate in the invasion, would be sent to Pusan, where it would be held in "floating reserve" and available to Walker in case of need. He also told Walker the 65th Regiment of the 3rd Division, scheduled to arrive in the Far East on September 18–20, would be diverted directly to Pusan and Eighth Army.[22]

Doubtless this mollified Walker somewhat, although a "floating reserve" of a completely green and untested regiment was not the same thing as the battle-tested 5th Marines. The September days leading up to this September 4 denouement had been extremely trying for General Walker. Although the 9th Regiment and 5th Marines counterattack in the Naktong Bulge was going well, the North Koreans were pressing hard north and west of Taegu and were still threatening near Masan. The success of these NK attacks had created a crisis of confidence in the American command at Taegu, and the question was recurring in Eighth Army headquarters—as well as back at the Pentagon—whether the Naktong line could hold.

General Walker was faced with an imminent and far-reaching decision, and loss of the 5th Marines did nothing to lessen it: should Eighth Army withdraw to the so-called Davidson Line, the army's last-ditch defensive positions just north of Pusan, which had been hastily laid out in August by Brigadier General Garrison H. Davidson, an engineer officer?[23] The line would have contained a perimeter larger than Dunkirk's, but it would have clearly created a Dunkirk situation. And retreat to it, with the decision on Inchon still not final—despite the fact that the assault force and the protective armada were already loading and moving out—could have spelled disaster for Eighth Army and for MacArthur's counteroffensive before the cold winds began to come down from Siberia. A war of swift retribution could be turned into a war of slow attrition.

Walker knew a great deal was riding on this decision. Yet it was his responsibility as army commander to ascertain the safety of his command. And no one else could do it, not even MacArthur. It appears, at first sight, that Walker's anxieties were ill-founded: the subtraction of some four thousand marines from his force left it still numerically superior to the North Koreans, who, besides, had suffered devastating losses in the first days of their offensive; in terms of firepower the UN force was overwhelmingly superior. But Walker was looking at some facts that sobered him: despite UN superiority, the North Koreans were on the offensive and they were penetrating American positions.

Walker on September 5 talked over the matter of retreating with his top staff and other high-ranking officers, as well as most of his division commanders. Walker reached no final decision while talking with them. Eighth Army G-3, just in case, prepared orders for the retreat to start at 5 a.m. September 6. But sometime during the night General "Bulldog" Walker decided to stay: there would be no withdrawal.[24]

CHAPTER 27

The Joint Chiefs
Get Cold Feet

FAR AWAY IN THE PENTAGON, fears about the safety of Eighth Army had been magnified far beyond the reality that General Walker faced. For the Joint Chiefs the threat that the North Koreans should throw the United Nations out of the perimeter seemed real, and Chairman Bradley felt MacArthur's orders to release the 5th Marines increased the danger.[1]

Furthermore, the Chiefs had heard nothing from MacArthur since their August 28 message to him concurring in planning for the Inchon landing, but asking for more information. (See page 180.) After reading the reports on North Korean advances and possible withdrawal to the Davidson Line, the Chiefs became greatly alarmed. On September 5 they signaled MacArthur they wanted information: "Pursuant to the request ... desire to be informed of any modification which may have been made in your plans for the mid-September amphibious operation."[2] The reminder brought forth only a casual rejoinder. MacArthur replied that "the general outline of the plan remains as described to you," and promised that by September 11 he would send them a detailed description of his planned operations by way of officer courier.[3]

This really was not an adequate response to the Chiefs, and on September 7 they decided to send MacArthur a final warning of the disastrous consequences if the Inchon landing failed, or if it failed to produce a quick victory. The Chiefs' message:

"While we concur in launching a counteroffensive in Korea as early as feasible, we have noted with considerable concern the recent trend of events there. In light of all factors including apparent commitment of practically all reserves available to Eighth Army, we desire your estimate as to the feasibility and chance of success of projected operation if initiated on planned schedule. We are sure that you understand that all available trained army units in the United States have been allocated to you except the 82nd Airborne Division and that minimum of four months would elapse before first of partially trained National Guard divisions could reach Korea in event that junction of main Eighth Army forces with X Corps bridgehead should not quickly be effected with forces now available to FECOM [Far East Command]."[4]

MacArthur later declared this message "chilled me to the marrow of my bones," because it implied strongly that "the whole movement should be abandoned."[5] There was no evidence of this chill, however, in MacArthur's prompt reply:

"There is no question in my mind as to the feasibility of the operation and I regard its chance of success as excellent. I go further and believe that it represents the only hope of wresting the initiative from the enemy and thereby presenting an opportunity for a decisive blow. To do otherwise is to commit us to a war of indefinite duration, of gradual attrition and of doubtful results, as the enemy has potentialities of reinforcement and buildup which exceed those of our own availability....The situation within the perimeter is not critical. It is possible that there may be some contraction and defense positions have been selected for this contingency. There is no slightest possibility, however, of our force being ejected from the Pusan beachhead. The envelopment from the north will instantly relieve the pressure on the south perimeter and, indeed, is the only way that this can be accomplished....The success of the enveloping movement from the north does not depend upon the rapid juncture of the X Corps and the Eighth Army. The seizure of the heart of the enemy distributing system in the Seoul area will completely dislocate the logistical supply of his forces now operating in South Korea and therefore will ultimately result in their disintegration.... Caught between our northern and our southern forces, both of which are completely self-sustaining because of our absolute air and naval supremacy, the enemy cannot fail to be ultimately shattered through disruption of his logistical support and our combined combat activities. The prompt junction of our two forces, while it would be dramatically symbolic of the complete collapse of the enemy, is not a vital part of the operation. For the reasons stated, there are no material changes under contemplation in the operation as planned and reported to you. The embarkation of the troops and the preliminary air and naval preparations are proceeding according to schedule. I repeat that I and all of my commanders and staff officers, without exception, are enthusiastic and confident of the success of the enveloping operation."[6]

MacArthur's assertion that all of the officers involved in Inchon approved was a bit of hyperbole, and Bradley upbraids him in his autobiography, saying naval and marine officers especially held grave reservation.[7] However, MacArthur's signal to the Chiefs was a brilliantly cogent summary of the reasons for Inchon and why it would succeed— and should have laid their fears to rest. It didn't.

The Chiefs had a final discussion of Inchon on September 8, including a morning conference with President Truman to review MacArthur's response. "It was really too late in the game for the JCS to formally disapprove Inchon," Bradley said.[8] The Joint Chiefs told the President they endorsed Inchon, and the same day flashed MacArthur: "We approve your plan and President has been so informed."[9]

MacArthur had carefully arranged that the Joint Chiefs have no grounds for disapproving his plans simply by not delivering them into their hands until literally hours before the troops began assaulting the beaches.[10] Lieutenant Colonel Lynn D. Smith, the courier bearing the operations order for Inchon with all the details, did not leave Tokyo for Washington until the morning of September 10. MacArthur told him, probably only partly in jest, "Don't get there too soon." The General further told Colonel Smith to deliver the following message to the Joint Chiefs: "If they say it is too big a gamble, tell them I said this is throwing a nickel in the pot after it has been opened for a dollar. The big gamble was Washington's decision to put American troops on the Asiatic mainland."

Colonel Smith reached Washington at 11 p.m. on September 13 and appeared before the Joint Chiefs at 11 a.m. September 14. By the time Smith had completed his presentation and answered questions, it was too late for the Chiefs to have cancelled the plan. H-Hour was 6:30 a.m. September 15 Far East time, or 4:30 p.m. September 14 Washington time.[11]

* * * * * * * *

While the top brass discussed whether Inchon was going to occur, the marines, sailors, soldiers and airmen who were to carry out the operation loaded on ships or planes and started the massive movement toward Inchon, although none but the most completely initiated knew the destination. There was much speculation, but no hard information.

Meantime, the battle to hold the Pusan Perimeter continued. And General Walker need not have worried about the safety of Eighth Army. The 9th NK Division in the Naktong bulge had suffered a total and terrifying defeat at the hands of the 5th Marines and the 9th Regiment. Although the weak 4th NK Division moved across the Naktong to support the 9th NK Division, neither had enough strength even to push against the 9th Regiment, left alone at Cloverleaf and Obong-ni ridge.[12] It was the same elsewhere in the perimeter, though fierce battles continued. U.S. counterattacks forced back the 2nd NK Division, which had penetrated the 23rd Regiment positions north of the Naktong bulge. The British 27th Brigade also was committed to battle for the first time. General Walker placed it north of the 2nd Division to block NK movement across the Naktong at the Yongpo bridge on the Koryang-Taegu road. The professional English and Scottish soldiers performed excellently, as expected. Fortunately for the British and the Americans in that sector, the 10th NK Division ineptly failed to advance strongly against either the British or the 38th Regiment, although the way was open to drive into the almost trackless mountains east of the Naktong and debouch north on Taegu or south on 2nd Division's rear.[13]

North of Taegu, things went badly for a few days. A U.S. effort to recapture Ka-san (Hill 902) failed, with heavy casualties (an engineer company used as infantry suffered almost 50 percent losses). North Koreans advanced past Ka-san to set up a roadblock two miles south of Tabu-dong and to occupy Hill 570 overlooking Taegu, only eight miles away. First Cavalry Division counterattacks were under way when, on September 8, North Koreans threatened Hills 314 and 660 even closer to Taegu. First Cavalry attention then focused on Hill 314, which it captured September 12 after some of the severest fighting in the war. The assault force, 3rd Battalion, 7th Cavalry, which had arrived in Korea at the end of August, suffered 229 casualties in the first two hours of the attack; the battalion had only 535 men. After Hill 314, the North Koreans backed up slowly, and the pressure on Taegu ended.[14]

On the southern front west of Masan, a reinforced battalion of the 27th Regiment was sent in the afternoon of September 1 to plug the huge gap left in the American line at Haman by the disintegration of two battalions of the 24th Regiment. The 27th Regiment's assault was aided by repeated attacks by air force fighters and navy planes from the *Valley Forge* and *Philippine Sea*, two hundred miles away, but steaming toward the battlefield at twenty-seven knots. By nightfall on September 1 troops of the 27th had secured most of the position abandoned earlier in the day by the 24th. NK troops counterattacked in the morning under cover of fog, but the 27th soldiers held on in an all-morning fight that was aided greatly, after the fog lifted, by napalm strikes which burned many North Koreans to death. The next morning the North Koreans tried again, but met a perfectly timed air strike directed from the battalion CP and by heavy artillery, mortar and tank-fire barrages. After the attack was repulsed, hundreds of North Koreans lay dead about the battalion position. Meanwhile the 35th Regiment, which had been cut off by NK troops moving behind it, refused to budge. At first one battalion and later two battalions of the 27th Regiment fought toward the 35th through an estimated three thousand North Koreans operating in rear areas. Although Americans suffered high casualties in some of the confused engagements, U.S. firepower eventually overwhelmed the North Koreans. By September 7 survivors of the 7th NK Division were escaping across the Nam river. The 25th Division buried more than two thousand North Korean dead found behind its lines; this did not include the enemy soldiers killed in front of the division positions. Despite some severe scares, the American line held in the south.[15]

There was one ironic event in the southern battle. The bridge over the Naktong at Namji-ri had been faithfully protected throughout "the days along the Naktong" because it was the only way the 25th Division could maintain direct contact with the divisions to the north. First Platoon of Company F, 35th Regiment, had effectively defended the bridge in almost nightly sallies by NK troops trying to capture it in order to drive toward Pusan. At one time, more than one hundred North Korean bodies lay on the northern approaches. The battle was over, and the Namji-ri bridge had survived intact. Then on September 9, a flight of American F-82s dropped out of the clouds and spotted the bridge. How the pilots got turned around, no one knows, but the F-82s raced in on a bombing run and one 500-pound bomb landed on an eighty-foot center span and blew it into the river below.[16]

In the final North Korean offensive in the perimeter, several gruesome atrocities against American troops occurred. These cases of mayhem, mutilation and callous killing appeared to be random and affected relatively few individuals, giving rise to the belief they were perpetrated by single North Koreans or small groups of NK soldiers. On Hill 314 north of Taegu on September 12 an American officer's body was found, bound hand and foot; gasoline had been poured over him and lighted. Two days later, the bodies of four American soldiers were located with their hands tied; their bodies bore evidence that the men had been bayoneted and shot while bound.[17] During the fighting behind the 35th Regiment's positions in the south, a mess truck was caught in a North Korean roadblock; one of the crew members was captured and mutilated and murdered while other crew members, hiding in a haystack, heard his screams. The man's body was recovered later; he had been castrated and his fingers cut off before he was killed. Later, many 25th Division soldiers saw bodies of Americans lying in a ditch in the 35th Regiment area, their hands tied and their feet cut off. Other Americans saw bodies with their tongues cut out. Members of the 7th NK Division apparently committed these atrocities. On the night of September 3–4, about fifteen

NK guerrillas, including one woman, attacked a radio relay station about four miles from Masan. The seven Americans and two South Koreans inside a tent were captured; the guerrillas tied up the Americans and took documents from the files, and then the woman shot all the prisoners with a tommy gun. Two wounded Americans lived to report the atrocity.[18]

CHAPTER 28

Inchon

INCHON WAS THE LAST great amphibious invasion undertaken by the United States. Because it also took place with the help of U.S. allies Britain, Australia, New Zealand, Canada and the Netherlands, it possessed a drama and excitement of great assemblages of men and means brought together to carry out huge common purposes. In the grim, dirty and costly war which Korea had become, the Inchon invasion, with its hundreds of ships, its aircraft sweeping the skies, its expectant marines and soldiers waiting for H-Hour, evoked memories of more idealistic days when total national efforts drew together men intent on a mutual goal to destroy evil. It had elements of a great and inspiring moment; but the automatic responses it brought forth were already anachronisms of a dead past and strangely unreal. For Inchon, unlike the invasions of Normandy and the Pacific islands in World War II, was essentially a mere military operation aimed at a limited strategic purpose of defeating an invading army. Although MacArthur was to demonstrate his own plans extended beyond military victory to the destruction of North Korea, no such vision transcended the reality of the Inchon mud flats for the men about to land there. Even if they had known MacArthur's plan, it is doubtful whether eliminating a little buffer state and incorporating it into a country run by a dictatorial Syngman Rhee would have been enough to stir ideals of democracy and freedom and elevate Inchon from an uninviting but necessary operation into a great and noble enterprise. For the men in and around the peninsula, as for most Americans and their allies, Korea had become a limited war for limited national aims, and even the great Inchon armada could not bring back the great sense of purpose and destiny that motivated men and nations on the Allied side in World War II.

Nevertheless, Inchon demonstrated the immense strength of the

United States and the tremendous savvy of the U.S. Navy. Unlike the grueling and more nearly even ground battles between American and North Korean soldiers in the perimeter, the Inchon invasion displayed the overwhelming imbalance between the United States and a wholly outclassed North Korea. It was as if a world champion heavyweight had stepped into the ring with a high-school lightweight. This was what was so astonishing about the fears of the Joint Chiefs; once American naval and air power was combined with well-equipped and well-trained amphibious assault forces, there was not a shadow of a doubt about the invasion's success. One example should suffice to show the disproportion between forces: the North Koreans had nineteen piston-driven aircraft; the United States had so much air power, jet and piston, there literally was not enough airspace over the battlefield and its approaches to accommodate it. In the more than two hundred ships assembled at Inchon, Admiral Struble had available the two marine-support escort carriers *Badoeng Strait* and *Sicily*; the attack carrier *Boxer*, steaming at forced speed from California with 110 aircraft on board; the attack carriers *Philippine Sea* and *Valley Forge*, plus, if needed, hundreds of air force fighters and bombers. In addition, Admiral Struble had the British light carrier *Triumph*, striking arm of the blockade and covering force, also composed of two British light cruisers (*Ceylon* and *Cockade*), and one British, one Dutch, two Canadian and two Australian destroyers. Included in the screening force were two British and two New Zealand frigates.[1]

To check on conditions of Inchon harbor and approaches, the navy on August 31 sent Lieutenant Eugene F. Clark to Yonghung, an island at the mouth of the ship channel, about sixteen miles south of Inchon. Clark and his two interpreters were carried from Sasebo on Kyushu on the British destroyer *Charity*, which transferred the party to a South Korean frigate. Lieutenant Clark commandeered the only motorized sampan on the six-by-three-mile island and organized teenaged boys into parties that watched the island coast. He set up two machine guns facing the adjacent island of Taebu, occupied by North Koreans, and for two weeks hung to this perilous perch, fighting sampan battles with NK vessels from nearby islands and capturing infiltrators who crossed from Taebu-do at low tide. At night Clark sent South Korean youngsters into Inchon harbor to measure the mud flats, water depths and heights of the seawall, and to spy on North Korean strength and fortifications. During his adventures Clark and his aides captured thirty small vessels, a few including policemen or soldiers. There were two remarkable aspects of Clark's operation: none of the South Koreans betrayed him, and his less-than-secret movements failed to tip off the North Koreans to preparations for an invasion of Inchon.

Clark was still in place when the invasion fleet entered the channel. In fact, Clark repaired a main navigation light for the deceitful Flying Fish Channel leading up to Inchon. And at midnight of September 14, Clark lighted this important navigational beam on the tiny islet of Palmi to help guide the invasion fleet up the channel. For his bravery and accomplishment, Lieutenant Clark won the Navy Cross.[2]

The key to a successful assault on Inchon was neutralization of tiny, 1,000-foot-wide Wolmi, an island just off Inchon and known to conceal high-velocity guns in deep revetments. To keep the location of the invasion secret from the North Koreans to the last minute, naval planners considered waiting until the morning of the assault to bombard the island. But the experts said no: the lessons from preinvasion bombardments of Japanese-held islands in the Pacific were too plentiful and recent; to expect to neutralize Wolmi in a single morning would be dangerously optimistic.[3]

This forced the navy to carry out a series of deceptive moves designed to prevent, said Admiral Struble, the finger of suspicion being pointed directly at Inchon.[4] The battleship *Missouri* shelled the east coast, including the rail center and port of Samchok. In addition, carrier aircraft struck not only Wolmi-do, but Kunsan, one hundred miles to the south, and possible landing sites near the North Korean capital of Pyongyang in the north.[5] Then, on September 7, Struble ordered an amphibious feint at Kunsan, which was carried out by the British frigate *Whitesand Bay* and a group of U.S. Army and Royal Marine commandos.[6]

On September 10 came the first devastating blow at Wolmi-do: F4U Corsairs from the *Badoeng Strait* and *Sicily* burned the island with napalm. The Corsairs dropped ninety-five tanks of napalm that destroyed most buildings and extinguished virtually all vegetation.[7] The aircraft struck the island again over the next two days.

At the end of August, the Japanese ports of Kobe and Yokohama on Honshu and Sasebo on Kyushu became centers of intense fitting out for the invasion. In the midst of frenetic preparations, Typhoon Jane swept over Kobe on September 3, bringing winds of 110 miles an hour and forty-foot waves. Seven American ships broke their lines, and the cables of a two hundred-ton crane snapped. Despite the damage, the port of Kobe and the marines loading there met their deadline of September 11. The 47 LSTs of the marine convoy departed Kobe on September 10 (37 of them manned by Japanese crews), and by the next day 66 cargo vessels cleared the port for Inchon. Simultaneously the 7th Division sailed from Yokohama, and on September 12 the 5th Marines departed Pusan to rendezvous at sea.[8]

The ships sailed just ahead of a second typhoon, Kezia, which had been brewing near the Marianas and was expected to pass over the Korea Strait September 12–13. The U.S. commanders hoped Kezia would follow the normal pattern and veer north, and therefore Admiral Struble ordered the fleet out to sea to get ahead of it. Struble himself departed Yokosuka September 11 on his flagship, the heavy cruiser *Rochester.* Rear Admiral Doyle, commander of the attack force, left Kobe the same day aboard the flagship *Mount McKinley,* with the marine commander, General Smith, and his staff on board. MacArthur had elected to observe the assault from the *Mount McKinley* because it would be closer to the action than the *Rochester.* MacArthur was accompanied by General Almond, X Corps commander; General Wright, FEC G-3; Major Generals Alonzo P. Fox and Courtney Whitney of his staff, and Lieutenant General Lemuel C. Shepherd, Pacific Fleet Marine Force commander, whom MacArthur had invited along as an advisor. They flew to Itazuke air base, then drove to Sasebo. *Mount McKinley* turned into Sasebo about midnight, September 12, having plowed through the heaviest seas Admiral Doyle had ever encountered; MacArthur and his party went on board, and the ship departed for Inchon half an hour later.[9]

Part of the armada encountered extremely rough seas off the southern tip of Kyushu early on September 13. There winds reached sixty miles an hour, and green water broke over the ships' bows. But during the day Typhoon Kezia shifted northeast, and as the force passed the island of Cheju off the southern tip of Korea, the Yellow Sea ahead was relatively calm.[10]

Although it gave away the impending attack, MacArthur and Struble had decided to send in the preliminary-bombardment force (Gunfire Support Group) on September 13 to silence the 75mm guns they had learned were emplaced on Wolmi-do behind deep revetments. These guns, more than anything else, were the object of the navy's concern. Unsilenced, these high-velocity weapons could have caused havoc with the light-skinned assault craft as they approached the beaches.[11]

With Struble's approval, the Gunfire Support Group commander, Rear Admiral J. M. Higgins, had decided on a bold move: instead of approaching Inchon at night, he would enter Inchon in broad daylight and at low water. His conservative argument for this was to avoid the dangers of a night-time approach: the possibility of ship collisions and running aground in the two shallow (thirty to sixty feet) approach paths.[12] But there also was an audacity in sailing right to an enemy-held shore in plain view: it displayed supreme confidence and panache, a flamboyant awareness that the U.S. Navy, with its old ally, the Royal

Navy, not only had command of the sea and the air, but dared any third-rate foe to contest it. It was the kind of quiet arrogance the admirals would have found unseemly in their subalterns, but which they themselves wore secretly but proudly behind their stern official demeanors and gold braid. Nobody else, they seemed to say, was going to spit in *their* ocean. (See Map 7.)

Admirals Struble and Higgins, in fact, *wanted* to draw fire from the revetted 75s in order to flush them out and smash them.[13] The bombardment group—the two U.S. heavy cruisers *Toledo* and *Rochester*, the two British light cruisers *Kenya* and *Jamaica*, and six U.S. destroyers—entered the approaches to Inchon at midmorning September 13, and moved up the Flying Fish Channel. Just before noon the group sighted a North Korean minefield, exposed at low water in the vicinity of Palmi-do, where the channel narrows. The discovery was an unexpected bonus to a daylight approach at low tide. The destroyers and cruisers opened fire on the mines, and the destroyer *Henderson* remained behind temporarily to hunt for and destroy any others.

As the cruisers anchored seven to ten miles offshore, the five remaining destroyers—*Mansfield, De Haven, Swenson, Collett* and *Gurke*—sailed on up the channel until the *Gurke* anchored just eight hundred yards off the Wolmi-do shore and the others strung out behind. An eerie silence descended. Every sailor's eyes searched Wolmi-do for the ominous humps that would reveal concealed North Korean gun positions. The silence continued for fifteen minutes. There was not a movement on the island. At last, at 1 p.m., Captain Halle C. Allan, the squadron commander, flashed the signal: "Execute assigned mission."

The destroyers unleashed all guns on Wolmi-do. The cruisers also dropped salvo after salvo on the island with their six- and eight-inch guns. The incredibly heavy fire rolled for three minutes, and still the five Wolmi-do guns had not fired. One wonders what went through the mind of the North Korean artillery commander: there in plain view and easy range stood five U.S. destroyers actually inviting fire; yet if he opened up, he thereupon spelled the doom of his guns and his crews. The North Korean commander weighed his choices and his duty—and opened fire.

The high-velocity 75mm shells struck *Collett* four times. One armor-piercing shell broke into two pieces. One piece penetrated to the engine room and fractured a steam line. The other broke into the plot room where it damaged fire-control equipment and wounded five men. The *Gurke* was hit in two places, neither seriously. The *Swenson* took a near miss that caused the death of Lieutenant (J.G.) David S. Swenson, the only man killed in the bombardment.[14]

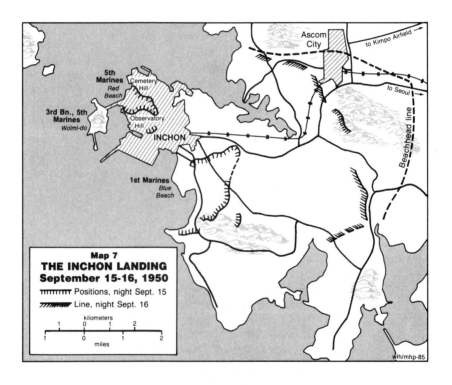

Map 7
THE INCHON LANDING
September 15-16, 1950

Positions, night Sept. 15
Line, night Sept. 16

The destroyers got what they came for: the locations of the 75s. The gunnery officers made quick adjustments. The destroyers' guns turned. Like cool and careful sharpshooters, the gun crews laid elevations and azimuths with hairbreadth accuracy. The North Korean guns fired only a few more rounds. Then the destroyers let go with salvo after salvo aimed past the deep revetments and directly onto the North Korean guns. The Wolmi-do guns fell silent.

The destroyers withdrew down Flying Fish Channel. On the way, they discovered eight more mines and destroyed them; these proved to be the only remaining mines sown on the Inchon approaches.[15] The Wolmi-do reduction continued the next day (September 14). But prior to standing up Flying Fish Channel, the advance force hove to with flags flying at half-mast, conducted a funeral service aboard the *Toledo* for Lieutenant Swenson, and buried his body at sea.[16]

At 11 a.m. naval aircraft delivered heavy strikes against Wolmi-do, and sixteen minutes later the cruisers began their second bombardments, this time taking targets within Inchon itself under fire. While navy planes made another strike on the island, five of the destroyers sailed back up the channel. After the aircraft had left a smoking pall over the tiny island, the destroyers began another bombardment, sending 1,700 five-inch shells into Wolmi-do and Inchon.[17] There was no return fire. The island was a seared landscape of shell-plowed earth and skeletonized trees.

The assault plan called for the 3rd Battalion, 5th Marines, to land on Wolmi-do at 6:30 a.m. September 15, during high tide. It was hoped the battalion would secure the island quickly, because there could be no reinforcement until afternoon on account of the lowering tide. At the next high tide, about 5:30 p.m., the remainder of the 5th Marines was to land at Red Beach—at the fifteen-foot-high heavy gray stone seawall directly against the heart of the city itself—while the 1st Marines simultaneously were to assault Blue Beach—a semiopen mud-flat area at the southern edge of the city and also protected by the seawall.[18] The Red and Blue Beaches likewise would be cut off from reinforcement until high tide the next morning. Meanwhile, the landing craft would be literally stuck in the mud. Therefore, the marines needed to gain total tactical success while the battlefield was completely isolated from NK reinforcements by the navy guns and planes.

The purpose of sending the 5th Marines directly into the built-up city was to secure Observatory Hill, one thousand yards inland, and Cemetery Hill, 130 feet high and to the left of the landing area, upon which three guns reportedly were emplaced. To secure the city, the marines felt these points should be taken quickly. The principal advantage in sending the 1st Marines over the mud flats at Blue Beach was that the railroad and main highway between Seoul and Inchon lay only a little more than a mile inland, and quick capture of these would cut off avenues of escape or access.[19]

An early objective of the marine division after securing the beachhead was Kimpo airfield, sixteen road miles northeast of Inchon. Thereafter the plan called for crossing the Han river and driving on Seoul. MacArthur wanted to attain both these objectives as quickly as possible. Kimpo was important because its six thousand-foot paved runway and heavy weight capacity would greatly increase air capability against Seoul; more important, it would be a base from which to disrupt supply of the NK army. Capture of Seoul, of course, would cut the main supply lines to the NK army in the south.

At 2 a.m. September 15, the Advance Attack Group, under naval Captain Norman W. Sears, started up the Flying Fish Channel, navigating the twisting corridor by radar, and guided by the still-burning flames of Wolmi-do and the navigation light on Palmi-do, atop which sat Lieutenant Clark, shivering inside a blanket, watching the invasion ships glide by.[20] The small convoy consisted of three high-speed transports carrying Lieutenant Colonel Robert D. Taplett's 3rd Battalion, 5th Marines, one landing ship dock bearing nine M26 Pershing tanks, and three rocket ships. It anchored quietly so as to place Wolmi-do between itself and the NK batteries, if any, along the Inchon waterfront.[21]

At 5 a.m. eight marine Corsairs lifted off their escort carrier to strike at Wolmi-do, and the first two planes caught an armored car crossing the causeway from Inchon and destroyed it. As the Corsairs bombed the ridgeline of the island, there was no life visible. At 5:50 a.m. the marines began loading into seventeen landing craft (LCVPs—landing craft, vehicle, personnel); the tanks loaded into three landing ships (LSUs—landing ship, utility). Naval gunfire and air strikes raked Wolmi-do, then the three squat rocket ships moved in close and laid down an intense barrage on the unfortunate island. The landing craft, which had been moving in circles waiting for H-Hour, straightened out into lines and struck for the island. Just as a voice announced over the *Mount McKinley's* loudspeaker, "Landing force crossing line of departure," General MacArthur came on the bridge to watch the craft approach Wolmi-do, one mile away.

There was no fire from the island. The first wave of marines reached the bathing beach on the north arm of Wolmi-do at 6:33 a.m., with marine Corsairs flying only fifty yards ahead of them and spraying the ground with machine-gun fire. The infantry moved rapidly against almost no resistance as the second wave hit the beach unopposed. Then the LSUs arrived; three of the tanks carried dozer blades for breaking up barbed wire, filling trenches and sealing caves; three other tanks mounted flamethrowers. The marines moved quickly across the island, blocking the causeway leading to Inchon and capturing the high ground. They secured the island at 7:50 a.m. Shortly thereafter, Colonel Taplett sent a squad with three tanks over the causeway that appended the tiny teardrop-shaped islet of Sowolmi to Wolmi-do. There they destroyed a platoon of NK troops; some surrendered, some swam into the sea and others were killed.

The entire operation cost the North Koreans 108 men killed and 136 captured. In addition, 100 more men refused to surrender and were sealed by tank dozers into their caves. U.S. intelligence reports had been approximately correct: NK prisoners said 400 soldiers guarded the island. Most were recent conscripts with little training and no experience. The marine casualties were light: 17 men wounded, none killed.

Now began the period of anxiety. The tide fell. No support could come until afternoon, and an enemy-held shoreline loomed ahead. Ever since Admiral Higgins's bombardment group had arrived two days before, whatever doubts the NK command may have entertained about UN intentions had vanished. The diversion of the *Missouri* to the Sea of Japan and the feint at Kunsan were seen to be what they were; the real thrust was coming at Inchon. If the invasion was to be stopped, the North Koreans had to get strong forces to Inchon, and fast. It was at this time that the awesome power assembled at Inchon and the brilliance of MacArthur's thrust into the rear became most clearly manifest: naval gunfire in steady drumfire covered all the closer approaches to the city; despite the rain which had begun to fall in the afternoon, navy and marine aircraft ranged up and down the roads and over the countryside to a depth of twenty-five miles behind the city, blocking any possibility of major reinforcement of Inchon, even if the NK command had any troops within striking distance. Although the isolated marines on Wolmi-do were nervous, they need not have worried: Inchon was sealed off; only the battered and frightened North Korean garrison of 1,600 men was in the city to oppose an invasion force of almost 70,000 Americans and ROKs. Some soldiers from Seoul moved to reinforce the Inchon garrison before dawn on September 15, but they moved back to the capital after dark.[22] The NK command evidently concluded it could not hold Inchon, and concentrated its few available troops at Seoul.

At 3:30 p.m. assault troops of the 1st and 5th Marines began going over the sides of their transports and into landing craft. The navy ships made another bombardment of the landing area and behind it. Then the rocket ships moved in close to Red and Blue Beaches and fired two thousand rockets on the landing area. At 4:45 p.m. the landing craft crossed the lines of departure and forty-five minutes later they landed on the beaches—the 1st Marines hitting at 5:32 p.m., the 5th Marines at 5:33 p.m.[23]

On Red Beach the 5th Marines climbed over the seawall with scaling ladders. A few boats put their troops ashore through holes in the wall made by the naval bombardment. It was a first-ever operation for the U.S. Marine Corps: the first assault into the heart of a city, the first landing on seawalls.[24] On the left flank, a platoon met North Koreans in trenches and a bunker just beyond the seawall. The marines charged. A vicious fire fight developed. The marines lost eight men killed and 28 wounded, but they wiped out the NK defenses and moved straight inland. Company A reached the top of Cemetery Hill, where the dazed North Koreans threw down their weapons and surrendered. Twenty-two minutes after landing, the company fired a flare signaling it held Cemetery Hill. By midnight other elements of the 1st Battalion had penetrated against sporadic resistance to the top of Observatory Hill.

On Blue Beach most of the men had to climb a high seawall to get inland. In the smoke and confusion, one group of marines went astray and landed at the seawall to the left of the beach. In some places, marines had to use dynamite to blast holes in the seawall. Admiral Struble and General Almond, observing the assault, approached Blue Beach in a barge as the landings were under way. Just as the barge neared the seawall, a marine sergeant ashore yelled out: "Boat there! Get the hell out of the way!" Admiral Struble, recognizing a proper order when he heard one, promptly ordered the coxswain to turn the barge away fast. Just as the barge turned, a huge explosion blew a hole in the wall, but the barge and occupants were unharmed.[25]

The 1st Marines moved inland quickly. The 2nd Battalion, under Lieutenant Colonel Allan Sutter, lost one man killed and 19 wounded in reaching the Inchon-Seoul highway a mile away, but by shortly after midnight the 1st Marines, too, had attained their D-Day objectives.

Because there could be no reinforcement during the low tide at night, the navy followed up the assault troops quickly, sending eight specially loaded LSTs onto Red Beach just before high tide. Unloading of equipment to support the next day's advance continued all through the night. Sadly, putting the LSTs ashore resulted in a tragedy. Just after 6:30 p.m. the beached LSTs received some enemy mortar and machine-gun fire. The gun crews on three of the LSTs began firing wildly with 20mm and 40mm cannon. Before they could be stopped, they had killed one and wounded 23 men of the 2nd Battalion, 5th Marines.[26]

At 7:30 a.m. September 16, the two marine regiments ashore made contact. Inchon was sealed off. Any North Koreans remaining in the city could not likely escape. A regiment of ROK marines, brought along with the invasion force, was assigned the job of mopping up the city. They went to work with a will, making Inchon unsafe for friend and foe until the task was completed.

Early on September 16, a flight of eight Corsairs lifted off the *Sicily* and spotted six T34 tanks on the highway three miles east of Inchon and heading toward the city. The Corsairs struck immediately with napalm and five-hundred-pound bombs, hitting three T34s and scattering the infantry going with them. The North Koreans shot back and brought down one Corsair, killing the pilot.[27] A second flight of Corsairs assaulted the tanks. Though the marine pilots believed they had destroyed them, three of the six T34s moved when an advance platoon of marine infantry approached. M26 Pershings shattered them.

That was the extent of the North Korean counterattack. The marines advanced quickly against light resistance. By evening they had reached the Beachhead Line, six miles inland. The Inchon landing was secure. NK artillery no longer could reach the beaches and docks where equipment and men were pouring ashore. The marines likewise were in place to assault Kimpo airfield and Yongdungpo, a large industrial suburb of Seoul on the south bank of the Han. Lieutenant Colonel Raymond L. Murray's 5th Marines were aimed toward Kimpo, Colonel Lewis B. (Chesty) Puller's 1st Marines toward Yondungpo.

At 5:45 a.m. September 17, an advance platoon of Company D, 5th Marines, occupying a forward roadblock watched as six NK T34 tanks moved past, accompanied by infantry, some riding on the tanks. The North Koreans in the dim early morning did not see the marines. At a range of seventy-five yards, a bazooka team fired a rocket at one NK tank and set it on fire. M26s and recoilless rifles opened up. Within five minutes the six T34s had been destroyed and 200 of 250 NK infantry killed. The marines suffered one man slightly wounded.[28]

Shortly afterward, General MacArthur, accompanied by a whole string of brass— Admiral Struble and Generals Almond, Wright, Fox, Whitney and others—and followed by a group of reporters and photographers, came to the forward marine positions. They passed the six T34s destroyed the day before and the six T34s still burning from the morning attack. MacArthur's jeep stopped at a culvert, and the other vehicles pulled up behind. The General got out, looked at the destroyed T34 tanks, examined some of the North Korean bodies, and said enthusiastically he was gratified. After MacArthur's procession moved back, the marines relaxed. Then they heard a suspicious noise and quickly flushed out six North Koreans hiding under the culvert on which

MacArthur's jeep had parked. A few rifle shots persuaded them to surrender.[29]

The 5th Marines reached the edge of Kimpo by 6 p.m., and within two hours they had seized the southern part of the field. The approximately four hundred North Koreans holding Kimpo appeared to be astonished by the appearance of the marines. They had not even mined the runway. That night, however, several company-sized NK attacks supported only by rifle and submachine-gun fire struck the marine perimeter; they were timid attacks and were repulsed with high casualties.[30] The North Koreans ran away to the northeast. Marines secured Kimpo on the morning of September 18. That same day the 5th Marines reached the Han. At 2:09 p.m. a marine Corsair landed at Kimpo and advance elements of Marine Air Group 33 supporting the invasion began arriving by air from Japan. Kimpo was in operation; by September 20, Corsairs based at Kimpo were making air strikes. (See Map 8.)

The morning of September 17, two NK Yak aircraft made two bold bombing runs against the cruiser *Rochester* lying in Inchon harbor. The first drop of four hundred-pound bombs fell too far astern, although one ricocheted off the cruiser's airplane crane without exploding. The second drop missed off the ship's port bow, and caused only minor damage. One of the Yaks strafed the HMS *Jamaica*, which shot down the plane, but suffered three casualties.[31]

The North Korean response to the Inchon invasion was fast, but the limitations imposed on the NK command by MacArthur's strategy and the tremendous U.S. air power began to tell almost immediately. The North Korean commander made one very smart decision: he did not inform his troops fighting on the Pusan Perimeter that UN troops had landed in their rear, although he began moving back some forces facing the perimeter three to four days after the landing.[32] The effect was that the Eighth Army did not break out of the perimeter on September 16 as planned, because the North Koreans facing the UN troops were still looking forward, not over their shoulders. As a result, they resisted fiercely. It was nearly a week before news of the landing began to reach the troops at the front.[33] And then the debacle ensued. The NK troops began streaming backward in panic. But before this happened, the North Korean command had a little time to try to retrieve a desperate situation.

By chance, the 18th NK Division was on the point of moving from Seoul to the Naktong front when the Inchon assault came. The NK command immediately ordered this green division to retake Inchon, and its advance elements checked the 1st Marines' progress on September 17 from hills three miles short of the village of Sosa, halfway between Inchon and Yongdungpo. There also was an NK regiment (the 70th) at

Suwon, about twenty miles south of Seoul, and this unit also moved up to join the battle.[34]

Except for the garrisons already there, and forces which by happenstance were near, the North Koreans encountered almost insuperable difficulties in getting reinforcements to the Inchon-Seoul front. The 87th Regiment of the 9th NK Division was located in the vicinity of Kumchon, west of the Naktong line and about 150 miles south of Seoul. Ordered to reinforce Seoul, the regiment departed Kumchon by rail on September 16, but took four days to get there; to avoid UN aircraft, it had to hide in tunnels during the day.[35] The twenty-five-hundred-man 25th NK Brigade, formed a month earlier at Chorwon, about 55 miles north of Seoul, started moving by train on September 15, the day of the invasion, but took four days to arrive in Seoul.[36]

North Korean resistance finally began to develop on September 18 against the 1st Marines, largely from the 18th NK Division. The marines passed around and through Sosa at midmorning, but east of the village NK artillery, which neither ground nor aerial observers could locate, caused many marine casualties in the afternoon. The North Koreans had also mined the highway. Marine tank spearheads stopped on September 19 when mines damaged two tanks. This forced engineers to begin the slow job of lifting the mines. And without tank support, the infantry advance slowed, though by nightfall forward foot soldiers had reached just west of Yongdungpo.[37]

The 7th Infantry Division started unloading at Inchon on September 18, and began moving rapidly on the 1st Marine Division's right to secure that flank and to establish a blocking position on the road leading south in the event the NK command was able to extricate a force from the Pusan Perimeter and send it north.[38] On September 19, the battleship *Missouri*, which had completed its diversionary attack on the east coast, arrived at Inchon and directed its huge 16-inch guns inland in support of the 7th Division.[39]

By September 19, the 5th Marines held the south bank of the Han just north of Kimpo and were poised for a crossing on September 20.[40] The assault on Seoul was about to begin. Capture of this city was top priority, and MacArthur, wanting to believe it, had predicted to General Almond that X Corps would capture Seoul five days after the landing. A less sanguine and more realistic Almond had countered: "I cannot do that, but I will have the city in two weeks."[41] Almond came closer to being right.

Americans were to advance on Seoul from two directions: the 5th Marines were to cross the Han north of Kimpo, then swing east along the north side of the river and attack Seoul in flank. The 1st Marines were to secure Yongdungpo, then cross the river immediately north of the suburb and join the 5th Marines in a flanking attack. The 7th Marines, who were to go into the line north of the 5th Marines, meanwhile arrived in Inchon on September 21. (See Map 8.)

The 5th Marines assault across the Han began early on September 20 against strong automatic-weapons and small-arms fire from a small hill north of the river. Company I took the hill by 9:40 a.m., suffering heavy casualties, but this broke the back of the NK defense. Marines, still riding in the LVTs they had used to cross the river, quickly moved a mile inland and cut the Seoul-Kaesong railroad and highway, thus blocking supplies and reinforcements from that direction. Then the 5th Marines swung east and, against increasing resistance, by the evening of September 21 were just west of Seoul along a series of hills running generally north and south. Here they stopped for the night; here the North Koreans had elected to make their stand for the western approaches to the city.[42]

Meanwhile, the 1st Marines moved up on the approaches to Yongdungpo, the 1st Battalion suffering many casualties in capturing a hill (85) guarding the northern approach to the suburb near the Han, and the 2nd and 3rd Battalions to the south blocking a desperate battalion-sized NK attack with five tanks along the Inchon highway. Two of the tanks were destroyed by bazooka fire, and marine arms all but annihilated the North Korean battalion: nearly three hundred bodies were found strewn in front of the marine positions.[43]

General Almond, seeing that a heavy fight was likely to develop to capture Yongdungpo, authorized shelling and bombing of the suburb. This continued for a full day. Yongdungpo was approachable best on the north next to the river and on the south along the road from Inchon. In the center the suburb was edged by rice paddies and dikes along the wide, north-south-running Kalchon creek. On the morning of September 21, the 1st Battalion moved on the north and the 2nd Battalion attacked along the Inchon road. Both battalions suffered high casualties and encountered heavy going. In the afternoon the 3rd Battalion passed through the 2nd and continued the attack under cover of heavy artillery fire.[44]

On this day, a 1st Battalion company commander, Captain Robert Barrow, carried out a brilliant move.[45] On a tactical scale it was as unexpected and decisive as Inchon had been on a strategic scale. Captain Barrow's Company A, emplaced on a hill west of Yongdungpo, was committed, in hopes of surprise, to the center of the line by the battalion commander, Lieutenant Colonel Jack Hawkins. Company A moved behind some low hills that masked the company's approach, and reached a high dike near the center of the line and thus faced the virtually undefended rice paddies and mud of Kalchon creek, which appeared to be impassable.

Not knowing what lay ahead, Company A formed into a long assault line behind the dike, climbed up and over it, and then descended into the rice paddies flanking Kalchon creek ahead. The company walked through the chest-high rice to the creek, plowed through the water and deep mud of the waterway, and reformed under the protection of another dike on the far side. Not a shot had been fired at the company. The North Koreans had not seen them approach. Captain Barrow's company walked right into the center of Yongdungpo. They had struck precisely at an empty and totally unguarded sector. The marines could hear heavy firing north and south of them, but only silence around them and in front of them. Another commander might have been terrified to find his company deep inside an enemy position and with no contact with or possible support from other units; and he might have made tracks to get his isolated and surrounded troops out of there. Captain Barrow saw the situation rather as a marvelous and unexpected opportunity. He realized he could drive unopposed straight into the North Korean rear. He radioed the battalion CP for instructions. Colonel Hawkins told him to keep going.

Company A passed right through Yongdungpo, and by about noon Barrow stopped his men at the eastern side of the suburb. There Barrow's men spotted an NK column marching toward the line; the North Koreans had no idea the marines were there and were singing as they marched. A platoon of Company A opened up with all available weapons on the column and cut it to pieces. At the same time, other platoons of the company began firing on individuals and small groups in the streets. These men, astonished at seeing a large U.S. force in the middle of their position, took to their heels. Finally the marines reached open ground at the eastern extremity of Yongdungpo. There, on a thirty-foot-high dike where a surfaced road joined the main Seoul-Inchon highway, Captain Barrow set up a hundred-yard-long defensive perimeter. Tactically, there could hardly have been a more crucial position. Looking north, Barrow saw a large group of North Koreans withdrawing from the battle line. He immediately directed machine guns to open up on the enemy, who, before they could fan out and seek cover, suffered heavy losses.

Throughout the afternoon small parties of North Koreans made repeated, but unsuccessful, forays against the levee, where Company A sat guarding the best exit route out of the city for the North Koreans. Communication of the company with the battalion CP ended because of a weak battery in the SCR-300 radio. This meant the isolated marines

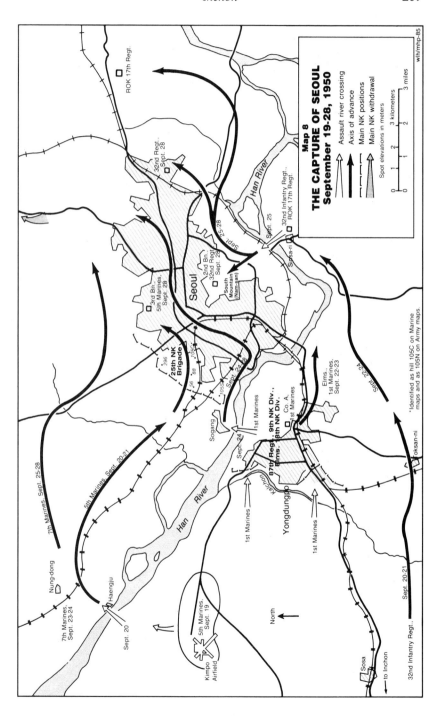

Map 8
THE CAPTURE OF SEOUL
September 19-28, 1950

Assault river crossing
Axis of advance
Main NK positions
Main NK withdrawal
Spot elevations in meters

0   1   2   3 kilometers
0   1   2   3 miles

wih/mhp-85

*Identified as hill 105C on Marine
maps and as 105N on Army maps.

were on their own. And at dusk their first great challenge came: five T34s made a fierce sortie out of Yongdungpo against the company. Bazookas destroyed one tank and damaged two others, but the two undamaged T34s, machine guns firing and cannons roaring, made five runs at thirty yards' range along a road running below the levee. The marines' deep foxholes protected them against the machine-gun bullets and the high-velocity 85mm shells imbedded deep into the earth of the levee before they exploded, causing no hurt to the marines. Unable to dislodge the marines, the tanks withdrew back into Yongdungpo. At 9 p.m. an NK company-sized force attacked the northern end of the perimeter, and before midnight the North Koreans had made four more such separate attacks. All to no avail. Captain Barrow's men held like rocks, though they were getting dangerously low on ammunition. The next morning, 275 NK soldiers lay dead in front of the marine positions.

The North Koreans, unnerved by the sudden appearance of the company in their rear and discouraged by their failure to break into the company's perimeter, completely abandoned Yongdungpo during the night of September 21–22 and fell back north of the Han. They left four T34s in the town. The main defending force at Yongdungpo had been the 87th Regiment of the 9th NK Division, which had just arrived from the Naktong front when the marines invested the city. The 87th was shattered in the battle. Prisoners revealed that one battalion suffered 80 percent casualties.[46]

Meanwhile, the 7th Division moved south of the marines, protecting their flank and blocking any NK troops moving up from the Naktong front. The division's 32nd Regiment was held up by minefields as it attacked to Anyang-ni, about seven miles south of Yongdungpo, but by afternoon on September 21 division elements had captured Anyang-ni.[47] This, plus the capture of Yongdungpo, cut the main supply lines to the NK troops in the south. Thereafter the enemy had only the less accessible and inadequate secondary routes to the east. The North Korean army's umbilical cord was cut, and the army, already panicking as word of what had happened seeped back, began to die.

By September 22, 7th Division troops had captured Suwon airfield after several engagements with NK tanks. This field, twenty-one miles south of Seoul, had a 5,200-foot runway, and it aided U.S. supply as C-54s began to land.[48]

CHAPTER 29

The Assault on Seoul

THE MARINE ATTACK on the western approaches to Seoul from from north of the Han river got under way on the morning of September 22. General Almond, who wanted to capture the city quickly, added a battalion of ROK marines to the effort.[1] The marine attack proceeded along an extremely narrow front: from north to south it measured less than three miles. And it was a frontal assault.[2] (See Map 8.)

The 5th Marines, already in place, made the major effort, and the 1st and 7th Marines joined them in the later stages. Arrayed against the marines and the ROKs was the newly formed and newly arrived 25th NK Brigade, plus the 78th Independent Regiment, perhaps 5,000 men in all. The North Koreans had moved hastily to emplace along the hills west of Seoul, digging trenches and foxholes, setting up coordinated fields of fire with more than fifty machine guns, and emplacing artillery and mortars.[3]

The 3rd Battalion, 5th Marines, was assigned to take Hill 296 on the north. In the center the ROK marines were to capture the west-to-east Hills 56, 88 and 105 Center. These were peaks of ridges that, like tentacles of an octopus, dangled south from the higher Hill 296. On the far south, the 1st Battalion, 5th Marines, was to secure Hill 105 South, which rose close to the Han.

In the north, the 3rd Battalion captured Hill 296 with only slight resistance, but did not secure the southern slopes where the NK strength was concentrated. In the center, NK fire stopped the ROK marines in their tracks, and U.S. marine Corsairs struck time after time all day trying to destroy the NK positions on the ridgeline, but in vain. Prisoners later said the 25th NK Brigade suffered 40 percent casualties that day. On the south, the 3rd Battalion was held up for a while, but late in the day it took Hill 105 South.

211

The next day, September 23, the ROK marines started their assault against Hill 56, but again suffered heavy casualties and made little headway. In midafternoon, the 5th Marines' 2nd Battalion took over from the ROKs, and this American battalion also suffered high losses and gained little. By night the assault units (Companies D and F) dug in for the night, but were short of the NK-held ridgeline. Along the rest of the attack front north of the Han the regiment had been locked in place all day. Meanwhile, the 7th Marines moved up behind the 5th Marines.

The extremely stubborn defense of the western gateway was holding up X Corps, and General Almond was becoming increasingly anxious to capture the city. Seoul already was masked, and its main communications lines to the NK army now folding away from the Naktong were cut. But Seoul was important politically and psychologically, and MacArthur earnestly desired its capture.[4] Equally important, the longer the remaining North Koreans had to build defenses within the city, the harder and more costly it would be to dislodge them.

Almond, dissatisfied with the marine progress, told General Smith on September 23 that he could continue his frontal assaults, but that he thought Smith should use the wide open space south of the Han to envelop the NK line and drive into the city behind it. General Smith was unwilling to do this. He said he was sure the North Koreans would wage a street-by-street fight for the city regardless of a flanking movement. He also wanted to consolidate his entire division north of the Han, and did not want parts deployed on both sides of the river.[5]

Almond told Smith pointedly that the marines had one more day to make progress in this head-on battering against emplaced North Korean positions. If not, Almond said, he would bring the 7th Infantry Division into place to envelop NK defenses from the south.[6]

At first light on the next morning of September 24, Companies D and F of the 5th Marines moved out in heavy mist to attack the ridgeline of Hill 56. Company F reached high ground and took cover to exchange fire with the enemy; Company D, however, remained pinned down by heavy fire for two hours. A grenade fight developed at extreme arm-throwing range, and both sides attempted to break the deadlock by flanking movements. Casualties were heavy on both sides. Sergeant Robert Smith led a squad of twelve marines on a wide end sweep to the north that was wiped out except for three wounded men who escaped. To try to break the deadlock, marine Corsairs came in repeatedly, disregarding their own safety to reach NK positions. In two Corsair strikes, NK antiaircraft fire damaged five of the ten planes engaged. The battle was degenerating into a bloodbath.

On the afternoon of September 24, General Almond called an open-air conference at Yongdungpo with General Smith and the 7th Division commander, Major General David G. Barr, plus other officers, and directed the 7th Division's 32nd Regiment, with the ROK 17th Regiment attached, to attack across the Han into Seoul at 6 a.m. the next day, September 25. The meeting was brief, and the commanders departed quickly to make their plans.

In the early afternoon, Company D, 5th Marines, had only 30 effective infantrymen left in its rifle platoons and 14 other men in its weapons platoon facing Hill 56. The company commander, Lieutenant H. J. Smith, decided on a desperate move: 33 men were to make the assault up the final 150 yards of the slope, while the 11 others were to follow with machine guns and ammunition. Corsairs came over on a final strafing run, dropping bombs and napalm on the NK positions. On a prearranged signal, the Corsairs made a dry-run pass, without firing, to keep the NK defenders down while the marines jumped up and charged forward in a hundred-yard-wide line. Lieutenant Smith was killed leading his men, but the others kept going, and 26 made it to the crest. The dry run of the Corsairs had been entirely successful, and the marines utterly surprised the North Koreans. Some panicked and ran down the reverse slope, others feigned death, and still others fought back. But it was soon over. North Korean dead were stacked up in foxholes and bunkers and other NK bodies were strewn over the landscape. Company D suffered 176 casualties out of 206 men—36 killed, the rest wounded.

It had been a gruesome series of battles, but the action of Company D on Hill 56 was the final effort that broke the North Korean defenses north of the Han. From the captured hill, marines moved north, south and east against little resistance. Most North Korean defenders lay dead or wounded. More than 1,200 NK bodies lay in their positions, and marine estimates of total NK troops killed was 1,750. Air strikes and artillery and mortar fire had done most of the killing and maiming.

While the final desperate battles of the 5th Marines were going on, the 1st Marines crossed the Han river on the morning of September 24 to form the right wing of the marine drive against the city. The 7th Marines moved up on the left flank of the 5th Marines with the mission to drive across the northern limits of Seoul to block escape routes north. A battalion of the 187th Airborne RCT, which had reached Japan, was airlifted to Kimpo and assumed responsibility for defending the airfield, though there were virtually no NK troops left anywhere near to attack it.[7]

The 32nd Regiment and the ROK 17th Regiment were to cross the Han at the ferry site of Sansa-ri, three miles east of the main rail and road bridges over the river. First objective was Nam-san, nine hundred feet high, the highest peak in the city and extending two miles from the Han shore right into the heart of the city. Urban structures wrapped around the base of Nam-san (South Mountain) on the west, north and east. The mountain was like a dagger pointing directly into Seoul's heart.

Other objectives of the U.S. and ROK soldiers were hills two and five miles east of Seoul that dominated the highway and rail lines entering the city from that side.[8]

After a heavy artillery and mortar barrage, the assault force, the 2nd Battalion, 32nd, mounted in marine amphibious vehicles brought in especially for the crossing, churned over the river without the loss of any men or equipment. The infantrymen moved quickly up on Nam-san and captured it with little loss; the North Koreans had been surprised by the sudden X Corps move, and South Mountain was only lightly manned.

The 1st and 3rd Battalions of the 32nd moved across the Han behind the assault force, then turned eastward toward the nearest hill objective, while the ROK regiment following behind drove to the farther hill target, which it captured in an all-night attack.

While the 7th Division and the ROK 17th Regiment were assaulting Seoul from the south, the 1st Marine Division was moving on the city from the west. The 1st Marines on the right flank turned north into the city and pointed toward the main business section, while the 5th Marines entered from the northwest and aimed generally at Government House two miles away, with Changdok Palace and the Royal Gardens just beyond.[9]

The North Korean commander evidently concluded that the reduction of the western-approach defenses and the sudden capture of Nam-san doomed Seoul. He ordered withdrawal to begin on the evening of September 25, sending north his major unit, the 18th NK Division, down to about 5,000 men. He left other detachments with the task of delaying the advance of the marines and soldiers.[10]

An air observer apparently spotted some of this northbound evacuation just before nightfall, because he reported North Koreans were streaming out of the city. General Almond immediately flashed the Far East Air Force to ask for a flare mission to illuminate the roads so marine night fighters could attack these fleeing troops. A B-29 quickly lifted off and dropped flares for several hours, and marine aircraft struck at two NK columns in the night.[11]

Almond also flashed the marine division and ordered it to "attack now" to try to destroy some of these NK troops as they fled. General Smith protested, but was told to go ahead as ordered.[12] But before the marine attacks could get under way, NK troops detailed to delay the marines struck in reinforced battalion strength against the 1st Marines and in reinforced company strength against the 5th Marines. The leathernecks shattered these attacks with great NK losses (the 1st Marines captured 83 prisoners and counted 250 NK bodies). But the North Korean attacks spoiled the marine advances, and at daybreak the marine positions were about where they had been the night before.[13]

The NK counterattack against the 32nd Regiment on Nam-san came a little later than those against the marines, but at 5 a.m. North Koreans struck in a vicious and violent stab with tanks and about a thousand foot soldiers. On the higher western point of Nam-san, Company G was able to hold its position, but the North Koreans overran Company F on the lower eastern knob. Lieutenant Colonel Charles W. Mount, battalion CO, pulled out every reserve soldier he could find and threw a desperate attack against the eastern knob. The Americans finally succeeded in two hours of heavy battle; the North Korean survivors fled down the slopes. The cost to the enemy was staggering: 394 men had been killed, an unknown number wounded, and 174 had surrendered.[14]

The 3rd Battalion of the 32nd, advancing eastward from Seoul to secure dominating hills, came upon a large column of NK troops on the highway leaving Seoul in this direction. Lieutenant Harry J. McCaffrey, Jr., CO of Company L, hardly believing his luck, immediately ordered his company to attack. The surprised North Korean force was virtually wiped out: Company L killed about five hundred men, destroyed five tanks, and destroyed or captured forty vehicles, three artillery pieces, seven machine guns, and much ammunition, oil products and clothing. It was probable that McCaffrey had shattered a large NK headquarters of corps size, which may have been directing the Seoul defense. McCaffrey received the Silver Star.[15]

By midafternoon on September 26, the ROK 17th Regiment had captured the hills east of Seoul, thus closing off the rail and highway lines going east from Seoul. The city was sealed now on the west, south and east, and the 7th Marines were moving to seal it on the north.

The main North Korean forces had evacuated Seoul, but the fight for the city was not over, although General MacArthur claimed it was captured on September 26. Although the Americans had two full divisions in and around the city, plus a regiment of ROKs, small detachments of North Koreans at barricades hindered the capture of the city. The North Koreans in Seoul were isolated from outside except by infiltration, and the certainty of UN capture of the city was never in doubt. But reduction of Seoul became a series of nasty little fights which took a toll on both sides. The North Koreans had stretched barricades all the way across the streets at many places in the middle part of the city, generally at intersections. The barricades, most of them about chest high, were composed of rice and fiber bags filled with earth. From behind the barricades and to the sides, North Koreans manned antitank guns and machine guns which swept the streets and made movement highly dangerous. Other NK soldiers hid in nearby buildings and fired from windows and doors. In front of the barricades, the enemy had put down antitank mines.[16]

The scenario was as if written for the destruction of a city. The marines and army soldiers quickly developed a method of destroying these barricades. But in the process they destroyed much of the neighborhood with them. When they encountered a barricade, U.S. troops ordered in marine or navy aircraft to rocket and strafe the positions. Then mortars and artillery established bases of fire to keep the North Koreans down and to cover the engineers while they exploded the mines. Then two or three medium tanks, usually M26 Pershings, advanced against the barricade, destroying the antitank guns and machine guns, and breaching the barricade. Infantry following after provided the tanks with protection and dealt with snipers. It sometimes took an hour to break a barricade. When the battle was done, a twisted, burning section of Seoul, along with many dead bodies, was left behind.

At 3:08 p.m. on September 27, Company G of the 5th Marines, which had advanced north up the half-mile-long Kwang Who Moon boulevard, arrived at Government House, the Korean capitol, and immediately pulled down the North Korean flags flying from either side of the Court of Lions in front of the building, and raised an American flag. Except for scattered snipers, the last North Korean troops filtered out of the city the night of September 27–28. By the evening of September 28, the 1st Marines had taken hills dominating the road leading north to Uijongbu and Chorwon. The great Inchon invasion had ended in total victory. The North Korean survivors were streaming northward by every unguarded road and path.

MacArthur's vision had been proved accurate; the doubts raised by the Joint Chiefs proved to have been unfounded. MacArthur's stature rose precipitously. President Truman sent the General a message glowing with sincere congratulations. The Joint Chiefs acknowledged that "your transition from defensive to offensive operations was magnificently planned, timed and executed."[17]

On September 29, MacArthur led Syngman Rhee through cheering South Korean throngs to Government House. There, before selected South Korean notables and high U.S. officers, MacArthur conducted Rhee to the dais, with an American flag on one side and a ROK flag on the other. MacArthur, looking for all the world like a kingmaker placing the crown on his favorite's head, personally returned Rhee to the center of power in South Korea. "In behalf of the United Nations Command,"

MacArthur said in his sonorous and unhurried voice, "I am happy to restore you, Mr. President, the seat of your government that from it you may better fulfill your constitutional responsibilities." MacArthur expressed hope a beneficent Providence would give Rhee and his officials wisdom and strength, and he asked the assemblage to join him in reciting the Lord's Prayer. Apparently everyone did—American and Korean, Christian and Buddhist, Confucian and Chondo-gyoist.[17] Both the State and Defense Departments protested because of the great prominence given the American flag and the emphasis on the war as a United States, rather than a United Nations, operation.[18] But MacArthur got world attention and credit for restoring Rhee, and the Washington complaints were drowned out by the flood of congratulations on his Inchon victory.

Preinvasion estimates of the number of North Korean troops available to counter the invasion proved to be low. The North Korean command had about 8,000 troops in Seoul, instead of the estimated 5,000, and 5,000 more in the Yongdungpo area. Reinforcements hurried to the battlefront ultimately increased the total number of soldiers in and around Seoul to at least 20,000 and the NK command was able to assemble 10,000 men between the Han and Suwon, twenty-one miles south.[19] Although these were still fewer than half the troops X Corps deployed, and most were green and little-trained, they were more than the American planners had bargained for. Even so, the North Koreans never were able to concentrate enough strength in any one place to achieve even parity of numbers, much less superiority. The reason was that the NK command had been so dislocated and unbalanced by the unexpected place of the invasion that it found itself forced to commit the troops it could scratch together in piecemeal blocking actions against U.S. and ROK forces that at each point were vastly superior.

Despite incredible effort, the North Koreans that were able to get to the new front were totally inadequate to affect the outcome. In order to try to retrieve a hopeless situation, North Korean commanders repeatedly ordered suicidal counterattacks right into the muzzles of American and ROK guns, and they tenaciously held their troops on the western approaches to Seoul against murderous U.S. air strikes and artillery barrages.

The North Koreans were defeated consecutively in detail and could never concentrate for a decisive counterstroke.[20] Thus, at Wolmi-do, naval and air power and the marine assault battalion completely outclassed the 400 defenders. At Inchon, a regimental assault at two separate points enveloped the 1,600-man garrison and left it to be mopped up by ROKs. At Kimpo, a full regiment overwhelmed the 500 confused defenders. At Yongdungpo, a brilliant coup de main into the rear by Captain Robert Barrow's company dislocated the defenders, but the North Koreans were desperately feeding troops in unit by unit to shore up a faltering line; they were not dictating the action themselves. Only on the western approaches to Seoul north of the Han were the North Koreans briefly able to achieve near parity, and this was facilitated by General Smith's decision to attack frontally on an extremely narrow front, thereby allowing the NK command to concentrate its forces. General Almond's move to flank the western position by sending an army and a ROK regiment into Seoul from the south unbalanced the NK position and immediately convinced the enemy commander to evacuate the city. The determined NK defense of the barricades in Seoul itself was more an act of defiance than of tactical purpose. Each barricade force was largely isolated from the others. Thus the Americans were able to reduce each barricade independently with no fear that the enemy could develop a coordinated counterattack or pose any threat to possession of the city.

With this evidence of careful calculation by MacArthur to eliminate any possibility of a dangerous North Korean response, it is surprising that the Joint Chiefs chairman, General Omar Bradley, still called Inchon "the luckiest military operation in history."[21] Hardly any operation could have involved less luck and more meticulous elimination of chance. Bradley at least owned up: "In hindsight, the JCS seemed like a bunch of nervous Nellies to have doubted."[22]

Secretary of Defense Louis Johnson lost his job in September, 1950, partly because he exasperated President Truman by trying to avoid ordering General MacArthur to withdraw a highly damaging statement implying Taiwan should become a U.S. base.

Presidential advisor W. Averell Harriman visited General Douglas MacArthur in early August, 1950, to try to get the General's agreement with administration policy on Taiwan. Harriman told Truman he could not convince MacArthur.

During the North Korean offensive in the summer of 1950, an American F-80 jet strafes an enemy T34 tank and jeep in the road and vehicles and troops in the village.

A Corsair shepherds part of the armada assembled for the Inchon invasion on September 15, 1950, the world's last great amphibious landing.

General Douglas MacArthur watches bombardment of Inchon from the bridge of the USS Mount McKinley. *He is flanked by (from left) Vice Admiral A. D. Struble, Major General E.K. Wright, and Major General Edward M. Almond, X Corps commander.*

Four LSTs unload on the beach at Inchon as marines gather equipment to move rapidly inland on September 15, 1950. Landing ships were stuck in the deep mud flats between one high tide and the next.

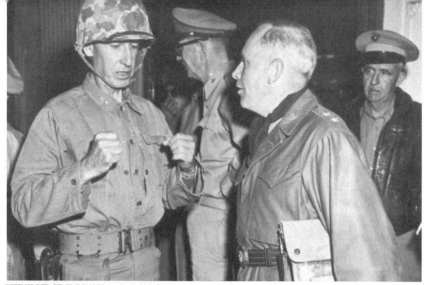

The commander of the 1st Marine Division, Major General Oliver P. Smith (left), discussing action immediately after Inchon landing, September 15, 1950, with his boss, army Major General Edward M. Almond, X Corps commander. At right is Major General Field Harris, commander of the marine air wing that provided close support to attacking units.

General Douglas MacArthur (in leather jacket) and an entourage of press and brass examine bodies of North Korean soldiers at advanced marine positions east of Inchon on September 17, 1950. The marine in camouflage helmet holds a Russian-made submachine gun known to Americans as a burp gun.

Marines carry back a wounded comrade while other marines hold positions in the assault on the outskirts of Seoul, September, 1950.

A marine infantryman keeps cover as he looks over the Han river valley near Seoul four days after the flanking movement against Inchon.

Much of Seoul was destroyed in vicious street battles in September, 1950. Here marine infantry lead an M26 tank in the attack.

A marine tank supports South Korean soldiers guarding North Korean prisoners captured in the assault on Seoul, September, 1950.

U.S. 7th Division infantry wait as an army M4A3 Sherman tank clears a gap in a barricade during the street-by-street North Korean defense of Seoul in September, 1950.

Breakout from the Pusan Perimeter: Koreans move back to their homes at Waegwan as U.S. infantrymen advance after the fleeing North Koreans. Soldier in foreground is carrying a Browning Automatic Rifle.

The legacy of war: 1st Cavalry Division troops move on north in the fall of 1950, leaving a shattered Korean village behind.

When a single vehicle moved on one of the narrow dirt roads that served as practically the only arteries in Korea, it usually raised a column of dust. When convoys such as this passed with artillery prime movers and trucks, the dust cloud could be choking.

CHAPTER 30

Breakout from the Perimeter

T HE EIGHTH ARMY plan to crack the Pusan Perimeter called for the 5th RCT and the 1st Cavalry Division to seize a bridgehead over the Naktong at Waegwan on September 16, the day after Inchon, and for the 24th Division then to drive through to Kumchon and on to Taejon and northward. Other elements of Eighth Army were to attack to hold the North Koreans in place until the 24th Division could get entirely through the North Korean defenses.[1] Although the Americans, ROKs and Britons in the perimeter had learned about the Inchon landing almost immediately and were excited, encouraged and raring to go, the North Koreans "on the other side of the hill" simply were not told by their high command about Inchon, and they fought on with their customary doggedness and ferocity.[2]

The idea that the NK command could or would withhold such stunning news from their troops had not occurred to Far East Command or Eighth Army. General Walker had asked that the perimeter breakout take place the day after Inchon not only to hold the main NK combat strength in the south and prevent the moving of reinforcements to Inchon-Seoul, but also to gain by the effect the invasion would produce on the North Koreans.[3] Evidence is strong, however, that the dazed North Korean command did not even resolve finally on withdrawal from the perimeter until three or four days after the landing and after Seoul already had been masked and communications to the south cut.[4]

The immediate result of the Eighth Army attack, therefore, was generally to encounter a stone wall of NK resistance that produced high U.S. casualties. The main point of the move, toward Waegwan, got virtually nowhere the first couple of days. The only substantial gains were made by the 2nd Division when two regiments broke through weak and exhausted NK troops on the lower Naktong. The only hint of

North Korean reaction to the news at Inchon was the commencement on the night of September 18–19 of the withdrawal of the most dangerously exposed NK divisions, the 6th and 7th, which were positioned west of Masan in the extreme south. Until September 19, however, the North Koreans everywhere put up most determined resistance, and there was not a hint of voluntary withdrawal. U.S., ROK and British advances, therefore, were minor and came only at the cost of heavy losses.[5]

On September 19 Waegwan fell to the 5th RCT, and that same day the ROK 1st Division penetrated the mountains north of Taegu to positions behind the 1st and 13th NK Divisions. These divisions then started withdrawing. The next day the ROK 3rd Division recaptured Pohang-dong on the east coast and the 5th NK Division began falling back northward rapidly. Meanwhile, in the mountains west of the coast, ROK troops began making sweeping advances. But the 1st Cavalry Division was not able to recapture Tabu-dong, in the old Bowling Alley battlefield, until September 21 and west of the Naktong the 2nd Division fought an extremely stubborn enemy as late as September 22.

For its part, the British 27th Brigade ran into a tragedy, but not entirely due to North Korean action. The British brigade was across the Naktong before daylight on September 22 and was moving toward Songju. Its route took the brigade along the main retreat route of the 10th NK Division. At dawn the English Middlesex battalion occupied a small ridge (the men called it Plum Pudding Hill) three miles short of Songju; then, on September 23, it attacked northeast to higher ground (Point 325 or Middlesex Hill), which it seized before dark. The Scottish Argyll battalion meanwhile attacked neighboring Hill 282 before dawn, moving up so unexpectedly that the Scots surprised the North Korean force at breakfast. Another NK unit, on Hill 388, nearly a mile southwest, started across a saddle to attack the Argylls, supported by heavy artillery and mortar fire. Shortly before noon, U.S. artillery, which had been blocking the NK advance, was withdrawn without warning, and the American tank fire, also in support, could not reach the attacking North Koreans. The Argylls called in an air strike on NK-held Hill 388. Soon three F-51 Mustangs arrived and circled the Argylls on Hill 282. The Scots displayed their white recognition panels. The North Koreans on Hill 388 also displayed white panels. The air force tactical-control officer could not reach the F-51s by radio. Suddenly the Mustangs attacked the wrong hill—with napalm and machine guns. The tragedy was over in two minutes: Hill 282 was enveloped in a sea of orange flame; survivors plunged down the slope to escape the burning napalm. A few wounded men still held the hill, and Major Kenneth Muir, second in command, quickly assembled thirty men and led them back through the dying flames to the crest before approaching North Koreans reached the top from the other side. Major Muir was mortally wounded by a burst of automatic-weapons fire, and the survivors, realizing the situation was hopeless, fell back to the foot of the hill. The Argylls suffered 90 casualties, 60 of them caused by the mistaken air attack.[6]

By September 23, the word was fully out to the North Korean troops about the Inchon landing, and NK units were in full flight northward. Signs of panic and disintegration began to appear quickly.[7]

Eighth Army, now just equipped with two new corps headquarters, I and IX ("Eye" and "Nine" Corps), bounded away from the Naktong line—IX Corps on the south with the 2nd and 25th Divisions attached, I Corps on the north with the 24th and 1st Cavalry Divisions and ROK 1st Division attached.

The pursuers moved out with extreme rapidity on practically every highway leading away from the perimeter. In some places North Koreans formed blocking parties that held tenaciously while their comrades escaped from encircling nets. In other places the Americans were slowed by blown bridges and antitank mines laid in the roads[8] (70 percent of all U.S. tank losses in Korea were caused by antitank mines, as compared to 20 percent from mines in all theaters in World War II[9]). In still other cases, North Koreans laid down their arms and walked meekly into POW camps, while others melted away into the hills and mountains, avoiding combat and trying to walk back to North Korea. Some of them made it. The North Korean divisions quickly evaporated as organized units, and the members, as individuals or in small groups, tried to get away as best they could. As might be expected, there were incredible contradictions and intense disorder. In some cases North Korean rear-guard units fought with all the ferocity for which the NK army had become known; in other cases North Koreans simply watched the Americans drive by in their tanks and vehicles and made no attempt to stop them. In one instance northeast of Kunsan on the west coast, the pilot of an air force mosquito spotter airplane saw a bunch of about two hundred North Koreans and dropped a note to them to throw away their arms and assemble on a nearby hill. They did so, and the mosquito pilot led ground patrols to the patiently waiting North Koreans.[10] But this occurred on October 1, and by that time total demoralization had set in.

Americans were now in their element: behind the wheels of trucks or the steering levers of tanks, with official Eighth Army sanction to ignore their flanks and with the horizon as their destination.[11] There were many spectacular stories of units advancing at least as fast as Patton's Third Army raced across France in 1944 after the breakout from Normandy. But perhaps the most spectacular was the odyssey of Task Force Lynch, the arrow point of the 1st Cavalry Division.

The task force was organized around the 3rd Battalion of the 7th Cavalry Regiment, commanded by Lieutenant Colonel James H. Lynch, augmented by an engineer company, seven M4A3 medium tanks, a reconnaissance platoon, a tactical air-control party to call in air strikes, and artillery and mortars.[12]

First Cavalry Division commander Hobart Gay launched Task Force Lynch at 8 a.m. September 22 from near the Bowling Alley and Tabudong, north of Taegu. With General Gay himself riding in the column and with five tanks in the lead, TF Lynch brushed aside scattered NK groups and started northwest toward the Naktong. Ahead of the column flights of aircraft, directed by the tac-air party, coursed up and down the road attacking anything in sight.

Near Naksong-dong, at the river, the road curved over a hill crest. The first M4A3 Sherman tank over was hit by an NK antitank shell. The tank was stopped. Since nobody could find the antitank gun, General Gay ordered the four remaining tanks to rush over the crest at full speed and with all guns blazing. It worked: the tanks overran two antitank guns. The force originally had been directed to cross the Naktong at a ferry site ten miles south of Naktong-ni, but orders were changed. And at 7 p.m. Colonel Lynch, bidding goodby to General Gay, headed north under a bright three-quarters moon to Naktong-ni, where the North Koreans had built an underwater bridge. It was to be a fortuitous change of crossing site.

Passing burning villages and retreating North Koreans who surrendered without even attempting to fight, TF Lynch reached Naktong-ni at 10:30 p.m. The lead tanks stopped on a bluff overlooking the river at the underwater bridge. Ahead the tankers saw an antitank gun pointed at them, and they fired at it. The shell struck a concealed ammunition truck, which exploded and set fire to everything around it, immediately lighting up abandoned NK tanks and trucks—and several hundred North Korean soldiers who were in the process of crossing the river on the underwater bridge. The task force began firing down on the unfortunate North Koreans, killing about two hundred of them.

A patrol reported that the waist-deep river was fordable and the far side was empty of North Korean emplacements. Colonel Lynch sent two companies of infantry across through the cold water at 4:30 a.m. September 23, and they secured the western side. Meanwhile engineers put into operation a ferry and raft capable of carrying over tanks and trucks. The next day four hundred laborers also improved the underwater bridge. Before noon tanks were across the river. They immediately moved to join the rest of the task force, which had reached Sangju.

The 1st Cavalry was held up west of the Naktong for a day because of an I Corps order; but just before midnight on September 25 General Gay reached Eighth Army headquarters and got permission to go all out for a linkup with X Corps if he could do so. Early on September 26 Gay called a commanders' conference and ordered the division to move out at noon and to keep going day and night until it reached 7th Division troops, who had advanced twenty-seven miles south of Seoul, to a point about three miles north of Osan.

The leading unit again was Task Force Lynch, now at Poun, thirty miles farther up the road. Led by tanks, it broke out with orders to move at maximum tank speed and not to fire unless fired upon. The detachment drove on for mile after mile, cheered on by waving South Koreans in each village it passed. Lieutenant Robert W. Baker, leading the tank platoon, reached a point past deserted Chongju, sixty-four miles beyond Poun, at 6 p.m. There the tanks ran out of fuel—because the refueling truck somehow had not joined the column and no one had thought to send it up. Officers searched through vehicles in the column and found enough gasoline cans to refuel three tanks. All at once three NK trucks approached in the near darkness, and one of the trucks ran into a reconnaissance platoon jeep. The North Koreans quickly made themselves scarce, and the Americans discovered the trucks carried enough gasoline to refuel the other three U.S. tanks.

By 8 p.m. the advance was started once again, the tanks and vehicles driving with their lights on. Three tanks under Lieutenant Baker took the lead, and the other three tanks were posted at the rear of the column. By 8:30 p.m. the point of the column had reached the main Seoul-Pusan highway just south of Chonan and moved north on it. Task Force Lynch was then about thirty miles from the 7th Division positions.

Chonan was full of North Korean soldiers. Not knowing which way to turn at an intersection, Lieutenant Baker stopped, popped his head out of his turret and spotted a North Korean soldier on guard. Pointing down one street, Baker asked the North Korean: "Osan?" The soldier idly nodded yes, then, thunderstruck, recognized Baker as an American. He quickly ran away. The rest of the column followed Baker through Chonan without opposition. The North Korean soldiers simply stood around and watched the Americans drive through.

North of Chonan, Baker's tanks caught up with a group of North Koreans marching north, and fired on them, but kept on going. Frequently they passed NK vehicles on either side, and the column moved on. Soon Baker's three lead tanks got ahead of the rest of the column, and Colonel Lynch was unable to reach them by radio to slow them down. Baker, now several miles in front of the rest of TF Lynch, encountered enemy fire about three miles north of Osan. Baker's tanks ran through this fire, but shortly thereafter encountered increased fire. An antitank shell sheared off the machine-gun mount of the third tank and killed a crew member. Baker's tanks were approaching U.S. lines and started receiving American small-arms and 75mm recoilless rifle fire. The 7th Division tankers standing guard on the road held their fire because of the high speed of Baker's tanks, the use of headlights and the sound of the motors. The tankers doubted they were NK armor. One tanker with the 7th division let the first of Baker's tanks go through, intending to fire on the second tank, when a white-phosphorous grenade exploded and lighted the white American star on the side of Baker's tank. Thus a tragic American-American battle was avoided. Baker stopped inside the lines of the 31st Regiment at 10:26 p.m.: he and his tanks had traveled 106 miles that day.

Unknown to Baker, however, he and his three tanks had slipped right past a strong North Korean tank force at Habong-ni, a couple of miles south of Osan. The NK tankers apparently thought Baker's Shermans were North Korean armor, and did not fire on them. But the rest of Task Force Lynch was not so lucky.

Now running without lights, TF Lynch approached Habong-ni about midnight and two T34s opened fire with cannon and machine guns. A bazooka team destroyed one of the NK tanks, but the second moved down the road where the column was strung out, firing into the American vehicles and running over several of them. It finally ran off the road into a rice paddy, but continued to fire at the column, even after an American 75mm recoilless rifle shell immobilized it. Captain James B. Webel, 7th Cavalry S-3, accompanying the task force, climbed on top of the tank and poured a five-gallon can of gasoline directly on the back and into the engine hatch. The resulting explosion blew Webel twenty feet from the tank; he got away with minor burns and two broken ribs, but he destroyed tank and crew.

At this moment two more T34s rumbled up from the north to the head of the TF Lynch column. The tanks halted and a voice called out in Korean: "What the hell goes on here?" The NK commander's words were drowned by a hail of American small-arms fire. The two T34s immediately slammed hatches and opened fire with cannon and machine guns. The task force truck blocking the road burst into flames. The three M4A3s still with Task Force Lynch meanwhile moved to the head of the column and engaged the T34s. But the North Korean tanks were joined quickly by eight more T34s, and although the American

Shermans destroyed one NK tank, two of the American tanks were shattered by North Korean fire. Captain Webel, running forward, found a 3.5-inch bazooka carried by some GIs and immobilized two tanks. In a tank-infantry battle that raged for more than an hour, Sergeant Willard H. Hopkins sneaked up on a T34 tank and dropped grenades down an open hatch, and that silenced the crew. He then organized a bazooka team that destroyed or helped to destroy four more tanks. One of the T34s ran through the task force column, shooting up and smashing into vehicles as it went. It got all the way to the southern end of the column, where gunners had hurriedly unlimbered a 105mm howitzer and, at a range of twenty-five yards, destroyed the enemy tank. Sadly, the exchange of fire between tank and howitzer also claimed the life of Sergeant Hopkins, who was in the act of attacking the T34 personally. Both Captain Webel and Sergeant Hopkins won the Distinguished Service Cross.

The three surviving T34s withdrew from the vicious fire fight, but the battle had claimed two American dead, 28 wounded, and two tanks and fifteen vehicles were destroyed. At 7 a.m., September 27, the task force, now on foot, advanced, ready for action. The point soon ran into a T34, which a bazooka team destroyed, and when an NK machine gun opened up, Lieutenant William W. Woodside and two men overran the position and killed the NK machine-gunners. At 8:26 a.m. the task force met a company of the 31st Regiment, 7th Division. The linkup of Eighth Army and X Corps had been achieved.

All across South Korea, desperate North Korean soldiers behaved in varying ways as their army and all sense of cohesion disintegrated. About 3,000 North Koreans, most of them members of the 6th and 7th Divisions, retreated into the almost impassable Chiri mountains in extreme southern Korea west of Chinju and north of Hadong. Another group of about sixty NK riflemen, using antitank and dummy mines, established a roadblock across the main Seoul-Pusan highway fifteen miles northwest of Kumchon and held it for ten hours, permitting about 2,000 6th Division soldiers to escape northward, still carrying their mortars and machine guns, but having discarded all their heavier weapons.[13] Many of these 6th Division soldiers reached the north. Yet only about 200 survivors of the 2nd NK Division were still with the division commander north of Poun at the end of September; the rest of the division had scattered into the hills. About 1,000 to 1,800 men of the 3rd NK Division were able to reach North Korea in the central mountains, and about 2,000 members of the 1st NK Division also got out through Wonju and Inje. On the night of October 1–2, a force of more than 1,000 North Koreans who had been bypassed in the eastern mountains broke out in an attempt to get north and overran the ROK II Corps headquarters at Wonju. The North Koreans killed many ROKs and then went berserk in the city, killing between 1,000 and 2,000 South Korean civilians before fleeing northward.[14]

All across South Korea, advancing American troops found grisly evidence of North Korean killings of political and military prisoners, murdered before the North Koreans retreated. At Sachon, near Chinju in the extreme south, North Koreans set fire to a jail where 280 captive South Korean police and government officials and landowners perished. At Anui, Kongju, Hamyang and Chonju, American soldiers found mass-burial trenches in which hundreds of people, including women and children, were buried.

But around Taejon the horrors were the most staggering because they involved thousands of persons. Near the Taejon airstrip, bodies of about 500 ROK soldiers, their hands tied behind their backs, lay in mass graves. After Taejon had fallen to the North Koreans on July 20, North Korean soldiers and officials arrested between 5,000 and 7,000 South Korean civilians and packed them into the city jail and the Catholic Mission. After the first U.S. troops crossed the Naktong in the counteroffensive, the North Korean security police at Taejon began executing these prisoners. They were taken out in groups of one hundred and two hundred, their hands tied behind them and bound to each other. They were led to previously dug trenches and shot. As the Americans neared Taejon, the executions were speeded up, and the last killings took place just before the city feel on September 28. Included in the killings were at least forty American and seventeen ROK soldiers. Only six persons survived this holocaust: two American soldiers, one ROK soldier, and three South Korean civilians. They had been wounded; feigning death, they were buried alive, but the dirt was spread so hastily and lightly over them they were able to breathe enough to stay alive until they could punch holes to the surface. One of them did it with a lead pencil. The six survivors were still wired to the dead beneath the soil when 24th Division soldiers rescued them.[15]

It was probable from the first that the polarization of politics in Korea into two extreme governments—one communist and the other far right-wing—would lead to horrible cruelties. Korea was engaged in a civil war, and neither side was in a mood to tolerate the views of the other. There is reason to suspect wholesale executions were also carried out by South Koreans. A Reuters dispatch published in the New York Times on July 14, shortly after the war began, reported Kim Tai Sun, chief of the South Korean National Police, as saying 1,200 communists and suspected communists had been executed by South Korean police since the outbreak of hostilities because they were considered "bad security risks."[16] *People's China*, an English-language official publication of the Beijing government, published accounts of alleged mass killings of political prisoners by South Korean police in the weeks just after the start of the war. An account by the Chinese Hsinhua news service dated July 31 reported that political prisoners were hauled to open pits near Taejon and systematically shot and buried in the weeks prior to the evacuation of Taejon. The article, published in the September 1 issue of *People's China*, also charged that South Korean police drowned 1,000 persons at sea after they had been arrested in Inchon a few days after the war started, and that other killings occurred at Suwon and Phyongtak (Pyongtaek?). Another article in *People's China* on March 16, 1951, also charged that mass killings by ROKs occurred in Seoul after the city was recaptured on September 28.[17]

CHAPTER 31

The United States Decides to Conquer

AFTER THE FRIGHTFUL LOSSES the North Korean army suffered in the first half of September in trying to crush the Pusan Perimeter, approximately 70,000 soldiers were left facing Eighth Army when the breakout began. Of these, between 25,000 and 30,000 eventually reached North Korea.[1] With few exceptions, the escaping North Korean units lost all of their heavy weapons and vehicles (most of these ran out of fuel). In some cases the soldiers kept their small arms; a few retained their automatic weapons and mortars. But the great majority of the North Koreans arriving back in the north were disorganized, dispirited and weaponless.

Although the North Korean army was woefully shattered, it had not quite experienced a Cannae. There were two reasons why not: one was the determination to escape; many North Koreans, especially those who were located near or in the eastern mountains, walked through rugged country for days and sometimes weeks to reach North Korea. The other was that, despite the brilliance of the Inchon invasion, there were literally no plans for exploitation of the thrust into the North Korean rear. At Cannae, Hannibal had blocked retreat of the Roman army by placing his heavy Carthaginian cavalry on the entire Roman rear. The 1st Marine and the 7th Infantry Divisions essentially halted after Seoul was captured, for MacArthur made no effort to drive all the way across Korea to the east coast and thereby cut off the surviving North Korean forces trying to get back to safety. The result was that most of the North Koreans who escaped got through roads east of Seoul, where no blocking forces stood in their way. Although the invasion force was held up for several days by the Seoul barricades, this battle could have been left to the marines, and the 7th Division might have been unleashed to rush straight across Korea from Seoul. There were few organized North Korean troops to stop such a thrust.

MacArthur and the Joint Chiefs simply had not produced a plan of how to exploit an Inchon victory. Perhaps part of the reason can be explained by the controversy surrounding Inchon itself, a controversy so consuming that careful consideration of what to do after Inchon was not made. There is evidence for this, for despite the fact that the National Security Council started working on the matter in mid-July, MacArthur did not receive authorization from the President or the Joint Chiefs to go beyond the 38th parallel in pursuit of North Korean forces until September 27.[2] This was twelve days after Inchon. Any invasion of the magnitude of Inchon should have included contingencies for breakout and exploitation and for pursuit and encirclement of defeated forces. Since Seoul is only about twenty-five miles south of the parallel, the possibility of and the need for movement over the 38th to destroy enemy remnants should have been considered and made part and parcel of the Inchon plan, not something decided on an opportunistic basis after Inchon. In short, the decision whether or not to cross the 38th parallel should have been made *before* Inchon, not *after*. Many political questions would have been made simpler if this decision had been made.

Leaving aside the political problems for a moment, the military problem of destruction of the North Korean army would have been made more difficult if the UN Command had adhered rigidly to its original purpose of driving the North Koreans back to, but not over, the 38th parallel. However, if the political decision to stop at the parallel had been made before Inchon, then plans could have been developed to net the maximum number of North Korean survivors while they were still south of it. This could have been done by planning to send, at the first possible moment, flying columns of 7th Division troops to Chunchon and Hongchon and from there across mountain roads eastward to block paths of retreat. This would not have cut off all of the fleeing North Koreans, but if it had been done immediately after Seoul was masked, the flying columns could have captured most of them. Alternatively, if the political decision had been made to pursue the North Korean survivors into the north (whatever the ultimate disposition of the North Korean state), then a more sweeping net could have been flung by a fast thrust to the northeast, up the Seoul-Chorwon-Pyonggang corridor straight for Wonsan on the east coast. This route, immediately after Seoul was invested, was virtually clear of strong North Korean forces (the 18th Division had withdrawn northward in disorder). A quick drive up this corridor by American tanks and motorized columns could have cracked right through what was to become known as the "Iron Triangle"—the area bounded by Chorwon, Kumwha and Pyonggang (not Pyongyang, the North Korean capital). It was in the Iron Triangle and in the Hwachon-Inje region southeast of it that most of the North Korean soldiers assembled after the retreat.[3] Thus a thrust up the Seoul-Wonsan route would have sealed off the vast majority of the survivors from retreat to and succor from the rest of North Korea.

In the event, a campaign which might have been a Cannae became merely a great victory (*merely*, of course, by comparison with what could have been achieved). It was a glaring error on the part of MacArthur and the Joint Chiefs not to take advantage of the overwhelmingly favorable strategic position of American forces at Seoul and to *complete* the encirclement of the North Korean army by a swift drive to the east coast.

If this had been done, the scattered, disorganized and poorly armed North Korean survivors could have been cut off below or near the 38th and the North Korean command would have had few experienced soldiers left upon which to build a military force. This would have reduced the strength of any argument that North Korea had to be occupied to guarantee the South's protection against renewed attack from the North.

Because the issue of the 38th parallel was not settled before Inchon, there developed immediately afterward three separate but related issues which became intermingled and confused leaders and the public alike.

One was a belated plan, which flowered as a result of the unexpected Inchon victory, for absorption of North Korea into a unified Korea, which, under the circumstances, could have been ruled by none other than Syngman Rhee and his right-wing followers. The second was MacArthur's military plans for destroying the remnants of the enemy army by occupying North Korea. And the third was how Red China and the Soviet Union would react—this being the key question, of course. If the Russians and Red Chinese could be discouraged from intervening, then the other two matters—the setting up of a U.S.-dominated state covering the entire peninsula and the destruction of the remaining North Korean armed forces—could be taken care of at leisure and with certainty of success. It was precisely on the third point that the American failure came. The primary reason was that American policy-makers continued to believe until too late that the danger of intervention was from the Russians. Their analysis was that the Russians were unlikely to intervene, and they believed the Chinese Communists would not respond independently.

For example, JCS Chairman Omar Bradley's appraisal at the time was that Red China was a Soviet satellite under tight control of Moscow, that "the Russians were not ready to risk global war over Korea," and that no unilateral move by Red China was likely because it lacked the military power. "Therefore," Bradley said, "there would be no Soviet or Chinese Communist intervention in Korea."[4]

Bradley also said that if the Chinese Reds were going to make a decisive military move, Taiwan was the more likely target. "We did not believe the Chinese Communists were likely to rush in to help solve Russia's problem in North Korea...."[5]

This reveals a thorough misunderstanding of Red China's real interest in Korea. It was not to pull the Soviet Union's chestnuts out of the fire, but to protect what Beijing felt were vital Chinese concerns. These can be summarized as avoiding the presence of an antagonistic world power on the Yalu and Tumen rivers, which form China's boundary with Korea. An army placed on the Yalu would be within easy striking distance of the North China plain.

When the invasion of North Korea was being contemplated, there were insufficient assurances given Beijing that the United States intended no harm to Red China. But whatever protestations of good faith the United States might have offered, Red China could not have been expected to accept so potentially dangerous a foreign presence on its frontier.

After the American Civil War, the United States faced a similar but far less dangerous situation when France occupied Mexico and French troops stood on the Rio Grande. Yet this situation evoked a sharp response by Washington, and that led to the abandonment by France of its puppet emperor in Mexico and to his ultimate execution.

MacArthur has been charged with bellicosely driving for the Manchurian border while loftily assuring Washington the Red Chinese would not enter Korea, and that, if they did, only a few thousand could get in. But this does not relieve the Joint Chiefs or the Truman administration—most especially Secretary of State Acheson—from sharing in the blame.

Even as late as October 12, the Central Intelligence Agency continued to focus on the Russian threat, to assert that full-scale Chinese Communist intervention in Korea was not probable in 1950, and to declare that "intervention will probably be confined to continued covert assistance to the North Koreans."[6] This conclusion evidently was accepted by the administration and was not challenged in Tokyo despite vast amounts of contradictory intelligence.[7]

Bradley also revealed a key to Washington's misunderstanding of Red China: that the Communist Chinese, if they acted at all, would move to restore North Korea instead of serving their own security directly. This, then, was unlikely, Bradley felt, because "the most favorable time militarily for intervention" had passed while the Americans and ROKs were holding on in the Pusan Perimeter.[8] Thus, Chinese concern for their own borders played a small role in American thinking, locked as American policy-makers were on the idea that any Russian or Red Chinese aid could only be to help the North Koreans. In the event, the Russians decided to cut their losses and essentially abandon North Korea, and Red China moved into North Korea for its own purposes and, in the process, established North Korea as its *own* satellite—thus recreating Korea's historic role with China as a "civilized tributary state" and buffer.

The flaws in American logic, plus a complete misreading of the actual situation, led to the tragedy that lay ahead.

"I would very much like to write," Bradley said, "that the military establishment had seen the flaws in this logic and held a different view. Such was not the case. Our military intelligence estimates had contributed substantially to the CIA's conclusions. We wrongly continued to focus too much emphasis on enemy intentions and not enough on his capabilities."[9]

If the United States had analyzed the situation in Korea from the viewpoint of the Red Chinese, it would have realized the absurdity of expecting Beijing to acquiesce to a forcible unification of North and South Korea. Any such UN-sponsored government would have been both dominated by the United States and almost certainly antagonistic to Communist China. Already, by its quarantine of Taiwan, the United States had shown itself in Red China's eyes to be an enemy. The Red Chinese had not reacted militarily to this quarantine, perhaps because they had no navy, but they could not logically be expected to accept the establishment of the U.S. military on the Yalu, with all the attendant chance of an American and Nationalist Chinese invasion of mainland China over this route.

The Red Chinese made it painfully clear that they wanted a reliable buffer in front of the Yalu. At least as far back as the Han Dynasty, in the time of Christ, the Chinese emperors had sought to keep Korea as a shield in front of the North China plain. The unchanging sameness of Chinese strategic concerns in Korea is shown by the astonishing fact that, about 100 B.C., the Han Emperor Wu-ti extended Chinese control over Korea down to a line that almost traces the modern 38th parallel.[10]

A drive by the United States and the United Nations to occupy all of North Korea would eliminate this strategic buffer. Therefore, the reasonable-sounding plan to reunite Korea in a UN-supervised election was viewed in Beijing as an extreme provocation.

It would have been much more realistic for the United States to have faced this problem squarely and decided where American national interests lay. However dazzling the prospect of conquering a communist state for the West, American strategic defenses would not have been appreciably improved thereby, and American national interests in no way would have been served if Red China resisted. The United States had no incentive, given its huge concerns in Europe and elsewhere, to get involved, as Omar Bradley so eloquently phrased it,"in the wrong war, at the wrong place, at the wrong time, and with the wrong enemy."[11] Therefore, the case was extremely strong for abiding by the original U.S. intention and merely restoring the frontier between North and South Korea at or somewhere near the 38th parallel. Although Red China doubtless would have squawked, it probably would not have argued greatly if UN forces had been sent temporarily across the parallel in short punitive incursions or to round up remnants of the North Korean army. It also is doubtful whether Red China would have done more than complain if the United Nations had ignored the parallel itself and set up a more defensible boundary in the vicinity of the 38th.

However, the glittering prize that seemingly offered itself with the success at Inchon muddled American thinking and made American leaders misconstrue reality. Much of the problem was that administration officials could not distinguish the interests of Red China from those of the Soviet Union. Although the United States had openly challenged the People's Republic in June by neutralizing Taiwan and was contemplating marching up to Red China's frontier with extremely powerful forces, it apparently occurred to few American policy-makers that the world's most populous country with the world's oldest civilization could be anything but an obedient satellite of the Soviet Union. And since they figured the Soviet Union would not risk war over Korea, they decided ipso facto Red China would not either.

While the United States was moving toward the idea of conquering North Korea, Secretary of State Acheson, according to his biographer David McLellan, "does not seem to have expressed any serious misgivings about the consequences of Chinese intervention."[12] That wishful thinking played a big role in administration decision-making is probable, especially as public opinion in the United States after Inchon began to swing toward its traditional one-dimensional desire for total victory. On September 21 Senator William Knowland, a major Republican leader, said a stop at the 38th parallel would be appeasement.[13] Senators Robert A. Taft and Arthur Vandenberg, other prominent Republicans, apparently did not disagree. Republican Representative Hugh D. Scott of Pennsylvania accused the State Department of calling a halt at the 38th parallel and said it was planning "to subvert our military victory in Korea." On September 18, the New York *Times* took an editorial position demanding the North Korean aggressors be destroyed and the 38th parallel be ignored. On September 25 *Time* magazine predicted the United States would urge the United Nations to sanction crossing the line and two weeks later listed six reasons why it should be crossed. After Inchon, the *U.S. News and World Report* also urged that the parallel be crossed. However, a prescient Hanson W. Baldwin, military writer for the New York *Times,* on September 27 observed the military need for continuing the attack against remaining North Korean forces, but said that, if United Nations troops crossed the line, "we will surely be accused of aggression and the Chinese Communists might well be provoked to action."

The United States came late to the decision to occupy North Korea, and this may account for, though it does not excuse, the failure to produce a more sensible and reasoned policy. According to Dean Acheson, U.S. policy in going into Korea was solely to restore South Korea to its status prior to the invasion and to re-establish the peace broken by that invasion.[14]

A study of this policy began July 17 when President Truman instructed the National Security Council to make proposals regarding recommended U.S. courses "after the North Korean forces have been driven back to the 38th parallel."[15] This directive led to a series of studies embodied in NSC 81 which were not circulated until September 1, an unconscionably long time given the fact that amphibious operations were in the offing and decisions were required urgently.

NSC 81 drafters concluded the UN Security Council resolutions provided a legal basis for military operations north of the 38th, but only "to compel the withdrawal of the North Korean forces behind this line or to defeat these forces." In the event the United Nations forces went beyond the 38th and the Soviet Union or Red China moved forces into North Korea or announced an intention to do so, MacArthur should halt at the 38th and await action of the UN Security Council.[16] NSC 81 recommended that plans for occupation of North Korea be drafted, but that they be carried out only with the approval of President Truman after consulting with the United Nations. NSC 81 suggested that, to reduce the confrontation level, only South Korean troops should be used north of the 38th and in no event should U.S. or other UN forces be used near the Soviet or Manchurian borders. In the event major Soviet or Red Chinese units were openly employed *south* of the 38th or major Soviet forces *north* of it, MacArthur should stand on the defensive and refer the problem to Washington. Thus NSC 81 drafters did not anticipate a unilateral Red Chinese move in North Korea, but only a possible unilateral Red Chinese move to help the North Koreans during the battle of the Pusan Perimeter. However, the NSC 81 drafters went completely beyond the idea of re-establishing the status quo ante. They held that the United States should seek unification of Korea through free elections by the United Nations and that the ROK government of Syngman Rhee should be recognized by the United Nations as the only lawful government in the country.

When NSC 81 made the rounds of Washington, it got only two significant changes: Acheson demanded and got a requirement that MacArthur had to clear operations north of the 38th with Truman,[17] and "it should be the policy" to avoid using non-ROK forces close to the northern Korean borders, but the document no longer prohibited them there.[18] These revisions (NSC 81/1) were approved by President Truman on September 11.[19]

The United States had committed itself to the unification of Korea, thereby changing its original purpose in entering the war. At first, there was a vague idea that unification was seen as an objective and did not necessarily imply an invasion of North Korea.[20] As late as September 21, Truman's mind was apparently not made up completely, because he told a reporter the decision to cross the parallel with troops would be left to the United Nations.[21] However, on September 27, before the matter was even submitted to the United Nations, Truman must have recognized Korea was not going to be unified without force. He therefore approved a JCS directive to MacArthur which specifically approved military action north of the 38th.[22] This directive, based on NSC 81/1, stated that MacArthur's objective was destruction of the North Korean armed forces. It authorized him to conduct military operations north of the 38th, "provided that at the time of such operation there has been no entry into North Korea by major Soviet or Chinese Communist forces, no announcement of intended entry, nor a threat to counter our operations militarily in North Korea." The directive prohibited sending MacArthur's forces or aircraft across the Manchurian or Soviet borders, and "as a matter of policy, no non-Korea ground forces will be used in the northeast provinces bordering the Soviet Union or in the area along the Manchurian border."

Despite the security classification of the Chief's authorization order to MacArthur, a State Department official was quoted the same day by the Associated Press as saying that MacArthur had been authorized to continue the attack into North Korea, but longer-range political questions "must be decided by the United Nations." Legal authority, the official said, had been established by the June 27 UN Security Council action (authorizing UN forces "to repel armed attack").[23]

The focus now shifted to the United Nations. The Soviet Union had returned to the Security Council on August 1, and Soviet Ambassador Jacob Malik subsequently vetoed a U.S. resolution condemning North Korea's continued defiance of the United Nations.[24] Knowing another resolution on Korea faced a sure Russian veto, the United States turned to the General Assembly to get approval of its plan to unify Korea by UN elections while trying to avoid announcing that the United Nations was thereby endorsing a forcible takeover of North Korea. The fact the United Nations would be doing precisely what it had gone to war to prevent North Korea from doing raised a moral cloud over the decision—and created a strong disinclination among member states to face up to the uncomfortable realities of the implications.

However, there was considerable support among UN members for the American policy as approved in NSC 81/1. On September 4, the UN Commission on Korea, headed by an Indian diplomat, reported that "unification can be the only aim regarding Korea." And at the end of the month British Foreign Secretary Ernest Bevin called for an end to the "artificial" division between the two Koreas.[25]

The question of whether unification should be sought by military means or through negotiation was never faced clearly by the world body, although unification through diplomacy appeared to be unlikely. Therefore, at the end of September, Secretary-General Trygve Lie declared the United Nations had "no alternative to an advance north of the 38th parallel."[26]

The case was building in and out of the United Nations for what General MacArthur already had received permission from the President and the Joint Chiefs to do: advance beyond the 38th parallel. However, instead of appraising coldly the political effects of destroying North Korea, the United States rather tried to obscure the fact it was calling for such destruction. The planners in Washington hoped to present a *fait accompli*, thinking perhaps a UN-occupied North Korea would be accepted when it became a fact. The specific case to this point was a September 29 "for-his-eyes-only" message to MacArthur from Secretary of Defense Marshall in response to news reports that General Walker had said he would halt at the 38th for "regrouping," and presumably await permission from the United Nations to cross. The key part of Marshall's message was as follows: "We want you to feel unhampered tactically and strategically to proceed north of the 38th parallel. Announcement above referred to may precipitate embarrassment in the UN where evident desire is not to be confronted with necessity of a vote on passage of 38th parallel, rather to find you have found it militarily necessary to do so."[27]

Marshall's message was neatly phrased: if MacArthur simply would move across the parallel without fanfare, the United Nations would find itself with an accomplished fact, and would not have to act formally one way or the other.

MacArthur tried to avoid playing the hand so close to his vest, missing Marshall's subtle inferences on the way. Responding next day to Marshall, MacArthur said "parallel 38 is not a factor in the military employment of our forces," and "I regard all of Korea open for our military operations," which was not precisely what Marshall had said.[28] MacArthur then informed the Chiefs he planned to announce these views publicly, which was precisely what Marshall had *not* said. MacArthur, for one, was not interested in hiding this hot card face down on the table.

The more politically sensitive Chiefs flashed him back immediately that it would be "unwise" to issue any such statement. Instead, he should proceed "without any further explanation or announcement and let action determine the matter. Our government desires to avoid having to make an issue of the 38th parallel until we have accomplished our mission of defeating the North Korean forces."[29]

The time had come for the United Nations to act, and on September 30 the British representative introduced a General Assembly resolution jointly sponsored by seven other countries, but not the United States, although Acheson probably drafted it.[30] In keeping with the sponsors' fear of saying frankly what they wanted to do, the resolution was misleading and ambivalent. It recommended that "all appropriate steps be taken to ensure conditions of stability throughout Korea," and that "all sections and representative bodies of the population of Korea, South and North, be invited to cooperate with the organs of the United Nations in the restoration of peace, in the holding of elections and the establishment of a unified government."[31]

Now, clearly, the communists were not going to agree to a UN election in 1950 if they had barred elections in 1948. Thus the "invitation" to cooperate with the United Nations was not likely to be accepted except at the point of a bayonet.

On October 7 the resolution passed forty-seven to five, with seven abstentions. Although it was deliberately ambiguous, the mailed fist within the velvet glove was apparent to anyone who could pick up fine diplomatic distinctions.[32] That it really took in any UN member is doubtful; however, it soothed sensitive officials unable to stomach reality.

It's interesting to show the different coloration official Washington placed on the resolution, compared to that which MacArthur placed on it, as reported in testimony during Senate committee hearings in the spring of 1951. MacArthur said: "My mission was to clear out all North Korea, to unify it and to liberalize it."[33] Secretary of Defense George Marshall, on the other hand, said the resolution authorized "in a somewhat oblique fashion" military operations north of the 38th, but did not require them, and set forth unification "as a political, rather than a military, objective."[34] Acheson said later that MacArthur "at once stripped from the resolution of October 7 its husk of ambivalence and gave it an interpretation that the enacting majority in the General Assembly would not have accepted."[35] Precisely. To be ambivalent was, after all, why the resolution was written as it was. But that by no means shows MacArthur misunderstood its real meaning.

Acheson himself disclosed the motive in the 1951 Senate hearings, despite an involuted method of phrasing that implies he was trying to hide the harsh truth. He said the hope in Washington and the United Nations had been that movement of troops across the 38th parallel to round up remnants of the North Korean army "would result in the carrying out of the UN resolution of the 7th of October, which was to hold elections in the north and, under the United Nations aegis, try and bring that whole country together."[36] The UN resolution itself in its preamble cited other UN resolutions of 1947, 1948 and 1949 calling for the unification of Korea and made a point that the goal had not been attained. As James F. Schnabel and Robert J. Watson say in their history of the Joint Chiefs of Staff, "Reading these provisions along with the vaguely worded operative portion of the resolution, General MacArthur could readily conclude that the Assembly meant for him to impose unity on Korea by the sword."[37]

It's unfortunate the United States did not face up to the implications of the invasion instead of pussyfooting around with a deliberately obscurantist resolution designed to gather as many votes as possible in the General Assembly. The outcome was that Red China suspected the United States was hiding a great deal more than its embarrassment in attempting to join the two Koreas by force. Red China feared actual aggression by the United States.

This is especially true because, in the run-up to the decision to cross the parallel and hold UN elections in all Korea, high American officials had assumed highly aggressive positions, and not all of them were repudiated by the Truman administration.

First, General MacArthur had visited Taiwan for two days, beginning July 31, igniting new fears in Beijing that the United States and Chiang Kai-shek were entering into an alliance (see page 164). Then, on August 10, U.S. Ambassador Warren Austin in the UN Security Council had said

American determination for a unified Korea "had never wavered," and on August 17 he had said the United Nations should see to the elimination of a Korea " 'half-slave' and 'half-free'."[38] On August 25, Francis P. Matthews, secretary of the navy, had openly advocated a preventive war "to compel cooperation for peace."[39] On this same day, General MacArthur's blockbuster message to the Veterans of Foreign Wars was released to the public stressing Taiwan's strategic importance and implying it should be a U.S. base (see page 176). Less than a week later, Major General Orvil A. Anderson, commandant of the Air War College, had asserted that the United States was already at war and boasted he could "break up Russia's five A-bomb nests in a week."[40] Statements of both Navy Secretary Matthews and General Anderson were promptly repudiated by the U.S. government, and both men were removed from office.[41] However, General MacArthur kept his job, although Washington had an impossible task trying to pass off his visit to Taiwan as nonpolitical, and the "withdrawal" of the General's VFW statement convinced few communists. Likewise, Ambassador Austin's unify-Korea comments in the United Nations were not disowned.

Allen S. Whiting writes in his study of China's entry into the Korean War: "The top-level denial of aggressive intentions may have been interpreted in China as a crude effort to conceal the true aims of American imperialism, inadvertently 'revealed' by military figures of high standing."[42] Beijing publicized Navy Secretary Matthews's "aggressors-for-peace" speech and MacArthur's VFW message as proof of American aggressive intentions, and dismissed the White House repudiation as a cover-up.[43]

The fact is that the United States had made its decision. Despite the woolly language in which the UN declaration was wrapped, the United States determined to employ naked power to compel a reunion of the northern and southern halves of Korea under a government that would be friendly to and dependent upon the United States. The Chinese, therefore, did not have to puzzle over labyrinthine meanings contained in public statements by U.S. officials. Taken together and read with the UN resolutions, the implication was crystal clear: Red China faced the imminent destruction of its Korean buffer.

CHAPTER 32

Red China Warns
the United States

O N SEPTEMBER 29, MacArthur reported to Washington his plans for
invasion of the north. He expected the offensive to get under way
between October 15 and 30, although it actually began October 9.[1]
MacArthur doubtless waited until after passage of the UN resolution to
move his troops, although he never admitted it. ROK troops on the east
coast had crossed the 38th parallel on September 30 and kept on going.
The ROKs were following the orders of Syngman Rhee, who said on
September 19 that, irrespective of what action UN forces took, "we will
not allow ourselves to stop." This was the first of several courses Rhee
pursued in the war without regard to UN policy.[2]

MacArthur came up with an astonishingly bad and ill-thought-out
plan to occupy all of North Korea and to destroy the remnants of the
North Korean army. Instead of sending some forces in hot pursuit
straight for Pyongyang, the North Korean capital, or dispatching strong
forces overland northeast to Wonsan to seal off North Korean soldiers
assembled in the Iron Triangle and Hwachon-Inje, MacArthur withdrew
his only fresh force, X Corps, already concentrated at Seoul, and sent it
on a long circuitous and time-consuming voyage to an amphibious
landing at Wonsan. Eighth Army, exhausted and out of supplies after
having driven up from the Naktong line, got the task alone of attacking
north toward Pyongyang.[3]

Thus, instead of sending X Corps quickly to shatter the demoralized
and poorly equipped survivors of the debacle in the south, MacArthur
ordered both the 1st Marine Division and the 7th Infantry Division to
withdraw to Inchon and Pusan and to embark from these ports for the
amphibious invasion. These were the only ports which could handle the

delivery of the supplies necessary for the offensive. The result was that both divisions were eliminated for weeks from the order of battle, and Inchon and Pusan and the roads and rail lines to and from them were clogged up exactly when they should have been dedicated wholly to bringing up supplies for the offensive.

Because of the delay in deciding whether to invade North Korea, the offensive was late to begin with. The amphibious landing at Wonsan was so late that ROK soldiers got to Wonsan on foot on October 10, before the marines in the assault force even got into their ships. MacArthur's original idea of sending X Corps from Wonsan and Eighth Army from Seoul on a huge pincers movement to seize Pyongyang and seal off NK army survivors in the Iron Triangle and Hwachon-Inje miscarried completely. Eighth Army captured Pyongyang long before X Corps landed at Wonsan, while the last few trained North Korean troops were able to get away and reform the North Korean army.

Omar Bradley later said that if a major at the Command and General Staff School had turned in this solution to the problem, he would have been laughed out of the classroom.[4] Nevertheless, the Joint Chiefs, of which he was the chairman, posed no objections to MacArthur's plan and cleared it September 29 with Secretary Marshall and President Truman.

* * * * * * * *

With ROK forces already across the 38th parallel and American and British Commonwealth forces preparing to invade, the attention of Western leaders and UN military commanders turned toward the Soviet Union and Red China to find out what they might do.

Intelligence services, thankfully, had picked up little indication of any activity in Siberia by Soviet forces. Although the Red Chinese in July and early August had had about 115,000 regular troops and 360,000 militia in Manchuria, close scrutiny in this period failed to show much interest in regard to Korea; rather, Beijing was preoccupied with Taiwan.[5]

Things had changed in mid-August, however. The apparent motivating force was U.S. Ambassador Austin's statements urging the unification of North and South Korea.[6] Approximately coincident with Austin's first statement regarding Korea on August 10, Mao Zedong met with Soviet Vice Premier V. M. Molotov, according to an August 17 New York *Times* article datelined Hong Kong. The *Times* article said the People's Republic agreed to enter the war with Soviet material help if the United Nations crossed the 38th parallel.[7] On August 20, three days after Austin's " 'half slave' and 'half free' " speech in the Security Council, Red Chinese Premier and Foreign Minister Zhou cabled the United Nations:

"Since Korea is China's neighbor, the Chinese people cannot but be especially concerned about solution of the Korean question, which must and can be settled peacefully." Zhou's message was broadcast in English from Beijing and also appeared in the English-language *People's China* published there.[8]

On August 22, Jacob Malik, Soviet representative in the United Nations, warned that any continuation of the war would lead inevitably to widening of the conflict, "and the responsibility for this would lie fully upon the government of the United States." Malik's statement marked a turning point: from then on Red Chinese public journals and official statements began to hint darkly that the People's Republic would defend the Yalu.[9]

Chinese reinforcements began moving into Manchuria after mid-August, and Red Chinese anxiety became manifest after Inchon. The Military Intelligence Section of the Far East Command estimated that Red Chinese People's Liberation Army (PLA) regulars in Manchuria rose to 246,000 by August 31 and to 450,000 by September 21.[10] U.S. intelligence sources also began to get specific reports that Red Chinese leaders were contemplating intervening in North Korea or that Chinese troops had already moved into North Korea.[11]

The steadily increasing evidence of PLA troop buildup in Manchuria was reported daily in teleconferences between G-2 section of the Far East Command and the Department of the Army, and each day the United Nations Command Daily Intelligence Summary (DIS) went to the Department of the Army by courier, arriving several days later at the Pentagon.[12] On September 8, the intelligence summary from MacArthur's headquarters contained this observation: "If the North Korean forces are unsuccessful in driving UN forces from Korea within a reasonable period of time, or if success of the North Korean army appears doubtful, the forces of General Lin Biao's Fourth [Field] Army will probably be committed."[13]

Nevertheless, the Pentagon discounted the likelihood of Red Chinese intervention. However, the Truman administration sought through the Indian government to find out Red China's intentions; according to Dean Acheson, the Indian ambassador to China, Kavalam Madhava Panikkar, reported at first that Zhou Enlai emphasized China's peaceful intentions.[14] This seems a strange report, because Ambassador Panikkar in his memoirs remarks that there were rumors of large-scale troop movements from Beijing north shortly after Inchon. Panikkar also said on September 25 that General Nie Yen-rung, China's acting chief of staff, had told him China would not "sit back with folded hands and let the Americans come up to their borders." Omar Bradley reported that

Washington had received a report from the British on this or some other conversation on September 27, but the report was not taken seriously because the British felt Panikkar was a "volatile and unreliable reporter,"[15] and had shown communist leanings and anti-American feelings in the past.[16]

On October 1, only four days after MacArthur received his authorization to enter North Korea, Red China's Premier Zhou Enlai made an official speech in Beijing that crossing the parallel was a possible cause for war. This had followed a September 24 cable to the United Nations protesting a new case of alleged strafings by U.S. aircraft that had occurred previously in Manchuria (all of which were probably accidental but which had roused Chinese tempers). In the October 1 speech Zhou denounced the "frenzied and violent acts of imperialist aggression of the United States," and declared the United States was "the most dangerous foe of the People's Republic of China." The Chinese people, Zhou asserted, "absolutely will not tolerate foreign aggression, nor will they supinely tolerate seeing their neighbors being savagely invaded by the imperialists."[17]

Red China's strongest warning came shortly after midnight on the night of October 2–3. Indian Ambassador Panikkar was summoned to the residence of Zhou Enlai, who informed the Indian emphatically that the People's Republic would intervene in Korea if American troops crossed the 38th parallel, but not if ROK forces did so alone. Panikkar immediately reported this to his government, and on the following day Panikkar also informed the diplomatic representatives of Britain and Burma.[18]

Zhou Enlai's warning reached Washington through British channels on the morning of October 3.[19] The State Department passed it on to Secretary Marshall and the Department of the Army notified MacArthur.[20]

Panikkar's warning was not given the attention it deserved. Truman discounted the Indian's word, because he observed that Panikkar had "played the game of the Chinese Communists fairly regularly." Instead, Truman suspected Zhou's warning might be a propaganda ploy or an attempt to keep the UN General Assembly from approving the North Korean intervention resolution, then being debated.[21] Alexis Johnson, the State Department's Far Eastern expert, responded, however, that while Zhou's message "undoubtedly contains a large element of bluff," he did not feel the United States could assume it was all bluff, and recommended ROK forces be used exclusively in North Korea, with UN air and naval support.[22] But Secretary Acheson thought Zhou's statement was part of a Soviet-Chinese effort to bring about the withdrawal of UN forces.[23] Both Acheson and Truman doubtless were influenced by the Central Intelligence Agency, which as late as October 12 was suggesting that, despite Zhou's statement and troop movements to Manchuria, "there are no convincing indications of an actual Chinese Communist intention to resort to full-scale intervention in Korea."[24]

In like vein, the October 14 Far East Command daily intelligence summary, presumably the official view of Major General Charles A. Willoughby, MacArthur's intelligence (G-2) chief, accepted a total of thirty-eight Red Chinese divisions (at about ten thousand men to a division) in Manchuria. The summary said, however, that recent threats to enter North Korea if American forces were to cross the 38th parallel "are probably in a category of diplomatic blackmail." However, the summary said twenty-four of these divisions were disposed along the Yalu at crossing points.[25]

The only direct U.S. action taken as a result of Ambassador Panikkar's messages was a notification to MacArthur from the Joint Chiefs, with Truman's approval, that in the event of "open or covert employment anywhere in Korea of major Chinese Communist units" he was to continue action as long as there seemed a "reasonable chance of success," and to take no actions against objectives within China itself unless he received prior authorization from Washington.[26]

Looking back, the misconceptions on both sides in these indirect exchanges between Beijing and Washington are sad to behold. The Red Chinese leaders doubtless felt they had dealt with the United States in a fully responsible and official manner, given the fact neither nation had diplomatic representation in the other's capital. India was a leading neutral nation and was known to have, through its excellent contacts with Britain, immediate access to the highest official levels in the United States. Zhou also must have chosen Panikkar because India had tried to remain uncommitted regarding Korea, and was respected by both sides. It was, however, Panikkar's pro-Red reputation, not his official position as ambassador of a major neutral nation, that was most noticed in Washington and that negated his influence there.

The chronology of Red China's steady drumbeat of warnings, beginning August 20, coupled with massive troop movements that were not hidden from intelligence agents, proves Washington had ample notification of China's anxiety and likely response. The responsibility for evaluating the war threats of other nations and determining the proper course for the United States was the Truman administration's, not MacArthur's and not the Chiefs'. Whether MacArthur wanted the United States to fight China or whether he downplayed the Chinese menace is not the point. Official Washington had the decision to make, not MacArthur, and Washington did not need to rely upon MacArthur for information or guidance. It received undiguised threats directly from China through reliable diplomatic channels as well as by means of radio and press announcements. It received intelligence information from many sources, including MacArthur's Far East Command. The Truman administration, especially the State Department, chose to ignore these warnings and to discount ominous intelligence reports. The administration, not MacArthur and not the Chiefs of Staff, was responsible for weighing the dangers to the United States and deciding whether to invade North Korea or seek an accommodation with Beijing. The errors of MacArthur and the Chiefs were devastating, but they were entirely military: MacArthur walked into an ambush not once, but twice, and the Chiefs let him do it. But if the Truman administration had hearkened to Chinese Communist threats, there would have been no traps into which MacArthur could have fallen.

Exactly what sort of accommodation the United States could have made with Beijing is unknown. Although Chinese Premier Zhou Enlai cited the mere crossing of the 38th as a possible *casus belli*, he had, significantly, left a large loophole by telling Indian Ambassador Panikkar that the movement of South Korean troops over the border did not matter, and only an invasion by American troops would encounter Red Chinese resistance. ROK troops were capable of completing the destruction of the North Korean army remnants, especially if they had been given more artillery, tanks and air support.

Even after UN troops moved northward, there is a possibility that the Chinese might have been satisfied with a judicious halt of UN forces at the narrow waist of Korea above Pyongyang, thus leaving them with a modest buffer in front of the Yalu. This was not what Beijing was broadcasting to the world, and Allen Whiting believes it was crossing of the 38th which prompted the Red Chinese to intervene.[27] Nevertheless, the Chinese acceptance of ROK invaders north of the parallel and their waiting until UN and ROK forces were virtually on Manchuria's doorstep before finally responding argues strongly that the United States could have achieved more by negotiation with Beijing after Inchon than it ultimately was to achieve by two and a half years more of bloody war.

It appears that a major contributing reason to the Truman administration's decision not to seek an accommodation with Beijing was the domestic political situation in the United States at the time. The November elections were imminent, and Republican leaders were loudly urging a continuation of the U.S. attack, while some were describing any plans for a halt as appeasement of communists. This was the period when McCarthyism was emerging as a powerful political force, and the Truman administration was already the target of the right-wing charges of a "communist conspiracy" in the State Department. However, few Americans would have elected for war in late 1950 against Red China, and a courageous administration that laid out the circumstances frankly to the voters would have found solid support for a course to restore the two Koreas, eliminate the chance for renewed aggression, and avoid a war with China.

* * * * * * * *

The UN offensive against North Korea had just got under way when President Truman, worried about the Chinese Communist threat to intervene and hoping he would have better success than others in conveying to MacArthur his administration's foreign policy, decided he and MacArthur needed a face-to-face meeting.[28] It was to be one of the strangest encounters in history between the chief executive of a nation and a subordinate military field commander, not least because Truman sought out MacArthur and in the process seemed to elevate the General into the President's political equal.

The date of the meeting, October 15, fell shortly before the November elections. Therefore, it is probable Truman also hoped a public showing of solidarity between himself and the Far East commander might bolster his administration's stature and help the Democratic cause in the elections.

Many persons in the State Department were opposed to the meeting, and Dean Acheson, who declined to go, summed up his objections as follows: "While General MacArthur had many of the attributes of a foreign sovereign . . . it did not seem wise to recognize him as one."[29]

Truman made it plain he would go to MacArthur. He at first considered meeting MacArthur in Korea, but security considerations made this impossible. Then he chose Hawaii, but at the suggestion of Secretary of Defense Marshall, the meeting place was shifted to Wake Island, a tiny U.S.-owned atoll 2,300 miles west of Honolulu and 2,000 miles southeast of Tokyo. The idea was to keep MacArthur from having to travel far while offensive operations against North Korea were at a high pitch.

At first, Truman wanted all the Joint Chiefs to accompany him, but they objected on the grounds it would be inadvisable for them all to be absent at once (Bradley said they also didn't want to go). Bradley volunteered to represent all the Chiefs. Others in the group included Dean Rusk, assistant secretary of state; W. Averell Harriman, special assistant to the President; Frank Pace, secretary of the army; Philip C. Jessup, ambassador-at-large; John J. Muccio, U.S. ambassador to South

Korea (flown in by MacArthur), and Admiral Arthur W. Radford, Pacific Fleet commander.

MacArthur arrived before Truman's aircraft, the *Independence,* set down, and the General was at the foot of the ramp when the President came down it. It was their first meeting (and it was to be their last), and it was cordial. Truman and MacArthur climbed into a battered old car and drove off to an hour's private conference at a Quonset hut beside the beach. According to the President's account, they discussed the situation in Korea and Japan, and MacArthur gave assurances the Korean conflict was won and Chinese intervention unlikely.

The President and the General then moved to another building for a larger conference with military and diplomatic advisors. There was no official transcript of this meeting, but Bradley reported at least seven persons took notes, including Bradley himself. However, a controversy developed later about shorthand recordings taken by Vernice Anderson, Jessup's secretary, who listened to the meeting from an adjacent room. MacArthur later objected that he had had no knowledge a verbatim transcript was being taken, or, indeed, that any record of the conference was kept. General Bradley reported that five copies of this transcript were sent to MacArthur on October 19 and that an aide to the General signed for them on October 27. It seems strange that MacArthur or anyone should object to records being kept of a formal meeting to discuss critical military questions that took place between the President of the United States, some of his chief advisors, and the commander of the military force currently engaged in combat.

Perhaps the real reason for MacArthur's unhappiness was that the record showed how wrong he could be. He told the conference he believed that formal resistance of the North Koreans would end by Thanksgiving. He said it was his hope to be able to withdraw Eighth Army to Japan by Christmas, leaving the U.S. 2nd and 3rd Divisions and detachments from other countries as an occupation force. Truman asked: "What are the chances for Chinese or Soviet interference?"

"Very little," MacArthur responded. "Had they interfered in the first or second months it would have been decisive. We are no longer fearful of their intervention. We no longer stand hat in hand. The Chinese have 300,000 men in Manchuria. Of these probably not more than 100,000 to 125,000 are distributed along the Yalu river. They have no air force. Now that we have bases for our air force in Korea, if the Chinese tried to get down to Pyongyang there would be the greatest slaughter."

As for Russian intervention, MacArthur said it was not feasible and would not take place, because there were no Soviet troops readily available for Korea, and it would take six weeks to get them to Korea, "and six weeks brings the winter."

General MacArthur later had a chance to comment on this statement. In reviewing Roy Appleman's official army history of the first five months on the war, on November 15, 1957, MacArthur said his opinion about Chinese or Soviet intervention was purely speculative and derived from the military standpoint, and assumed the United Nations would retaliate against Chinese lines of communication and bases of supply (i.e., in Manchuria). He said the question posed by Truman fundamentally was one requiring a political decision.[30] This, of course, is true. MacArthur was wrong about Chinese intervention, but no more wrong than the top American leadership, including the man who asked him the question, the President of the United States. And it was Truman's job, not MacArthur's, to determine Red China's intentions.

One cannot help believing, however, that Truman did attach great importance to MacArthur's opinion regarding Chinese Communist intentions. MacArthur had become bigger than life because of his success at Inchon, and his views were received with great respect and accorded great weight. This is shown by the fact that MacArthur's opinions were not questioned by the President or anyone else present, who, as Appleman says, "must be assumed to have had knowledge of the highest level of intelligence bearing on the matter."[31]

The Wake Island conference ended amicably. Truman released a statement that it had been highly satisfactory and that "there is complete unity in the aims and conduct of our foreign policy."[32] This, of course, implied MacArthur was a joint maker, with the President, of American foreign policy—a remarkable and possibly inadvertent admission on Truman's part. Whether Truman believed it or was dissembling for the folks back home, his statement claiming unity was wrong. A great storm was brewing.

CHAPTER 33

Up to the Chongchon River

MACARTHUR ISSUED two surrender orders to the North Koreans in preparation for his offensive beyond the 38th parallel, though no one seriously thought the NK command would entertain any idea of negotiation, much less surrender. The first proclamation, drawn up by the State Department, was broadcast by MacArthur on October 1.[1] There was no response. The second was broadcast on October 9, the day Eighth Army's attack started. The message, broadcast and printed on leaflets and dropped by air, included the text of the United Nations resolution of October 7 and contained a final warning to North Korean forces to cease resistance "in whatever part of Korea situated." It had been directed by the Joint Chiefs. Premier Kim Il Sung of North Korea replied the next day in a defiant message to his troops ordering them to fight to the end.[2]

The Eighth Army advance, led by the 1st Cavalry Division, moved from the vicinity of Kaesong, north of Seoul, in the direction of the North Korean capital of Pyongyang. The ROK 3rd Division had already crossed the 38th parallel on the east cost on September 30, and the ROK 6th Division crossed it on October 6 in the vicinity of Chunchon on the central front.[3] By October 10 the ROK 3rd and Capital Divisions had entered Wonsan and by the eleventh had secured this east-coast port city, while X Corps was still laboriously mounting an amphibious expedition to storm it by sea. While the ROK 3rd Division remained in the Wonsan area to secure it and to greet X Corps when it arrived, the Capital Division moved on up the coast fifty air miles. On October 17 it captured both Hamhung and its port, Hungnam.

Meanwhile, the 1st Marine Division at Inchon and the 7th Division at Pusan completed their loading onto ships on October 16. The marines sailed from Inchon on the seventeenth, but were held up in landing because of delay in lifting about three thousand mines laid in Wonsan

249

harbor under Russian supervision.[4] The sailing of the 7th Division was delayed for nearly two weeks, while the marines steamed back and forth for six days in the Sea of Japan in what the leathernecks called "Operation Yo-Yo." Finally, on October 25, the marine LSTs went into Wonsan harbor, and the next morning they unloaded troops. By October 28, the marine division was ashore at Wonsan, two weeks and three days after the city had been secured by the ROK army.[5]

Meanwhile, Eighth Army had driven deep into North Korea. By October 14, the 1st Cavalry Division, after a series of hard fights, had enveloped Kumchon and broken the thin North Korean defensive line north of Kaesong. Thereafter a coordinated NK defense virtually ceased.[6] I Corps moved on all southern corridors for Pyongyang, while ROK forces flanked the North Korean capital to the southeast and east. By October 17, four ROK Divisions, two American divisions (1st Cavalry and 24th) and the 27th British Commonwealth Brigade were all racing for Pyongyang. The British brigade meanwhile had been joined by a battalion of the Royal Australian Regiment.[7] The 1st Cavalry reached Pyongyang first on October 19, closely followed by the other units.[8] MacArthur flew into Pyongyang on October 21 and, during his brief visit, reviewed Company F, 5th Cavalry Regiment, the first unit to enter the North Korean capital. In a poignant scene, MacArthur asked all the men who had landed with the company in Korea ninety-six days before, when it numbered almost two hundred men, to step forward. Five men did so, and three of them had been wounded.[9]

With Pyongyang captured and North Korean opposition reduced to isolated actions by individual units, the way was open for Eighth Army to continue northward toward the Yalu. Since X Corps on the east coast had lost its original purpose of moving west to link up with Eighth Army, MacArthur changed its mission and ordered it to drive east of the Nangnim-sanmaek mountains to the Yalu, while Eighth Army west of it drove separately toward the river.[10]

There was now no need for 7th Division, still idly floating aboard ships in Pusan, to land at Wonsan. MacArthur accordingly diverted it to Iwon, 150 miles up the coast from Wonsan.[11] This small port had been captured earlier by a flying column of the ROK Capital Division, which was rushing up the east coast road. By October 28, two days after the marines unloaded at Wonsan, the ROKs had moved through Iwon and captured Songjin, 105 air miles northeast of Hungnam, and kept on going.[12]

The 7th Division began landing over the beaches at Iwon on October 29 and completed most of its debarkation by November 9. In the meantime, MacArthur ordered the Far East Command's only theater reserve force, the 3rd Infantry Division, to land at Wonsan to protect the

Wonsan-Hungnam coastal strip. This greatly understrength division had received 8,500 Korean draftees. It began arriving at Wonsan on November 5 and completed its redeployment on November 17.[13]

MacArthur had created two separate commands, Eighth Army to the west and X Corps to the east of the high mountainous spine of North Korea (some heights reached over six thousand feet). The lack of contact between the two forces across the twenty- to thirty-five-mile gap raised some concern in Eighth Army and among the Joint Chiefs, but little either to X Corps or MacArthur.[14] This mountainous spine of Korea was virtually without roads and had only rugged, steep trails. The fact that these mountains effectively separated the two UN commands because UN troops could not operate in them assured that enemy troops also could not carry through a major envelopment in them. MacArthur set up the separate commands in the first place because of the forbidding terrain and the lack of communication between the western and eastern parts of northern Korea. Enemy forces did not use these mountains for extensive or decisive military operations because they could not do so, any more than UN forces could do so.

The criticism that might be leveled at MacArthur is that he did not concentrate his forces in the face of the enemy. When MacArthur changed the mission of X Corps and directed it to occupy northeastern Korea, this became a wholly separate campaign using three American and two ROK divisions. If the capture of northeastern Korea had been left to ROK forces and the American divisions of X Corps had been consolidated with those of Eighth Army on the Chongchon river, the defeat of Eighth Army might have been prevented or mitigated. Until the Chongchon front was stabilized, ROK forces could have continued to advance in northeastern Korea close to the safety of the sea. This is what the ROKs did anyway, and they were never in danger of being surrounded.

* * * * * * * *

With the North Korean capital captured, Eighth Army started a drive October 20 up the western side of Korea to the Chongchon river, which flows in the same southwesterly direction as the Yalu and about sixty miles to the south of it. The Chongchon, forty-five air miles north of Pyongyang, was the preliminary objective of Eighth Army preparatory to the final lunge to the Yalu.[15]

The attack was commenced by an airdrop of the 4,000-man 187th Airborne RCT at two separate points, both about twenty-six miles north of Pyongyang: Sukchon and Sunchon. MacArthur hoped the paratroopers could cut off North Korean officials and enemy troops and rescue American prisoners of war reportedly being moved northward by a train that ran only at night and hid in tunnels by day. The airdrops went off well. The army also for the first time in war dropped heavy equipment, vehicles and guns by parachute.

But the 187th failed to catch any North Korean officials, the main body of the North Korean army or the train carrying the American POWs. The force making the Sukchon drop, however, did land behind the 2,500-man 239th NK Regiment, the last North Korean force to leave Pyongyang and assigned the mission of delaying the UN advance. Now this regiment found itself attacked from the north instead of the south. The surprised NK force put up a fierce fight and withdrew into a line of hills. During the night the regiment tried to break through the paratroopers to the north, but suffered immense losses in direct assaults into the muzzles of paratroop guns.[16] On October 22, the trap was sprung on the 239th NK Regiment, as the 27th British Commonwealth Brigade closed up on the south side of the enemy.

There the newly arrived 3rd Battalion of the Royal Australian Regiment distinguished itself. Just north of Yongyu the Australians, acting as the advance point and riding on medium tanks of the attached U.S. 89th Tank Battalion, came under fire from an apple orchard on both sides of the road. The Australian commander, Lieutenant Colonel Charles H. Green, ordered Company C under Captain A. P. Denness to flush out the North Koreans in the orchard. The U.S. tankers had orders not to fire because of the proximity of the paratroopers. Therefore, the Aussies fixed bayonets and charged into the orchard with an élan that drew admiration from all who witnessed it. Soon Colonel Green ordered his other three companies into the fight, and then he moved his own small headquarters group after them. It was a curious fight: the Australians relied on the rifle, grenade and bayonet; the North Koreans drew in mortar fire and automatic weapons. But the Aussies thoroughly bested the North Korean soldiers. As soon as Colonel Green's headquarters group got into the orchard, it was assailed by a sizable group of NK troops; the headquarters group quickly killed thirty-four enemy soldiers, while the Australians suffered only a few wounded, including three men of Colonel Green's personal staff. An Aussie platoon, passing out of the orchard and into a harvested rice field, kicked over stacks of straw and shot North Koreans they found hiding in them. In this fierce, hand-to-hand infantry fight, the North Koreans lost 270 men killed and 200 captured. The Australians, incredibly, suffered only seven wounded. The NK survivors fled, and the English Middlesex Battalion passed through the Aussies and joined the 187th Airborne. The NK regiment was virtually ground away between paratroops and

Australians. Practically all members were killed, wounded or captured.

The Eighth Army advance force moving up the road from Pyongyang to Sunchon encountered few enemy soldiers. But the assistant commander of the 1st Cavalry Division, Brigadier General Frank A. Allen, Jr., and his party discovered a sad and sickening sight: around a railroad tunnel near Myongucham, about five miles northwest of Sunchon, were the bodies of sixty-six American POWs who had been murdered and seven more American POWs who had either starved to death or died of disease. In addition, General Allen and his party found twenty-three Americans who had escaped from their North Korean captors, some of them critically wounded (two died during the first night).

The survivors told the story: two trains, each carrying about 150 American POWs, left Pyongyang on October 17, crawling slowly and repairing the heavily broken tracks as they went. These were survivors of a group of 370 Americans the North Koreans had marched north from Seoul shortly after the Inchon landing. Each day five or six Americans died of dysentery, starvation or exposure. Their bodies were removed from the train. A few Americans escaped along the way. On October 20, while the paratroop drop was in progress, the second of the two trains remained in the Myongucham tunnel. It still had about 100 Americans, crowded into open coal gondolas and boxcars. That evening, the North Korean guards took the Americans in three groups to get their evening meal. The North Koreans shot them down as they waited for it. Most of the Americans who survived did so by feigning death. The guards and the train left that night.[17]

CHAPTER 34

Destination: The Yalu River

EIGHTH ARMY INTELLIGENCE (G-2) predicted on October 21 that the North Koreans were incapable of making more than a token defense at the Chongchon river. G-2 forecast the NK remnants would retreat in two directions: up the Chongchon valley into the high central mountains near the Manchurian border centering on Kanggye and Manpojin, and northwest from Anju and Sinanju on the lower Chongchon toward Sinuiju, opposite the Manchurian city of An-tung (Dandong) near the mouth of the Yalu river. (See Map 9.)

The region around Kanggye and Manpojin was well suited to a defensive battle because of high, almost roadless mountains. This had been the Korean guerrilla stronghold during Japanese rule, and this was where the North Korean government and the bulk of its tiny remaining military power were trying to move.

To keep as many North Koreans as possible away from this potential sanctuary, Eighth Army on October 22 sent a column of tanks (Task Force Elephant: Company C of the 6th Medium Tank Battalion) on roundabout routes to Kujang-dong on the Chongchon river. There two railways joined: a line coming up from Anju on the lower Chongchon and another threading through central North Korea. Now broken, these rail lines no longer could be used by NK forces to flee into the high mountains. The tanks reached Kujang-dong in the late evening, followed by the ROK 1st Division. Task Force Elephant then turned southwest to Kunu-ri, twenty miles downstream on the Chongchon. On the way, the ROKs rescued forty-two escaped American POWs.[1]

The ROK 6th Division, having turned northeast at Kunu-ri, pressed up the Chongchon valley on the road leading past Kujang-dong to Huichon. On the way, a sergeant of the division found the bodies of twenty-three

254

American POWs on the railway track four miles north of Kujang-dong, plus three Americans still alive.[2] East of the ROK 6th Division, the ROK 8th Division reached Tokchon at midnight on October 23, and reached Kujang-dong two days later.

On October 23, Major General Paik Sun Yup, commander of the ROK 1st Division, led his troops down the Chongchon valley to Anju and Sinanju. Sinanju had been deserted by NK forces, but, before they departed, they had destroyed the bridges across the river there. However, ROKs captured a damaged but still intact wooden bridge over the Chongchon three miles northeast of Anju. Repair of the bridge started at once and continued throughout the night. By 9 a.m. October 24 trucks could cross it, and the same morning a reconnaissance patrol discovered a tank ford three miles upstream from the bridge. The U.S. 6th Medium Tank Battalion crossed there in support of all three regiments of the ROK 1st Division, which, by October 24, were over the Chongchon and attacking northeast toward Unsan. There was little North Korean resistance. And the Yalu was only fifty-five miles away.[2]

Meanwhile, the 27th British Brigade reached Sinanju only a few hours after a ROK 1st Division tank patrol entered the town, and the next day the Middlesex Battalion crossed the wide, tidal Chongchon in assault boats, while the rest of the brigade crossed that night over the ROKs' bridge at Anju.

The ROK 6th Division reached Huichon on the night of October 23, driving through extremely moutainous and rugged country, with even higher mountains in front of it. Signs of total North Korean disintegration were everywhere. At Huichon the division captured twenty T34 tanks needing only minor repairs. At this town the 6th Division turned west and later north. Its objective: Chosan on the Yalu, fewer than fifty air miles away. The ROK 6th Division was now far ahead of any other UN force.

It looked to the UN troops in Korea as if the war was almost over, and only hard driving was now needed to press to the Yalu and eliminate the last vestiges of the North Korean army. Despite all the threats by Red China, there was no evidence of Chinese troops in front of the American, British Commonwealth and ROK soldiers pressing eagerly forward.

On October 24, General MacArthur cancelled an order he had issued October 17 restricting all but ROK forces north of a line generally thirty to forty miles south of the Manchurian border. This restriction had been in keeping with the letter of his instructions of September 27 from the Joint Chiefs not to use non-ROK forces close to the border. (See page 235.) MacArthur now removed all restrictions on the use of UN ground forces south of the border, and he instructed his commanders to press to the northern limits of Korea with all forces.[3]

MacArthur thus abruptly and without prior warning to the JCS abandoned the carefully worked out plan to keep UN forces, especially American forces, away from the Yalu and a direct confrontation with the Red Chinese. It was astonishing beyond belief that he could have forsaken such a delicate policy without discussing it with Washington. After several top-level conferences the Joint Chiefs queried MacArthur why he had done this.[4] Given the provocation, the Chiefs' query was mild. They said they knew he had "sound reasons" for his action, but what he had done was "a matter of concern here." MacArthur replied matter-of-factly that ROK forces were not strong enough to secure North Korea alone and that their commanders often were highly emotional and unreliable. Therefore, he had made the change as "a matter of military necessity."[5]

Anyway, MacArthur said, Secretary of Defense Marshall in his September 29 message had said MacArthur was to "feel unhampered tactically and strategically to proceed north of the 38th parallel." (See page 236.). This, of course, was stretching the intent of Marshall's message to the limit and beyond. Marshall's intention was not to grant MacArthur authority to go as far as he wanted in Korea north of the 38th parallel, but merely to *cross* it with as little noise as possible. MacArthur must have felt his use of Marshall's letter for authority strained his credibility, because he followed it up with a sharp conclusion: "This entire subject was covered in my conference at Wake Island."

Now the record of the Wake conference contains no reference to any such authority having been given MacArthur. The only possible way it could have been conveyed without the knowledge of the Joint Chiefs and the administration was in MacArthur's private conference with Truman in the Quonset hut beside the beach. And it would have been odd indeed for the President of the United States to have granted such authority in secret to a field commander and not to have informed anyone else, most especially Secretary Marshall or the JCS.

There is no record that the Joint Chiefs went to Truman to thrash out the matter. Indeed, the Chiefs threw up their hands and let the order stand.[6] Bradley said, "it was really too late for the JCS to do anything about the matter."[7] This was not true. There still had been no contact between Red Chinese and UN forces, even ROK forces. A few days later the Chiefs were to act with great dispatch to cancel a MacArthur order literally minutes before it was to be carried out.

There have been innuendoes that MacArthur actually invited a Chinese Communist attack in an attempt to force the United States into a war of destruction against the Red Chinese government. Some persons

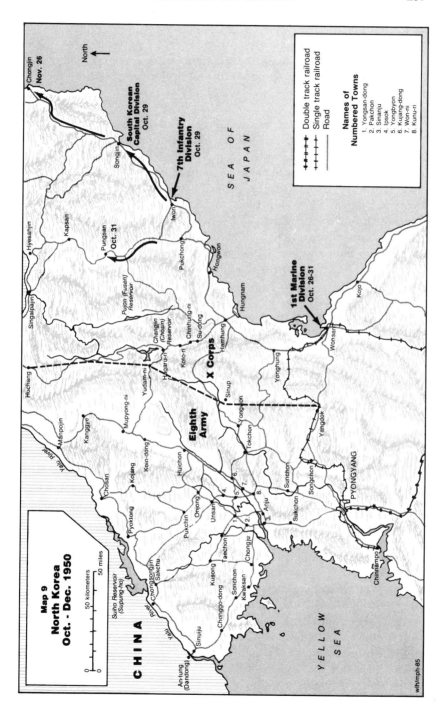

Map 9
North Korea
Oct. - Dec. 1950

Double track railroad
Single track railroad
Road

Names of
Numbered Towns
1. Yongsan-dong
2. Pakchon
3. Sinanju
4. Ipsok
5. Yongbyon
6. Kujang-dong
7. Won-ni
8. Kunu-ri

see evidence of this intent in his decision to send American forces to the Yalu.

An example of innuendo is this statement by I. F. Stone: "If MacArthur was . . . gambling that penetration of the buffer zone by non-Korean troops would be sure to provoke Chinese intervention, he won that gamble. . . ."[8]

There is little to support this in the record of the time, however. The evidence rather supports the idea that MacArthur sincerely believed, as did most of the Americans in Korea, that the Red Chinese threats were a bluff and that the war would be over in a few days. One example of this is that on October 22 MacArthur approved a request by General Walker to divert to Japan all bulk-loaded ammunition ships due to arrive thenceforth in Korea, because he felt there was enough ammunition in Korea to satisfy future needs. MacArthur also took steps to have six ammunition ships en route to the Far East diverted to Hawaii or returned to the U.S.[9] If MacArthur really had thought his action would precipitate a violent Chinese Communist reaction, it is unlikely he would have wanted to deny his troops any ammunition they could possibly expend.

MacArthur can be accused of blindness to the Chinese Communist threat, but it is not probable that he secretly conspired to draw the Red Chinese into the war. He, like the Central Intelligence Agency and the Joint Chiefs, apparently believed Beijing would not respond to provocation because the time for intervention in Korea had passed with the ending of the Pusan Perimeter. More likely MacArthur was looking at the longer haul: a strong American presence on the Yalu and an American alliance with Chiang Kai-shek with U.S. bases on Taiwan. Then if Red China displayed intransigence or expansionist ideas, the mainland would be vulnerable to powerful air strikes, and, if need be, use of atomic bombs, while a strong ground offensive always could be threatened from Korea straight on Beijing by American or Nationalist forces.

MacArthur made it plain he wanted to deal with Red China from a position of strength. And there is a possibility he favored a pre-emptive strike against mainland China if it could not be brought to terms. But this is quite different from saying he was trying to draw the Chinese into the Korean War. Of course, the Chinese were looking at the matter from the other side of the hill, and they saw that Americans could be denied a position of strength against Red China by denying them North Korea. Thus a strange sort of Catch-22 situation developed: by insisting on a unified Korea to bring peace to that country the United States forced the Red Chinese into the war—which had the same effect as, but a different origin than, a conspiracy to drag the Chinese Communists into the war.

Whether the movement of non-ROK forces to the Yalu actually precipitated the Chinese Communist intervention is questionable anyway. The Chinese Communist Forces (CCF) struck ROKs first, not Americans or Britons. And the ROKs were struck when they had penetrated the farthest of any UN forces. More likely than a direct design to block non-ROK (especially American) forces was a Chinese decision to attack *any* forces that got too close to the Yalu. Since no attack occurred on any forces south of the Chongchon river, the question arises as to whether the Chinese thought this river line was a sufficient buffer in front of the Yalu. This hypothesis cannot be verified. The Chinese always publicly insisted that the crossing of the 38th parallel was the cause for intervention. Yet they waited until UN forces were fewer than fifty miles from the Yalu before striking.

The Chinese Communists maintained strongly that the U.S. invasion of North Korea was merely a pretext for an invasion of China itself. But the Beijing leadership clearly did not want a confrontation with the United States. Perhaps this explains the hesitation to strike until the UN forces were virtually on the Yalu's banks.

The Chinese actually made their position on the matter indisputable in a widely disseminated joint declaration November 4, 1950, by the Communist Parties of China. This statement, "Aid Korea, Protect Our Homes," summarized the Chinese Communist position as follows:

"The situation today is very clear. The U.S. imperialists are copying the old trick of the Japanese bandits—first invading Korea and then invading China. Everyone knows that Korea is a small country, but that its strategic position is very important. Just as with the Japanese imperialists in the past, the main objective of the U.S. aggression on Korea is not Korea itself, but China. History shows us that the existence of the Korean People's Republic and its fall and the security or danger of China are closely intertwined. The one cannot be safeguarded without the other. It is not only [the] moral duty of the people of China to support the Korean people's war against U.S. aggression, [but also it] is closely related to the direct interests of all the Chinese people. It is determined by the necessity of self-defense. To save our neighbor is to save ourselves. To defend our fatherland, we must support the people of Korea....We hold that the Korean question should be solved in a peaceful way and that the aggressive forces of the imperialists should be withdrawn from Korea. But the American imperialists and their accomplices were not only unwilling to withdraw their aggressive forces, halt the war of aggression and settle the Korean question in a peaceful way, but, on the contrary, frenziedly pushed the aggressive war northward across the 38th parallel toward the Chinese border—the Yalu and the Tumen rivers. Thus we have been forced to realize the fact that if lovers of peace in the world desire to have peace, they must use positive action to resist atrocities and halt aggression...."[10]

This totally revealing statement occurred at a critical moment: it was directly after the Chinese Communists had struck a stunning warning blow at UN forces moving to the Yalu and just before they withdrew from contact again. The Chinese message was plain. But the Americans were not listening.

There are two recorded comments on Chinese intentions in Korea by Chairman Mao Zedong which shed some light on the subject, but not much. One of them was made in a speech in Beijing on October 23, 1951, while the war was still going on. "As everyone knows," Mao said, "the Chinese people would not be fighting the U.S. forces if they had not occupied our Taiwan, invaded the Democratic People's Republic of Korea and pushed on to our northeastern frontiers."[11] The other, made on September 12, 1953, after the war ended, was in an address to the Central People's Government Council. Mao said: "The victory in the war to resist U.S. aggression and aid Korea is a great one and has major significance. First, together with the Korean people, we have fought our way back to the 38th parallel and held on there. This is very important. If we had not fought back to the 38th parallel and our front lines had remained along the Yalu and Tumen rivers, it would have been impossible for the people in Shenyang, Anshan and Fushun [cities in Manchuria] to carry on production free from worry."[12]

Both the statement by the communist parties and the two Mao statements place emphasis on the presence of U.S. forces on the Yalu as precipitating factors in the Chinese intervention, while also indicating that crossing the 38th parallel was important. Since the statements make specific references to the U.S. drives to the Manchurian border, the question must remain whether the passage of UN forces into North Korea alone would have provoked the Chinese into active opposition, or whether the kindling point occurred when U.S. troops approached the Chinese border. However, the statements also place importance on restoring North Korea to its previous borders (and Mao mentions Taiwan). It may be that the Chinese leadership hoped UN forces could be induced to stop at the Chongchon, whereupon negotiations on a permanent cease-fire line could have been undertaken. When this failed, the Chinese leadership probably decided to try to push UN forces back to the vicinity of the 38th in order to negotiate from a position of greater strength.

CHAPTER 35

The Warning Blow Falls

MACARTHUR'S OCTOBER 24 ORDER dropping restrictions on non-ROK forces moving north opened the gates for Eighth Army to rush toward the Yalu and what everyone hoped was the end of the war. On the west, the 27th British Commonwealth Brigade led the way out of the bridgehead over the Chongchon at Sinanju, with the U.S. 24th Division coming up behind. The ROK 1st Division, in the center around Yongsan-dong and Ipsok, pressed toward Unsan. On the right, the ROK 6th Division moved rapidly through mountainous terrain in the vicinity of Onjong, with the division's 7th Regiment far in the vanguard and striking for Chosan on the Yalu itself. The ROK 8th Division meanwhile moved up the Chongchon valley toward Huichon to join the ROK 6th Division.[1] (See Map 9.)

This was no coordinated army-wide steamroller on all corridors, however. Instead, the attack resembled a series of rapier thrusts of individual units along roads that promised the swiftest penetration. There was little physical contact between the various columns. Each was free to advance as fast and as far as it could, without considering the gains (or problems) of the others.

Eighth Army expected little organized opposition, and General Walker emphasized to his troops they were to make speedy advances to the northern border.

On the west, the actions of the 24th Division and the attached 27th Brigade constituted a separate and unrelated operation from the actions unrolling on Eighth Army's eastern flanks. Led by the Middlesex Battalion, the 27th Brigade on October 25 encountered severe North Korean opposition after crossing the Taeryong river near Pakchon. Aided by artillery and air strikes, the English infantry cracked the NK defensive line, knocking out ten T34 tanks and two self-propelled guns.

On October 29 the Australian battalion took the lead and the 27th Brigade drove toward Chongju. Just before the town the Australians gained a pass and nearby ridgelines, which the North Koreans attacked during the night with tanks and SP guns. The Aussies stopped this NK assault, though losing thirty-nine killed and wounded, and the next day the Argyll Battalion entered Chongju. This day the much-admired Australian commander, Colonel Green, was mortally wounded by NK artillery fire.

The British Commonwealth brigade was exhausted by its hard battles, and General Church, 24th Division commander, passed the U.S. 21st Regiment into the lead on October 30. At 2 a.m. on October 31, seven T34s and about five hundred NK infantry tried to ambush the U.S. column a couple of miles west of Kwaksan, but fierce return fire by the Americans stopped them, and at dawn the enemy fled. Resistance collapsed, and by noon of November 1 the regiment's 1st Battalion under Lieutenant Colonel Charles B. Smith had reached Chonggo-dong, eighteen miles from Sinuiju and the Yalu river. This was to be the farthest penetration of American forces in Eighth Army, and by coincidence it was achieved by the same battalion (Task Force Smith) that had first engaged the North Korean forces near Osan of July 5. At Chonggo-dong, seven NK tanks and about five hundred infantry attacked the battalion, but the Americans smashed the effort and the North Koreans backed off.

Meanwhile the 5th Regimental Combat Team moved north from the Chongchon crossings and by November 1 had cracked through stubborn North Korean delaying forces and reached a point about ten miles north of Kusong.

* * * * * * * *

While the American and British Commonwealth forces on the west had hard but successful going against fierce but deteriorating North Korean opposition, the ROKs on the central and eastern fronts encountered a wholly new situation. It happened on October 25, the day after MacArthur opened up the front to non-ROK forces. That day of October 25 was cold and a small flurry of snow fell early.

The day opened auspiciously for the ROKs. The night before, most of the ROK 7th Regiment, heading for Chosan, passed through Onjong before turning north to reunite with the regiment's advance battalion, which meanwhile had walked northwest over a cart trail. The road was clear ahead, there was no sign of any enemy, and the regiment confidently mounted on its trucks and headed north for Chosan, fifty air miles away on the Yalu. Late in the afternoon the regiment reached

Kojang, eighteen air miles south of Chosan, and bivouacked there for the night. Officers later could not determine how, whether by design of the enemy or pure happenstance, this regiment slipped easily and without incident through what they realized afterward was the eye of a needle. For behind this far-in-advance ROK regiment a trap of massive and overwhelming proportions was about to snap shut.

The first jaw was sprung at 11 a.m. while the 7th Regiment was peacefully driving north up the road to Kojang. The ROK 1st Division's 15th Regiment, with a company of the U.S. 6th Medium Tank Battalion in the lead, having passed through Yongbyon, continued on without opposition through Unsan, and reached a bridge a mile and a half beyond the town. There the tanks were halted by mortar fire which was falling on the bridge. ROK troops fanned out on both sides of the bridge and moved toward the unseen enemy. Half an hour later they reported three hundred Chinese troops in the hills ahead of them. Shortly thereafter, the ROKs captured the first Chinese soldier taken prisoner by UN forces in the war.

The sudden, fierce contact and the Chinese prisoner were shocking beyond belief. ROK officers quickly called in a Chinese-speaking interrogator and learned even more shocking news. The Chinese soldier said there were 10,000 Red Chinese soldiers north and northwest of Unsan (facing the ROK 1st Division) and another 10,000 to the east toward Huichon (facing the ROK 6th Division). Although the ROKs and the Americans were inclined to dismiss these claims as ridiculously high, they were probably accurate. It took some time for UN officers to credit the fact, but even the lowest-level soldiers in the Chinese People's Liberation Army or, as they came to be called universally in Korea, the Chinese Communist Forces (CCF), were given comprehensive and accurate briefings on UN troop dispositions and their own army's battle plans.[2]

Unbelievable or not, the news of the first contact with Chinese troops spread along the battlefront quickly. The U.S. Air Force tactical air party controller with the ROK forces at Unsan radioed the news to a mosquito spotter plane overhead, and the pilot immediately signaled Eighth Army headquarters. Headquarters of U.S. I Corps, which had tactical charge of the western front, also got a detailed message that evening, and special arrangements were made to fly the Chinese POW to the Eighth Army advance command post of Pyongyang for interrogation the next morning. (By midafternoon of October 26 three more Chinese POWs arrived at Pyongyang.)

Throughout the twenty-fifth the fighting gradually intensified north of Unsan, with the ROK 15th Regiment getting nowhere. The ROK 12th

Regiment, following behind the 15th Regiment, turned west when it reached Unsan and just outside the town in this direction it also was stopped by Chinese troops.

Meanwhile, the second jaw of the CCF trap was sprung the same morning west of Onjong, this time on the 3rd Battalion of the ROK 6th Division's 2nd Regiment. This battalion passed through the village of Onjong and headed for Pukchin as a way station on its drive to Pyoktong on the Yalu. The remainder of the regiment followed behind. Eight miles west of Onjong the battalion came under enemy fire. The ROKs dismounted from their vehicles, thinking they had encountered a small delaying force of North Koreans.

Army records of the engagement at Onjong are fragmentary, but this is apparently what happened: the ROKs had struck a Chinese roadblock, and shortly after they were stopped by it, the Chinese threw another roadblock behind the battalion, between the ROKs and Onjong. Evidence is strong that the ROK battalion panicked from the unexpected attack and its fierceness. About 350 ROK soldiers died or were captured, including the KMAG advisor, Lieutenant Glen C. Jones, who succumbed later in a prison camp. The remaining members of the battalion, however, infiltrated in the afternoon back into Onjong, minus heavy weapons and vehicles.

When the ROK 2nd Regiment's 2nd Battalion arrived at Onjong and learned the 3rd Battalion ahead was caught in a heavy fire fight, it moved out to support it. While this battalion was traveling west on the road, however, members saw enemy troops moving about on the hills to the north of the road. Patrols sent out to investigate came back with a Chinese prisoner. He told the interrogator the Chinese force had been waiting around Pukchin since October 17. The 2nd Battalion never reached the beleaguered 3rd Battalion. It, too, was caught in a Chinese trap: CCF troops threw up a roadblock between this battalion and Onjong, but the men of the 2nd Battalion were able to escape by moving southward across country. The 2nd Battalion, along with the 3rd Battalion survivors, rejoined the regiment during the night hours at Onjong.

Anxiety was now high among ROKs at Onjong. With seeming ease the unidentified CCF unit had been able to penetrate through the mountains and establish roadblocks behind the ROK units which the South Koreans could not break. To the ROK soldiers, their flanks now became objects of dread, because CCF troops might materialize from them at any moment. At 3:30 a.m. on October 26 it happened: Chinese soldiers penetrated this new position as well, and the ROKs broke again, rushing eastward to the rear. They had gone only three miles when they came to still another

Chinese roadblock. The whole regiment was cut off. Not a single company remained intact. The ROKs, completely routed, scattered into the hills and made for the Chongchon river as best they could.

There is little doubt the ROK 2nd Regiment failed to fight hard in its first encounter with the Chinese. Perhaps one cause was unreasoning fear developing from the surprise and violence of the CCF blows; another may have been a result of the traditional fear of Chinese soldiers instilled in Korean minds. Whatever the reason, 2,700 of the 3,100 members of the 2nd Regiment eventually escaped to the Chongchon, a firm indication they had run more than they had fought.

By midafternoon on October 26, the ROK position at Onjong had been completely vacated. Practically every heavy weapon and every vehicle belonging to the 2nd Regiment had been abandoned. Meanwhile, at the ROK 1st Division sector at Unsan the situation on the morning of October 26 was ominous. By daylight it was obvious the Chinese had nearly surrounded the town during the night. To the north the ROK 15th Regiment retreated under enemy attack, and at 10:30 a.m. the commander of the U.S. 6th Tank Battalion, fearing his armor was in danger of being overrun, ordered the tanks to move back southeast of Unsan. West of the town the ROK 12th Regiment held fast. But the ROK 1st Division's third regiment, the 11th, which had moved up to assist the 12th Regiment, had to move south of Unsan almost at once because the Chinese had cut the main supply route in an envelopment from the west. Instead of breaking this Chinese roadblock, however, the 11th Regiment itself was pressed northward to the edge of Unsan. The ROK 1st Division was virtually surrounded. With the ROKs at Unsan were Americans in two tank companies, the 17th Field Artillery Battalion (eight-inch howitzers) and the 10th Antiaircraft Artillery Group (155mm howitzers and 90mm AAA guns).

Eighth Army's reaction to the startling developments at Unsan and Onjong was astonishing. Instead of quickly blowing the whistle and alerting Far East Command to a new and fearsome threat to the UN position in Korea, the army periodic intelligence report (PIR) of October 26 merely said the presence of Chinese troops at Onjong and Unsan indicated "some further reinforcement of North Korean units with personnel taken from the Chinese Communist Forces, in order to assist in the defense of the border approaches."[3] General Walker and the Eighth Army staff at Pyongyang had been studying the many reports of CCF attacks, but intelligence officers did not accept all the information from the Chinese prisoners at face value.[4]

The Far East Command was as little stirred up as Eighth Army. The FEC G-2, Major General Charles A. Willoughby, after reporting the news of Chinese troops to Washington, added on October 28: "From a tactical standpoint, with victorious United States divisions in full deployment, it would appear that the auspicious time for intervention has long since passed; it is difficult to believe that such a move, if planned, would have been postponed to a time when remnant North Korean forces have been reduced to a low point of effectiveness."[5]

The shocking events at Onjong and Unsan on October 25 and 26 apparently were not conveyed to the 7th Regiment of the ROK 6th Division, exposed now in a precarious position far to the north at Kojang, with CCF forces ranging at large behind them. Therefore, on the morning of October 26, the 7th Regiment's Reconnaissance Platoon, accompanied by Major Harry Fleming, KMAG officer with the regiment, drove to Chosan and stopped at the Yalu. This ROK platoon, with a single American officer along, was to be the only unit operating under Eighth Army command to reach the Yalu. The platoon discovered North Korean soldiers fleeing across the river into Manchuria on a narrow floating footbridge, and the ROKs quickly set up machine guns to fire at them, making sure the bullets did not reach the Manchurian shore opposite. After scouting the town and leaving a small detachment to guard it, the Recon Platoon and Major Fleming drove back to Kojang. The plan still was to move the entire regiment to Chosan the next day. That evening, finally, a radio message came from ROK 6th Division headquarters ordering the regiment to abandon its plans and to turn around and rejoin the division. Major Fleming replied the regiment could not move unless it was resupplied with gasoline, food and ammunition. This set in motion a hurried effort to get U.S. Air Force transports loaded up and dispatched to Kojang for an airdrop. The drops finally were made at 11 a.m. on October 28. Meanwhile, the 7th Regiment lay immobile in what was now obviously the heart of enemy-held territory.

On the morning of October 27, the situation at Unsan was critical. The Chinese still had the main supply route closed off south of town, and the supply situation for the ROK 1st Division was getting desperate. At 11 a.m., however, ten C-119 transport planes flying from Ashiya Air Base in Japan made a successful airdrop, and eased the supply situation. With a fresh supply of ammunition, the ROK 15th and 12th Regiments attacked and made slight gains north and west of Unsan, and, to the south, the 11th Regiment cleared the main supply road. The ROKs found the Chinese exceptionally well camouflaged and well dug-in, and therefore extremely hard to locate.

This day General Paik, the ROK 1st Division commander, who had been absent when the CCF attack came, had returned, and he examined the bodies of the enemy dead. Paik had served with the Japanese army in Manchuria in World War II and knew the Chinese well. His report to I Corps: all the bodies were Chinese, and all the troops in front of him (he estimated 10,000) were Chinese, and not individual Chinese mixed in with North Korean units.[6]

By the morning of October 28, General Walker had become sufficiently alarmed to order the U.S. 1st Cavalry Division at Pyongyang up to Unsan to pass through the ROK 1st Division and attack to the Yalu. The 1st Cavalry's 8th Cavalry Regiment departed Pyongyang on the morning of October 29 and went into an assembly area at Yongsan-dong that night. The 5th Cavalry Regiment followed.

Meantime, in the Onjong sector, the ROK II Corps commander, Major General Yu Jae Hung, decided to attempt at least to retrieve the vehicles and artillery pieces abandoned by the 6th Division's 2nd Regiment at Onjong. When the Onjong attack took place, the ROK 6th Division's 19th Regiment (less one battalion) and the ROK 8th Division's 10th Regiment were at Huichon. General Yu ordered one battalion of the 10th Regiment to remain on guard at Huichon, and the other four battalions, plus supporting arms, to attack westward to Onjong and recapture the equipment.

On October 28, the leading elements of the two ROK regiments reached a point where they could look down on Onjong and see some of the abandoned guns and trucks. That was as far as they got. On October 29, the Chinese shattered these ROK forces, and the survivors fled in panic, leaving their vehicles and all their artillery. By now, with devastating speed, most of three ROK regiments had been destroyed as combat units.

On the morning of the same day (October 29), the isolated ROK 7th Regiment at Kojang started off to rejoin the division. About twenty miles south of Kojang the regiment ran into a Chinese roadblock. Within a short time the whole regiment had been committed. Because of effective close air support by American fighters called in on the Chinese positions, the 7th Regiment was able to hold its own during the day. But that night, with the aircraft gone, the CCF forces penetrated the ROK positions and they largely disintegrated. During the night large numbers of the ROKs scattered into the hills in an attempt to get away, although a few South Koreans stayed in their positions to the end. By daylight, resistance had ended. Remarkably, according to a hand-drawn map captured much later, a single battalion of Chinese troops carried out this ambush and destroyed the ROK 7th Regiment. A total of 875 officers and men of the regiment eventually escaped to Kunu-ri and rejoined the division. This meant that almost 2,700 men were killed or captured. The only American to survive was Major Fleming, who was wounded in fifteen places and became a prisoner.

CHAPTER 36

Disaster at Unsan

BY THE END OF OCTOBER 29, all three regiments of the ROK 6th Division had been virtually destroyed, as well as one regiment of the 8th Division. The ROK 1st Division position at Unsan was now floating with both of its flanks in air: the 6th Division at Onjong on the right had ceased to exist, and there was a gap of fifteen air miles between the 1st Division and the nearest elements of the U.S. 24th Division on the left. Survivors of shattered units and the remaining operating elements of the ROK II Corps on the right flank, the 8th and 7th Divisions, were now retreating southwest down the Chongchon river valley. By November 1 they were almost south of Unsan, about four or five miles northeast of Kunu-ri, on both sides of the Chongchon.[1]

On the morning of October 29, the ROK 1st Division commenced an attack north and west from Unsan, but the fighting quickly developed into a bitter battle against emplaced Chinese troops using mortars, automatic weapons and small arms. Despite heavy artillery concentrations and repeated strafing runs by Fifth Air Force aircraft, the Chinese could not be dislodged. Heavy CCF fire, including shelling by powerful 120mm mortars, forced U.S. supporting tanks to withdraw.

Air support soon was reduced, however, because at the end of October Chinese troops set fire to the forests north and northeast of Unsan. The fires, at least ten separate ones, sent great clouds of smoke into the air which for days obscured UN aerial observation and shielded Chinese troop movements.

On November 1, the U.S. 8th Cavalry Regiment relieved the ROK 12th and 11th Regiments north, west and south of Unsan, while the ROK 15th Regiment continued to hold its positions to the northeast of Unsan. (See Map 10.) The ROK 11th Regiment was shifted to blocking positions east of Unsan, and the 12th Regiment was sent into reserve at Ipsok, south of Unsan.

The same day, on I Corps order, the 3rd Battalion of the U.S. 5th Cavalry Regiment moved six miles northeast of Yongbyon astride the Yongbyon-Kujang-dong road to bolster the disintegrating ROK II Corps lines. The same afternoon, the 1st Battalion of the 5th Cavalry was flung against a Chinese roadblock that had been discovered southwest of Unsan on the Yongsan-dong-Unsan road.

By November 1, evidence of large CCF troop movements was clear. In the morning, a Korean civilian reported two thousand Chinese soldiers were in a valley nine miles southwest of Unsan with the mission to move eastward and cut the road below the town. At noon, air and artillery fire dispersed an enemy column eight miles southeast of Unsan that was approaching ROK 11th Regiment positions, and killed about one hundred horses and an unknown number of men. During the afternoon, aerial observers reported sighting large columns of Chinese in motion northeast and northwest of Unsan, and an air strike hit the northeast column, which contained twenty-one vehicles loaded with troops.

During the afternoon, the 1st Cavalry Division CP at Yongsan-dong picked up a conversation from an observer in an L-5 spotter plane to the fire-direction center of the 82nd Field Artillery Battalion (155mm howitzers): "This is the strangest sight I have ever seen. There are two large columns of enemy infantry moving southeast over the trails in the vicinity of Myongdang-dong and Yonghung-dong [points west of Unsan]. Our shells are landing right in their columns and they keep coming."

General Hobart Gay, commander of the 1st Cavalry, who had become uneasy about the dispersion of his division, called I Corps and asked permission to move the 7th Cavalry Regiment, south of the Chongchon, to join him at Yongsan-dong, and to withdraw the 8th Cavalry Regiment from Unsan. General Gay also protested use of the 3rd Battalion, 5th Cavalry, as a blocking force on the east. All of his requests were denied by I Corps.

On the afternoon of November 1, General Walker telephoned Major General Frank W. Milburn, commander of I Corps, and told him the ROK II Corps had ceased to exist as an organized force and that his right flank was unprotected. Walker told Milburn to take over command of any ROK II Corps troops he found. Milburn immediately set off for Kunu-ri to see the ROK corps commander and directed his chief of staff, Brigadier General Rinaldo Van Brunt, to organize a blocking force on the Kunu-ri-Anju road southwest of Kunu-ri. Van Brunt sent a group composed largely of engineer and ordnance troops to this position; its major purpose was to protect the I Corps right flank and the pontoon bridges over the Chongchon river.

In their retreat down the Chongchon river, the remaining units of the ROK II Corps had largely fallen apart. When General Milburn reached Kunu-ri, the ROK corps commander said he had lost contact with most of his units, that they were disorganized, and that, so far as he knew, he had only three battalions of the ROK 7th Division in the vicinity of Kunu-ri capable of fighting. Milburn told the ROK commander he must hold Kunu-ri and that the blocking force west of town would support him.

Meantime, two companies of the 1st Battalion, 5th Cavalry, had been unable to break the roadblock the Chinese had established southwest of Unsan on the Yongsan-dong-Unsan road. In the evening, the battalion CO got permission to commit his third rifle company, but before it arrived the Chinese troops in the roadblock attacked one of the American companies and forced it out of its positions. The other company also withdrew on order of the battalion CO, and the whole battalion concentrated at a defensive position south of the roadblock. This was serious news. It meant the Chinese were in position to block the 8th Cavalry and the ROK 15th Regiment at Unsan and had invested these regiments on the north, west and south. Only to the east was there a small sector open.

During the afternoon of November 1, the Chinese attack north of Unsan gained strength against the ROK 15th Regiment. The Chinese gradually extended their attacks west into the zone of the 8th Cavalry Regiment, the first probing attacks coming about 5 p.m. All of the Chinese attacks thus far had used only automatic weapons, rifles and mortars (mostly 60mm and 81mm, but a few heavy 120mm). However, in the early evening of November 1, the Chinese for the first time fired rockets from launchers mounted on trucks. These 82mm Russian Katyushas were located and quickly forced to move by U.S. artillery, but not before the rockets hit an ammunition truck.

At dusk, the 8th Cavalry's 1st Battalion was emplaced directly north of Unsan, with its right flank on the Samtan river, but its left was dangling in air. Between it and the 2nd Battalion positions on the west was a gap of nearly a mile where a ridge extended from the north toward Unsan. To the southwest of Unsan the 3rd Battalion was emplaced along the Nammyon river and guarded the bridge over the river on the Yongsan-dong–Unsan road—this being the same road where, a few miles south, CCF troops were holding the roadblock the 1st Battalion, 5th Cavalry, was unable to crack. (See Map 10.)

On the 8th Cavalry's right flank, across the Samtan river, the ROK 15th Regiment was under heavy attack. About 7 p.m. the U.S. 10th Antiaircraft Group supporting the ROKs issued a march order and, with tension rising by the minute, began packing its equipment. At 8:30 p.m.

the group closed its fire-direction center, and at 9 p.m. its motor convoy moved south under blackout. The group's 90mm guns, which were tractor drawn and could be moved quickly, remained behind and fired for an hour or two longer, but they, too, withdrew on corps order. After 11 p.m. the ROK 15th Regiment disintegrated rapidly, and shortly after midnight ceased to exist as a combat force. Few ROKs escaped; most were killed or captured.

The 1st Battalion of the 8th Cavalry sustained a strong attack at 7:30 p.m. all along its line. The attack forced the right flank back four hundred yards, and the left flank then withdrew two hundred yards. The battalion CO, Major John Millikin, Jr., rushed fifty men from the Engineer Platoon and Heavy Mortar Company to bolster the right flank, and it held. But at 9 p.m. the Chinese discovered the gap between Millikin's battalion and the 2nd Battalion on the west and began moving through it along the ridgelines to the rear of the 2nd Battalion.

At 10 p.m. the tanks holding the bridge over the Samtan river northeast of Unsan reported large groups of Chinese had crossed the river and were moving south. Millikin, sensing the ROK 15th Regiment was buckling, sent his assistant operations officer across the river to find out. The officer got across, was fired upon, but returned with the bad news: the 15th, indeed, was folding. It was now apparent the Chinese were passing Millikin's battalion on the east. Millikin therefore ordered the battalion trains and all noncombat vehicles to a road fork south of Unsan and to be prepared to move from there southeast across the Kuryong river ford to Ipsok. About the same time, Lieutenant Colonel William Walton, CO of the 2nd Battalion, ordered his motor-pool vehicles to evacuate by the same route. Vehicles of both battalions arrived safely at Ipsok.

The Chinese now extended their attack to the 2nd Battalion, using bugle calls and whistles. These were eerie and unnerving to the American soldiers, who thought of them as some sort of psychological warfare. Actually, they were forced on the Chinese as a means of communication because their radio net went down only to regiments and phones only to battalions; below battalions the Chinese largely relied on bugles, whistles, flares and flashlights for signals.[2]

The CCF attack on the 2nd Battalion soon penetrated its right and encircled its left in a double-envelopment movement. The attack on the 1st Battalion meanwhile continued heavy. Company A, near the battalion boundary, fell into a hand-to-hand fight with Chinese approaching in two directions and withdrew to the next ridge. Along the river, the tanks holding the bridge were forced back. By 11 p.m. both the 1st and 2nd Battalion positions had been penetrated by the Chinese. The

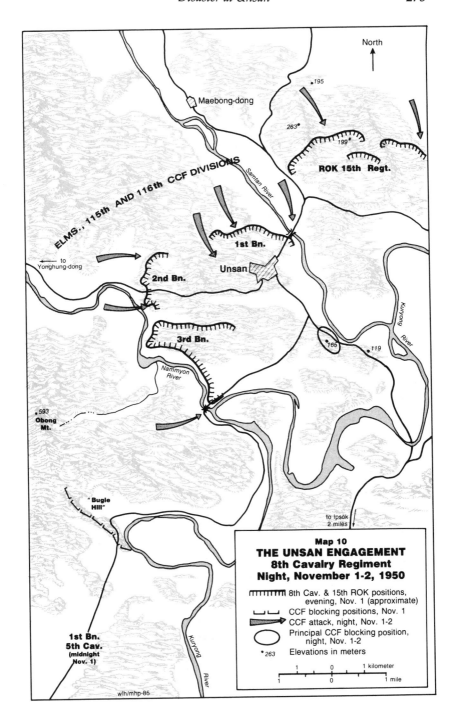

North

Maebong-dong

*195

263*

199*

ROK 15th Regt.

ELMS., 115th AND 116th CCF DIVISIONS

Samtan River

to
Yonghung-dong

1st Bn.

Unsan

2nd Bn.

3rd Bn.

Kuryong River

*166

*119

Nammyon
River

*593
Obong
Mt.

"Bugle
Hill"

to Ipsök
2 miles

1st Bn.
5th Cav.
(midnight
Nov. 1)

Kuryong River

wlh/mhp-85

Map 10
THE UNSAN ENGAGEMENT
8th Cavalry Regiment
Night, November 1-2, 1950

8th Cav. & 15th ROK positions,
evening, Nov. 1 (approximate)

CCF blocking positions, Nov. 1

CCF attack, night, Nov. 1-2

Principal CCF blocking position,
night, Nov. 1-2

* 263   Elevations in meters

1   0   1 kilometer

1   0   1 mile

1st Battalion had used up most of its original supply of ammunition and the reserve supply had been rushed forward. Millikin reported by radio to the regimental commander that his situation was increasingly desperate and he was running out of ammunition.

While this battle was going on, the I Corps commander, General Milburn, was holding a conference at Anju with his division commanders. In this meeting, Milburn ordered I Corps to go from attack to defense at once, and for the 8th Cavalry and the ROK 15th Regiment to withdraw from Unsan immediately. Likewise, he ordered the 24th Division on the left to halt its advance units, now only a few miles from the Yalu.

The 1st Cavalry commander, General Gay, telephoned from Anju to tell his chief of staff, Colonel Ernest V. Holmes, to issue the withdrawal order. Colonel Raymond D. Palmer, 8th Cavalry CO, got the order about 11 p.m., and forty-five minutes later he issued a warning order alerting all battalions and the regimental trains for withdrawal south. The only exit route possible was the ford over the Kuryong river to Ipsok, five miles south. Major Millikin telephoned Colonel Walton of the 2nd Battalion that he would try to hold Unsan until Walton's battalion cleared the road junction south of the town; then he would withdraw. The 3rd Battalion, southwest of Unsan, was to bring up the regimental rear.

The 1st Battalion's Company A had been forced from its left-flank position, and Chinese troops were infiltrating south along the ridgeline into Unsan behind the battalion. The Chinese also were attacking Company B on the right and the tanks along the river. The tankers soon reported they had been forced back to a road junction at the northeastern edge of Unsan; there they told Millikin they would try to hold until the 1st Battalion withdrew past them. When Millikin arrived at this junction, he found two tanks and the Company D mortar vehicles; the other four tanks had passed into Unsan, where the sound of heavy small-arms fire showed the Chinese were already there. These four tanks reached the road junction south of town.

It was a few minutes later (about 12:30 a.m.) when elements of Companies A and B arrived at the road fork where Millikin was waiting. Chinese troops in the town saw them and fired, causing some casualties. Millikin told the two companies to move around to the east of the town and wait for him on the road south. Millikin and most of his staff remained at the junction, hoping to direct the rest of the battalion along the escape route. He also planned to send the mortar carriers, with the two remaining tanks as escort, through Unsan to the road fork, a mile and a half south of town.

After fifteen minutes, Millikin told the two tanks and the mortar trucks, now loaded with wounded, to try to get through Unsan. As the small convoy headed into the town, a burning truck at the first turn forced the column to halt. In attempting to get around this truck, the first tank slid into a shell crater and got stuck. Chinese soldiers killed the tank commander as he tried to free the tank, and other Chinese placed a satchel charge on the tracks of the second tank and disabled it. Of the ten tank crewmen, two were killed and five were wounded. None of the wounded men on the mortar carriers escaped.

About 1 a.m., while Millikin was still waiting at the road junction northeast of Unsan, various isolated individuals—men from Company C, South Koreans attached to the 1st Battalion, stragglers from the ROK 15th Regiment *and* Chinese soldiers—arrived there. Chaos promptly ensued. The ROKs and Americans tried to escape in small groups, and Millikin and some others went westward north of Unsan and then around to the southwest where, at 2 a.m., they met parts of the 2nd Battalion that were also trying to reach the road fork south of Unsan.

This fork was critical to the retreat of the 8th Cavalry, and Colonel Palmer placed protection of it in the hands of Lieutenant Colonel Hallett D. Edson, regimental executive officer. There the junction was guarded by two squads of the Reconnaissance Platoon and a platoon of Company I, 3rd Battalion. The regimental trains passed through, then several groups from the 1st Battalion and some from the 2nd Battalion. The four tanks that had passed through Unsan got there at 12:30 a.m., and Colonel Edson placed them in defensive positions at the junction; when two more tanks arrived a while later, Edson ordered the first four to go on to the ford over the Kuryong and to protect it for the last part of the withdrawal. He kept the newly arrived tanks at the road junction.

Now artillery supporting the regiment came through and headed toward the Kuryong. Headquarters and Battery B of the 99th Field Artillery Battalion (105mm howitzers) passed through without incident. Next came Battery C, commanded by Captain Jack Bolt, about 2:20 a.m. Bolt's battery, in twenty vehicles, proceeded through the junction with Bolt's jeep in the lead. About two hundred yards beyond, Bolt had to wait because the second vehicle in the convoy had made a wrong turn and had to stop and back up. While waiting, Captain Bolt glanced at some paddy land to his left and saw in the moonlight a line of men coming toward the road. He thought they were Americans, but when they were about fifty yards away, they opened fire on Bolt. The captain shouted to his driver to get going; when the vehicle rounded a curve, it lost sight of the battery behind and encountered fifteen or twenty Chinese soldiers standing in the road. They opened fire on the jeep, and Bolt returned fire with his .45-caliber grease gun. The Chinese scattered and Bolt's jeep hurtled past, passing two smaller groups of Chinese soldiers. Captain Bolt soon caught up with the tail of the regimental column; he tried to get one of the tanks to go back and break up the developing roadblock, but the tank commander said he was out of ammunition.[3]

The Chinese roadblock force apparently had come down the west bank of the river and emerged below the road junction. As Bolt's jeep disappeared around the bend, the Chinese opened fire on the next vehicle as it approached. This firing caused the driver to lose control of the truck, and it upset over the side of an embankment and dragged the 105mm howitzer it was towing crosswise in the road, blocking it. One of the two tanks at the roadblock tried to break the roadblock, but the truck and howitzer obstructed the way—and the tank came under fire. The crew abandoned the tank. There is some evidence a Chinese satchel charge broke the tank's treads. This was the end of the movement of vehicles: the Chinese had cut the only remaining escape road from Unsan.

The men at the road junction were bewildered and frightened. Colonel Edson apparently made an effort to get men together to break the roadblock, but it failed. A few Chinese soldiers came down among the stalled vehicles and threw grenades, but most remained at the roadblock. Soon, Chinese mortar and machine-gun fire began falling on the road junction. The Americans and ROKs still north of the block moved off singly or in small groups and tried to infiltrate to the rear.

Both Colonel Walton, leading survivors of the 2nd Battalion, and Major Millikin, with men from the 1st Battalion and some from the 2nd, arrived at the road junction and found a jumble of wrecked vehicles and equipment. Walton led his men southward across the hills and arrived at Ipsok after daylight with 103 men. The rest of the 2nd Battalion never succeeded in reaching the road fork, because a Chinese force cut them off a half-mile west of Unsan with another roadblock. Among the units stopped at this roadblock was Battery A of the 99th Artillery and a platoon of tanks from the 70th Tank Battalion. The infantry caught in this roadblock scattered for the most part into the hills, and many reached Ipsok. Others went into the positions of the 3rd Battalion, 8th Cavalry, on the Nammyon river southwest of Unsan.

When Major Millikin got to the road fork he found Major Robert J. Ormond, CO of the 3rd Battalion, who was there with the platoon of Company I, which earlier had been posted at the intersection. Ormond's orders had been to hold the junction open until the 1st and 2nd Battalions got through before moving out his 3rd Battalion. Ormond told Millikin he believed large portions of the 1st and 3rd Battalions had already passed to the rear. Therefore, Ormond decided to go back to his own battalion and start its withdrawal.

The road junction now was getting small-arms fire from points to the *south* other than from the Chinese roadblock; this indicated enemy soldiers were moving at large between the Americans still north of the junction and the sanctuary of Ipsok. Millikin collected any soldiers he could find around the junction, about forty of them; after an abortive effort with the last remaining tank to crack the roadblock, Millikin's party separated into small groups and infiltrated through the Chinese lines. Millikin and a small group with him crossed the Kuryong river before daybreak and reached Ipsok about 8 a.m.

CHAPTER 37

The Lost Battalion

A S MAJOR ORMOND MOVED BACK to his 3rd Battalion position along the Nammyon, he realized it would be impossible to evacuate the battalion by way of the road junction south of Unsan. Equally impossible was the use of the direct route that led over the bridge at his battalion position and south to Yongsan-dong. The 5th Cavalry Regiment had been unable to break the Chinese roadblock on this road, about three air miles south of the Nammyon (see page 271). Instead, with his executive officer, Major Veale F. Moriarty, Ormond drew up a cross-country route and sent the motor officer off to find a ford over the Kuryong where battalion vehicles could cross.[1]

While this was going on, the battalion, which so far had seen no action, partially consolidated for movement. The battalion trucks, along with some of the men, were drawn up at the battalion CP just north of the bridge over the Nammyon.

Still along the Nammyon and guarding the bank was Company L. Still at the bridge were two squads of riflemen and an attached platoon of 70th Tank Battalion armor. The time was about 3 a.m. A column of men—a platoon or possibly a company—approached the bridge from the south and the guard at the bridge let it pass, believing the men to be ROKs. The column moved up to the battalion CP. When it was even with the CP, one of the men in the column pulled out a bugle and sounded a call. The column which had *marched* right into the center of the 3rd Battalion was Chinese. The bugle call was the signal for a massive and completely unexpected attack on the battalion from all sides.

At the same time, other Chinese troops attacked Company K, holding a ridgeline northwest of the CP, and Company L along the river. Other Chinese attacked the tanks on the road near the bridge. One tank was quickly damaged by a satchel charge and soon blew up. But the remaining tanks backed up the road toward the battalion CP and, from there, held off other Chinese troops trying to cross the river from the south.

Great confusion developed at the CP. Hand-to-hand encounters between Americans and Chinese took place over the entire head-quarters area. The Chinese unit fanned out through the area, firing at anyone they saw moving in the bright moonlight and tossing grenades or satchel charges into the massed vehicles, setting many on fire. Major Ormond rushed off to see how Company L was doing, while Captain Filmore W. McAbee, battalion operations officer, started for the U.S. roadblock at the river. As Captain McAbee approached the bridge, a bullet knocked off his helmet and another shattered his shoulder blade. McAbee turned back toward the CP and got into a fight with a small group of Chinese soldiers, with both using a jeep as a shield. After this brief encounter, McAbee saw about thirty CCF soldiers trying to set a tank on fire, and he emptied his carbine at them. Now weak from loss of blood, the captain turned toward the CP dugout. A few steps along, three Chinese soldiers jumped from a roadside ditch and prodded McAbee with their bayonets. They did not, however, attempt to disarm him; rather they jabbered at him, apparently in confusion. McAbee pointed down the road, and after a little argument among themselves, the Chinese soldiers walked away. This same strange event occurred a second time to Captain McAbee on his way back to the dugout, and again the Chinese walked away, leaving him alone. McAbee staggered to the dugout, where Major Moriarty thrust him inside and, hearing a frantic call for help, rushed out and found the battalion S-4 officer grappling on the ground with a Chinese soldier. Moriarty shot the Chinese with his pistol and another who was crouching nearby. A center of resistance developed around a tank commanded by Staff Sergeant Elmer L. Miller. Soon, however, Chinese mortar fire began landing around the tank, and Major Moriarty took the twenty men who were at the tank and led them across the stream to destroy a small group of enemy at the river bank. The group then proceeded southeast and, joined by about eighty men from different units of the regiment, reached ROK lines near Ipsok after daybreak.

The Chinese at the battalion CP were finally driven off after about half an hour. Meanwhile, most of Company L had withdrawn to the CP area, as had the remnants of Company K. This company had been ambushed on the way to the CP and lost its command group and a platoon. The Chinese followed close on the two companies, but the men of the battalion held off the enemy, forming a defense perimeter around the three tanks left with the battalion, and another defense sector around the

CP dugout. Three men who fired a machine gun at the dugout were killed in succession by Chinese grenades, and, by daylight, only five of the twenty men assembled there were left. After daybreak, however, the Chinese attacking the dugout withdrew, and the survivors joined the others in the perimeter around the tanks.

An hour after daylight, a mosquito airplane came over and called in fighter-bomber strikes all day against the Chinese. This kept the enemy troops under cover and permitted the battalion to organize and to bring in the wounded. They found Major Ormond badly wounded and the remainder of the battalion staff either wounded or missing. About 170 wounded were brought inside the perimeter. Only six officers and 200 men were still able to function. Apparently the dead were not counted. The men used the daylight hours to dig trenches and to retrieve rations and ammunition from the vehicles. An L-5 airplane dropped a mail bag of morphine and bandages, and a helicopter hovered briefly over the battalion position to pick up the most seriously wounded, but drew off without landing when it was hit by Chinese fire. A mosquito plane radioed the battalion group a relief column was on the way.

This column was the 5th Cavalry, which, after having been stopped the previous day at the roadblock south of the 3rd Battalion position, resumed the attack at daybreak, November 2. Lieutenant Colonel Harold K. Johnson, 5th Cavalry commander, placed his 1st Battalion on one side of the road and his 2nd Battalion on the other and sent them in a direct assault against the Chinese-held ridgeline—quickly dubbed Bugle Hill—through which the road to the beleagured 3rd Battalion, 8th Cavalry, ran. Colonel Johnson hoped to break open enough of a hole for his 3rd Battalion, held in reserve and spearheaded by a tank company, to crack through and rescue the cutoff battalion. Johnson had a personal interest in saving this battalion: it had been part of the 3rd Division in the U.S., and he had brought it to Korea to augment the 8th Cavalry Regiment and had commanded it throughout the Pusan Perimeter period.

To assist the 5th Cavalry, General Gay, division commander, also attached the 1st Battalion of the 7th Cavalry Regiment, which had now moved up, with instructions for it to strike out left across country in an effort to outflank Bugle Hill while the 5th Cavalry struck the front. The two assault companies of the 5th Cavalry failed to reach their objectives on Bugle Hill, although the regiment suffered 350 casualties. The 7th Cavalry battalion merely moved off into rugged country and contributed nothing to the fight.

Higher headquarters had vetoed moving up 105mm howitzers to support the 5th Cavalry, and only longer-range 155mm howitzers could reach the Chinese positions. Repeated strikes by air force fighters and fighter-bombers probably did little damage because the heavy haze created by the Chinese firing of the forests obscured targets. The dug-in Chinese, reported by a prisoner to be five companies, did not move from Bugle Hill.

At 3 p.m. General Milburn, I Corps commander, after talking with General Gay, told the 1st Cavalry commander to withdraw the division. Both agreed that, with the forces available, the division could not break the roadblock. At dusk, after receiving confirmation of the order from I Corps, General Gay made what he called his most difficult decision: he ordered the 5th Cavalry to withdraw and to leave the isolated 3rd Battalion, 8th Cavalry, to its fate.

A division liaison plane flew over the battalion's small perimeter and dropped a message ordering the men to withdraw as best they could under cover of darkness, an order also confirmed over Sergeant Miller's tank radio.

As the last protecting air force planes withdrew at dark, the Chinese opened up on the perimeter with 120mm mortars that had been brought into position during the day. The infantry decided that the three U.S. tanks under command of Sergeant Miller would be lost if they remained, and Miller led the tanks off to the southwest, where the crews had to abandon them in the valley of the Kuryong; Miller and a few of his men survived to reach friendly lines.

At the 3rd Battalion perimeter, the Chinese followed up the heavy mortar barrage with an infantry attack, which the Americans repulsed by setting fire to their vehicles with bazooka shells. Silhouetted by the light from the fires, the infantry shot down the Chinese attackers in great numbers. But the Chinese kept coming: six times they repeated the attacks, each time using about forty men, and each time the Americans threw them back. During the night about fifty men from the Eighth Cavalry's 2nd Battalion, who had been hiding in the hills, broke through to join the 3rd Battalion in its little island.

During this heavy action, the Chinese overran the old CP dugout where between fifty and sixty badly wounded men were being kept. The Chinese took fifteen of these who were able to walk, including Captain McAbee and Chaplain Emil J. Kapaun, and removed them to the Nammyon river outside range of fire. These wounded men had to climb over the bodies of Chinese dead, which were piled three high in places where they had been killed by American fire.

On the morning of November 3, a patrol from the battalion perimeter went to the CP dugout and gave rations to the wounded men still there. There was no U.S. air support this day, and Chinese fire kept everyone under cover. The night was a repeat of the night before: but the Chinese were working closer. After each attack, the Americans crawled out and took weapons and ammunition off the Chinese dead, because their own ammunition was almost gone.

At daylight on November 4, there were under 200 Americans able to fight and about 250 wounded. A discussion reached the conclusion the able-bodied men should attempt to escape. Captain Clarence R. Anderson, the battalion surgeon, volunteered to stay with the wounded.

About 2:30 p.m. the able-bodied Americans withdrew to the east side of the perimeter just as the Chinese bombarded the area with white-phosphorous shells, which obscured the perimeter and approaches with thick smoke and screened the Chinese assault, which this time met no resistance. The unwounded Americans moved all night east and northeast, then south and southwest. On the afternoon of November 5 the group went south through hills and crossed the Kuryong river valley. The next afternoon, within sight of bursting American artillery shells, the group was surrounded by Chinese troops and the American officers decided to break the group into small parties in the hope that some, at least, might escape. It was a forlorn hope; most of the men were either killed or captured that day in the vicinity of Yongbyon.

At first, losses to the 8th Cavalry were reported to be a thousand men, but men straggled in for days, friendly Koreans saved others, and on November 22 the Chinese themselves, in a propaganda move, released twenty-seven Americans, nineteen of them captured at Unsan. Final 8th Cavalry losses were tallied at about six hundred men, though additional men were lost in supporting artillery and tank units. The regiment also lost much of its equipment.

CHAPTER 38

The Chinese Back Off

THE 1st CAVALRY and the ROK 1st Divisions withdrew to the south side of Chongchon. It was clear Eighth Army had suffered severely. Not only had the 8th Cavalry been mauled, but the 5th Cavalry had suffered heavily in its failed attempt to break through the Bugle Hill roadblock. The 15th Regiment of the ROK 1st Division and the 10th Regiment of the ROK 8th Division had disappeared as effective units, and the ROK 6th Division had virtually ceased to exist.

At least as significant as the loss of men and materiel was the disintegration of the ROK II Corps. The remaining elements of its three divisions retreated in confusion down the Chongchon river to the vicinity of Kunu-ri before some semblance of order could be restored.[1] This area was only thirteen miles from the only permanent bridge crossing the Chongchon, the ROK-captured wooden structure three miles northeast of Anju.

This threat to the single reliable means of crossing the Chongchon dictated a decision by General Walker to withdraw Eighth Army across the river, except for a bridgehead north of the Sinanju crossing of the river on the west, held by the 27th British Commonwealth Brigade, and another bridgehead above the wooden bridge, held by the U.S. 19th Regiment.[2]

To guard against another collapse of the ROK II Corps, Walker on November 3 placed the 5th RCT at Kunu-ri behind the ROKs, and moved the 9th Regiment of the 2nd Division south of Kunu-ri to protect the vital road south to Sunchon.[3] The Chinese were not long in attacking the ROKs. The next day, CCF units broke the 3rd Regiment of the ROK 7th Division on a hill three miles northeast of Kunu-ri, and the South Koreans began streaming back through the 5th RCT. The ROK 8th Regiment was committed, and though the hill (622) changed hands several times during the day, at dark ROKs were in possession. The 5th RCT was also attacked strongly by the Chinese, and the American regiment had to withdraw about a thousand yards. But by evening the Chinese were repulsed, and Eighth Army remained in possession of Kunu-ri. The right flank of the army held.

The Chinese also struck the 19th Regiment's bridgehead north of the bridge over the Chongchon on November 4. About a thousand CCF troops succeeded in getting behind the 1st Battalion of the 19th, emplaced about seven miles northeast of the bridge. The American force quickly retreated across the Chongchon without putting up much of a fight and lost its heavy equipment and vehicles. An effort by the 3rd Battalion of the 19th to drive through to the 1st Battalion's former positions failed when strong Chinese forces on the road stopped it. The worsening situation caused the 24th Division commander, General Church, to order the 21st Regiment to cross the river during the night and attack on November 5 to restore the bridgehead line. This attack succeeded.

The Chinese likewise moved on the night of November 4–5 against the 27th Brigade bridgehead position just south of Pakchon and about five miles north of the river crossing at Sinanju. About a battalion of Chinese circled east around Pakchon toward the 61st Field Artillery Battalion of the 1st Cavalry Division, which was emplaced a couple of miles south of Pakchon in support of the British. The Chinese aim was to cut the road behind the 27th Brigade, and especially to demolish a critical bridge over a stream at the artillery position. If this bridge were blown, no brigade tanks or vehicles could get out.

When the Chinese opened up with mortars and small-arms fire against the artillery, each battery commander immediately placed all his men, except the gun crews, in a tight perimeter around the battery position, with every automatic weapon available manned. Word of the attack reached the brigade, and Company A of the Argylls started south immediately to aid the artillerymen. The heaviest Chinese attack fell on Battery C. The battery commander, Captain Howard M. Moore, wheeled one 105mm howitzer around and fired point-blank at enemy troops in rice paddies to the east. Later, he got another howitzer turned around; the two pieces fired 1,400 rounds at the Chinese, most of them at 300 yards range, some as close as 50 yards. The gunners kept the Chinese away, and also stopped their efforts to demolish the bridge. The artilleryman killed one member of the demolition squad who got to within twenty yards of the bridge. In supporting the artillery, the Argylls lost two men killed and eighteen wounded, while the artillery battalion suffered two killed and thirty-five wounded.

In tribute to Battery C of the artillery battalion, Brigadier Basil A. Coad, 27th Brigade commander, commented: "I would like to say how magnificently these American gunners fought. Dead Chinese were lying thirty yards from the gun shields.... It was up to the very highest traditions of any artillery regiment."

It had become clear that a large Chinese force had virtually surrounded the 27th Brigade bridgehead. An attempt to crack the constricting band was made by the Australian battalion to the north; the Aussies in a desperate battle lost twelve killed and sixty-four wounded. But it was now apparent that the brigade could not hold the bridgehead, and both the brigade and the artillery withdrew south under fire toward the Chongchon on the road that had been cleared by the Middlesex Battalion while the Australians were attacking to the north.

That evening the brigade held a perimeter on the first line of hills about two miles north of the river. The Chinese attacked this position shortly after dark, and the attack continued without pause for four hours, the CCF losing several hundred men in the process. By dawn of November 6, however, the Chinese had withdrawn from contact.

During this same night the Chinese also attacked the left-hand side of the 19th Regiment bridgehead, which was located about four miles north of the bridge over the Chongchon. At least part of the Chinese force crept up on the U.S. position from the rear by following a field telephone wire. The Chinese caught many Americans asleep in their sleeping bags and killed them where they lay. Despite heroic action by several men, the battalion was forced to withdraw more than half a mile and was only barely able to maintain itself until daylight, when the Chinese broke off contact.

On this day, November 6, one of the strangest events in the history of warfare took place. The Chinese army, in the full flush of victory, suddenly broke off contact with the UN forces and, for no apparent reason, withdrew entirely from the fight. Australians in their positions north of the Chongchon could see the Chinese forces marching northward immediately after the predawn attacks against the 27th Brigade had ended. Aerial spotters reported many sightings of Chinese forces moving away from the battleground. By the end of the day, all were gone—back into the mountains.

It was as if the Chinese command had determined to deliver a series of stunning blows to the UN forces immediately after they crossed the Chongchon river and, as soon as they were driven back to the river, to leave them alone. Whether this was, indeed, the Chinese plan is not known. Yet the Chinese remained wholly out of contact with the UN forces thereafter until MacArthur launched the "end-the-war" offensive on November 24, and they only attacked after the UN troops advanced again across the Chongchon and attempted to reach the Yalu.

The same thing occurred in the X Corps sector on the east. But because Chinese and American troops were engaged in a heavy battle on November 6, it was not until the next day that the withdrawal occurred. On October 28 ROK forces had encountered Chinese troops near Su-dong, about twenty-eight air miles north of Hungnam, and about fourteen air miles below the southern end of the Changjin (Chosin) reservoir. The Chinese stopped a regiment of the ROK 3rd Division.[4] After the 7th Marine Regiment of the 1st Marine Division relieved the ROKs on November 2, preparatory to attempting to drive to the Changjin reservoir, Chinese troops attacked the marines fiercely when they moved north. The attacks left seven hundred Chinese dead in front of marine positions.[5] When the marines attempted to move north again on November 5, Chinese troops blocked them on Hill 750 (How Hill), a half-mile north of Chinhung-ni, and stopped repeated marine attacks cold. On the morning of November 7, however, marine patrols found the Chinese had withdrawn.

CHAPTER 39

A Time to Reconsider

I T IS NOT KNOWN whether the Chinese leadership deliberately attacked the UN forces as a warning, and then withdrew in hopes the United Nations would reconsider its northward movements and stop. This is the only plausible explanation that has been advanced.[1] Whatever the Chinese intention, the reaction to the attacks in Tokyo and Washington is baffling. There no longer could be any doubt about the possible danger of a Chinese intervention: it had occurred. There no longer could be any question about what the Chinese could do: they had destroyed several major military components.

The Chinese First Phase Offensive had provided MacArthur and the Joint Chiefs of Staff with a deadly warning. The attacks had been massive, shocking and decisive. The Chinese had threatened they would attack if the Americans advanced; and they had delivered on this threat. How the American military command could discount this warning and walk a second time into the lion's mouth is incomprehensible.

Unfortunately, Eighth Army and the Far East Command were reluctant to believe the UN forces were facing organized Chinese units (see page 265). The report of the UN Command for the period October 16–31 reported the capture of Chinese prisoners but concluded "there is no positive evidence that Chinese Communist units, as such, have entered Korea."[2] Likewise, the Central Intelligence Agency, on October 26, got the results of Eighth Army's interrogation of the first Chinese prisoner captured at Unsan, but sent it forward with the lowest possible appraisal of both source and content.[3]

No one in Washington challenged the interpretation placed on the evidence in the field.[4] At last, on November 3, the Joint Chiefs asked General MacArthur for an "interim appreciation" of the situation regarding Chinese troops (Truman in his memoirs says he instigated this query).[5] MacArthur's response the next day showed he was as unaware as the Chiefs of the significance of the Chinese intervention. He confessed it was "impossible at this time to authoritatively appraise the actualities of Chinese Communist intervention in North Korea." Thereupon, MacArthur listed a wide choice of possible courses of action the Chinese *might* take—full military intervention, covert assistance, sending of volunteers, and opportunistic seizure of the extreme north in the belief that none but ROK forces would penetrate to the Yalu.[6] This response, of course, was equivalent to no appraisal at all.

Even the United Nations did not respond. On November 5, MacArthur sent a special report to the United Nations, saying that UN forces "are presently in hostile contact with Chinese Communist military units." MacArthur submitted twelve pieces of evidence of Chinese involvement. In response to a special U.S. request, the Security Council assembled on November 6 in a special session at which Ambassador Warren Austin presented MacArthur's report. The council, however, took no action and postponed discussion for two days.[7]

The inescapable conclusion must be that the leadership in Tokyo and Washington failed to heed the Chinese warning and consequently failed to halt before a great catastrophe occurred.

The evidence of extremely powerful Chinese forces blocking the UN advance was overwhelming and unequivocal. A three-division ROK corps had been shredded into small, frightened fragments. An additional ROK regiment had vanished from the order of battle, with all of its equipment and most of its men lost. An American regiment had been shattered, forced into precipitate retreat, and one of its battalions abandoned for lost. Blame has been heaped on MacArthur because he obstinately refused to credit the evidence in front of his eyes and insisted on returning to the offensive. But this same evidence was before the eyes of the Chiefs of Staff and the administration leaders in Washington. And despite a great deal of talk, they did nothing to avert the calamity. These men in Washington must share with MacArthur the responsibility for what was to happen. They were, indeed, MacArthur's superiors, and they had the power to override MacArthur's obsession with total victory.

As James F. Schnabel and Robert J. Watson say in their history of the Joint Chiefs during the Korean War, "Whatever its explanation, the ensuing three-week lull on the battlefield between what the Chinese later called their 'First Phase' and 'Second Phase' offensives provided the United States with a breathing space in which to readjust its policy and strategy to a changed situation. Through indecision, vacillation and faulty judgment this opportunity was lost."[8]

Secretary of State Acheson later said: "This government missed its last chance to halt the march to disaster in Korea. All the President's advisors in this matter, civilian and military, knew that something was badly wrong, though what it was, how to find out, and what to do about it they muffed."[9]

It was far more than a muff; it was an abdication of responsibility. When men in positions of power recognize something is badly wrong, they are obligated to call immediately for caution, not for continuation of the policy which brought on disaster. The President's advisors did not confront MacArthur, although they were to be presented shortly with evidence that MacArthur himself had radically changed his estimate of the Chinese threat: he had ordered aerial destruction of all the bridges over the Yalu river to slow reinforcements streaming into Korea. In two crucial matters—continuation of the UN offensive and bombing the Yalu bridges—the Chiefs of Staff and the administration, after initially balking, ended up by backing down and letting MacArthur have his way.

MacArthur's order to bomb the Korean ends of the Yalu bridges (as well as all factories, means of communication, cities and villages between the UN lines and the Yalu) came on November 5, only a couple of days after he had told the Joint Chiefs it was impossible to "appraise the actualities" of the Chinese intervention. Now he ordered a two-week effort by the full power of the Far East Air Force to knock the North Koreans and their Chinese allies out of the war. "Combat crews are to be flown to exhaustion if necessary," MacArthur commanded Lieutenant General George E. Stratemeyer, commander of the Far East Air Force.[10]

MacArthur did not even tell the Joint Chiefs about this highly provocative order, which could be construed by Beijing as nothing but a direct confrontation. But General Stratemeyer, recognizing the potential impact, alerted his air force superiors in the Pentagon, and defense officials got to Acheson three hours before the bombers were to lift off the fields. Acheson went to Truman, who said his main concern was the safety of the troops, but that MacArthur should justify the attack before it was made. Thus the Joint Chiefs on November 6 flashed MacArthur to cancel immediately all bombing within five miles of the Manchurian border, and to respond as quickly as possible with reasons for ordering the bridges bombed.

MacArthur's bristling response not only demonstrated beyond a shadow of a doubt that he was determined to go on with the offensive whatever the consequences, but that MacArthur himself had reached a far more ominous appraisal of the Chinese danger than he had indicated before. This latter disclosure, if nothing else previously had done so, should have raised a red flag to the Chiefs and the Truman administration and caused them to stop everything in its tracks until the dangers could be assessed. Instead, the Chiefs and the administration succumbed to the verbal bullying of MacArthur; at the precise moment when they should have exerted decisive leadership, they allowed a disastrous policy to continue on to its sad denouement.

Here was MacArthur's message to the Chiefs: "Men and material in large force are pouring across all bridges over the Yalu from Manchuria. This movement not only jeopardizes but threatens the ultimate destruction of the forces under my command. The actual movement across the river can be accomplished under cover of darkness and the distance between the river and our lines is so short that the forces can be deployed against our troops without being seriously subjected to air interdiction. The only way to stop this reinforcement of the enemy is the destruction of these bridges and the subjection of all installations in the north area supporting the enemy advance to the maximum of our air destruction. Every hour that this is postponed will be paid for dearly in American and other United Nations blood. The main crossing at Sinuiju was to be hit within the next few hours and the mission is actually already being mounted. Under the gravest protest that I can make, I am suspending this strike and carrying out your instructions. What I have ordered is entirely within the scope of the rules of war and the resolutions and directions which I have received from the United Nations and constitutes no slightest act of belligerency against Chinese territory, in spite of the outrageous international lawlessness emanating therefrom. I cannot overemphasize the disastrous effect, both physical and psychological, that will result from the restrictions which you are imposing. I trust that the matter be immediately brought to the attention of the President as I believe your instructions may well result in a calamity of major proportion for which I cannot accept the responsibility without his personal and direct understanding of the situation. Time is so essential that I request immediate reconsideration of your decision pending which complete compliance will of course be given your order."[11]

General Bradley in his autobiography says neither he nor anyone else in Washington was "prepared for the ferocity of the blast that came back from MacArthur," nor for the "complete about-face of his forces estimate of November 4," which caused a "profound shock in Washington."[12]

It was just at this time (November 6) that MacArthur issued a special bulletin full of bombast charging the communists with having "committed one of the most offensive acts of international lawlessness of historic record by moving without any notice of belligerency elements of alien communist forces across the Yalu river into North Korea." The communiqué also charged the Chinese Reds with massing a great concentration of troops within the sanctuary of Manchuria.[13] The Chinese, of course, *had* warned they would strike if the United States invaded North Korea.

The staggering news contained in MacArthur's message and his public communiqué was not that the Yalu bridges had to be bombed but that a wholly new and immensely greater danger to UN forces was now being posed by the Chinese. If Chinese troop movements actually threatened the destruction of UN forces and if the Chinese were massing troops in Manchuria, then bombing the Yalu bridges was a relatively small problem; what to do about the Chinese threat was the enormous problem. The Chinese could throw up pontoon bridges very quickly over the Yalu. In any event, the Yalu was going to freeze over soon, and the river then would become an avenue, not a barrier. After all, the French cavalry in 1794 rode into Amsterdam on the ice.[14] Bombing the bridges was not going to stop the movement of Chinese troops. The great question was what to do about the danger to UN forces. The obvious answer was not to persist in preparations for an offensive, but to make immediate plans to protect UN troops, either by digging in in place or moving back to a more defensible line.

The Chiefs, however, did not immediately address this issue; instead they dealt only with the matter consuming MacArthur: the bridges. They called Truman and read MacArthur's message to him. Truman, boxed in a corner with his field commander calling for bombing and the Joint Chiefs offering no alternative, had no choice but to approve the air offensive.[15]

MacArthur had won. The bombings got under way on November 8, but the attacks on the bridges did not have great success. The pilots had only limited approach paths because they could not violate Manchurian air space, and Chinese antiaircraft fire and jet aircraft appeared. The first all-jet battle in history was fought over the Yalu on November 8, when Lieutenant Russell Brown in a U.S. F-80 shot down a Russian-built and probably Chinese-piloted MIG-15. By December 5, when the air offensive was called off, only four of the twelve rail and highway bridges linking Korea to Manchuria had been broken.[16]

Secretary Acheson has an apologetic passage in his memoirs about the drift of events in Washington during this critical period from the first appearance of Chinese troops to MacArthur's final announcement of his "end-the-war" offensive. It summarizes the excuses that were being made along the Potomac but also, perhaps inadvertently, silhouettes the continuing failure of leadership. Here is what Acheson said:

"All the dangers from dispersal of our own forces and intervention by the Chinese were manifest. We were all deeply apprehensive. We were frank with one another, but not quite frank enough. I was unwilling to urge on the President a military course that his military advisors would not propose. They would not propose it because it ran counter to American military tradition of the proper powers of the theater commander....If General Marshall and the Chiefs had proposed withdrawal to the Pyongyang-Wonsan line and a continuous defensive position under united command across it—and if the President had backed them, as he undoubtedly would have—disaster would probably have been averted. But it would have meant a fight with MacArthur, charges by him that they had denied him victory—and his relief under arguable circumstances. So they hesitated, wavered, and the chance was lost. While everyone acted correctly, no one, I suspect, was ever quite satisfied with himself afterward."[17]

EASTFOTO

Zhou Enlai (left), Communist Chinese premier and foreign minister, stands with Chairman Mao Zedong and Lin Biao (right), one of Red China's outstanding commanders.

This battalion of The Royal Australian Regiment distinguished itself in Korea in a number of engagements. In its first fight the Aussies, using mainly rifles and bayonets, routed a North Korean regiment.

BRITISH COMMONWEALTH OCCUPATION FORCES JAPAN PHOTO

EASTFOTO

Red Chinese Premier Zhou Enlai receives Mme. Vijayalakshmi Pandit, with an Indian cultural delegation, and K.M. Panikkar, Indian ambassador to Beijing.

President Harry Truman bids goodbye at Wake Island on October 15, 1950, to General MacArthur and his political advisor, Brigadier General Courtney Whitney (right).

WIDE WORLD PHOTO

EASTFOTO

Chinese Communist infantry moving to an attack in Korea.

General George C. Marshall (left), secretary of defense after September, 1950, and Dean Acheson, secretary of state, were responsible for many of the decisions on Korea. Acheson especially failed to counter General MacArthur's plans to drive to the Yalu in face of Chinese threats to intervene if he did so.

A Chinese soldier displays knocked-out U.S. tank of 1st Cavalry Division in the early months of the Chinese intervention.

CHAPTER 40

Empty Rhetoric on the Potomac

T HOUGH THE CHINESE ATTACKS produced no change in plans at MacArthur's headquarters, they at least brought on a discussion of American policy in Washington. On November 8, the Joint Chiefs, in response to a request from the State Department, asked MacArthur for a discussion of the Korean situation, with the implication that the General should abandon his planned offensive and fall back on the defensive.[1]

But MacArthur rejected any idea of giving up his attack, though he had acknowledged in a November 7 message that "the introduction of Chinese Communist forces in strength into the Korean campaign has completely changed the overall situation."[2] In response to the Chiefs, MacArthur said:

"It would be fatal to weaken the fundamental and basic policy of the United Nations to destroy all resisting armed forces in Korea and bring that country into a united and free nation." MacArthur said he was confident U.S. air power could halt Chinese reinforcements from Manchuria and destroy those in Korea. He planned to start his offensive of November 15 and proceed to the northern borders of Korea. "Any program short of this would completely destroy the morale of my forces and its psychological consequence would be inestimable. It would condemn us to an indefinite retention of our military forces along difficult defense lines in North Korea and would unquestionably arouse such resentment among the South Koreans that their forces would collapse or might even turn against us."

An idea of setting up a buffer zone in extreme North Korea between the Chinese and the UN forces, which the British were rumored about to propose, was rejected out of hand by MacArthur as equivalent to giving the Sudetenland in Czechoslovakia to Nazi Germany in 1938. Rather, MacArthur urged, the United Nations should condemn Red China for defiance of its resolutions and should threaten military sanctions if Chinese forces were not withdrawn.

MacArthur's damn-the-torpedoes drive for unconditional surrender in war was summarized in his concluding remark: "I recommend with all the earnestness I possess that there be no weakening at this crucial moment and that we press on to complete victory which I believe can be achieved if our determination and indomitable will do not desert us."[3]

Part of MacArthur's optimism doubtless was based on his view, expressed in various ways, that U.S. air observation could spot Chinese troop movements, and, this being so, aircraft could destroy those troops. This was despite the fact that the North Koreans for months had been moving troops and equipment almost wholly at night to avoid aerial detection. It also is at odds with the position MacArthur himself took when he demanded the bombing of the Yalu bridges as the only way to stop the Chinese because they were moving over the river under cover of darkness. Nevertheless, on November 9, MacArthur informed the Joint Chiefs that U.S. air power could "deny reinforcements coming across the Yalu in sufficient strength to prevent the destruction of those forces now arrayed against me in North Korea."[4] And on November 17, he told John J. Muccio, U.S. ambassador to Korea, that the Chinese could not have infiltrated more than thirty thousand men into North Korea because any larger numbers would have required overt troop movements that would have been detected by air.[5] Yet at that moment there were more than six times that many Chinese soldiers already in Korea.[6] On November 18, MacArthur assured the Joint Chiefs that intensified air attacks over the preceding ten-day period had been successful in isolating the battle area, stopping troop reinforcements by the enemy and greatly reducing his flow of supplies.[7] It became obvious later that the Chinese Communist soldiers' skill in counteracting aerial surveillance contributed to General MacArthur's low evaluation of the Chinese threat in North Korea. However, MacArthur's own messages to the Joint Chiefs were contradictory. This inconsistency alone should have been warning enough that the real extent of the Chinese troop buildup was not being ascertained, and that UN forces were facing a threat of unknown proportions.

After mulling over MacArthur's messages, the Joint Chiefs on November 9 sent a report to Secretary of Defense Marshall in preparation for a meeting that day with the National Security Council. In this analysis, the Chiefs said the Chinese might be in Korea protecting hydroelectric power complexes along the Yalu, tying down American forces in a war of attrition, or trying to drive UN forces out of Korea entirely. The UN Command had three choices of action, the Chiefs said: to press on to the

Yalu, to hold a line short of the Yalu, or to withdraw. They did not recommend a specific course, but they implied a preference for holding positions below the Yalu "pending clarification of the military and political problems raised by Chinese intervention."[8] If firmly adhered to, it would have been a reasonable policy; but the Chiefs were not firm.

It was at the NSC meeting on November 9 that there was a chance to adopt a cautious policy, and here the abdication of responsibility in Washington was most clear; for here nothing was done. At this meeting, presided over by Acheson in the absence of Truman, there was much discussion of the Chinese intervention and of several potential U.S. courses of action, including holding a line below the Yalu. In the end, however, the NSC agreed not to change MacArthur's orders. The Far East commander was to act at his discretion, and was constrained only by the prohibition against attacking Manchuria.[9] MacArthur had been handed a virtual carte blanche. The Joint Chiefs did not protest.

In the United Nations, members likewise talked a lot but arrived at no conclusion. A resolution introduced on November 10 would have declared "the Chinese frontier with Korea inviolate," but the session ended before a vote could be taken. The Chinese meanwhile had rejected a Security Council invitation to send a representative to hear the discussion on MacArthur's report on Chinese intervention. This refusal, plus the withdrawal of Chinese forces from battle in Korea, apparently convinced most of the Security Council members that no immediate action was necessary.[10]

The Security Council also failed to act because Red China announced it had accepted a two-months-old UN invitation to attend a Russian-sponsored debate on "U.S. aggression" toward Taiwan, and members hoped they could discuss the whole Far East situation when the Chinese arrived. By the time of the debate, however, the military situation in Korea had changed profoundly; thus the Security Council forfeited whatever influence it might have had on the course of events.[11]

Sanguine feelings that a settlement could be worked out were not shared by everyone, however. The Australian prime minister on November 13 informed United States through diplomatic channels that the consequences of a Chinese-United Nations confrontation would be grave and urged the Americans to ignore the Chinese "provocation to the extent possible."[12] The Swedish ambassador to Beijing reported in mid-November that Chinese Communist movements toward Korea were on a large scale. The Burmese embassy in Beijing reported the Chinese were prepared to go to any length to aid North Korea. The Netherlands on November 17 passed on to the U.S. government information that the Chinese intervention was motivated by fear of aggression against Manchuria, and if the UN forces halted fifty miles south of the Yalu there would be no further intervention.[13] Most important of all, the Chinese Communist parties in a widely disseminated announcement on November 4 signaled to the world China's intention to use force to "support the Korean people's war against U.S. aggression" (see page 259).

But the National Security Council action of November 9 giving MacArthur a free hand precluded much attention being paid to these statements—either the Chinese Communist parties' warning, the Dutch suggestion to halt below the border, or a British proposal finally advanced around the middle of the month for UN forces to withdraw to a line across the narrow part of Korea with the territory north of the border to be administered by a UN body upon which Red China would be represented. Although Acheson thought the idea of a buffer had merit, he persuaded the British to withhold introduction of the proposal at the United Nations, partly because he wanted the Chinese to demilitarize *their* side of the border, too, and expected difficulty in getting the Chinese to agree.[14]

Meantime, Acheson and the State Department pursued the idea of a buffer with the Defense Department and set up a joint State-Defense meeting on November 21 to discuss the possibility of negotiating with the Chinese to establish a demilitarized zone on both sides of the border.[15] This State move was too little and too late. MacArthur already had informed the Joint Chiefs on November 18 that the Eighth Army offensive would get under way on November 24.[16] Moreover, on November 20, Major General Charles L. Bolté, the U.S. Army's G-3, produced a blistering report on the State proposal in which he recommended categorical rejection of the idea of a demilitarized zone and said "the establishment of such a zone prior to the attainment of the destruction of all resisting armed forces in Korea would weaken the fundamental and basic policy of the United Nations to make Korea a united and free nation."

The conference was attended by Secretaries Acheson and Marshall, the Joint Chiefs, Deputy Secretary of Defense Robert A. Lovett, and other high-ranking State officials. They came to the conclusion that General Bolté already had advanced: no change in MacArthur's authorization to advance to the Yalu. However, after discussions on the difficulty in getting the Chinese to agree to a neutral zone at the border, Deputy Secretary Lovett suggested that MacArthur—after reaching the Yalu with his troops—create a de facto demilitarized zone by unilateral action by withdrawing to a defensible position south of the river. Most of the people at the conference favored Lovett's idea, and General Collins traced a possible line ten to twenty-five miles south of the river. In indirect and diplomatic language, the Chiefs on November 24 suggested to MacArthur the general idea of such a line, and also suggested that ROK troops hold this line.

This hopeful proposal by the State and Defense officials and the Joint Chiefs seems pathetic and unrealistic in light of the actuality of United States confrontation of China in advancing to the Yalu, and in light of the enormous Chinese military buildup in Manchuria and North Korea. After all, a pullback ten to twenty-five miles from the Yalu would be less than nothing in Chinese eyes: they already had attacked UN forces fifty miles from the river.

In any event, the proposal was immediately demolished by General MacArthur.[17] The General responded to the message just after he returned to Tokyo after a visit to the Eighth Army front, where the offensive was beginning. During this visit, MacArthur flew over the Yalu in a "personal reconnaissance," and he told the Chiefs the terrain south of the river could not be easily defended, whereas the river line itself had natural defense features to be found nowhere else. Aside from the military foolishness of such a move, MacArthur said, the political results would be "fraught with most disastrous consequences," because any failure to keep going until the "public and oft-repeated" objective of destroying all enemy forces in Korea would be viewed by the Korean people as betrayal, and the Chinese and all other Asians would view a halt as weakness and appeasement of the Communist Chinese and Russians.

MacArthur also said that completing the UN mission of occupying all Korea provided "the best—indeed only—hope that Soviet and Chinese aggressive designs may be checked before these countries are committed to a course from which for political reasons they cannot withdraw."

So, there it was: MacArthur maintained the *only* way to keep the Chinese from entering the war was to advance to the Yalu. No better evidence of MacArthur's divorce from reality could be offered. After reading this message, Admiral Sherman, chief of naval operations, commented: "He seems very disdainful of our concern over the major conflict with the Chinese."[18]

But the time for the Truman administration and the Joint Chiefs to have stopped the offensive was before it began. In one way MacArthur was dead right: it made no sense to assume all of the risk of a Chinese attack, drive out all opposing troops, finally attain the international boundary, and *then* unilaterally withdraw ten or twenty-five miles. This November 21 conference and MacArthur's response to it demonstrates that both Washington and MacArthur had failed to face the realities of the Chinese threat. They were, however, to face the consequences of this failure.

CHAPTER 41

A Different Kind of Army

NEITHER THE FAR EAST COMMAND nor the authorities in Washington were willing to acknowledge it, but an immense and remarkable military force was now facing the United Nations troops. The men in this force were always called volunteers by Beijing, apparently in order to perpetuate the myth (on both sides) that the Korean War was a local dispute. In fact, they were members of regular Chinese People's Liberation Army (PLA) units, which were deployed as units in Korea. As such, the men were part of a singular military organization which developed from Chinese Communist guerrilla groups that fought the Nationalists. The PLA still retained in 1950 the informal, though effective, manners and practices inherited from its guerrilla past. These set the PLA apart from every other army in the world.

One extremely unusual thing about the Chinese forces was that they possessed no distinctive, separate officers corps, although there was a strong "cadre," or leadership group, at all military levels which served the role of an officers corps. There were no military ranks as such in the PLA below the general officer level. Commanders were called by their job titles, such as "squad leader," or "company commander." And in keeping with the army's guerrilla origin and the egalitarian theory of communism (notably practiced *only* in the Chinese army and not in other communist armies), everyone wore basically the same uniform—unlike their North Korean comrades, whose officers, following their Soviet models, sported distinctive epaulets and possessed a full panoply of military ranks. The only distinctions between officers' and ordinary soldiers' uniforms in the PLA were subtle and not very obvious differences in the cut of the tunics, and officers' uniforms sometimes carried red piping at several points (around the collar, across the cuff).[1]

Chinese winter uniforms were a heavily quilted cotton of mustard brown color (though some were dark blue), under which the men wore their summer uniforms or whatever other clothing they might have. The quilted uniforms were not very "military" looking, but they were warm, though hard to dry if they got wet. Chinese soldiers wore cloth, rubber-soled shoes (some had acquired fur-lined boots). Headgear was a heavy cotton cap with ear flaps.

Alexander L. George's study of PLA forces in Korea, based on extensive interviews of captured Chinese prisoners,[2] showed that the Chinese actively discouraged a military caste system, not only by recruiting leaders from the ranks but also by encouraging efforts of the rank and file to discuss, solve and administer various everyday problems. This is what led, among other things, to extensive precombat briefing of ordinary soldiers about the tactical situation and battle plans for the unit. The information given these largely illiterate men contributed greatly to the soldiers' sense of responsibility to work as part of the larger operation, but it disconcerted UN interrogators, who couldn't believe common soldiers could have so much precise knowledge.[3]

The Chinese units were formed around small combat groups and founded on the idea that comradeship was good for morale and that social behavior was governed by intimate face-to-face relationships. Thus rifle squads were organized on a "three-times-three" system in which three men comprised a team with each man assigned to watch (and watch out for) the other two, and with three teams making up a squad. This team system meant a team leader had only three men to control and helped to solve the problem, present in all armies, of getting the individual soldier actually to fight.[4] Because camaraderie was considered to be so important, men in divisions were drawn as much as possible from the same provinces or regions, and companies were formed of men from a single village. In a country like China, where there are many dialects and subcultures, this was important. Whenever feasible, an entire unit, when reassigned, was returned to the home province for rest and recruitment, a policy that faintly resembled the British army's regimental system. This system broke down in Korea because of intense pressures there, and unit solidarity declined when it occurred.[5]

One PLA improvement over the Nationalist Chinese army was the official ban on beatings and abuse of the men. There was a sincere effort to eliminate arbitrary treatment, discrimination and sadistic features of army discipline. The PLA attempted to avoid gross disparities of food by rank, required leaders to address men in polite language, reduced extreme forms of military courtesy, and encouraged comradeship between officers and men. Discipline and performance were promoted by an elaborate system of awards and honors for good conduct and brave actions and by "group shaming" at unit criticism meetings for bad conduct and poor combat performance.[6]

An astonishing fact about the Chinese Communist Forces (CCF) in Korea was that they defeated American troops with the heaviest firepower of any army in the world and with total command of the air—and the Chinese did it almost wholly with weapons no larger than mortars. Their rifles and machine guns were a mixed lot from many sources, including American weapons captured from the Nationalists, or World War II Japanese weapons confiscated in Manchuria at the war's end. The few artillery pieces they had, they mostly left in Manchuria. But they employed their mortars very effectively. Most of them were American, though they had acquired a few Soviet pieces, especially the highly effective Russian 120mm heavy mortar.[7] They also relied on hand grenades and, as a weapon against tanks, satchel charges of TNT explosives. Satchel charges of about five and twenty pounds each were carried by antitank sections. If laid on the tracks or under a tank, a satchel charge could disable it.

In addition to a poverty of heavy weapons, the Chinese were limited by their primitive logistical system. Some attempts were made to bring reserve stocks up to forward dumps about thirty miles behind the front, but not much could be accomplished forward of the railheads because the CCF relied for supplies on human and animal transport. One result was that they fired mortars only on the most lucrative targets, and troops normally depended upon small arms, machine guns and grenades in their attacks.[8]

Although extremely limiting in some respects, the CCF dependence upon the backs of animals and soldiers liberated them from roads and permitted troops to fight anywhere they could walk, whether in front, on the side, or behind the UN lines. United Nations forces, on the other hand, were tied to the roads because their supplies arrived by truck on these roads, which thus were vulnerable to being cut by roadblocks. There is a curious parallel between these Chinese Communist armies and the revolutionary armies exploited a century and a half before by Napoleon Bonaparte. Like Napoleon, the Chinese cut themselves free from supply bases in their rear (called magazines in Napoleon's time). The result: Napoleon and the Chinese Communist forces achieved great local mobility and could practice audacious tactics, while their enemies, still tied to supply bases, were locked into protecting their lines of supply. As an example, the Chinese Communists expected each soldier to carry on his back the food he required for a long period, perhaps six days or longer. This food generally was in concentrated form, like cooked rice, soybean curds and the like. In similar manner, Napoleon in the Marengo campaign of 1800 sent his troops across the Alps into Italy with no food but hard biscuits, a compact, durable nutriment that needed no cooking.[9]

The Chinese were extremely disciplined in fire fights, especially in night fighting. They were so good at camouflage that UN aircraft seldom could find them. They generally marched at night, averaging extremely high march rates (eighteen miles a day for eighteen days in the case of one CCF force). During the day, every man, animal and piece of equipment was concealed and camouflaged, and during the daylight only scouting parties generally moved, unless troops were engaged in combat. When CCF outfits were compelled to march by day, they were under standing orders, if an aircraft appeared overhead, for every man to stop in his tracks and stand motionless. Officers were authorized to shoot down any man who violated this order.[10]

Chinese tactics were similar to North Korean tactics, and they were pursued with vigor and determination. Their general method of attack was to get a force to the rear of enemy positions and to cut off escape routes and supply roads, and then to send in both frontal and flank attacks to bring the enemy to grips. They also employed a related defensive tactic ("hachi shiki") in which they allowed an attacking enemy force to move forward in a V-formation whose sides they closed and then sent a force behind the mouth of the V to halt any troops coming to relieve the trapped unit.[11]

The Chinese Communists had learned their military lessons in battles against the materially superior Nationalist Chinese, and they had developed a pattern of attack which was effective against an enemy with better arms and equipment. Night attacks were the rule, and any deviation from them was a surprise. The advancing units generally followed the easiest and most accessible terrain in making their approaches: valleys or draws or stream beds. As soon as they met resistance, they deployed against this resistance, peeling off selected small units of the main column to engage the opposition. However, if they met no opposition, the whole column often moved in the darkness right past defensive emplacements deep into the rear of UN positions. There are many examples of this. In some cases entire CCF regiments marched in column formation into the UN rear in this manner. Once engaged, CCF units closed on small troop positions, usually platoons, with grenades, rifles and submachine guns (the old American Thompson was their favorite, though they also used the cruder Russian burp gun extensively).[12]

Once fired upon, attacking CCF troops hit the ground, but rose during any lull and advanced again. Once fully committed, they seldom halted their attack even when suffering heavy casualties. Other Chinese came forward to take the place of those killed or wounded, and the buildup continued, often on several sides of the position, until a penetration was made—either by destroying the position or forcing the defenders to withdraw. After consolidating the newly won position, the CCF troops then crept forward against the open flank of the next platoon position. This combination of stealth and boldness, executed in darkness against small units, could result in several penetrations of a battalion front and could be devastating.

Occasionally the Chinese used mortars to inflict casualties and, by watching closely for movement in removing these casualties, to locate the front line of a UN position. After establishing what they believed to be the front, the CCF dropped white phosphorous mortar rounds on the lines as markers, while assault troops crawled as close as possible and, in skirmish formation, rushed the front line.

The Chinese doctrine was based on cutting the defending force into small fractions and attacking these fractions with local superiority in numbers. Thus the ambush was the favorite CCF method of fighting, and this ambush technique was employed whether the attack was directly to the front, by means of infiltration or movement to the flanks, or by setting up roadblocks to the rear of UN positions. Attacking forces as a rule ranged in size from a platoon to a company (50 to 200 men) and were built up continually as casualties occurred.

The best defense for American troops against the Chinese tactics was somehow to maintain their positions until daybreak. Then, with visibility restored, the Chinese attacks ceased, and the American superiority in weapons and dominance in the air usually could restore the situation by blasting known CCF positions.[13] However, Chinese night attacks were so effective that this counsel often went unheeded, and UN troops retreated from enemy troops attacking from all sides or their positions were simply overrun or destroyed.

The Chinese had some tactical problems, however. Perhaps the worst was the rigidity that developed from their poverty of communications equipment. Since their radio nets went down only to regiments and telephones only to battalions, the CCF below battalion level generally had to rely on runners, bugles, whistles, flares or flashlights for signaling. The resulting tactical inflexibility sometimes was fatal. Commanders below the battalion level apparently had few or no options, and a battalion once committed to an attack sometimes kept it up as long as the ammunition lasted, even though it might be futile and could result in tactical suicide.

On October 6, 1950, the Chinese Communist party's Politburo held an emergency session and decided to send "volunteers" to Korea, although no one actually volunteered but was sent in regular Peoples Liberation Army units in Red Chinese uniforms. Nevertheless, being called volunteers, they preserved the fiction that the war was limited to the Korean peninsula, thereby not challenging the U.S. directly. The Politburo also adopted a new slogan, "Resist U.S. aggression, aid Korea."[14]

Two days later the Communist central committee and Mao Zedong appointed General Peng Dehuai as commander of the "volunteers." Peng was a famous soldier, whose service reached almost to the foundation of the Red army in the late 1920s. He began assembling twelve PLA advance divisions along the Yalu. On October 11 he returned to Beijing to meet with North Korean representatives. While there, Peng, Mao and other Politburo members became alarmed at the speed of the American advance and decided to send forces into North Korea immediately. On the night of October 18 the movement commenced.[15] Following their practice of marching by night and hiding by day, the Chinese forces moved in the west to blocking positions on the southern faces of the high mountain mass fifty air miles south of the Yalu and a few miles north of the Chongchon, and on the east to positions below the Changjin (Chosin) reservoir.

The Chinese forces were organized in armies, generally composed of three 10,000-man divisions, thus approximately equaling an American corps in size.[16] The 30,000-man armies were attached to army groups generally having four armies in an army group, and several army groups made up a field army. Elements of the fourth field army, the best combat force of Red China were those first committed in the Korean War.[17] The Fourth Field Army was composed of five army groups and sixty divisions, or about 600,000 men in all. Parts of this field army had participated in the capture of the southern Chinese island of Hainan in the spring of 1950, but the army had concentrated in the summer of 1950 back in its permanent home in Manchuria. Likewise, late in the summer and in the early fall the Third Field Army moved into Manchuria. By mid-October the PLA had massed 400,000 in both field armies close to the Korean border.

As Eighth Army moved across the Chongchon river on October 25, three Chinese armies, the 39th, 40th and 38th, each of three infantry divisions were deployed from the west to the east—the 39th above Unsan, the 40th around Onjong, and the 38th northwest of Huichon. Two additional armies, the 66th and the 50th, also of three divisions each, lay hidden in reserve in the mountains and were not committed during the First Phase offensive.

On the X Corps front, one Chinese army, the 42nd, was deployed south of the Changjin reservoir, but only one of the 42nd Army's three divisions (the 124th) engaged ROK or marine troops in the first phase, the other two divisions (the 125th and 126th) being emplaced farther north.[18] However, elements of the 125th CCF Division apparently engaged and virtually destroyed the 7th Regiment of the ROK 6th Division after it had been cut off in its attempt to reach the Yalu at Chosan (see page 267).[19]

Thus, on the Eighth Army front, fifteen CCF divisions with 150,000 men were arrayed, though only about 90,000 were committed in the first phase. On the X Corps front, three CCF divisions, with 30,000 men, were arrayed, though only about 10,000 men were committed at first. This gave a total of 180,000 CCF troops in Korea when MacArthur on October 24 gave the order for a full-scale drive of all forces to the Yalu.[20]

By use of a code the Chinese were successful for a while in disguising the identity and size of the forces they had committed to Korea. Most captured Chinese soldiers at first identified themselves as being from the 54th, 55th, 56th, 57th and 58th Units. When questioned further, they indicated they were with, say, the 1st Battalion of the 55th Unit. For a while, UN interrogators believed them and thought the units were token Chinese groups sent into Korea. In fact, the units identified Chinese armies. For example, the 55th Unit was the 39th Army and the 56th was the 40th Army. The 1st Battalion, 55th Unit, designated the 115th Division, 39th Army. The Chinese soldiers were rather quick to give the game away under questioning, but the interrogators were reluctant to abandon the fiction that these actually were token units. This contributed to the low estimates of Chinese troops deployed in Korea. By November 1 Eighth Army G-2 had changed its view and declared the units were regimental-sized; and by November 4 and 5 it had raised them to division-sized, still only a third their actual size.[21]

In its battles with the Nationalists the CCF never had faced the enormous firepower exhibited by UN forces, especially in the form of artillery and aircraft. This concentration of fire was not only unparalleled in CCF experience, but it forced the Chinese to develop alternatives quickly (night marches, resupply only at night), and caused heavy constraints on troop mobility and great psychological effects.[22]

This appreciation of American power was expressed graphically in a pamphlet, "Primary Conclusions of Battle Experience of Unsan," produced November 20 by the 66th CCF Army after the fight with the 8th Cavalry Regiment.[23] The conclusions were complimentary to American firepower, citing the coordination of U.S. mortars and tanks, activity of artillery, the great hazard to Chinese transportation of aircraft strafing and bombing, the excellence of U.S. transportation, and the heavy infantry rate of fire, especially at long range.

The conclusions were less complimentary to American infantrymen themselves. When cut off from the rear, the pamphlet says, American soldiers "abandon all their heavy weapons, leaving them all over the place, and play opossum....Their infantrymen are weak, afraid to die, and haven't the courage to attack or defend. They depend on their planes, tanks and artillery. At the same time, they are afraid of our firepower. They will cringe when, if on the advance, they hear firing. They are afraid to advance farther....They specialize in day fighting. They are not familiar with night fighting or hand-to-hand combat....If defeated, they have no orderly formation. Without the use of their mortars, they become completely lost....At Unsan they were surrounded for several days, yet they did nothing. They are afraid when their rear is cut off. When transportation comes to a standstill, the infantry loses the will to fight."

The judgment the Chinese came to in dealing with Americans was that a Chinese unit had to fight its way rapidly around the Americans into their rear, that attack routes should avoid roads and flat terrain in order to keep away from U.S. tanks and artillery, and that night warfare in mountains required the Chinese to have a definite plan, with liaison between platoons, and with small leading patrols attacking, then sounding the bugle so larger Chinese forces could move up in column to attack.

CHAPTER 42

Attack into the Unknown

W HILE U.S. LEADERS in Washington and Tokyo talked, the American and other soldiers in Korea prepared for the test that lay ahead. Eighth Army, held up by supply difficulties, got MacArthur's authorization to postpone the offensive date from November 15 to November 24. In the X Corps area, however, the advance continued, slowly by the marines, fast by the ROKs and the 7th Infantry Division whose troops faced largely North Koreans.[1]

From the beginning of the X Corps operations in the northeast, General Smith, the 1st Marine Division commander, had been unhappy with the dispersal of his division, spread out in various assignments along the east coast. On November 7 he asked General Almond to allow the division's consolidation. The experience of the marines with the Chinese south of the Changjin reservoir (see page 286) apparently caused Almond to agree.[2]

After the leading marine elements on November 10 reached the Koto-ri plateau, eleven miles below the southern end of the reservoir, General Smith showed no inclination to hurry the advance. (See Map 9.) He was concerned because his task was to advance to the reservoir and from there to drive on to the Yalu—and his forces were not going to be supported by troops on either side. Smith was worried about his exposed western flank, the high, almost trackless extension of the Taebaek mountains that separated X Corps from Eighth Army on the west. He also wanted to improve the atrocious crooked road up the high mountain pass from the division railhead at Chinhung-ni, and he wanted to develop a secure base at Hagaru-ri, at the south end of the reservoir. But most of all, Smith wanted to concentrate his division in the Hagaru-ri area before attempting to advance farther toward the Yalu. As he said, he didn't like the idea of stringing his division along "a single mountain road for 120 air miles from Hamhung to the Yalu." Therefore, Smith deliberately stalled his division's advance.[3]

The day the marines reached the 4,000-foot-high Koto-ri plateau, bitter weather struck the high uplands of North Korea with temperatures below zero degree Fahrenheit. From that day onward, the men in the northeast were to be involved in a winter campaign that placed immense stress on men and equipment. Marine patrols sent out from Koto-ri on November 11 and 12 found only small, scattered enemy groups in the hills, and on November 14 the 7th Marine Regiment, now wearing arctic parkas, walked in subzero weather through snow toward Hagaru-ri, eleven miles beyond. When they reached the village, burned out by previous U.S. air attacks, it was practially deserted. On General Almond's urging, two days after the marines entered Hagaru-ri, General Smith and Major General Field Harris, commander of the 1st Marine Air Wing, selected a site there for an airstrip to bring in supplies and evacuate casualties. It was a wise move. Engineers got to work on the airstrip on November 19, and other engineers improved the road through the pass from Chinhung-ni. Smith held up the marine advance at Hagaru-ri while this work continued.

Meanwhile, ROK troops, with U.S. air and naval support, moved along the east coast against persistent North Korean defenses, getting close to Chongjin, the last major city before the Siberian border. The army 7th Division, which had landed at Iwon, pushed north toward the Yalu, in an area the Chinese Communists had not occupied. But North Koreans did contest the 7th Division advance, beginning at Pungsan, about halfway from the coast to the Yalu. An engagement there on November 2 and 3 ended with the withdrawal of the NK force. While the 17th Regiment of the division continued northward, the 31st Regiment advanced westward toward the Pujon (Fusen) reservoir, and on November 8 encountered Chinese troops on Paek-san, a 7,700-foot peak twelve miles east of the Pujon reservoir; after an inconclusive engagement, the Chinese withdrew and the U.S. patrols continued westward.[4]

On November 19 against some NK opposition, the 17th Regiment seized Kapsan, about twenty-one air miles from the Yalu at Hyesanjin, and drove on about eight miles north of Kapsan. The next day the regiment, in a column of battalions, advanced on foot nineteen miles through and over the mountains to a point only a few miles from the Yalu. NK opposition was fleeting and light. On the morning of November 21, the regiment entered Hyesanjin without a shot being fired. There, in a village mostly destroyed by previous air attacks, American soldiers at last stood on the banks of the Yalu and looked over at the bleak Manchurian hills beyond. Cold as it was, there was something of a celebration. General Almond and the 7th Division commander, Major General David D. Barr, accompanied the 17th Regiment into the village, and it was an occasion for everyone to congratulate one another and speculate on the imminent end of the war.

The day after the 17th Regiment reached Hyesanjin, the 7th Division's 32nd Regiment, having arrived at Kapsan, dispatched a small task force northwest with the mission of reaching the Yalu at Singalpajin, about twenty air miles west and downstream from Hyesanjin. This detachment was commanded by a determined second lieutenant, Robert C. Kingston, twenty-two years old, who drove his small force against persistent North Korean delaying forces until November 29 when he reached Singalpajin. Kingston's small group and the 17th Regiment were the only American troops to reach the Yalu.[5]

* * * * * * * *

While UN troops continued to move in northeastern Korea against generally light NK resistance and while Eighth Army built up supply depots and men along the Chongchon river in the west, the Chinese Communist Forces were concentrating large forces in the mountains south of the Yalu. The first real tip-off on what was occurring came on November 23, when marines captured two Chinese deserters seven miles west of Hagaru-ri. These Chinese soldiers said they had crossed the Yalu ten days earlier and were members of the 89th CCF Division. This was startling news, because, if true, it indicated they were members of a new CCF army, the 20th, and of a new Field Army, the Third, which in the summer had been in the Shanghai area.[6] On November 13, ROK troops on the eastern flank of the Eighth Army positions had captured Chinese prisoners who said they were from the 42nd CCF Army. This army, whose troops had engaged the marines south of the Changjin reservoir, was sideslipping westward to join other elements of the Fourth Field Army.[7]

Taken together, the evidence provided by these prisoners indicated the elements of the CCF Fourth Field Army were consolidating on the western side of the high mountain spine of Korea to oppose Eighth Army, while an entirely new force, parts of the CCF Third Field Army under Chen Yi were gathering east of the mountains to oppose X Corps.[8] Although UN intelligence officers understandably were unable to detect this shift fully at the time, the Fourth Field Army concentrated eighteen divisions, or 180,000 men, in the west, while a reinforced twelve-division army group (the IX) of the CCF Third Field Army, with 120,000 men, assembled in the east.[9]

Against these 300,000 Chinese troops and an imprecisely known number of North Koreans, the UN Command had assembled seven American divisions, six ROK divisions, two British Commonwealth brigades, a Turkish brigade, as well as battalions from the Philippines and Thailand and a British commando company.[10] Altogether the UN Command had the equivalent of fourteen divisions. However, these divisions averaged substantially more men than the CCF divisions, and thus the disparity in numbers was not as great as may have appeared. U.S. army and marine divisions had about 124,000 men (including some 18,000 ROKs), the ROK divisions had about 82,000 men, and other UN troops totaled about 12,000 men. There were also about 29,000 men in U.S. Army separate combat units, mostly tank and artillery detachments. UN combat forces, therefore, totaled about 247,000 men, not counting air combat personnel.[11]

The UN forces, especially American, had much higher firepower than the CCF forces, notably in artillery and tanks. They had, in addition, complete command of the air and high mobility because of great numbers of vehicles. The Chinese had little artillery and were stronger in infantry. In light of the relative strengths of the two sides, it is surprising at first glance that the Chinese, who generally walked into battle, were able to achieve such devastating success against a highly mobile army with extremely heavy firepower. The primary reason was that Chinese tactics of night infiltration, attack to the front, envelopment to the sides and roadblocks to the rear were stunning in their effect and time and after disarrayed or routed UN forces. The original Chinese appraisal of U.S. troops after the first battle with Americans at Unsan (see page 305) was borne out: when cut off from the rear, Americans tended to become disorganized, and they relied upon their transportation, planes, tanks and artillery.

In the matter of supply the differences between the Americans and the Chinese were extreme and illustrative. Americans mostly depended upon their numerous trucks to bring up supplies to forward areas. When these failed because of bad or blocked roads, they called for air supply, either drops by parachute or ferrying of supplies to forward airfields. Air supply was costly and subject to the vagaries of ill-aimed drops and bad weather. However, the general abundance of supply permitted Americans to be wasteful in their expenditure of ammunition, a habit which was disastrous when CCF roadblocks cut off trucks and air supply was not feasible.

The Chinese had to rely largely on human or animal transport to move up supplies to forward areas.[12] The ubiquitous A-frame wooden racks which Koreans and Chinese used to haul loads on their backs was a common mode of carriage. The Chinese, therefore, got much less resupply than the Americans, but what they did get was not dependent upon the roads. As a consequence, the Chinese could move through the mountains on steep tracks and through roadless valleys and emerge behind UN forces to set up roadblocks and cut off or envelop forward troops. Americans, largely tied to their main supply routes (MSRs), were thus especially vulnerable to the semiguerrilla tactics of the Chinese forces. Where Americans could establish a line that could not be flanked and where their supplies were assured from the rear, they were practically invincible: here their artillery, air-strike capability and infantry firepower were without peer. But Chinese doctrine did not call for fighting slugging matches with the Americans, because they would lose. Although there were many stories about the Chinese using "hordes of troops" in "human-wave tactics" to storm UN positions, it was not mass attack but deception, surprise and stealthy infiltration at night which made the Chinese formidable. The Chinese did use "human waves" with platoons and companies to overrun well-chosen tactical positions in order to make critical penetrations, but these were usually to hold defending troops in place while other Chinese units flanked the enemy positions and set up roadblocks in the rear. The official U.S. Marine Corps history of the war cited the derisive comment of one marine: "How many hordes are there in a Chinese platoon?"[13]

CHAPTER 43

The "Home-by-Christmas" Offensive

THE "HOME-BY-CHRISTMAS" UN offensive jumped off in the west along the Chongchon river on the morning of November 24. The offensive got its ironical name during MacArthur's visit to the front just prior to its start when he flew over the Yalu river. During this trip he made a casual remark to reporters that he hoped to have the troops "home by Christmas."[1] It was an unfortunate comment and totally unrealistic, and reporters doubtless knew it. But it was news and the name naturally stuck.

On the far western flank, the 24th Infantry Division, ROK 1st Division, and the 27th British Commonwealth Brigade made up I Corps; in the center the 25th and 2nd Divisions and the newly arrived 5,200-man Turkish Brigade formed IX Corps; on the east the the ROK II Corps (6th, 7th and 8th Divisions) constituted the right wing. The 1st Cavalry Division was in reserve.[2] (See Map 9.)

Everything went well at first. The 24th Division, on the extreme left, advanced about four miles in the first couple of hours, and, by the end of November 25, had passed Napchongjong and was within a mile of Chongju. In this section, Americans encountered only poorly organized North Korean troops. The ROK 1st Division was less successful. It was driven back by a counterattack southeast of Taechon.

The first real blow fell on the ROK 8th Division, on the extreme right. Fully aware that the ROKs were the weakest link in the Eighth Army chain, Chinese forces attacked this division on the night of November 25–26 in the vicinity of Tokchon, a town located in the high mountains about twenty-five miles east of the main U.S. positions along the Chongchon river. Strategically, this was a flanking move against the entire UN position on the Chongchon, and it achieved instant and total success. The Chinese, using their standard tactics of infiltration, envelopment and roadblocks in the rear, were soon moving at will throughout the ROK sector. By November 26 and 27, CCF troops from this now-open eastern flank had penetrated into the IX Corps rear as far back as supporting artillery units, and were threatening to unhinge the entire Eighth Army line.[3]

Shortly thereafter on the X Corps front the same thing was happening: on November 27, when the eastern offensive began, the 5th and 7th Marine Regiments, which had moved northwestward from the southern end of the Changjin reservoir at Hagaru-ri to Yudam-ni, attacked westward with the aim of severing the Chinese-North Korean supply route. During the night, Chinese troops cut the marine line of retreat and also slipped all around them. By the following day, the attacking marines had become besieged.[4] At the same time, three battalions of the 7th Infantry Division, which had advanced northeast from Hagaru-ri up the eastern shore of Changjin reservoir, also were attacked on all sides.[5]

On the Eighth Army front along the Chongchon, Chinese troops on the night of November 25–26 attacked the 25th and 2nd Divisions. The 25th Division, on and across the Chongchon, was able to withdraw across the river and thus miss the heaviest of the CCF blows, though it was hard-pressed and suffered substantial losses. The 2nd Division, on the right, was not so lucky: it caught the full tide of the Chinese attack.

The 2nd Division's positions were centered a few miles northeast of the town of Kujang-dong on the Chongchon, about fifteen air miles northeast of Kunu-ri. The division's 9th Regiment was on the left and the 38th Regiment on the right, with the 23rd Regiment in reserve north of Kunu-ri. CCF troops hit the 9th Regiment on front, flanks and rear, and the regiment staggered under the blows. The division commander, Major General Laurence B. Keiser, on November 26 committed two battalions of the 23rd Regiment on the 9th's right and threw the 2nd Engineer Combat Battalion into the line on the left to keep the division front intact. The division now was in extreme danger. The collapse of the ROKs on the right flank and the movement of the Chinese to the right rear eliminated any possibility of retreat by way of Tokchon, now occupied by the CCF. There were no north-south roads leading away from the river in this area. This left only one line of withdrawal open to the division: southwest along the river valley from Kujang-dong to Kunu-ri. From Kunu-ri there were two routes: a tiny road winding through mountains, then along the course of the Taedong river to Sunchon, eighteen air miles south, and a road continuing on the Chongchon valley to Anju and Sinanju, where other roads led south.

Most of Eighth Army's forces still along the Chongchon were in position to use the routes leading south from Anju and Sinanju. But for the 2nd Division, it was imperative that it be able to withdraw at least to Kunu-ri—and this meant the road from Kujang-dong had to be kept open. If this road were cut, the entire 2nd Division would be blocked above it.

The Chinese attacked 2nd Division positions on the night of November 26–27 with the same persistence and ferocity as the night before. They overran the command post of the 23rd Regiment, but troops rallied and retook it. Several division units held their ground until they were overrun or the defenders had run out of ammunition. CCF troops infiltrated through and around the right flank of the 38th Regiment, forcing it to pull back rapidly to the southwest and change front to block the Chinese now coming from the east.

By the daylight of November 27, with the right flank of 2nd Division in danger of collapse, the commander of IX Corps, Major General John B. Coulter, committed the Turkish Brigade to drive east on the Kunu-ri–Tokchon road in hopes of slowing the Chinese advance. The Turks, located near Kunu-ri, moved off immediately. But they had gone only eight miles east of Kunu-ri before they clashed in a fierce and bloody battle with the Chinese troops. The Chinese quickly surrounded the Turkish Brigade, and it appeared the entire force might be lost.

With Chinese troops within eight miles of Kunu-ri, and thus behind 2nd Division, it became clear the division had to get out of its cul-de-sac immediately or it would be destroyed. General Walker already had ordered his army reserve, the 1st Cavalry Division, to move to the collapsed eastern flank to prevent the Chinese from cutting in behind Eighth Army and severing all the main routes of withdrawal to the south. First Cavalry moved resolutely to the vicinity of Sunchon and stemmed the Chinese flood. Walker also detached the 27th British Brigade from I Corps and sent it east to help.

Walker directed the withdrawal of the entire Eighth Army on November 28, and all units but the 2nd Division and the Turkish Brigade were in position to comply quickly. During the day, however, the Turks broke out of their encirclement and pulled back toward Kunu-ri; they had suffered severely in the battle, but they had held their key positions: unless the Turks blocked this route, Chinese troops could drive through to Kunu-ri and seal off the 2nd Division's retreat from the northeast.

Second Division's 23rd Regiment, along with 2nd Battalion of the 9th and the 72nd Tank Battalion, set up positions at Kujang-dong to keep CCF forces from rolling up the division down the Chongchon valley. The 38th Regiment, however, was still above Kujang-dong, and it withdrew under heavy Chinese pressure through Kujang-dong while the blocking force held open the road junction. Meanwhile, the remainder of the 9th Regiment withdrew down the Chongchon valley road to Won-ni, five miles northeast of Kunu-ri, to cover the withdrawal. The 9th set up defensive positions facing northeast, its left flank secured by the river. Virtually every vehicle of the 2nd Division, except those belonging to the holding forces, now moved down the valley road to Kunu-ri. Traffic on this narrow, dirt route became extremely congested and slowed at times to a crawl. But the delaying force at Kujang-dong held resolutely and prevented the closely pressing Chinese from slipping around it and blocking the road. As the 2nd Division vehicles finally moved south, the blocking force backed down the road to the 9th Regiment's holding position at Won-ni, and went into a line to the right of the 9th, along with remnants of ROK forces that had fled the ROK II Corps debacle. The 38th Regiment had moved into the mountains southeast of Won-ni to link up with remnants of the Turkish Brigade, which were still holding the CCF on the Tokchon-Kunu-ri road. Unfortunately, the Chinese reached the assigned defensive positions of the 38th Regiment *before* the Americans got there. The 38th had to take up alternative positions, but it still was able to touch the Turks.

On November 29, the 2nd Division was holding precariously at Won-ni, under heavy attack, while division headquarters was making urgent preparations to displace the division to Kunu-ri and from there to retreat down the narrow lane of a road to Sunchon. During the morning, the division headquarters got shocking news: a Chinese roadblock had been set up about ten miles south of Kunu-ri on this lifeline.

General Keiser immediately dispatched the 2nd Reconnaissance Company to eliminate this block. The company tried, but failed, and division then sent Company C of the 38th Regiment. The combined efforts of both companies were fruitless, and division asked IX Corps to send a force from the south to crack open the roadblock. IX Corps dispatched a battalion of the 27th Brigade, but it could not immediately reach the block. Shortly after nightfall, General Keiser directed the 9th Regiment to attack south astride the Kunu-ri–Sunchon road at 7:30 a.m. the next day. The 9th Regiment CO, Colonel Charles C. Sloane, Jr., pulled together his pitifully reduced regiment, now down to four hundred men, less than an eighth its normal strength, and made preparations for the attack. Meanwhile, the remainder of the division withdrew to the high ground south of Kunu-ri.

By now, all of the Eighth Army units except 2nd Division and the attached remnants of the Turkish Brigade had successfully withdrawn except for rear-guard units, and the 1st Cavalry Division was holding Sunchon open for 2nd Division to come through. The big question now was whether the Kunu-ri–Sunchon road could be reopened. If not, the only route left was to continue fourteen air miles on down the Chongchon valley to Anju, where the 5th RCT was holding a blocking position, and from there to turn south. Either route had its perils. The Kunu-ri–Sunchon road was much shorter and only relatively few Chinese troops were thought to have been able to infiltrate through to set up the roadblock. The road to Anju ran just on the southern side of the Chongchon river and Chinese troops could be expected to begin encircling a retreating column and cutting it into pieces with roadblocks.

The decision was complicated by conflicting reports coming back from the 9th Regiment: it was making slow progress against fanatical Chinese resistance, and the estimated strength of the roadblock rose with each report. Nevertheless, a decision had to be made, and division decided on the Kunu-ri–Sunchon road. Headquarters decided to begin withdrawal at noon and ordered all units except the 23rd Regiment to assemble at the division CP, located six miles south of Kunu-ri on the Sunchon road. The 23rd Regiment and the Engineer Battalion were designated the rear guard. The 23rd was to remain in its position near Kunu-ri until the rest of the division made its getaway, while the Engineer Battalion was to hold the high ground immediately south and southwest of the division CP to shield the division column as it moved through.

Division units and attached outfits assembled on order while division headquarters received increasingly desperate reports. The 23rd Regiment guarding the rear said pressure was increasing on the front and flanks. The 9th Regiment, assaulting the Chinese blocking the Sunchon road, reported the enemy was still firmly astride the exit route. Intense sniper fire from all directions began to fall into the division CP area. The 2nd Division War Diary described the situation as follows: "By 1300, the remaining known alternatives were limited to either fighting south to break the roadblock or to button up in the vicinity of the division command post for a futile last-ditch stand. The decision was made to fight out to the south and at 1330 the column moved out."

The leading elements of the division column had traveled about three-fourths of a mile south when heavy CCF fire rained down from both sides of the road. Vehicles were bumper to bumper and the pace was slow and intermittent. The roadblock obviously had not been broken. And as the men soon discovered, it stretched for seven miles: it was not a roadblock at all, it was an avenue of death and mayhem. Whenever firing would commence from the hidden CCF soldiers on the sides, the men in and on the vehicles would hit the ditches and their abandoned vehicles would stall the column. The men of the 17th Field Artillery Battalion, an eight-inch howitzer unit attached to the division, reported a twin-40mm

AAA halftrack came up and started spraying the roadsides with fire. but they reported the biggest reason the column was somehow able to run this bloody corridor was that U.S. aircraft ranged constantly up and down the road, shepherding the column and savaging anything on the sides of the road that looked suspicious. When the aircraft were on their runs, the Chinese mortars and guns fell silent. But as soon as the nose of an attacking plan turned up after a strafing run, the Chinese gunners opened fire again. Thus progress came in short spurts followed by halts caused by CCF fire or a blocked road caused by burning or disabled vehicles. These vehicles had to be bypassed or pushed aside. Vehicles soon became loaded with wounded. The dead were of necessity left strewn along the sides of the road.

Instead of the troops seeing an overall picture of what happened to the column, individuals and small groups experienced a series of vignettes. In this gauntlet of panic, death and destruction only what individual soldiers witnessed and participated in had any reality or validity. As an example, some of the men of the 17th Artillery remembered vividly that a jeep carrying a military police lieutenant attempted to pass their vehicles on the road. A sniper hit the driver and killed him instantly, and the lieutenant, badly shocked, was placed by members of the battalion atop a jeep trailer. Other soldiers noticed that ROK and Turkish soldiers joined the column from the left (eastern) flank, and climbed up on vehicles. After a while, a howitzer turned over and eight ROKs riding on the piece were crushed to death.

As the column moved on south and night fell, Chinese troops closed in on the rear of the column using bayonets, small arms, grenades and mortars. The Engineer Battalion continued to hold two critical hills southwest of the old division CP until well after darkness; not a man escaped from the northernmost of the two hills. The hopelessness of getting all the heavy equipment out became apparent, and some small groups began to abandon vehicles and heavy weapons on the road and move across-country.

About 8:15 p.m. the head of the 17th Artillery column, driving through the darkness with no lights except blackout lamps, reached a stream where the bridge had been blown. A bypass across a ford had a good approach from the north, but a steep approach over terraced rice paddies on the south. There three vehicles had been stuck and had restricted passage. The first 17th Artillery tractor through uncoupled in order to pull out the stuck trucks. As this was taking place, two U.S. tanks drove up from the south with their lights on and illuminated the 17th Artillery men working at the bypass. At once Chinese 60mm mortars, machine guns and individual snipers opened up on the bypass. About five mortar rounds landed in the area. A Chinese sniper was standing in the road only thirty feet from Captain Roland D. Judd, executive officer of Battery A, and was aiming his rifle at him when a cannoneer shot him down. The tanks quickly shut off their lights and fired their cannons and machine guns in the general direction of enemy fire, and the 17th Artillery at last was able to go through the bypass. That was the end of the Chinese firing. By 9:30 p.m. the battalion had cleared the last blockade. "I never felt so relieved in my life when I looked at the head of the column and saw the lights come on," said First Sergeant Jack E. Williams of Battery A.

The division moved into Sunchon with wounded on top of trailers, on howitzers, and on fenders. An estimated 400 dead UN troops had been counted along the sides of the road in the seven-mile gauntlet, and many more men had been wounded and carried along.

While the majority of the division moved south through the Chinese roadblocks, the 23rd Regiment held off Chinese troops near Kunu-ri. When the regiment got the order to withdraw, the CO, Colonel Paul L. Freeman, Jr., told his tanks and artillery to fire off their reserves of ammunition while the other troops got a motorized column together to move out fast. The tankers and gunners quickly fired off more than three thousand rounds during a twenty-two-minute concentration.

This terrific volume of fire led the Chinese to believe the regiment was about to counterattack. They started to dig in, and when the regiment moved out the Chinese made no effort to come after them. Colonel Freeman realized there was no hope of going through the Sunchon road. Therefore, he led the regiment out by way of Anju, where it cleared the 5th RCT blocking position and had a safe road back.

The 2nd Division had got through, but at heavy cost. When it assembled south of Sunchon it had lost five thousand men and was exhausted and combat ineffective. Eighth Army withdrew the division entirely and sent it to the Seoul vicinity to rest and rebuild with replacements and new equipment.[6]

* * * * * * * *

General Walker thrust the newly arrived British 29th Independent Brigade into defensive positions north of Pyongyang in an attempt to form a defensive line along the east-west road from Pyongyang to Wonsan across the narrow waist of Korea. But the Chinese cut this road at Songchon, about twenty-five miles northeast of Pyongyang while UN forces were still north of the city. Walker, therefore, ordered the evacuation of the North Korean capital, now burning from numerous fires, and left the 29th Brigade as the rear guard. This brigade consisted of battalions of the Gloucestershire Regiment, Royal Ulster Rifles and Royal Northumberland Fusiliers, along with tanks of the 8th Hussars and a detachment of Royal Artillery.[7] Joining in the covering force were the 27th British Brigade and the 25th Division and ROK 1st Division.[8]

Within a week after the CCF counteroffensive started Eighth Army had backtracked more than fifty miles from the Chongchon, virtually broken contact with the Chinese force, and kept going. The Chinese were unable to maintain the pace of Eighth Army's retreat. They could only advance as fast as they could walk over the snow-covered mountains and the ice-bound rivers. The UN forces, however, had motor transports, and they could retreat at speed. Following them were hundreds of thousands of Korean refugees.

By the middle of December, Eighth Army was nervously in place below the 38th parallel and along the frozen Imjin river south of Kaesong on the west. The debacle had ended at last. The army was awaiting the next CCF offensive. The initiative had passed over entirely to the Chinese. It had been the longest retreat in American history. Eighth Army had withdrawn precipitously more than 120 air miles (and many more miles by road) from the Chongchon to the Imjin. Most of the way it had fled of its own volition, not to escape enemy pressure. The Chinese had merely followed on foot, far behind motorized columns of the United Nations forces.

CHAPTER 44

The March to the Sea

A T THE CHANGJIN RESERVOIR on the X Corps front there was extreme crisis. In most of the northeastern sector the ROKs, the 3rd Division and most of the 7th Division were positioned out of range of the Chinese attack and were able to scurry to safety on the coast. But most of the 1st Marine Division and elements of the 7th Division were completely cut off on the 4,000-foot-high plateau around the Changjin (Chosin) reservoir. With no bolt-hole open, the marines and the soldiers appeared to be threatened with annihilation.[1]

The focal point of the entire Changjin operation was the village of Hagaru-ri, near the south end of the reservoir. (See Map 11.) This village was at the junction of one road that led fourteen miles northwestward to Yudam-ni on the western shore of the reservoir, and another road that led northeastward up the eastern shore of the reservoir. Hagaru also was at the end of the road, much of it unbelievably steep and difficult, that stretched sixty-four miles north from Hungnam and the sea. This road was the only one traversing this mountainous country, and thus it became the Main Supply Route, or MSR, of the marine division and the army troops on the plateau.

These three narrow highways, nowhere wider than an American country dirt lane, many of the stretches mountain-shrouded and twisting, were to become the avenues of an incredible campaign that had poignant similarities with the legendary March to the Sea of the ten thousand Greek soldiers under Xenophon in 400 B.C. It also possessed a unique and unforgettable drama of its own, in which deeds of extreme bravery and endurance were the common currency of both sides.

From Hagaru, two regiments of marines with attached artillery were assigned the mission of moving to Yudam on the northwest and from there striking west-northwest to Mupyong-ni, about thirty-six air miles away, and then by way of Kanggye to Manpojin on the Yalu. Also from Hagaru, one artillery and two infantry battalions of the 7th Infantry Division were to move northeastward up the eastern reservoir shore to clear enemy troops and prevent flank attack on the marines from the east.

Hagaru was to be the base for these attacks. Therefore, supplies had to be stashed here and a hospital established. General Almond, X Corps commander, and General Smith, marine commander, believed an airstrip long enough to land C-47 two-engine transport planes was also needed to insure resupply and the evacuation of wounded in an emergency.

Neither medium tanks nor the bulldozers needed to build the airstrip could negotiate the hairpin turns of the road leading from the foot of the mountains at Chinhung-ni to the beginning of the four thousand-foot plateau at Koto-ri, ten miles north. Engineers started to improve this road on November 16 and had made enough progress by November 18 that six M4A3 Sherman tanks got up on the plateau, although it took more work to widen turns before the M26 Pershings were able to move up. Work had proceeded on the road sufficiently by November 19 for five large bulldozers to get up to Hagaru and begin hacking out a runway on ground frozen as hard as granite.

Plans were to create a 3,200-foot runway, a monumental task, given the conditions. The field manuals called for a 3,600-foot runway for C-47s at *sea* level, plus another 1,000 feet for each 1,000 feet of altitude. At Hagaru, 4,000 feet above sea level, that meant a 7,600-foot runway. Not only was there insufficient level ground for such an airfield, but the sub-zero temperatures made such a project impossible.

X Corps therefore fell back on the incredible adaptability of the C-47 (the military version of the DC-3 airliner). This already had become the practice in Korea. This fabulous aircraft not only was the workhorse of the military forces in Korea, but was required to perform under conditions and on fields that were ludicrously tiny—either carved out of broken ground like the strip at Hagaru, or laid out on the floors of minuscule valleys with towering mountains ranging on all sides. And the C-47 produced. Any passenger who flew often in Korea (and it was the only means of rapid travel available) came to think it perfectly normal for a heavily laden C-47 to drop over a high mountain ridge, fall like a stone toward a postage-stamp field, brake almost the moment the craft hit the ground, and then come to a shuddering rest within a dozen or a score of yards of the end of the runway. Hairy as this experience was, it was as nothing compared to a takeoff: the pilot revved the engines until the craft fought to break away; then, when it seemed the plane would tear itself apart from the strain, the pilot released the brakes and the C-47 burst down the short runway, got quickly aloft, and, its engines straining for every ounce of power, climbed just above the rapidly rising ground and over the final ridgeline. Often the planes cleared the last ridge by a few feet. Of all the men in Korea who earned respect for their skill and daring, none were held in higher esteem than the pilots of the C-47s.

While the marine engineers were working twenty-four hours a day to construct the airstrip, quartermaster and truck units were building up a supply base, and medical units were establishing a field hospital. Meanwhile, the 7th Marine RCT moved out toward Yudam from the Toktong pass, about eight miles west of Hagaru, and on November 25 seized Yudam. Most of the 5th Marine RCT simultaneously began to move in stages to Yudam, preparatory to passing through the 7th Marines to lead the X Corps offensive toward Mupyong on November 27.

At the same time the 1st Battalion of the 7th Division's 32nd Regiment reached Hagaru and moved up to the eastern side of the reservoir and emplaced November 26 near the shore about thirteen miles northeast of Hagaru. Following behind this battalion was the 3rd Battalion of the 7th Division's 31st Regiment, supported by the 57th Field Artillery Battalion.

Everything was funneling through Hagaru, and the supply base, hospital and airstrip destined the village to be the only sanctuary for marines and army forces on the plateau. However, no one really anticipated a massive Chinese attack, and the need to establish a strong defensive force at Hagaru was not felt by anyone in authority. Therefore, the 1st Marine RCT, which had been designated to garrison Hagaru, was also ordered to protect the MSR with positions at Koto and Chinhung. In addition, the intense pressure on available transportation to get the assault forces into position dictated that the garrison force for Hagaru got lower priority. Consequently, by the evening of November 26, only a little over two-thirds of the 3rd Battalion, 1st Marines, had been able to get up to Hagaru. This force—Companies H and I and all but a platoon of the Weapons Company—was under the command of Lieutenant Colonel Thomas L. Ridge. It was about the only combat force at Hagaru except for two batteries of marine artillery and a few remnants of the 7th Marines which had not yet got through to Yudam.

There were, however, dozens of supply, transportation, engineer, headquarters and other special detachments at the village, including all but a small part of 1st Marine Division headquarters.

Colonel Ridge quickly found himself named commander of the entire Hagaru defense force. At first this seemed a routine job, and there was little sense of urgency when Ridge began making plans for establishing a

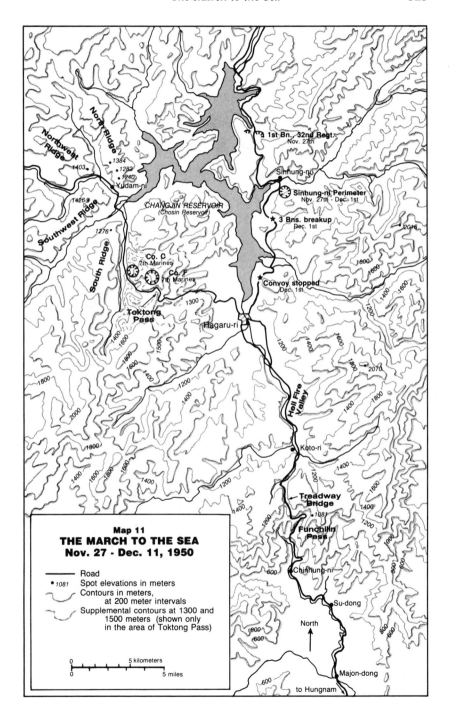

Map 11
THE MARCH TO THE SEA
Nov. 27 - Dec. 11, 1950

——— Road
• *1081* Spot elevations in meters
Contours in meters,
at 200 meter intervals
Supplemental contours at 1300 and
1500 meters (shown only
in the area of Toktong Pass)

0   5 kilometers
0   5 miles

perimeter defense. However, on November 27 and 28 the reality of a Chinese attack had manifested itself all over the Changjin plateau. By November 28 any lingering doubts were dispelled when marine pilots reported enemy roadblocks had cut off Yudam, Hagaru and Koto from each other. Now no 1st Marines reinforcements could be rushed forward, and Ridge had to make do with the troops he had available and those he could scrape together.

Intelligence reports indicated Chinese forces would approach the natural amphitheater of Hagaru from the south. This was just south of the open area where engineers were working all day and, under floodlights, all night to complete the airstrip. For this reason, Colonel Ridge posted his two rifle companies south of the airstrip on the most likely avenues of CCF attack. He distributed the other units he had available around a narrow perimeter. Most of these were engineer, service or headquarters detachments.

The Chinese attack came, as expected, against the two rifle companies. It struck about 10:30 p.m., November 28, against carefully prepared marine positions. The Chinese were staggered by the power of the marine small-arms, mortar and artillery fire and lost men heavily. However, about 12:30 a.m. a group of CCF soldiers broke through the Company H positions and penetrated as far back as the company CP. A few Chinese got beyond the marine infantry and began peppering the marine engineers still working under floodlights on the airstrip. A detachment of engineers counterattacked and cleared the airstrip, and the engineers resumed work under the floodlights while the battle raged on. The Chinese also succeeded on the northern part of the Hagaru perimeter, on so-called East Hill, against headquarters troops and army engineers. Although the CCF achieved a breakthrough here, they did not exploit it, indicating this was a diversionary attack in limited strength.

The Chinese penetration of Company H positions was not as dangerous as it seemed at first, either, because the Chinese fell to looting and wandering about in small groups without purpose. Apparently because the frontline troops had no radio contact with their rear, the CCF commanders did not realize a complete breakthrough had been attained and did not rush in new troops to exploit it. By morning, the Chinese still inside the marine perimeter had been hunted down and destroyed.

Chinese troops had set up roadblocks south of Hagaru, cutting it off from Koto, and penetrated as far south as Chinhung, where they exchanged shots with marine outposts, but were driven away by an expedition. At Koto, where the 2nd Battalion, 1st Marines, had moved on

November 24 and set up a perimeter, patrols established on November 27 that CCF troops were in the vicinity. On November 28, General Smith ordered the 1st Marines CO, Colonel Lewis B. Puller, to send a force from Koto up the MSR to make contact with a tank force that Smith ordered to move south from Hagaru. The relief force ran into a hail of Chinese fire less than a mile north of the Koto perimeter. Since it was obvious the Chinese were in greater strength than believed, the relief force returned to Koto.

That evening three additional combat units arrived at Koto from the south. These were Company G of the 1st Marines, Company B of the 31st Regiment of the 7th Division, and the newly arrived 235 officers and men of the 41st Independent Commando of the British Royal Marines. Colonel Puller organized the newcomers as a task force under the command of the Royal Marines CO, Lieutenant Colonel Douglas B. Drysdale. The task force's orders: fight through to Hagaru the following day (November 29). Going with the task force were seventy men of the marine division headquarters and signal battalion.

Task Force Drysdale moved out early on November 29 but ran into well-entrenched Chinese a little north of the perimeter, and Drysdale waited until seventeen medium tanks moved up. Drysdale put the marine tanks at the head of this column, with the vehicles carrying the three combat units following and the division headquarters group trailing at the rear. Progress up the road was slow because the M26 Pershings had to halt frequently to blast Chinese in emplacements and houses with their 90mm guns and then to spray the enemy with machine-gun fire after they were flushed out. Chinese mortar fire began to land on the column; one round scored a direct hit on a marine truck, wounding every man in it.

The task force had reached a point about four miles north of Koto when the tank officers told Colonel Drysdale and Captain Carl L. Sitter, CO of Company G, 1st Marines, they thought the tanks could get through to Hagaru, but it was inadvisable to move the trucks farther because Chinese resistance was increasing. Colonel Drysdale radioed General Smith for instructions. It was a difficult decision for Smith, but because of the urgent situation at Hagaru, he ordered the task force to continue.

The task force resumed its move northward. But it stopped abruptly about halfway to Hagaru when increased Chinese fire hit it in a mile-long valley flanked closely on the right (east) by a sharp rise of ground and on the left by a frozen creek and low grounds several hundred yards wide stretching to a small river and wooded hills beyond. This is the place Colonel Drysdale called Hell Fire Valley. It deserved the name.

The British and American marines and the U.S. soldiers piled out of their vehicles once more. A Chinese mortar round set one of the trucks afire in the southern part of the column, thus splitting the force. Chinese troops on the hills poured small-arms and mortar fire on the column, preventing removal of the damaged truck. During this time, the head of the column under Drysdale started advancing once more, thinking the others would follow. But that portion behind the burning truck could not get around it and had to remain. The advance group under Drysdale included the tanks, about three-fourths of the Royal Marines, Company G of the 1st Marines, and a few of the army infantrymen. Left behind in Hell Fire Valley were sixty-one British commandos, most of the army infantry company, and practically all of the marine division headquarters section.

Lieutenant Colonel Arthur A. Chidester, assistant marine division G-4 (supply) and senior officer caught south of the burning truck, ordered the blocked vehicles to turn around and attempt to get back to Koto. Before this could happen, however, Chinese forces split the blocked column in two again and began pouring fire on the troops now divided into two isolated pockets. Colonel Chidester was wounded and captured and apparently died of wounds.

The cutoff Americans and Britons sought shelter in the road ditches and around an unused narrow-gauge railway line, but there was little cover because the Chinese on the elevations above could send down plunging fire. At first, while marine Corsairs ranged over the area firing at any CCF who showed themselves, the Chinese fire was light. But with darkness the enemy got bolder, although they waited several hours before moving within grenade-throwing range. The isolated members of the column, spread along a 1,200-yard stretch of road, formed one large defense perimeter in the north pocket, and three small perimeters in the south pocket.

There was some hope that twelve marine tanks that meanwhile were moving up from Koto to assist the task force would be able to break through and aid the surrounded column. But the marine armor ran into heavy opposition and could not advance, showing that Chinese troops had moved in behind the column after it passed north. The tanks closest to Koto got back fairly soon. Another group farther north was cut off but finally got back in a few hours. The farthest-advanced tank group was unable to move, however, and remained the night boxed inside a protective perimeter formed by artillery concentrations fired from Koto. With daylight this tank group also moved back to Koto without mishap.

At the stalled column, no determined Chinese attacks occurred until about midnight. Rather, the Chinese looted the now-abandoned trucks, and the Chinese leaders merely kept the perimeters pinned down and enveloped. In the early hours of November 30, CCF soldiers began small probing attacks using grenades. The situation got increasingly desperate, especially in the larger northern pocket, which was under the command of Major John M. McLaughlin. Frank Noel, an Associated Press photographer, and two other men attempted to run the CCF gauntlet about 2 a.m. but were captured before they had gone a hundred yards. At 4:30 a.m. the Chinese commander sent the prisoners to the perimeter with a surrender demand. McLaughlin, with a British commando, went out to parley in hopes of delaying a renewed Chinese attack while some of the men escaped. The Chinese parley team would not be taken in, however, and threatened to overrun the perimeter in an all-out attack. They gave McLaughlin ten minutes to decide whether to surrender. McLaughlin went from one to the other of the forty able-bodied men he had left. None had more than eight rounds of ammunition left. Finally, the major consented to surrender on condition his seriously wounded were evacuated. The Chinese agreed, and the fight in Hell Fire Valley ceased. McLaughlin's long parley permitted the men in the three smaller perimeters to the south to escape on foot. The Chinese did not keep their promise to evacuate the seriously wounded: however, they did allow them to be moved to a Korean house, and when the Chinese moved back into the hills for a day, an opportunity was found to evacuate the men to Koto.

The head of Task Force Drysdale did not know the tail of the column had been left in Hell Fire Valley and made fairly good progress until, about two thousand yards from Hagaru, it ran into heavy CCF fire. A Chinese team got close enough to one of the tanks to damage it so severely with a satchel charge that it had to be abandoned, and several vehicles were set on fire. Colonel Drysdale was wounded in this fight and command passed to Captain Sitter, CO of Company G. Sitter led the battered head of the task force into the Hagaru perimeter.

Losses in the task force were heavy: 61 for the Royal Commandos, 48 for Company G, 1st Marines; 119 for Company B of the army 31st Regiment; 50 for marine division headquarters and 43 in tank, truck and signal units—a total of 321 men out of 922 engaged, or 35 per cent. In addition, 75 vehicles were lost.

Nevertheless, Hagaru gained the bulk of the Royal Marines Commando and Company G, 1st Marines, and it no longer was in serious danger of being overrun, although the Chinese continued their attacks.

CHAPTER 45

The Agony of the Three Battalions

T HE EXPERIENCES of the 7th Division troops on the eastern side of
Changjin reservoir and the marines on the western side were
unrelated to each other tactically or to the fights at Hagaru or along the
MSR to Koto, as close as they were. Although they occurred
simultaneously, their stories have to be told separately.

When the 1st Battalion, 32nd Regiment, emplaced November 26 near
the reservoir shore about thirteen miles northeast of Hagaru, temperatures were well below zero degree Fahrenheit, and men already were
suffering from frostbite. The next day, the start of the X Corps offensive,
the battalion moved farther north to blocking positions and relieved the
last small detachment of 5th Marine Regiment troops, although most
marines had moved back on November 25. Meanwhile, the 3rd Battalion
of the 31st Regiment, now coming forward, was to attack through the
32nd Regiment's battalion and drive north, supported by the 57th
Artillery.[1] (See Map 11.)

The 32nd's battalion took up positions on the high ground on both
sides of a pass on the north-south road running a short distance east of
the reservoir. Company A occupied the left-hand (western) side of the
road with its 3rd Platoon and also outposted the 1st and 2nd Platoons
eight hundred yards north of the position. Company C emplaced just
east of the road and Company B formed a flank-protection position on
the east side of the battalion position.

Shortly after midnight on November 28, one Chinese force flanked
the western positions of Company A in the main emplacement position
on west side of the road. By the time the penetration was discovered,
some CCF had got back as far as the company's mortars in the rear. At

the same time another CCF force attacked Company A's right flank and also penetrated the pass on the road. As soon as the Company A commander, Captain Edward B. Scullion, learned about the attack on his left, he moved to that flank to reorganize the platoon. There he was killed by an enemy grenade, and the platoon leader, Lieutenant Raymond C. Densfield, was wounded in the knee.

The CCF double-envelopment disorganized the left flank of the battalion's position, and cut off the two Company A outposts eight hundred yards north. But the Company A executive officer, Lieutenant Cecil G. Smith, was able to establish a skirmish line to protect the company's right flank by using command-post personnel and mortarmen who had climbed up on the ridge after their mortar positions had been overrun. At the same time, Lieutenant James O. Mortrude's platoon of Company C on the immediate east side of the road at the pass fired effectively at the CCF below them.

When the battalion commander, Lieutenant Colonel Don Carlos Faith, Jr., learned of Captain Scullion's death, he sent his assistant operations officer (S-3), Captain Robert F. Haynes, to take command of Company A. Accompanied by Captain Erwin B. Bigger, CO of Company D (Heavy Weapons Company), Haynes started up the road from the south toward the Company A position. At a curve in the road a Chinese group, which had infiltrated behind the frontline positions, opened fire. Haynes was hit and fell, and Bigger returned to the battalion CP and told Sergeant Jeremiah Casey, the Company A mess sergeant, to take a patrol and get Captain Haynes out. Casey gathered some men from the CP and departed. The patrol returned and reported Sergeant Casey killed and Captain Haynes dead. Colonel Faith then phoned Lieutenant Smith at Company A and told him to take command. "It's your baby now," Faith said.

During the night Chinese troops also overran the right-flank platoon of Company C and two platoons of Company B. The Company C men on the right flank faced east to meet the CCF attack and for the next two hours the beleaguered 32nd Regiment men defended their positions while Chinese intermittently tried to climb the slopes. A 75mm recoilless rifle with the Weapons Company produced excellent sharpnel effects by firing into the trees; but the machine guns could fire only one shot at a time because of the extreme cold.

The battalion held. With daylight Americans moved down toward the mortar positions abandoned the night before and encountered four Chinese soldiers. They killed three and took the fourth prisoner. The U.S. mortars were still in place and undamaged. The two platoons of Company A on the outpost eight hundred yards ahead of the battalion had not been discovered by the Chinese and had not fired a shot. During the day, however, the new Company A CO, Lieutenant Smith, moved the two platoons back to the main company perimeter and also across the road to Lieutenant Mortrude's Company C platoon position. Mortrude led a force of Company C in a counterattack to the east in the morning, and, with the excellent assistance of carrier-based marine Corsairs, was able virtually to re-establish the battalion perimeter by nightfall. But just before dark, Corsairs warned the battalion they had spotted an estimated enemy battalion on the road 5,000 yards to the north and marching toward the positions of the 32nd's 1st Battalion.

Meanwhile on this day, November 28, the 3rd Battalion of the 31st Regiment and the 57th Artillery moved into a perimeter on the road east of the reservoir at Sinhung-ni and about four miles south of the 32nd's battalion.

At 8 p.m. November 28 in the positions of the 32nd's battalion an estimated CCF company descended the ridgeline from the north where the two Company A platoons had been outposted the night before and struck Company A. Other CCF simultaneously attacked again along the road on the right flank of the company. A machine gun and a 75mm recoilless rifle stopped the first Chinese attack, but CCF soldiers worked around the flank and struck a platoon from the west, killing the platoon leader, but did not have enough strength to exploit the advantage. Battalion headquarters scraped together thirty men and sent them to support Company A.

Sporadic CCF mortar and small-arms fire began to come into the Company C sector. At 11 p.m. Lieutenant James G. Campbell, a Heavy Weapons Company platoon leader attached to Charley Company, heard a shout and saw a group of men running off a knoll that he knew was held by a squad of five men. Campbell counted five figures and shot the sixth, who, by this time, was ten feet from Campbell's foxhole. Campbell yelled to a machine-gunner to open fire on the just-evacuated small knoll. At that moment Campbell was knocked down. He thought someone had hit him in the face with a hammer: a bullet had penetrated his cheek and lodged in the roof of his mouth.

Although the Chinese attempted for some time to organize a strong point from which to launch an attack on Company C, the 1st Battalion's 81mm mortars prevented the Chinese from assembling, and about 2:30 a.m., November 29, the area became quiet. The situation, however, was getting critical, for Chinese soldiers were all around the battalion. Between 3 and 4 a.m. the battalion made preparations to evacuate its position and move back to join the 31st's 3rd Battalion and the 57th Artillery at Sinhung-ni. There was some panic as the 1st Battalion withdrew. Although the Chinese recognized what was happening and increased their fire, the Americans and attached ROKs had no difficulty drawing away and assembling on the road to move south. Soldiers unloaded kitchen equipment from the trucks to make room for the wounded.

While Chinese surrounded the 1st Battalion, 32nd Regiment, other CCF soldiers did the same to the other two American battalions at Sinhung. By morning these two battalions had suffered heavy losses of men and equipment and were invested on nearly all sides. The two firing batteries of the 57th Artillery were down to a total of four 105mm howitzers (instead of the normal twelve). The defense perimeter—1,000 yards across east to west, 600 yards north to south—was in a pocket of low ground beside the reservoir and was vulnerable to attàck. Except for a small sector along an inlet of the reservoir on the northwest, the two battalions were surrounded.

The Chinese had set up a roadblock about halfway between the 1st Battalion and the two battalions at Sinhung, but the battalion CO, Colonel Faith, and elements of Company A assaulted the block and destroyed it. The Chinese commander investing Sinhung, seeing the approach of the battalion from the north, dispatched a strong CCF force up the road to block it. From their positions on the high ground at the just-demolished roadblock, the Americans saw the Chinese force coming. Colonel Faith's Company A group quickly moved out on the ice of the reservoir a short distance west of the road, circled around to the rear of the advancing Chinese, and slaughtered them. The area was littered with the bodies of 130 dead Chinese soldiers. The battalion thereupon moved down into the valley and joined forces with the two battalions at Sinhung.

Although the American forces were now consolidated, they were still in a precarious position. Not only was the perimeter open to attack, but food supplies were almost exhausted. Ammunition and fuel were in low supply. It was bitter cold. Even the few men who had managed to keep their bedrolls were afraid to fall asleep for fear of freezing. In order to keep blood circulating, men had to be constantly moving their limbs and shifting their body positions. All automatic weapons had to be fired every half-hour to keep them working.

Three factors kept the situation from being hopeless: airdrops of food and ammo, hope that a relief force would come to their aid from the south, and the warm security of the marine black Corsairs, which remained constantly overhead, attacking any enemy troops that dared to show their heads.

The airdrops came in on the afternoon of November 29. The first drop landed on high ground to the east. Americans had to fight their way to it, but recovered many of the bundles. The second drop went entirely to the Chinese, falling outside the perimeter to the southwest. The third drop was successful. Lieutenants Smith and Campbell believed the CCF had set out captured panels in order to divert the lost drop to the Chinese, but Lieutenant Mortrude believed the C-54 pilot, worried about ground fire, had dropped his load without making a practice pass.

The hope that a relief force was coming had validity. Brigadier General Henry I. Hodes, assistant 7th Division commander, formed a company-sized task force, supported by tanks, of army troops at Hagaru. This task force moved out on the afternoon of November 29, but was quickly hurled back by Chinese troops with the loss of two tanks and a large number of men killed and wounded.

The black Corsairs, however, were not a disappointment. Controlled from the perimeter by marine Captain Edward P. Stamford, the Corsairs napalmed, rocketed and machine-gunned any targets observed. The air support continued on into the night of November 29–30 because of bright moonlight. Marine pilots later reported that so many Chinese troops were around the perimeter they could drop their loads anywhere with good chances of hitting Chinese.

November 30 passed quietly for the beleaguered American battalions. The relief force had failed and no other was coming. But the officers inside the perimeter developed no alternative plan to extricate the battalions. The men improved their positions and tried to keep warm.

At 10 p.m. November 30, about one hundred Chinese attacked Company A of the 1st Battalion, 32nd. A machine-gunner asked for a flare to light the area. When it was sent out, the Americans could see a column of Chinese troops marching up the road. The column was quickly dispersed with machine-gun fire. Failing to penetrate the perimeter at Company A's positions, the Chinese maneuvered to the east and struck Company C, announcing their attack by a heavy volume of small-arms, machine-gun and mortar fire. One mortar round hit a machine-gun position, killing two men, wounding three, and perforating the gun's water jacket. Shortly after midnight the Chinese hit another sector of the perimeter held by the 3rd Battalion, 31st.

The Chinese tactics of infiltration and assault on small frontline positions were not working so well because of the tight perimeter the soldiers had created. Even so, about 3 a.m., December 1, individual Chinese soldiers did get into the perimeter on the northeast. These CCF troops were still inside the perimeter at daylight. To kill or capture them, Lieutenant Robert D. Wilson, executive of Company D, 1st Battalion, led a group of mortarmen and artillery gunners against them. Lieutenant

Wilson was wounded twice, but kept on until he was finally hit again and killed. But the counterattack restored the perimeter.

Shortly after daylight the Chinese attacked on the west, moving through a narrow ravine at the base of a hill. It was an unusual move, because it was sprung in daylight, and the U.S. troops gave way; but the line held around a 75mm recoilless rifle. Lieutenant Campbell was locating people to move ammunition to the hard-pressed gunners defending against the attack. A mortar round landed ten feet from Campbell and a group of other men, wounding Campbell in the side and two other men. Campbell was carried to an aid station tent, which was full, with about twenty-five patients inside. At least fifty more wounded lay outside.

Dazed with shock, Campbell lay outside for about half an hour. Colonel Faith appeared and asked all men who could possibly do so to come back on the line. "If we can hold out forty minutes more," Faith said, "we'll get air support." There was not much response, because most of the men were seriously wounded. Campbell, however, responded; he could not walk, but he crawled toward the west. Before he got to the line, however, he collapsed into a foxhole. Someone helped Campbell back to the aid station. This time he got inside for treatment. Much medical equipment had been lost in withdrawing from the first position. The medical personnel had no more bandages. There was no more morphine. The medics cleaned Campbell's wounds with disinfectant. The seriously wounded patients were fed hot soup and coffee to keep them from freezing.

Colonel Faith, in command of the whole perimeter after the death of Colonel Allan D. MacLean, 31st CO, decided the survivors would have to make a break for Hagaru, eight miles to the south. Hope that a relief force would come through had vanished. And the battalions would be torn to pieces by the continuing attacks and the steady mortar barrage if they remained much longer.

Ammunition supply had diminished again. Some men had only one clip left. The artillery howitzers had exhausted their shells. Lieutenant Mortrude's platoon, the unit least hurt, was designated advance guard, supported by a tracked M16 (twin-40mm AAA guns). Mortrude's task was to clear the road in front of the column of vehicles as it moved south toward Hagaru. Lieutenant Smith's Company A, 1st Battalion, 32nd, followed by Company B, were placed as advanced flank security guard on the east, while the reservoir itself hopefully would provide security on the west.

The column started south about noon, and almost immediately encountered Chinese small-arms and burp-gun fire. Four U.S. aircraft (identification unknown), dropping napalm in close support, struck, not the Chinese, but Mortrude's advance guard and Smith's flank guard. Several men were burned to death. Five men, their clothes on fire, tried frantically to beat out the flames. The M16 in which Mortrude was riding was set ablaze. Everyone scattered.

This, Lieutenant Smith said later, was the beginning of the end. Until the mistaken napalm attack, units had maintained organizational structure. Now they began to fall apart. Units intermingled in panic as key personnel were killed or wounded. No one had slept for several days. One thought now drove the men onward: to keep going or they would be lost. Smith said several times he was tempted to lie down, go to sleep, and play dead. But he knew that would be the end. He and all the other men continued moving, because, whenever a man stopped, a Chinese waiting in ambush was able to draw a bead on him and hit him with a bullet.

Lieutenant Mortrude, though wounded in the knee, gathered ten men around him and proceeded to carry out his orders. Firing as they advanced, the men dispersed twenty Chinese soldiers. As Mortrude and his men ran down the road screaming obscenities at the Chinese, they met scattered small groups of CCF soldiers and killed them or drove them away. Mortrude and his group soon passed beyond CCF fire from the flanks, and the lieutenant and the men began to believe they were in the clear. Then, about two miles below the former perimeter at Sinhung, they encountered a bridge that had been blown.

Mortrude and his group were joined by a platoon of Company A, and together they crossed under the bridge and moved up a ridge east of the road to reconnoiter. It quickly became clear this was another Chinese ambush site. CCF fire from higher ground to the east began to rake the Americans. A bullet hit Mortrude in the head and knocked him unconscious for half an hour. When the lieutenant regained his senses, he noticed American troops continuing up a hill south of the blown-out bridge. Corporal Alfonso Camoesas bandaged Mortrude's head, and the lieutenant followed after the troops, seeing many American dead and wounded on the slope as he passed. Mortrudge was dazed and in shock, but he reached the road again south of the blown bridge and followed after a group of men he could vaguely distinguish moving out ahead of him on the ice of Changjin reservoir.

Meanwhile, the main body of Americans and ROKs with the vehicles reached the blown bridge in the late afternoon. The bridge had to be bypassed, but the banks of the stream were steep and drivers had to exercise extreme care to avoid overturning the vehicles. The situation was made more desperate because the Chinese lying in ambush had not been scattered by Mortrude's group and the Company A platoon. The few men who had survived the earlier ambush had continued on southward around the bridge without attacking the Chinese.

If the trucks were going to get across the stream, they would have to be towed by a halftrack. As this operation commenced, Chinese fire began to fall on the men and vehicles bunched up at the broken bridge. The truck in which Lieutenant Campbell was riding with other wounded men reached the middle of the stream bed, and there it stalled. CCF fire struck some of the wounded men in the truck, and Campbell decided it would be better for him to get out and move under his own power. After crossing the stream he realized his head was clear and the shock had vanished. Although his leg and side pained him and his cheek had swelled up, he felt reasonably good. Campbell hailed a three-quarter-ton truck, one of fifteen vehicles that had got past the destroyed bridge.

This truck did not go far, however, before it and the other vehicles were halted by another Chinese roadblock. Colonel Faith, a blanket wrapped around his shoulders, organized a group to assault the enemy, who were now firing from positions west of the road, while sporadic fire also came in from east of the road. The Americans and the ROKs crouched in the ditches alongside the vehicles and returned fire, although cautiously, because of the ammo shortage. It was getting dark, but U.S. aircraft were still overhead delivering fire.

Captain Bigger, blinded in one eye by a mortar fragment and wounded in the leg, led an assault on the Chinese west of the road with about seventy-five men, most of whom were walking wounded. A U.S. airplane came in on a strafing run, but fired short into the Americans and nearly demoralized the attack. But the men continued doggedly on and succeeded in knocking out the CCF positions. However, by the time they got to the high ground, other Chinese soldiers had circled in behind them and the column on the road. Captain Bigger and his group, seeing little chance of getting back to the men on the road, elected to turn west out on the reservoir ice and walk on it back to Hagaru.

Another group of about fifteen Americans, including Lieutenant Smith and an infantry and an artillery lieutenant, also climbed up the ridge on the west. The artillery lieutenant knocked out a Chinese machine gun with two grenades, and the group, reaching the crest, looked back north and saw trucks still stopped at the blown-out bridge. Troops also were strung out on the road south of the bridge. Looking west, Lieutenant Smith's group saw Captain Bigger and his men walking toward the ice. The American forces were scattering into small detachments and isolated individuals. Debacle had set in. The men now were merely trying to save themselves.

Smith and his group debated what to do. They were now without ammunition. They decided there was no point in going back to the road. They, too, decided to move west and try to get back to Hagaru on the reservoir ice. About twenty-five Chinese soldiers, seeing the path the Americans were taking, tried to head them off. But Smith and his group reached the reservoir before the Chinese and moved out on it. The Chinese standing on the bank, fired at the Americans without effect, but one Chinese soldier came out on the ice and bayoneted an American who had lagged behind. Strangely, this was the only known instance of a Chinese coming on the ice after the fleeing Americans and the few ROKs. For some inexplicable reason the Chinese seemed to regard the men who had gained the ice no longer to be fair game.

Lieutenant Campbell, still back at the roadblock with the stalled vehicles, got out of the three-quarter-ton truck and started forward. He met his platoon sergeant, Harold Craig, who had been wounded in the back. Craig was about to toss his carbine away because he planned to make a break for safety when darkness came and prefered to rely on his bayonet. Lieutenant Campbell gladly accepted the carbine, since he had no weapon. The carbine had a thirty-round "banana" clip in it; this promised some security.

As the men in the ditches around the vehicles established a base of fire, Colonel Faith led an assault on the roadblock and cleared it. But Faith was mortally wounded in the kidney in this attack, and the commander was placed in a jeep, where he quickly turned blue from the cold and the wound.[2] Additional wounded were placed in the truck and across the hoods of the vehicles. By now it was dark, and the fifteen-vehicle column moved south at about ten miles an hour.

A mile below the roadblock the vehicles passed two knocked-out U.S. tanks. Campbell reasoned they had been part of the 7th Division task force that had tried and failed to rescue the battalions on November 29. The men began to believe they were safe. But about a mile past the destroyed tanks the column halted again. The lead truck and jeep were fired upon as they entered a small village. The truck driver was killed and the truck overturned and spilled out the wounded. A few wounded men managed to work back up the road and warn the column.

An artillery major, the ranking officer in the group, collected all the men he could find who could walk and fire a weapon, about seventy soldiers, and he led them down the road toward the village. They bore little resemblance to a military unit: they had no designated subordinate leaders, no formation, no plan, and a great percentage were walking wounded. This mob of men entered the village and immediately began to receive small-arms and automatic-weapons fire from high ground south of the village and east of the road. The Americans returned fire for a few minutes, but discouraged and without resolution, they picked up several wounded men from the overturned truck, plus several more wounded in the desultory engagement, and returned to the trucks. By this time it was 10 or 11 p.m., December 1.

A group of officers, none of whom Lieutenant Campbell recognized, decided they should wait where they were. Word of the situation, they reasoned, would surely have got to Hagaru by that time, and aid undoubtedly would arrive soon. Major Robert E. Jones, S-1 of 1st Battalion, 32nd Regiment, however, recognized the plight of the men and instructed any who could walk to move off in groups of two and three across the reservoir, three-quarters of a mile away, and try to get to Hagaru on their own. Some of these men departed. About one hundred men remained with the vehicles. They waited for about an hour. Then the tail of the column began to receive small-arms and mortar fire. The column commander decided to try to make a run for it through the village. It was a hopeless move, and Lieutenant Campbell despaired that the column could get through.

The column approached the village. Enemy fire quickly killed the drivers of the first three trucks. The column halted. Chinese machine-gun fire raked the column at point-blank range. Campbell jumped off the tailgate of the third truck and dived into a ditch. He heard the wounded moan as they received additional wounds. Campbell fired his carbine at the machine-gun flashes on the hill. Someone yelled: "Look out!" Campbell turned and saw a three-quarter-ton truck hurtling toward him. He scrambled out of the way, but the truck ran over his foot and bruised the bones, then crashed into the three stopped lead vehicles. Someone had decided to try to push these vehicles through the village or off the road. The three lead trucks, their drivers dead, jammed together and rolled into the ditches, overturned, spilled the wounded on the ground, and crushed many of them—and blocked the road completely. Meantime, the Chinese closed on the rear of the column, throwing white phosphorous grenades. Campbell fired the last three rounds in his carbine at the machine-gun flashes and dived into a culvert underneath railroad tracks that ran alongside the road. It was 1:30 a.m. December 2.

The wounded who could not move remained where they were. Everyone else scattered. Corporal Camoesas found himself with thirty-five other men; carrying six wounded men, the group reached the reservoir. Camoesas walked out on the ice and looked back: the trucks were burning. Campbell crawled through the culvert. He found a man wounded in the leg who could not walk. Two other soldiers joined Campbell; together they dragged the wounded man across a rice paddy to a lumber pile where two ROKs joined them. At the edge of the reservoir several other Americans joined the group, making seventeen all told. The men walked out on the reservoir ice. Campbell was not sure where Hagaru was, but he felt certain they would reach it if they followed the shoreline. Coming to a house still occupied by North Koreans, one of the ROK soldiers asked where the marines were. The North Koreans told the ROK that American jeeps came up the road every day. Although some of the men were suspicious of the North Koreans, Campbell believed he recognized the road. He led off southward, and the rest followed. Two miles down the road, the group met a marine tank outpost. The tankers directed the men to the nearest CP and from there a truck took them to the marine hospital at Hagaru. They arrived at 5:30 a.m. December 2.

Lieutenant Smith and his group reached a marine supply point at Hagaru at 9:30 p.m. December 1. Captain Bigger and his band of mostly wounded men got to the village at 10 p.m., and Camoesas and the men with him, after hiding on the reservoir shore for a while to rest, got to the marine tank outpost at 8 a.m. December 2. Other men drifted in for a while longer, in ones and twos and occasionally in small groups.

Before dawn, about 670 7th Division men had been taken into the hospital or the warming tents at Hagaru. Lieutenant Colonel Olin L. Beall, CO of the marine 1st Motor Transport Battalion at Hagaru, however, was not satisfied that all the 7th Division survivors could get into Hagaru because of wounds and the extremely cold weather. At daylight, he went out personally in his jeep to look for men, and he quickly found more than his jeep could carry. Hurrying back into Hagaru, Beall organized a task force of trucks, jeeps and sleds and led it out to rescue as many soldiers as the marines could find. The only opposition they encountered came from long-range sniping, which grew so troublesome in the late afternoon that the marines set up a machine gun on the reservoir ice to give protection. Strangely, the Chinese soldiers, far from hindering the escape of the 7th Division survivors, actually assisted in some cases. Beall and his men rescued 319 soldiers on December 2, nearly all of them suffering from frostbite or wounds. Some were found to be wandering in aimless circles on the reservoir ice, in a state of shock.

A company-sized force of the 31st Regiment at Hagaru moved out with tanks on December 2 to attempt to bring in any organized units of the three battalions that might have been left behind. This force met heavy opposition, and was recalled when it became obvious that only stragglers of the three shattered battalions remained.

Colonel Beall and his men kept at their rescue work until an estimated

1,050 survivors of the original 2,500 men in the three battalions had been saved. Only 385 of the survivors were able-bodied. A marine reconnaissance patrol counted more than 300 dead in the abandoned trucks of the battalions. Many more were missing in action and presumed dead.

CHAPTER 46

An Act of Defiance

T HE MAIN FORCE of the X Corps offensive, the marines at Yudam-ni, were moving into place on November 26, but the 7th Marines there that day received sobering news in the persons of three Chinese soldiers they captured. These men said three CCF divisions had reached the Yudam area on November 20, and were planning to move south and southwest from there to cut the MSR after the 7th and 5th Marine RCTs had passed. The 7th Marines immediately relayed this information to division and division to corps. Although X Corps had identified six CCF divisions in northeast Korea (out of twelve actually there), intelligence estimates regarding possible Chinese reaction still were optimistic. The corps decision: go ahead with the offensive.[1]

The assault unit of the marines, the 2nd Battalion of the 5th Marines, reached Yudam on the evening of November 26, and set up for the start of the attack the next morning.

Yudam lies in the center of a deep valley about a mile and a quarter northwest of a small inlet of the Changjin reservoir. It is about 3,500 feet above sea level, and is surrounded by five great ridges which press closely against the valley. (See Map 11.) For example, one of these ridges is peaked by Hill 1426 (that is, 1,426 meters above sea level, or about 4,700 feet), and it is only a mile and a half southwest of the village, but 1,200 feet above it.

Despite an overnight temperature that dropped to zero degree Fahrenheit, accompanied by fierce north winds, the 2nd Battalion, 5th Marines, on the morning of November 27 attacked westward out of Yudam on a road squeezed between Northwest Ridge (Hill 1403) and Southwest Ridge (Hill 1426). To provide flank security Company H of the 7th Marines assaulted Hill 1403 on Northwest Ridge and Company G of the 7th Marines attacked Hill 1426 on Southwest Ridge. Company

340

H reached its objective without opposition. But Company G, after capturing Hill 1426 without encountering any Chinese, almost immediately thereafter came under strong Chinese fire from a peak on the ridgeline five hundred yards farther southwest.

The 5th Marines' lead assault force (Company F) moved westward on the road between the steep walls of Northwest and Southwest Ridges. When it reached a point a little over a mile west of Yudam, the assault company was struck by long-range small-arms fire from the westernmost parts of Southwest Ridge. About the same time, a marine spotter pilot radioed that Chinese positions were all across the western front, north and south of the road.

Company F climbed partway up the slopes of Hill 1403, then turned west again through a draw and up toward the ridge closest to the road from which some of the Chinese fire had come. Meanwhile the unit following behind Company F, Company D of the 5th Marines, edged westward along the road. As soon as this unit came within sight of the Chinese on the ridges, it, too, met a hail of fire. Marine 105mm howitzers emplaced south of Yudam, plus close-support 81mm and 4.2-inch mortars, sent concentration after concentration onto the closest Chinese-held ridge. Then marine Corsairs flashed in and rocketed and bombed the CCF positions.

Company F assaulted the enemy emplacements from the north and drove the Chinese away, but were slowed by heavy CCF machine-gun fire that swept the ridge from a peak a thousand yards farther west. At the same time, Company D filed around the road bend at the southern end of the ridge and there came face to face with tiers of entrenchments the Chinese had dug on the eastern slopes of a mountain about a mile to the west-southwest. Heavy Chinese fire from the mountain converged on the marine company.

Faced with this formidable barrier, the CO of 2nd Battalion, 5th Marines, Lieutenant Colonel Harold S. Roise, called off the attack for the day. He ordered Company F to remain on the ridge for the night, and for Company D to set up a block on the road and a defensive perimeter on a spur of Southwest Ridge near the road. Colonel Roise placed his third rifle company, Company E, in a draw between Company F and the 7th Marines' Company H on Hill 1403.

While the Chinese to the west and southwest of Yudam had spent the day indicating their intentions to stop any movement in that direction, other Chinese forces had materialized to the north and northeast of the village: a patrol from the 7th Marines moving on North Ridge ran into heavy fire about four thousand yards north-northeast of the village and withdrew to the southern tip of North Ridge, a little more than a mile north of Yudam.

During the day and early evening the other two battalions of the 5th Marines arrived at Yudam and formed perimeters for the night near the village. A great deal of marine firepower was concentrated the night of November 27 in and around Yudam: two marine regiments, nearly three-fourths of the marine division's artillery (thirty 105mm and eighteen 155mm howitzers emplaced south of the village), plus substantial numbers of heavy 4.2-inch mortars and 75mm recoilless rifles. Supplies of food, ammunition and motor fuel were not high, but the 7th Marines CO, Colonel Homer L. Litzenberg, on November 27 got fifteen truckloads of supplies delivered over the fourteen-mile route from Hagaru.

* * * * * * * * * * *

When night fell on November 27, the marines occupied a substantial perimeter. On Northwest Ridge, they held the southernmost elevations, Hill 1403 and the high ground closest to the road leading westward. On Southwest Ridge they held Hill 1426 and the terrain between it and Yudam itself. On South Ridge they held the high ground (Hill 1276) nearest the road leading back to Hagaru, and on North Ridge they held two of the peaks immediately northeast and east of Yudam (Hills 1282 and 1240).

There also were two marine companies posted outside this perimeter to protect the vital MSR leading back to Hagaru. One of these was Company C, minus one platoon, of the 7th Marines, emplaced a little over four miles south of Yudam on the lower slopes of Hill 1419 near the road. The other was Company F of the 7th Marines, reinforced with heavy machine guns and 81mm mortars and numbering 240 officers and men, emplaced about three miles by road beyond Company C on an isolated elevation (quickly dubbed Fox Hill for Fox Company) just north of the MSR at Toktong pass.

When one looks at a map of the area, the insecurity of the marine positions becomes immediately apparent. First, the heavy wheeled equipment of the marine infantry and their artillery dictated a dependence upon the MSR leading back to Hagaru, while the Chinese, carrying their small arms, machine guns and mortars on their backs, could walk over the ridgelines and valleys and block the MSR almost wherever they wished. Second, the great bulk of marine strength was lodged in the deep valley of Yudam itself. Possession by the Chinese of any of the high ridges immediately above this valley would permit the Chinese to pour fire down on the massed marines and their equipment. Either eventuality—blockage of the MSR south to Hagaru or capture of commanding heights above Yudam—could spell destruction of the entire force.

On the moonlit night of November 27, three Chinese divisions set out to accomplish just this destruction. They used their familiar system of a frontal attack accompanied by a double-envelopment. While the 89th CCF Division moved up two regiments for a massive direct assault against the marines holding the southern eminences of Northwest Ridge, the 79th CCF Division slipped down North Ridge and invested the marine positions on Hills 1282 and 1240. At the same time, the 59th CCF Division completed a wide circuit to the southeast and drove in across the southern parts of South Ridge and around Toktong pass to cut the MSR to Hagaru.

The marines had not anticipated such an immense Chinese response. The CCF movements had largely been concealed from air observation, thanks to Chinese skill at camouflage by day and their practice of moving into advanced positions by night. A third Chinese skill, at infiltration of enemy positions, also quickly made itself known to the marines. Within a few hours after nightfall, CCF soldiers were all over the Northwest and North Ridges, and they quickly encircled the positions of the isolated Companies C and F on the MSR south of Yudam-ni and took over wide sections of the MSR itself.

It was no night anyone would choose to fight a battle. Two hours after the sun set, the temperature dropped to twenty degrees below zero Fahrenheit. The marines outposted on the hills were especially numbed by the cold. Carbines and Browning Automatic Rifles (BARs) froze and became unreliable or unserviceable. The basic U.S. rifle, the M1 (Garand), and the .30-caliber heavy machine gun remained operable, however, though some weapons showed quirks.

The CCF investment of Northwest Ridge provided a perfect example of the Chinese method of attack. It was practically the opposite of the "human-wave" tactics over wide fronts attributed to them in the press. On Northwest Ridge, small groups of CCF soldiers, beginning about 9 p.m., made probing attacks against marine positions, withdrawing as soon as contact was made. Having located the outpost and front lines, the Chinese then threw in heavy concentrations of mortar fire on the U.S. positions, and the CCF infantry opened fire with machine guns emplaced all across the ridge. After about twenty minutes of this concentrated fire, the CCF mortar concentrations began to move progressively toward the marine rear in walking fire. Chinese whistles began to blow, the CCF machine guns fell silent, and the first Chinese assault forces, hoping to achieve a complete breakthrough, struck on an extremely narrow front in the draw at the juncture of Companies E and

F. The Chinese advanced in column formation to within grenade range, then deployed quickly into skirmish lines that advanced right on the marine positions. The Chinese attackers threw grenades and fired their weapons and moved forward without regard to losses. Although marine machine-gunners piled up Chinese attackers, the enemy finally broke through into this gap. The Chinese, attempting to roll back the newly exposed flanks, overran part of the right-hand platoon of Company F, 5th Marines, but the left-hand platoon of Company E, 5th, reinforced by a machine-gun section and a reserve squad rushed from the rear, held fast and bent back its left to prevent envelopment from the rear. Meanwhile, hastily called in mortar fire laid barrages on the salient in the draw. The heavy marine fire eliminated any chance the Chinese could make a breakthrough at this point. Furthermore, some men of Company E had the idea of turning their machine guns on a hut two hundred yards up the draw and setting it ablaze. The resulting fire exposed the Chinese troops in the narrow corridor and offered the marines a turkey shoot. This virtually eliminated the Chinese attackers. Hundreds were killed or wounded, and the CCF commander ordered his remaining troops to withdraw. Incredibly, Companies E and F lost only seven men killed and twenty-five wounded, although the severe weather caused sixty men to fall out from frostbite.

Company H, 7th Marines, emplaced on Hill 1403 and seven hundred yards northeast of the salient, was less fortunate. Chinese troops made probing attacks on the company from all sides. About 10 p.m. they launched a strong assault against the company's right-flank platoon; in the space of minutes, the right flank collapsed. The Company H commander, Captain Leroy M. Cooke, quickly called for artillery and mortar barrages, and the prompt response stopped the Chinese advance and gave Cooke a chance to reorganize his platoons. When the supporting fires stopped, Cooke personally led an assault to restore the right flank, but CCF machine guns and grenades smashed the counterattack, and Cooke was killed at the head of his men. The CO of the 3rd Battalion, 7th Marines, Lieutenant Colonel William F. Harris, dispatched Lieutenant H. H. Harris (no relation) to take over the company, and it held under a second major CCF attack that came after a lull. However, at 4 a.m. November 28, Colonel Harris ordered the hard-pressed company to pull back toward the rear of Company E, 5th Marines.

Hill 1403, sitting directly above Yudam on the northwest, was now lost, and like a dagger pointed into the entire marine perimeter. The CCF were in an excellent position to isolate Companies D, E, and F of the 5th Marines, emplaced west of Hill 1403, and also to attack the rear and flanks of the units on North and Southwest Ridges. In addition, at daylight they would be able to look right down on the marine artillery and the two battalions of the 5th Marines in the valley floor around Yudam.

The CCF attack against North Ridge also got under way in the early hours of November 28. The first strike came in several assaults against Company E, 7th Marines, on Hill 1282, about 1,200 yards northeast of Yudam. These attacks were made by two CCF companies of the 235th CCF Regiment, 79th Division. The first assault struck around midnight at a marine platoon on the northeastern arc of the company perimeter on the ridge crest. Failing because of heavy fire, the Chinese attempted to slip around and behind the marine position, but ran headlong into another platoon on a spur leading southward from the peak. Because of the poor communications of battalions with higher headquarters, this CCF force apparently got no orders to call off its attacks. As a result, two CCF companies, totaling more than two hundred men, for two hours charged time after time right into the mouths of the marine guns and were destroyed almost to the last man. Marine casualties also were heavy, but Company E, 7th Marines, remained in possession of the hil.

The second strike on North Ridge took place on Hill 1384, about 1,200 yards north of Yudam. This hill was not occupied by marines until after dark on November 27. By then the 3rd Battalion, 5th Marines, had arrived at Yudam and was emplaced in the valley just north of the village. The battalion CO, Lieutenant Colonel R. D. Taplett, learning that the hill directly north of his battalion was devoid of friendly troops, dispatched a platoon of Company I five hundred yards up the slope. About three hundred yards behind this platoon a platoon of South Korean police set up two machine guns. About 2:30 a.m. November 28, a CCF force overran the Company I platoon and came on down the ridgeline and attacked the ROK police, who fired on the Chinese but vacated their positions. The Chinese then spread out along the hillside and poured fire down on the 3rd Battalion in the draw below. It was a frightening situation. The Weapons Company, on the far side of the draw, held its ground, but the Headquarters and Service Company, directly under the Chinese guns, fell back across the road, leaving the battalion CP blackout tent isolated, with bullets flying all around. Colonel Taplett elected to remain in the tent in order to keep telephone contact with his companies. Few CCF soldiers descended from the ridge, and apparently none paid any attention to Taplett's blackout tent, which they probably thought was unoccupied. Major John J. Canney, the battalion executive, however, left the CP to retrieve the Headquarters and Service Company, and was killed as he approached the road.

The third enemy strike on North Ridge was directed against Hill 1240 where, about 1 a.m., the Chinese hit Company D, 7th Marines, in a savage assault. One platoon on the northwest sector fought off three attacks before being overrun about 2:30 a.m. About 3 a.m. the Chinese overran the company CP. Captain Milton A. Hull, company commander, though wounded himself, rallied his few remaining troops on a lower slope and led a counterattack against the crest. The surprised Chinese retreated, but quickly struck the front, right flank and rear of the small counterattack force. Captain Hull was wounded again, but the small group, now down to sixteen fighting men, continued to hold in a hazardous position below the crest of Hill 1240.

Meanwhile the situation on Hill 1282 worsened. About 3 a.m. the CCF commander moved up another company of about 125 men to renew the attack against the crest. Two platoons of Company A, 5th Marines, had been dispatched about 1 a.m. to reinforce Company E, 7th Marines, on the hill, but it took this detachment two hours to climb the icy ridges in minus-twenty-degree weather, and it did not arrive until the new assault against 1282 was in full fury. Both Chinese and marines suffered crippling losses in the assaults. The Chinese commander, using squads of eight to ten men, struck time after time, and both Chinese and marine forces eroded away in the short-range exchanges of fire and grenades. The Chinese finally drove a wedge between the marines defending the summit and two platoons on a southern spur. On the summit, the three marine platoons were in the throes of a last stand. All of the officers were killed or wounded, and by 5 a.m. the surviving marines had been driven to the reverse slope on the west while the two other platoons still clung to the crest of the southern spur. Chinese losses by now totaled about 250, while marine losses were about 150.

The situation on North Ridge was desperate for the entire marine position at Yudam. If the Chinese could emplace directly above the valley on the North Ridge, the plunging fire they could send down on the infantry and artillery below would make Yudam immediately untenable for the marines. If the marine forces were to remain intact, the Chinese had to be forced away from the Yudam valley.

The first marine counterattack got under way at 3 a.m. against Hill 1384 on the north. Colonel Taplett, still in his blackout tent directly under the Chinese guns, ordered two platoons of his Company G to counterattack up the Hill 1384 spur. These platoons moved forward aggressively and kept going against slender CCF resistance, indicating the Chinese had not realized the advantage achieved by their deep penetration and had not rushed in heavy reinforcements. By daybreak the two platoons were almost at the top of 1384, and Colonel Taplett brought them back to a position on the high ground directly above Yudam.

To restore the situation on Hills 1282 and 1240, the 5th Marines' Company C and the third platoon of Company A were dispatched up the ridgeline spurs in the early hours of November 28—one Company C platoon heading off to help hold 1240 and the remaining marines moving to 1282. The Company C force arrived at 1282 about 4:30 a.m., and the CO, Captain Jack R. Jones, quickly deployed his men to attack while 81mm mortars from Yudam valley opened up in a preparatory barrage. Jones led his men in a direct frontal assault against about fifty Chinese soldiers on the crest armed with machine guns and grenades. The marines met a hail of fire, but overran the Chinese in a gruesome, hand-to-hand clash. Only about half a dozen Chinese survived this attack by retreating. With other marines, the company was able to establish a connection between troops on the crest and two isolated pockets of marine survivors of the earlier fight.

They were just in time. The Chinese, as quick to recognize the significance of this hill as the marines, already had dispatched a new rifle platoon to reinforce the position. The new CCF platoon was approaching the crest from the east as Captain Jones and his men were winning the top. The Chinese platoon therefore confronted the guns of the triumphant marines as they neared the summit. The CCF platoon leader, surprised to see Americans on top, immediately ordered his force to charge before it had time to spread into a skirmish line. The Chinese soldiers, bunched closely together, met a withering fire and grenades when they were about ten yards from the top, and the Chinese platoon virtually melted away in killed and wounded. The Chinese commander immediately ordered another platoon up 1282, and this unit, too, was destroyed by American fire. The 1st Battalion of the 235th CCF Regiment was now down to a single platoon. Incredibly, this last detachment doggedly climbed the hill and assaulted the Americans. All but a half-dozen of these men, too, fell dead or wounded into the blood-soaked snow. Total Chinese casualties on 1282 were about four hundred men, virtually all of them dead, because evacuation of the wounded was practically impossible, since marines held the summit for the next twenty-four hours. Marine losses were heavy, too: more than two hundred dead and wounded.

The small relief force that had been sent to help the beleaguered men on Hill 1240 arrived after daylight and, aided by the sixteen men still left with Captain Hull, cleared the crest of Chinese. Radios with the marines on 1240 were out, however, and they were unable to call in Corsairs or mortars. When Chinese counterattacked about 11 a.m., they forced the marines to withdraw about 150 yards down the slope. Here the marines held until 5 p.m., when they were relieved by Company B, 5th Marines. The cost: practically all the men of Company D, 7th, and half of the platoon of Company C, 5th.

When November 28 ended, the Chinese on North Ridge held the crests of Hills 1384 on the north and 1240 almost due east of Yudam, but had been pushed to the lower slopes of Hill 1282, which was located between these other two peaks. The immediate danger to the marines' position at Yudam had been prevented by U.S. possession of 1282, but the longer-term prospects on this flank were not encouraging.

While the 79th and 89th CCF Divisions assaulted the Northwest and North Ridges on the night of November 27–28, the 59th CCF Division carried out its wide enveloping movement to the southeast and took absolute possession of long stretches of the MSR south of Yudam. CCF troops also encircled the two isolated marine forces guarding the road: Companies C and F, 7th Marines.

The attack against Company C was fierce and raged until daybreak. Then, with the help of artillery concentrations, the company drove the Chinese back into the hills. However, the company remained pinned down by CCF fire coming from every direction. The company radio was destroyed by fire and could not call in Corsair air strikes, although the aircraft were overhead. With ammunition running low, Company C could do nothing but close up in a tight perimeter and await help from Yudam.

About 2:30 a.m. November 28, Chinese troops struck Company F from three directions on Fox Hill just north of Toktong pass. Two squads on the summit were overwhelmed almost immediately, losing fifteen men killed, three missing and nine wounded out of thirty-five men. Repeated CCF attacks were thrown back with heavy casualties. A big part of the reason was the determined stand of three men who refused to be budged: Privates First Class Robert F. Benson and Gerald J. Smith and Private Hector A. Cafferatta. These men were credited with annihilating two CCF platoons. Although Company F suffered 20 dead and 54 wounded in the night attacks, by daybreak it was in control of the situation and the Chinese made no attempt to attack during the day. An estimated 450 Chinese dead lay on the approaches to the company position.

* * * * * * * * * *

The situation called for the marines to fall back on defense and cancel plans for any advance. The 7th Marines CO, Colonel Litzenberg, and the 5th Marines commander, Lieutenant Colonel Raymond L. Murray, agreed to pull marines entirely off Northwest Ridge and back to Southwest Ridge, thereby establishing a smaller perimeter around Yudam. This constriction also removed the marines from direct fire from the Chinese now holding Hill 1403 on Northwest Ridge.

Meantime, the 1st Battalion of the 7th Marines moved south on the morning of November 28 to rescue Companies C and F on the MSR. After five hours of effort, the battalion was stopped cold three miles south of Yudam-ni and still a mile short of the Company C perimeter. A renewed attack against the enemy, aided by Corsair strikes and mortar concentrations, drove the Chinese away, and permitted the battalion to join up with Company C. But Company F, three miles farther away and burdened with many wounded, could not move. The 1st Battalion, along with the rescued Company C, went back to Yudam. Company F had to fend for itself. It was a bitter disappointment. A series of probing attacks and mortar concentrations on the night of November 28–29 cost Company F five more men killed and twenty-nine wounded. But air drops on November 29 brought in adequate ammunition and supplies. And a marine helicopter dropped into the perimeter to deliver needed batteries for the company's radios. Although hit by long-distance fire, the helicopter got away safely.

Back at Yudam, there were not enough tents in the medical aid station to shelter more than the seriously wounded. The others were protected from freezing by being placed side by side outdoors on straw and under tarpaulins. By November 30, however, enough tents had been erected to care for about five hundred wounded.

The 5th Marines surgeon, navy Lieutenant Commander Chester M. Lessenden, told Keyes Beech, a press correspondent, that plasma could not be used because it would not go into solution at the low temperatures and the tubes would clog with particles. Medics could not change dressings because they had to work with gloves on to keep their hands from freezing. The corpsmen did not cut men's clothes off to get at wounds because the men would freeze to death.[2]

General Smith, marine division commander, by radio ordered another effort on November 29 to rescue Company F, as well as an effort to open the MSR to Hagaru. The two regimental commanders, believing all their units holding the Yudam perimeter were needed in place, formed a composite battalion out of reserve units under command of Major Warren Morris, executive of the 3rd Battalion, 7th Marines. This force moved out early November 29 and got only three hundred yards beyond the perimeter before heavy machine-gun fire hit the column from both sides of the road. Chinese troops could be seen plainly on the ridges, and soon mortars, 75mm recoilless rifles and Corsairs were firing at them. The battalion reached a point about two and a half miles down the road when Corsair pilots dropped messages that CCF forces were entrenched ahead in heavy force on both sides of the MSR. Colonel Litzenberg told Major Morris to call off the effort to get through to Hagaru, but to continue to try to reach Company F and return to Yudam by nightfall.

By this time the composite battalion was engaged with large numbers of Chinese, while more were moving on the battalion from all directions through draws that largely masked them from air observation. Air observers spotted some of this movement and relayed it urgently to Litzenberg. He radioed Morris to extricate the force immediately and get back to Yudam.

That afternoon, Captain William E. Barber at the Company F perimeter called his platoon leaders together and told them not to expect relief for another day. The attacks that night, however, were beaten off at the cost of only one wounded. The night of November 29–30 was a turning point both for the besieged men of Company F and the garrison at Yudam. Everyone felt the Chinese had shot their bolt without achieving more than local gains at the cost of many men killed and wounded. However, it was obvious that the two regiments and their supporting arms had to get out of the trap and back to Hagaru.

On X Corps orders, the Yudam force broke off action on November 30 and prepared to move back to Hagaru. The plan called for 1st Battalion, 7th Marines, to strike out cross-country on the night of December 1 to relieve Company F and to secure the vital Toktong pass before the arrival of the main column. It would be impossible to carry the wounded over the mountains, and in any event the regiments needed their vehicles and heavy weapons for the trials that lay ahead. Therefore, the main body had to fight its way along the MSR to Toktong pass.

In preparation for the cross-country trek to relieve Company F, the marines had to capture Hill 1419 to the east of the MSR about halfway between Yudam and the Fox Hill perimeter. Company H of the 7th Marines got this assignment, but ran into heavy CCF defenses, and the cross-country force itself had to help win the peak. Thereupon Company H was attached to the force, and thus four rifle companies formed the cross-country unit.

This force adopted the movement techniques of the enemy: not only did it march under cover of darkness, but the men left their vehicles and heavy equipment for the battalion walking wounded and frostbite victims to drive out, and took only what the able men could carry on their backs.

Meanwhile, the main force on the MSR led off with the only tank that had been able to get through to Yudam, while an artillery battery followed close behind in order to unlimber near the pass and provide covering fire for the rear guard while the rest of the artillery displaced from Yudam.

The cross-country force, though heavily laden with extra ammunition, walked through rough mountains and through snowdrifts and got into several fire fights along the way, but on the morning of December 2 it broke the siege of Company F. This company had suffered greatly during its ordeal: of 240 men, 26 had been killed, 3 were missing and 89 had been wounded; in addition, practically all the rest suffered from frostbite or digestive ills. The men of the cross-country force, now calling themselves the Ridgerunners of Toktong pass, moved on the secure the pass itself.

The main force, spearheaded by the 3rd Battalion, 5th Marines, ran into repeated and heavy Chinese opposition, but continued to advance along the MSR, aided by attacking Corsairs, which repeatedly broke up Chinese blocking positions. Chinese also attacked the marine rear guard but were unable to make a breakthrough. The chief problem of the main force was to keep Chinese troops far enough away from the MSR to prevent them from firing effectively on the retreating vehicles and men. The vehicle train made slow progress on the afternoon of December 2 because Chinese soldiers infiltrated back into areas on hills vacated by marine riflemen as they moved out. Excellent air support kept most of these efforts to local harassing attacks, but the Chinese singled out the drivers of vehicles with their fire, and several were shot.

The marines broke through CCF positions at Toktong pass on December 3 in a converging attack by the Ridgerunners and the main body's spearhead. Several more fights engaged the spearhead force, but the last major barrier was cracked at Toktong pass. The lead position had taken a heavy toll of the spearhead 3rd Battalion, 5th Marines. On December 1 there were 437 men in the three rifle companies; by December 4, the companies were down to 194 men—a loss of 243 men in four days.

The marine column moved on to Hagaru, with large numbers of wounded required to walk; because there were so many, only the seriously wounded could be carried on vehicles. And some of these had to be strapped to the hoods. The column was met by the Royal Marines commandos, reinforced by a platoon of U.S. tanks, who moved out from Hagaru on the afternoon of December 3 to drive away the Chinese on the road. The long marine column continued all through the night hours to move slowly into Hagaru. Although the Chinese continued to hover around the column's flanks and to fire at it whenever possible, the marines had little difficulty until 2 a.m. on December 4. Then the prime movers of eight 155mm howitzers ran out of diesel fuel. The troops ahead of the howitzers moved on ahead, unaware of the break in the column. Shortly after the 155s stopped, a Chinese platoon attacked, but the artillerymen drove it off. The gunners were soon joined by other marines, and they hastily organized an attack against the now-gathering Chinese. In the confusion, a CCF force got to the MSR ahead of the 155s and blew a small bridge. While engineers repaired it, two waiting truck drivers were killed by Chinese snipers. Other truck drivers bypassed the bridge and made a dash for Hagaru by crossing the small stream on the ice. At 8:30 a.m. a platoon of marines overran the blocking Chinese position while other troops cleared the high ground above the MSR. The 155mm howitzers meanwhile had been pushed off the road, and the remainder of the marine column pressed on through to Hagaru. It had been assumed the 155s would be retrieved, especially since a cache of diesel fuel had been dropped only a thousand yards eastward along the road. But it was not to be. The British marines tried to recover the howitzers but failed because of heavy enemy fire, and marine commanders reluctantly ordered aircraft to destroy the eight stalled howitzers, plus a ninth which earlier had been abandoned after skidding off the road.

At 2 p.m. December 4 the last men of the rear guard entered the Hagaru perimeter and the four-day retreat ended. About fifteen hundred casualties were brought into Hagaru, about a third of them frostbite and other nonbattle casualties. Every man of the Yudam force was exhausted. Scarcely any had had sleep for days. All had been under severe nervous strain. What little food they had been able to snatch had usually been crackers and canned rations thawed by body heat. No unit of the marine force was more worn out than the Ridgerunners, the four-company 7th Marines force that had marched cross-country to rescue Company F at Toktong pass, and which had protected the column ever after. A few hundred yards before reaching the edge of the Hagaru perimeter, the men of the Ridgerunners halted, closed themselves into a compact column, dressed ranks, and *marched* into the perimeter, their shoulders thrown back and their shoepacs beating a steady cadence on the frozen road. It was a *beau geste* in the finest tradition of the U.S. Marines, a defiance of adversity. No body of soldiers, however polished and resplendent their uniforms, ever looked grander and more admirable than this group of dirty, bearded, weary—and dauntless—men.

Members of the Turkish Brigade move into position in December, 1950, shortly after suffering severe casualties attempting to block encirclement of the U.S. 2nd Division at the Chongchon River in North Korea.

Frozen bodies of American marines, British commandos and South Korean soldiers are gathered for group burial at Koto-ri.

Marine Corsairs have just struck Chinese positions in the Changjin reservoir area of northeast Korea with jellied gasoline napalm. Close air support was a key to the successful retreat to the sea in December, 1950.

Marines take up temporary defensive positions in the retreat from the Changjin reservoir.

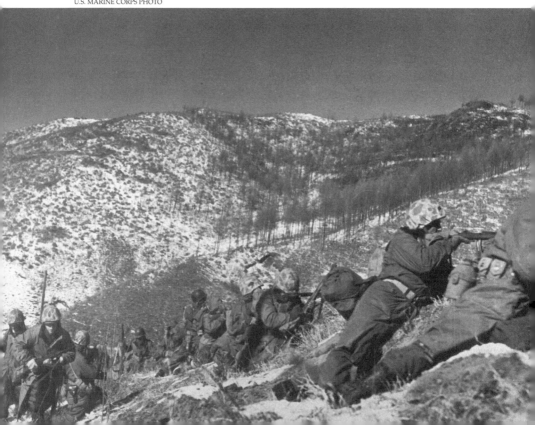

*Marines in the retreat from Changjin reservoir halt while leading elements clear
a Chinese roadblock.*

This C-47 is being unloaded at the tiny Hagaru-ri airstrip at Changjin reservoir. From here 4,312 wounded and frostbitten men were evacuated by air in the five days before the retreat to the sea began.

The marine and army retreat from the Changjin reservoir in December, 1950, occurred in temperatures around zero degrees Fahrenheit.

Marines reclaimed all their dead on the retreat from Changjin reservoir. Infiltrating Chinese soldiers stripped clothing from some of the bodies.

This sixteen-foot hole was blown by Chinese soldiers in the single road from Changjin reservoir to the sea. Bridge sections dropped by air permitted this gap to be spanned and men and equipment to get out.

These are some of the 385 able-bodied survivors of 2,500 7th Division men caught in a series of Chinese ambushes along the eastern shore of Changjin reservoir in late November, 1950.

Marines move toward evacuation ships at Hungnam harbor in December, 1950, as the United Nations abandons northeast Korea.

When United Nations troops began evacuating northeast Korea after the Chinese offensive of November, 1950, many North Koreans wanted to go along. Here at Hungnam some of the 98,000 civilians carried to South Korea board ships for the journey.

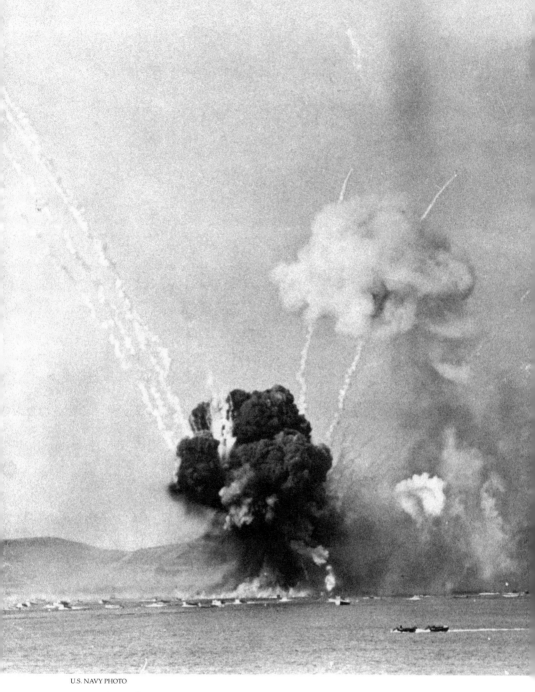

U.S. ordnance teams detonated great stocks of American ammunition at Hungnam as the last troops of X Corps withdrew in landing craft and abandoned the effort to conquer North Korea.

CHAPTER 47

The Breakout

A GREAT SURGE of confidence rushed through the marines and soldiers around the Changjin reservoir when the men from Yudam-ni broke through the Chinese and arrived at Hagaru-ri. Despite the frightful casualties suffered by marines and soldiers, spirits were lifted up, because the officers and men decided the Chinese had hit them with everything they had—and it had not been enough to defeat them. While the headlines in the United States were screeching with fear that the entire American force would be destroyed, the men on the scene lost the anxiety of trapped men and gained an easy assurance that they would make it to the sea.

Perhaps not all had the aplomb of the marine commander, General Oliver Smith, who argued with a British correspondent that there could be no talk of retreat. After all, Smith contended, the marines and soldiers were surrounded, and therefore there was no rear, thus nowhere to retreat *to*. Instead he preferred to call it a breakout to the coast.[1]

Of course, it *was* a retreat, and Smith knew it as well as anyone. In traditional marine style, he preferred to emphasize the positive. But despite the returning self-confidence the "breakout to the coast" was going to be an enormous and perilous undertaking. It also would represent a huge and terrible American defeat which could not be washed away with euphemisms.

Nevertheless, there was good cause for American optimism. The Chinese had shown their Achilles' heel—their inability to sustain and to exploit a successful offensive. Despite the immense success of their Changjin attacks, the Chinese had been unable to press through to decisive victory, except in limited engagements, as in the overwhelming of the small column in Hell Fire Valley. The reason could be traced to their primitive supply and transportation system. It relied upon the

353

backs of men and upon beasts of burden, and attacks were thereby limited to brief engagements requiring relatively small amounts of ammunition which could be carried to the battle scene. Stockpiling of great quantities of supplies, in the American tradition, was impossible. Thus Chinese decisions had to be quick and overwhelming, and in the nature of the situation, they had to be essentially *local*. Given the Chinese logistics and their dependence upon footpower for mobility, breakthroughs of United Nations lines could not be exploited decisively by swift and massive motorized penetrations aimed at complete victory on a grand tactical or strategic scale.

The Chinese possessed no great logistical system based on roads and trucks which could feed vast quantities of supplies to rapidly advancing columns, as was available to American forces. On the contrary, Chinese forces, however great their tactical victories, had to stop, regroup and resupply before they could advance again. Because of the effects of UN artillery, mortars and air power, this restrengthening could best be achieved by retiring from the battle lines, alleviating the danger and simultaneously reducing the distances to supplies in the rear. Thus the Chinese offensives quickly assumed a pattern of advance, attack, withdrawal, advance, attack, withdrawal.

The essentially unlimited numbers of men that China could bring into the field if the need arose meant that Chinese forces could achieve a great many local victories that could have overall disastrous effects upon a foe, especially his morale. But however many local victories the CCF achieved, they could not destroy a modern army led by determined commanders and possessed of great mobility and firepower.

The marines learned quickly that, no matter how shattering, demoralizing and costly a typical Chinese night attack might be, the defenders need only hold their positions until daylight to survive. With visibility restored, ground-support aircraft and observed artillery and mortar fire could quickly drive the Chinese to cover. And even if the marine force remained surrounded and unable to move, it could be resupplied from the air, and could be worn down only be repeated costly attacks which used up precious Chinese ammunition and bled the attacking units white. Thus it was that, though marine units in such situations often suffered heavy losses, the attacking Chinese units nearly always suffered greater losses, often to the point of complete destruction. Likewise, marine assaults on Chinese roadblocks took the form of shattering attacks of rocketing, machine-gunning and napalming by close-support aircraft, of direct tank and machine-gun fire, and of heavy indirect mortar and artillery fire. Although the marine infantry often had a difficult time ousting determined Chinese defenders from hill positions covering the

MSR, they could get the columns through, even if they could not prevent the Chinese from closing back over the MSR after they had departed.

Korea, therefore, exhibited the strange case of the encounter of two kinds of armies, each different from the other and each emphasizing its advantages and reducing its disadvantages as best it could. The great Chinese advantage was the marvelous ability of individual soldiers to move over difficult terrain; this was made possible by their reliance upon their own feet and upon the weapons, food and ammunition they could carry with them; this meant CCF units could go where they wished, materializing far behind UN lines or flanking or cutting off frontline units. This advantage was accentuated by the Chinese skill at silent infiltration of even the most closely held positions and their ability, despite having to rely upon bugles, whistles and flares, to maneuver and fight at night. The great American advantage was astonishing firepower, which could defeat virtually any enemy force if it could be brought it bear. Because firepower implies great (and sometimes wasteful) expenditure of ammunition and reliance upon heavy weapons like tanks, artillery, and tracked and wheeled vehicles, American operations inevitably were tied to the MSRs which carried the ammo and the vehicles.

Since the Chinese found they could not destroy the emplaced American forces, even though they might surround them, their strategy came quickly to center on blocking the vital American MSR in the hope of denying the cutoff Americans sufficient resupply and thus forcing them to surrender. American strategy in normal circumstances, of course, would have been to reopen the MSR and keep it open. In the case of the MSR running from Hagaru back to Hungnam, however, the Chinese mobility meant this MSR could be cut at will wherever the Chinese decided to cut it, especially in the rough, high country between Hagaru and the last major marine bastion at Chinhung-ni, twenty-one miles to the south.

It was this inability to open the MSR and keep it open which dictated the American decision to abandon northeast Korea. Although the work of building the C-47 strip continued without cease, there was no possibility that two-motored transports could bring in enough supplies to sustain a continued operation using one small strip at Hagaru. Likewise, airdropped supplies could not be delivered in sufficient tonnage to sustain a single regimental combat team, must less a whole marine division. The Far East Air Force's Combat Cargo Command estimated it could deliver seventy tons a day by airdrop, using C-119 and C-54 cargo planes. Although in practice Cargo Command raised the total to one hundred tons a day, a remarkable achievement, it was still five tons short of the full needs of a single RCT. Fortunately, supply officers earlier had laid in six days of rations and additional ammunition at Hagaru before the Chinese encirclement. But time was running out, and the marines and army soldiers had to depart soon.

Meanwhile, there were thousands of marine and army wounded and frostbite cases at Hagaru. To take these men down the treacherous and dangerous MSR in trucks in the retreat to Hungnam would have led to tragedy, even if enough vehicles could have been found to carry them. Now the great foresight of Generals Almond and Smith, who had insisted an airstrip be built at Hagaru, and the incredibly determined work of the marine engineers came to be appreciated.

By December 1, the strip was 2,900 feet long and 50 feet wide, an absurdly tiny landing place when construction manuals called for a runway 7,600 feet long at Hagaru's elevation. Nevertheless, the over-crowding of the wounded in the hospital had become critical, the men from Yudam were coming with their many wounded and frostbitten, and the UN forces had to evacuate within days—whatever the disposition of the wounded. General Smith elected to authorize a trial run at the airstrip. Groups of parka-clad marines watched anxiously at 2:30 p.m. on December 1 as an air force C-47 dropped with flaps full down onto the frozen, snow-covered strip, and bounced and braked across the rough, uneven surface. But it made it. Half an hour later, the real test came. Now loaded with twenty-four wounded men, the C-47 strained as the pilot set the throttles at full power, released the brakes at last, and allowed the craft to roar down the runway: for a single, frightening, agonizing moment it appeared that the plane would not be able to get airborne in the short run; then, while the men on the ground cheered wildly, the pilot forced the tail up and the wings gained enough lift to rise and slowly clear the hills to the south. Thus was born the Hagaru airstrip. In its short existence it gave birth to one of the great legends in man's conquest of the air, a testament to American determination. Before the day was out, three more C-47s landed, and two of them took off again, carrying sixty more casualties. The third craft remained: it came in heavily loaded with ammunition, and when it hit the runway, its landing gear collapsed. It had to be dragged off and abandoned.

The next day, the C-47s commenced an amazing shuttle between Hagaru and Yonpo airfield, a few miles southwest of Hungnam. Most men went from Yonpo to the 1st Marine Division Hospital at Hungnam, the army 121st Evacuation Hospital at Hamhung, or the USS *Consolation* hospital ship in Hungnam harbor. A few critical cases were evacuated directly from Hagaru to Japan. Returning to Hagaru, the C-47s brought not only needed fragile equipment and medical supplies, but also 537 marines who had recovered from wounds in hospitals in Japan.

On December 2, air force and marine C-47s flew out 914 casualties. On December 3, 700 more went out. On December 4, the figure rose to about 1,200. Still, by the morning of December 5, there were more than 1,400 wounded and frostbitten men remaining in the Hagaru hospital, and the breakout was ordered to commence the next morning. Faced with this imperative deadline, the C-47 pilots stepped up their shuttle, and they got all the casualties out by nightfall. When the last craft rose over the mountains and disappeared toward Yonpo, air and medical personnel counted up the accomplishments: 4,312 men had been flown out of the airstrip in five days—3,150 U.S. marines, 1,137 army soldiers, and 25 British marines. The C-47 pilots had done it without losing a man, although one air force craft lost power on takeoff and came down just outside the defense lines, but without further harm to the casualties. Troops rushed out immediately and rescued the men, but the aircraft had to be destroyed.

* * * * * * * * * *

X Corps, the marine division, the navy, the air force and the 1st Marine Air Wing planned the retreat to Hungnam carefully. Combat Cargo Command began emergency airdrops of supplies on both Hagaru and Koto-ri. Generals Almond and Smith decided to drop only enough supplies at Hagaru to provide for the breakout to Koto. The supplies for the haul to the rear marine perimeter at Chinhung-ni were assembled at Koto-ri. Because the marine and army troops would be required to move in long columns on the roads and therefore would have a difficult time deploying mortars and artillery constantly in support, the commanders hastily assembled one of the heaviest concentrations of combat aircraft in American history. Every available land-based fighter and fighter-bomber of the Far East Air Force, plus the Australian F-51 squadron, was ordered to support the retreat. FEAF's medium and heavy bombers were assigned urgent targets to interdict or slow the movement of Chinese supplies and reinforcement to the Changjin reservoir front. The heaviest tactical support job was laid on the marine and navy fighters and fighter-bombers. The navy quickly moved its fast-carrier force—*Leyte, Valley Forge, Philippine Sea* and *Princeton*—off the Hungnam shore, with their planes poised to attack all observed targets on the MSR and its approaches. In addition to the land-based marine Corsair squadron VMF-312, the marine Corsair squadron (VMF-214) at Yonpo airfield flew missions out of the field until December 7, when the squadron casually transferred back between sorties to the escort carrier *Sicily*, which had hurried to a station offshore. The baby flattop *Badoeng Strait* was already on station off Hungnam with its marine Corsair squadron (VMF-323), and on December 4 the third marine Corsair squadron (VMF-212) departed Yonpo for Itami air base in Japan, where it hastily re-equipped for return to battle on the just-arrived light aircraft carrier *Bataan*. Thus, four fast fleet carriers, two escort carriers and one light carrier were offshore and in direct support of the breakout. These, plus the FEAF, represented an awesome assemblage of air power, and assured the marines and army soldiers an air umbrella and a reliable overhead attack platform for the entire retreat. Although the ground troops on the long trek back to the coast justifiably gained renown for their bravery and their endurance, their efforts would have been far more costly had it not been for the sacrifice, courage and determination of the airmen and the crews. The aircraft climbed into the skies in terrible weather conditions. Glazed ice and snow accumulated on the flight decks of the carriers and had to be laboriously chipped away. Only in the direst of circumstances were sorties scrubbed. On one such rare occasion the marine 214th squadron had to cancel flight operations because 68-knot winds, heavy seas, and freezing temperatures had covered the *Sicily's* flight deck and aircraft with ice. Ditching in the sea was at least as dangerous as crashing on land: the water was so cold it would kill a man in twenty minutes. Pilots wore bulky survival clothing, but the danger remained.

The breakout from Hagaru was set for December 6. The 7th Marines were to lead the way. Attached to the 7th was a provisional battalion of 490 soldiers of the 7th Division, 385 of them the able-bodied survivors of the three army battalions shattered on the eastern shore of the reservoir. The 5th Marines were assigned the mission of covering the movement of the 7th Marines out of Hagaru and forming the rear guard. Attached to the 5th was the one battalion of the 1st Marines (the 3rd) which had reached Hagaru. The remainder of the 1st Marines at Koto and Chinhung were to join this force when it arrived there and then form the rear guard for the rest of the way into Hamhung.

While the 7th Marines broke out toward Koto on the morning of December 6, the 2nd Battalion of the 5th Marines attacked the so-called East Hill, to the north of Hagaru, behind mortar and artillery fire and Corsair strikes. The CCF forces had penetrated to the hill on the first night of their attack and had not been dislodged. This enemy salient was a threat because the hill looked over the road leading to Koto. The battalion succeeded in gaining the two peaks on East Hill after considerable resistance, but in the afternoon Chinese troops foolishly began to mass for a counterattack in the saddle between the two peaks. They were promptly caught between fires from the marines on the two peaks and were set upon by Corsairs. The Chinese in the saddle quickly surrendered, 220 of them, by far the largest group of enemy captured in the entire Changjin operation. That night other CCF forces returned time after time to attack East Hill, enduring frightful casualties against marine fire. Although the Americans suffered considerable casualties from CCF mortar and machine-gun fire and from a few Chinese who reached grenade-throwing range, nearly eight hundred Chinese were dead in front of the marine positions when daylight came. This exercise demonstrated how vulnerable the Chinese were when they attacked well-emplaced American positions that could not be easily infiltrated and flanked and that were supported by heavy weapons.

The attack of the 7th Marines down on the MSR to Koto was designed around the sound concept of clearing the hills and ridges on both flanks of the road, pushing forward on the road with a strong tank-led vanguard, distributing a company (G) along both flanks of the road as close-in security for vehicles of the regimental train, and bringing up the rear with a strong defensive force. The 7th Marines and the provisional army battalion thus formed a moving hedgehog, bristling with guns and firing in all directions at anything that moved. The hedgehog was formed as follows: the 2nd Battalion constituted the advance guard on the MSR; the 1st Battalion cleared the high ground on the right (west) of the MSR; the army provisional battalion cleared the ground on the left (east) side, and the 3rd Battalion formed the rear guard.

When the movement south started at first light, the lead tank took three hits from a CCF-fired 3.5-inch bazooka, but the column moved on without further incident for twenty minutes, when it came under heavy fire from CCF positions from high ground on the left. A heavy fog prevented air support at first, but when it lifted air controllers called in marine Corsairs and 81mm mortar fire fell on the enemy position. Even so, it took a coordinated attack by two vanguard infantry companies with tanks to end resistance and permit the column to start moving at noon.

About 4,000 yards south of Hagaru the column encountered the next CCF hill position. After an artillery barrage and on-target firing by the tanks, Company F cleared this position by 3 p.m., aided by a flanking attack by Companies D and E and by the army battalion.

On the right flank, the 1st Battalion pushed methodically across the hills looking down on the MSR, but encountered no serious opposition during the daylight hours. The army battalion on the left also continued to move, although it got into several fire fights, indicating the main CCF defensive effort was centered on this side of the MSR.

By dark, the 7th Marines column had advanced 5,000 yards south of Hagaru. Everyone knew Chinese resistance would increase as night fell and the close air support departed. Since CCF reinforcements were known to be moving in to try to block the retreat, U.S. commanders decided the column should keep on going, despite darkness. The 7th Marines hedgehog proceeded without incident for another 3,000 yards. By 10 p.m. it had reached the notorious Hell Fire Valley. There a Chinese machine gun opened up on the vanguard. The advance was held up until midnight, when an army tank knocked out the machine gun. The column moved on for another 1,200 yards to a bridge the CCF had blown. It took marine engineers until 2 a.m. to make repairs, then the column met another blown bridge that took an hour and a half before a bypass for it could be created. Meanwhile, Chinese troops tried to attack the rear of the column, but determined marine resistance forced the enemy troops to move back. However, about 2 a.m., while the column was halted for the bridge repair, Chinese troops infiltrated back onto the high ground around the column and began to fire down on the vehicles. Several officers and men of the regimental command post were killed, but marines deployed and stopped the attack. Around 5:30 a.m., however, the commander of the rear-guard 3rd Battalion, Lieutenant Colonel William F. Harris, disappeared, and it was later determined he had been killed. The battalion executive, Major Warren Morris, took command.

The 7th Marines got to Koto without further incident. Directly behind the 7th was the first column of the division trains. The breakout planners had hoped the advance of the 7th would open the MSR for this column, but because of the 7th Marines' delays, the Division Train No. 1 did not move out of Hagaru until 4 p.m. In the early darkness about 2,000 yards south of Hagaru the train was hit by CCF mortar and small-arms fire, and marine artillerymen deployed and repulsed the CCF attackers. About 1,500 yards farther on, Chinese mortar rounds set several vehicles afire, blocked the road and brought the column to a halt. At daybreak on December 7 the Chinese attacked the train and the marine artillerymen unlimbered their howitzers in direct fire at ranges from 500 yards down to 40 yards. They killed or wounded all but about fifty of the five hundred or so Chinese attackers, and these survivors fled.

The division headquarters company convoy accompanying the division train also had to fight its way through the night, being stopped several times by mortar fire which set trucks aflame. Just before daylight a company-sized group of Chinese approached within a few yards of the headquarters company, but was held off by marine fire. Night-fighter aircraft, coming in as close as thirty yards from the marine troops, pinned down the Chinese until daybreak when four Corsairs dropped about four tons of bombs and napalm on the Chinese, who ran. Just forward of the division headquarters column, the Military Police Company was guarding about 160 Chinese prisoners, who were lying in the road when the CCF attack came. The attacking Chinese appeared to concentrate their fire on the huddled POWs; when some of them attempted to break free, the marines as well as CCF fired into them, and 137 were killed. The division train and headquarters convoys reached Koto without further attacks.

Division Train No. 2, with support of the 3rd Battalion, 5th Marines, had been unable to leave Hagaru until after dark on December 6 and by midnight had reached a point only a short distance south of the village. The late start proved fortunate, however, because the column completed most of its movement in daylight on December 7 under continuous air cover and received only scattered and light Chinese resistance.

The 1st Battalion, 5th Marines, and the 3rd Battalion, 1st Marines, left Hagaru, accompanied by the British 41st Commando, on the morning of December 7 and moved down the MSR, also under air cover for much of the day, and arrived at Koto without mishap.

By 10 a.m. December 7 no Americans were left in Hagaru except the division rear guard, the 2nd Battalion, 5th Marines, along with a platoon of tanks and a group of marine engineers and ordnance demolition teams charged with blowing up equipment and supplies the marines could not remove. As the force pulled out of the village, where great stocks of Americans goods and equipment were burning, the engineers set off one last tremendous explosion that destroyed the bridge over the Changjin river south of town. The rear guard, followed by thousands of fleeing Korean refugees, moved on south, blowing bridges as it went. The rear guard got less air and artillery support than any of the detachments, but Chinese opposition was limited to scattered rifle fire and a few desultory mortar rounds in Hell Fire Valley. By midnight the rear guard was within the Koto perimeter.

It had been a highly successful effort: more than 9,000 marines, 800 army troops, 125 British marines and 40 ROK police had got through to join the Koto garrison. At Koto, marine Colonel "Chesty" Puller was in command of 2,600 U.S. and 25 British marines, along with 1,500 army troops of the 7th Division, mostly artillerymen and members of the 31st Regiment, who got through before the Chinese closed the MSR. Thus, there were now almost 11,700 marines, 2,300 army troops, 150 Royal Marine commandos and some ROKs—14,000 men—at Koto.

A Koto, a small 1,750-foot airstrip permitted liaison planes and old World War II torpedo bombers pressed into service as flying ambulances to fly out several hundred wounded and frostbitten men. Even one C-47 miraculously landed in a snowstorm and took off with nineteen casualties.

The next stage on the journey was Chinhung-ni, only ten miles farther south, but by far the most precipitous and dangerous section of the MSR. It ran through the high Funchilin pass between steep mountains and practically nowhere along its entire snaking length was the road more than one lane wide. Once committed to the road, vehicles had to keep going or back up: there were few places where a vehicle could turn around or pull off the road.

Because the road was ideal for Chinese roadblocks, especially at Funchilin pass, halfway between Koto and Chinghung, division planners decided the 1st Battalion, 1st Marines, located at Chinhung, had to attack northward up the MSR to clear this pass. To protect Chinhung, X Corps authorized dispatch of so-called Task Force Dog from the coast. This consisted wholly of army troops—a battalion of the 7th Regiment, 3rd Division; an armored artillery battalion; and detachments of engineers, and antiaircraft and signal troops. Task Force Dog brushed aside Chinese roadblocks and reached Chinhung on December 7.

There was one other potentially disastrous problem facing the evacuation: about three and a half miles south of Koto the one-lane road had been built around a sheer mountainside at a point where penstocks or pipes of a Japanese-built hydroelectric system carried water to turbines in the valley below. The one-lane bridge built over these penstocks already had been blown twice by the Chinese, and army engineers had repaired it twice. Now word came that the Chinese had blown it again—creating a sixteen-foot gap. There was no way to bypass this point, nor the equipment or time to cut off a side of the mountain to create a bypass. Neither was there time to build a timber trestle bridge. Yet if the evacuation force's vehicles, tanks and guns were to be brought out, this gap had to be spanned. Without vehicles and heavy weapons the force would be highly vulnerable to Chinese attacks.

Fortunately, there were at Koto two operative army treadway-bridge (Brockway) trucks which could carry sections to the broken bridge, but there were no prefabricated treadway sections. How to get them to Koto? The only answer was to drop them by air. That was not exactly a school solution, for neither the army nor the marines had ever air-dropped these 2,500-pound, six-foot-long bridge elements. But to test the idea engineers hopefully hooked some parachutes to a treadway section, loaded it on an air force C-119, and dropped it on Yonpo airfield on December 6. The test was a failure: the section was badly damaged.

Air-delivery experts studied the problem and hastily ordered larger parachutes flown in from Japan with a special crew of army parachute riggers. A work detail at Yonpo worked all night to ready a treadway section in each of eight C-119s, along with a plywood center piece so a vehicle of any width could travel over a completed span. The engineers required only twenty-four feet of bridge, but decided they needed to drop double this amount in case of damage. At 9:30 a.m. December 7, three C-119s appeared over Koto and dropped their loads: they all came down safely, slowed by the bigger chutes. At noon, five more drops came: one of them fell into the hands of the Chinese and one was damaged, but the other three landed safely.

The breakout from Koto started on the morning of December 8 with the 7th Marines and the provisional army battalion moving to secure hills east and west of the MSR immediately south of Koto, while the 5th Marines went forward to seize a dominating peak (Hill 1457) 5,000 yards south of the village and about 1,700 yards east of the MSR.

At 2 a.m. the 1st Battalion, 1st Marines, already had departed Chinhung in a swirling snowstorm to move north to capture the peak commanding the MSR over Funchilin pass, the great Hill 1081, just east of the pass. While 81mm and 4.2-inch mortars and five army quad-50s and twin-40mm self-propelled weapons moved up to support them, the marines walked in snow-muffled silence up on the mountain. The snow and the absence of air cover, because of the snowstorm, gave the marines almost total surprise, and they achieved great success. They came upon one bunker complex so unexpectedly that a kettle of rice was still cooking on the stove: the surprised defenders were killed or routed.

The 7th Marines moving out of Koto were slowed when the regiment's 3rd Battalion ran into strong CCF small-arms fire on its first objective, Hill 1328 on the west side of the road about 2,000 yards south of Koto. When, at 11 a.m., the 7th Marines CO, Colonel Litzenberg, suggested to the 3rd Battalion commander, Major Warren Morris, that he commit his third company to the attack, Major Morris responded sharply: "All three companies are up there—fifty men from George, fifty men from How, thirty men from Item. That's it." A chastened Colonel Litzenberg, reminded that the entire battalion had been worn down in the bitter campaign to fewer men than in a normal marine company, committed his reserve, the 2nd Battalion, in a flanking attack against the Chinese, and by 6 p.m. the two battalions had joined on the slopes of the hill. Meanwhile the army battalion on the east of the MSR captured its hill objectives without opposition and moved on to join up with the 5th Marines, who had traveled down the MSR and then deployed eastward toward their objective, Hill 1457. The army and marine troops drove the Chinese off this high ground about 4 p.m. and repulsed a weak CCF counterattack.

The snow clouds departed on the night of December 8–9, and the morning of December 9 dawned clear, bright and cold. It also disclosed a disappointment to the 1st Battalion, 1st Marines, on Hill 1081: the day before they had reached all but the final dominating knob of this hill mass. While the other companies supported, Company A assaulted this bare, wind-swept peak, behind mortar concentrations and a strike by four Corsairs. The Chinese, knowing possession of this peak would crack their entire position dominating the MSR, resisted to the last gasp. By 3 p.m. the marines were in possession of 1081, but Company A now was down to 111 able-bodied men out of 223 who had started out from Chinhung. But they held the key height of Funchilin pass, and they counted 530 enemy dead on the mountain.

The advances continued on December 9 behind excellent air and artillery support, and a force soon reached the site of the broken bridge, which it secured after a short skirmish with Chinese. One marine platoon crossed over the heights behind the bridge and discovered fifty Chinese soldiers in foxholes. "They were so badly frozen," said Major W. D. Sawyer, CO of 1st Battalion, 7th Marines, "that the men simply lifted them from the holes and sat them on the road."

The Brockway trucks loaded with the treadway bridge sections now moved to the broken bridge. By 3:30 p.m., three hours after work started, the engineers had the sections in place. Everything looked great as the first few vehicles drove over the span. Then a tractor towing an earth-moving pan broke through the plywood panel that had been laid down in the center of the span between the outside treads. This threatened disaster, not only because the huge piece of equipment was left on the bridge, but because trucks and other equipment having narrower treads would be unable to cross at all.

An expert tractor driver, Technical Sergeant Wilfred H. Prosser, managed to back the machine off the wrecked bridge, a stupendous undertaking in itself. Then Lieutenant Colonel John H. Partridge, commander of the marine 1st Engineer Battalion, arrived. He quickly calculated and found that, if the treadways were placed as far apart as possible, 136 inches, M26 tanks would have two inches to spare and jeeps, riding the lips of the inboard edges of the treadways, 45 inches apart, would have one-half of an inch. The changes were quickly made. As darkness came, the first jeep, guided by flashlights held by engineers, successfully negotiated the chasm, riding eerily inside the treadways, with its tires scraping both edges. Colonel Partridge's solution for narrow-gauged vehicles worked. All night long vehicles and troops poured across this fabulous span without incident. Accompanying the soldiers were thousands of Korean refugees, many of them leading oxen.

The columns met no serious opposition from the Chinese, who appeared to be stunned by the cold. The few prisoners the Americans captured were mostly suffering severely from frostbite and prolonged malnutrition. They confirmed that the battle and nonbattle casualties of the Chinese forces had been crippling. Only in the early morning hours of December 10 was there any significant CCF activity, and this came when marines stopped an attack on Hill 1328, the first objective of the breakout south of Koto. Marine observers believed the Chinese were sideslipping southward, parallel to the MSR, a suspicion confirmed when troops on Hill 1081 spotted Chinese moving in small columns in the low ground only a thousand yards east of this mountain. Although artillery and air strikes immediately were unleashed against these columns, they continued on marching stoically through the fire for an hour.

As infantry began arriving at Chinhung, as many as possible were put on trucks and driven back to Hungnam, though many had to continue walking. It appeared the entire evacuation would proceed without further loss or holdup. The MSR was now under the protection of Task Force Dog and two battalions of the 3rd Infantry Division's 65th Regiment in the vicinity of Su-dong, six miles south of Chinhung, and at Majon-dong, seven miles south of Su-dong. However, on the night of December 10, a small group of Chinese infiltrated into the village of Su-dong and started a wild fire fight that blocked movement for some time before soldiers and marines broke up the attack and set fire to the house serving as the Chinese stronghold.

Another reverse occurred after midnight on December 11 at the tail of the column. The forty tanks of the evacuation force had been placed at the rear to prevent the halting of the entire retreat in the event of a tank breakdown. As the tanks, guarded by the marine Recon Company, clanked southward down the MSR, thousands of Korean refugees trailed behind, approaching as close as they dared. Chinese soldiers had mingled among them, hoping for a chance to strike. About 1 a.m. when the tail of the column was about 2,000 yards above the treadway bridge, the brakes froze on the ninth tank from the rear and the last nine tanks came to a halt. The remainder of the tanks rolled on forward and disappeared, leaving the nine tanks and a twenty-eight-man platoon of the Recon Company guarding them.

During the delay, five CCF soldiers emerged from among the refugees and one called in English that they wanted to surrender. Lieutenant Ernest C. Hargett, the Recon Platoon leader, went forward suspiciously while Corporal George A. J. Amyotte covered him with a BAR. All at once the lead Chinese stepped aside and revealed the other four Chinese suddenly brandishing burp guns and grenades. Hargett pulled the trigger of his carbine, but it would not fire in the extreme cold, and Hargett rushed at the Chinese, swinging his carbine like a club. He crushed the skull of one Chinese but a grenade exploded and wounded him. Hargett was saved by Amyotte, who shot down the Chinese. But other enemy troops began firing from high ground on flank and rear while Hargett's platoon slowly fell back. The last tank was lost to the Chinese, along with the crew. A Chinese explosive charge stunned Hargett and blew Private First Class Robert D. DeMott over the sheer drop at the side of the road; DeMott fell unconscious on a ledge some feet down. The other men of the platoon thought he had been killed and moved on backward. Two other Recon Platoon men were missing and presumed killed in the melee. Amyotte, wearing experimental new fiberglass-plated body armor, was firing his BAR to cover the withdrawal when a grenade landed squarely on his back and exploded, but it did him no harm, though twelve other members of the platoon were wounded in the wild fight. Meanwhile, tank crewmen managed to free the locked brake and drove the two front tanks down the road. The other tanks were lost to the enemy or abandoned by their crews.

The engineers at the treadway bridge were waiting to destroy the bridge as soon as the last elements of the division passed over. After the two tanks had passed, followed by the Recon Platoon, dragging their wounded with them, the engineers believed all the Americans who could get out had done so. They set off the demolitions. They were not quite correct: PFC DeMott, blown onto a precarious ledge below the MSR by the satchel-charge explosion, recovered consciousness after a while, and, slightly wounded, climbed back up on the road. There he saw only Korean refugees. Hearing a huge detonation ahead, he realized the treadway bridge had been destroyed. He remembered, however, that pedestrians could cross through a gatehouse above the hydro plant's penstocks, and traveling with the refugees, DeMott arrived in Chinhung, the last man out.

At 11:30 p.m. December 11, the tanks, with their Recon Company mother hens, reached assembly areas in the Hamhung-Hungnam area. They were the final elements. The "breakout to the coast" had succeeded. Considering the immense dangers the troops had faced, the costs had been comparatively small. Nevertheless, about 1,000 men had been killed, wounded or reported missing in the breakout alone, most of them marines. In the battles around the Changjin reservoir before the breakout, the marines had suffered 2,665 casualties—383 killed or dead of wounds, 159 missing, and 2,123 wounded. The three 7th Division battalions cut off and shattered east of the reservoir had lost over 2,000 killed, missing or wounded men, while 100 army troops were killed or wounded in other engagements. Thus, including the losses to the British marine commandos and the few ROKs, about 6,000 of the approximately

25,000 troops in the campaign were killed, wounded or captured in the Changjin reservoir operations.

* * * * * * * * * *

While the forces were coming down the MSR from Hagaru, General Almond ordered the remainder of X Corps to concentrate in the vicinity of Hungnam. From the far north at Chingjin, the ROK 3rd and Capital Divisions withdrew to Songjin, about eighty miles south, where some were evacuated by ship and others carried by truck and rail to Hungnam. All the elements of the U.S 7th Division not around the Changjin reservoir and on the MSR leading to it were deployed to defend the Hamhung-Hungnam sector. The U.S. 3rd Division meanwhile evacuated Wonsan and joined in the defense of Hamhung-Hungnam.

To evacuate X Corps, a huge 193-vessel fleet assembled and, beginning December 11, began removing troops, equipment and supplies. In the two-week evacuation, 105,000 troops and 98,000 Korean refugees were taken aboard ships and carried to South Korea. In addition, 350,000 tons of cargo and 17,500 vehicles were hauled away. While the evacuations went on, the 3rd and 7th Divisions defended a constantly shrinking perimeter, while naval craft bombarded and air force, marine and navy planes made regular strikes against CCF and North Korean positions. The Chinese and North Koreans lacked artillery, and sent few shells into the perimeter, and they did not risk major infantry attacks in the face of U.S. firepower. On the day before Christmas, 1950, the last troops of the 3rd Division still on shore fired off their last rounds, climbed into waiting landing craft, and pulled away to protecting warships. Ordnance and engineer troops fired off the stocks of shells that could not be removed and set fire to supplies that had to be left behind. At 2:36 p.m. December 24, the U.S. fleet turned away from Hungnam and steamed south.

The great effort to conquer North Korea had ended in failure.

CHAPTER 48

MacArthur Panics

MACARTHUR'S RESPONSE to the Chinese attacks was full of outrage and querulous complaint at the effrontery of the Chinese in spoiling his careful plans. On November 28 he radioed the Joint Chiefs that "all hope of localization of the Korean conflict to enemy forces composed of North Korean troops with alien token elements can now be completely abandoned....We face an entirely new war."[1]

The General's peevish attitude—in total contrast to his easy confidence of a few days before, when he had said UN air power could stop Chinese reinforcements in North Korea—was shown in his assertion that the Yalu river had frozen over and this opened up "avenues of reinforcement and supply which it is impossible for our air potential to interdict." It was evident, MacArthur told the Chiefs, that the present UN force was "not sufficient to meet this undeclared war by the Chinese....The resulting situation presents an entirely new picture which broadens the potentialities to world-embracing considerations beyond the sphere of decision by the theater commander. This command has done everything humanly possible within its capabilities but is now faced with conditions beyond its control and strength."

The reaction in Washington to the Chinese attack was to talk frantically—and do nothing. President Truman called a meeting of the National Security Council. In the meeting Secretary of Defense Marshall read a hastily prepared memorandum from the secretaries of the military services urging the United States to act through the United Nations and not unilaterally. The Joint Chiefs said the United States had no more ground forces to send. Secretary Marshall said the United States must not get "sewed up" in Korea, but must get out without loss of prestige. General Collins said he believed MacArthur could "hold the line in the narrow neck of Korea" (that is, the Wonsan-Pyongyang corridor, a position already threatened because of Chinese attacks on the rear of Eighth Army). Secretary of State Acheson raised an alarm by asserting the United States was much closer to general war and there was danger the Soviet Union would get involved. The United Nations, Acheson said, had to uncloak Chinese aggression without pointing a finger at the Soviets, and also should seek to "make life harder" for the Chinese Communists. Air Force Secretary Thomas K. Finletter warned of air attack by China or the Soviet Union or both. Admiral Sherman said that, if Chinese air forces attacked from Manchuria, "we must hit back or we cannot stay there." President Truman agreed, but said "we will meet that when it comes."[2]

The only positive action to result from the discussions was the Joint Chiefs' agreement that MacArthur should go over to the defensive, something that was occurring by itself anyway.[3] MacArthur, meanwhile, asked the Chiefs to permit Chinese Nationalist troops to be committed to Korea.[4] In light of the enormous pressures on the Truman administration at the moment, it is remarkable that MacArthur's proposal received a courteous reply. The message, cleared with Acheson and Marshall, once again stated the elementary facts about use of Chiang Kai-shek's forces: it probably would disrupt the united position of the allies, the British Commonwealth countries would find it wholly unacceptable, hostilities might extend to Taiwan, and the U.S. position of leadership in the United Nations would be seriously compromised.[5] Perhaps an extension of the war was precisely what MacArthur had in mind, however.

In the meantime, MacArthur summoned his two field commanders to Tokyo on the evening of November 28 for a "council of war." This resulted in a decision that Eighth Army should withdraw as far as necessary to keep it from being outflanked by Chinese forces, and that X Corps should withdraw to the Hamhung-Hungnam area.[6] MacArthur announced his decision on X Corps to the JCS on November 30, and then proceeded to assert that the dispositions of X Corps threatened the main supply lines of the enemy forces attacking Eighth Army. (This was said at the very moment the 1st Marine Division and elements of the 7th Division were fighting for their lives in the Changjin reservoir area!) MacArthur also told the Chiefs that a continuous line across the narrow part of the peninsula was impracticable owing to the distance involved, the numerical weakness of his forces, and the logistical problems posed by the mountains between east from west.[7] Setting up a line across the narrow waist of Korea was becoming a moot point, because Chinese forces were moving behind the hurriedly retreating Eighth Army to sever the Pyongyang-Wonsan highway at Songchon. However, MacArthur's argument that he had too few troops to man such a line is strange in light of the fact that this was the narrowest part of Korea, and withdrawal farther south inevitably would result in an even longer defensive line. JCS Chairman Bradley certainly believed such a line was possible.[8]

The fact is MacArthur was succumbing to panic. Less than two hours after his message on X Corps, MacArthur sent another flash to the Chiefs asserting the Chinese were reinforcing their troops rapidly and further withdrawals of Eighth Army were inevitable because the Chinese had as their objective "the complete destruction of United Nations forces and the securing of all Korea."[9] He did not explain how he had come to this conclusion.

This message from MacArthur caused extreme anxiety among the Joint Chiefs. They feared the retreat of Eighth Army would leave X Corps precariously "huddled in a beachhead between Hungnam and Wonsan." Therefore, the Chiefs, with the approval of Secretary Marshall and President Truman, told MacArthur "the entire region northeast of the waist of Korea should be ignored except for strategic and tactical considerations relating to the security of your command."[10] In other words: forget about a bridgehead; get the troops out.

The United States meanwhile was barely holding its own in the United Nations. A special emissary from Communist China, General Wu Xiuzhuan, sent in response to the Security Council's invitation (see page 295), arrived on November 27. The Security Council for three days— during the height of the initial Chinese Communist assaults in Korea— engaged in an acrimonious debate on two Soviet resolutions that would have condemned the U.S. for interfering in both Korea and Taiwan. The Security Council defeated these resolutions. Then the members voted on a six-nation resolution introduced several weeks earlier, assuring Communist China that its interests would be protected and asking it not to aid North Korea. This resolution received nine favorable votes (India abstained), but the Soviet Union vetoed it.[11] The United States kept its friends in line in these two votes, but UN support was wavering. Said James Reston in the New York *Times* on November 30: "There is no doubt that confidence in General Douglas MacArthur, even on Capitol Hill, has been shaken badly as a result of the events of the last few days. Similarly, there is no doubt that United States leadership in the Western world has been damaged by President Truman's acceptance of the bold MacArthur offensive."[12]

Matters were scarcely helped by a proposal by the U.S. ambassador to the United Nations, Warren Austin. On November 30 he suggested to his British and French colleagues that a much stronger resolution condemning Red China as an aggressor be put before the General

Assembly. Both countries reacted strenuously; they wanted no part of a resolution that would commit the United Nations to fight against the Chinese while leaving Europe wide open to possible Soviet attack.[13] Likewise, some Asian and Latin American countries made it clear that public opinion would not support a war with Communist China. The United States was becoming dangerously isolated. The situation was in no way improved by an ill-considered remark by President Truman at a November 30 press conference. Truman issued a statement that UN forces had "no intention of abandoning their mission in Korea." Reporters began to question the President, leading Truman to say that the United States would take any steps necessary to meet the military situation, including use of "every weapon that we have." Did this mean, a reporter asked, that use of the atomic bomb was being considered? The President answered that "there has always been active consideration of its use," and he went on further to imply the decision to drop the A-bomb would be left to General MacArthur.[14] Truman's remarks were potentially a disaster. He had been led along this path by reporters' questions, but he had said the unsayable: that the United States, when it suffered a military reverse, might use the atomic bomb to redress the situation. In the swelling worldwide moral opposition to atomic weapons and the agonizing fear of an atomic confrontation now that the Soviet Union had exploded its own bomb, such a statement, however casually offered, could have only the most chilling effects everywhere. Truman's error was vastly compounded by his implication that, not he, but General MacArthur might decide on its use—and MacArthur already had developed a reputation throughout the world as trigger-happy and determined on the destruction of Red China's ability to make war. To leave the decision in the hands of this warrior was frightening beyond all measure.

Reaction was swift, both within the U.S. government and without. Before the day was over, Secretary Acheson had hastily assembled a "damage-control party" and released a statement, on behalf of the White House, assuring the world that only the President could authorize the use of nuclear weapons, that the more possession of any weapon necessarily entailed "consideration" of its use, and that the situation regarding the weapons had in no way changed as a result of the press conference. It was a brave effort, but lame compared with the electric effect of Truman's utterance throughout the world. The reaction in the British House of Commons was so fierce that Prime Minister Clement Attlee, after a quick telegraphic consultation with the U.S. government, assured the members he would fly to Washington to confer with Truman.[15]

Washington quite obviously was getting hysterical and irrational. Acheson, for example, at a big meeting of the administration's major political and military advisors on December 1, suggested the United States might offer to withdraw from Korea if Red China withdrew its military forces from Manchuria![16] A proposal for joint withdrawal of UN and Chinese forces from Korea had some promise, but to expect China to pull its troops out of an integral part of its own country—and that part considered by its leaders to be the most threatened—was nonsense.

This meeting brought forth a lot of other discussion and proposals, but the only definite decision was to send General Collins to Tokyo the same day to talk things over with MacArthur. On December 2, Truman met with Acheson, Marshall and Bradley, and they considered two ways of seeking a cease-fire: a UN resolution or a diplomatic approach to the Soviet Union or Red China. The men decided to wait on Collins's return and Attlee's conference with Truman to make a decision.[17]

On December 3, the Joint Chiefs got a dismal report from MacArthur saying that, unless he got substantial reinforcements, the UN Command would be forced into a series of withdrawals, its strength diminishing with each retreat, or else driven into beachheads where troops could only hang on. The United Nations, MacArthur reported gloomily, was "facing the entire Chinese nation in an undeclared war," which would lead, unless something were done, to "steady attrition leading to final destruction."[18]

It was in this context that a joint State-Defense conference was held on December 3, with all the major officers in both departments, plus the Joint Chiefs (except Collins), in attendance. MacArthur's report, however, far from sending the military men in the conference into despair, had the reverse effect: it go their backs up. General Bradley did not like the idea of the United States being expelled form Korea: it would lose prestige around the globe. The Germans, he said, already were muttering that the United States had proved weak. Admiral Sherman was adamantly opposed to asking for a cease-fire. And if China wanted war, the United States should get down to the business of defeating China, he said. Otherwise, Sherman maintained, other countries would "push us around." A more realistic Acheson, however, pointed out the United States then would be "fighting the second team," and the first team, the Soviet Union, would be delighted to see the United States bogged down with Red China. Finally, Dean Rusk, assistant secretary of state, proposed confining any cease-fire to an agreement to re-establish a line at the 38th parallel, and this idea got general agreement. The group also agreed that MacArthur meantime should concentrate his troops into beachheads.

Immediately upon adjournment of the meeting, Acheson, Marshall and Bradley went to the White House to report to Truman.[19] The result was a message sent the same day to MacArthur by the Chiefs: "We consider that the preservation of your forces is now the primary consideration. Consolidation of forces into beachheads is concurred in."[20]

Clearly, MacArthur's pessimistic appraisal of the situation in Korea had caused American military leaders and the Truman administration to come to the somber conclusion that American forces were in danger of annihilation. This, of course, by no means was the attitude of the soldiers and marines in Korea, defeated and bloodied as they were. Already some army and marine commanders in Korea were beginning to realize the Chinese were hamstrung by their primitive supply system and would have a difficult, if not impossible, time driving the United Nations out of Korea. They could inflict fearsome casualties; and they could deflate puffed-up ideas of Western superiority; but they could not sustain an offensive long enough to push a determined UN army into the sea, unless they were prepared to sustain losses of inconceivable size.

This was not the viewpoint of General MacArthur, however, when General Collins sat down with him in Tokyo on December 4. MacArthur estimated the Chinese had 500,000 troops in Korea and the North Korean army was back up to 100,000 men. Having grossly underestimated CCF strength before the offensive started on November 24, MacArthur now grossly overestimated Chinese strength. This meant, MacArthur said, the enemy could envelop any static UN defensive line and force Eighth Army back to the Seoul-Inchon area, while X Corps already was creating another beachhead around Hamhung. Collins was alarmed, but not convinced, and when he got to Korea, he found the situation serious but not desperate.[21] Meantime, MacArthur ordered Eighth Army to hold Seoul as long as possible, but to withdraw in successive positions to Pusan, if forced, while X Corps would be removed from Hungnam and placed under Eighth Army when it landed in the south.[22]

CHAPTER 49

Back to the 38th Parallel

WHILE GENERAL COLLINS was in the Far East, President Truman was seeing British Prime Minister Attlee (December 4–8). Before he left for Washington, Attlee received a quick visit on December 2 from Réné Pleven, the French prime minister, and they achieved a "general identity of view." Attlee therefore carried the views of both Britain and France with him when he and his deputation arrived in Washington.[1]

Americans and Britons did not come to a complete understanding, though they papered over most of their disagreements. Part of the problem with the British, and with virtually all of the U.S. allies, was the continuing public complaint by MacArthur about the "privileged sanctuaries" of China and the failure of European countries to support an aggressive stance in the Far East. Finally, on December 5 Truman issued a directive generally to all U.S. officials—but clearly meant for MacArthur—requiring all public statements relating to foreign or military policy to be cleared in advance by the Department of State and Defense.[2] This directive, transmitted to MacArthur the next day, was to assume massive significance later.

In the Truman-Attlee talks, the British pulled away from the position they had brought with them, that Taiwan should be ceded to Red China as a price of peace; but they continued to favor admission of Red China to the United Nations.[3] In regard to the use of nuclear weapons, which the British wanted the Americans never to use without consulting the United Kingdom, the two sides finally decided on a statement in the joint communiqué that mentioned President Truman's hope "that world conditions would never call for the use of the atomic bomb," and his desire to keep the British prime minister at all times "informed of developments which might bring about a change in the situation."[4]

General Collins got back in time to attend the last session of the Allied leaders on December 8, and his report was somewhat reassuring, namely, that he believed it unlikely UN forces would be driven out of Korea, and that, with X Corps joining Eighth Army, the combined forces could hold a Pusan perimeter indefinitely.[5]

The most important point emerging from the conference, however, was that Americans and Britons agreed to end the war on the basis of the old border, the 38th parallel. The crusade to unify Korea by force had ended. This decision led immediately to an effort in the United Nations. The Indian delegate, Sir Benegal N. Rau, with U.S. and British support, led an effort by thirteen Asian and Arab states asking the Chinese and the North Koreans not to cross the 38th parallel.[6] There was no direct response from Beijing or Pyongyang. But a great deal of diplomatic discussions and closed-door meetings took place for days; the Indians notably explored with Beijing the possibility of a cease-fire and the New York *Times* on December 8 reported that "responsible officials" in Washington gave assurances UN forces would not renew their invasion of North Korea if communist forces stopped at the parallel.[7]

On December 11, the thirteen Arab-Asian states began a movement in the United Nations to get a cease-fire agreement to be handled by a three-man commission. After much discussion in Washington, the Truman administration agreed to cease-fire terms essentially as proposed by the Joint Chiefs: limitation of the agreement entirely to Korea, establishment of a twenty-mile-wide demilitarized zone with its *southern* boundary generally following the 38th parallel, a ban on introduction of new troops by either side, and prisoners of war to be exchanged on a one-for-one basis.[8]

The thirteen-nation proposal for a cease-fire passed the UN Political and Security Committee (the First Committee) on December 13 and the full General Assembly on December 14, in both cases with U.S. support.[9]

The thirteen-nation group immediately asked Beijing to keep at the United Nations its special ambassador, General Wu Xiu-zhuan, who had been at the earlier UN meetings to discuss Soviet resolutions trying to condemn the United States (see page 370). The group also assured China of a "clear understanding" that negotiations on Far Eastern problems would take place immediately after a cease-fire had been arranged.

Now the Beijing government, in the flush of victory and after already winning its primary aim, the re-establishment of a buffer state between the Americans and the Yalu, made a major and costly error. On December 21, the Red Chinese rejected the UN proposal on the grounds that all UN actions taken without Communist China's participation were illegal.[10] On December 23, Foreign Minister Zhou Enlai sent a telegram to the thirteen-nation group, and its text was broadcast by Beijing radio, in which he assailed the United States actions, and declared the 38th parallel had been obliterated forever by the UN invasion of North Korea. He asserted Red China would not consider a cease-fire unless there also was an agreement on the withdrawal of foreign troops from Korea, settlement of Korean affairs by "the Korean people themselves," withdrawal of "American aggression forces" from Taiwan, and the seating of Red China in the United Nations.[11]

Apparently the Chinese Communist government decided its military successes in Korea were sufficient to force all these demands down the throat of the United States. They were wrong, not only because this renewed the resolve of the United States to defend its position in Korea, but also because—if the Chinese had accepted a cease-fire—their stock in the United Nations would have risen so high it would have been extremely difficult for the United States subsequently to bar Red China's admission to the world body. World opinion also would have made it politically unwise for the United States to continue, over a long period, to support Chiang Kai-shek on Taiwan. Thus the Red Chinese, by demanding too much, got nothing. And the war nobody wanted went on its bloody way.

December 23 was a major turning point in the Korean War. The reason was not just the decision of Red China to continue the fighting in hopes of forcing the United States to abandon Taiwan and acquiesce to Beijing's admission to the United Nations. The other reason was that on this day Lieutenant General Walton H. Walker, commander of Eighth Army, was killed while driving northward from Seoul when his jeep was struck by a truck. Walker's successor was Lieutenant General Matthew B. Ridgway, then army deputy chief of staff for administration, and an officer who had created a shining image for himself as a fighter when he commanded the 82nd Airborne Division and a corps in World War II, and who won high marks after the war as a leader within the Joint Chiefs of Staff organization.

Ridgway brought to Eighth Army a new spirit that reflected its pugnacious, offensive-minded commander. Ridgway arrived at Eighth Army, now incorporating X Corps as well, at a crucial time: both forces had been thoroughly defeated and, after deep and seemingly unstoppable retreats, were suffering from a crisis of confidence. Ridgway quickly recreated a sense of pride in the officers and men of Eighth Army by stopping all talk of defeat and retreat and emphasizing attack and victory. He strapped a grenade on his combat jacket—an affectation that drew snickers from the weary combat veterans of Korea—but this very flamboyance and aggressive assertiveness created a respect for the man, though no one expected him to have occasion to throw a grenade at an enemy. The men of Eighth Army seemed to sense immediately that the grenade was not displayed as some sort of symbol of bravado and braggadocio to draw attention to himself, but as a device to emphasize to the officers and men that the business of an army is fighting and Eighth Army was being run by an officer who intended to employ that army in its proper role.

UN forces in Korea were transformed by Ridgway from a retreating, ready-for-peace group of men into a responsive military instrument. No doubt the individual man still wished for an end to the war, but a pervasive attitude that the army was beaten quickly dissipated when Ridgway took command and a sense of military professionalism and purpose returned. At the moment when the Chinese Communists decided to exploit their gains by rejecting a cease-fire and undertaking a powerful new offensive, they encountered a commander on the UN side who would fight the Chinese for every inch of ground and every advantage. General MacArthur himself gave Ridgway a free hand. In an interview with MacArthur immediately after he arrived in Tokyo from Washington, Ridgway asked MacArthur whether it would be permissible to attack if the opportunity offered. General MacArthur responded: "The Eighth Army is yours, Matt. Do what you think best."[12]

As General Ridgway was taking over control, the question in Washington was whether the United Nations could hold out in Korea. On December 29, the Joint Chiefs sent a directive to MacArthur, approved by Truman, stating that all available estimates indicated the Chinese possessed the capability of forcing UN forces out of Korea if they chose to exercise it. The directive went on:

"It is not practicable to obtain significant additional forces for Korea from other members of the United Nations. We believe that Korea is not the place to fight a major war. Further, we believe that we should not commit our remaining available ground forces to action against Chinese Communist forces in Korea in face of the increased threat of general war. However, a successful resistance to Chinese-North Korean aggression at some position in Korea and a deflation of the military and political prestige of the Chinese Communists would be of great importance to our national interests, if this could be accomplished without incurring serious losses."

The directive instructed MacArthur to defend successive positions in Korea, but if the line were forced back to the Kum river near Taejon, and if the Chinese massed large forces, "it then would be necessary, under these conditions, to direct you to commence a withdrawal to Japan."[13]

In MacArthur's reply on December 30, the General argued strongly for a totally different policy which would force the war on the Chinese. Because most of China's military forces had been concentrated in Manchuria and Korea, MacArthur argued, other parts of China were vulnerable. He therefore suggested four actions that might be undertaken "in case" the Truman administration decided "to recognize the state of war which has been forced upon us by the Chinese authorities": blockade China's coast, destroy China's war-making capacity by air and naval bombardment, reinforce the UN Command in Korea with Chinese Nationalist forces, and allow Nationalists to carry out diversionary attacks against the mainland.[14]

This was a proposal for expanding the war far beyond Korea and risking a world war. It was precisely what the Truman administration wanted to avoid, yet there were many people in the United States who would support such a policy, which was later to be described as "hawkish." It was a policy based on the traditional American concept that war demands fighting to total victory. MacArthur's message of December 30 exemplified this attitude to perfection and thereby drew a sharp contrast between those who advocate war to the finish, whatever the consequences, and those who advocate war limited to carrying out recognized and clearly delineated national aims.

MacArthur acknowledged that such a course of action had been rejected earlier as likely to provoke a major war. But China now was fully committed, he argued, and "nothing we can do would further aggravate the situation" as far as China was concerned. Whether the Soviet Union would intervene, he said, was a "a matter of speculation."

The chief of naval operations, Admiral Sherman, emerged as a limited supporter of MacArthur's aggressive position. He advocated a naval blockade of the China coast "as soon as our position in Korea is stabilized or when we have evacuated Korea," removal of restrictions on Nationalist troop operations, logistical support for guerrillas in China, and naval and air attacks on targets within China "at such time as the Chinese Communists attack any of our forces outside of Korea."[15]

CHAPTER 50

The New Year's Eve Offensive

W HILE OFFICIALS IN WASHINGTON were agonizing over
MacArthur's provocative and extremely dangerous proposals to
extend the war to China, the Chinese Communist Forces, now with the
backing of some reorganized North Korean troops, unleashed a New
Year's Eve offensive against Eighth Army. The Chinese had been slowly
building up their troops and supplies behind the line where Eighth
Army finally had stopped its retreat from the Chongchon river—along
the Imjin river in the west and extending approximately along the 38th
parallel eastward to the Sea of Japan. The recently evacuated X Corps
troops still were reorganizing in the southern part of Korea, and the first
blows of the CCF offensive again landed on Eighth Army.

General Ridgway had placed the bulk of his forces in the relatively
lower western and central sectors because it had become clear by
observation that the Chinese were concentrating strong forces north of
Seoul. I Corps, under Major General Frank W. Milburn, held the Imjin
river line with the 25th Divison, ROK 1st Division, the Turkish Brigade,
and the British 29th Brigade. IX Corps, under Major General John B.
Coulter, held the central sector with the 1st Cavalry Division, 24th
Division, ROK 6th Division, 27th British Commonwealth Brigade, and
the recently arrived Greek and Philippine Battalions. In the eastern
mountains, where heavy attacks were not expected, Ridgway had
concentrated ROK forces.[1]

The communist offensive struck all along the line, but was most
powerful against I and IX Corps. Seven CCF armies and two North
Korean corps penetrated deeply toward Seoul in the west and toward
the rail and road center of Wonju in the central sector. The offensive

rapidly gained momentum, and Ridgway ordered UN forces to pull back to the south bank of the Han river, now filled with cakes of floating ice, except for an arc around Seoul. Ridgway hoped to delay the Chinese capture of Seoul in order to deny them the bridges there. With the UN line under extreme pressure, Ridgway on January 2 committed X Corps on the eastern flank of IX Corps. General Almond's corps assumed control of three ROK divisions already in the line, the U.S. 7th Division, the just-reorganized and re-equipped U.S. 2nd Division, and the 187th Airborne RCT.

The Chinese, now less anxious about the opposition they would encounter, pressed forward much faster than during the November attack along the Chongchon. The attack set off a debacle among the ROK forces in the west. General Ridgway found the scene especially depressing. He wrote: "On New Year's morning I drove out north of Seoul and into a dismaying spectacle. ROK soldiers by the truckloads were streaming south, without order, without arms, without leaders, in full retreat. Some came on foot or in commandeered vehicles of every sort. They had just one aim—to get as far away form the Chinese as possible. They had thrown their rifles and pistols away and had abandoned all artillery, mortars, machine guns, every crew-served weapon."[2]

Ridgway leaped out of his jeep and stood in the middle of the road waving his arms to flag down an approaching truck. The first few dodged by him without slowing down, but he did succeed in stopping a group of trucks carrying ROK officers. "The group in the advance truck listened without comprehension and would not obey my gestures," Ridgway reported. "Soon the whole procession was rolling again." Ridgway, the fighting man's general, stood helplessly on the road and watched the ROKs run away. He quickly set up a program, however, to stop the rout: he established straggler posts far to the rear, manned by U.S. military police, to regain control. It worked. The fleeing ROKs were reorganized into units, rearmed and sent off under their own officers to new sectors. "Most of them," Ridgway reported, "thereafter fought well, as do most courageous men when they are well-trained and properly led." In general, Eighth Army retreated in good order, although Ridgway was unhappy that a battalion of the U.S. 19th Regiment "had also been caught up into an untidy retreat when the ROKs next to them had broken." (See Map 12.)

Ridgway realized it would be impossible to hold the bridgehead arc around Seoul, and on January 3 he ordered the evacuation of the city. He told the U.S. ambassador to Korea, John Muccio, to inform Syngman Rhee that, from 3 p.m. on, the bridges and main approach and exit roads over the Han would be closed to all but military traffic, although a single footbridge across the river had been spared for civilians. He placed Brigadier General Charles D. Palmer, assistant division commander of the 1st Cavalry Division, in charge of the two pontoon bridges over the river, with full authority to use Ridgway's name to keep military traffic flowing. While military police under Palmer guarded the northern approaches and kept the swelling tide of Korean refugees at bay, long, slow lines of infantrymen, trucks, tanks, artillery and carriers moved over the pontoon bridges to the south bank. At last the heaviest equipment of all moved: eight-inch howitzer batteries and Centurion tanks of the British 29th Brigade. The Centurions exceeded the rated tonnage of the bridges, and the pontoons sagged deeply into the ice-choked river as they moved onto the bridges. But the pontoons held, and the last of the Eighth Army forces crossed safely.[3] Directly behind them came the horde of refugees, now freed to go.

Ridgway ordered Eighth Army to fall back in the west to the vicinity of the 37th parallel, on a line running from Pyongtaek on the Seoul-Taejon highway east through Ansong, northeast to Wonju, and from there in a curving line to the east coast town of Samchok. This necessitated the rapid evacuation of Kimpo airfield, where 500,000 gallons of fuel and 23,000 gallons of napalm were set afire to deny them to the communists.

Close behind the military forces came endless steams of refugees. Many died of exposure in the bitter cold. Nevertheless, they pressed on, many trying to reach Pusan, which already was jammed with homeless people. The mass movement of people endangered military operations, clogging highways and railroads and permitting spies and guerrillas to infiltrate into the south along with the refugees. At last, Eighth Army officials established control points at key road and rail junctions to channel the people into the southwestern provinces, away from the military lines of communication.

As Eighth Army withdrew, the familiar Chinese weaknesses, their need to move on foot and their primitive supply arrangements, slowed the advance, especially in the west. Few Chinese pushed south of Seoul, and, as Eighth Army withdrew farther south, contacts with the Chinese diminished sharply. Even as early as January 7, a task force built around the 27th Regiment of the 25th Division pushed north from Pyongtaek toward Osan without finding an enemy soldier.

In the central and eastern fronts, however, heavy fighting continued. The II North Korean Corps in late December had passed through the eastern mountains to place large numbers of NK troops behind the lines. When the January offensive continued, these guerrilla forces increased their disruptive activities and raided military installations. During the first days of January, the situation in the X Corps sector was confused. X Corps lost contact entirely with ROK 5th and 8th Division troops in the mountains on the east, and the ROK 2nd Division had virtually disintegrated. With only isolated pockets of ROKs operating east of X Corps, an estimated 18,000 enemy troops poured through the resulting gap. To counter this threat, Ridgway formed a defensive line facing east and northeast on the X Corps right flank and another to block the enemy movement from the north. But communist troops already had penetrated so deeply and in such force that it appeared UN troops might be pushed still farther south.

But X Corps under General Almond was not interested in retreating. The X Corps Command Report described the action thus: "X Corps literally absorbed the Red attack, and a very unusual situation developed with large bodies of the enemy operating inside the corps zone without being able to force the withdrawal of X Corps. There was no real front line in the generally accepted sense and units eighty miles behind the most forward elements of the corps were officially awarded battle credits for engagements with infiltrating enemy units. In general, the U.S. 2nd and 7th Divisions held the forward portion of the corps zone and the 2nd, 5th and 8th ROK Divisions, together with the 187th Airborne RCT, held the rear portion of the corps zone. Each X Corps command having area responsibilities patrolled its area aggressively and, after fixing enemy locations, organized attacks to eliminate these units. Small-unit action and ambushes by both sides characterized the fighting in the corps zone."

The key to the defense of the central front was the decision by Ridgway to hold Wonju. The 2nd Division got the assignment, along with the newly arrived French and Netherlands battalions, and the division's spirited defense frustrated the communist effort to drive down the road corridor from Chunchon through Wonju and thereby split Eighth Army. Although North Korean forces drove 2nd Division troops below Wonju, the Americans held the road corridors and soon began to move back into Wonju with patrols. Because of this, the main communist effort was diverted mostly into the mountains southeast of Wonju, where it lost momentum and finally was smashed.

Wonju assumed great importance because it was the junction of five main roads as well as a railway from Seoul to Pusan. The force that controlled Wonju had gone a long way toward controlling central Korea. Possession of Wonju would have put the communists in a position to move southwestward behind I and IX Corps, and thus require them to withdraw still farther south to the Kum river line, the last defensible position before a retreat to a new Pusan perimeter. To meet the threat of possible NK movement through the mountains east of 2nd Division, Ridgway ordered the 1st Marine Division to the vicinity of Andong to prevent enemy infiltration and to protect the ROK supply road to Yondok on the east coast.

* * * * * * * * * * *

The results of the New Year's Offensive were not as dire as the doomsayers had predicted, and in Washington a new spirit of optimism arose. Specifically, the Truman administration and the Joint Chiefs decided to back off from MacArthur's urging to carry the war to the Chinese mainland in hopes of keeping hostilities confined to Korea. As James F. Schnabel comments in his study of command in the first year of the war, "Thus far, the Chinese government had not declared war against the United States and had, in fact, disclaimed responsibility for the actions of Chinese armies in Korea. While this was purely a technicality it was an important one. Confining the fighting in Asia to a limited arena in Korea and preserving the unity of the bloc of nations allied with the United States against communist aggression were basic principles of established national policy."[4]

Therefore, on January 9, 1951, the Joint Chiefs sent MacArthur an interim reply to his message of December 30. The Chiefs said MacArthur's four proposals for retaliation against China would be "given careful consideration," but there was little possibility of change in American policy regarding the war. In addition, the Chiefs said any blockade of the China coast would require negotiations with the British, because of their trade through Hong Kong, as well as approval by the United Nations (which manifestly would not be forthcoming). The Chiefs said any naval or air attacks against China proper could be approved only if the Chinese attacked U.S. forces outside of Korea. The Chiefs also once more turned down MacArthur's bid to get Nationalist Chinese troops sent to Korea and said two partially trained U.S. National Guard divisions might be sent to Japan as a garrison, but only if UN positions in Korea could be stabilized; otherwise, forces withdrawn from Korea in an evacuation would have to be used.[5]

The Chiefs therefore ordered MacArthur to defend successive positions in Korea as previously directed, while attempting to inflict maximum damage to communist forces, "subject to primary consideration of the safety of your troops and your basic mission of protecting Japan." The Chiefs added that, "should it become evident in your judgment that evacuation is essential to avoid severe losses of men and material you will at that time withdraw from Korea to Japan."

MacArthur's hopes for extending the war to China were dashed. He took out his pique in a pettifogging request for "clarification" of the directive. MacArthur chose to interpret the alternative—to hold out in Korea if possible, otherwise to withdraw—as being contradictory.[6] It was "self-evident," he said, that UN forces were not strong enough both to hold Korea and to protect Japan. Strategic dispositions "must be based upon overriding political policy establishing the relativity of American interests in the Far East," MacArthur said. A beachhead line (later defined after JCS questioning as the old Naktong river line) could be held for a time, but with inevitable losses, he said. "Whether such losses were regarded as 'severe' or not would to a certain extent depend upon the connotation one gives the term," the General wrote.[7]

Then MacArthur made a devastating evaluation of the morale of the troops in Korea. If true, the potential ability of the forces to fight the communists was doubtful. It was not the kind of charge a theater commander makes off the cuff about his troops; yet MacArthur leveled the charge without substantiation. Here is what he said:

"The troops are tired from a long and difficult campaign, embittered by the shameful propaganda which has falsely condemned their courage and fighting qualities in misunderstood retrograde maneuver, and their morale will become a serious threat to their battle efficiency unless the political basis upon which they are asked to trade life for time is clearly delineated, fully understood, and so impelling that the hazards of battle are cheerfully accepted."

In conclusion, MacArthur tried to lay upon Washington the responsibility for deciding immediately whether or not to remain in Korea. He said the decision was "of highest national and international importance, far above the competence of a theater commander....My query therefore amounts to this: is it the present objective of United States political policy to maintain a military position in Korea—indefinitely, for a limited time, or to minimize losses by evacuation as soon as it can be accomplished? As I have pointed out before, under the extraordinary limitations and conditions imposed upon the command in Korea, its military position is untenable, but it can hold for any length of time up to its complete destruction if overriding political considerations so dictate."

In effect, MacArthur was saying the national policy of the United States—to hold Japan and to maintain South Korea—was not feasible, and, furthermore, the morale of the troops was in perilous jeopardy. President Truman called a meeting of the National Security Council for January 12 to draw up an answer to the General.[8] To Secretary Acheson the message was a "posterity paper" to place the blame on Washington if things went wrong. It was a sign to Acheson that MacArthur was "incurably recalcitrant and basically disloyal to the purposes of his commander in chief."[9]

The MacArthur message galvanized the Joint Chiefs, with the approval of Secretary Marshall, to send General Collins back to Korea once more to obtain first-hand information on the morale and fighting efficiency of Eighth Army. General Vandenberg, the air force chief, decided to go as well, to review air force evacuation plans. They left the afternoon of January 12. Before departing, however, they attended the National Security Council meeting Truman had called. At this session the President approved a draft JCS message to MacArthur.[10] This JCS message, sent immediately thereafter, spelled out to the Far East commander that he was to follow national policy. The Chiefs accepted MacArthur's views that it would be infeasible to hold out in Korea, especially if the Chinese continued their major offensive efforts, but "it would be to our national interest, and also to the interest of the UN, to gain some further time for essential diplomatic and military consultations with UN countries participating in the Korean effort before you issue firm instructions for initiation of evacuation of troops from Korea. It is important also to United States prestige worldwide, to the future of UN and NATO organizations, and to efforts to organize anti-communist resistance in Asia that Korea not be evacuated unless actually forced by military considerations, and that maximum practicable punishment be inflicted on communist aggressors."[11]

Thus the monkey was placed firmly on MacArthur's back: defend Korea as long and as hard as you can, and withdraw only under the most severe pressure. The Chiefs rejected MacArthur's contention that a decision on evacuation of Korea had to be made *before* UN troops were forced to evacuate. Rather, the Chiefs said in effect: make the Chinese prove they can push us out of Korea; don't decide they can do it in advance and act accordingly.

Of course, the reality of the situation in Korea itself already was vindicating the position of the Chiefs. While MacArthur in Tokyo was maintaining UN forces could not hold out in Korea, UN forces were doing just that. The immediate reason was that the Chinese once more had outrun their supplies, and in the west already were in the withdrawal phase of their standard practice of advance, attack, withdrawal, advance, attack, withdrawal. The only way the Chinese could have driven the UN forces out of Korea would have been to commit an overwhelming mass of men time and after against the guns and planes of the UN Command. The fact is the Chinese did *not* commit this overwhelming mass of manpower. This raises the question as to whether the Chinese indeed ever had the real intention of forcing UN troops out of Korea entirely, or whether they were bluffing and were intent actually on merely forcing Eighth Army back into South Korea. Although the Chinese refusal in December to accept a United Nations plan for a cease-fire along the 38th parallel raised suspicions that the Chinese in fact did wish to push the Eighth Army into the sea, this decision should be seen more realistically as a huge error on the part of Beijing to try to parlay a battlefield victory into a capitulation by the United States in regard to Taiwan and a Red Chinese seat in the United Nations.

CHAPTER 51

Acheson's Calculated Risk

EIGHTH ARMY slowly was stemming the Chinese-North Korean January offensive, and the Joint Chiefs were resolving to fight as long as possible in Korea. Meanwhile Secretary of State Acheson was attempting to isolate Red China in world opinion. With Truman's approval, Acheson was considering a resolution in the UN General Assembly declaring Communist China an aggressor.[1]

The UN cease-fire commission, however, had not accepted China's earlier rejection as final and drew up a new peace plan intended to meet some of the demands of Beijing. The plan was presented to the UN First Committee on January 11 only hours after U.S. officials learned about it. It proposed a six-step program for peace: an immediate cease-fire, exploration of further measures to promote peace, withdrawal of armed forces from Korea, "appropriate arrangements" for the Korean people to express their views on their government, interim arrangements for the unification of Korea, and establishment of an "appropriate body" to settle Far Eastern problems, including the status of Taiwan and China's representation in the United Nations. This "appropriate body" was to be composed of representatives of the United States, United Kingdom, the Soviet Union and Communist China.[2]

It was a shattering package because the proposal for an appropriate body clearly stacked the deck against the United States: Britain would be reluctant to side with the United States in rejecting Red China's admission to the United Nations, and once Red China was admitted, the American position of support of the Nationalists on Taiwan would be weakened. Even if the United States could stop any formal action by the appropriate body, it would inevitably lose in world opinion.

If the Chinese Communists had had their wits about them, they would have jumped at this open invitation to world acceptance and to achievement of all their major aims in Korea, the United Nations, and, ultimately, Taiwan. Acheson recognized this instantly when he saw American choices as "murderous": to accept the plan would open the administration to violent criticism at home by Republicans and the China Lobby; to oppose it would brand the United States as an opponent of peace.[3]

Acheson decided to take a calculated risk. He believed the Chinese had demonstrated their intransigence (and lack of political savvy) in their rejection of the December cease-fire proposal. Therefore, he reasoned they would reject this one as well. Acheson recommended to Truman: agree to the proposal, and when China rejects it, other nations will join the United States in censuring Chinese aggression. Truman bought the idea.

Although, as Acheson expressed it, "the political roof fell in," especially in the Senate, the UN First Committee quickly approved the plan after Ambassador Warren Austin praised it and said the United States would vote for it. The First Committee asked the UN secretary-general to transmit it to Beijing. The Chinese reply came on January 17: a cease-fire without political negotiations was wholly unacceptable. Beijing's counter-proposals were essentially what it had called for in December: admission to the United Nations and removal of U.S. forces from Taiwan. Acheson had won. The Red Chinese leaders had thoroughly demonstrated their amateurishness in international politics. Acheson gained the upper hand in the United Nations on the strength of Beijing's dumb response. "We must now face squarely and soberly the fact that the Chinese Communists have no intention of ceasing their defiance of the United Nations," Acheson pronounced.[4]

It was the opening the United States needed: on January 20, Ambassador Austin submitted a resolution to the UN First Committee which frankly called the Red Chinese aggressors. Although some UN members were hesitant to place this label on Beijing, the resolution was approved by the First Committee on January 30 and by the General Assembly on February 1. The resolution called for a UN subcommittee to consider "additional measures" to meet Chinese aggression and another committee to try to end the war.[5] It had been a neat finesse by Acheson. As some UN members complained, the United States had got the best of both worlds—Red China was thrust into the pariah status of aggressor, and no political repercussions resulted at home from having to accept a stacked UN four-power commission to settle Far Eastern problems.

* * * * * * * * *

Generals Collins and Vandenberg arrived in Tokyo on January 15, and after a conference with MacArthur, they flew on to Korea. The biggest question they wanted answered on the ground was whether MacArthur's gloomy appraisal of Eighth Army's morale was correct. While Vandenberg toured air force bases, Collins, in company with General Ridgway, visited the headquarters of a number of U.S., UN and ROK units. Collins found that MacArthur had been wrong. Morale in Eighth Army was good, and was improving daily under Ridgway's vigorous, offensive-minded leadership. The ROKs were shakier, largely because the Koreans had a traditional fear of the Chinese. Collins came to the conclusion the ROKs might collapse if the United States indicated it might pull out of Korea; if the United States remained resolute, the ROKs could be held in line, he felt. Ridgway further told Collins he didn't believe the Chinese could drive the United Nations out of Korea entirely. Although he thought, with determined pressure, they could force UN troops back to a beachhead position around Pusan, Eighth Army then could hold with its flanks resting on the sea and Chinese supply lines harassed by air.[6]

Meanwhile, General Vandenberg, while making an aerial reconnaissance by helicopter, flew twelve miles in advance of the UN positions, landed, and joined a ground patrol. As Schnabel says in his study of policy in the first year of the war, this spoke well for Vandenberg's courage, but reflected "some doubt on his judgment." The Chinese would have found the capture of the top air force officer of the United States and a member of the Joint Chiefs of Staff to be a bonanza beyond compare, and Vandenberg clearly risked capture in venturing out with a patrol.[7]

Collins sent back to the Joint Chiefs an optimistic report indicating Eighth Army could hold out in Korea, at least for a while. This in turn moved the National Security Council on January 17 to postpone any decision on direct actions against Red China.[8] Collins repeated this reassuring prognosis to the Joint Chiefs when he and Vandenberg arrived back in Washington on January 18. The military leadership of the United States breathed a collective sigh of relief. "For the first time since the previous November, responsible authorities in Washington were no longer pessimistic about our being driven out of Korea," Collins wrote afterward.[9]

The Collins appraisal of UN morale in Korea, gainsaying MacArthur's views, was a watershed of the Korean War. As Schnabel and Watson say in their study of the Joint Chiefs, during the weeks after beginning of the Chinese counteroffensive November 25, "there had been an invisible but important alteration in the command relationships involved in the Korean conflict. The organizational charts remained unaltered, except for the insertion of a new name in the box representing the commanding general Eighth Army. But the imposing figure in Tokyo no longer towered quite so impressively. In every previous decision of crucial import—commitment of U.S. troops in Korea, selection of the Inchon landing site, separation of X Corps from Eighth Army, advance of UN forces to the Yalu—the recommendations of General MacArthur had proved decisive. Now, however, his prestige, which had gained an extraordinary luster after Inchon, was badly tarnished. His credibility suffered in the unforeseen outcome of the late November offensive, and declined further when General Collins contradicted his assertions about the sinking morale of Eighth Army. There was indeed some reason to believe that General MacArthur's own morale had been affected. Certainly his frequently changing appraisals of the military prospects in Korea seemed difficult to account for on any other basis. And his superiors, their patience tried by numerous arguments necessitating the sending of emissaries to Tokyo, no longer reposed full confidence in him."[10]

* * * * * * * * * *

On the ground in Korea, the battlefront had become relatively quiet. The Chinese were in the withdrawal phase of their offensive and were building up reserves and supplies and bringing up thousands of replacements for the casualties suffered in the first days of the attack. Chinese troops set up light screening forces between their withdrawal positions far to the rear and the Eighth Army front. Contact between the two armies virtually ceased.[11]

Ridgway was dissatisfied with the intelligence reports he was getting from his G-2, primarily because, as he wrote, "all our vigorous patrolling, all our constant air reconnaissance had failed to locate any trace" of the Chinese forces. Major General Earle E. (Pat) Partridge, commanding the Fifth Air Force, offered Ridgway an old AT-6 advanced trainer, and with Partridge himself at the controls, the two generals meticulously searched, often at treetop height, a sector twenty miles deep in advance of Eighth Army's positions. "Hardly a moving creature did we spot," Ridgway wrote, "not a campfire smoke, no wheel tracks, not even trampled snow to indicate the presence of a large number of troops."

The only way to find out what was out there was to advance cautiously into it, Ridgway decided—but an advance, Ridgway said, "far different from the reckless and uncoordinated plunge toward the Yalu," which MacArthur had ordered on November 24. On January 20, Ridgway directed his subordinate commanders to create opportunities for brief, violent actions to disrupt enemy preparations for his new offensive. On January 22 a task force of the 1st Cavalry Division advanced several thousand yards in the vicinity of Ichon on the western front, meeting only scattered resistance. This showed the Chinese did not occupy in strength any positions close to the front lines of I and IX Corps. Therefore, Ridgway scheduled a larger reconnaissance force, Operation Thunderbolt, on January 25, with each corps using a U.S. division and a ROK regiment. The operation was designed to be a methodical, coordinated push north to seek out the enemy. Ridgway insisted on a doctrinaire U.S. Army attack formula: tanks, antiaircraft automatic weapons and artillery covered a certain number of hills with fire; under this cover the infantry advanced and swept the ground clean of any enemy troops before moving on to the next objective. Any enemy force flushed out was set upon by air force or marine fighters. Ridgway also insisted on something rare in Korea: advancing forces had to keep in a solid front, with units maintaining contact left and right with other units as they moved forward. The old-style method in Korea of advancing columns down roads with or without flank support by infantry moving through bordering hills was abandoned. The purpose, of course, was to prevent the Chinese from flanking roadbound columns or moving behind them to set up the devastating roadblocks that had damaged UN forces so badly in the past. Eighth Army's strength in men and weapons made this practice feasible.

The carefully staged advance of I and IX Corps encountered little resistance, although the Turkish Brigade east of Osan faced an estimated CCF regiment briefly before the Chinese faded backward. During the first days of the advance, some Chinese forces launched a few small night counterattacks. Generally, however, they engaged only in outpost actions before they withdrew.

In the X Corps sector, however, it was a different story. While the two westernmost corps were moving methodically forward in Operation Thunderbolt, Ridgway ordered X Corps to create diversionary actions to the north. X Corps armored patrols reached Wonju, now deserted by North Koreans and Chinese, then moved on to Hoengsong ten air miles north. As part of this advance, the 2nd Division's 23rd Regiment, with the French Battalion attached, moved January 31 into the "twin-tunnels" area near Chipyong-ni, about twenty miles northwest of Wonju. The Chinese contested this advance fiercely and repeatedly attacked French and American positions, until finally driven away by air attacks. The cost to the 23rd was 105 men and to the French Battalion 125 men, but estimated losses on the Chinese side ran into the thousands.

Meanwhile, in the I and IX Corps sectors, armored spearheads probed northward against stiffening resistance, but still limited to delaying actions. UN columns began to encounter roads heavily mined, and CCF mortar and some artillery fire began to drop into UN lines. The intensity of Chinese resistance increased steadily until February 9 and then suddenly evaporated. UN patrols penetrated to a point three miles east of Inchon and reported no enemy activity. Other patrols rushed through a heavy snowstorm to the banks of the Han river without contact. Task forces of the 25th Division advanced almost six miles on February 10 and seized Inchon and Kimpo airfield without firing a shot. By nightfall I Corps had closed up to the south bank of the Han and looked across at Seoul.

Ridgway now ordered X Corps and the ROK III Corps to the east to attack northward to envelop Hongchon, thirteen air miles north-northwest of Hoengsong, in order to disrupt efforts by North Korean forces to regroup south of Hongchon. Other ROK units in the mountains to the east were to advance to protect the right flank of X Corps. This operation, called Roundup, began of February 5, with the ROK 5th and 8th Divisions attached to X Corps moving to envelop Hongchon. They were supported by special armor, artillery and infantry teams from the U.S. 2nd and 7th Divisions and the 187th Airborne RCT. On February 6 the ROKs began meeting heavy resistance, with the ROK 8th Division on the right particularly suffering in its movement northeast of Hoengsong. The ROK III Corps on the east could not keep pace with the X Corps advance, and by February 8 strong NK forces were hitting the right flank of X Corps. The ROK 5th Division thereupon shifted over, faced east, and prepared to block the North Korean flanking thrusts. The ROK 3rd Division got the assignment to continue the left-hand flanking attack toward Hongchon. X Corps soon began to see a steady buildup of enemy forces on its front. Minefields and booby-trapped foxholes appeared. There was evidence the North Koreans were attempting to entice the UN and ROK forces to attack, while air observers reported large enemy groups moving south and east above Hoengsong. Intelligence reports indicated the Chinese had shifted most of their troops to the west-central front, and were likely to launch a counteroffensive while I and IX Corps moved up on the west to the Han river.

The expected counterstroke came on the night of February 11–12, when elements of the 40th and 66th CCF Armies and the North Korean II and V Corps struck the three ROK divisions (3rd, 5th and especially the 8th) north of Hoengsong in a violent attack. The Chinese and NK troops made immediate penetrations and forced the ROKs to backtrack quickly. This permitted enemy troops to move through the snow-covered mountains to set up roadblocks behind UN lines. The situation deteriorated rapidly, and an effort of the three ROK divisions to set up a defensive line north of Hoengsong collapsed. The ROK 8th Division was shattered. One regiment of the ROK 3rd Division was surrounded. The special U.S. armor-artillery-infantry support teams found their positions untenable when the units they were supporting were overwhelmed. These forces suffered heavy casualties during their attempts to withdraw to U.S. perimeter positions in and around Hoengsong.

Meanwhile, the 23rd Regiment and the French Battalion which had advanced slightly to the north of Chipyong-ni encountered strong Chinese resistance and on February 14 elements of three Chinese armies attacked in this sector. They forced U.S. troops east of Chipyong-ni to withdraw to the south and the 23rd RCT and the French Battalion to pull into a closed perimeter at Chipyong-ni, emplacing on a ring of hills immediately around the town. The decision of the UN Command to hold Chipyong-ni was crucial. If the village fell, a corridor would be opened to Yoju, about ten miles to the southwest and thereby enemy troops would be able to sweep behind X Corps by moving southeast along the upper Han corridor. To prevent a breakthrough, Ridgway attached the British Commonwealth 27th Brigade and the ROK 6th Division to the 2nd Division and moved them into blocking positions along the Yoju-Wonju road. By the end of February 14, most elements of X Corps had successfully withdrawn to a line running from Chipyong-ni to Wonju and from there to the mountain village of Pyongchang, twenty-three miles east of Wonju.

But the 23rd RCT and the Frenchmen at Chipyong-ni were under fanatical attack. They held, mowing down hundreds of Chinese who assaulted the tightly closed perimeter. On February 15 the Chinese tried again, and again failed. As a result, the communist command shifted its main thrust to the east, using the II and V North Korean Corps to try to reach the communications and supply center of Chechon, about twenty-two miles southeast of Wonju. Troops of the ROK I Corps and the U.S. 7th Division stopped this attack.

The rocklike stand of the 23rd RCT and the French Battalion in the Chipyong-ni perimeter played a major role in stopping the CCF advance. The Chinese suffered an estimated five thousand casualties in their assaults.

An armored task force of the 5th Cavalry Regiment ran through a curtain of CCF fire to join the Americans and Frenchmen at Chipyong-ni and to break the enemy investment of the village, and the following day the weary defenders found the Chinese troops had slipped away. Both the French Battalion and the 23rd Regiment and supporting troops were awarded the American Distinguished Unit citation.

By February 16, it was apparent the CCF-NK offensive had been contained, and units of X Corps commenced aggressive patrolling to prevent the enemy from consolidating his gains. Although Operation Roundup had failed to reach Hongchon and three ROK divisions had been severely mauled, the communist counteroffensive likewise had been stalled, and the Chinese and North Korean casualties greatly exceeded UN and ROK losses.

At the same time on the western front I and IX Corps were gradually occupying all the ground up to the Han. Several ROK patrols tried to slip across the river, but were driven back, and prisoner-of-war reports indicated Seoul was filled with Chinese and NK troops. The enemy also maintained a bridgehead south of the Han to the east of Seoul, and on the night of February 13–14 a strong force attacked southward toward Suwon, but was swiftly halted with severe casualties: 1,152 enemy bodies were counted and 353 prisoners captured.

Far behind the lines American and ROK troops also were slowly reducing large concentrations of guerrillas and remnants of North Korean army units cut off by earlier UN advances. These guerrillas disrupted communications and were a constant source of unease and danger, but they were difficult to defeat because they faded back into the mountains when they were attacked. The 1st Marine Division, assigned to flush out guerrillas, developed a successful tactic: before marines attacked, they surrounded a guerrilla band, if possible, and then assaulted with mortars and artillery support. Gradually these and other efforts reduced the size of the guerrilla forces.

The collapse of the Chinese and North Korean attack against X Corps resulted in the enemy's returning to his standard procedure—withdrawal from the battle line to replenish supplies and replace casualties. The Chinese were suffering greatly from cold, hunger and disease, a product of their crude supply system, inadequate medical care, and the devastation which air force, marine and navy aircraft had wreaked on virtually all of the towns and villages behind UN lines. Few buildings were left standing, and any suspected of harboring enemy troops were immediately blasted or napalmed. Troops outdoors were seldom able to construct adequate shelters because of fear of giving away their positions. Later, the Chinese developed underground chambers capable of protecting large numbers of men, as well as the standard bunkers dug into mountains and covered with heavy logs and earth. But in this first winter of the war, in which the Chinese were mostly advancing, these refinements were large absent, and the Chinese soldiers suffered accordingly.

On February 18, Major General Bryant E. Moore, new commander of

IX Corps, told General Ridgway some troops of the 24th Division had found enemy positions in front of them vacant; patrols quickly sent out confirmed that enemy forces along the entire Eighth Army central front were beginning a general retreat. Ridgway immediately ordered X Corps to attack eastward to destroy the nasty NK salient reaching almost to Chechon, and also directed IX Corps to move northward to the Han.

Recognizing that the enemy relied upon withdrawal to regain his strength before advancing again on the offensive, Ridgway hit upon a method of countering the enemy: a general, but cautious, advance upon the heels of the withdrawing enemy to give him neither rest nor a chance to restock his supplies. Ridgway planned this operation, code-named Killer, on February 18, two days before a visit by MacArthur to the front. He planned for IX and X Corps to advance to deny important positions to the enemy, keep him off balance and to destroy as many enemy troops as possible. Ridgway ordered the 1st Marine Division attached to IX Corps and directed it to move north toward Hoengsong and Hongchon. He shifted X Corps into the mountains east of Wonju with instructions to drive north in tandem with the marines.

MacArthur arrived in Korea on February 20, the eve of the attack. He and Ridgway went up to the front. Ridgway describes what happened: "Standing before some ten or more correspondents met at the X Corps tactical command post, with me leaning against a table in the rear, MacArthur said calmly: 'I have just ordered a resumption of the offensive.' There was no undue emphasis on the personal pronoun, but the implication was clear: he had just flown in from Tokyo, had surveyed the situation, discussed it with his subordinates, and had then ordered the Eighth Army to attack."[12] Thus MacArthur managed, before the press corps, to take credit for an offensive wholly thought up and already ordered by General Ridgway.

Operation Killer was slow, and it encountered few enemy troops, who withdrew before the UN advance. UN troops continued northward all along the two-corps front, and by February 24 the marine division had seized the high ground just to the south of Hoengsong. The same day, General Moore, IX Corps commander, died of a heart attack after the helicopter in which he was riding crashed into the Han river. General Smith, marine division commander, took temporary command until the arrival March 5 of Major General William H. Hoge.

The biggest obstacle to the advance of both corps was a thaw accompanied by heavy rains, which turned roads and land into mud and raised stream levels to flood stages in some places. Although CCF and NK troops contested the advance, their mission was to delay, not hold in place. On the western front, the Chinese also withdrew their bridgehead on the south side of the Han, most likely because they wanted to evacuate equipment and supplies over the river before the ice on it broke up.

Operation Killer had not killed a great number of enemy troops. But it had set the UN forces advancing, and morale and a new sense of purpose rose in Eighth Army. By March 1 the UN line had reached points between the 37th and 38th parallels, and the Chinese and their relatively few North Korean allies were still in no mood for a fight. Everyone knew this was the lull to recoup strength before the storm of the spring offensive, but the gloom and prophesies of disaster just prior to and after the Chinese New Year's offensive had vanished.

One important reason why morale in Eighth Army had improved so dramatically was that, starting around the first of the year, the army inaugurated a new program of five-day Rest and Recuperation (R&R) leaves to Japan, for which the lowliest GI and the highest officer were eligible. The program got started slowly—at first only about two hundred men per division per week were able to go—but it quickly accelerated, and it soon became an extremely significant factor in the capacity of American and other UN soldiers and marines, as well as airmen and sailors, to endure the loneliness, exhaustion and danger of their assignments.

The transition of a war-weary soldier or marine from a foxhole in Korea to the dazzling lights of Tokyo or other Japanese cities was staggering. But the hope for R&R buoyed many a man whose morale otherwise would have sunk. GIs quickly dubbed the R&R leaves I&I (Intercourse and Intoxication), or, more vulgarly, A&A (Ass and Alcohol). There were, indeed, great opportunities for both in Japan. Clubs for officers, noncoms and enlisted men abounded in Japan, but the many excellent commercial nightclubs run by Japanese claimed the attention of most of the R&R men. These clubs offered superb Japanese beer, professional Japanese combos with female vocalists singing American pop tunes and generally a plethora of Japanese girls waiting to be picked up. Americans and other UN troops were overwhelmed by the often beautiful but always extremely polite and *clean* Japanese women. The Japanese ran official red-light districts, providing, in typical Japanese fashion, offerings for any taste—from raucous and bawdy to restrained and refined. Some men frequented these houses, but the greatest and most sought-after sources of feminine company were found right on the streets of the cities. Generally the Japanese girls and young women were not prostitutes in the traditional sense; rather they were working women who were attracted to the excitement and comparative high life that a man on R&R could offer. Almost without exception the Japanese women stood shyly on the streets, seldom calling or hustling, and responded to inquisitive glances or nods by Westerners with embarrassed giggles and polite responses in generally bad broken English. To the hollow-eyed young men from Korea, badly in need of solace, comfort and affection, these young Japanese women were apparitions come to life. There were a lot of American women in Japan: wives of officers and noncoms on duty in Japan or sent to Korea who remained in their excellent apartments and quarters in Japan, a few female military personnel and nurses, and many civilian women who held jobs in the U.S. occupation. These civilian women, universally called DACs (for Department of the Army civilians, whether they worked for the army or not), were by far the most visible American females in Japan. But despite nostalgic glances at long American legs by many a veteran from Korea, the DACs attracted little attention as compared to the Japanese women. Sometimes this was because DACs played American boy-girl games and acted coy when they encountered young men, and soldiers who had been through the ordeal of Korea often found themselves unable to readjust their thinking on short notice to this sort of play-acting. Another reason was that many young American women in Japan seemed surprisingly unaware of and unaffected by the agony going on in Korea. Because they spoke English, they conveyed this indifference or ignorance to men on R&R, for whom Korea by no means was a matter of indifference, though they seldom wanted to dwell on the subject. The Japanese girls may have had no more understanding of or interest in Chosen, as the Japanese called Korea, than the typical American DAC, but their English was generally limited. The extent of their discussion of the problems and policies of the Korean conflict was usually restricted to some statement such as, "You Chosen go?" accompanied by a look of great sympathy. This meant, "Have you been, are you going, or are you going back to Korea? How sorry I am for you!" While American women were expected to understand the trauma of Korea, Japanese women were not; or they were given credit, whether deserved or not, for deeper insights which their poor English prevented them from expressing.

Whatever the other reasons, the principal reason why American women were not pursued more persistently was that the Japanese women answered every possible need of young men who wanted to get away from the reality of Korea and had little time in five days to explore lasting or deep relationships. The ready availability of modest, demure and extremely feminine young Japanese women seemed to them a heaven-sent gift. Strangely, however, the very muteness that the barrier of language placed between Westerner and Japanese often forced them into expressions of real feeling which a mutually intelligible language might have masked or prevented. However short they were, many of the encounters between GI or officer and Japanese girl-san left deep and lasting emotions on both sides. Although the reconciliation of the Japanese people with the American people began in the years of the occupation before the Korean War, it was the war itself, with its hundreds of thousands of young American men who briefly visited Japan and briefly encountered Japanese people in bars, clubs, hotels and on the streets, that slowly turned a World War II-spawned antagonism for the Japanese into an affection for the Japanese. It was a rare American who visited Japan, even on a five-day R&R, who came away with anything but admiration for the Japanese people.

While the men in Korea joked about I&I or A&A, and many of them practiced both (and most of those who did not lied about it when they got back to their outfits, young men not wishing to be ridiculed by their peers), the fact is Rest and Recuperation leave was well-named. The majority of men from Korea with any sophistication at all immediately abandoned the spartan quarters provided for them on military bases and removed themselves to small Japanese inns. At the inn the young man was met by a solicitous, bowing proprietor (usually a mature female and always called Mama-san), who directed him to remove his shoes at the door and led him to a scrupulously clean and neat room with tatami mats on the floor and spotless bedroll likewise spread on the floor. Subsequently the Westerner was directed to the rear of the inn where a traditional Japanese bath was installed: that is, a hot tub which was used exclusively for soaking, the washing and rinsing having to be done in advance with a tiny wash basin, soap and rag. The effect of this cleanliness and this peace on the mind and body of a young soldier or marine after months of dirt and weariness in foxholes was likely to be devastating. Despite all the talk (and some action) regarding wine, women and song, the most lasting and happy memories that most men carried back from their R&Rs were remembrances of being clean and of being able to lie down in peaceful sleep untroubled by mortars or wet or cold. Few veterans of Korea would ever admit it among their associates, but a great many of them *slept* away great portions of their R&Rs.

CHAPTER 52

North to the Kansas Line

BY THE BEGINNING of March, a curious military situation had
developed in Korea: Eighth Army was methodically moving northward, step by step, while the communist forces, largely Chinese, were
delaying the Eighth Army movement by means of a light screen of
soldiers who fought hard, but pulled back after making UN troops send
in artillery and mortar preparations, deploy infantry and then attack.
Behind this cloud of skirmishers, the communist troops withdrew,
keeping their formations intact, though the delaying units often suffered
heavily. On the map it looked like a giant retreat by the Chinese and
North Koreans, especially as defensible pass after pass and ridgeline
after ridgeline were abandoned to Eighth Army after short actions or
after no opposition at all.

The communists were a long way from being beaten, however, and
every Eighth Army commander from Ridgway on down knew it. It
became increasingly clear as the communists withdrew that they were
recoiling for a massive counterstroke: the spring offensive.[1] The focal
point of this counterstroke was the Iron Triangle—the mountain-flanked
area a few miles north of the 38th parallel bounded by Chorwon,
Kumwha and Pyonggang. (See Map 12.) Here the Third CCF Field
Army was massing, and here the Chinese were able to use the railways
and highways coming in from their rear to build up a large base of
supplies. Immediately south of the Iron Triangle and extending eastward
into the Taebaek mountains there was only a limited road net that could
be used by UN troops approaching the huge communist buildup.
Farther south, much better road nets would have given Eighth Army
more opportunity to move up equipment and supplies and to shift
troops than would be available in the high, rough country bordering the
Iron Triangle and the region to the east around Hwachon reservoir and

399

Inje. By pulling their forces into the rough, almost roadless mountains just north of the 38th parallel, the Red commanders put UN forces at a maximum disadvantage, with supply limited to a few approach roads and all of these expected to be in bad shape with the spring rains and thaw.

The Chinese strategy followed closely a CCF training directive captured in IX Corps during the winter. "Warfare must not be conducted hastily," the directive stated. "In combat, it is absolutely necessary in all cases to establish accurate and detailed plans after serious consideration. Rash attempts to defeat the enemy by quick battles without knowledge of changes in his situation nor the degree of our combat readiness will always result in reverses. Therefore, there must absolutely be no hasty nor impatient attitude toward warfare....Engagements must be conducted only when the situation is entirely to our advantage."

As sensible as this Chinese strategy was, it still gave Ridgway the chance to occupy most of the remainder of Red-dominated South Korea, and Ridgway jumped at the chance. Ridgway's attack plan was excellent. Instead of trying to advance all along the front, he ordered a powerful thrust, primarily by IX Corps and X Corps, in the center of the line, with the aim of capturing Chunchon. This city was the major road junction in central Korea, and its capture would cut off most easy routes of enemy withdrawal, leaving only routes through rugged mountains. Capture of Chunchon also would flank the enemy troops occupying Seoul and the western banks of the Han in front of I Corps, as well as the mostly North Korean troops in the eastern mountains. Ridgway had great hopes this stroke also could catch large numbers of Chinese troops facing the UN advance, and he planned to air-drop the 187th Airborne RCT on Chunchon to cut off the enemy's retreat. The Chinese withdrew so rapidly, however, that Ridgway cancelled the airdrop, and also failed to capture any substantial number of Chinese troops.

The UN attack, which Ridgway code-named Ripper, began on March 7 and aimed at reaching the Idaho line, which represented the expected deep penetration into the center of the communist front. Operation Ripper in the I Corps sector began with a tremendous artillery barrage and the assault of the 25th Division across the Han river near its confluence with the Pukhan river, about twenty miles east of Seoul. The ROK 1st Division and the U.S. 3rd Division created diversionary attacks in the vicinity of Seoul in an attempt to draw Chinese attention away from the 25th Division. The Chinese contested the 25th Division penetration for three days of heavy fighting and then withdrew in some disorder. Elsewhere along the attack front, UN troops made strong gains from the first day. Opposition continued to be what it had been previously: small units delayed at passes, roadblocks and ridges; when they were invested or assaulted by air, artillery and mortar fire, the survivors withdrew. This method of slowing the UN advance was excellent, because the Chinese selected the least-accessible places to fight—where roads were few or hills were steep and approaches difficult or open to fire from defenders' positions. A strong Chinese ally was the weather. The roads suffered badly in the rains and from the thousands of wheels that had to run over them. Although army and marine engineers, along with thousands of Korean civilians, worked constantly on the roads, delays slowed Eighth Army's advance. This sort of slow, slogging progress continued for the next six weeks, and it worked in recovering South Korean real estate from the communists, though it was less successful in destroying enemy troop formations.

The most spectacular result of Operation Ripper was that the advance, by moving northward on both sides of Chunchon, left the Chinese in and around Seoul in danger of being cut off if Ridgway elected to thrust west to sever the roads leading north out of the capital. The Chinese did not wait to allow Ridgway this opportunity, but withdrew around March 13 and 14. A ROK patrol on the night of March 14–15 found the city almost deserted by Chinese forces, and ROK and UN troops quickly moved in without opposition. The capital had changed hands for the fourth time in nine months of war.

During this period, an unusual event occurred in the east in the Taebaek mountains. The 10th NK Division had been operating for some time behind the UN lines in the Chungbong mountains, west of the east-coast town of Samchok. Though it was harried by as many as four ROK divisions, and had suffered high casualties, the division was still intact. On March 17 and 18 this NK division fought its way from the south through the ROK 3rd and 9th Divisions and disappeared to the north—a breakthrough from the rear *into* the front.

In the IX Corps sector more and more antitank mines were found in the roads, and bunkers and trenches with overhead covers began to appear on the ridgelines, as well as innumerable machine-gun nests. The days of grinding positional warfare were already being foreshadowed. Although Chinese opposition south of Chunchon was stiff and enemy soldiers had sometimes to be driven off in hand-to-hand combat, the progress of IX Corps was steady, with all the corps forces moving: 1st Marine, 1st Cavalry, 24th and ROK 6th Divisions and the 27th British Commonwealth Brigade. Attached to the 1st Cavalry were the Greek and Thai Battalions, and the 27th Brigade had recently been augmented with the 2nd Battalion of the Princess Patricia Canadian Light Infantry, the New Zealand 16th Field Artillery Regiment and the Indian 60th Field

Ambulance and Surgical Unit.

By March 19, IX Corps patrols had entered the Chunchon valley and it became apparent that the airdrop of the 187th Airborne RCT would not be necessary. The Chinese already had slipped the trap. Ridgway had an immediate alternative plan: on March 23 he ordered the 187th RCT dropped at Munsan-ni, on the Imjin river about twenty miles northwest of Seoul. The idea again was to trap large bodies of Chinese troops between I Corps forces north of Seoul and the Imjin. The trap was sprung, but again the quarry had flown.

By the end of March Eighth Army stood generally just below the 38th parallel, although ROKs on the east coast had moved a few miles above it. It is ironic, but this old political division now became a battle line. But not for long. President Truman decided the 38th had lost much of its significance. On March 15, he answered a reporter's query about whether UN forces would be allowed to advance over the line: "That is a tactical matter for the field commander. A commander in chief 7,000 miles away does not interfere with field operations. We are working to free the Republic of Korea and set it up as the United Nations wants it. That doesn't have anything to do with the 38th parallel."[2] The decision ultimately was left to Ridgway. With MacArthur's approval, Ridgway elected to continue the advance over the 38th in hopes of achieving maximum destruction of the communist forces.

Red troops in heavy numbers were now in the Iron Triangle and in the Hwachon reservoir-Inje areas, and were preparing for their spring offensive. Eighth Army came *up* to the Chinese offensive. Ridgway and other commanders were left in doubt only about when and where the attack would come. One definite clue that the communists planned no retreat behind the Iron Triangle: they had built no defensive positions farther to their rear. By the first week of April intelligence sources had identified nine CCF armies (27 divisions) and had tentatively identified ten more CCF armies (30 divisions), along with 18 NK divisions and 6 brigades. Although losses to all these forces had been heavy and it was unlikely the Chinese would employ anything like 57 divisions, communist strength was great, and the potential for an offensive was obvious.

Ridgway decided, under the circumstances, it would be better for Eighth Army to move forward than to stand in place. Therefore, on April 5 he set in motion a follow-up attack to Ripper. This assault was code-named Rugged and called for a general advance to a new objective line, Kansas. (See Map 12.) This new line ran along commanding ground just north of the 38th parallel, except along the Imjin river in the west, where UN forces were to remain in position. Including fourteen miles of tidal

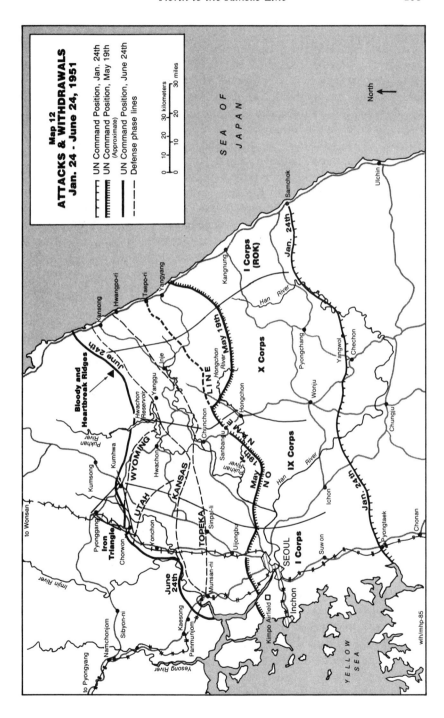

Map 12
ATTACKS & WITHDRAWALS
Jan. 24 - June 24, 1951

UN Command Position, Jan. 24th
UN Command Position, May 19th (Approximate)
UN Command Position, June 24th
Defense phase lines

water of the Han river before it emptied into the Yellow Sea and a ten-mile water barrier of the Hwachon reservoir (the source of Seoul's water and electric power), the line ran 115 miles. In the east the extremely mountainous terrain was practically roadless, limiting action by both sides; along the remainder of the line Eighth Army could occupy positions of considerable strength and depth.[3]

The advance to the Kansas line was rapid: by April 9 all units except X Corps and the ROK III Corps in the high Taebaek mountains had reached the line, having been held up more by rugged terrain than by enemy action. Even so, these two corps were rapidly drawing up to the line. On this day the North Koreans opened several sluice gates of the Hwachon reservoir in an attempt to flood the lower Pukhan river, which flowed southwest out of the reservoir. Within an hour the water level in the river had risen several feet, one engineer pontoon bridge was broken and engineers had to swing a second one back to one bank. This event caused Eighth Army to organize a hasty task force of the 7th Cavalry and the 4th Ranger Company to seize the dam and immobilize the gate-opening machinery. This task force failed for a variety of reasons, one of which was insufficient supply of landing craft to get across the reservoir. Anyway, it did not matter greatly, because the water level soon fell in the Pukhan. The effect on UN operations was negligible.

The quick success in getting to the Kansas line encouraged Ridgway to add another objective line on the west. This line was designated Utah and was essentially a northern bulge of the Kansas line in the west. (See Map 12.) Its purpose was to thrust UN troops to a point just south of Chorwon, the southwestern anchor of the Iron Triangle. I Corps and the westernmost element of IX Corps were engaged in this movement, and it went forward rapidly. Meantime, other things had been happening elsewhere.

Infantry of the 19th Regiment, 24th Division, retreat ten miles south of Seoul on January 3, 1951.

South Korean President Syngman Rhee urges courage at a meeting in Seoul in December, 1950, shortly before the city was lost in the Chinese New Year's Eve offensive.

Korean refugees pack the roads south of Seoul on January 5, 1951, trying to get away from Chinese troops.

An American F-80 jet attacks North Korean vehicles caught in the open. The F-80 was armed with six .50-caliber machine guns and could carry rockets and bombs.

Winter battle: a machine-gun crew rests above a Korean village after assaulting a Chinese position.

A wounded soldier of the French Battalion is readied to be carried back for medical care. The French Battalion gained renown and suffered high losses at Chipyong-ni in early 1951 and on Heartbreak Ridge in the fall of 1951.

Men of the 25th Division observe an artillery concentration beginning to land on a Chinese position in central Korea in March, 1951.

Infantry of the 25th Division advance in central Korea in late March, 1951.

Four white-phosphorous artillery shells drop on Chinese positions in front of the 25th Division on the Western front in February, 1951.

Chinese soldiers captured near Hwachon reservoir in central Korea await shipment at 24th Division headquarters.

CHAPTER 53

MacArthur Finally Does It

THE APPROACH to the 38th parallel gave the Truman administration an opportunity to offer the Chinese a cease-fire. The status quo ante had effectively been restored, and the UN Command had advanced to the parallel, not retreated to it, and thus was in a position where it could negotiate, if not from dominance, at least from strength.

President Truman decided to issue a public declaration that the UN Command was willing to consider a cease-fire, and on March 19 the Joint Chiefs and Secretaries Acheson and Marshall discussed a draft declaration that had been prepared by the Department of State. In the next few days this draft was circulated to some United Nations governments for their reaction and approval.[1]

The American plan again was to offer a cease-fire without prejudicing the U.S. position in regard to Taiwan or the admission of Red China to the United Nations. But the administration and the Joint Chiefs saw a cease-fire as a strong possibility for a political solution in Korea at least and a likelihood that fighting would not resume.[2]

Truman planned to state that other United Nations objectives than liberating South Korea—especially unification of Korea and establishment of a free government in all of Korea—could be accomplished without more bloodshed. As Schnabel says in his study of policy in the first year of the war, "The Chinese Communists were, in effect, to be invited to cease fire and to negotiate a settlement of the outstanding issues. They were also to be warned that if they refused to negotiate, the United Nations would be forced to continue fighting."[3]

On March 20, the Joint Chiefs alerted General MacArthur as to what was happening with the following message: "State planning Presidential announcement shortly that, with clearing of bulk of South Korea of

405

aggressors, United Nations now prepared to discuss conditions of settlement in Korea. Strong UN feeling persists that further diplomatic effort towards settlement should be made before any advance with major forces north of the 38th parallel. Time will be required to determine diplomatic reactions and permit new negotiations that may develop. Recognizing that parallel has no military significance, State has asked JCS what authority you should have to permit sufficient freedom of action for next few weeks to provide security for UN forces and maintain contact with enemy. Your recommendations desired."[4]

MacArthur responded with a complaint about any restriction on his operations, along with a non sequitur on his inability to conquer North Korea, which was specifically not being asked of him. He also scarcely noticed the specific request in the JCS message. MacArthur's reply: "Recommend that no further military restrictions be imposed upon the United Nations Command in Korea. The inhibitions which already exist should not be increased. The military disadvantage arising from restrictions upon the scope of our air and naval operations coupled with the disparity between the size of our command and the enemy ground potential renders it completely impracticable to attempt to clear North Korea or to make any appreciable effort to that end. My present directives, establishing the security of the command as the paramount consideration, are adequate to cover the two points raised by the State Department."[5]

That is where matters lay. MacArthur knew the United States was seeking a cease-fire and was diligently searching out the views of its allies. The President of the United States was preparing to broadcast a message to the Chinese Communists offering peace and a measure of conciliation. A chance to end the war seemed to be at hand.

Three days later, without notice to anyone in the United States, General MacArthur issued his own statement: it ranks among the most blatant acts in history of a field commander defying the instructions of superior authority and the established policy of the nation he serves.

MacArthur's statement was released to the public on March 24 Far East time. Besides usurping the authority of the President of the United States, MacArthur put down the Chinese with an arrogant, belittling statement which could only be interpreted by Beijing as a virtual ultimatum threatening extension of the war unless Red China sued for peace.

MacArthur's message proclaimed that, "even under inhibitions which now restrict the activity of the United Nations forces and the corresponding military advantages which accrue to Red China, it has been shown its complete inability to accomplish by force of arms the conquest of Korea." MacArthur said, however, "the fundamental questions continue to be political in nature and must find their answer in the diplomatic sphere." MacArthur continued: "The enemy therefore must now be painfully aware that a decision of the United Nations to depart from its tolerant effort to contain the war to the area of Korea through expansion of our military operations to his coastal areas and interior bases would doom Red China to the risk of imminent military collapse....Within my area of authority as military commander, however, it should be needless to say I stand ready at any time to confer in the field with the commander in chief of the enemy forces in an earnest effort to find any military means whereby the realization of the political objectives of the United Nations in Korea, to which no nation may justly take exception, might be accomplished without further bloodshed."[6]

MacArthur had found a way to torpedo Truman's peace initiative, and he used it. Truman's offer could not now be made, especially as a flood of inquiries poured in from allies asking whether U.S. policy had changed.[7]

Although MacArthur disclaimed it, the evidence is preponderant that MacArthur deliberately decided to hazard making national policy on his own. He had argued in favor of expanding the war against China. He knew the Truman administration opposed this course, and he saw the new Truman initiative would close that door. His virtual ultimatum to China was issued only days after he learned of Truman's plans. The coincidence is too great to ignore.

In his memoirs, MacArthur spoke of the statement as a "routine communiqué" in the "local voice of a theater commander." He said that twice before he had called upon the enemy to surrender without "the slightest whisper of remonstrance" from Washington.[8] He failed, however, to mention that both of those statements, on October 1 and 9, were issued on the eve of the UN invasion of North Korea, and he had made them at the direction of the Joint Chiefs of Staff.

MacArthur's March 24 statement, in fact, was an unbelievable presumption of authority by a theater commander. As Truman later wrote, "It was an act totally disregarding all directives to abstain from any declaration on foreign policy. It was in open defiance of my orders as President and as commander in chief...."[9]

Truman's first reaction was to instruct MacArthur to abide by the President's instructions regarding statements (see page 374). The Joint Chiefs accordingly sent this priority message to MacArthur: "The President has directed that your attention be called to his order as transmitted ... 6 December 1950. In view of the information given you ... [on] 20 March 1951 any further statements by you must be coordinated as prescribed in the order of 6 December. The President has also directed that in the event communist military leaders request an armistice in the field, you immediately report that fact to the JCS for instructions."[10]

It seems inconceivable, but that is not *all* that MacArthur did shortly after the ides of March, 1951, to destroy his own position. On March 20, MacArthur answered a letter written on March 8 by Representative Joseph W. Martin, Jr., the minority (Republican) leader of the House of Representatives. Martin wrote MacArthur seeking the General's endorsement of Martin's views that Nationalist Chinese troops should be used in the war. MacArthur's requests for these troops already had been rejected several times by the Truman administration, and MacArthur had been told each time of the political problems of using Chiang Kai-shek's forces. Yet General MacArthur, in his reply to Martin, indicated his agreement with Martin regarding Nationalist troops, and also repeated his familiar contention that the policy of the Truman administration favored Europe at the expense of Asia. He ended the letter, in which he criticized the strategy of a limited war, with the statement: "There is no substitute for victory."[11] This phrase, often repeated, became identified with MacArthur in the public mind—and justifiably so. As late as 1962 MacArthur said this to the graduating class at West Point: "Your mission remains fixed, determined, inviolable. It is to win our wars ... the will to win, the sure knowledge that in war there is no substitute for victory."[12] Thus, MacArthur personified the idea that wars are to be fought to the finish, to total victory, to unconditional surrender. The Clausewitzian concept that wars are extensions of national political aims and should be pursued only as far as national interests can be seen and not a step further was not MacArthur's view. MacArthur, with his concept of war to the bitter end, could only be at odds with national policy in the Korean War, which manifestly was being fought only for limited national goals and not to embroil the United States in a full-scale war with China, a war whose outcome could scarcely be conceived.

For a theater commander to write such a letter to the leader of the opposition in the House is almost inconceivable. Having delivered himself into the hands of the Truman administration's opponents on the most politically explosive issue in the Far East—protection of Taiwan and support of the Nationalists—MacArthur should not have been surprised by what Martin did: on April 5 he read the letter on the floor of the House and thereby announced to the public MacArthur's opposition to administration policy. MacArthur's side in the dispute was thereby broached publicly, but not the administration's counterarguments. There are indications that MacArthur was being used by Republicans in order to get at Truman and Acheson, especially as the Republicans nominally were isolationists and MacArthur was calling for a wider war in Asia. The questions that MacArthur's letter raised contributed to the administration's decision to lay out the whole issue of the war's purpose in Senate committee hearings that followed.

On April 6, Truman called a meeting in his office.[13] Attending were Secretary of State Acheson, Secretary of Defense Marshall, Special Assistant W. Averell Harriman, and General Bradley. Truman wanted an answer to the following question: What action should he take regarding MacArthur's continued defiance of his directives? Harriman: relieve him. Marshall: be cautious, give him (Marshall) some time to reflect. Bradley: he deserves to be relieved, but the JCS should discuss it first. Acheson: relieve MacArthur, but it would be the biggest fight in Truman's administration. Acheson advised Truman: act on the carefully considered advice "and unshakable support" of all his civilian and military advisors. He urged Bradley and Marshall to discuss the matter fully with the Joint Chiefs, free of any prior conclusions of the President.

Truman did not discuss his own feelings, but merely instructed the four men to confer among themselves later in the day and be prepared the next morning, Saturday, April 7, to discuss the matter again with the President. That afternoon, in Marshall's office, the four senior advisors talked for nearly two hours, coming up with several ideas but reaching no conclusions except to recommend to Truman that he make no decision until the following Monday, April 9. This they told Truman on Saturday morning, urging the President to confer over the weekend with congressional leaders of both parties.

Bradley called a meeting of the Joint Chiefs on Sunday afternoon. All were present. Four hours later, the Chiefs, a "sad and sober group," according to Collins,[14] moved to Secretary Marshall's office, where Marshall asked each officer separately what to do. Collins reported he felt the President was entitled to have a commander whose views fitted better with his own and who was more responsive to the will of the commander-in-chief.[15] Sherman felt the President had to have a commander "in whom we can confide and on whom we can rely."[16] All the Chiefs felt MacArthur should be relieved.

Monday morning, April 9, Acheson, Marshall, Harriman and Bradley appeared again in the President's office. Truman told them he had discussed the matter over the weekend with congressional leaders. Now he wanted his four advisors' recommendations. Bradley said the Joint Chiefs felt MacArthur should be relieved. Marshall agreed with the Chiefs' conclusions. Acheson and Harriman emphatically recommended dismissal. Truman thereupon announced his decision:

MacArthur would be relieved of his command, and then, and only then, did he disclose to the four men that he had made his decision to fire MacArthur after the General's statement of March 24.

Who was to replace MacArthur? Bradley and Marshall thought it should be Ridgway. Truman approved, and immediately after the meeting Marshall and Bradley met with Collins and instructed him to prepare draft messages to MacArthur, Ridgway and Lieutenant General James A. Van Fleet, who already had been designated as Ridgway's successor if the need arose.

An era was ending. An eminence on the American scene since World War I, in which, at age 38, he commanded a brigade in the 42nd (Rainbow) Division, MacArthur was a great and splendid figure in the American pantheon of heroes. Less than seven months previously, his star had reached its zenith with the great success of the Inchon invasion. Now MacArthur, his military reputation sullied within the administration and among top military leaders after his insistence upon attacking into massed Chinese armies on November 24, was felled, not for military failures, but for political ineptitude. He somehow had missed, for all his brilliance, the essence of the American political system: that decisions, right or wrong, are largely arrived at by political consensus or compromise and by a political process based upon democratically elected representatives, and any substantial deviation from this process threatens the American political balance. Whether MacArthur had been right or wrong made little difference; by taking it upon himself to make policy unilaterally, he was operating outside the American political system, and he therefore isolated himself. The inevitable isolation of persons who do this has kept men on horseback and would-be dictators from gaining great power in the United States.

Nevertheless, MacArthur's dismissal was deeply shocking to the American people, indeed to most people in the Western world. The public knew nothing of MacArthur's perfidy in usurping the President's role in the peace overture and in destroying any possibility of success of the President's cease-fire plan. Only a few people understood the enormity of MacArthur's military error in falling twice into a Chinese Communist ambush. Likewise, the arguments for and against use of Nationalist Chinese troops seemed esoteric to some Americans, and those who agreed with the administration's position knew little of MacArthur's intransigence on this matter and of his refusal to accept the official U.S. position. Finally, MacArthur's answer to Joe Martin's letter on the subject put him firmly into the camp of Truman's opponents and guaranteed that his dismissal would result in partisan repercussions. To Americans who did not understand the whole situation, the matter now smacked somehow of political in-fighting and decisions on American security tied in some way to political considerations. This was totally false, but in the highly divided atmosphere of Washington in 1951 the answer to Martin identified MacArthur with Truman's Republican opponents and clouded an issue that otherwise could have been clarified. Beyond all this, the dismissal of a war hero in the midst of war disturbed Americans greatly.

Acheson had advised President Truman wisely. Unless he had the firm backing of all his civilian and military leaders, the political damage to the administration could be fatal. Now that Truman had got his backing, all of the leaders who had joined Truman's camp had willy-nilly vacated MacArthur's camp. Therefore, there was great concern and anxiety in Washington among these leaders and great care that the matter be handled gingerly, as well as en bloc, in order that no one be caught outside the solid Truman phalanx. Consequently, on Tuesday afternoon, April 10, the principals met again in Truman's office, and there Joseph Short, the presidential press secretary, was directed to prepare a news release announcing MacArthur's removal. Bradley assisted in the preparation of this announcement.

The administration also worked out a plan to deliver the message to MacArthur as discreetly as possible. The plan was for Frank Pace, the secretary of the army, who was in the Far East at the time, to carry the notice to MacArthur's home in the U.S. embassy in Tokyo at 10 a.m. April 12, Tokyo time (8 p.m. April 11, Washington time) prior to the General's departure for the Dai Ichi building.

At about 3 p.m. on April 10, Washington time, Truman received and signed the orders, and gave them to Acheson for transmittal to Ambassador Muccio in Pusan for delivery to Secretary Pace, then at the front with General Ridgway. Upon receipt of these orders, Pace was to fly to Tokyo and give the news directly to MacArthur face-to-face. However, the commercial communications facilities used by the State Department broke down, and the message did not get to Secretary Pace. Then, while Pace was at the front, press secretary Short informed General Bradley that somehow the Chicago *Tribune* had got wind of the firing and was preparing to print the news in the next morning's edition. Bradley immediately went to Blair House to tell the President, who decided at once to send the orders to MacArthur directly, using the army communications system. He also directed that a press conference be held quickly; thus, at the strange hour of 1 a.m. April 11, reporters were handed the announcement. Unfortunately, this botching of the administration's best-laid plans gave MacArthur a great deal more public sympathy.

The President's order went on the army wires about an hour before the press conference. Signed by General Bradley, it read: "I have been directed to relay the following message to you from President Truman: I deeply regret that it becomes my duty as President and commander in chief of the United States military forces to replace you as supreme commander, allied powers; commander in chief, United Nations Command; commander in chief, Far East, and commanding general, U.S. Army, Far East. You will turn over your commands effective at once to Lieutenant General Matthew B. Ridgway. You are authorized to have issued such orders as are necessary to complete desired travel to such place as you may select. My reasons for your replacement will be made public concurrently with the delivery to you of the foregoing order, and are contained in the next-following message. Signed Harry S. Truman."[17]

The "next-following message" was: "With deep regret I have concluded that General of the Army Douglas MacArthur is unable to give his wholehearted support to the policies of the United States government and of the United Nations in matters pertaining to his official duties. In view of the specific responsibilities imposed upon me by the Constitution of the United States and the added responsibility which has been entrusted to me by the United Nations, I have decided that I must make a change of command in the Far East. I have, therefore, relieved General MacArthur of his command and have designated Lieutenant General Matthew B. Ridgway as his successor.

"Full and vigorous debate on matters of national policy is a vital element in the constitutional system of our free democracy. It is fundamental, however, that military commanders must be governed by the policies and directives issued to them in the manner provided for by our laws and Constitution. In time of crisis, this consideration is particularly compelling.

"General MacArthur's place in history as one of our greatest commanders is fully established. The nation owes him a debt of gratitude for the distinguished and exceptional service which he has rendered his country in posts of great responsibility. For that reason I repeat my regret at the necessity for the action I feel compelled to take in his case. Signed Harry S. Truman."[18]

Even though Truman had the orders sent by army communications, the fastest means available to the government, commercial news services still got the story to Tokyo first. Before the official message reached MacArthur, the results of the news conference in Washington had been broadcast over Tokyo radio. An aide to the General, hearing the broadcast, telephoned Mrs. MacArthur, and it was she who informed MacArthur of his relief.[19]

General Ridgway also got the news first from a correspondent, who asked him whether he was due for congratulations.[20] Getting official confirmation of the news, Ridgway flew immediately to Tokyo in Secretary Pace's Constellation, which was much faster than his own B-17. He landed at Haneda airport and went directly to the Dai Ichi building, where MacArthur received him at once. "I had a natural human curiosity to see how he had been affected by his peremptory removal from his high post," Ridgway wrote later.[21] "He was entirely himself—composed, quiet, temperate, friendly, and helpful to the man who was to succeed him. He made some allusions to the fact that he had been summarily relieved, but there was no trace of bitterness or anger in his tone. I thought it was a fine tribute to the resilience of this great man that he could accept so calmly, with no outward sign of shock, what must have been a devastating blow to a professional soldier standing at the peak of his career."

MacArthur met Ridgway at the airport for a brief farewell, then Ridgway flew back to Korea in Secretary Pace's borrowed four-engine Constellation to turn over his command to General Van Fleet, who was flying there himself. Pace's pilot was supposed to fly into K-2 airport at Taegu, a large base with a runway long enough for the biggest aircraft. Unfortunately, the pilot dropped into a light-plane landing strip by mistake, barely missed a mountain, laid on his brakes the instant he realized he was on the wrong field, and ended tail-high in a rice paddy with four tires blown.[22]

Returning to Tokyo after exchanging command with Van Fleet, Ridgway moved into the Imperial Hotel until MacArthur left Tokyo, "out of courtesy to my old commander in chief, to stay away from his headquarters."[23] MacArthur returned to the United States, arriving in San Francisco on April 17. There he received a hero's welcome. From the west coast the General proceeded to Washington, where he landed shortly after midnight on April 19 and was greeted by Secretary Marshall and members of the Joint Chiefs. The welcoming party, however, was nearly overwhelmed by spectators who broke through restraining ropes. Later, on April 19, he spoke eloquently to a joint meeting of Congress. It was a subtle point, but the Democrats kept the event from being a joint *session* of Congress and thus not a formal state function but rather a courtesy to a distinguished hero. MacArthur closed his address with a quotation from an old army ballad: "Old soldiers never die, they just fade away." The song, resurrected by music producers, enjoyed brief popularity within the United States. It got less attention in Korea, where young soldiers were dying. MacArthur went on to New York, where his welcoming parade drew the largest crowds ever.[24]

CHAPTER 54

The MacArthur Hearings

I T WAS INEVITABLE that the firing of MacArthur would arouse severe criticism of the Truman administration by its opponents, and the manner in which the dismissal itself went awry gained MacArthur additional sympathy.[1]

The controversy culminated when two committees of the Senate, Armed Services and Foreign Relations, decided to conduct hearings. They began on May 3, but the initiative for them came on April 13 when the Armed Services Committee invited MacArthur to appear and give his views on the military situation in the Far East, together with the circumstances leading up to his dismissal. General MacArthur accepted this invitation; thereupon the Senate Committee on Foreign Relations asked to take part. From this request came the decision that the two committees would meet jointly in continuous hearings to question MacArthur and those involved in his dismissal, as well as other individuals who could shed light on the general situation in the Far East.

The Senate committee hearings were a turning point in American attitudes about the war. With MacArthur gone, there was no major advocate of an extended war in Asia on the scene. Some Republicans hoped to use the hearings to embarrass Truman and to attack Acheson, as well as to illuminate what they considered to be inadequate American support of Chiang Kai-shek. But there was little indication they were prepared to take up a crusade to drive the communists out of China and the Far East.

At the end of the hearings, which ran through June 27, after more than two million words of testimony from fourteen witnesses, including MacArthur, the secretary of state, the secretary of defense, and all the Joint Chiefs of Staff, the results were far less damaging to the administration than many feared and ended up rather damaging to

MacArthur's reputation instead. On the first three days of the hearings, devoted to MacArthur's testimony, the General gave the Republicans every indication the Joint Chiefs agreed with his views on the war. There was great disappointment in the extreme Republican ranks when the JCS revealed, not endorsement of MacArthur's views, but fundamental support of the Truman administration and the concept of a limited war. The JCS felt that MacArthur's proposals for ending the war by assaulting China would involve great danger and emphasized that existing American strength was not sufficient to withstand possible intervention by the Soviet Union. General Bradley finally put the entire concept into a single short statement: "The course of action often described as a 'limited' war with Red China would increase the risk we are running in engaging too much of our power in an area that is not the critical strategic prize....Frankly, in the opinion of the Joint Chiefs of Staff, this strategy would involve us in the wrong war, at the wrong place, at the wrong time, and with the wrong enemy."[2]

Secretary of State Acheson, for whom some Republicans were gunning, also came out of the hearings in good shape, although he was subjected to ferocious assault. He was able to explain the Truman administration's policy and to elucidate for the committee and the American public the error of bogging the U.S. down in a campaign which was strategically useless, which threatened Soviet intervention, and which virtually guaranteed loss of support by U.S. allies.[3]

Although the hearings were officially closed to the public, each day's transcript was reviewed for security and facts that might affect national security were deleted. These cuts were kept to the absolute minimum, however, to prevent criticism by committee members who might otherwise have called for open hearings.[4]

MacArthur was treated with great deference during his testimony (May 3–5). The General denied that any of his actions had been improper or that he was ever guilty of insubordination, though he did not question the authority of the President to remove him. None of the other witnesses accused MacArthur of insubordination, either. The key recommendations that MacArthur had made in his address to Congress were similar to the ones he had proposed to the Joint Chiefs: intensification of the economic blockade of Red China, blockading the China coast, permitting air reconnaissance of Manchuria and the China coast, and removal of restrictions on operations by the Chinese Nationalists. On the witness stand, MacArthur implied the Joint Chiefs agreed with him on these matters, and they must have been vetoed by Truman or Secretary of Defense Marshall.[5] MacArthur also implied the Chiefs agreed with him that cease-fire terms should not include acceptance of Red China in the United Nations or abandonment of Taiwan to Beijing, but that the JCS views had been "disapproved by the secretary of defense who said that he believed that those two items might well be considered at the conference, the peace conference."[6]

When Marshall followed MacArthur to the stand, he denied he had overruled the Joint Chiefs and emphasized that the policy of the United States was to deny Taiwan to Communist China and to oppose seating Red China in the United Nations. Though the Truman administration would be willing to discuss the matters, he said, it had not wavered in excluding the issues from the armistice terms.[7] Marshall also denied that he or the President had vetoed proposals of the Joint Chiefs for widening the war.[8] Marshall pointed out that the Joint Chiefs, the secretary of defense and the President had to be responsible for U.S. security around the globe, whereas MacArthur's mission was limited to a particular theater and a particular adversary.[9] His most crushing comment on MacArthur, however, was the following: "It became apparent that General MacArthur had grown so far out of sympathy with the established policies of the United States that there was grave doubt as to whether he could any longer be permitted to exercise the authority in making decisions that normal command functions would assign to a theater commander. In this situation, there was no other recourse but to relieve him."[10]

General Bradley also denied MacArthur's charge that he and the Chiefs had been overruled by the President or the secretary of defense. Rather, the Chiefs were in thorough agreement with the administration's policy toward the war. Bradley said the fundamental military consideration was "whether to increase the risk of a global war by taking additional measures that are open to the United States and its allies." He explained that MacArthur had believed the measures he had suggested would not increase the risk of global war, while the Chiefs of Staff disagreed, holding that "such a risk should not be taken unnecessarily."[11]

Bradley testified that Collins, Vandenberg and Sherman all had favored relieving MacArthur for three reasons: he had made it clear he was not in sympathy with the decision to limit the conflict to Korea, he had failed to comply with the President's directive to clear statements on policy in advance, and the JCS members "have felt and feel now that the military must be controlled by civilian authority in this country."[12]

The Chiefs in their testimony corroborated Marshall's and Bradley's statements.[13] By the time all the witnesses had appeared, on June 25, ten weeks had elapsed since MacArthur's removal. UN forces in Korea clearly were holding their own, and the issue of MacArthur's relief had lost much of its popular emotional appeal. The committees decided not to produce a formal report of findings, though eight of the twenty-six senators issued their own report, which praised MacArthur and criticized the administration.[14]

The hearings had not vindicated MacArthur. The General's star fell after this long public bloodletting, because the American public had learned through the hearings that the Truman administration was attempting to limit U.S. commitment to Korea and to the Far East in general, and the public as a whole supported this view. Acheson had the last word: the hearings, he said, "exhausted both committees, bored the press and the public, publicized a considerable amount of classified material, and successfully defused the explosive 'MacArthur issue.' "[15]

Meanwhile, the war in Korea had reached a new crisis.

CHAPTER 55

The Spring Offensive

WHEN GENERAL VAN FLEET took command of Eighth Army on April 14,[1] UN troops had occupied the Utah line, the northward extension of the Kansas line in the sector just below Chorwon, the southwest anchor of the Iron Triangle. (See Map 12.) It was obvious the Chinese were recoiling in order to unleash their spring offensive, however, and Van Fleet, with Ridgway's approval, decided to move the line in the west even farther north to the Wyoming line, which ran right below Chorwon and Kumwha, then fell south to the Kansas line from Hwachon reservoir to Taepo-ri on the east coast.

By April 19, all I and IX Corps units were in position along the Utah line and preparing to attack. But portents of an enemy offensive were great. The Chinese became extremely sensitive to light observation planes flying over their lines, and began firing on them with machine guns and light cannon, a sure sign they did not wish to be spied on. Beginning on April 13, in the IX Corps sector in the center, the Chinese commenced burning straw and setting wood and brush fires in the mountains. By April 15 a belt of smoke extended six to ten miles deep across the IX Corps front, effectively ending air reconnaissance flights and giving the Chinese an opportunity to redeploy without risk of detection. As the winds at this time were from the south, southwest and west, the smoke screen kept drifting away from the CCF front, however; and the enemy command dispatched guerrillas south of the UN positions to set fires to forests and brush in the mountains.[2]

Eighth Army and I and IX Corps planners already had decided approximately where the main enemy attacks would come. On the west in the I Corps sector, the U.S. 24th and 25th Divisions were advancing to the Wyoming line in the deepest penetration of any troops into the communist front. G-3 (operations) planners expected the Chinese to strike hard against these extended divisions to hold them in place, and to send their strongest offensive thrust on the left (western) flank of I Corps against the ROK 1st Division, emplaced along the Imjin river, and against the U.S. 3rd Division and British 29th Brigade, holding positions immediately west of the 25th Division. In the IX Corps central sector, G-3 expected the major push south from Kumwha to Kapyong, a village on the main east-west communications route in central Korea: the Seoul-Chunchon highway. Kapyong is about twelve air miles west of Chunchon, and a valley leads northward into high and rugged mountains to Panam-ni, about nineteen miles north of Kapyong. The valley was being defended by the ROK 6th Division. There were three main reasons why G-3 expected the enemy thrust there: the mountains kept UN forces from using tanks, severely limited artillery, and prevented lateral movement of UN troops to counterattack; the Chinese tended to attack ROK troops and along major unit boundaries, and a successful drive to Kapyong would sever east-west communications between I and IX Corps. IX Corps already had anticipated trouble by positioning the British Commonwealth 27th Brigade at Kapyong as a blocking force, with a company of U.S. tanks in support.

The enemy attacks came as predicted: the biggest assault headed straight south toward Seoul, and the secondary, but still massive, attack drove through the ROK 6th Division toward Kapyong. It was a double-envelopment offensive designed to pinch off Seoul. At the same time, mostly North Korean units commenced a smaller effort in the eastern mountains around Inje. Radio Pyongyang announced its objective: the destruction of the UN command, and predicted the goal would be achieved rapidly. This was bombast, because the Chinese committed only roughly half the 700,000 troops they had available in Korea. They also used little artillery, few tanks and no close air support, although Chinese and North Korean air power had been growing ever since the entry of the Red Chinese in the war. Instead, the CCF followed their standard offensive tactics of night attacks, assaults to the front to hold UN troops in place, envelopment of the flanks, and attempts to set up roadblocks in the rear. Although some artillery had begun to appear, the CCF largely used their standard weapons: mortars, small arms, machine guns, grenades and satchel charges (against tanks). When daylight came, the CCF broke contact and ran for cover from UN aircraft and artillery fire.

Attacks started on the night of April 22 by the light of a full moon. The ROK 6th Division north of Kapyong at Panam-ni reported about 9:30 p.m. an estimated regiment of CCF troops had infiltrated its front-line positions at three points, and the two regiments occupying the front line were heavily engaged and withdrawing. The ROK division fell back ten miles the first day (April 23) and even more the second. The April IX Corps Command Report commented drily: "The [ROK] regiments were reported to have established defensive positions at various points, but when the distance covered in the 36-hour period is considered it is obvious that at best these defense stands could be little more than token resistance." The 27th Brigade stood firm in its blocking positions three miles north of Kapyong, and the 1st Marine Division on the right and the 24th Division on the left in I Corps held and refused penetration of their exposed flanks. During the early morning hours of April 24, the Chinese made contact in force with all forward elements of the 27th Brigade and quickly surrounded the Australian Battalion. The Aussies held their positions, however, and late in the afternoon the attached American company of tanks (72nd Battalion) opened a path for the Australians so they could withdraw to the main brigade positions, now just north of Kapyong.

In the I Corps sector, the Chinese and some North Koreans made several crossings of the Imjin river against the ROK 1st Division and the U.S. 3rd Division, but heavy artillery fire and rapid and frequent air strikes contained these advances, although some Chinese troops were able to penetrate into rear areas. The 24th and 25th Divisions, holding the advanced UN position a few miles south of Chorwon, caught the full brunt of the Chinese frontal assault. The attached Turkish Brigade, on the left, endured several penetrations, while some elements of the 25th Division's 24th Regiment, in the center, withdrew. Even so, the frontal assault generally was contained. In the 24th Division the situation was the same: some penetrations, but the line held. Nevertheless, the enemy advances on the left, along the Imjin, and the gaping hole blasted by the Chinese at Panam-ni, where the ROK 6th Division had disintegrated, left the 24th and 25th Divisions dangerously exposed, and both units withdrew about six miles to more defensible positions. The Chinese quickly followed up these withdrawals, and assaulted the Turkish Brigade and the forward regiments of the 3rd and 24th Divisions. The Chinese made considerable inroads in both the Turkish and 24th Division sectors, forcing I Corps to withdraw its troops again to positions running generally along the 38th parallel.

Meanwhile, IX Corps was frantically trying to block the huge breach in its line created by the breakup of the ROK 6th Division. While the British 27th Brigade held its positions just north of Kapyong, the 5th Cavalry RCT was attached to the British and directed to seize positions north of the 27th Brigade's line. The 5th Cavalry moved forward, engaged large groups of Chinese and inflicted about 175 casualties, but disengaged after it ran out of ammunition.

At this time the 27th Brigade was redesignated the 28th Brigade, and the battalion of Argyll and Sutherland Highlanders returned home and was replaced by a battalion of the King's Own Scottish Borderers.

Despite the valiant defensive stands of the British Commonwealth Brigade and the 5th Cavalry RCT, the Chinese on April 26 cut the Seoul-Chunchon highway, and General Van Fleet pulled IX Corps back to the Hongchon river, about ten miles south of Kapyong. In the I Corps sector the ROK 1st Division, on the extreme left, gave way and exposed the left flank of the 1st Battalion, Gloucestershire Regiment, of the British 29th Brigade. The English battalion held its position gallantly for several days, even though isolated and virtually overrun. Only a few of the soldiers of the battalion got back safely to UN lines.

Having cut the Seoul-Chunchon road, the Chinese now turned their main effort against Seoul, outflanking Uijongbu on April 27 and forcing the 3rd Division to pull back to positions only four miles north of Seoul. ROK forces meanwhile withdrew southeast toward Seoul from Munsan-ni, and other positions along the Imjin. On April 29, UN aircraft spotted about six thousand enemy troops attempting to ferry over the Han river to the Kimpo peninsula northwest of Seoul. The air attacks were so devastating that only a small number of these troops survived, and these were contained by ROK marines. Enemy troops also attempted to outflank Seoul on the east near the junction of the Pukhan and Han rivers, but 24th and 25th Division troops held them to the north bank of the Han.

On April 29 Van Fleet established a new line, which he did not name, and thus it naturally became known as the No-name line. It was the line Eighth Army's commander expected his forces to hold. It extended from the 3rd Division's defensive arc just north of Seoul eastward along the Han to a point near its junction with the Pukhan and thence northeast-ward to Sabangu, just north of Hongchon, and from there northeastward to the east coast at Taepo-ri. Van Fleet also redeployed troops to defend against the major CCF attack toward Seoul. To I Corps he attached the ROK 1st Division, the 1st Cavalry and 25th Divisions, with the 3rd Division in reserve and with the British 29th Brigade holding Kimpo peninsula. To IX Corps, to the east of I Corps, Van Fleet attached the 28th Commonwealth Brigade, the 24th and 7th Divisions, the ROK 2nd and 6th Divisions, and the 187th Airborne RCT in reserve. In the east center X Corps got the 1st Marine Division and the U.S. 2nd Division and the ROK 5th and 7th Divisions. Farther east in the high mountains and along the coast the ROK I and III Corps defended.

By the end of April, Eighth Army had stopped the offensive and was holding a strong, continuous line across the peninsula. Characteristically, the CCF drive had petered out, and the Chinese moved back into their withdrawal phase for resupply and replacements. To intelligence officers it was clear this was another lull before another storm, and Van Fleet decided to take advantage of the CCF supply weaknesses and resume the initiative. In the first week of May, frontline divisions established patrol bases more than seven miles in advance of the No-name line, and armored patrols ranged ten to twelve miles forward. The 29th Brigade cleared the Kimpo peninsula. The ROK 1st Division turned back up the Munsan-ni road toward the Imjin. The Chinese abandoned Uijongbu to the 1st Cavalry Division on May 6. A 25th Division task force drove up a parallel road leading northeastward from Seoul toward Kumwha. In IX Corps, an armored patrol pushed Chinese troops off the Seoul-Kapyong road. In X Corps, U.S. marines on May 7 knocked North Korean troops out of camouflaged bunkers on the road leading north from Hongchon and recaptured Chunchon. At the same time a 2nd Division task force (French Battalion, plus Rangers, a 9th Regiment force and tanks) pressed up the road from Hongchon toward Inje. The ROKs in the mountains on the extreme right advanced as well.

But the Chinese and North Koreans resistance increased dramatically after May 10, and it became clear that the withdrawal phase was ending and that the advance and attack phases were about to recommence. During the first days of May, it appeared the CCF would concentrate their main offensive effort against Seoul by striking west of the Pukhan-Han river junction. During the next five days, however, G-2 detected the movement of five Chinese armies eastward and their deployment in front of Chunchon-Inje, a sector held by X Corps and the ROK III Corps. Van Fleet did not have time to redeploy his army to meet this unexpected move of the enemy, and only alerted the 3rd Division, in I Corps reserve on the west, to move out on his order. Fortunately, the extremely mountainous and rough terrain in the east gave X Corps and the ROKs good defensive positions, although UN armor and artillery could not operate as well, and UN air power had more difficulty hitting targets.

Along the No-name line itself, troops had used their time to construct strong, interlocking positions, minefields, booby-trapped barbed-wire entanglements, and dug-in emplacements with overhead cover. The enemy attack came on the night of May 15–16. As expected, it struck X Corps and the ROK III Corps between Naepyong-ni, ten air miles east of Chunchon, and No-dong, ten air miles west of Taepo-ri on the east coast. Into this sector, thirty-two air miles wide, the enemy poured twenty-one Chinese and nine North Korean divisions. The most intense blows fell on the ROK 5th and 7th Divisions of X Corps, located in the high mountain country along a twenty-mile front in the vicinity of Hangye-ri, a village ten miles northeast of Inje. The two ROK divisions held their positions for a while, then, penetrated and disorganized, they fell back broken.

To the left of the ROK divisions, the U.S. 2nd Division, with the French and Netherlands Battalions attached, stood its ground in the face of fierce and unrelenting attacks. A strong factor in the success of the defense was the tremendous aid of the artillery. During the twenty-four hours of May 17, corps and division artillery supporting the division fired almost 38,000 rounds. At the same time, UN aircraft flew 174 close-support sorties, including 12 sorties by B26 bombers, which napalmed, bombed and strafed enemy troop concentrations. Strikes came immediately in front of the main line of resistance and sometimes within one hundred yards of dug-in troops. G-2 estimated casualties from this tremendous aerial attack alone at five thousand.

On May 18, Van Fleet, recognizing that the disintegration of the ROK 5th and 7th Divisions posed a severe danger to the UN line, shifted the 2nd Division and the marines eastward to fill the gap, and ordered IX Corps to extend eastward to fill the sector vacated by the marines and 2nd Division. Van Fleet also dispatched the 15th RCT of the 3rd Division from Seoul to shore up the western flank of the enemy salient and sent the other two regiments of 3rd Division, the 7th and the 65th, to blocking positions at the southernmost stretches of the penetration.

Second Division was continually and heavily engaged throughout this dramatic eastward movement and also drove right into the sector where the Chinese were making their major effort. In effect, the 2nd Division pinched off the deep enemy salient by driving from the west into its base. The few elements of ROK units that had remained on the No-name line now were completely disorganized and had been driven from the line before 2nd Division troops reached them. On this day, more than 41,000 rounds of artillery were fired, and in the corps sector UN aircraft flew 137 sorties during the day and 28 more radar-controlled attacks at night on enemy assembly points.

While the battle raged in the eastern mountains, a strong enemy force struck down the Pukhan river toward the Han on May 17, but 25th Division and ROK 6th Division soldiers halted this attack after three days of violent action.

By May 20 the UN troops had stopped the enemy offensive, and X Corps started back to wrest the initiative again from the Chinese and retake its positions on the No-name line. Van Fleet had already started the counteroffensive movement on May 18 when he ordered I and IX Corps, along with the 1st Marine Division, on the X Corps left, to send out strong patrols to prepare to attack to a new phase line (Topeka), about halfway between No-name and Kansas lines. The next day, after attaching the newly arrived Canadian 25th Brigade to the U.S. 3rd Division, he enlarged the counterstroke by directing all three corps and the ROK I Corps on the east coast to advance (the ROK III Corps having been deactivated).

Once more the enemy pulled back to replenish his supplies and troops, and once more Eighth Army moved forward against generally light resistance. Within a few days, I Corps troops reached the Imjin river north of Munsan-ni and entered Uijongbu and other points north of Seoul. IX Corps pushed toward Kapyong, drove the Chinese armies across the Hongchon river and moved toward the western end of the Hwachon reservoir. In the X Corps sector, the 187th Airborne RCT captured Inje and the marines were making a final push toward the eastern end of the Hwachon reservoir. By the end of the month, X Corps was deployed along the Soyang river and ROK troops to the east had captured the port town of Kansong. Eighth Army was now back about to the old Kansas line, and, except in the west, where it ran along the Imjin, the line lay north of the 38th parallel. South Korea again had been cleared of enemy troops.

On June 1, Van Fleet directed I and IX Corps to continue their advance to the Wyoming line, running just south of Chorwon and Kumwha at the Iron Triangle. This advance (code-named Piledriver) went off with little difficulty, except along the approaches to the Iron Triangle, where the enemy resisted strongly. Eighth Army troops pressed on. By June 10, aided by night-and-day air support, the 3rd Division, the ROK 9th Division and the 10th Philippine Battalion had gained the high ground south of Chorwon, while the 25th Division and the Turkish Brigade fought to within three miles of Kumwha. The next day the enemy abandoned Chorwon and Kumwha. The base of the Iron Triangle had been captured. On June 13, two tank-infantry task forces, one from Chorwon and the other from Kumwha, reached Pyonggang, the apex of the triangle, and found it, too, deserted. However, UN forces discovered that the enemy lay in strength on the high ground north of Pyonggang. The task forces therefore departed rapidly. Units of IX Corps also pushed northeast from Kumwha toward Kumsong and likewise found this line heavily occupied by enemy troops, who were establishing a strong defensive line. These UN units, too, pulled back to Kumwha. Because the Iron Triangle was dominated by surrounding heights, neither side attempted thereafter to hold the low ground in strength, though Chinese troops struck back on June 17 and recaptured Pyonggang.

In the X Corps sector, troops advanced north of Inje to the lower lip of "the Punchbowl," a large circular depression, about three miles wide at the bottom and six at the top. On the east coast, ROK troops moved up the coast about eleven miles north of Kansong.

Behind the front, the Chinese and North Koreans were establishing heavily dug-in emplacements laced with bunkers and underground rooms covered with tree trunks and earth and all but impervious to anything but direct hits by 155mm guns. Every bunker became a strongpoint and every hill a fortress. In the warm June days of 1951, United Nations troops looked out on the enemy positions in the steep and complex mountains of central Korea and realized soberly that positional warfare had come to Korea. The successful UN defense of the No-name line with reinforced artillery fires and interconnecting machine-gun and small-arms fires of units on each flank already had proved the Chinese and North Koreans would suffer heavily if they tried to crack it. The Chinese and North Koreans now were creating their own version of such an entrenched line, echeloned in great depth and invulnerable to all but the most powerful and devastating attack.

The time had come for peace in Korea. The United States, China, and the Soviet Union wanted it, and virtually all the rest of the world longed for it, with the exception of the President of South Korea, Syngman Rhee. He was still pressing the United Nations to conquer North Korea for him.

CHAPTER 56

Talking Peace and Practicing War

WITH THE RELIEF OF MACARTHUR the most articulate advocate of extending the war had departed. The Senate committee hearings were showing that the Truman administration and the Joint Chiefs strongly supported limiting the war and bringing it to as rapid a close as possible. By the first of June, with nearly all South Korea clear of communists, the time seemed ripe to end the fighting through some form of negotiated settlement.

United Nations Secretary-General Trygve Lie reflected this sentiment when he announced on June 1 that a cease-fire approximately along the 38th parallel would fulfill the main purposes of the United Nations, provided peace could be brought to the troubled peninsula.[1] At about the same time, Secretary of State Acheson, in his testimony before the Senate committee, expressed a willingness to settle on the 38th parallel. It was a position that was going to cause trouble later.

Acheson, having decided that cease-fire approaches through the United Nations would not succeed, elected instead to pursue direct approaches with the Soviet Union. In May, the United States made some overtures to Russian diplomats in France and Germany, with no success. Likewise, an attempt to approach the Beijing government through Hong Kong was a failure. Additional fruitless efforts were made in Moscow by Swedish and U.S. diplomats. Finally, in mid-May, Acheson asked for help from George Kennan, an authority on Soviet history and government then on State Department leave at Princeton University. Kennan chose as his contact Jacob Malik, deputy foreign minister of the Soviet Union and Soviet delegate to the United Nations. Kennan called Malik, who invited Kennan to his home on Long Island, New York, for an exploratory meeting on May 31. Kennan said the United States wanted neither confrontation nor continuation of the war. The meeting produced no result, but Malik got in touch with Moscow, and at their second meeting, on June 5, he told Kennan his government wanted a peaceful solution in Korea as soon as possible. But he said the Soviet Union could not itself take part in negotiations and advised Kennan to approach the North Koreans and the Chinese. "No doubt existed in any of our minds that the message was authentic," Acheson wrote. "It had, however, a sibylline quality which left us wondering what portended and what we should do next."[2]

Two weeks later, on June 23, Ambassador Malik did a remarkable thing: he appeared on a UN-sponsored radio broadcast available to UN members for public statements and declared the people of the Soviet Union believed the conflict in Korea could be settled. As a first step, he recommended that discussions should commence between the belligerents aimed at a cease-fire and an armistice providing for mutual withdrawal of forces from the 38th parallel. If both sides had a "sincere desire" for peace, Malik said, this withdrawal would not be too great a price to pay.[3]

Acheson immediately asked the United States ambassador to the Soviet Union, Alan G. Kirk, to approach the Foreign Office in Moscow and find out whether Malik's proposal represented Soviet policy. Andrei Gromyko, Soviet deputy foreign minister, confirmed that Malik, indeed, was expressing official Soviet views. Gromyko went further and advised Kirk that a *military* armistice should be concluded between military representatives, that the settlement should be limited to military matters, and that no political or territorial matters should be discussed.

Gromyko allowed as how he knew nothing of Red China's attitude on a cease-fire, but it was clear that messages had passed between Moscow and Beijing, because the men of the Kremlin would never have put themselves into a position of saying peace was possible without clearing it with the Chinese. Sibyls they might, on occasion, be; Pollyannas never.[4]

With this green light, Acheson proposed to have negotiations conducted at the military level, as per Gromyko, and at a JCS-State meeting on June 28, Dean Rusk, assistant secretary of state, recommended that General Ridgway broadcast an invitation to the enemy commanders to send representatives to a conference. Generals Bradley and Collins approved this approach, but General Vandenberg thought this indicated the United Nations was suing for peace. He challenged the wisdom of ending the fighting now that the enemy was suffering at UN hands. He got no support from his JCS colleagues, however. Not only did U.S. allies with troops in Korea unanimously favor negotiations, but General Bradley saw problems in getting continued support from the American people if the United States failed to take this opportunity to end the fighting. The joint meeting concluded that a working group should prepare a message for General Ridgway incorporating the text of a broadcast to the enemy calling for opening negotiations.[5]

The group quickly drafted a message which was approved at a second JCS-State meeting and sent to Ridgway for review. Ridgway submitted a few minor changes, which went through channels up to Truman, who approved them, and at 8 a.m. June 30 Tokyo time Ridgway addressed the following radio message to the commander in chief of communist forces in Korea: "As commander in chief of the United Nations Command I have been instructed to communicate to you the following: I am informed that you may wish a meeting to discuss an armistice providing for the cessation of hostilities and all acts of armed force in Korea, with adequate guarantees for the maintenance of such armistice. Upon the receipt of word from you that such a meeting is desired I shall be prepared to name my representative. I would also at that time suggest a date at which he could meet with your representative. I propose that such a meeting could take place aboard a Danish hospital ship in Wonsan harbor."[6]

Meanwhile, in Washington, the Joint Chiefs, Secretary Marshall, Secretary Acheson and their staffs produced a blueprint of the American position, though not without some initial doubts being raised by advisors who mistrusted the communists. This blueprint was hashed over at a JCS-State meeting on June 29, and that evening Bradley, Marshall and Acheson showed it to Truman. The President approved it, and the JCS promptly sent it to General Ridgway.[7]

This position paper became the basis for American bargaining with the communists. Its key provisions were as follows: the principal military interest in an armistice was ending hostilities, assuring against resumption of fighting and protection of UN forces; arrangements reached were to "be acceptable to us over an extended period of time, even though no progress is made in reaching agreement on political and territorial questions"; discussions were to be "severely restricted to military questions" and not to involve any political or territorial matters; a demilitarized zone on the order of twenty miles in depth was to be established across Korea "based generally upon the positions of the opposing forces at the time the armistice arrangments are agreed upon"; supervision of a cease-fire was to be controlled by a Military Armistice Commission with equal membership by both sides; no reinforcements were to be introduced by either side; prisoners of war were to be exchanged on a one-for-one basis as expeditiously as possible.

The JCS-State meeting already had anticipated trouble because UN forces were generally north of the 38th parallel, and the United States had to deal with Acheson's public reference that the United States would be agreeable to a settlement based on the parallel. Therefore, the instructions to Ridgway on this point were explicit: "If the communist commander refers to statements attributed to United States government officials that the United States is prepared to accept a settlement on or around the 38th parallel, you should take the position that such statements are not applicable to an armistice in the field but are properly the subject for governmental negotiation as to a political settlement. Further you should state that in any event the military arrangements you propose involve certain areas under communist military control south of the 38th parallel [Onjin and Yonan peninsulas in the west, and the area west of the Imjin river] and certain areas under UN control north thereof."

The question of American instransigence in insisting that the armistice line had to be the battle line was to assume major proportions in the months to come, because the communists argued that the settlement line had to be the 38th. It is, therefore, important that the Chinese response to Ridgway's message did not mention the 38th parallel as a cease-fire boundary.

The communist answer came on July 1 Tokyo time. Ridgway flashed the Joint Chiefs the following message regarding the Chinese response:

"Several versions of a reply to my message to the commander in chief, communist forces in Korea, have been received. In order to insure coordination, I recommend that the following be agreed upon as the official reply and that the JCS confirm to me that in their deliberations they will use this version: 'Peking—Here is important news from the Korean front. After consultations held today between General Kim Il Sung, commander in chief of the Korean army, and General Peng De-huai, commander in chief of the Chinese Peoples Volunteers, a joint notice was sent to General Ridgway, commander in chief of the United Nations forces, in reply to the broadcast message from General Ridgway on June 30 in which he expressed a willingness to dispatch delegates to hold cease-fire talks with our delegates. The contents of the notice are as follows: "General Ridgway, commander in chief of United Nations forces: Your broadcast message of June 30, regarding peace talks, has been received. We are authorized to tell you that we agree to suspend military activities and to hold peace negotiations, and that our delegates will meet with yours. We suggest, in regard to the place for holding talks, that such talks be held at Kaesong, on the 38th parallel. If you agree to this, our delegates will be prepared to meet your delegates between July 10 and 15, 1951. Signed, Kim Il Sung, commander in chief of the Korean Peoples Army, and Peng De-huai, commander in chief of the Chinese Peoples Volunteers." ' "[8]

It was a conciliatory response. For whatever the reasons, it was evident that Chinese wanted peace, and had convinced (or coerced) the North Koreans into going along. The spring offensive had been extremely costly to the Chinese, who had lost thousands of men in trying to breach the UN defensive line. Nevertheless, the Chinese had accomplished their major national purpose: to drive the Americans back from the Yalu and to the vicinity of the 38th parallel, leaving North Korea a secure buffer against American incursions in the future. The Chinese had thoroughly frightened the American military establishment with their great and unexpected victories, and they also had at least partially convinced American leaders they were serious in their threats to drive the UN forces into the sea.

Up to this point the Chinese had spurned efforts at a cease-fire. Now they not only agreed to talk about an armistice, but, of paramount importance, in the version Ridgway and the Far East Command were convinced was accurate, they agreed *in advance* to suspend military operations (but see below); that is, they announced in the messages monitored by the Far East Command their willingness to stop the fighting entirely while the talks went on. In effect, the Chinese and North Koreans agreed to the very conditions which American leaders had insisted upon: a cease-fire along the battle line, not the 38th parallel.

It is at this point that American suspicion of the Chinese—expressed specifically by General Ridgway but backed by the Joint Chiefs, the State Department and the President—rose to the fore and destroyed the possibility of ending the war at a stroke by mutual agreement.

Shortly after Ridgway received the response from Beijing, he dispatched a message to the Joint Chiefs which referred to the Chinese broadcast and said: "Their intent is clear that military action shall be suspended from beginning of armistice negotiations. Such action might gravely prejudice safety and security of United Nations forces. I consider this wholly unacceptable, and unless otherwise instructed, I shall categorically reject it."[9]

Ridgway thereupon gave the Chiefs a number of reasons why he wanted military operations to continue while the peace talks went on. The primary ones he listed were as follows: "buildup of hostile offensive capability" was continuing; enemy vehicular and rail movements were up substantially; there was an unverified report of a "CCF mechanized army" in Koksan, about forty-five air miles east of Pyongyang; there were reports "only partly confirmed" of Soviet antiaircraft materiel and personnel in Korea; there were unconfirmed reports of the presence in Korea of an international brigade "of substantial strength"; prisoner-of-war interrogations had "repeatedly referred to next offensive as scheduled on or before 15 July" with weather conditions expected to deteriorate about the same time; enemy efforts to build new and rehabilitate old airfields in North Korea were proceeding.

Ridgway's message to the Chiefs continued: "To summarize, intelligence to date reveals a clearly developing pattern of capability to exercise an increasing offensive potential at any time from 10 July on. It is to be expected that if exercised optimum advantage will be taken of weather. It is further to be expected that enemy will intensify his efforts to increase this offensive potential throughout the period of negotiations, if conducted as he suggests they be conducted. If negotiations so conducted, we would be incapable of checking his military activities in Korea, particularly his preparation for major offensive actions by ground and air. Request your approval of my proposed actions soonest. Immediately upon receipt of your reply, I plan to answer the communist commanders' message accepting Kaesong as the location, making provision for cessation of hostilities along the Munsan-Kaesong road and in the Kaesong area, but urging that the date be advanced."

Despite his almost hysterical tone, Ridgway is to be lauded for his concern about the possibility of another communist offensive. But this capability existed anyway: the Chinese were ending their withdrawal phase and were completing resupply of arms, ammunition and food and replacement of lost personnel. Not knowing the intentions of the UN Command any better then Ridgway knew the intentions of the communist command, the Chinese were preparing to stop the further advance of UN forces in the only way they could: by attacking. If Ridgway was suspicious of the Chinese, the Chinese had reason to be suspicious of the UN Command. The potential for military buildup after suspension of military operations existed on both sides of the line.

In Ridgway's version of the communist response, the Chinese were willing to take the chance and halt all military operations during the armistice talks. That this was a good-faith gesture and not duplicity to mask a buildup for a new offensive is indicated by the fact that thereafter the Chinese never attempted another offensive in Korea. From the moment they announced a willingness to cease military operations, their military posture was that of defense of the existing line.

Ridgway, of course, could not know Chinese policy in the future. However, he was not willing to take the chance that cessation of fighting once agreed upon would stick. No one knows whether it would have or not; the likelihood is that it would, because both sides were weary of war and neither would have had much to gain by its resumption. But the Joint Chiefs decided to go along with Ridgway's request (and presumably the President agreed, since he did not countermand the Chiefs' instructions). Therefore, the question as to whether a cease-fire would have held cannot be answered, because the fighting did not end. What influence American insistence on this point had on Chinese intransigence is not known, but it assuredly soured the atmosphere of the cease-fire talks from the outset for the communists.

The Chiefs responded on July 2 Washington time in a single message to Ridgway's July 1 message (CX 66183) regarding the communist radio response and to his following message (CX 66188) asking that military operations continue during the talks.[10] The Chiefs simply ignored Ridgway's request that they agree on the version of the Chinese-North Korean response which he had transmitted to Washington. Instead, the Chiefs said the following: "Reference your CX 66183, the version transmitted in Mandarin from Peiping, as translated in Washington before Peiping broadcast in English, is in agreement with version later transmitted in English from Peiping, and is accepted as official by State and Defense. It reads as follows: 'Your statement of June 30 this year concerning peace talks has been received. We are authorized to inform you that we agree to meet your representative for conducting talks concerning cessation of military action and establishment of peace. We propose that the place of meeting be in the area of Kaesong on the 38th parallel; if you agree, our representatives are prepared to meet your representatives between July 10 and 15, 1951.' "

An extremely important part is missing from the version Washington decided to accept as official: it makes no reference whatsoever to the communist agreement to suspend military activities first and then to hold peace negotiations, as the Far East Command's version contained. Quite significantly, the Chiefs made no comment to Ridgway on this crucial discrepancy between Washington's and Tokyo's version. No point was raised that, since there was a discrepancy, the true contents of the Chinese-North Korean message should be ascertained, by flashing back a clarification query to Beijing, for instance. Instead, the Chiefs, in the message to Ridgway, went directly to the next point, which agreed, also without discussing the point at all, with Ridgway's request that fighting continue while the peace talks were being held. Thus, Ridgway got what he wanted, and the difference between his and Washington's "official" version was not raised again.

The inference is clear: Washington elected to conclude that the Red message omitted a call for an immediate cease-fire, and thus Washington avoided the criticism that would have arisen in insisting on continuation of the fighting in the face of the communist offer to stop.

The Chiefs instructed Ridgway not to appear eager to advance the date of the meeting and to reply to Kim Il Sung and Peng De-huai along the following lines: "I have received your reply to my message of 30 June. I am prepared for my representatives to meet yours at Kaesong on July 10 or at an earlier date if your representatives complete their preparations before that date. Since agreement on armistice terms has to precede cessation of hostilities, delay in initiating the meetings and in reaching agreement will prolong the fighting and increase the losses."

The Chiefs did not leave the matter at that. They told Ridgway "there must be no relaxation in military effort on our part until proper arrangements for cessation of hostilities have been agreed upon as contained in the armistice terms."

Thus, American suspicion of Chinese motives insured that the fighting would go on until such time as both sides could agree on a settlement. Consequently, the peace talks from the beginning became precisely what Soviet Deputy Foreign Minister Gromyko suggested they not be: political negotiations. If Gromyko's suggestion for a strictly military settlement had been followed to the letter, the Chinese proposal for cessation of hostilities (assuming Ridgway's version was correct) would have effectively ended the war immediately in the way it was ultimately to end two years later: along the battle line. Thereafter both sides could have talked and negotiated to their heart's content without affecting the reality of the peace. More important, young men on both sides would have ceased to be killed and maimed, for the losses after the peace talks began were far greater than they had been before the talks began.

* * * * * * * * * *

A cease-fire agreement without willing cooperation and a sincere desire to end the fighting on both sides always holds the potential for veiling military buildups. The problem was that each side approached an armistice from different points of view.

The American position for peace hinged around a demilitarized zone along the existing battle line, and an armistice commission with unrestricted inspection within Korea by military observer teams to monitor troop and weapons buildup. The communist position was based on withdrawal of all foreign troops from Korea, both Chinese and United Nations, and the demarcation line along the 38th parallel.[11] It is no wonder the peace talks got off to a bad start and that disagreements were rife.

Immediately after the chief UN negotiator, Vice Admiral C. Turner Joy, led his team to the first meeting with the communists on July 10, the two sides got into a controversy on agenda items.[12] The communists insisted the agenda include discussion of the 38th parallel as a demarcation line and the withdrawal of all foreign troops. The UN negotiators refused to admit either of these as agenda items. The matter of the 38th parallel was resolved temporarily on July 16, when the communists agreed to an agenda item on the demarcation line that did not specifically mention the parallel, although they had not given up on the idea.[13]

But the issue of foreign troop withdrawals became the critical problem. As Schnabel and Watson state in their history of the Joint Chiefs in the war, "The enemy's insistence that all foreign troops leave Korea became the main hindrance to agreement."[14] It is no wonder the Chinese felt the Americans were not dealing honestly with them. After all, this was exactly what the United States had endorsed after the UN cease-fire commission on January 11 had introduced a peace plan in the United Nations (see page 387). This UN plan specifically called for the withdrawal of all armed forces from Korea. The United States publicly had praised this plan and had voted for it. The Chinese doubtless did not know the United States had agreed to the peace plan only because Acheson was convinced the Chinese would reject it, as Beijing did. In their naiveté, the Red Chinese probably thought mutual withdrawal of foreign troops at a cease-fire was acceptable to the United States.

Now it was not acceptable, either to Ridgway or the Pentagon. The reason was a fear that, if UN forces were pulled out of Korea, the Chinese could send massive reinforcements to North Korea from Manchuria.[15] The United States completely altered its previous public position and became adamant when communist negotiators made it plain they wanted foreign troops out of Korea. This in turn increased Chinese suspicion that the U.S. wanted to keep troops for possible aggression in the future. The communists probably used the issue of the 38th parallel demarcation line primarily as a bargaining position and to embarrass the United States rather than holding to it as a firm demand. But they were anxious about continued occupation of South Korea by a strong UN force; this force was bound to be wholly American, because the other UN members with troops in Korea had no intention of maintaining permanent military establishments in the peninsula. If the United States was afraid the Chinese would take advantage of a foreign troops pullout to threaten South Korea with Chinese troops rushed from the Yalu, the Chinese were equally afraid American forces remaining in South Korea could threaten North Korea once again, and thereby endanger China's buffer in front of its frontier.

Therefore, both sides went into the peace talks with highly opposed positions that guaranteed conflict. The American insistence upon continued hostilities while the talks went on added to the intensity of this conflict. Consequently, the talks quickly ceased to be discussions by military commanders in the field trying to come to an armistice, and became an arena which both sides used in a fierce propaganda war against the other. That both sides were utterly suspicious of the other is shown in each side's requiring assurances against resumption of hostilities—the United States by the demand for an armistice commission and a demilitarized zone, the communists by the demand for UN troops to exit Korea.

Far better would have been the strictly military agreement recommended by Andrei Gromyko. The United States probably could have achieved in July, 1951, a simple cease-fire along the existing battle line and no withdrawal of troops by either side. The communists likely would have complained about the perfidy of the United States in advocating a return to the 38th and not carrying through, but a battle-line frontier had as much to recommend it to the communists as to the United Nations, because the communists had built a strong main line of resistance (MLR) along it and would not have had such a defensive line along the 38th. The communists might have agreed to a withdrawal of two kilometers by each side from the battle line to form a demilitarized zone, as ultimately was agreed upon two years later.[16] In this way, the MLR defensive positions of either side would not have had to be abandoned, only extended backward another two kilometers. A simple cease-fire would not have answered the UN concern about a potential buildup of communist forces in North Korea, but it also would not have prevented additional UN buildup in Korea. The UN Command would have possessed the same insurance against resumption of fighting as the communist command. Ultimately, any cease-fire rests upon the sincerity of each party to it.

A simple cease-fire also would not have solved the prisoner-of-war issue that was to consume nearly the last year and a half of the negotiations. But discussions on this issue, if they had been argued while the guns were silent, would not have occurred while young men were being killed and wounded in battle.

Nevertheless, the suspicious American leadership refused a simple cease-fire, and the armistice talks went their prolonged, bitter, propagandistic way while the fighting went its bloody sad way. All wars are tragic, but the last two years of the Korean conflict were tragic beyond measure, because nothing was gained by either side in all the fighting that went on after the peace talks began. Although the time would come when General Van Fleet would order massive attacks against individual hill masses and positions, the UN Command did not wish to sustain the huge losses it involved in moving the whole line substantially farther north. Likewise, the Chinese declined to sustain the even greater losses required to drive Eighth Army out of its prepared positions and into South Korea again.

Instead, a stalemate developed almost immediately, a stalemate that mournfully resembled the horrible years of trench warfare on the western front in Europe in World War I. This stalemate was punctuated by continual shelling of opposing lines, of individual battles and engagements, of patrols and sorties, almost in repetition of the fighting in World War I. And, like the Great War, this kind of fighting demanded a steady and unrelenting letting of blood.

In a real sense, the Korean War ended when the peace talks started at Kaesong. Both the Chinese and the Americans had obtained what they had originally set out to get, and they were never to obtain anything more. What followed was two years of doleful, almost inconceivable battle that could scarcely be called a war, because it was pursued essentially without purpose, though the cost on both sides in men and treasure was immense. Neither side sought a decision in these two years of conflict. The defense and capture of a hill mass could cost literally thousands of casualties but the engagement did not materially strengthen one side's position or weaken the other side's. These numerous and sanguinary battles for ridgelines affected local tactical situations, but the overall strategic position of both hostile sides remained unaffected. For this reason, there was a peculiar, almost palpable, sense of desperation among participants in the last two years of conflict, as if the two sides were groping in darkness toward an outlet that neither side could find, but meanwhile continued blindly to bludgeon one another as they felt their way along.

The feelings within Korea were accentuated by an increasing sense of indifference to the conflict by people outside of Korea. When the peace talks quickly produced an impasse and the great offensives ended and were replaced by local actions on mostly nameless ridgelines, Korea dropped out of the headlines. Because the United States had not gone on a true war footing and because only a relatively small number of men were involved, compared to the huge national effort in World War II, Korea soon became known as the Forgotten War. Long before Vietnam, American soldiers, sailors and airmen were to experience at home uninterest and uninvolvement in the war their nation was committed to fighting. Unlike Vietnam, Korea did not even develop an active opposition to the war at home sufficient to cause demonstrations or petitions. Rather, most Americans went on with their lives almost unaffected by the war; only those families whose sons were involved appeared deeply concerned. And as a system of rotation of troops got started in strength in late 1951 and accelerated in 1952, families with men in Korea began to focus on the time when their men would get home rather than to search for ways to end the war for everyone. Perhaps one of the reasons Korea did not evoke the emotional response that Vietnam later was to bring forth was that the Pentagon resisted all efforts to escalate the war and to increase the number of men in Korea. This, of course, was abetted by the Chinese refusal to undertake another offensive. Korea also did not evoke the emotional response of Vietnam because it was the first U.S. war against communists and many Americans believed vaguely that communism was being contained in Asia by the battle lines. In part, this was because no major American leader dared to rise in this flood tide of McCarthyism to oppose Americans fighting communists anywhere. The vast and continued spasm of fear of communism at home virtually assured that no one in authority in the United States would be willing to advocate accommodation with the communists, especially communists who were fighting "our boys." As a result, American concessions were few. Chinese concessions likewise were few. In part, this intransigence by the Chinese was due to the great importance in the Orient of "face," and therefore the Chinese wanted to put forward the impression they were dictating events. It also was due in part to the Red Chinese decision to use the peace negotiations for propaganda purposes to shore up their newly established and still somewhat shaky position inside China and to bolster their prestige among the uncommitted nations of the world. Another reason was a mirror image in Beijing of the intransigence manifested in Washington: some leaders pushed strongly for hard-line positions against the United States because die-hard communists were as suspicious of capitalist motives as capitalists were of communist motives; and each episode of intransigence by one party evoked a disproportionately severe counterresponse by the other party. Intransigence built upon intransigence until, at one point in the peace talks (August 10, 1951), both sides sat silently across the table from each other for two hours and eleven minutes before adjourning because the UN Command refused to discuss the 38th parallel as a basis for demarcation and the communists refused to discuss any other line.[17]

CHAPTER 57

The Bloody Ridges

I T TOOK UNTIL JULY 26, 1951, for the two delegations at Kaesong to agree upon an agenda. At that time, the communists dropped their insistence on troop withdrawal from Korea as an agenda item in exchange for a vaguely worded recommendation to the governments on both sides. The agenda consisted of five items: (1) adoption of the agenda; (2) fixing a military demarcation line and a demilitarized zone; (3) concrete arrangements for a cease-fire and armistice, including a supervisory organization; (4) arrangements relating to prisoners of war; and (5) recommendations to the governments on both sides.[1]

The discussions on Item 2 of the agenda, the demarcation line, immediately caused conflict, the Reds returning to their insistence on the 38th parallel. The disputes at the table in Kaesong were accentuated by disputes away from it over admission of UN newsmen and limiting the UN delegates' freedom of movement. The result was an agreement to create a five-mile neutral circle around Kaesong and to allow freedom of movement by both sides to and from Kaesong. The communists almost immediately began accusing the UN Command of violations by air strafing and ground fire, while the UN complained that a company of fully armed Red soldiers marched within a hundred yards of the UN delegates. Each side denied culpability, and suspicion accelerated.[2]

On August 19, a force in the neutral zone fired on a communist military police patrol and killed the leader. The Reds accused the UN Command, which replied it was the work of a guerrilla band. On August 23, the communists called off the meetings for several weeks and charged UN aircraft had bombed Kaesong. The UN Command said the evidence was fabricated and decided the Chinese and North Koreans were engaged in a propaganda campaign to discredit it.[3] Then on September 10, a U.S. airplane did strafe the Kaesong area in error. The

UN Command apologized, which surprisingly brought forth an almost friendly response from the communists and a proposal to resume the talks.[4] Liaison officers met again on September 23, but by this time General Ridgway had decided he did not want to meet any longer at Kaesong, and the liaison meetings got entangled in disputes over selecting a new site. It took until October 7 to agree on the tiny village of Panmunjom, about six miles east of Kaesong and about midway between the two front lines.[5]

The Joint Chiefs meanwhile were having some difficulty with General Ridgway, who had become thoroughly exasperated with the communist tactics of argument, invective and harassment. He recommended the United Nations "get tough" with the Reds, and said diplomatic language was useless in these military talks. "To sit down with these men and deal with them as representatives of an enlightened and civilized people," he complained to the Chiefs on August 6, "is to deride one's own dignity and to invite the disaster their treachery will inevitably bring upon us." He wanted to tell the UN delegates to "employ such language and methods as these treacherous savages cannot fail to understand, and understanding, respect."[6] The Chiefs calmed Ridgway down and the talks went on.

So did the fighting. Ridgway got permission from Truman to make a major air strike on the North Korean capital of Pyongyang, which took place on July 30, and he also sought a combined naval and air attack against the North Korean port city of Rashin (Najin), only a few miles from the Soviet border. The decision on Rashin also went all the way up to the President, who approved a JCS recommendation for an air strike, but not naval bombardment. The attack against Rashin was carried out August 25 by thirty-five B-29 bombers under navy fighter escort.[7]

Ridgway also approved General Van Fleet's Operation Talons, a proposed attack designed to straighten out the Eighth Army line from Kumwha to Kansong (on the east coast) in the central and eastern sectors.[8] Talons ultimately never was attempted because the evidence of what such an operation would cost became gruesomely evident as a result of a limited attack which Van Fleet ordered in the X Corps area. This attack, which acquired the highly appropriate, if journalistic, name of the Battle of Bloody Ridge, was to demonstrate the true nature of battle between armies deeply emplaced on heavily defended main lines of resistance.

Van Fleet was concerned about the will to fight of Eighth Army as a result of the slowdown of operations upon start of the peace talks.[9] He felt combat efficiency had slipped; patrols were conducted indifferently and failed to bring in prisoners. As he said later, "A sitdown army is subject to collapse at the first sign of an enemy effort....As commander of the Eighth Army, I couldn't allow my forces to become soft and dormant."[10]

Van Fleet wanted to eliminate a sag in the line in the Taebaek mountains in eastern Korea. North Koreans held commanding terrain on the west, north and east of the so-called Punchbowl, a large circular depression twenty miles northeast of Hwachon reservoir. From these heights, the North Koreans could observe UN defenses and troop movements and could direct artillery fire on the main line of resistance. If UN troops could seize these positions, they would lessen the threat of attacks developing from these heights, and Eighth Army could shorten and straighten its line.

On July 21, shortly after the peace talks started, Van Fleet directed X Corps to produce plans for seizing the western rim of the Punchbowl. (See Map 13.) Near the end of the month, 2nd Division, under Major General Clark L. Ruffner, captured a foothold on the western edge of the Punchbowl with a patrol base on Hill 1179. Rains prevented much more activity until August 18, when ROK troops attacked a J-shaped ridge just southeast of the Punchbowl. North Koreans were dug into strongly fortified positions there, and it took bitter fighting until August 27 to clear this ridge. Also on August 18, the ROK 36th Regiment of the 5th Division, now attached to the U.S. 2nd Division, attacked Hill 983, southwest of the Punchbowl, the big two-mile-wide and three-mile-deep mountain mass that was to acquire the name of Bloody Ridge from *Stars and Stripes*, the service newspaper.

The preliminary to this assault on Hill 983 was a days-long concentration of artillery fire which gradually eliminated practically every trace of vegetation upon the ridgeline, turning it into a brown landscape with skeletons of trees clawing the air. The ROKs attacked frontally up the fingers leading to the peak. The ROKs quickly established the pattern of battle that was to predominate in Korea for the next two years in hundreds of battles, engagements and sorties on mountains and ridges all across the front. The heavy artillery bombardments and air strikes had eliminated trees and underbrush, but had not destroyed the communist bunkers or all the thick minefields protecting the emplacements. The bunkers, constructed of heavy timbers, and usually covered with deep layers of rock and earth, were so massive that generally only a direct hit by the heaviest-caliber artillery was able to destroy them. Such direct hits were difficult, because the bunkers were hard to find in the torn-up ground. The most effective weapon against them was the 155mm Long Tom rifle. There were relatively few Long Toms available, and they could not always be placed

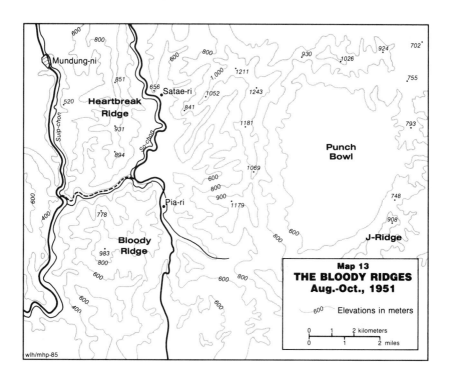

Mundung-ni

Heartbreak
Ridge

Sulp-chon

So-chon

Satae-ri

Pia-ri

Bloody
Ridge

Punch
Bowl

J-Ridge

Map 13
THE BLOODY RIDGES
Aug.-Oct., 1951

600 Elevations in meters

0   1   2 kilometers
0   1   2 miles

wlh/mhp-85

in position for direct, low-trajectory fire. As a result, as soon as the ROKs got within range of the bunkers, the North Koreans struck at them with automatic-weapons fire and clouds of hand grenades, which they threw or rolled down the ridgelines at the attacking troops.

After five days of repeated frontal assaults against Bloody Ridge, the ROKs finally took it, but then had to withdraw because of heavy NK counterattacks. General Ruffner had to commit parts of the 2nd Division's 9th Regiment to support the ROKs, but still the North Koreans refused to budge. The heavy casualties the ROK 36th Regiment suffered led to a sharp decline in morale, and on August 27 some units of the regiment broke and ran. This spread panic among parts of the 9th Regiment as well.

The new X Corps commander, Major General Clovis E. Byers, decided to apply pressure against the Reds across the whole corps front in hopes of forcing the enemy to disperse his firepower and prevent the steady buildup of troops on Bloody Ridge. He assigned to the ROK 5th Division the mission of seizing the northwest rim of the Punchbowl and directed the 1st Marine Division to capture the northeast rim. The 2nd Division meanwhile got the assignment to take Bloody Ridge, while the ROK 7th Division was to attack and capture terrain to the west of Bloody Ridge.

The marines were fortunate in attacking while NK units were in the process of being exchanged, and the leathernecks' forceful assaults carried through and won control of the northern lip of the Punchbowl.

The 2nd Division's attacks on Bloody Ridge again were direct assaults. Although they were fierce and sustained, they failed to dislodge the North Koreans. The leading unit, the 9th Regiment, suffered heavy casualties, but could not drive the NK defenders away. Brigadier General Thomas E. de Shazo, who had taken command of the 2nd Division temporarily, laid out a double-envelopment plan, using the division's 23rd and 38th Regiments, while the 9th Regiment continued the direct assault on the ridge. On September 4 and 5 the resolution came suddenly: the North Koreans, weakened by heavy losses, evacuated Bloody Ridge, leaving the bodies of five hundred dead comrades on the heights. In almost three weeks of fighting, the ROKs and Americans had suffered more than 2,700 casualties, while the communists had sustained an estimated 15,000.[11]

Van Fleet evidently took a close look at the casualty figures on Bloody Ridge, because on September 5 he informed Ridgway that the contemplated Operation Talons, on a much larger scale than Bloody Ridge, was not worth the probable cost in lives and materiel. Instead, Van Fleet said he favored "tidying up" the Eighth Army eastern flank during the remainder of September, and around October 1 he planned to launch an attack in the west by I Corps. If this I Corps attack was successful, Van Fleet planned to make an amphibious landing near Tongchon, on the east coast about thirty miles south of Wonsan, which would link up with a proposed land advance northeast from Kumwha. Ridgway approved these major operations only for planning purposes, and they ultimately were not carried out, because they involved an unacceptable risk of failure.[12] But Ridgway offered no objection to continued limited-objective attacks on an opportunistic basis. Van Fleet swiftly issued a directive on September 8 to his corps commanders emphasizing limited-objective attacks, reconnaissance and patrolling. On the same day, he directed X Corps to take the ridge just north of Bloody Ridge.

This ridge was similar in size and height to Bloody, and the 2nd Division again got the assignment to attack. This mountain ranks with its neighbor, Bloody Ridge, in the chronicle of the costliest ridgeline battles in Korea. It quickly earned its name: Heartbreak Ridge, as news correspondents called it. When the North Koreans withdrew from Bloody Ridge, they fell back to Heartbreak, where they had established bunkers, trenches and gun positions that were every bit as strongly fortified and well camouflaged as those on Bloody. The United States attack again was to be made into the very teeth of the enemy main line of resistance.

The assault on Heartbreak began eight days after the end of Bloody on September 5. This gave the North Koreans time to strengthen their defenses and to reinforce the units guarding the ridge and approaches. The 2nd Division's acting commander, General de Shazo, decided to use a single regiment, the 23rd, in the assault force, and to approach from the Satae-ri valley on the east and cut Heartbreak between the middle peak (Hill 931) and the southern peak (Hill 894). One battalion then was to turn north along the ridge-line and seize the northern peak (Hill 851), while a second battalion would seize 931 and 894. As soon as the assault force captured Hill 894, the 9th Regiment was to advance and capture a hill about a mile west and slightly south of Hill 894. The 38th Regiment was emplaced, along with the attached French Battalion, on the heights a couple of miles east of Heartbreak and just west of the Punchbowl.

On the morning of September 13, after a half-hour artillery barrage on Heartbreak, the 23rd Regiment advanced north up the Satae-ri valley. The North Koreans quickly spotted the force and laid down heavy artillery and mortar fire on it. Despite casualties, the 23rd pressed on. As the assault battalion arrived at an east-west spur that led up to the top of Heartbreak, it ran into a regiment of NK troops manning concealed bunkers covering the approach ridge with machine guns and small arms. The withering fire forced the assault battalion to dig in at the foot of the spur, and the prospects of a quick capture of the mountain mass immediately vanished.

General de Shazo, realizing he needed more force to seize the ridge, ordered the 9th Regiment to redirect its assault against the southern peak of Heartbreak (Hill 894), in order to relieve some of the pressure on the 23rd Regiment. On September 14 the 9th's 2nd Battalion drove up the southwest fingers of Hill 894 and, supported by tank and artillery fire, by nightfall had reached within 650 yards of the crest of 894 against light NK resistance. The next day the 2nd Battalion, 9th, seized the crest of 894, having suffered only eleven casualties. In the next two days, however, against repeated and vain counterattacks, the battalion lost more than two hundred men.

The 9th Regiment's attack failed to solve the 23rd Regiment's problem. North Korean fire kept the 23rd's assault forces pinned down on the lower slopes, and on September 16 the 23rd's commander, Colonel James Y. Adams, ordered his other two battalions to attack abreast on either side of the assault battalion in an attempt to force the peaks. The attacks made little headway against the curtain of fire the communists laid down.

Attrition now began to play a heavy role in the battle. American vehicles were jammed up in the narrow valley southwest of Heartbreak and exposed to enemy artillery and mortar fire. Korean porters who had the task of carrying ammo and supplies up the mountain to the troops began to drop their loads and bolt for cover. This forced Americans to take over much of the task. It could take up to ten hours to bring a wounded man down on a litter.

The stalemate led the 9th Regiment's CO, Colonel John M. Lynch, to suggest on September 19 that the attack be broadened by sending his 1st Battalion to attack ridgelines across the Suipchon river southwest of Heartbreak. Lynch hoped this would lead the North Koreans to believe the Americans were trying to envelop Heartbreak from the west and to divert some of their men and weapons in this direction. Major General Robert N. Young, the new 2nd Division commander, arrived on September 20, and deciding Lynch's plan was sound, he ordered the attack on September 23. Meanwhile, Van Fleet ordered General Byers, X Corps commander, to advance the western flank of his corps to bring it into phase with IX Corps on his left. Thus, on September 23, Byers sent the ROK 7th Division to attack another hill about 2,000 yards northwest of the 9th Regiment's objective. This doubled-up flanking movement against Heartbreak on the west was thought to have the possibility of threatening NK forces on Heartbreak. These flanking attacks made good progress, and by September 25 the 9th Regiment had secured its objective and the following day the ROKs got theirs.

Although the North Koreans shifted a regiment to contain these flanking movements, they were not weakened on Heartbreak. The 1st Battalion of the 23rd Regiment briefly got up on Hill 931 on September 23, but could not withstand an NK counterattack which shattered the American battalion and, when ammo ran out, forced it back down to lower heights.

The French Battalion was moved to relieve the 23rd's 2nd Battalion, and it tried to drive south along the ridgeline while the 1st Battalion, 23rd, moved north toward the crest of 931. But the North Koreans fought off Americans and Frenchmen.

On September 26, after almost two weeks of futile and costly battle, Colonel Adams told General Young it was suicidal to continue with the original plan. His 23rd Regiment had sustained more than 950 casualties and the division total over the period was 1,670. Adams favored broadening the attack in an effort to disperse the communists' resistance. Young and the corps commander, Byers, agreed with Adams, and they called off further assaults on Heartbreak by the 23rd.

The 2nd Division G-3, Major Thomas W. Mellon, developed a new plan by which all three regiments would launch tank-supported attacks up the Suipchon river valley toward the village of Mundung-ni west of Heartbreak, while an American-French tank-infantry task force would operate to the east in the Satae-ri valley as a decoy. The 9th Regiment was to clear the western side of the Mundung-ni valley, the 23rd Regiment with the French Battalion attached was to move onto the Heartbreak peak (Hill 931), while the 38th Regiment was to provide support. In order to get M4A3 Sherman medium tanks into the narrow Mundung-ni valley, the division's engineer battalion had to sweep up enemy mines and rebuild the rough track that ran up it. It was a huge task, but the engineers set about it. They exploded enemy antitank mines by placing blocks of tetranol in a chain at fifty-foot intervals along the track and setting them off. The explosions detonated the mines nearby.

On October 4, fighter-bombers attacked targets in front of the division, and the American-French task force raided up the Satae-ri valley. The rest of the division concentrated for the move up the Mundung-ni valley. On the afternoon of October 5, the division's artillery began a heavy pounding of the three NK regiments facing the Mundung-ni valley. These three regiments, as a result of their heavy engagement, were down to fewer than a thousand men each. That evening, before the UN attack began, marine Corsairs struck the North Korean positions with napalm, rockets and machine-gun fire.

The 9th Regiment advance on the west side of the Mundung-ni valley reached its objectives on October 7 against only light resistance, then the regiment swung northwest. The 38th Regiment moved up the valley behind tank support, while on Heartbreak the 23rd Regiment also made progress. The 23rd's 1st Battalion created a diversion north against Hill 851, the French Battalion feinted south toward Hill 931, while the 2nd Battalion struck 931 from the south, with the 3rd Battalion in reserve behind the 2nd. To preserve surprise, the 2nd Battalion, 23rd, under Lieutenant Colonel Henry F. Daniels, approached Hill 931 without a preliminary artillery barrage; once the attack started, division artillery opened up on all known NK mortar positions. This helped greatly, and the battalion closed on 931 with only light losses and routed the enemy from bunkers with flame throwers, grenades and small arms. By 3 a.m. October 6 the 2nd and 3rd Battalions had captured the southern half of 931, and beat off the inevitable counterattack. As daylight broke, the Americans continued forward, while the French Battalion moved in from the north. By noon, 931 was secured.

The 3rd Battalion continued on north to aid the 1st Battalion in its attack against Hill 851, the last enemy bulwark on Heartbreak. Below in the Mundung-ni valley, the division's tanks moved up behind the engineers as they continued to build a passable road, raced through the village of Mundung-ni and beyond and inflicted heavy casualties on Chinese troops moving in to reinforce the North Koreans. This tank thrust surprised the enemy and cut off supply and replacement routes to the NK troops on Heartbreak and also opened the way for 38th Regiment troops to drive northward.

On October 10, the 2nd Battalion of the 23rd Regiment moved off 951 and took possession of the lower slope of an east-west finger southeast of Mundung-ni leading up to the summit of Hill 851. This peak was now being approached from west and south, as the 23rd's 1st Battalion and the French Battalion inched northward along the ridgeline toward 851, bunker by bunker, in bitter fighting. The North Koreans, along with Chinese who had joined them, had to be killed or wounded. None surrendered. The regiment's 3rd Battalion also shifted to the spur on the west to continue pressure.

Finally, at daybreak on October 13, the French Battalion stormed the peak of 851 and took possession of the last pinnacle on Heartbreak. After thirty days of vicious combat, the UN forces had captured Heartbreak Ridge.

The cost was staggering. The 2nd Division had suffered more than 3,700 casualties over the Heartbreak Ridge period. The 23rd and the Frenchmen incurred almost half of these losses. Estimates of Chinese and North Korean casualties went as high as 25,000.[13]

What was attained? A small sag in the line was eliminated. Behind Heartbreak there loomed another mountain, and this mountain bristled with the same kind of bunkers and firepower that had cost so much on Bloody and Heartbreak. The men on both sides exhibited extraordinary heroism and determination. But the battles they fought resembled so sadly the destructive battles of attrition in World War I that the question arose whether the modest gains were worth the cost. The final judgment, on both sides, was that they were not.

There were many other engagements along the front during the fall of 1951. In September a series of local attacks, counterattacks and combat patrols occupied both I and IX Corps. These led into a general UN movement in October to a new front on the west known as the Jamestown line, which extended the MLR a few miles over the Imjin in the west and north of Chorwon in the center. In the east-central sector, the U.S. 24th Division and the ROK 2nd and 6th Divisions in IX Corps created a northward bulge by approaching just south of Kumsong. Some of the engagements in I and IX Corps were fierce and bloody, though none was as long and sustained as the Bloody and Heartbreak battles. The 1st Cavalry Division caught the brunt of the enemy's resistance in its move northwest from the Yonchon area, about twelve air miles southwest of Chorwon. The 1st Cavalry suffered about 2,900 casualties in the seventeen-day operation that pushed the line about five miles westward. Another costly engagement was fought by the 3rd Division in the Battle of the Bloody Angle (September 28–October 6) just west of Chorwon. The division sustained more than five hundred casualties in securing ridgelines flanking the Seoul-Chorwon railway, which was reopened to supply the front.[14]

Despite all the hopes for peace which had blossomed when the cease-fire talks commenced in July, the period from their start until November, when stalemate had settled over the battle line, was one of the bloodiest and most costly in the entire war for both sides. During this period, but especially September and October, the UN forces suffered nearly 60,000 casualties, more than 22,000 of them American.[15] By comparison, from the start of the war until the Chinese launched their great offensive on November 25, 1950—that is, counting all of the battles of the July and August retreat, the Pusan Perimeter, the Inchon landing, the breakout from the perimeter, and the advance almost to the Yalu—total American casualties were fewer than 28,000.[16] Estimated Chinese and North Korean losses during the July-November, 1951, period were almost 234,000.[17] There could scarcely be more graphic proof of the extreme toll demanded by battles on the ridge lines.

By the end of the fighting in October, it had become clear that any further major advances against the enemy main line of resistance would require unconscionable losses. Since the UN Command retained control of the sea, it could flank the communist line with amphibious landings in the rear. But with the vast quantity of Chinese manpower available to the Reds (much of it not used and distributed in the interior of North Korea), a decisive blow like Inchon could not be repeated. Also, the Chinese now had begun to contest American air supremacy over the Yalu, though not over the battle front. Beginning in September, UN air interdiction began to encounter increasingly strong resistance from Chinese MIG-15 Russian-built jets (which the Chinese had to buy from the USSR)..In November, the UN Command was forced to cancel daylight raids north of the Chongchon river close to the Yalu, and Red jets were sighted for the first time on fields south of the Yalu. In November, the Chinese also deployed Russian-made TU-2 twin-engine light bombers. Although the Chinese did not enter into an all-out battle for the air over North Korea, the presence of Red high-performance aircraft posed an increasing threat to American air superiority, and raised questions as to what the United States should do if the peace talks failed.[18]

A 3rd Division twin-40mm antiaircraft artillery weapon fires direct support against Chinese positions on the Western front near the 38th parallel.

Soldiers of the English Gloucestershire Regiment battalion stop for afternoon tea. In April, 1951, this battalion was overrun by a massive Chinese attack and only a few of its members reached UN lines.

A battery of self-propelled 155mm Long Tom rifles fire north of Seoul in May, 1951, as United Nations troops move up behind withdrawing Chinese.

Major General William M. Hoge (right), commander of IX Corps, studies map at Chunchon airstrip, May, 1951, with General Matthew B. Ridgway (left), Far East commander, and Lieutenant General James A. Van Fleet, Eighth Army commander.

A U.S. 3rd Division medic gives blood plasma to a wounded North Korean soldier.

To protect against American artillery fire and air attacks, the Chinese and North Koreans created deep underground tunnels, rooms and bunkers nearly impervious to all but direct hits by heavy-caliber weapons. These Chinese soldiers are armed with "potato masher" grenades.

An American F-80 Shooting Star stands on its wing tip in June, 1951, to avoid smoke from an earlier aerial attack against a communist-held hilltop.

Men of the 9th Regiment, 2nd Division, climb a steep slope on Bloody Ridge on September 5, 1951. This regiment suffered severe casualties in this and the subsequent Heartbreak Ridge battles.

Red Chinese soldiers cover Americans emerging from a cave to surrender.

This is Bloody Ridge, occupied by survivors of the 9th Regiment, after it was captured on September 5, 1951. It cost 2,700 American and South Korean casualties and an estimated 15,000 North Korean casualties. The battle of Heartbreak Ridge, which followed Bloody Ridge, claimed 3,700 American and French casualties and an estimated 25,000 North Koreans and Chinese.

U.S. ARMY PHOTO

Two Chinese Communist soldiers in their standard padded cotton uniforms stand guard on the edge of the neutral zone at Panmunjom, midway between the communist and United Nations lines, where the two-year truce talks were largely held.

U.S. NAVY PHOTO

The essence of ridgeline battle conditions in Korea: marines in trenches crouch for cover as a Chinese 82mm mortar round lands on their positions. Most casualties on both sides were caused by mortar and artillery fire.

An enemy mortar round lands directly on a marine ridgeline position.

CHAPTER 58

Another Try for Peace

HOPES FOR PEACE in Korea rose again when the delegates assembled October 25 at a large conference tent at Panmunjom. The UN Command submitted a proposal that called for a demarcation line based on the line of contact between the two sides. The Reds turned down the proposal, but finally stopped insisting on the 38th parallel as a dividing line. It looked as if real progress would be made, until the UN Command insisted that the ancient Korean capital of Kaesong be included on the UN side of the line. General Ridgway felt Kaesong was important strategically, but because of the approaching armistice talks he had given up plans in June, 1951, to seize the city. Now he changed the UN position and demanded Kaesong, although it was plainly inside Red lines, and the UN had insisted all along that the demarcation line be the battle line.[1] Ridgway's attitude got little sympathy, even in the United States. On November 6 the Joint Chiefs told Ridgway public sentiment would not support breakdown of the talks over Kaesong.[2]

The big breakthrough came on November 7. The communist delegation proposed that the existing line of contact be the demarcation line and that both sides withdraw two kilometers to form a demilitarized zone. Ridgway, however, rejected this proposal and insisted the line should be the line of contact as of the effective date of the armistice.[3]

The communist delegation reacted angrily to Ridgway's position and the Joint Chiefs also felt the Far East commander was being intransigent. Ridgway complained the Reds were seeking only a de facto cease-fire. The Chiefs, backed by the State Department and the President, told Ridgway he should accept the present line of contact, but that it had to be renegotiated if other issues were not settled in a month or so.[4]

The communists insisted that the demarcation line not be revised, even after a one-month period passed, until all other agenda items had been settled, and the UN delegates reluctantly agreed. By November 23, staff officers had begun tracing the battle line on maps, and four days later the demarcation line was established.[5]

The negotiators had disposed of Item 2 on the agenda, the demarcation line. They still had three items to go. They moved to Item 3, the concrete arrangements for an armistice, including methods of supervision. Ridgway wanted free inspection of Korea by joint observer teams at ports of entry and centers throughout Korea, joint aerial observation and photographic reconnaissance over all Korea, and complete joint observation of the demilitarized zone (DMZ). His major aim was to prohibit introduction of reinforcements after a cease-fire so that the Reds would not be able to build up their power secretly.[6]

The Chiefs did not agree with Ridgway. They told him on November 16 that ground and air observation was desirable, but not at the expense of breaking off the talks. Anyway, the Chiefs said, the State Department was exploring an alternative to local inspections: a joint announcement by all UN nations with forces in Korea that punitive action would be taken against Communist China if a major violation of the armistice occurred. This was the "greater sanction" statement that came to have considerable significance in American thinking, especially after the United Kingdom in late 1951 agreed to issue it with the United States.[7] Carried to its logical conclusion, a "greater sanction" threat implied a violent widening of the war in the Far East if the Chinese decided to advance again in Korea after an armistice. This was a subject the Chiefs, the State Department and Truman had been discussing for some time as a course of action if the peace talks failed.[8] In a real sense, a "greater sanction" statement would have been as good a guarantee as inspections to insure Red China's compliance with an armistice. Even if they desired to do so, the Communist Chinese might think twice before attacking in Korea again if they feared the consequences would be a naval blockade of their coast and air attacks on China and Manchuria, with the inevitable implication that atomic weapons might be used.

Ridgway was insistent on inspections and controls within Korea, however, and the UN and communist delegations were heading for a conflict when they convened on November 27 to discuss Item 3. The Reds called for each side to designate an equal number of members for an armistice commission that would supervise the armistice. The UN team demanded no increase in military forces by either side after an armistice and also demanded that military armistice commission teams have free access to all Korea.[9] The UN Command also refused to consider withdrawing from some small islands off the west coast of Korea occupied by UN forces that were above the demarcation line. The

Reds made clear after the armistice they would accept no restriction on rehabilitation of roads, railways, buildings and other facilities in Korea, including airfields. Furthermore, they indicated, if foreign troops on both sides simply evacuated Korea after an armistice, there would be no need for inspections, observation and so on.[10]

Seeing the adamant stand of the UN Command, the Reds on December 3 made a concession: an organization made up of neutral nations would carry out inspections in Korea to insure compliance with the no-reinforcement provisions. However, they coupled this with a requirement that both sides not introduce *any* additional military forces, thereby prohibiting even the normal rotation of troops, or the sending of men to Japan on R&R. The United Nations wanted routine one-for-one replacements.[11]

In the midst of these delicate negotiations, with each side bringing up highly sensitive issues virtually certain to cause clashes, President Truman stepped into the arena and took an extremely hard stand on the rehabilitation of North Korea after an armistice. Truman was looking over a Joint Chiefs proposal that would withdraw UN objection to rehabilitation of all facilities except airfields (this because of the fear that the Reds would establish air bases that could threaten UN forces; the UN Command, of course, also insisted on *no* closing down of UN air bases in South Korea).

Truman demanded to know "why we should allow rehabilitation of roads, railroads and other facilities except airfields. We have expended lives, tons of bombs and a large amount of equipment to bring these people to terms. They have been able to give us a bad time even in the crippled condition of their communications and they have been able to operate effectively even without airfields."[12]

The Joint Chiefs patiently explained to the President that, since they expected no political settlement in Korea, an armistice would have to last a long time, and "it would be impossible to deny for any appreciable time the right to rehabilitate those facilities upon which the economy of the country depends." As for airfield rehabilitation, the Chiefs felt this presented a real threat. The President accepted the Joint Chiefs' viewpoint.[13]

Therefore, airfield rehabilitation became a major issue. Whatever the Joint Chiefs' fears, it was unrealistic to expect the communists to accept an unequal arrangement like this—with UN aircraft emplaced in South Korean fields, but communist craft denied use of North Korean fields.

Other disputes on Item 3 were painfully worked out by compromise over a long period, but the airfield issue, especially fields that could accommodate jet aircraft, threatened to disrupt the talks completely. The

UN team backed off aerial inspections and proposed finally to allow the rehabilitation of civil airfields, but the Reds completely rejected this.[14] On January 25, 1952, the delegations decided to set aside the airfield issue and work up agreements on other aspects of Item 3.[15]

Finally, the two sides came down to the issue of what to do with the prisoners of war each held (Item 4 on the agenda). They directly addressed the issue on December 11, and then only after the UN delegation had forced the Reds' hand. Five months had gone by since the peace talks had started, five months of agonizingly slow progress, and at last the two sides got down to the issue that would drag the talks on for a further year and a half.

The POW dispute became clouded with so much invective and emotion and was oppressed with so many strange turnings and dead ends, that it is difficult to realize the issue was very simple: the United States refused to return any POW who did not want to go back to communist rule, while the Reds wanted all their men brought home.

The United States used the POW issue for propaganda against the communists by showing to the world that many citizens of communist countries would "forcibly resist" returning to communist rule. This grew out of the American hatred of things communist, and, though it had a high moral flair (by showing Americans believed in freedom of choice), it carried a tremendous amount of questionable baggage with it.

In the first place, the United States had signed the Geneva Convention of 1949, containing Article 118, which stated: "Prisoners of war shall be repatriated without delay after cessation of hostilities."[16] The United States had not ratified the convention, but had informed the Red Cross on July 4, 1950, that it intended to abide by it.[17] The Geneva provision on prisoners had been aimed directly at preventing a recurrence of the action of the Soviet Union after World War II: it had kept thousands of POWs in slave-labor camps for years. The Geneva Convention delegates had not addressed the possibility that large numbers of prisoners might not wish to go home after a war. The United States, in the early stage of the cease-fire process, had taken the position that prisoners of war should be exchanged on a one-for-one basis as quickly as possible.[18] Since the UN Command held several times as many POWs as the Reds, it could not have adhered to this one-for-one concept; however, no one thought then that POWs should be interviewed by their captors and asked whether they would rather not be sent home at war's end. This came later.

The U.S. position on POWs unquestionably delayed the armistice. Admiral Joy, the first chief of the UN truce team, claimed the U.S. position on voluntary repatriation of POWs "cost us over a year of war."[19] During this period the UN Command suffered far more casualties in battle than there were POWs who did not wish to be repatriated. Therefore, there was a very narrow moral issue posed: should troops be expected to fight and some to die in order to honor their nation's feelings for the possible fate of former enemy soldiers? Leaving aside the American agreement to abide by the Geneva Convention, should Americans have died to give former enemies freedom of choice?

In addition, the U.S. position insured that *all* POWs—American, other United Nations, North Korean, South Korean and Chinese—had to endure additional months of confinement until the matter could be resolved.

The idea of allowing POWs a choice came from Brigadier General Robert A. McClure, army chief of psychological warfare. He proposed to General Lawton Collins that Chinese prisoners who were former Nationalist soldiers (and there were many of these) might fear punishment by the communists for having surrendered. He suggested they might be repatriated to Taiwan. Collins passed this along to the JCS, maintaining that, since Taiwan was still legally a part of China, it would be within the bounds of the Geneva Convention! Collins added a suggestion that no enemy POWs be required to return to communist control. Meanwhile, General McClure asked General Ridgway whether POWs could be classified according to their wishes, clearly the first stage of applying a policy of voluntary repatriation.[20]

Ridgway was not very sympathetic. In the event of a full peace settlement, he pointed out, the Geneva Convention would require repatriation of all POWs. Because of this, Ridgway said, he was preparing to screen, for release to the South Korean government, about forty thousand South Koreans being held as captives who had been captured and impressed into the North Korean army before they were again captured by the UN Command. These men were not regarded as prisoners by South Korea.[21] This procedure was the obvious solution for individuals who were of questionable POW status. The plan would not be legal for bona-fide enemy soldiers held as POWs, whatever their personal wishes as to repatriation.

Meanwhile, General Collins's suggestion had been referred to the JCS Joint Strategic Survey Committee, which drafted a message to Ridgway on July 18, 1951, asking whether he approved of not repatriating POWs without their "full consent." Ridgway responded that such a policy would be humanitarian but would establish a precedent contrary to the Geneva Convention and could prevent the return of U.S. prisoners in future wars while providing propaganda for the present enemy.[22]

The Chiefs decided to submit the issue to the secretary of defense. It went to Robert A. Lovett, still deputy secretary but named to replace George C. Marshall after he resigned as defense secretary on September 12. Lovett sent the proposal to Secretary of State Acheson, who responded August 27 discouraging voluntary repatriation for the same reason advanced by Ridgway: it was contrary to the Geneva Convention. Acheson, the devious thinker that he was, thereupon muddied the waters by suggesting any prisoners not wanting to return home be *paroled* and released. Parole was provided for in the Geneva Convention, but hardly in the form Acheson was proposing, and this idea mercifully was allowed by other American leaders to fade away.[23]

Secretary Lovett was of the opinion that, while the United Nations had to take into account humanitarian concerns for prisoners, it had to avoid any solution which involved "bargaining with the welfare of our own prisoners."[24] Collins, after reading Acheson's reply, changed his mind and convinced his other JCS colleagues the voluntary-repatriation idea should be withdrawn, because the best hope for getting back prisoners of the Korean War and future wars was through firm adherence to the Geneva Convention.

The whole idea of voluntary repatriation of POWs appeared to be fading rapidly until President Truman unexpectedly entered the picture on October 29. Talking with the then acting secretary of state, James E. Webb, Truman said he thought a plan that would exchange all of the UN Command's POWs for all of the communists' would be inequitable, because the United Nations held several times as many POWs as the Reds. In addition, Truman feared many of the communist prisoners, especially those who had surrendered willingly or who had cooperated with their captors, would be "immediately done away with" if sent back home. Truman did not come to a decision regarding a policy for returning Red POWs, but he did reject an all-for-all settlement unless the UN Command received "some major concession which could be obtained in no other way."[25]

Truman's views influenced the State and Defense Departments in their draft of a POW exchange plan in December which contained the germ of voluntary repatriation. The plan directed Ridgway to seek a one-for-one POW exchange and, if this could not be obtained, to seek agreement for prisoners to express their wishes regarding repatriation.[26]

The communists naturally insisted that both sides release all POWs held by them immediately after signing an armistice, while the UN delegation demanded as a first step a full exchange of lists of POWs. On December 18, the Reds yielded on this point, and both sides exchanged lists. The figures the United Nations received were shocking. They showed the communists held only 11,559 POWs (3,198 American, 7,142 ROKs, the remainder other UN soldiers). The UN Command was carrying 11,500 Americans and 88,000 ROKs on the missing list, and fully expected the communists to be holding many more prisoners.[27]

The UN Command gave the Reds 132,474 names, 95,531 North Koreans and 20,700 Chinese, plus 16,243 former ROKs who had been resident in South Korea when the war started and had been captured and impressed into the North Korean army. But the United Nations had committed a major error: it had reported earlier as POWs another 44,000 persons. The names of these persons had been sent to the International Committee of the Red Cross (ICRC) in Geneva. Most were former South Korean residents who had been captured while fighting for the communists, and they had been screened and reclassified. (See page 453.) This gave the Reds an immediate propaganda issue, which they exploited, charging the UN Command was withholding 44,000 of their men. The UN Command, equally shocked at the low figures of UN troops being held by the Reds, accused the communists of withholding the names of 50,000 UN and ROK prisoners. The UN delegation based this figure on broadcasts by North Korea early in the war that boasted it had captured 65,000 ROK and American troops while driving into South Korea.[28]

The conflict over the lists of POW names raged for several days, but had simmered down by January 2, 1952, when Rear Admiral R. E. Libby, a UN delegate, submitted the basic UN Command proposal. It called for a one-for-one exchange of prisoners until all UN POWs who desired release had been let go, then a one-for-one exchange until certain South Korean and other foreign civilians held by North Korea were released, and then release from prisoner status of all other POWs who did not want to be repatriated. The next day the communists angrily rejected the UN plan in toto. They called it a shameful attempt for the United Nations to detain 160,000 of their men. Release and repatriation, they asserted, must not be a "trade of slaves." The communists attacked the UN plan from every possible angle, and the dispute raged for weeks.[29]

CHAPTER 59

The POWs Seize the Stage

C OMMUNIST ANGER about voluntary repatriation doubtless was sincere, and this possibly led to the Reds' worldwide propaganda campaign early in 1952 to brand the United States on charges of germ warfare. The opening salvo was fired February 2 in Paris by Jacob Malik, Soviet ambassador to the United Nations, who attacked the "Anglo-American bloc," and repeated an earlier North Korean charge that UN forces had used "toxic gases" spread by bullets. In late February, both Beijing and Pyongyang radio accused the United States of dropping bacteria-carrying insects in North Korea between January 28 and February 17. This charge was picked up by the communist press throughout the world, with variations added, such as firing harmful bacteria in artillery shells, and sending across infected flies, snails and rodents. The United States denied the charges, but the communist "hate America" campaign raged on even after Secretary Acheson asked the International Committee of the Red Cross to investigate the alleged epidemic in North Korea. The ICRC on March 12 offered the North Korean and Chinese governments a full scientific investigation, provided it was given free access to North Korea, an offer not accepted. Likewise the World Health Organization of the United Nations offered an investigation, but its offer was not acknowledged. The communists reached the peak of their attack on May 5 when they produced a confession from two U.S. flyers shot down in January that they had dropped "germ bombs" over North Korea.[1]

The germ-warfare campaign slowly faded in mid-1952, probably because by then the communists had another propaganda issue: alleged atrocities against communist POWs held by the United Nations. The POW-atrocity campaign began on February 18, while both sides were at the height of their dispute over voluntary repatriation. What, if any, role the communist command in Pyongyang or Beijing had in the incident is not known, but it was highly damaging to the UN case.

The incident occurred on Koje-do, an island near Masan, just off the southern coast of South Korea, where most of the communist POWs and newly designated civilian internees were housed in numerous closely adjacent compounds. U.S. troops entered Compound 62 in preparation for rescreening Korean prisoners already reclassified from POW to civilian internee status. The purpose was to correct errors and identify those who would accept repatriation. Between 1,000 and 1,500 of the 5,600 inmates in this compound attacked the U.S. soldiers, using compound-made steel-tipped poles, knives and barbed-wire flails as well as rocks. The Americans immediately began firing. In the melee that resulted, one American was killed and 38 wounded, while 55 Koreans were killed outright, 22 died later, and 140 were wounded.[2]

On February 23 the Red delegation at Panmunjom protested against "the sanguinary incident of barbarously massacring large numbers of our personnel." The UN delegates rejected the protests on the ground that the Koje-do incident was an internal affair, since it involved civilian internees, not POWs. This enraged the communists, and a new worldwide propaganda campaign was born. General Van Fleet replaced the camp commandant with Brigadier General Francis T. Dodd, but riots and incidents continued. The Far East Command later produced evidence that the riots and other problems on Koje and elsewhere were superintended by the communist high command. Prisoners got instructions from agents who allowed themselves to be captured and who took charge when they arrived at the camps, sometimes ordering murders of anticommunists being held in the compounds.[3]

Meanwhile, in Washington the question of voluntary repatriation was being debated throughout February, but the final decision was Truman's. As he wrote later, in his memoirs, "Just as I had always insisted that we could not abandon the South Koreans who had stood by us and freedom, so I now refused to agree to any solution that provided for the return against their will of prisoners of war to communist domination." He also later issued a statement, "We will not buy an armistice by turning over human beings for slaughter or slavery."[4]

There was little real progress for weeks on the key issues, airfield rehabilitation and voluntary repatriation of prisoners, and the communists added another bone of contention by demanding that the Soviet Union be a member of the Neutral Nations Supervisory Commission to make sure no increase in military strength came into North or South Korea after the end of hostilities. The UN Command would not accept Russia because it did not consider the Soviets neutral, though the delegates did not want to say so publicly.

On March 13 a second major clash occurred between guards and prisoners at Koje-do. A group of cooperative North Korean prisoners was marching past a compound filled with North Koreans hostile to the United Nations. In front of the marching detail a ROK army detachment, not connected with the detail, was moving along. From the compound prisoners suddenly began throwing stones at the cooperative NK soldiers and the ROKs alike. Without orders, the ROKs turned and began firing into the compound. They killed ten POWs outright, mortally wounded two and injured twenty-six, plus a passing U.S. officer. The Red delegation at Panmunjom immediately labeled this another "barbarous massacre."[5]

It was not until April 28 that Admiral Joy finally presented the UN Command's so-called "package proposal" to the communists at Panmunjom. The package was designed to break the deadlock, and had been weeks in preparation by the delegation, Ridgway, the JCS and officials in the Truman administration. The UN Command agreed to accept rehabilitation and reconstruction of airfields in North Korea without restriction, provided the communists agreed to no forcible repatriation of POWs and membership on the Neutral Nations Supervisory Commission that was acceptable to both sides. After a short recess, the chief Red delegate, General Nam Il, rejected the offer as being of no help, and Joy responded that it was the "final and irrevocable" UN stand. On May 6, Ridgway issued a statement saying responsibility for peace now rested with the communist leaders. Impasse had been reached.[6]

Almost as if on cue, trouble erupted again at Koje-do. It came just as General Ridgway was about to give up his Far East Command to replace Dwight D. Eisenhower as supreme allied commander in Europe. Eisenhower had resigned to run for President. Replacing Ridgway as Far East commander was General Mark W. Clark, who had commanded the U.S. Fifth Army in Italy in World War II. Clark arrived in the Far East on May 7 and was scheduled to take over from Ridgway on May 12. Just as he arrived came the news of what had happened at Koje.[7]

The camp commander, General Dodd, had gone to the gate of Compound 76 to meet with communist prisoners ostensibly to discuss grievances. General Ridgway wrote that Dodd did not use proper safeguards, apparently meaning he was not adequately guarded. The POWs seized Dodd and carried him into the compound. Immediately afterward, the prisoners hoisted a sign indicating Dodd's life was forfeit if guards used force to recapture him. They sent out word demanding that representatives from other compounds be brought in for a general conference. This demand was met by nonplussed American officers left in charge, and two POW representatives from each compound were sent to Compound 76 that evening.[8]

General Van Fleet directed that no force be used to free General Dodd unless he himself approved. The fear was not just for Dodd's life, but that a full-scale attempt at breakout might be imminent, and force might precipitate a pitched battle with severe loss of life.

Van Fleet also formally relieved Dodd as commandant of the camp and replaced him with Brigadier General Charles F. Colson, chief of staff of I Corps, who left immediately for Koje.

Before Colson arrived on May 8, the prisoners made several demands, the main one being that they be allowed to establish a formal association. Brigadier General Paul F. Yount, commander of the Second Logistical Command at Pusan, refused and demanded Dodd's release. When Colson arrived, he informed the Red leaders that Dodd no longer was camp commandant and that unless he was released unharmed troops would enter the compound and free him by force. The prisoners ignored Colson.

Meanwhile, Ridgway and Clark flew to Korea and conferred with Van Fleet and afterward with Admiral Joy. Ridgway authorized Van Fleet to take necessary action to get Dodd's release and to use whatever force he required. Van Fleet did not react swiftly or forcefully, out of fear for Dodd's life. He ordered a tank company of the 3rd Division to move the two hundred miles by road from its position in the north and to transship by LST to Koje. The 2nd Division's 38th Regiment and a battalion of the 9th Regiment also moved toward Koje by LST.

On the morning of May 9, General Colson demanded Dodd's release. Six hours later he issued a second demand. The prisoners refused and wanted to talk. Although this refusal should have resulted in an immediate assault on the compound, Colson decided to wait until the tanks arrived late that night, meaning no attack could be launched until the morning of May 10. In the meantime, Colson authorized the prisoners to hold a meeting.

A bizarre spectacle developed. The prisoners set themselves up a people's court, drew up a list of nineteen counts of death or injury to compound inmates, and required Dodd to answer each charge. As Walter G. Hermes says in his history of the last two years of the war, "Although [the prisoners] were generally disposed to accept his explanations and dismiss the accusations, the spectacle of prisoners, still captive and surrounded by heavily armed troops, trying the kidnapped commanding officer of the prison camp on criminal counts and making him defend his record was without parallel in modern military history."

In the early afternoon, Van Fleet flew into Koje to talk over the situation. He, Ridgway and Clark had decided to permit no press coverage of the emergency. He informed Colson that the negotiating period with the POWs should end at 10 a.m. on May 10, and that Colson had authority to use all the force he required. Meanwhile, Dodd's kangaroo court trial dragged on into the night, and Dodd, who had been supplied with a telephone, asked Colson for an extension until noon on May 10. With Van Fleet's order still in his ear, Colson refused. During the night twenty 3rd Division tanks, five equipped with flamethrowers, arrived on Koje and moved into position.

Early the next morning, with U.S. troops poised for the expected assault on Compound 76, the prisoners dispatched their latest demand to General Colson. Though the English was awkward and not always clear, it constituted a powerful propaganda document and was obviously phrased for a world audience. The POWs demanded:

"1. Immediate ceasing the barbarous behavior, insults, torture, forcible protest with blood writing, threatening, confinement, mass murdering, gun and machine gun shooting, using poison gas, germ weapons, experiment object of A-Bomb, by your command. You should guarantee PW's [prisoners' of war] human rights and individual life with the base on the International Law.

2. Immediate stopping the so-called illegal and unreasonable volunteer repatriation of NKPA [North Korean People's Army] and CPVA [Chinese People's Volunteers Army] PW's.

3. Immediate ceasing the forcible investigation (Screening) which thousands of PW's of NKPA and CPVA be rearmed and falled in slavery, permanently and illegally.

4. Immediate recognition of the P.W. Representative Group (Commission) consisted of NPKA and CPVA PW's and close cooperation to it by your command. This Representative Group will turn in Brig. Gen. Dodd, USA, on your hand after we receive satisfactory declaration to resolve the above items by your command. We will await your warm and sincere answer."

This remarkable POW document gave Colson pause. He had got a disturbing report from his intelligence officer that other compounds were ready to stage a mass breakout as soon as he launched his assault. Giving some credence to this fear was the fact that the Korean villages near the camp were deserted. Yet Colson had 11,000 troops available and could have quickly smashed any uprising. Nevertheless, he held up on the attack, and discussed the matter with General Yount, the Logistics Command chief.

Afterward, Colson replied to the POW demand. He denied the UN

Command committed the offenses alleged, asserted the matter of voluntary repatriation was being decided at Panmunjom, accepted a POW association, and said there would "be no more forcible screening of PW's in this camp, nor will any attempt be made at nominal screening."

The prisoners continued to haggle with Colson, but neither Van Fleet nor Ridgway received up-to-the-minute reports on what was happening. Ridgway was exasperated. Around noon Dodd phoned Colson and presented the prisoners' case. Dodd argued there had been incidents in the past when prisoners had been killed, whereas Colson's answer denied eveything. The problem, Dodd said, was mostly semantics, but the communists would not free him until these questions of meaning were cleared up. Then an astonishing thing happened: with the POW leaders sitting beside him, Dodd passed on their and his own suggestions to Colson to rewrite his reply in a form acceptable to the communists; Dodd even offered to write in the changes the prisoners considered mandatory. Colson then drafted a reply along lines demanded by the prisoners, and General Yount was informed of the general contents of the reply.[9] Here is the response Colson sent:

"1. With reference to your item 1 of that message, I do admit that there has [sic] been instances of bloodshed where many PW have been killed and wounded by UN Forces. I can assure in the future that PW can expect humane treatment in this camp according to the principles of International Law. I will do all within my power to eliminate further violence and bloodshed. If such incidents happen in the future, I will be responsible.

2. Reference your item 2 regarding voluntary repatriation of Korean Peoples Army and Chinese Peoples Volunteer Army PW, that is a matter which is being discussed at Panmunjom. I have no control or influence over the decisions at the peace conference.

3. Regarding your item 3 pertaining to forcible investigation (screening), I can inform you that after General Dodd's release, unharmed, there will be no more forcible screening or any rearming of PW in this camp, nor will any attempt be made at nominal screening.

4. Reference your item 4, we approve the organization of a PW representative group or commission consisting of Korea Peoples Army and Chinese Peoples Volunteer Army, PW, according to the details agreed to by Gen. Dodd and approved by me."

Having achieved this coup, it is no wonder that the communists asked to delay release of General Dodd until the next morning so that, in recognition of his services, he could be decked with flowers and escorted to the gate. But Colson had had enough. He demanded Dodd's immediate release, and at 9:30 p.m. May 10 Dodd walked out of compound 76 and immediately was taken to a place where he was kept incommunicado.

Because the press, excluded from Koje by FEC directive, was getting impatient for news, General Clark decided to publish a statement on the affair. Included in it were the prisoner demands and Colson's reply. The press also met Dodd and he issued a brief report on his capture and release.

Historian Hermes summed up the bitter harvest of the affair: "Colson traded Dodd's life for a propaganda weapon that was far more valuable to the communists than the lives of their prisoners of war."[10]

Van Fleet tended to discount the effects of Colson's letter, but General Clark and the leadership in Washington recognized its extreme damage at once. For an American general officer, whatever the circumstances, to admit mistreatment, killing and wounding of prisoners, and to promise in the future to give prisoners humane treatment was a political disaster. In Tokyo Clark denounced the Colson statement as "unadulterated blackmail," and said POWs had been killed only as a result of violence. In Washington there was talk about repudiating Colson's statement. Truman decided not to use the term, but to do the same thing in other words by having the JCS direct Clark to say Colson's exchange "has no validity whatsoever," as it took place under "duress involving the physical threat to the life of a UN officer." The entire incident, the statement said, was a propaganda effort to becloud the whole prisoner-of-war issue, and Colson had no authority "to purport to accept any of the vicious and false charges."

General Yount established a board to investigate the matter, and it found both Dodd and Colson blameless. General Van Fleet disagreed and recommended both officers be reprimanded. Clark went further. "It is beyond my comprehension how the board could have arrived at such conclusions in the face of the obviously poor judgment displayed by both of these officers," he told the JCS. He recommended both be reduced to the rank of colonel and that Yount be reprimanded because he knew of the damaging passages in Colson's letter but did nothing to have them removed. Clark's recommendations went all the way up to the President, who approved them. They were carried out.

Clark also quickly replaced Colson as camp commandant with Brigadier General Haydon L. Boatner, assistant commander of the 2nd Division. Clark sent in the 187th Airborne RCT and a tank battalion, raising total UN forces to almost 15,000. Boatner proved to be fully equal to the task of bringing Koje's recalcitrant prisoners to order.

At Panmunjom the Reds made the most of the Dodd affair. General

Nam Il said on May 9: "The endless series of bloody incidents occurring in your prisoner of war camps clearly proves that your so-called screening is only a means of retaining forcibly captured personnel of our side." The next day he denounced the UN Command for "systematically taking a series of barbarous measures to attain your long-deliberated objective of forcibly retaining our captured personnel."

The Reds, in world opinion, threatened to push the Americans off the moral high ground they had taken when Truman decided against forcible repatriation. Now the issue was no longer clear.

However, the potentially disastrous situation at Koje-do had to be eliminated, whatever the problems the UN Command had with world opinion. On Koje were more than 80,000 prisoners, including the most extreme elements. Because of the closeness of the compounds to one another, a general prison uprising was possible, and would have been extremely difficult to stop without staggering casualties. Clark's plan was to disperse the prisoners to small 500-man compounds on Koje, on the mainland, and on the island of Cheju, some eighty miles below the southwest coast of the mainland.[11]

When the breakup of the Koje compounds started in earnest on June 10, resistance centered once again on the 6,000 prisoners in Compound 76. General Boatner was not going to negotiate, however, and he sent his troops in armed with tear gas and concussion grenades. The resulting violent clash cost the life of one American soldier and left 14 wounded. The Reds lost 31 killed and 139 wounded. After that, the other compounds submitted without resistance. When the compounds were cleared, guards found 3,000 spears, 1,000 gasoline grenades, 4,500 knives, a large number of barbed-wire flails, clubs and other weapons. In one compound they found the bodies of sixteen prisoners who had been murdered.[12]

CHAPTER 60

Rhee the Despot, Clark the Hawk

WHILE THE UN COMMAND was preoccupied with the extremely bad repercussions of the Dodd kidnapping, South Korea's President Syngman Rhee produced an exhibit of dictatorial and arbitrary behavior that raised widespread doubts about the kind of government the United Nations was supporting in South Korea.

The South Korean constitution required the president to be elected by the National Assembly. Rhee's term as president ended in the summer of 1952, and Rhee knew he stood no chance whatsoever of being re-elected by the Assembly because of the intense opposition to his autocratic methods and his refusal to tolerate any opposition to him. Rhee, therefore, conceived a simple solution: change the constitution to provide for a popular election of the president. Rhee was confident he could sway the people to vote for him. Rhee's many opponents in the National Assembly, however, refused to accept a constitutional change. Rhee thereupon on May 27 declared martial law in the Pusan area, where the ROK government was operating, and arrested some members of the National Assembly on obviously trumped-up charges of treason and complicity with the communists. Other Assembly members, fearful of being arrested, went into hiding.[1]

This clear demonstration of Rhee's contempt for orderly government and his determination to knock down anyone who stood in his way led to turmoil in South Korea, sardonic glee among the communists, and all sorts of wild and extreme plans by the UN Command and the Truman administration to force Rhee back into lawful line, including action by the UN Command to take over martial law in the Pusan area and get Rhee (or if he refused, Prime Minister Min Chang Taek-sang) to end martial law. All these plans came to nothing, however. On July 2, ROK police rounded up scores of South Korean legislators who had been boycotting the sessions and escorted them to the Assembly Hall, along with seven assemblymen on trial in the communist-conspiracy case. The assemblymen spent consecutive nights in the hall working on amendments to the constitution. On July 4 the cowed Assembly voted 163–0 with 3 abstentions to permit direct election of the president and vice president, a bicameral legislature and (as a sop to Assembly feelings) greater cabinet responsibility to the Assembly.[2] In August Rhee won re-election by a landslide, but the affair left a terribly sour taste in the mouths of Americans and allies, and foreshadowed the far greater trouble the UN Command was going to have with this antidemocratic leader of a supposedly democratic republic.

Meanwhile, at Panmunjom, Major (later Lieutenant) General William K. Harrison, Jr., on May 22 replaced Admiral Joy as senior UN delegate upon Joy's reassignment, but Harrison had no better success in bringing the Reds to an agreement than Joy. General Clark, frustrated by the communists' obstinate refusal to budge, decided on an action that American leaders were to employ again in Vietnam: launching massive air attacks in an effort to force the Reds to agree to American demands on peace. Since practically everything of military value in North Korea that could be flattened by bombs had already been flattened, Clark had to search for targets that could hurt North Korea. He found them in eleven hydroelectric generating and two transformer stations that had not been bombed earlier because General Ridgway had vetoed attacks on the ground the electricity generated was used primarily for North Korea's civilian economy, not military purposes, and their destruction would not induce the communists to accept an armistice.

General Clark reversed Ridgway's position and, after getting approval of the Joint Chiefs, the secretaries of defense and state and President Truman, he ordered navy and air force craft on June 23 to undertake a huge, sustained three-day onslaught against the stations. The two services launched more than 1,400 sorties against the targets, and severely damaged the plants. North Korea was thrown into a power blackout for two weeks, and it took a long while for power supplies to be restored.[3]

To the great surprise of Clark and officials in Washington, bombing the power plants caused an enormous uproar throughout the world, not least among American allies. Acheson, in London at the time attending a meeting of foreign ministers, caught a full charge of outrage at close range from British Foreign Secretary Anthony Eden and French Foreign Minister Robert Schuman. Eden was particularly incensed because the

British government had not been notified in advance, and Schuman complained of heavy criticism of the bombings among the French people and lawmakers. There were open expressions among both allies and neutral states that the United States was trigger-happy and committed to a policy of military irresponsibility. Jawaharlal Nehru, prime minister of India, summed up a strong current of world opinion by asserting he was "disturbed at the thought that the future of the United Nations and of war and peace might be decided without proper consultations, and might ultimately depend on the discretion of military commanders who would naturally think much more of local military objectives than of large questions affecting the world."[4] In other words, Nehru reiterated the old saw that wars are too important to be left to the generals.

The United States, therefore, went into the summer negotiations at Panmunjom with two black eyes: bombing the power plants and the Dodd affair, which clouded American motives on voluntary repatriation.

General Clark added to the growing dissatisfaction among the allies by ignoring both world criticism and violent communist outrage and actually stepping up the air attack on North Korea in the summer of 1952. UN aircraft carried out a sustained assault on Pyongyang in July and August which left the NK capital largely flat and totally without military worth. UN aircraft also hit targets along the Yalu and, in one case, struck an oil refinery within eight miles of the Soviet border.[5]

The sustained air attacks on North Korea failed utterly to bring the communists to terms. Although American policy makers had worked throughout the summer to explore various possibilities for breaking the deadlock, nothing succeeded. The Reds and the Americans had reached a complete standstill on the issue of forced repatriation. Other nations privately began offering suggestions on the issue as well, and on September 2 the president of Mexico, Miguel Aleman, sent to the UN secretary-general a proposal that all POWs desiring to be repatriated be sent home at once and that each UN member agree to accept a percentage of the POWs resisting repatriation. This proposal soon was released to the public.[6] Finally, on September 24, President Truman met with all of his top civilian and military advisors to come to some decision on the problem. After his advisors argued a number of proposals, including the Mexican suggestion, Truman came to a firm decision: at Panmumjom General Harrison would lay down three quite similar choices on the POW issue. If the Reds rejected all three, Harrison would declare an indefinite recess and the UN Command would then "be prepared to do such other things as may be necessary," with the implication the war might be extended to China itself if everything else failed.[7]

On September 28 Harrison met the communist delegates and asked them to select from three choices on the prisoner issue: (1) transfer all prisoners to the demilitarized zone (DMZ), where, upon checking, they would be considered to be fully repatriated, except that any prisoner who indicated a desire to return to the side that detained him could do so; (2) transfer to the DMZ those prisoners opposing repatriation, where they would be interviewed on their wishes by a neutral group; (3) transfer these same prisoners to the DMZ, where they would be free to go to the side of their choice.[8]

On October 8 the two delegations assembled again at Panmumjom, and General Nam Il informed the United Nations all three proposals were unacceptable. General Harrison answered with a formal statement calling the communist position unreasonable, inconsistent and inhuman and concluded that the UN Command had no further proposals to make and therefore was calling a recess. Total impasse finally had been reached—one year and three months after the truce talks had begun.[9]

In Tokyo General Clark issued a statement that the UN Command had striven to end the war, but that the enemy had refused to allow the POW issue "to be resolved in accord with moral dictates which most of humanity holds to be fundamental." In Washington Acheson asserted: "We shall not trade in the lives of men. We shall not forcibly deliver human beings into communist hands."[10]

The collapse of the truce talks brought immediate reaction on the battle line and in the POW camps. On cue the prisoners stepped up their rioting and other disorders, deliberately courting harsh measures from the guards seeking to control them. This resulted in the killing and wounding of prisoners by UN guards, and gave the communists opportunities to charge that their men were being subjected to continued murders and other atrocities.[11] The communist POWs, excellently directed by orders from the communist high command, were serving their countries in the continuing war against the United Nations.

On the battlefront a series of small but bloody engagements had been going on since September as the Reds attempted to improve their positions before winter set in. On October 8, the day General Harrison unilaterally recessed the peace talks, General Clark authorized General Van Fleet to launch Operation Showdown, designed to seize the hills of the Iron Triangle north of Kumwha. Van Fleet predicted he could capture the objective in about five days at a cost of some two hundred casualties. But the attack by IX Corps, launched October 14, ground on for weeks in gruesome fighting against fierce Red resistance. It cost 9,000 U.S. and ROK and 19,000 communist casualties. When the attacks petered out on November 18, the UN Command had achieved only a slight improvement in its position, and the cost had been excessive. Direct assaults on enemy main lines of resistance to achieve limited objectives were futile.[12] In an attempt to draw the Reds out of their prepared defenses along the MLR, Eighth Army on October 15 faked an amphibious landing by the 8th Cavalry Regiment at Kojo, on the east coast about twenty-five miles below Wonsan. But the Reds would not be decoyed out of their positions, and the simulated assault was a flop.[13]

With no prospects of breaking the communists' determination at Panmunjom, the Far East Command and the Pentagon began to consider seriously a course of action if the peace talks failed. Military operations officers had been coming up with plan after plan ever since the talks had started running into snags, but nothing had been decided definitely. Then, on October 16, eight days after the Reds rejected Harrison's final offer on prisoners, General Clark forwarded to the Joint Chiefs his Oplan 8–52, which was designed to turn the war around abruptly by seeking a military decision. Oplan 8–52 called for a major amphibious assault, enveloping attacks to destroy the maximum number of enemy troops, airborne assaults on targets of opportunity, and—most significantly—air and naval attacks on targets in China and Manchuria and a naval blockade of China.[14] Thus Clark, who only two weeks after assuming command in the Far East had asked the Joint Chiefs to approve sending Nationalist Chinese divisions to fight in Korea,[15] wanted to follow MacArthur's belligerent course further and launch vindictive blows against mainland China. The theory that the communists could be encouraged to accept American peace proposals if only they were bombed enough was being carried to its ultimate conclusion.

In a letter going along with the plan, Clark pointed out that Oplan 8–52 made no provision for the use of atomic weapons, but he urged that serious consideration be given to removing the restriction on employing A-bombs. Clark said he believed nuclear weapons would be essential if he was to make the most effective use of his air power against targets of opportunity and to neutralize enemy air bases in Manchuria and North China.[16]

There it was: a blueprint for a greatly widened war in Asia with the possibility of expanding it into a nuclear holocaust.

Clark's plan got opposition form Secretary of the Army Frank Pace on the grounds of cost and manpower, but there was a far more cogent reason for the Joint Chiefs of Staff to sit on his proposal: the election of the President of the United States was going to take place in a little more than two weeks, and neither of the candidates for that election was Harry S. Truman.[17]

The Joint Chiefs had reason for pause regarding expanding the war because, almost from the start of the 1952 presidential election campaign, national policy about Korea was under intense scrutiny—and from the Republicans was under severe attack. Although Adlai Stevenson, the Democratic candidate, loyally defended the Democratic Truman administration's record, he agreed with Dwight D. Eisenhower, the Republican candidate, on seeking an end to the fighting by political means. Neither candidate advocated achieving a clear-cut military victory.[18]

The strong possibility of a Republican victory promised a likelihood of a change in the direction of the war. The screeching stop to any decision on expanding the war, however, came on October 24—eight days after Clark submitted his Oplan 8–52—when General Eisenhower made his climactic speech on Korea in Detroit. Whether this speech was what pushed Eisenhower over to victory is not certain, but it very likely was the catalyst, because it confirmed in many Americans the feeling that they had, in Eisenhower, the man who somehow would make everything right. Analyzed carefully, Eisenhower's Detroit speech offered nothing new and promised nothing. But it was just what many Americans wanted to hear, and it created a new and exciting hope that commonsensical Ike could work it out where Truman and his supersophisticated and devious secretary of state, Acheson, had failed.

Eisenhower at Detroit pledged that his one goal would be to bring the Korean War "to an early and honorable end." He said he would begin with a simple resolution: "to forego the diversions of politics and to concentrate on the job of ending the Korean War—until the job is honorably done. That job requires a personal trip to Korea. I shall make that trip. Only in that way could I learn how best to serve the American people in the cause of peace. I shall go to Korea."[19]

"I shall go to Korea." It had an electric and conclusive ring to it, as if Ike could fly out to Korea, ride around the roads and talk with the generals and the GIs, and somehow in a few days discover the secret key to peace which had eluded everyone else. Of course it was absurd. And Eisenhower, one of the most experienced field commanders of the twentieth century, knew better than almost anyone else that his trip was to be only a public-relations tour to impress the folks at home. But to many American people it promised precisely what they had hoped for: thumbs down on the war-hungry men who clamored for a vengeful extension of the war to China, and, in Korea, peace.

It is no wonder that General Collins was less than commital when he responded to Clark's battle plan on November 7—three days after Eisenhower had won 442 electoral votes to Stevenson's 89 and had secured a 5–4 margin in the popular vote. Collins told Clark the Chiefs were studying Oplan 8–52 and would consider his views on the use of atomic weapons, but "our worldwide commitments for personnel and logistical support are extremely heavy, and I cannot give you any indication at this time as to what action may be taken."[20]

CHAPTER 61

Others Take a Hand

THE UNITED STATES was already deeply suspect by many moderate nations because they perceived American bellicosity was growing with increased American frustration at Panmunjom. This, plus the abrupt breakdown of the truce talks, made it inevitable the United Nations would attempt to take into their hands the responsibility for ending a war that was ostensibly a UN affair, though it had been virtually dictated from the start by the United States. When the seventh General Assembly of the United Nations convened in New York on October 14, the State Department tried to head off the takeover movement by rallying support for the U.S. position. During the next few weeks several members introduced proposals to end the war, including the Mexicans, who offered Aleman's suggestion. But it was an Indian initiative in November which quickly overshadowed all the others. The Indians proposed a four-nation Repatriation Commission to take charge of all prisoners. Those individuals desiring to return home would be allowed to do so. Each side then would be given access to the remaining prisoners to "explain" their right to be repatriated; those who, after ninety days, still opposed going home would be dealt with at the post-armistice political conference. Any disputes within the Repatriation Commission would be resolved by an umpire.[1]

The Indian plan quickly gained widespread support, especially from Britain, Canada and France, and the United States could only get the draft amended to assure that no force would be used against prisoners, and that, if the postwar political conference made no decision on nonrepatriates in thirty days, they would be turned over to the United Nations. The Indian resolution passed on December 3. It was quickly rejected by Red China and North Korea, but its ideas were by no means dead.[2]

471

President-elect Eisenhower arrived in Korea on December 2, accompanied by his secretary of defense designate, Charles E. Wilson, and by General Omar Bradley and Admiral Arthur W. Radford, commander of the Pacific fleet. Generals Clark and Van Fleet conferred with Eisenhower and conducted him on tours of the combat zone and other areas during his three-day stay. There was, naturally, nothing new Eisenhower could learn from the generals about achieving peace, and the talks were largely about increasing the ROK army to twenty divisions, using Nationalist Chinese troops in Korea, and various military matters. Eisenhower endorsed eventual expansion of the ROK army, but made no commitment on use of Nationalist Chinese troops. However, after becoming President, Eisenhower did cancel President Truman's 1950 order prohibiting any Nationalist Chinese action against mainland China. Clark's Oplan 8–52 was not discussed, though Ike was aware of it. Eisenhower was seeking an honorable truce in Korea, not an expansion of the war in search of a military victory. As Clark later wrote, "The question of how much it would take to win the war was never raised."[3]

Meanwhile, the issue of alleged UN atrocities in the prison camps would not go away as the Reds continued to orchestrate disturbances. On December 14, communist civilian internees on the small island of Pongam near Koje-do staged a well-organized uprising which drew prisoners and ROK guards into a confrontation. Guards fired into massed prisoners and killed 85 and wounded 113 seriously. To many people the toll seemed too high. The Red Cross complained, and the Soviet Union made an effort in the United Nations to condemn the United States for "mass murder" of prisoners at Pongam-do. The Soviet effort failed, however, by a 45–5 vote, but ten nations abstained, indicating considerable dissatisfaction with the prisoner situation.[4]

* * * * * * * * *

It is strange, but an event little noticed at the time and wholly extraneous to the Panmunjom peace talks was the stimulus that finally broke the prisoner deadlock and led to the decision on both sides at last to reach an agreement. The event took place in December, 1952, at a meeting in Geneva of the executive committee of the League of Red Cross Societies. By a vote of 15–2 (Soviets and Chinese Communists opposed) the committee urged, as a "goodwill gesture," that both sides in Korea immediately repatriate sick and wounded prisoners.[5]

In Tokyo General Clark read a news report of the Red Cross group's action, and proposed such an exchange—not because he thought the Reds would agree, but because it had propaganda advantages. Clark's suggestion fell on deaf ears in Washington, however, and it was not until February 22, 1953, that it was approved, because the State Department had learned the Red Cross proposal might be introduced into the UN General Assembly, which was scheduled to meet shortly.[6]

The communists did not respond until March 28. Then the North Korean and Red Chinese commanders accepted the offer of an exchange and went further: the exchange should lead to a settlement of the entire POW question.[7] Two days later there was an even more significant breakthrough: Premier Zhou Enlai repeated the commanders' offer over Radio Beijing. "The time should be considered ripe for settling the entire question of prisoners of war in order to insure the cessation of hostilities," Zhou broadcast. His solution was similar to the Indian proposal passed December 3 in the General Assembly. After all prisoners desiring repatriation had been exchanged, Zhou said, the remaining prisoners should be handed over "to a neutral state so as to insure a just solution to the question of their repatriation."

Next day the Chinese telegraphed the proposal to the president of the UN General Assembly, Lester Pearson of Canada. It was endorsed by North Korea, and on April 1 was lauded over Radio Moscow for its "entire fairness" by V. M. Molotov, Soviet foreign minister.[8] No one knows what influence, if any, the death on March 5, 1953, of Soviet Premier Stalin had on the sudden melting of communist intransigence. Whatever the reason, Red obstructionism was replaced by Red cooperation, and by April 20 the exchange had started at Panmunjom. Called Little Switch by the UN Command, the transfer of sick and wounded prisoners went off without serious difficulty and was essentially completed by May 3. The United Nations returned 5,194 North Korean and 1,034 Chinese POWs, plus 446 civilian internees. In exchange, the UN Command received 471 ROK soldiers, 149 Americans, 32 Britons, 15 Turks and 17 other UN prisoners (total: 684).[9]

The thaw resulted in resumption of the truce talks at Panmunjom on April 26, but the delegates immediately bogged down in an effort to name the neutral nation that would supervise the prisoner exchange. This dispute lasted until May 7, when the Reds abruptly abandoned the idea of a single neutral nation and proposed a Neutral Nations Repatriation Commission (NNRC), similar to the Indian proposal in the United Nations in the fall. This commission would be made up of a representative from India and by members of the Neutral Nations Supervisory Commission that had finally been named previously (Poland, Czechoslovakia, Switzerland and Sweden). Each was to provide equal numbers of troops to control the repatriation. This proposal was close to the American requirements. The UN Command wanted, however, for all troops used to be Indian, the commission to operate only on the basis of unanimous (not majority) vote, and for prisoners not disposed of within thirty days by the postwar political conference to be released to civilian status. The Reds balked at these demands, and the talks went on.[10]

The two sides were extremely close to an agreement; the remaining issues were relatively minor and could be resolved by compromise. At this time, however, the irrational obstructionism of the old autocrat Syngman Rhee erupted to threaten the prospects of an armistice. Running like a Wagnerian leitmotiv through the entire truce talks had been Rhee's frequently repeated opposition to an armistice of any kind. Rhee wanted to conquer all of Korea, with American help, he hoped, and he never wavered from this aim. When the talks started, Rhee demanded as a price of his approval the complete withdrawal of Chinese troops and the disarmament of North Korea, among other things. He made radio broadcasts trying to torpedo the talks, staged mass meetings, and issued official press releases opposing the UN negotiations. A typical Rhee statement was this one on April 14, 1952: "I cannot understand the sentiments of those who believe cease-fire talks will succeed. I am still opposed to any cease-fire which leaves our country divided. No matter what arguments others may make, we are determined to unify our fatherland with our own hands."[11]

In April, 1953, however, with Operation Little Switch under way and the prospects strong for final agreement on an armistice, Rhee became more and more outspoken in his opposition to peace and he indicated that South Korea might go it alone against the communists if the United Nations agreed to a cease-fire.[12] On May 12 Rhee informed General Clark he would not allow North Korean nonrepatriates to be released to neutral states, and, moreover, did not consider India a neutral state, and would allow no Indian troops in South Korea. Trying to accommodate Rhee, Clark attempted to get the Reds to allow all Korean POWs who did not want repatriation to be released immediately upon the signing of an armistice, a proposal which the Reds naturally rejected on May 13. This led to another period of unproductive argument and a recess until May 25.[13]

Meanwhile Clark, still convinced that continued air attacks would bring the Reds to terms, decided to bomb North Korean dams that held back water to irrigate the farmers' rice paddies. These dams, Clark believed, would be legitimate military targets because breaking them would send flood waters over roads and railways and thus disrupt enemy communications. He ordered the first bombing May 13 against a dam near Toksan, north of Pyongyang. The resulting flood took out six miles of railway lines, five railway bridges and two miles of road. It also destroyed or damaged 3,200 acres of rice paddies. During the next ten days, UN aircraft attacked two other dams, but the Reds reacted quickly after the first bombing and lowered the water levels in the reservoirs, thus preventing floods.[14]

It was during this period of recess in the talks at Panmunjom that the Joint Chiefs of Staff met with the National Security Council on May 20 and presented their recommendations on the course the United States should take in the event the talks broke down completely—*and* the United States made a determination to extend the war to reach a decision. This may be the origin of the often repeated assertion that President Eisenhower finally brought the Reds to heel only by threatening to use the atomic bomb on them. The Chiefs' plan, however, by no means committed the United States to any such action, and the Reds were not handed an ultimatum. Rather, the JCS recommendations were only contingency plans that had long been considered for possible use if the Far East situation deteriorated to such a degree that the United States would be willing to risk global war. Eisenhower had already indicated he was seeking a peaceful solution to the Korean impasse, not a wider war. Therefore the Chiefs recommended in a dire emergency intensified air and naval operations against mainland China and "extensive strategical and tactical use of atomic bombs," but urged their employment so as to obtain "maximum surprise and maximum impact." This call for surprise eliminated the possibility that the Reds might be delivered an ultimatum.[15]

By mid-May 1953 the major deterrent to an armistice was, in any case, not the communist leadership in Pyongyang and Beijing, but the South Korean leader himself, Syngman Rhee. It is ironic, but the ultimate obstacle to peace in Korea was posed, not by the enemy, but by an ally.

Clark thought Rhee was bluffing, and felt that if South Korea was offered a mutual-security pact by the United States, along with economic aid and help to build the ROK army to twenty divisions, the South Korean president could be brought to terms.[16] As a result, when the Panmunjom talks began again on May 25, U.S. officials decided to drop the Rhee-appeasing demand to release all Korean POWs immediately after an armistice.[17]

An hour before the delegates met at Panmunjom, President Rhee received General Clark and Ellis O. Briggs, who had replaced John J. Muccio as U.S. ambassador to Korea the previous November. Clark and Briggs tried to soften the blow by assuring Rhee that if he cooperated fully with the armistice agreement the United States would support him militarily, economically and politically. Rhee's response was total rejection: "You can withdraw all UN forces, all economic aid. We will decide our own fate. We do not ask anyone to fight for us. We made our mistake perhaps in the beginning by relying upon democracy to assist us. Sorry, but I cannot assure President Eisenhower of my cooperation under the present circumstances."[18]

At Panmunjom, in pleasant contrast, the atmosphere was positively rosy. General Harrison presented the UN Command's terms: no force could be used against prisoners by the neutral commission; India must provide all the troops; all persuasion ("explanations") to prisoners who did not want to return home had to be completed in ninety days; and if the postarmistice political conference could not agree within thirty days on the fate on nonrepatriates, the nonrepatriates' disposition would be referred to the UN General Assembly. Instead of attacking the UN Command again, the Reds only mildly criticized it, and the two sides recessed until June 4. On that date, the communists agreed to an armistice and presented an agreement which varied from the UN document only in giving no role to the UN General Assembly in regard to nonrepatriates. The Red proposal provided simply that those not disposed of by the political conference would be released. On June 5 the UN delegation approved the communist version, subject to clarification of a few points.[19]

On June 8, both sides signed the repatriation agreement. It set up the Neutral Nations Repatriation Commission (NNRC), provided that all prisoners who wished to return home would be permitted to do so within sixty days, and then picked up the agreement worked out regarding nonrepatriates.

The central valley of Koje-do, where most of the compounds housing North Korean and Chinese prisoners of war were located. Near here also is where Brigadier General Francis T. Dodd, camp commandant, was captured by POWs and released only after another U.S. general issued a highly damaging statement indicating POWs had been killed and abused.

Extremely crowded POW enclosures on Koje-do reduced United Nations control and permitted Red POW leaders to direct riots and other violence by prisoners.

A Fifth Air Force F-51 Mustang drops napalm jellied gasoline tanks on an industrial target in North Korea in August, 1951.

As the Korean War went on, American air power methodically demolished virtually everything in North Korea having any military significance whatsoever. Here supply warehouses at the east-coast port of Wonsan are bombed in July, 1951.

A marine F4U Corsair pulls up from a bombing run on a Chinese-held hill in western Korea in October, 1952.

President-elect Dwight D. Eisenhower (left) *watches as a South Korean lieutenant points out on a sand table the location of his division's units. Eisenhower's promise to voters that "I shall go to Korea" helped his election in November, 1952, but he learned little on his visit in December to guide him in ending the war.*

A widely distributed photo showing a child killed in what the Red Chinese called a 1953 U.S. B-29 attack on the Manchurian border city of Antung, opposite Sinuiju on the Yalu River.

General Mark W. Clark, Far East commander, signs the Korean armistice agreement on July 27, 1953, after two years of negotiation, during which hundreds of thousands of men were killed and wounded in continued hostilities.

North Korean Premier Kim Il Sung prepares to sign armistice document handed to him July 27, 1953, by General Nam Il, head of the communist delegation at Panmunjom.

Chinese Communist commander Peng Deh-huai signs Korean armistice at Kaesong.

CHAPTER 62

The Final Crisis

PEACE SEEMED TO BE only a few days away. But Syngman Rhee already had thrown a monkey wrench into the armistice works. On June 6 he announced the UN agreement was unacceptable and called instead for mutual withdrawal of all United Nations and communist forces, to be preceded first by a U.S.-ROK mutual-defense treaty. If neither was acceptable, then, Rhee said, "we must be allowed to continue the fighting."[1]

Still trying to placate the South Korean strong man, Eisenhower sent a letter which promised to continue to seek peaceful unification of Korea, prompt negotiation *after* the armistice of a mutual-defense treaty, and economic aid. "Even the thought of separation at this critical hour," Eisenhower wrote "would be a tragedy."[2] General Clark and Ambassador Briggs presented Eisenhower's letter to Rhee, who showed no interest in it. He declared again he would not permit Indian troops in his country and Korean prisoners would not submit to "indoctrination" by communist persuaders. As General Clark told the JCS, "Rhee was utterly unreasonable and gave no ground whatsoever. He himself is the only one who knows how far he will go but undoubtedly he will bluff right up to the last."[3]

Rhee immediately ordered the return of all ROK officers training in the United States and recalled the ROK delegate on the UN armistice delegation. Throughout South Korea demonstrations erupted with unprecedented anti-American feelings. Rhee and other government officials continued to make threatening remarks.[4]

Meanwhile, on the battle front, Lieutenant General Maxwell D. Taylor, who had taken over February 11 as commander of Eighth Army upon Van Fleet's retirement, had to contend with a series of communist attacks. It was a sure sign the communists were sincere about an

477

armistice, because they wanted to improve their positions prior to the end of the fighting.

The Red assaults started in earnest on the western front on May 25, the day the talks recommenced at Panmunjom. Early in June they shifted to the east-central part of the line where Chinese forces began to drive to eliminate a shallow UN bulge, about eight miles wide, which thrust up close to Kumsong. By June 18, when the attacks slackened, the ROK troops who held this sector had been driven back about two miles.[5] All along the line the Chinese concentrated their attacks largely against ROK units, as if to show the South Koreans how difficult it would be for them to fight a war alone.

In the face of Rhee's continued defiance, John Foster Dulles, President Eisenhower's secretary of state, decided to send Walter S. Robertson, assistant secretary of state for Far Eastern affairs, to see Rhee to clear up "misunderstanding as to our post-armistice policies." On June 17, Rhee told Ambassador Briggs he would be happy to see Robertson.[6]

That night Syngman Rhee ordered, and ROK troops carried out, an act of betrayal to South Korea's allies that caused many Americans to feel like throwing up their hands in despair and, as Rhee clearly hoped to do, cast doubt on Red acceptance of an armistice. Rhee directed ROK guards at four prison camps to assist in the breakout of North Korean prisoners who did not want repatriation. U.S. camp commanders and administrative personnel at these camps—at San Mu Dai, Nonsam, Masan and Pusan—were completely unable to stem the flow of this human tide, which quickly evaporated into the South Korean countryside, where the North Koreans were assisted by ROK government officials. About 25,000 of the 35,000 North Koreans who resisted repatriation escaped the first day and smaller numbers on succeeding days from these and four other camps. By the end of the month, the UN Command had only 8,600 North Korean nonrepatriates in custody.[7]

Rhee, having been turned down by the Americans on his demand that Korean prisoners not wishing to return home be released upon signing an armistice, took unilateral action to insure just this for most of the prisoners. This deed was an undeniable violation of the agreement the UN Command had made with the communists. Therefore, if it caused the Reds to refuse an armistice, so much the better, so far as Rhee was concerned.

Rhee frankly admitted his complicity with this statement: "I have on my own responsibility ordered the release of the anti-communist Korean prisoners on this day, June 18th, 1953. The reason why I did this without full consultation with the United Nations command and other authorities concerned is too obvious to explain. The governors and police officers in the various provinces have been instructed to take care of these released war prisoners to their best ability. We trust all our people and our friends will cooperate in this so that there will be no unnecessary misunderstanding anywhere."[8]

General Clark had predicted earlier that Rhee was capable of releasing the North Korean nonrepatriates. He even considered replacing the ROK guards with U.S. troops at the compounds holding these prisoners, but decided against it because it "would only irritate an already sensitive situation."[9]

At Panmunjom, General Harrison had the unenviable job of admitting frankly to the communist delegates what had happened. On June 18 he delivered to the Red liaison officers a letter making clear the ROK complicity in the escapes and assuring the Reds that U.S. troops were taking over guard duties at the camps and would make every effort to round up escapees (few were, however, given ROK government efforts to disperse them into the populace). The communists called for a meeting on June 20 in which they accused the UN Command of deliberately having connived with the "Rhee clique." But it was evident the Americans were more surprised at Rhee's action than the communists were, since they thoroughly distrusted Rhee. Therefore, after the obligatory rapping of the Americans' knuckles, the Reds went on to the crux of the matter: "Is the United Nations Command able to control the South Korean government and army? If not, does the armistice in Korea include the Syngman Rhee clique? If it is not included, what assurance is there for the implementation of the armistice agreement on the part of South Korea?" If South Korea was to be included, then the Reds said the UN Command had to recover the 25,000 North Korean POWs and guarantee such events would not recur in the future.[10]

Clark advised the Joint Chiefs the UN Command obviously could not control the ROK government or army and the armistice did not include South Korea.[11] With that the matter rested for the moment. Washington had decided to send Walter Robertson to negotiate with Rhee.

Accompanied by General Collins, Robertson arrived in Tokyo on June 24, and both at once went into a meeting with General Clark, Ambassador Robert D. Murphy, UN Command political advisor, and Ambassador Briggs from Korea. The men agreed that if Rhee remained uncompromising, Robertson should tell him the United Nations would get out of Korea. Implied in this would be readiness of the UN Command to make an agreement with the communists to withdraw all UN forces and release U.S. and UN prisoners, and leave everything else, including security of his country, to Rhee. The officials believed that if Rhee was convinced the United States meant business, he might change his mind.[12] Here was developing a giant game of "chicken," because the United States, after all it had invested and suffered in Korea and after deciding the peninsula was important to U.S. security after all, was not going to fold its tents and steal silently away, Rhee or no Rhee. The United States might threaten and posture, but it would not carry out the threat. The question was whether Rhee knew this.

Threatening withdrawal represented a change in American policy. Therefore, the officials queried Washington. On June 25 President Eisenhower met with Secretary of Defense Wilson, Secretary of State Dulles and the Joint Chiefs. Eisenhower decided to give Clark the authority to act as he felt necessary, except that Clark could not use force to make the ROKs comply with an armistice. Eisenhower also directed that Clark could not commit the UN Command to withdraw from Korea, but he was authorized to make ROK leaders believe a withdrawal would come if they did not comply with the armistice.[13]

Rhee meanwhile was tightening the screws himself. On June 21 he ordered surveillance of all Koreans working for UN personnel, a decision that at once dried up U.S. counterintelligence sources. Rhee ordered English-speaking linguists to be drafted into the army. At the ports of Pusan and Inchon, Korean workers suddenly stopped working for the UN Command. Korean drivers of embassy vehicles were afraid to go on the streets for fear they would be arrested by Korean National Police as draft dodgers. Even Koreans who performed housekeeping work for U.S. units were intimidated. Demonstrations broke out all over South Korea.[14]

Beginning June 26, Robertson commenced a series of meetings with Rhee that at first made little progress. General Clark began measures to create an impression of impending withdrawal of UN troops. He called conferences of high-level U.S. commanders, consolidated nonrepatriate Korean POWs into fewer compounds, slowed down shipments of supplies to Korea and halted shipment of equipment to four new ROK divisions being activated. On July 1 Rhee backed off to the degree that he agreed to moving of POWs to the DMZ so Indian troops and the Neutral Nations Repatriation Commission would not be in ROK territory. Then he added: "We are very near to an agreement not to obstruct the armistice, provided the U.S. definitely pledges to resume fighting with us, in case of a failure of the political conferences, until the unification of Korea is accomplished."[15] If the United States agreed to this, it would constitute a blank check for Rhee, and leave him no incentive at all to come to an agreement with North Koreans on anything at a postwar conference. Robertson came back, after Washington approval, essentially with a reiteration of the President's position: a mutual-defense treaty, provided the Senate approved; aid in building the ROK army to twenty divisions; economic aid to Korea, subject to congressional approval; and cooperation with Korea at the political conference.[16]

The ROK government responded with the request that the armistice be postponed until the Senate ratified the mutual-defense treaty. Robertson said such a delay could not considered, but the Eisenhower administration would move as quickly as possible to complete the treaty.[17]

The climax came on July 9 when Secretary Robertson was able to extract from Rhee a promise that, although South Korea would not sign the armistice, "we shall not obstruct it, so long as no measures or actions taken under the armistice are detrimental to our national survival." Rhee also said he would "endeavor to cooperate fully and earnestly in the political and peaceful achievement of reunification of our nation, which is our most fundamental national objective and necessity."[18]

It had been an exhausting fight. The United States had stopped Rhee's active opposition to an armistice, but had saddled itself with highly expensive commitments, not only in regard to a mutual-security treaty (ratified by the U.S. Senate in January, 1954) but in regard to long-term financial and military support of the ROK government. It also had locked itself to Syngman Rhee.

While American leaders were battling with Rhee, communist forces on the battle line began their last attacks. These were designed partly as a propaganda move to show the communists were winning militarily at the very last, partly to punish the ROK army, and partly to establish the best possible long-term armistice-line positions. The attacks started on June 24 in the eastern and central sectors, concentrating again in the Kumsong bulge. When both sides decided to go back to the bargaining table at Panmunjom on July 10 (Rhee having been placated), the fighting on the front reached its climax. By July 14 six Chinese divisions had pressed savagely against the ROK positions in the Kumsong bulge and had practically destroyed the ROK Capital Division and much of the ROK 3rd Division. Casualties on both sides were extremely heavy, because it was a stand-up fight directly on the main line of resistance with direct assaults by the communists into the heart of the ROK defensive positions. In this last, sad series of battles, thousands of young men died or were maimed for mere yards of territory. UN casualties for June and July, 1953, were more than 52,000 men, mostly ROKs. Estimated casualties for communist troops in the same period were 108,000.[19]

At Panmunjom both sides jockeyed for last-minute assurances, and in South Korea Rhee began to try to welsh on his deal, but got nowhere with a now thoroughly disgusted Eisenhower. On July 23 staff officers at Panmunjom agreed on the demarcation line and DMZ. Finally at 11 a.m. on July 27, in ceremonies characterized by frigid politeness, Generals Harrison and Nam Il each signed nine copies of the armistice and a brief supplementary agreement authorizing the turnover of nonrepatriates to the Neutral Nations Repatriation Commission in the DMZ. Later General Clark signed at his advanced headquarters at Munsan-ni, while Kim Il Sung, the North Korean chief, and Peng De-huai, the Chinese commander, signed in their headquarters. Twelve hours later the war finally ended, three years, one month and two days after it started.[20]

Afterward, the neutral-nations inspection teams were quickly shown to be a failure because the UN Command decided the Reds were bypassing them and secretly bringing arms and men into Korea. Therefore the great effort the UN Command had made to get inspection teams was nullified.[21]

The "greater sanction" statement, which the United States was relying on to discourage any renewed Far East aggression, was signed on July 27 in Washington by the nations having troops in Korea. But it was not released publicly for a week because American allies were less than enthusiastic about giving any pledges to Syngman Rhee's government. When it was released, it was buried, because of allied reticence, at the end of a special report of the UN Command on the armistice and history of the negotiations. Though the statement indicated a breach of the armistice might result in extending hostilities beyond Korea, it got little attention. One fact was clear to nearly everyone: the nations that had backed the United States in Korea—and had seen a police action escalate into an agonizingly long war of attrition—were not about to rush in once again without long and sober contemplation.[22]

Finally, the postarmistice political conference designed to bring North and South Korea together was not even held until April, 1954, and then only as part of a conference at Geneva which is notable for producing the partition of Vietnam that ended the first (French) Indochina War. Regarding Korea, nothing was achieved.[23]

The prisoners exchange (Big Switch) began at Panmunjom on August 5 and was completed by September 6. The Reds repatriated 7,862 ROKs who wanted to come home, 3,597 Americans, 945 Britons, 229 Turks, and 140 other UN soldiers. A total of 335 South Koreans, 23 Americans and one Briton refused repatriation. Of these, eight South Koreans decided later to return to their country, two went to India and the remainder went back to North Korea. Two Americans decided to return to the U.S. and twenty-one went back to North Korea, as did the lone Briton. On the communist side, 70,183 North Koreans and 5,640 Chinese went home as voluntary repatriates. A total of 14,704 Chinese refused repatriation; of these, 440 later decided to return to China, 12 went to India, 17 died, escaped or were missing, and 14,235 returned to South Korea and most ultimately went on to Taiwan. A total of 7,900 North Koreans refused repatriation; of these, 188 later went home, 74 went to India, 34 died, escaped or were missing, and 7,604 returned to South Korea.[24]

The final number of prisoners, repatriates and nonrepatriates, on both sides was 118,917. The dispute over their fate consumed more than a year, during which time many thousands of men died or were wounded in battle. In the last four months of the war alone, 200,000 UN and communist soldiers were battle casualties.[25]

The United States suffered 139,272 casualties in the entire war, not counting frostbite cases and other injuries. Of these 24,965 were killed, 101,368 wounded, and 12,939 were missing and presumed dead. South Korea suffered 272,975 losses: 46,812 killed, 159,727 wounded, and 66,436 missing and presumed dead. Other UN nations lost 14,103 men: 2,597 killed, 9,581 wounded, and 1,925 missing. On the communist side Joint Chiefs estimates were that the North Koreans suffered 620,264 casualties: 214,899 killed, 303,685 wounded and 101,680 missing. The Chinese sustained 909,607 casualties: 401,401 killed, 486,995 wounded, and 21,211 missing.[26]

Total battle casualties on both sides therefore were 1,956,000. More than two million civilians in North and South Korea were killed or injured. In addition much of South Korea and practically all of North Korea were shattered. It would take many years to repair the damage.

Perhaps leaders on both sides should have read and heeded Sun Tzu, who wrote in *The Art of War*, in 500 B.C.: "In all history, there is no instance of a country having benefited from prolonged warfare."[27]

CHAPTER 63

The Long Shadow of the Korean War

THE FAILURE OF THE UNITED STATES to win the Korean War so profoudly disturbed American leaders that they spent much effort over the next two decades attempting to hurt Red China, the country which had prevented victory.

This urge for revenge caused the United States to focus much of its strength and attention against a country that, in fact, posed practically no danger and was seeking virtually the same international goals in East Asia as the U.S.: peace, trade and keeping the Soviet Union at a distance.

American leaders vindictively refused to see this and maintained instead that Red China was obsessed with a desire to conquer all of East Asia. This was patently untrue. But American leaders to a large extent actually believed the charges of aggression which they had begun leveling at Beijing as soon as Red China intervened in the Korean War. Yet the wish was father to the thought, for American leaders were so incensed by the Chinese action that they required the existence of an aggressive China in order to justify their ardent longing to destroy the regime which had so thoroughly thwarted the United States.

The top political and military leaders conveyed to the American people an upbeat message when the guns finally stopped. They gave the impression that the U.S. had actually won because it had stopped the march of Communism. For a long time Americans as a whole accepted this judgment or a least the belief that the war had been no worse than a draw. Anyway, they were grateful the bloodletting had ceased and the war had not escalated into a world conflict.

But in their hearts and private counsels the top American leaders nurtured a deep sense of frustration, made all the more acute because they were unable to express it publicly. They knew they could have attained in 1951 virtually the same peace they finally achieved in 1953. They knew all the pain, sacrifice and losses in the intervening two years had gone for naught, that the final battle line of 1953 was only insignificantly different from the line in 1951 and that the terms the U.S. had accepted in 1953 could have been achieved two years previously.

Beyond that, they knew—although few of the American public had grasped the fact—that the Red Chinese had blocked their plans to conquer North Korea and consolidate it with Syngman Rhee's South Korea. This had been the sole reason for the invasion of North Korea after the Inchon invasion of September 1950, and when it failed they knew, as scarcely any of the public did, that the war had been pursued thereafter essentially without purpose.

Most frustrating of all was the realization that the Red Chinese, with pitifully poor weapons and a laughably primitive supply system, had halted the United States, the most powerful nation on earth with a glittering array of modern technology, sophisticated industry and advanced weapons.

To defeat the enemy which had bested the United States now became a major object of American foreign policy. Indeed, the animosity that flowed out of the frustrations of the Korean War elevated the anger toward the People's Republic into something resembling a blood feud, pursued with a passion, doggedness and irrationality all out of keeping with the danger and utterly unlike the far-cooler disputes it conducted with any other nation, including the Soviet Union.

Omar Bradley, when chairman of the Joint Chiefs of Staff in 1951, had stated eloquently that a conflict with Red China would be the "wrong war" against the "wrong enemy"—given the immense danger the United States faced from the nuclear-armed Soviet Union. Although American leaders recognized this reality and had in fact declined to attack the People's Republic directly, they harbored a far deeper resentment against Beijing than they ever entertained against the Kremlin.

This can be shown in two examples. First, the U.S. imposed sanctions which virtually prohibited trade with Red China, in an effort to slow or prevent development of a modern industrial state in China. These sanctions were stiffer than those imposed on the Soviet Union and were known as the "China differential." Washington pressured other countries to adopt similar sanctions and, though most countries relaxed them in the late 1960s, the United States continued them for two decades.[1]

The second proof of special U.S. animus was the decision of the National Security Council on November 5, 1953, less than four months after the Korean War ended, to adopt as official U.S. policy the destruction of the Chinese Communist regime, a resolve the NSC never made against the Soviet Union.[2]

To justify its extremely confrontational position, the U.S. had to maintain that the Red Chinese were incorrigibly aggressive. American leaders created in their minds three examples of such aggression: the Chinese intervention in Korea, Beijing's intent to seize Taiwan and Chinese support of the Communist Vietminh revolt which had been going on since 1946 against the French in Vietnam.

Yet none of these proved Chinese aggression. The move into Korea had been strictly defensive, to preserve the historical shield protecting the Chinese heartland around Beijing. The resolve to capture Taiwan was, to Beijing, an internal matter, since even Chiang Kai-shek maintained Taiwan was part of China. Beijing's support of the Vietminh was largely a counter to growing fear that the U.S. would intervene in Vietnam to destroy the Communists and create a U.S.-backed state on the southern Chinese frontier. And, compared to American backing of the reactionaries in Indochina, Beijing's support of the Communists was modest and aimed wholly at self-protection.

Nevertheless, American leaders refused to see pacific intentions in the Chinese and particularly misconstrued China's role in southeast Asia. It was here that President Eisenhower and his secretary of state, John Foster Dulles, believed the "falling-domino" theory was about to be tested. This theory dominated the Eisenhower administration and rested on the idea that, if the Communists gained any substantial part of Indochina, they would continue aggression against other free people of the region.[3]

The issue of southeast Asia came to a head the spring of 1954 when France was on the verge of losing an army surrounded by Vietminh at Dien Bien Phu in northwestern Vietnam. To get out of Vietnam while preserving a bit of French "prestige," Paris engineered a conference at Geneva to discuss the Vietnam and Korea issues. The talks on Korea got nowhere but the conference on Vietnam produced remarkable proof of Soviet and Chinese disinterest in aggression in the region—which the United States defiantly failed to heed.

The U.S. opposed anything but a military solution in Vietnam, theorizing that Communists had to be destroyed to prevent the ultimate loss of all southeast Asia. Yet the Soviet Union and China demonstrated they were willing to sacrifice Vietminh gains to achieve their own aims, proving there was no conspiracy of conquest. Although the Vietminh were about to overrun all of Vietnam, the Russians and Chinese forced their leader, Ho Chi Minh, to accept a "temporary" division of the country along the 17th parallel and withdrawal of all Communists to the north, leaving a separate South Vietnam supported by the U.S. The Soviet Union did this to prevent France from joining a supranational European army and China did it to prevent an American presence on its southern frontier.

Indeed, China revealed its sole concern at Geneva, stipulating that it required only a "small Communist buffer state in northern Indochina," and spelling out that it wanted "military protection of its southern borders."[4]

It is astonishing that the United States did not see that China's actions in Geneva were entirely defensive and sought precisely the same buffer or shield against U.S. aggression on the south that it had gained in Korea. This was conclusive proof that China was avoiding any adventure in southeast Asia.

Yet Secretary Dulles entirely missed the significance of the Chinese (and Soviet) actions and immediately set to work to create a barrier against Communist expansion. On September 8, 1954, he induced seven nations to join the U.S. in the Southeast Asia Treaty Organization (SEATO). Although advertised as a counterpart to the North Atlantic Treaty Organization (NATO), it was far weaker, without provisions for unified military command in response to an attack, thereby showing that signatories were not deeply convinced of danger. Only the major friends of the U.S joined: Britain, France, Australia, New Zealand, Pakistan, the Philippines and Thailand. But India, Burma, Ceylon (Sri Lanka) and Indonesia refused, demonstrating they were not worried about Communist subversion.

Dulles also missed the significance of a campaign launched in April 1954, when Zhou Enlai enunciated five principles of "peaceful coexistence" which became the foundation for China's foreign policy for the next two decades. The principles called for nations to exhibit "mutual respect for each other's territorial integrity and sovereignty, mutual nonaggression, mutual noninterference in each other's internal affairs, equality and mutual benefit and peaceful coexistence."[5]

The principles were aimed partly at showing that the U.S. was not following them but their major purpose was to convince China's neighbors of Beijing's peaceful intentions. Dulles and other American leaders considered the principles as propaganda and discounted them. Yet at a conference of unaligned countries at Bandung, Indonesia, in April 1955, Beijing gained much support when it promised to use them in its relations with other nations. This did much to alleviate fear regarding China's aims.

American hostility to Red China showed itself most cogently in regard to Taiwan and the approaches to it. Before the Korean War ended the U.S. had sent a military advisory group to Taiwan to help rebuild Nationalist Chinese forces and after the war the U.S. continued patrols of the Seventh Fleet in the Taiwan (or Formosa) strait to prevent Communist seizure of the island.

The United States resolved to protect Chiang Kai-shek and the Nationalists. To justify this decision the NSC announced in November 1953 that Taiwan was essential to the U.S. defense position in the Far East and the U.S. had to maintain the island "independent of communism."[6]

In 1949 the Joint Chiefs had decided it was not strategically vital. Now it was, not because its military importance had risen but because KMT possession of a bit of China could be stretched to preserve the fiction that it still constituted the legitimate government of the whole country. This gave the U.S. an excuse to continue blocking Red China's admission to the UN and a seat on the Security Council and denying Red China diplomatic recognition.

For a while there was some thought of covertly helping Chiang reconquer the mainland. This had been the theory behind the decision of President Eisenhower immediately after he became president in 1953 to "unleash" Chiang by no longer prohibiting the Nationalists from attacking mainland targets. This idea soon died, however, because KMT forces were manifestly too weak for such an enterprise.

Thoughts of a Nationalist offensive disappeared in May 1954 when Red Chinese forces began to make moves toward seizing a group of tiny islands off the coast of China which had remained in KMT hands when Beijing became preoccupied with the Korean War. The most important of these islands were Jinmen (Quemoy), just off the entrance to the harbor of Xiamen in southern Fujian province, and Mazu (Matsu), less than twenty miles off the Fujian coast opposite the port of Fuzhou.

Chiang Kai-shek had posted large garrisons on the offshore islands to defy the Reds. But they were clearly indefensible, had no military significance, and should have been evacuated. However, many American military and political leaders opposed giving the Chinese Reds the satisfaction of acquiring the bits of real estate and Admiral Arthur W. Radford, chairman of the Joint Chiefs of Staff, sent elements of the U.S. Seventh Fleet to visit the islands, thus preventing any action.

On September 4, 1954, however, Red onshore batteries commenced a heavy bombardment of Quemoy and Secretary Dulles reacted with a prophecy that loss of the island would jeopardize the Nationalists on Taiwan. This was nonsense. But Admiral Radford advocated American intervention, although the army chief of staff, General Matthew B. Ridgway, said losing Quemoy would make no difference to the defense of Taiwan.

For the next several months official Washington contemplated going to war over Quemoy. American leaders pulled away from a decision only because the Chinese Reds made no aggressive move and Eisenhower pointed out that a war would almost certainly expand far beyond the Taiwan strait and might become a nuclear confrontation with the Soviet Union. Yet, led by Dulles who pressed hard for a response, no matter what the consequences, American hostility against China grew so great that there remained a positive danger of American intervention if the Chinese Communists tried to take over the island.[7]

Meanwhile the Nationalists evacuated all of the other, more exposed, offshore islands they had occupied, some of which had been subjected to Chinese Communist air attacks. But, bolstered by U.S. support, Chiang Kai-shek resolved to remain on Matsu and Quemoy.

Early in 1955 the United States adopted Taiwan as a protectorate. In January Congress gave Eisenhower authority to use military forces to defend the Taiwan area and on February 9 the Senate approved a mutual-defense treaty with the island.[8] The U.S. thus formally adhered to a "two-Chinas" policy. Britain and other friends opposed the U.S. taking such a rigid position and from this point on American power was all that kept the Nationalists in the UN, not conviction of the majority of other UN members.

It was only the hesitation of Beijing that prevented a major confrontation in the Taiwan strait. Though the Chinese launched another, larger, bombardment against Quemoy in August 1958, the purpose was to exhibit fearlessness to the United States, not actually to invade the island. Although this bombardment brought on another period of great tension between Red China and the U.S., the Chinese did not attempt an invasion and thereafter the issue of Quemoy and Matsu slowly faded away. The first shelling occurred in 1960 on the occasion of a visit of President Eisenhower to Taiwan. Beijing since has left the islands alone, having decided their possession by the Nationalists poses no threat.

Beijing was preoccupied from the Korean War onward with socializing the nation's peasants and creating a modern industrial state. Hostility of the Eisenhower administration was so unrelenting that Mao Zedong and Zhou Enlai gave up hope of working out any settlement with it. With the U.S. having closed off normal international trade and assistance, Red China had to rely on help from the Soviet Union. But the Soviets were willing to give only modest aid, preoccupied as they were with their own recovery from World War II. To achieve as much as possible through China's own efforts, Mao Zedong conceived the Great Leap Forward, creating large rural communes in 1958 which sought to solve China's food shortages and break out of its centuries-old poverty by mobilizing the people into huge work "brigades" and teams. The Great Leap eliminated personal incentives and was a disaster, leading to an immense famine in 1959-61.

At the same time a fundamental conflict between China and the Soviet Union was about to turn these former friends into enemies. Russia was afraid of a thermonuclear holocaust and was seeking an accommodation with the West. Red China, however, had been cast beyond the pale of civilized nations by American action and was deeply distrustful of U.S. intentions. Beijing feared the Soviet Union was about to form an alliance with the United States at the expense of China.

In June 1959, Nikita Khrushchev, the Soviet premier, backed out of an agreement he'd made two years previously to assist China in developing the atomic bomb. Chinese leaders were convinced he did this to curry favor with Washington. Then Khrushchev launched a public attack on the communes. Soon after in Beijing for the tenth-anniversary celebrations of the founding of the People's Republic he advised Mao Zedong to accept the "two-Chinas" formula being pushed by the U.S., a wholly unacceptable proposal. In June 1960, Khrushchev withdrew all 1,400 Soviet techicians who were helping China develop its industry, taking their blueprints and know-how with them.[9] After this, neither country attempted to conceal its hostility to the other.

When John F. Kennedy became president in January 1961, he possessed a dazzling opportunity to exploit the schism between China and Russia and reach an understanding with the People's Republic, thus isolating the Soviet Union, the U.S.'s principal challenger. But Kennedy revealed that his bias against China was at least as great as that of Eisenhower and Dulles. Far from trying to come to a settlement with China, he sought an understanding with Russia and proposed in July 1963 that both countries join to make a preemptive strike against China's nuclear-bomb laboratories at Lop Nur in Xinjiang province. Khrushchev would have nothing to do with this.[10]

By the time of the Kennedy administration there was no longer even unproved suspicion of Chinese motives to justify continued isolation of Beijing. For over a decade the Chinese had operated extremely circumspectly with other countries, moving outside their borders only once (in Korea) and then only to protect their national interests.

In regard to Taiwan, the main bone of contention, U.S. leaders found themselves boxed into an intellectual impasse. Both the Nationalists and the Communists maintained the island was a part of China. This meant logically that Taiwan's status was an internal Chinese affair and the U.S. had no business interfering. Chiang Kai-shek knew, of course, that without the protection of the United States his long-discredited regime would disappear. The only way Chiang and the United States had been able to get around the logical inferences of Taiwan being a part of China had been to hold that the Chinese Communists were not indigenous elements but represented a conspiracy of world conquest directed by the Kremlin. In light of the Sino-Soviet split and Moscow's efforts at rapprochement with the West, the idea of the Chinese Reds being agents of a Krelim-directed conspiracy had become ludicrous. Yet the U.S. had no right to hold Taiwan if it acknowledged the truth. Kennedy overlooked the facts and continued to maintain the fiction of a conspiracy.

When Lyndon B. Johnson succeeded Kennedy after he was shot by an assassin on November 22, 1963, he continued his predecessor's hostility toward China. Johnson became increasingly preoccupied with the civil war in Vietnam which had resumed soon after the Geneva convention of 1954. Johnson mobilized enormous American strength in Indochina and commenced a huge bombing campaign against North Vietnam in late 1964 and in 1965. China protested but informed Washington privately that it would not go beyond material aid to the Communists, provided the U.S. did not invade North Vietnam with ground forces and threaten China's frontiers.[11]

Thus the reason China had gone to war in Korea and the requirement that it had announced at the Geneva conference emerged again: China would not tolerate an American army on its frontier. Johnson, who learned this much at least from the Korean War, never sent troops into North Vietnam, though his military advisors urged him to do so.

Meanwhile China exploded its own atomic bomb on October 16, 1964, and developed the hydrogen bomb on June 17, 1967. China thereby stepped fully upon the world's stage as a great power. This proved the American policy of isolating China had become extremely dangerous, for it was useless to talk about limiting nuclear weapons if the country continued to be treated as a pariah and denied admission to the United Nations. But Johnson reacted in precisely the opposite way when he learned of China's A-bomb, implying that China was threatening to use the bomb as blackmail when in fact Zhou Enlai informed Johnson that China would never be the first to use nuclear weapons.[12]

When Richard Nixon became U.S. president in January 1969, few persons thought he would change what had become a settled policy of hostility to Red China. Although China was now a nuclear power, Nixon had been Eisenhower's vice president and was a certified anti-Communist. However Nixon was the first president since Roosevelt to analyze American relations with China to any degree and he, along with his secretary of state, Henry Kissinger, realized that it was imperative to bring this enormuns nation with one-quarter of the earth's people back into the world communtiy.

By this time virtually no other countries, except those closely tied to the United States, any longer professed that China constituted a danger to world peace. In the absence of any provocation from China, most American people also had moved away from the hostility toward China which had ruled administrations through Johnson's.

There was overwhelming public support when Nixon and his wife visited Beijing in February 1972, and at last brought about a rapprochement between these two great nations. Had it not been for the Korean War, reconciliation would almost certainly have come much sooner. Thus was the shadow of this sad and painful conflict cast far into the future, to burden a whole generation.

Notes

In my research I have drawn largely from six major types of sources: original documents in the National Archives; the official histories of the war produced by the army, navy, air force, marines and Joint Chiefs of Staff (JCS); autobiographies and memoirs of major figures involved in the war; State Department and Archives publications of presidential and diplomatic messages, statements and decisions; scholarly studies on the war or political and diplomatic matters related to the war; and contemporary news reports, mostly from the New York *Times*, and articles in the English-language *People's China*, published in Beijing.

Most of the documents drawn from the National Archives, citations from periodicals and other sources are identified in the appropriate places in the chapter notes. However, a manuscript and a microfilm, both available in the Archives, are included below in a list of Frequently Cited Works. This list also includes all published works referred to often. These works are given in the chapter notes by the short titles assigned them in the list.

A brief discussion of the first three types of sources follows:

National Archives. The primary documents on the Korean War and diplomatic, executive and legislative matters related to the war are largely to be found in the Archives. The Modern Military History Headquarters Branch and the Legislative and Diplomatic Branch are in the main Archives building at Eighth Street and Pennsylvania Avenue, Washington, D.C., phones (202) 523-3340 (military history) and (202) 523-3174 (legislative and diplomatic). The other major Archives documents depository is in the Modern Military History Field Branch at the Washington National Records Center in Federal Building No. 1, 4205 Suitland Road, Suitland, Maryland, a Washington suburb (address: Washington, D.C. 20409; phone: (301) 763-1710).

Photographs of the war by all services are preserved in the Still Picture Division in the main Archives building and at the Defense Audiovisual Agencies, Still Photographic Depository, Building No. 168, Anacostia Naval Station, Washington, D.C. 20374, phone (202) 433-2168. Maps of Korea in the war period are preserved at the Cartographic and Architectural Branch, Special Archives Division, National Archives, 841 South Pickett Street, Alexandria, Virginia, phone (703) 756-6700.

The Modern Military History Headquarters Branch preserves the complete records of the Joint Chiefs of Staff, including the messages that passed between the JCS in Washington and the Far East Command in Tokyo; the Department of the Army G-3 (Operations) records; the battle and other studies of the eight Historical Detachments of Eighth Army operating in Korea; and various other documents that have a bearing on the war. The Legislative and Diplomatic Branch preserves messages, reports, statements and other documents concerning diplomatic and political decisions relating to the war. This branch also preserves the 3,600-page record of the hearings from May 3 to June 27, 1951, of U.S. Senate committees before which General Douglas MacArthur, the Joint Chiefs of Staff, Dean Acheson, George Marshall and other figures in policy-making roles testified in "an inquiry into the military situation in the Far East and the facts surrounding the relief of General of the Army Douglas MacArthur." At the Modern Military History Field Branch at Suitland, Maryland, are the War Diaries (through November, 1950) and Command Reports (after November, 1950), with supporting documents. These are monthly summaries of action prepared by all levels of command from the United Nations Command/Far East Command down to regiments and separate battalions. These papers provide much of the basic documentation of the war.

Each National Archives branch has an elaborate filing system to locate the millions of documents entrusted to its care. However, the researcher usually does not need file numbers, provided he can identify the source of the document and date. In most cases, researchers are not allowed to search for documents in the stacks; rather, they must ask for documents, and the archivists locate and bring them to researchers in reading rooms. I have provided in the chapter notes the information the archivists need to find documents cited. In the case of some Joint Chiefs of Staff records that otherwise might be difficult to locate, I have provided the JCS numbers by which they are filed in the Archives. Otherwise, I have omitted file numbers. A routine citation is this one: JCS 94933 to CINCFE, 24 Oct 50. This indicates a message of October 24, 1950, from the Joint Chiefs of Staff in Washington to the commander in chief, Far East (General MacArthur) in Tokyo. This and other Joint Chiefs messages are either in regular JCS files or in a series of message books containing messages exchanged with the Far East Command maintained by General Omar N. Bradley while he was chairman of the JCS and now making up part of the Chairman, Joint Chiefs of Staff (CJCS) files. They are in the Headquarters Branch in the main Archives building in Washington. Another citation: War Diary, "The 2d Infantry Division and the Korean Campaign," vol. 3 (p.1), 1 November 1950–30 November 1950, Historical Section G-2, Hq 2d Infantry Division. This and other war diaries and command reports are filed by unit and date in the Field Branch at Suitland.

Official histories. I have referred extensively to all of the official histories. They are cited fully in the list of Frequently Cited Works. The army's Office of the Chief of Military History (OCMH) has produced three of five projected volumes in the U.S. Army in the Korean War series. These are James F. Schnabel, *Policy and Direction: The First Year* (1972, reprinted 1978); Roy E. Appleman, *South to the Naktong, North to the Yalu* (1961, reprinted 1975); and Walter G. Hermes, *Truce Tent and Fighting Front* (1966). To this series has been appended another OCMH history by Major Robert K. Sawyer, *Military Advisors in Korea: KMAG in Peace and War* (1962). The fourth volume in the official OCMH series, *Ebb and Flow*, by Billy C. Mossman, is in the process of being written. It will cover the war from the United Nations offensive on November 24, 1950, to the start of the peace talks on July 10, 1951. The contemplated fifth volume, *Theater Logistics*, has not been undertaken so far.

The official U.S. Air Force history of the war is by Robert Frank Futrell, *The United States Air Force in Korea, 1950-53* (1961). The official marine study is by Lynn Montross and Captain Nicholas A. Canzona, *U.S. Marine Operations in Korea, 1950-1953* (1954). The U.S. Navy's history is by Commanders Malcolm W. Cagle and Frank A. Manson, *The Sea War in Korea* (1957).

James F. Schnabel and Robert J. Watson wrote *The History of the Joint Chiefs of Staff, The Joint Chiefs of Staff and National Policy*, vol. 3, *The Korean War*, part 1 (1978) and part 2 (1979).

The army OCMH produced two books, *Korea 1950*, anonymous (1952), and *Korea 1951-53*, by John Miller, Jr., Major Owen J. Carroll and Margaret E. Tackley (1956). These give an overall summary of the war and provide a large number of pictures. In addition, the Military History Section of Headquarters, Far East Command, produced a manuscript, "History of the Korean War, Chronology, 25 June 1950–31 December 1951," covering day-by-day events in the war during its most active period; it is available at the Modern Military History Headquarters Branch, National Archives.

While all of these works are important, the starting point for any serious study of the war must be three outstanding volumes: Roy Appleman's *South to the Naktong, North to the Yalu,* James Schnabel's *Policy and Direction: The First Year,* and James Schnabel and Robert Watson's history of the Joint Chiefs in the war. Appleman's book is by far the most complete and scholarly account of the military and related aspects of the crucial first five months of the war. It documents every major event in the period. I have drawn freely from this great well of information and have added to it largely in order to expand upon particular events and developments. I also have drawn heavily from Schnabel's learned analysis of the policies, strategies and command methods during the first year, especially leadership in Washington and Far East Command headquarters. The JCS history by Schnabel and Watson is an extremely skillful, thorough and exact study of the Joint Chiefs and Truman administration plans and actions and has added much to the understanding of the war. It provides a running documentation of messages and orders that passed between the Pentagon and the Far East Command.

Autobiographies and memoirs. The personal reports by the major figures involved in the war are important, especially those of Secretary of State Dean Acheson, President Harry Truman, General Douglas MacArthur, General Omar Bradley, General J. Lawton Collins, General Matthew B. Ridgway, General Mark W. Clark, and Indian ambassador to Beijing K. M. Panikkar. Most of these personal accounts are referenced in the Frequently Cited Works list. Others are given in the appropriate places in the chapter notes. I feel a special comment should be made regarding General Bradley's book, *A General's Life, an Autobiography,* by General of the Army Omar N. Bradley and Clay Blair (1983). This book was completed by Mr. Blair after General Bradley's death. However, because of Mr. Blair's close association with Bradley and his access to Bradley's files and records, and because the book is presented as an autobiography, I have chosen to treat references in this volume as direct quotes from Bradley himself.

FREQUENTLY CITED WORKS

Acheson	Dean Acheson. *Present at the Creation.* New York: W.W. Norton & Company, 1969.
Appleman	Roy E. Appleman. *South to the Naktong, North to the Yalu,* United States Army in the Korean War. Office of the Chief of Military History. Washington: U.S. Government Printing Office, 1961 (reprinted 1975).
Barnett	A. Doak Barnett. *China and the Major Powers in East Asia.* Washington: Brookings Institution, 1977.
Bong-youn Choy	Bong-youn Choy. *Korea: A History.* Rutland, Vt.: Charles E. Tuttle Co., 1971.
Bradley	Omar N. Bradley and Clay Blair. *A General's Life, an Autobiography.* New York: Simon & Schuster, 1983.
Cagle and Manson	Comdrs Malcolm W. Cagle and Frank A. Manson. *The Sea War in Korea.* Annapolis, Md.: United States Naval Institute, 1957.
Chronology	Military History Section, Far East Command. Manuscript, "History of the Korean War, Chronology, 25 June 1950–31 December, 1951." Available at Modern Military History Headquarters Branch, National Archives, Washington.
Collins	Gen. J. Lawton Collins. *War in Peacetime: The History and Lessons of Korea.* Boston: Houghton Mifflin Company, 1969.
Department of State *Bulletin*	State Department, Bureau of Public Affairs, Office of Communication. *Bulletin.* Published weekly. Washington: U.S. Government Printing Office.
Dulles	Foster Rhea Dulles. *American Policy toward Communist China, 1949–1969.* New York: Thomas Y. Crowell Company, 1972.
Foreign Relations, 1950, Korea	State Department. *Foreign Relations of the United States, 1950,* vol. 7, *Korea.* Washington: U.S. Government Printing Office, 1976.

Foreign Relations, 1951, Korea	State Department. *Foreign Relations of the United States, 1951,* vol. 7, *Korea and China,* parts 1 and 2. Washington: U.S. Government Printing Office, 1983.
Foreign Relations, 1952–54, Korea	State Department. *Foreign Relations of the United States, 1952–54,* vol. 15, *Korea,* parts 1 and 2. Washington: U.S. Government Printing Office, 1984.
Futrell	Robert Frank Futrell. *The United States Air Force in Korea, 1950–1953.* New York: Duell, Sloan and Pearce, 1961.
George	Alexander L. George. *The Chinese Communist Army in Action: The Korean War and Its Aftermath.* New York: Columbia University Press, 1967.
Hermes	Walter G. Hermes. *Truce Tent and Fighting Front,* United States Army in the Korean War. Office of the Chief of Military History. Washington: U.S. Government Printing Office, 1966.
Korea 1950	Anonymous. *Korea 1950.* Office of the Chief of Military History. Washington: U.S. Government Printing Office, 1952.
Korea 1951–53	John Miller, Jr., Maj. Owen J. Carroll and Margaret E. Tackley. *Korea 1951–53.* Office of the Chief of Military History. Washington: U.S. Government Printing Office, 1956.
MacArthur	Gen. of the Army Douglas MacArthur. *Reminiscences.* New York: McGraw-Hill Book Company, 1964.
McLellan	David S. McLellan. *Dean Acheson: The State Department Years.* New York: Dodd, Mead and Co., 1976.
Military Situation in the Far East	U.S. 82nd Congress, Senate. Committees on Armed Services and Foreign Relations. *Hearings, Military Situation in the Far East, 1951.* Microfilm version from Legislative and Diplomatic Branch, National Archives, includes all formerly classified testimony. The version published by U.S. Government Printing Office, Washington, 1951, omits the classified testimony.
Montross and Canzona	Lynn Montross and Capt. Nicholas A. Canzona (USMC). *U.S. Marine Operations in Korea, 1950–1953,* 5 vols. Washington: Historical Branch, G-3, Headquarters, U.S. Marine Corps, 1954.

Murphy	Lt.Col. E. Lloyd Murphy, U.S. Army. *The U.S./U.N. Decision to Cross the 38th Parallel, October 1950: A Case Study of Changing Objectives in Limited War.* Air War College Research Report No. 3660. Maxwell Air Force Base, Ala.: Air War College, 1968.
Paige	Glenn D. Paige. *The Korean Decision* [June 24–30, 1950]. New York: Free Press, 1968.
Public Papers, Truman, 1950	National Archives. *Public Papers of the Presidents of the United States, Harry S. Truman, 1950.* Washington: U.S. Government Printing Office, 1965.
Ridgway	Gen. Matthew B. Ridgway. *The Korean War.* Garden City, NY: Doubleday & Co., 1967.
Sawyer	Maj. Robert K. Sawyer. *Military Advisors in Korea: KMAG in Peace and War.* Office of the Chief of Military History. Washington: U.S. Government Printing Office, 1962.
Schnabel	James F. Schnabel. *Policy and Direction: The First Year,* United States Army in the Korean War. Office of the Chief of Military History. Washington: U.S. Government Printing Office, 1972 (reprinted 1978).
Schnabel and Watson	James F. Schnabel and Robert J. Watson. *The History of the Joint Chiefs of Staff, The Joint Chiefs of Staff and National Policy,* vol. 3, *The Korean War,* part 1 (1978) and part 2 (1979), produced in soft cover and by duplicator by the Historical Division, Joint Secretariat, Joint Chiefs of Staff, and available at Modern Military History Headquarters Branch, National Archives.
Truman, *Memoirs* 2.	Harry S. Truman. *Memoirs,* vol. 2., *Years of Trial and Hope.* Garden City, NY: Doubleday and Co., 1956.
Whiting	Allen S. Whiting. *China Crosses the Yalu: The Decision to Enter the Korean War.* Stanford, Calif.: Stanford University Press, 1960.

REFERENCE NOTES

CHAPTER 1. *June 25, 1950*
1. Appleman, pp. 16, 26.
2. 1st Lt. Bevin R. Alexander, "Enemy Materiel", 5th Historical Detachment, Eighth Army, 1952, National Archives, provides an analysis of North Korean and Chinese Communist weapons, uniforms and other equipment.
3. Appleman, p. 17.
4. Alexander, "Enemy Materiel".
5. Gen Heinz Guderian, *Panzer Leader*, New York: E.P. Dutton & Co., Inc., 1952, pp.162, 233–38; Maj Gen F.W. von Mellenthin, *Panzer Battles*, (Norman, Okla: University of Oklahoma Press, 1956), pp. 153–55.
6. Schnabel, p. 84; Appleman, pp. 69, 71.
7. Appleman, pp. 156, 163.
8. Schnabel, p. 36.
9. Sawyer, *Military Advisors in Korea*, p. 100.
10. Schnabel and Watson, p. 43; Appleman, p. 16; Sawyer, p. 100; Schnabel, p. 36.
11. Appleman, p. 35.
12. Ibid., pp. 7–18.
13. Ibid., p. 9.
14. Ibid., pp. 73, 92, 98, 101, 145, 154. In addition, War Diaries of combat units in the early months of the war give examples of this tactic.
15. James Chambers, *The Devil's Horsemen: The Mongol Invasion of Europe*, (New York: Atheneum, 1979), pp. 59–60.

CHAPTER 2. *How Did It Happen?*
1. Schnabel and Watson, pp. 49–53.
2. Schnabel, pp. 59–65.
3. Schnabel and Watson, p. 54.
4. *Korea 1950*, pp. 4–6.
5. Maj Gen J.F.C. Fuller, *A Military History of the Western World*, 3 vols. (New York: Funk & Wagnalls, 1956), pp. 3:599, 620–23; United States Strategic Bombing Survey, Summary Report (Pacific War), 1946, pp. 11, 17, 19.
6. Karl von Clausewitz, *On War*, O. J. Matthijs Jolles (New York: Modern Library, 1943), p. 16.
7. Ibid, p. 596.
8. Fuller, *Military History of the Western World*, 3: 623–28; B. H. Liddell Hart, *History of the Second World War* (New York: G. P. Putnam's Sons, 1971), pp. 692–98.

CHAPTER 3. *Partition*

1. Truman, *Memoirs,* 2: 317; Appleman, pp. 2–3; Schnabel and Watson, p. 3; Schnabel, pp. 7–8.

2. Schnabel, p. 9; Schnabel and Watson, p. 3.

3. Schnabel, pp. 10–11; Schnabel and Watson, p. 9.

4. Appleman, p. 4.

5. *Korea 1950,* p. 5; Schnabel, pp. 13–28. Bong-youn Choy gives a somewhat different view of the separation of North and South (chapters 8–12, pp. 199–302), in which he emphasizes the autocratic practices of Syngman Rhee and his advocacy of reuniting Korea by force.

6. Bong-youn Choy, p. 240.

7. Ibid., p. 241.

8. Ibid., p. 245.

9. Ibid., p. 242.

10. Ibid., p. 246.

11. Ibid., p. 67.

12. Ibid., p. 88.

13. Ibid., p. 249, cites *Facts on the Korean Crisis,* (New York: Committee for a Democratic Far Eastern Policy, n.d.), pp. 4–5.

14. *Korea 1950,* p. 7; Schnabel and Watson, pp. 11–12.

15. Bong-youn Choy, pp. 340, 351, 391.

16. Younghill Kang, "The Valley of Utopia," *Introducing Korea,* ed. Peter Hyun, (Seoul: Jungwoo-sa, 1979), p. 29.

CHAPTER 4. *Hands Off Taiwan and Korea*

1. Barnett, p. 175.

2. Dulles, p. 57. Chinese personal names throughout are romanized by use of the *pinyin zimu* (literally "spell the sound") system, adopted by Red China in 1958, rather than the older Wade-Giles system long familiar to Western readers. An exception is the Nationalist generalissimo and chief, who is rendered as Chiang Kai-shek (Pinyin: Jiang Jie-shi) because this is the name by which he is known in the West. Chinese geographical names are given in the text in both Wade-Giles and Pinyin, except Canton. Manchuria, which legally does not exist in Red China, is known to Westerners as the great northeastern region of China bordering on Siberia and Korea and is so used in the text.

Chinese names appearing in the text are rendered as follows in Pinyin (with the Wade-Giles versions in parentheses): Zhou Enlai (Chou En-lai); Mao Zedong (Mao Tse-tung); Lin Biao (Lin Piao); Nie Yen-rung (Nieh Yen-jung); Chen Yi (Chin Yi); Wu Xiu-zhuan (Wu Hsiu-chuan); Peng De-huai (Peng Teh-huai); Deng Hua (Teng Hua); Xie Fang (Hsieh Fang); Bian

Zhang-wu (Pien Chang-wu); Ding Guo-you (Ting Kuo-yu); Cai Zheng-wen (Tsai Cheng-wen). (Sources: George C. Hsu, Richmond, Virginia, and *Encyclopedia Britannica*, 15th edition, (1978), Macropaedia vol. 16, pp. 801-2.)

3. Ibid., p. 57–58.

4. Ibid., p. 58.

5. Ibid., p. 40. Dulles cites Marshall's testimony as given in *Military Situation in the Far East.*

6. Ibid., p. 41.

7. Dulles's *American Policy Toward Communist China, 1949–1969* gives a detailed summary and analysis of the development and execution of American policy in this period.

8. Schnabel and Watson, p. 34; Barnett, p. 171.

9. Dulles, p. 66; Schnabel and Watson, p. 37.

10. Schnabel and Watson, p. 37.

11. Ibid., p. 13-15.

12. Ibid., p. 29–35.

13. Barnett, p. 167.

14. Ibid., p. 167; Dulles, pp. 27–28.

15. Barnett, p. 171.

16. Dulles, pp. 42–44.

17. *Selected Works of Mao Tsetung,* 4 vols. (Peking: Foreign Languages Press, 1975), 4: 425–50.

18. Schnabel and Watson, p. 38.

19. Ibid., p. 36.

20. Ibid., p. 38. (Schnabel and Watson cites New York *Times* article 2 Mar 49, interviewer G. Ward Price.)

21. Schnabel and Watson, p. 55.

22. Nikita Khrushchev, *Khrushchev Remembers,* with an introduction, commentary and notes by Edward Crankshaw (Boston: Little, Brown and Company, 1970), pp. 367–73.

23. Schnabel and Watson, p. 54. Soviet advisors accompanied North Korean forces from the creation of the first armed units in 1946. In 1948 there were 150 Soviet advisors with each North Korean division. As North Korean military leadership developed, this number dropped to about twenty advisors per division in 1949 and to three to eight in 1950. Apparently the Soviet government withdrew the remaining advisors shortly before hostilities commenced in order to prevent them from falling into enemy hands. (Source: Schnabel, p. 37.)

24. Ibid., p. 55.

25. Sawyer, p. 105.

26. I. F. Stone, *Hidden History of the Korean War* (New York: Monthly Review Press, 1952).

27. Bong-youn Choy, pp. 259–60.
28. Stone, p.. 44.
29. Schnabel and Watson, p. 71.
30. Sawyer, p. 112.
31. Truman, *Memoirs* 2: 332–33; Schnabel and Watson, p. 74.

CHAPTER 5. *Attack across the 38th*
1. The account of the initial North Korean offensive is largely drawn from Appleman, pp. 19–35, which is based on extensive interviews with survivors and official documents.
2. Appleman, p. 26.
3. Schnabel and Watson, p. 85.
4. Appleman, pp. 38–39; Schnabel, p. 71.
5. Appleman, p. 42.
6. Ibid., p. 34.

CHAPTER 6. *Decision in Washington*
1. Schnabel and Watson, pp. 69–70.
2. Ibid., p. 67.
3. Ibid., p. 71.
4. Ibid., p. 66; Truman, *Memoirs* 2:332; Acheson, pp. 402–04.
5. Schnabel and Watson, p. 73.
6. Truman, *Memoirs* 2:332–33.
7. Acheson, p. 405.
8. Schnabel and Watson, p. 76.
9. Ibid., p. 76; Paige, pp. 116–21.
10. Schnabel and Watson, p. 86.
11. Ibid., pp. 79–80; Truman *Memoirs* 2:333–36; Paige, pp. 125–41, gives a full account of this meeting as well as all the decisions leading up to the U.S. intervention.
12. Schnabel and Watson, p. 79.
13. Ibid., p. 77.
14. Ibid., pp. 77–78.
15. Ibid., p. 80.
16. Ibid., p. 89; Acheson, p. 407.
17. Schnabel and Watson, p. 89.
18. Ibid., p. 90.
19. Ibid., p. 90.
20. Truman, *Memoirs* 2:337–38; Acheson, pp. 407–08; *Military Situation in the Far East*, pt. 2, pp. 949, 1049–50 (Bradley testimony); p. 1475 (Vandenberg); p. 1643 (Sherman), and pt. 4, pp. 2574–75, 2581–82 (Johnson).

CHAPTER 7. *War and the Quarantine of Taiwan*

1. Schnabel and Watson, p. 92.
2. Ibid., p. 93.
3. *Public Papers, Truman, 1950,* p. 492; Schnabel and Watson, p. 94.
4. Schnabel and Watson, p. 95.
5. Ibid., p. 95; Truman, *Memoirs* 2:338; Paige, pp. 187–91; Acheson, p. 409.
6. Schnabel and Watson, p. 40 cites CINCFE (Commander in chief, Far East) to DA (Department of the Army) for JCS (Joint Chiefs of Staff), 29 May 50, CM IN 4359, 4444 (this system of identification designates messages between the Far East Command and the Joint Chiefs and will be used throughout; messages are preserved in the National Archives) ibid., pp. 77–78, 514; Bradley, pp. 532–33.
7. Alexis de Tocqueville, *Democracy in America,* 2 vols. (New York: Alfred A. Knopf, 1966), pp. 1:239–40.
8. Ibid., 1:235.
9. Ibid., 1:355, 261 n.
10. McLellan, p. 277.
11. *People's China,* 2, no. 2, (July 16, 1950), p. 4.
12. Paige, p. 248.
13. Ibid., p. 248.

CHAPTER 8. *The Army of the United Nations*

1. Paige, pp. 195–200, 219; Public Law 599, 81st Congress.
2. Schnabel and Watson, p. 107; Truman, *Memoirs* 2:341–42.
3. Schnabel and Watson, pp. 95-96; Paige, pp. 202–06; Acheson, p. 408.
4. Schnabel and Watson, pp. 133–35; Appleman, pp. 110–11; Schnabel, p. 102.
5. Appleman, p. 44; Schnabel and Watson, p. 97.
6. Appleman, pp. 44–45; Schnabel and Watson, p. 110.
7. Appleman, pp. 12, 50.
8. Schnabel and Watson, pp. 111–13, cites MacArthur's message, CINCFE C 56942 to DA for JCS, 30 June 50, CM IN 8776.
9. Ibid., pp. 113–17.
10. Ibid., p. 118.
11. Ibid., p. 118; Truman, *Memoirs,* 2:342; Acheson, p. 412.
12. Schnabel and Watson, p. 118.
13. Ibid., p. 118.

CHAPTER 9. *Goodbye to the Good Times*

1. Appleman, p. 49, Schnabel, p. 54.

2. Schnabel, pp. 43–44; Appleman, p. 49.
3. McLellan, p. 168.
4. Ibid., p. 169.
5. Ibid., pp. 175–79.
6. Appleman, p. 48; Schnabel, pp. 43–45.
7. Schnabel pp. 159–60.
8. Ibid., pp. 45–46.

CHAPTER 10. *The Teenagers Stand and Fight*
1. Appleman, p. 56.
2. Appleman, p. 56–57; Sawyer, p. 134.
3. Appleman, p. 57; Sawyer, p. 134.
4. Appleman, pp. 55, 57.
5. Ibid., p. 58.
6. The narrative on Task Force Smith is based on Appleman, pp. 59–76.
7. Collins, p. 67.

CHAPTER 11. *Withdrawal in Disorder*
1. Appleman, pp. 77–79.
2. The narrative in this chapter on the 34th Regiment is based upon Appleman, pp. 77–78, and Capt Russell A. Gugeler, "Withdrawal Action," in *Combat Actions in Korea* (Washington, D.C.: Combat Forces Press, 1954), pp. 3–19, a detailed study of the action of Company A, 1st Battalion, 34th Regiment.
3. Gugeler, p. 6, cites Brig Gen George B. Barth, "The First Days in Korea," *Combat Forces Journal,* March, 1951.
4. Appleman, p. 82.
5. Gugeler, p. 14.
6. Appleman, pp. 84–85.

CHAPTER 12. *One Bonanza, Several Defeats*
1. The narrative on the retreat of the 21st and 34th Regiments to the Kum river is based on Appleman, pp. 88–100.
2. Appleman, p. 95.
3. The analysis of the battle situation in the ROK sectors of the front is based on Appleman, pp. 101–08.

CHAPTER 13. *The Kum River*
1. Appleman, pp. 110–11.
2. Ibid., p. 122.

3. The narrative on the action of the 34th Regiment and the 63rd Field Artillery Battalion is based on Appleman, pp. 123–30.
4. Appleman, p. 129.

CHAPTER 14. *Taepyong-ni*
1. The narrative on the 19th Regiment's engagement at Taepyong-ni is based on Appleman, pp. 130–45, and the afteraction report of Capt Martin Blumenson, 4th Historical Detachment, Eighth Army, "Kum River Defense, 19th Infantry Regiment, 16 July 1950" (National Archives).

CHAPTER 15. *Taejon*
1. The narrative on the battle of Taejon is based on Appleman, pp. 146–81, and upon the afteraction study by Capt Martin Blumenson, 4th Historical Detachment, Eighth Army, "Withdrawal from Taejon 20 July 1950" (National Archives).
2. Schnabel, p. 84.
3. Ibid., p. 84.
4. Appleman, p. 157.
5. Ibid., p. 156.
6. Ibid., p. 156.
7. Ibid., pp. 165–66.
8. Ibid., p. 166.
9. Ibid., p. 168.
10. Ibid., pp. 179–80.
11. Ibid., p. 180.

CHAPTER 16. *The Ghost Division*
1. The narrative on the movement of the 6th NK Division and the engagement of the U.S. 29th Regiment's 1st Battalion at Hadong pass is drawn from Appleman, pp. 210–20.
2. Appleman, pp. 222, 227.
3. Ibid., p. 247.
4. Ibid., p. 213.
5. Ibid., p. 211, 213.
6. Ibid., p. 233–34.

CHAPTER 17. *Retreat to the Naktong*
1. Appleman, p. 187. Much of the following narrative on the withdrawal of American and ROK forces to the Pusan Perimeter is drawn from Appleman, pp. 183–209.
2. Appleman, pp. 189-91.
3. Ibid., p. 197.

4. Ibid., p. 194.

5. Ridgway, pp. 191–93; Collins, p. 91.

6. Appleman, p. 200.

7. Ibid., p. 203.

8. Ibid., pp. 235–47.

9. Ibid., p. 197.

10. Ibid., p. 203.

11. Ibid., p. 207.

12. Ibid., p. 206.

13. Ibid., pp. 207–8.

14. Ibid., p. 251. Appleman cites letter, Gay to Appleman, 24 Aug 50; EUSAK [Eighth U.S. Army in Korea] War Diary, G-3 Journal, 3 Aug 50; EUSAK Periodic Operations Report 66, 3 Aug 50.

15. Appleman, pp. 239, 259.

16. New York *Times* 26 Jul 50, 30 Jul 50.

17. Appleman, pp. 259, 263.

18. Ibid., p. 264.

19. Ibid., p. 263.

CHAPTER 18. *The First Counteroffensive*

1. Appleman, p. 267. On August 6–7, 1950, the 25th Division War Diary gives total strength of 23,080 troops, including 11,026 attached; this included the 27th Regiment, which became army reserve on August 7. On August 9, 25th Division strength was given as 24,179, of which 12,197 were attached.

2. Futrell, p. 113.

3. Appleman, pp. 269–70.

4. Ibid., p. 256.

5. The account of Task Force Kean is drawn largely from Appleman, pp. 266–88, and from Montross and Canzona, 1: 99–156.

6. Appleman, p. 269.

7. Futrell, p. 112; Montross and Canzona, 1: 140–43.

8. Futrell, p. 115.

9. Appleman, pp. 285–86.

10. Ibid., p. 286.

11. Ibid., p. 287.

12. Ibid., pp. 364–75.

13. Ibid.

CHAPTER 19. *The Days Along the Naktong*

1. Appleman, p. 259 n.

2. Ibid., pp. 389-90. On August 26, 1950, due to the low strength of the 24th Infantry Division, Eighth Army Commander Walton H. Walker ordered the division's 34th Infantry Regiment, along with its supporting 63rd Field Artillery Battalion, to be reduced to paper status and the infantrymen reassigned to form third battalions to the division's 19th and 21st Infantry Regiments and the artillerymen to augment the division's 11th, 13th and 52nd Artillery Battalions. At the same time, Gen Walker assigned to the division the separate 5th Regimental Combat Team (with its supporting 555th Field Artillery Battalion). Of the 1,898 men who entered Korea with the 34th Regiment on July 6, only 184 were still in the regiment on August 26. The rest had been killed (98) or wounded (569) or were missing (773) or had suffered nonbattle casualties (274).

3. Ibid., p. 382; Schnabel and Watson, p. 172. In addition to the United States and South Korea, nineteen countries contributed personnel on the UN side in the Korean War. Four countries—India, Italy, Norway and Sweden—contributed noncombatant medical units only. South Africa provided no ground troops or naval craft but did contribute a squadron of aircraft (Canberras). The United States contributed by far the largest number of military personnel (ground, sea and air), followed by South Korea, Britain, Canada, Turkey, and Australia, in that order. In addition, the United States commitment of ships and aircraft far exceeded those of any other nation. South Korea contributed the second-largest number of naval craft, but most of these were small vessels. The British contribution of naval craft was second only to the U.S. in strength and power. *Ground forces.* Military ground personnel in Korea by country on June 30, 1951, were as follows, with the number on July 31, 1953, in parentheses: United States 253,250 (302,483); Republic of Korea 273,266 (590,911); Australia 912 (2,282); Belgium 602 (44 from Luxembourg)(944); Canada 5,403 (6,146); Colombia 1,050 (1,068); Ethiopia 1,153 (1,271); France 738 (1,119); Greece 1,027 (1,263); India (noncombatants) 333(70); Italy (non-combatants) 64 on June 30, 1952 (72); Netherlands 725 (819); New Zealand 797 (1,389); Norway (non-combatants) 79 (105);Philippines 1,143 (1,496); Sweden (non-combatants) 162 (154); Thailand 1,057 (1,294); Turkey 4,602 (5,455); United Kingdom 8,278 (14,198). *Air force squadrons.* Number of squadrons on June 30, 1951, and, in parentheses, on June 30, 1953, as follows: United States 58 (66); Australia 1 (1); Canada 1 (1); South Africa 1 (1). *Naval ships.* Number of ships on June 30, 1951, and, in parentheses, on June 30, 1953: United States 186 (261); Republic of Korea 34 (76). Number of ships on January 15, 1952, and, in parentheses, October 15, 1952: Australia 4 (4); Canada 3 (3); Colombia 1 (1); Denmark

1 (1); Netherlands 1 (1); New Zealand 2 (2); Thailand 2 (2); United Kingdom 22 (22). Source: Schnabel and Watson, Appendix VI.
4. Appleman, p. 259.
5. Ibid., pp. 289, 319–75.
6. Ibid., p. 333.
7. Ibid., p. 290.
8. Ibid., pp. 289–318; Montross and Canzona 1: 173–206. Much of the narrative on the Naktong Bulge battles is drawn from these two sources.
9. Capt Russell A. Gugeler, "Attack Along a Ridgeline," *Combat Actions in Korea*, (Washington, D.C.: Combat Forces Press, 1954), pp. 20–29.
10. Appleman, p. 310.
11. Ibid., p. 310.
12. Ibid., p. 312.

CHAPTER 20. *"We Are Going to Hold This Line"*
1. Appleman, pp. 339–42.
2. Ibid., pp. 342–45.
3. Futrell, p. 134.
4. Appleman, p. 263.
5. Futrell, p. 130.
6. Ibid., p. 131.
7. Ibid.
8. Appleman, p. 352.
9. Ibid., p. 353.
10. Futrell, p. 131.
11. Appleman, p. 353.
12. Futrell, p. 132.
13. Appleman, pp. 345–50.
14. Ibid., pp. 335–39, 345–63. Much of the narrative on the battle of the Bowling Alley is drawn from these sources.
15. Ibid., p. 351.

CHAPTER 21. *Forging a Sword of Vengeance*
1. Ridgway, p. 42
2. Polybius, *The Histories,* Book 3, Chaps. 107–18, The Loeb Classical Library, trans W. R. Paton (London: William Heineman; New York: G. P. Putnam's Sons, 1922), 2:263–93; Livy, *The War with Hannibal,* trans. Aubrey de Selincourt, (New York: Penguin Books, 1965), pp. 145–52; *Encyclopedia of Military History,* eds. R. Ernest Dupuy and Trevor N. Dupuy (New York: Harper & Row, 1970), pp. 65–66.
3. Appleman, p. 488.

4. Ibid., p. 493; Collins, p. 123; Schnabel and Watson, p. 208.

5. Ridgway, pp. 33, 40.

6. Ibid., p. 36.

7. B. H. Liddell Hart, *Strategy,* (New York: Frederick A. Praeger, 1954), p. 164.

8. Ibid., p. 25.

9. Ibid., pp. 45, 123, 199; *Encyclopedia of Military History,* pp. 64–65, 749, 987–88; Livy, pp. 95–102; Polybius, 2: 191–209.

10. Sun Tzu, *The Art of War,* edited and with a foreword by James Clavell (New York; Delacorte Press, 1983), pp. 15, 20.

11. B. H. Liddell Hart, *Strategy,* pp. 162–163.

12. B. H. Liddell Hart, *History of the Second World War* (New York: G.P. Putnam's Sons, 1971), pp. 498–513.

CHAPTER 22. *MacArthur v. the Joint Chiefs*

1. Bradley, pp. 552–53.

2. Schnabel and Watson, p. 178.

3. Ibid., p. 179.

4. Ibid., p. 179.

5. Ibid., pp. 180–82.

6. Ibid., pp. 183–85.

7. Ibid., pp.186–88.

8. Ibid., p. 189; Collins, p. 117.

9. Schnabel and Watson, p. 187.

10. Schnabel, p. 141; Collins, pp. 81–85; Schnabel and Watson, pp. 191, 202.

11. Collins, p. 81.

12. Bradley, p. 523.

13. Collins, p. 81.

14. Schnabel and Watson, p. 191.

15. Ibid., p. 191.

16. Collins, p. 83.

17. Ibid., p. 116.

18. Ibid., p. 85.

19. Schnabel, p. 141.

20. Collins, p. 116.

21. Schnabel and Watson, p. 192.

22. Bradley, p. 544.

23. Collins, p. 116.

24. Ibid., p. 117; Schnabel and Watson, p. 193; Bradley, p. 545.

25. Schnabel and Watson, p. 193.

26. Ibid., p. 193, cites CINCFE CX-58327 to JCS, 21 Jul 50, CM IN 14303.

27. Schnabel, p. 142, cites C 58473, CINCFE to DA for JCS 23 Jul 50.

28. Schnabel and Watson, p. 204.

29. Ibid., p. 204; Schnabel, p. 142.

30. Schnabel and Watson, p. 198.

31. Ibid., p. 194; Appleman, p. 491.

32. Schnabel and Watson, p. 194; Schnabel, pp. 169–71.

33. Schnabel, p. 146, cites chronicles by Maj Gen Oliver P. Smith, USMC; copy available in Historical Section; G-3, USMC Hq., Washington; Special Action Report (SAR) 1st Marine Div, 15 Aug–30 Sep 50, copy in same files; Malcolm C. Cagle, "Inchon, Analysis of a Gamble," *U.S. Naval Institute Proceedings* 80, no 1 (January 1954), pp. 47–51. See also James A. Field, Jr., *History of United States Naval Operations, Korea* (Washington, D.C.: U.S. Government Printing Office, 1962), pp. 171–83.

34. Schnabel, p. 146.

35. Ibid., p. 146.

36. Ibid., p. 144.

37. Ibid., p. 146.

38. Ibid., p. 147; Appleman, p. 504.

CHAPTER 23. *MacArthur Calls on Chiang Kai-shek*

1. Truman, *Memoirs* 2:355–56.

2. McLellan, p. 279.

3. Schnabel and Watson, p. 506.

4. Ibid., pp. 80–81, 506.

5. Ibid., p. 507; Schnabel, p. 368.

6. Schnabel and Watson, pp. 508–9; Schnabel, p. 368.

7. Schnabel and Watson, pp. 507-8.

8. Ibid., p. 509.

9. Ibid., p. 509.

10. Ibid., p. 508.

11. McLellan, p. 279.

12. Schnabel and Watson, p. 510.

13. Schnabel, p. 368.

14. Bradley, p. 549.

15. Truman, *Memoirs* 2:354; New York *Times* 10 Aug 50, p. 1; Schnabel and Watson, p. 510.

16. McLellan, p. 279; Schnabel, pp. 368–69.

17. Schnabel and Watson, p. 511.

18. Ibid., p. 512, and Schnabel, p. 369 cite SecDef WAR 88014 to CINCFE, 4 Aug 50.

19. Schnabel and Watson, p. 513 cites CINCFE C59418 to DA, 5 Aug 50, CM IN 18884.

20. Ibid., p. 513.

21. Ibid., p. 195.

22. Ridgway, p. 36.

23. Ibid.

24. Ibid., p. 37.

25. Truman, pp. 349–53.

26. Ibid., p. 354.

27. Ibid.; Schnabel and Watson, p. 514 cites *Public Papers, Truman, 1950*, p. 580.

28. Truman, *Memoirs* 2:351. Truman gives Ambassador Harriman's report on his visit with MacArthur verbatim on pages 349–53. It contains an observation by MacArthur that there was no need to change the South Korean constitution because it already provided 100 seats for the North.

29. McLellan, p. 284.

CHAPTER 24. *The Decision on Inchon*

1. Bradley, p. 546.

2. Collins, p. 121; Schnabel and Watson, pp. 197–98.

3. Collins, p. 121; Schnabel and Watson, p. 207.

4. Collins, p. 121.

5. Schnabel, pp. 144–45; Appleman, p. 491; 1st Lt Martin Blumenson, Monograph, "Special Problems in the Korean Conflict (Miscellaneous Problems and Their Solutions)," "The Augmentation of U.S. Units by Korean Troops, " Chapter 4, Eighth U.S. Army Korea, 1951, National Archives; see also Appleman, pp. 385–89.

6. Appleman, p. 492.

7. Ibid., p. 492.

8. Schnabel, p. 158.

9. Schnabel and Watson, p. 207; Schnabel, p. 149; Collins, pp. 121–27; Bradley, pp. 546–47.

10. Collins, p. 122–23.

11. Schnabel, p. 148.

12. The official accounts of the Inchon operation refer to the navy having located an alternative landing site at Posung-myon, a township-like small administrative district about thirty miles south of Inchon and due west of Osan. A close study of the 1:250,000 Army Map Service (LI551) terrain maps of the area dated 1950 (Inchon J52M and Sosan J52S) reveals no area named Posung-myon. There is, however, a Pusong-myon area on the Sosan map (coordinates 6364), located southwest of the town of Sosan and some 50 miles south of Inchon. I have, therefore, elected to identify the proposed landing site as Pusong-myon.

13. Schnabel, p. 148; Motross and Canzona, 2:44.

14. Schnabel, p. 148.

15. Ibid., p. 149; Schnabel and Watson, p. 210.

16. Bradley says in his autobiography (p. 547) that almost all the admirals and marine generals in the Far East had grave misgivings about Inchon. Secretary of Defense Johnson later said Collins did not favor Inchon and went to Tokyo "to try to argue General MacArthur out of it." (Schnabel, p. 149, cites *Military Situation in the Far East*, pt. 4, p. 2618.)

17. Schnabel, p. 149, cites Walter M. Karig, *Battle Report, The War in Korea*, (New York: Rinehart, 1952), pp. 166–67, Karig's work, described by Joy and Almond as substantially correct, is the basis of Schnabel's account of the August 23 briefing. See also Schnabel and Watson, p. 109. Appleman, pp. 493–94, twice gives the date of the meeting erroneously as July 23, perhaps through confusion with the earlier Collins-Vandenberg visit, which he does not mention. See also Collins, pp. 123–26, and Courtney Whitney, *MacArthur, His Rendezvous with History;* (New York: Knopf, 1956), pp. 345–50.

18. Collins, p. 123.

19. Schnabel, p. 149.

20. Ibid., p. 150.

21. Collins, pp. 124–25.

22. Ibid., p. 120.

23. Ibid., p. 125.

24. Appleman, p. 493.

25. Collins, p. 126.

26. Schnabel, pp. 171–72; Appleman, p. 503.

27. Appleman, p. 497.

28. Ibid., p. 500.

29. Ibid., pp. 545–46.

30. Ibid., p. 395.

31. Ibid., p. 546.

32. Ibid., p. 547.

33. Ibid., p. 548.

34. Ibid., p. 381.

35. Ibid., p. 545.

36. Schnabel, p. 150.

37. Bradley, p. 547.

38. Ibid., p. 547; Schnabel and Watson, p. 211 note.

39. Truman, *Memoirs*, 2:358–59.

CHAPTER 25. *MacArthur Alienates Truman*

1. Schnabel and Watson, p. 515. The text of the MacArthur message to the VFW is printed in *Military Situation in the Far East*, pt. 5, pp. 3477–80.

2. Ibid., p. 516. See *Military Situation in the Far East,* pt. 2., p. 1217.

3. Collins, p. 274.

4. Acheson, p. 423.

5. Truman, pp. 354–55; Schnabel, p. 370, John W. Spanier, *The Truman-MacArthur Controversy and the Korean War* (Cambridge, Mass.: Harvard University Press, 1959), pp. 73–77, gives a good analysis of the MacArthur message and its political and diplomatic impact.

6. Bradley, p. 551.

7. Schnabel and Watson, pp. 515–16, cites *Public Papers, Truman, 1950,* pp. 531–32.

8. Ibid., p. 516.

9. Ibid., pp. 516–17; Schnabel, pp. 369–70.

10. Truman, p. 356; Acheson, p. 423; Bradley, p. 551; Collins, p. 275; Schnabel and Watson, p. 517; Schnabel, p. 370.

11. Acheson, p. 423.

12. Ibid., p. 423.

13. Bradley, p. 551.

14. Truman, p. 356.

15. Bradley, p. 551; Schnabel and Watson, p. 517.

16. Schnabel and Watson, p. 517, cites SecDef DEF 89880 to CINCFE, 26 Aug 50, reprinted in *Military Situation in the Far East,* pt. 5, p. 3480; General Bradley later testified the order was sent without consulting the Joint Chiefs (*Military Situation in the Far East,* pt. 2, p. 880).

17. Schnabel, p. 370, cites Johnson's testimony in *Military Situation in the Far East,* pp. 2587, 3665.

18. Truman, pp. 355–56.

19. Schnabel, p. 371, cites C 61325, CINCFE to DA for SecDef, MacArthur (personal) for Johnson, 27 Aug 50; MacArthur, pp. 385–86, 389.

20. McLellan, p. 283.

21. Schnabel, p. 370; Schnabel and Watson, p. 518.

22. Schnabel, p. 370 cites *Military Situation in the Far East,* p. 2002.

23. Bradley, p. 552; McLellan, p. 285.

24. Schnabel and Watson, p. 218.

25. Bradley, p. 552; McLellan, p. 285.

CHAPTER 26. *The North Koreans Try Once More*

1. Schnabel and Watson, pp. 211–12 cites JCS 89960 to CINCFE, 28 Aug 50.

2. Ibid., p. 212.

3. Ibid., p. 212; Schnabel, p. 151; Collins, p. 126n says the JCS did not get copies of the Inchon invasion order until September 8.

4. The narrative on the North Korean September offensive is based on

Schnabel and Watson, pp. 212–13; Appleman, pp. 397–487; Montross and Canzona, 1: 209–25.

5. Appleman, p. 395–96.
6. Ibid., pp. 381–83.
7. Ibid., pp. 393–94.
8. Ibid., pp. 395–96.
9. Ibid., p. 438.
10. Ibid., p. 408.
11. Ibid., pp. 411–36.
12. Ibid., p. 422.
13. Ibid., pp. 443–51.
14. Ibid., pp. 445–46.
15. Ibid., p. 450.
16. Ibid., p. 452.
17. Ibid., pp. 437–43.
18. Ibid., p. 452.
19. Ibid., p. 453; Montross and Canzona, 1: 212–37, gives a detailed account of marine operations in the second battle of the Naktong Bulge.
20. Appleman, p. 496.
21. Ibid., p. 496; Montross and Canzona, 1: 210–11.
22. Appleman, p. 496–97.
23. Ibid., pp. 391–92.
24. Ibid., p. 416.

CHAPTER 27. *The Joint Chiefs Get Cold Feet*
1. Bradley, p. 555.
2. Schnabel, p. 152 cites, JCS 90639 to CINCFE, 5 Sep 50.
3. Ibid., pp. 152–53, cites C 62213, CINCFE to JCS, 6 Sep 50.
4. Schnabel and Watson, p. 213, cites JCS 90908 to CINCFE, 7 Sep 50; Schnabel, p. 153.
5. Schnabel and Watson, p. 213 cites MacArthur, p. 351.
6. Ibid., pp. 213–14, cites CINCFE C 62423 to DA for JCS, 8 Sep 50, CM IN 9304; Schnabel, pp. 153–54.
7. Bradley, p. 556.
8. Ibid., p. 556.
9. Schnabel and Watson, p. 214, cites JCS 90958 to CINCFE, 8 Sep 50.
10. Ibid., p. 215.
11. Ibid., p. 215 cites, Brig Gen Lynn D. Smith, USA (Ret.), "A Nickel After a Dollar," *Army*, September, 1970, pp. 25, 32–34.
12. Appleman, p. 466.

13. Ibid., pp. 469–70.
14. Ibid., pp. 421–36.
15. Ibid., pp. 470–85.
16. Ibid., pp. 478–79.
17. Ibid., p. 435.
18. Ibid., pp. 477–78.

CHAPTER 28. *Inchon*
1. Cagle and Manson, pp. 503–08; Appleman, p. 497.
2. Cagle and Manson, pp. 88–89; Appleman, p. 501, cites Walter M. Karig, *Battle Report: The War in Korea,* (New York: Rinehart, 1952), pp. 176–91, which relates the Clark mission in detail.
3. Cagle and Manson, p. 89.
4. Ibid., p. 89.
5. Ibid., p. 89; Appleman, p. 500.
6. Cagle and Manson, p. 89.
7. Ibid., p. 91; Appleman, p. 502.
8. Appleman, pp. 501–2.
9. Ibid., p. 502; Collins, p. 130.
10. Collins, p. 130; Appleman, p. 502.
11. Collins, p. 131.
12. Cagle and Manson, p. 90.
13. Ibid., pp. 90–93; Collins, p. 131; Appleman, p. 503.
14. Cagle and Manson, pp. 91–93; Appleman, p. 503.
15. Collins, p. 131.
16. Cagle and Manson, p. 93.
17. Ibid., p. 93; Appleman, p. 503.
18. Appleman, p. 499; Cagle and Manson, p. 97; Montross and Canzona, vol. 2, gives a complete and detailed account of the marine aspects of the Inchon landing and the capture of Seoul.
19. Appleman, p. 499.
20. Cagle and Manson, p. 93.
21. Collins, p. 132; Appleman, pp. 503–5; Cagle and Manson, pp. 93–101.
22. Appleman, p. 508.
23. Ibid., pp. 506–7.
24. Cagle and Manson, p. 94.
25. Ibid., pp. 99–100.
26. Appleman, pp. 507–8; Montross and Canzona, 2:110–111.
27. Montross and Canzona, 2:134.
28. Ibid., pp. 149–51; Appleman, pp. 509–10.
29. Montross and Canzona, 2:151–52; Appleman, p. 510.

30. Montross and Canzona, 2:159–64.

31. Appleman, pp. 511–12.

32. Ibid., pp. 544, 572.

33. Ibid., p. 571.

34. Ibid., p. 513.

35. Ibid., p. 519.

36. Ibid., p. 523.

37. Ibid., p. 512.

38. Ibid., p. 512.

39. Ibid., p. 513.

40. Ibid., p. 511.

41. Ibid., p. 515.

42. Ibid., p. 510.

43. Ibid., p. 571.

44. Ibid., p. 518.

45. Ibid., p. 518, Montross and Canzona, 2:225–32 provides a full description of Company A's operation.

46. Appleman, pp. 518–19.

47. Ibid., pp. 520–22.

48. Ibid., p. 522.

CHAPTER 29. *The Assault on Seoul*

1. Appleman, p. 520.

2. The narrative on the reduction of Seoul is largely drawn from Appleman pp. 515–41, and Montross and Canzona, 2:233–52.

3. Appleman, p. 523.

4. Ibid., p. 527.

5. Ibid., p. 527; Montross and Canzona, 2:244.

6. Appleman, p. 527.

7. Ibid., p. 526.

8. Ibid., pp. 528–29.

9. Ibid., p. 531.

10. Ibid., p. 533.

11. Ibid., p. 531.

12. Ibid., p. 532; Montross and Canzona, 2:261–64.

13. Appleman, p. 533.

14. Ibid., p. 530.

15. Ibid., p. 531.

16. Ibid., pp. 534–35; Montross and Canzona, 2:261–80.

17. Appleman, pp. 537–38.

18. Ibid., p. 537; Schnabel, pp. 184–85, cites W 92972, DA to CINCFE, 30 Sep 50.

19. Appleman, p. 540.
20. Montross and Canzona, 2:134.
21. Bradley, p. 556.
22. Ibid., p. 557.

CHAPTER 30. *Breakout from the Perimeter*
1. Appleman, pp. 542–43.
2. Ibid., pp. 571–72.
3. Ibid., p. 542.
4. Ibid., p. 572.
5. Ibid., p. 572.
6. Ibid., pp. 582–83.
7. Ibid., p. 572, The narrative summary of the breakout from the Pusan Perimeter is largely drawn from Appleman, pp. 542–606, which provides a detailed study of the entire operation by all participating units.
8. Ibid., p. 578.
9. Ibid., p. 602.
10. Ibid., p. 600.
11. Ibid., p. 573.
12. Ibid., pp. 590–98.
13. Ibid., p. 603.
14. Ibid., pp. 599, 603–04.
15. Ibid., pp. 587–88 cites the 25th Division War Diary, 5 Oct 50; 24th Division War Diary, Staff Sections, 29 Sep – 31 Oct 50 and G-1 Historical Report, 4 Oct 50; 2nd Division War Diary, Judge Advocate Staff Section Report, Sep-Oct 50; Interim Historical Report, War Crimes Division, Judge Advocate Section, Korean Communications Zone (cumulated to 30 Jun 53); New York *Times*, 3 Oct 50. National Archives photos in army files (by cities) show bodies of victims. Photos are located at Defense Audiovisual Agencies, Still Photographic Depository, Building 168, Anacostia Naval Station, Washington, D.C. 20374.
16. New York *Times*, 14 Jul 50, p. 2.
17. *People's China* Peking [Beijing], 2, no. 5 1 Sep 50; idem. 2, 16 Dec 50; idem. 3, no. 6 (16 Mar 51).

CHAPTER 31. *The United States Decides to Conquer*
1. Appleman, pp. 545–46, 604.
2. Schnabel and Watson, pp. 220–30.
3. Appleman, p. 604.
4. Bradley, p. 570.
5. Ibid., p. 564.
6. Schnabel and Watson, p. 262, cites Memo, Director CIA to President, 12

Oct 50, w/encl, OCJCS File 381 (1950).

7. Ibid., p. 262, cites FEC Daily Intelligence Summary No. 2957 of 14 Oct 50; Appleman, p. 759.

8. Bradley, p. 570.

9. Ibid., p. 570.

10. Charles O. Hucker, *China's Imperial Past* (Stanford, Calif: Stanford University Press, 1975), pp. 125–27.

11. *Military Situation in the Far East*, pt. 2, pp. 731–32, May, 1951.

12. McLellan, p. 291.

13. Murphy, pp. 41–42, cites Martin Lichterman, *To the Yalu and Back*, Inter-University Case Program 92 (New York: Bobbs-Merrill Company, 1963), p. 16; Robert A. Taft, *A Foreign Policy for Americans*, (Garden City, N.Y.: Doubleday and Company, 1951), pp. 106–7; Arthur H. Vandenberg, Jr., ed., *The Private Papers of Senator Vandenberg*, (Boston: Houghton Mifflin Company, 1952), pp. 544–45; New York *Times*, 18 Sep 50, p. 22; 30 Sep 50, p. 16; 1 Oct 50, p. 8E; *Time*, 25 Sep 50, p. 35; 9 Oct 50, pp. 34–35; David Lawrence, "Expose the Aggressors," *U.S. News and World Report*, 6 Oct 50, p. 52; 13 Oct 50, pp. 6, 8; Hanson W. Baldwin, New York *Times*, 27 Sep 50, p. 6.

14. Acheson, p. 450.

15. Schnabel and Watson, p. 220, cites Memo, ExecSecy, NSC to NSC, "Future United States Policy with Respect to North Korea," 17 Jul 50, *Foreign Relations, 1950, Korea*, p. 410.

16. Ibid., p. 224, cites NSC 81, 1 Sep 50, *Foreign Relations, 1950, Korea*, pp. 685–93.

17. Ibid., p. 226; Bradley, p. 560.

18. Schnabel and Watson, p. 227.

19. Ibid., pp. 226–27.

20. Ibid., p. 227.

21. Ibid., p. 228, cites *Public Papers, Truman, 1950*, p. 644.

22. Ibid., p. 230, cites JCS 92801 to CINCFE, 27 Sep 50.

23. Murphy, pp. 47–48, cites New York *Times*, 28 Sep 50, p. 14.

24. Schnabel and Watson, p. 240, cites Department of State *Bulletin*, 2 Oct 50, p. 559; 9 Oct 50, pp. 597–98.

25. Ibid., p. 241, cites New York *Times*, 30 Sep 50, p. 4.

26. Ibid., p. 242, cites Trygve Lie, *In the Cause of Peace* (New York: MacMillan, 1954), p. 345.

27. Ibid., p. 242, cites JCS 92985 to CINCFE, 29 Sep 50.

28. Ibid., p. 243, cites CINCFE C 65034 to JCS for SecDef, 30 Sep 50, CM IN 16966.

29. Ibid., p. 243, cites CINCFE C 65118 to DA for JCS, 1 Oct 50, CM IN 17229; JCS 93079 to CINCFE, 1 Oct 50.

30. Murphy, p. 44, cites New York *Times*, 26 Sep 50, pp. 1, 14.

31. Schnabel and Watson, pp. 244–45, cites text of resolution of 7 Oct 50 in Raymond Dennett and Robert K. Turner, eds., *Documents on American Foreign Relations,* vol. 12, January 1–December 31, 1950,(Princeton, N.J.: Princeton University Press, World Peace Foundation, 1951) pp. 459–60.

32. Ibid., pp. 244– 45; Acheson, p. 454; Department of State *Bulletin,* 9 Oct 50, pp. 596–97.

33. Schnabel and Watson, p. 247, cites *Military Situation in the Far East,* pt. 1, p. 19.

34. Ibid., p. 247, cites *Military Situation in the Far East,* pt. 1, pp. 361–62.

35. Acheson, p. 455.

36. Schnabel and Watson, p. 246, cites *Military Situation in the Far East,* pt. 3, p. 2258.

37. Ibid., p. 247.

38. Whiting, pp. 78–79; Murphy, p. 28.

39. Murphy, p. 30.

40. Schnabel and Watson, p. 260; Murphy, pp. 29–31.

41. Schnabel and Watson, p. 260 note; Murphy, p. 31; Whiting, p. 96.

42. Whiting, p. 96.

43. Ibid., p. 100; Murphy, p. 34.

CHAPTER 32. *Red China Warns the United States*

1. Appleman, p. 615.

2. Ibid., pp. 614–15, 623; Schnabel and Watson, p. 249.

3. Schnabel and Watson, pp. 233–38; Bradley, p. 565; Appleman, p. 609–14; Schnabel, pp. 187–92.

4. Bradley, p. 568.

5. Schnabel and Watson, p. 257.

6. Ibid., p. 258, cites Dept of State, Office of Intelligence Research (OIR), "Chinese Communist Propaganda on the Korean Conflict, June- October 1950," OIR Rpt No. 5409, 29 Nov 50, copy in G-2 files; Whiting, pp. 47–115.

7. Murphy, p. 34, cites New York *Times,* 17 Aug 50, p. 4.

8. Whiting, p. 79; Murphy, p. 34; *People's China* (Peking) 2, no. 5. (1 Sep 50).

9. Whiting, pp. 69–70, 92–94.

10. Schnabel and Watson, p. 258, cites the first of these figures is given in Charles A. Willoughby and John Chamberlain, *MacArthur: 1941–1951,* (New York: McGraw-Hill Book Co., 1951), p. 386; the source is not identified, but presumably is one of the FEC Daily Intelligence Summaries (DIS). Schnabel, p. 199, however, says the source is a manuscript, Col Bruce W. Bidwell, "History of the War Department Intelligence Division," pt. 7, ch. 5. The second figure is from Schnabel, p. 199, and is taken from

FEC DIS 2934 for 21 Sep 50; it is given as the number of troops Maj Gen Charles A. Willoughby, FEC G-2, speculated were "massed in Manchuria," but presumably refers to regulars rather than militia. Whiting, pp. 119–21, gives a tabulation, illustrated with maps, of major Chinese Communist forces between May and November 1950, which clearly bring out the shift to the Korean borders; the information is compiled from various secondary works.

11. Schnabel and Watson, p. 285, cites Willoughby and Chamberlain, p. 386; Appleman, p. 758.

12. Schnabel, p. 199.

13. Murphy, p. 39, cites Willoughby and Chamberlain, pp. 385–86.

14. Acheson, p. 542; Schnabel and Watson, p. 259.

15. K. M. Panikkar, *In Two Chinas: Memoirs of A Diplomat* (London: Allen and Unwin, 1955), pp. 107–8; Bradley, p. 569.

16. Schnabel, p. 198.

17. Murphy, p. 52, cites Richard P. Stebbins, *The United States in World Affairs, 1950*, (New York: Harper & Bros, 1951), p. 359; Whiting, pp. 107–8; New York *Times*, 2 Oct 50, p. 3; Appleman, p. 608. Harrison E. Salisbury reported in the New York *Times* (2 Oct 50, p. 3) that Zhou's statement had received big headlines in Moscow, something it did not get in the United States.

18. Panikkar, pp. 109–11.

19. Schnabel and Watson, p. 260, cites London 1934 to State, 3 Oct 50, CM IN 17782. This is in National Archives in JCS file CCS (Combined Chiefs of Staff) file No. 383. 21 Korea (3–19–45) sec. 34.

20. Ibid., p. 261.

21. Truman, *Memoirs*, 2:362.

22. Bradley, p. 569.

23. Acheson, p. 452.

24. Bradley, p. 570; Schnabel and Watson, p. 262, cites Memo, Director CIA to President, 12 Oct 50, w/encl., OCJCS File 381 (1950).

25. Appleman, p. 759; Schnabel and Watson, pp. 258, 262; Willoughby and Chamberlain, p. 386; Schnabel, p. 200. All cite FEC UN Command DIS No. 2957 of 14 Oct 50.

26. Schnabel and Watson, p. 261.

27. Whiting, pp. 108, 110.

28. The narrative on the Wake Island conference is drawn from the following sources: Schnabel and Watson, pp. 263–70; Truman, *Memoirs* 2:362–63; Bradley, pp. 572–77; Schnabel, pp. 210–14; Appleman, pp. 760– 61.

29. Acheson, p. 456.

30. Appleman, p. 760.

31. Ibid., p. 761.
32. Truman, *Memoirs,* 2:368.

CHAPTER 33. *Up to the Chongchon River*
1. Schnabel and Watson, pp. 232, 238; Appleman, p. 609.
2. Schnabel and Watson, p. 249.
3. Appleman, pp. 615–18, 622–31.
4. Ibid., pp. 634–35.
5. Ibid., pp. 618–21, 631–37.
6. Ibid., p. 630.
7. Ibid., p. 614.
8. Ibid., pp. 646–53.
9. Ibid., p. 635.
10. Ibid., p. 636.
11. Ibid., pp. 636–37.
12. Ibid., p. 729.
13. Ibid., pp. 738–41.
14. Ibid., p. 746; Schnabel and Watson, p. 237.
15. Ibid., pp. 654–66.
16. Ibid., pp. 658–60.
17. Ibid., pp. 661–63.

CHAPTER 34. *Destination: The Yalu River*
1. Appleman, pp. 664–65.
2. Ibid., p. 665–66.
3. Ibid., p. 670; Schnabel and Watson, pp. 274–75.
4. Schnabel and Watson, p. 275, cites JCS 94933 to CINCFE, 24 Oct 50.
5. Ibid., p. 276, cites CINCFE C 67397 to DA for JCS, 25 Oct 50, CM IN 4890.
6. Ibid., p. 276.
7. Bradley, p. 579.
8. I. F. Stone, *Hidden History of the Korean War* (New York: Monthly Review Press, 1952), p. 155.
9. Appleman, p. 699, cites CX67506, CINCFE to CG Eighth Army and CG JLC, 26 Oct 50, and CX 7702, CINCFE to DA, 28 Oct 50.
10. *People's China* (Peking) 2, no. 10 (November 16, 1950), pp. 4–5.
11. *Selected Works of Mao Tsetung,* 4 vols. (Peking: Foreign Languages Press, 1977), 4:61.
12. Ibid., 5:117.

CHAPTER 35. *The Warning Blow Falls*
1. The narrative on the Onjong engagements and the first engagements at

Unsan are drawn from Appleman, pp. 671–84.

2. Whiting, p. 125; Cagle and Manson, p. 168; George, p. 127.

3. Appleman, p. 677, cites EUSAK PIR 106, 26 Oct 50; I Corps Opn Dir 15, 26 Oct 50.

4. Ibid., p. 678.

5. Schnabel, p. 234, cites DIS, GHQ, UNC, 2971, 28 Oct 50.

6. Appleman, p. 677, cites I Corps War Diary, 27 Oct 50; New York *Times*, 27 Oct 50.

CHAPTER 36. *Disaster at Unsan*

1. Appleman, pp. 679–81. The narrative on the engagement of 8th Cavalry Regiment and supporting arms at Unsan is drawn from Appleman, pp. 689–700, and from Capt Edward C. Williamson, 4th Historical Detachment, Eighth Army, Narrative Report, "Unsan: Ambush of Battery C, 99th Field Artillery Battalion, 1st Cavalry Division, 29 October–2 November 1950," in Modern Military History Branch, National Archives.

2. George, p. 4.

3. Williamson, "Unsan: Ambush of Battery C."

CHAPTER 37. *The Lost Battalion*

1. The narrative on the action of 3rd Battalion, 8th Cavalry, is drawn from Appleman, pp. 700–708.

CHAPTER 38. *The Chinese Back Off*

1. Schnabel, pp. 234–35, cites a Gen Walker memo of 6 Nov 50 to MacArthur.

2. Ibid., pp. 235–36; Appleman, p. 709.

3. Appleman, p. 709–16.

4. Ibid., pp. 686–88. The Changjin reservoir was shown by its Japanese name, Chosin reservoir, on the Japanese maps the Americans used; likewise the nearby Pujon reservoir was shown as the Fusen reservoir; for this reason, many of the reports on engagements in this region call the reservoirs by their Japanese names (Appleman, p. 729 n.).

5. Ibid., pp. 741–45.

CHAPTER 39. *A Time to Reconsider*

1. Whiting, pp. 137, 160–62, speculates on Chinese reasons for withdrawing, but reaches no conclusions.

2. Schnabel and Watson, p. 281, cites *Military Situation in the Far East*, pt. 5, p. 3427.

3. Ibid., p. 281, cites CIA PD 430 and PD 432 to CSUSA et al., 26 Oct 50, CM IN 5569, and 27 Oct 50, CM IN 5570. Both messages bore "Routine" precedence.

4. Ibid., p. 282.

5. Ibid., p. 289 cites AC/S, G-3 WAR 95790 to CINCFE, 3 Nov 50; Truman, *Memoirs* 2:373.

6. Schnabel and Watson, pp. 289–90, cites CINCFE C 68285 to DA for JCS, 4 Nov 50, CM IN 8116; MacArthur's response is printed in Truman, *Memoirs* 2:373.

7. Ibid., cites Department of State *Bulletin,* 13 Nov 50, p. 792.

8. Ibid., pp. 300–301.

9. Acheson, p. 466.

10. Schnabel, p. 241; Schnabel and Watson, p. 290; Futrell, pp. 209–10.

11. Schnabel and Watson, pp. 292–94, cite CINCFE C 68396 to DA, 6 Nov 50, CM IN 8618; reprinted in Truman, *Memoirs* 2:375.

12. Bradley, p. 585.

13. Appleman, p. 762, cites GHQ FEC Communique 11, 6 Nov 50; see also New York *Times,* 6 Nov 50; Department of State Publication 4263, pp. 20–22. MacArthur's complaints, often repeated, about the "privileged sanctuary" of Manchuria for Chinese troops and aircraft drew a lot of support among some in the military, on Capitol Hill and in the U.S. at large. This was a spurious argument, because the UN forces also enjoyed a "privileged sanctuary" not only in Japan and Okinawa, where many aircraft were based, but on and behind the lines in Korea as well.
Commenting on this in the 1951 Senate committee hearing on the Far East situation, General Bradley said the communists "are not bombing our ports and supply installations, and they are not bombing our troops" (*Military Situation in the Far East,* pt. 2, pp. 878– 79). The UN forces actually enjoyed a far more privileged sanctuary than the communists because everything on and above the battle line in Korea was fair game for UN bombing and strafing raids, whereas the skies on the front lines and behind it were almost always clear of communist aircraft, except in a few isolated cases.

14. The really cold weather, which was to be as much of an enemy as the Chinese, struck on November 14 all across the front, dropping temperatures to 10°F. in the west to -20°F. in northeastern Korea (Schnabel, p. 272). The Yalu's surface had only a short time to remain liquid.

15. Truman, *Memoirs* 2:375–76.

16. Futrell, pp. 211–16; Schnabel, pp. 245–46; Appleman, p. 716. Despite urging that UN aircraft be permitted "hot pursuit" of Red aircraft a few miles into Manchuria, crossing the border remained forbidden, primarily because of the opposition of U.S. allies. See Schnabel and Watson, pp. 315–16; Schnabel, pp. 247–50.

17. Acheson, p. 468.

CHAPTER 40. *Empty Rhetoric on the Potomac*

1. Schnabel and Watson, p. 301, cites JCS 96060 to CINCFE, 8 Nov 50 (and JCS 96069, correcting an error in the original).

2. Ibid., p. 301, cites CINCFE CX 68436 to JCS, 7 Nov 50, DA IN 8684.

3. Ibid., pp. 301–302, cites CINCFE C 68572 to DA for JCS, 9 Nov 50, CM IN 9417.

4. Appleman, p. 765, cites CINCFE to DA for JCS, C68572, 9 Nov 50.

5. Schnabel and Watson, p. 308, cites Memo of Conversation of Ambassador in Korea (Muccio), "North Korean Military Action," 17 Nov 50, *Foreign Relations, 1950, Korea,* p. 1175.

6. Appleman, pp. 717–18.

7. Schnabel, p. 272, cites C 69211, CINCUNC to DA, 18 Nov 50.

8. Schnabel and Watson, pp. 302–4, cites Memo, JCS to SecDef, "Chinese Communist Intervention in Korea," 9 Nov 50.

9. Ibid., pp. 304–305, cites NSC action No. 387, 9 Nov 50; NCS 81/2, 14 Nov 50, filed in National Archives JCS records as CCS (Combined Chiefs of Staff) 383.21 Korea (3-19-45), sec. 39. At a meeting on November 8, 1950, of the National Security Council staff to draw up recommendations for the November 9 meeting, the CIA representative estimated there were 750,000 Chinese troops in Manchuria available for use in Korea. Two Defense Department officials said the UN situation would be serious if these forces intervened and no action were allowed against Manchuria. They said, without attacking Manchuria (which might set off a full-scale war), UN air power could only impede, not stop, Chinese progress. (Schnabel and Watson, p. 304, cites Memo, Finletter to SecDef [Marshall], 8 Nov 50, Office of the Secretary of Defense File, CD 092 [Korea] Folder 3.) Despite the responsibility residing in the Truman administration and the Chiefs of Staff, the Far East Command's estimates of Chinese capabilities and intentions were the determining factors in the estimates by MacArthur's superiors in Washington. Says Roy Appleman in his official history of the first five months of the war (p. 757): "Normally the intelligence evaluation of whether a foreign power has decided to intervene in a war in national force involves political intelligence at the highest level. Field and theater commanders could expect such an evaluation to be made by the government in Washington with the advice of its Central Intelligence Agency. The intelligence responsibility of Eighth Army and X Corps was tactical; strategic intelligence responsibility rested with the Central Intelligence Agency, the Department of the Army, and the theater headquarters, with the ultimate political intelligence the responsibility of the President and his immediate advisors. But apparently the Central Intelligence Agency and the administration generally did not evaluate the available intelligence so as to reach a conviction on the question of whether

the Chinese intended to intervene in the Korean War different from that held by General MacArthur. It must be inferred that either Washington was undecided or that its view coincided with that of the Commander in Chief, Far East, since it did not issue directives to him stating a different estimate. The conclusion, then, is that in the developing situation of November the views of the Far East Command were decisive on the military course to be taken in Korea at that time." The Far East Command (FEC) estimate of October 28 asserted that the auspicious time for Chinese intervention had passed. On October 31 the FEC daily summary mentioned ten Chinese prisoners had been captured and the ROK II Corps had suffered reverses, and this "may signify the commitment of Chinese Communist Forces in the Korean conflict." (Appleman, p. 761, cites FEC DIS 2974, 31 Oct 50.) But the United Nations command report to the Security Council for October 16–31 said there was no positive evidence the Chinese had entered Korea. (Appleman, p. 762, cites Dept of State Publication 4051, United Nations Command Eighth Report to the Security Council, 16-31 October 1950, p. 2.) By November 3 the FEC said there might be 34,000 Chinese in Korea, and added that 833,000 men were in Manchuria, of whom 415,000 were regular Chinese ground forces. (Appleman, p. 762 cites FEC DIS 2977, 3 Nov 50.) By November 9 the FEC had raised the probable total of Chinese in Korea to 76,800 men.(Appleman, p. 763, cites FEC DIS 2983, 9 Nov 50, and 2988, 14 Nov 50.) In November on a visit to X Corps, Maj Gen Charles A. Willoughby, MacArthur's G-2, discussed the danger of Chinese entry with General Almond and other officers. Asked how many Chinese troops he estimated were in Korea, Willoughby answered that only volunteers had entered Korea and probably only a battalion of each division identified was actually in Korea. Asked about the reverse suffered by the 8th Cavalry Regiment at Unsan, Willoughby reportedly said the regiment had failed to put out adequate security, had been overrun by a small, violent surprise attack, and had scattered during the hours of darkness. (Appleman, p. 764, cites Letter, Col William J. McCaffrey, X Corps deputy chief of staff, Nov 50, to Lt Gen Edward M. Almond, 1 Dec 54, and forwarded by Almond to Appleman.)

10. Schnabel and Watson, p. 311, cites G-3 DA WAR 96655 to CINCUNC, 15 Nov 50; Department of State *Bulletin*, 20 Nov 50.

11. Ibid., pp. 240, 313.

12. Schnabel, p. 266, cites Intelligence Report, 13 Nov 50, in G-2, DA files.

13. Ibid., p. 266.

14. Schnabel and Watson, pp. 314, 324, cite State to Supreme Commander, Allied Powers (SCAP) Tokyo (unnumbered), 17 Nov 50, CM IN 12347, which summarizes the British proposal; memo of conversation by

Ambassador-at-Large Philip Jessup, 21 Nov 50, *Foreign Relations, 1950, Korea*, pp. 1204–08; Acheson, p. 467.

15. Memorandum for the Chief of Staff, U.S. Army, "State-Defense High Level Meeting on Korea (Buffer State in North Korea)," by Maj Gen Charles L. Bolte, with addenda; message to MacArthur by CofS USA (Collins) to CINCUNC, WAR 97287, 24 Nov 50, on results of State-Defense meeting, in National Archives, Joint Chiefs of Staff, G-3 files. See also Schnabel, pp. 267–71; Schnabel and Watson, pp. 323–29.

16. Schnabel, p. 272, and Schnabel and Watson, p. 322, cite CINCFE C 69211 to DA for JCS, 18 Nov 50, CM IN 12368. The X Corps decision to attack on November 27 was approved November 24 by MacArthur: Schnabel, p. 266, cites CX 69661, CINCFE to CG X Corps, 24 Nov 50, X Corps Operations Order No. 7, 25 Nov 50.

17. Schnabel, p. 270, and Schnabel and Watson, pp. 330–31, cite C 69808, CINCUNC to DA for JCS, 25 Nov 50, CM IN 14393.

18. Schnabel and Watson, p. 331.

CHAPTER 41. *A Different Kind of Army*

1. Appleman, p. 688; 1st Lt Bevin R. Alexander, "Enemy Materiel," 5th Historical Detachment, Eighth Army, National Archives.

2. George, p. 36.

3. Ibid., p. 127.

4. Ibid., pp. 15, 51, 136.

5. Ibid., p. 40.

6. Ibid., pp. 36–7.

7. Alexander, "Enemy Materiel"; Appleman, pp. 688, 718.

8. Montross and Canzona, 3:93.

9. R. R. Palmer, in "Frederick the Great, Guibert, Bulow: From Dynastic to National War,'', in *Makers of Modern Strategy—Military Thought from Machiavelli to Hitler*, ed. Edward Meade Earle (Princeton, N.J.: Princeton University Press, 1943), p. 70.

10. Appleman, p. 770.

11. Ibid., p. 719.

12. The account of Chinese tactics is based on Alexander, "Enemy Materiel"; Montross and Canzona, 3:91–94, and a study by S. L. A. Marshall, "CCF in the Attack," Eighth Army Staff Memorandum, ORS-S-26, 5 Jan 51. See also S. L. A. Marshall, *The River and the Gauntlet*(New York: William Morrow & Company, 1953), which describes Chinese tactics in the defeat of Eighth Army by Chinese Communist Forces, November, 1950, in the battle of the Chongchon river.

13. Montross and Canzona, 3:107.

14. Wu Xuguang, Wang Yan, He Ding, Jiang Baohua, Zhang Xi,

Biographies of PLA Generals, Peng Dehuai, vol. 3, Beijing: Liberation Army Publishing House, 1986, chapter 6, translated by Ellis L. Melvin, Tamaroa, Illinois.

15. Ibid.

16. The CCF division sometimes averaged below 10,000 men in Korea, but divisions usually were brought up to strength after engagements. Normal CCF doctrine was to commit a division to combat for about six days and then withdraw it to replenish supplies and replace casualties. This procedure limited the capacity of CCF forces to sustain offensives and momentum of breakthroughs. In theory a CCF division had three infantry regiments and a battalion of artillery, though in 1950 in Korea Chinese artillery was extremely rare. After the beginning of the peace talks in the summer of 1951, however, the Chinese gradually built up artillery in a wide mixture of guns and howitzers (some captured American, some Russian, some Japanese) which began to approach parity with UN artillery. The CCF strength, however, always remained greater in mortars than in artillery. The ridges of Korea were ideally suited for mortars, anyway, because their high trajectory permitted rounds to be dropped on emplacements virtually wherever located, whereas artillery and tank gun shells, fired on a flatter trajectory, often could not reach enemy positions on the reverse slopes of hills or in positions masked by hills in front. Artillery howitzers, with a high trajectory, especially when fired at maximum elevation of the tubes, were better at reaching emplacements than flatter-trajectory guns, but neither were as good as mortars. Of course, high-velocity flat-trajectory weapons were ideal for shattering armor or bunkers, and the Chinese suffered in this respect. CCF infantry regiments, in addition to three 852-man infantry battalions (often averaging fewer men in combat), had a mortar and bazooka (rocket-launcher) company, guard company, transportation company, medical unit with attached stretcher personnel (often civilians pressed into service), and a combined reconnaissance and signal company. CCF infantry battalions had three companies of about 200 men each (often averaging fewer), plus a heavy weapons (mortars and machine guns) company, and a small headquarters. Each company had three rifle platoons, a 60 mm mortar platoon, and headquarters. (Montross and Canzona, 3:86, 89 n., 93 n.; Alexander, "Enemy Materiel.")

17. Appleman, p. 751, cites FEC MIS, Order of Battle Information, CCF, pp. 9, 171; FEC Intelligence Digest 10, 2 Nov 51.

18. Ibid., p. 718.

19. Ibid., pp. 766–67.

20. Ibid., pp. 717–18, cites Allied Translator and Interpreter Section (ATIS) *Enemy Documents*, Issue 47, pp. 139ff, booklet, "A Collection of Combat Experiences," issued by Hq XIX Army Group, CCF 29 Mar 51 (also par-

tially reproduced by Hq U.S. I Corps, G-2 Sec., Aug 51); Ibid., Issue 11, pp. 74–82, "Primary Conclusions of Battle Experiences at Unsan," issued by Hq 66th Army, 20 Nov 50; Ibid., Issue 6, 2 Sep 51, A-9 and 35, 1–15 Nov 52, p. 45; FEC Intel Digest, vol. 1, no. 4, p. 26 (17 Feb 53), XIII Army Group, CCF; FEC, Order of Battle Information, CCF, 15 Jun 51; Eighth U.S. Army Korea PIR 109, 29 Oct 50.

21. Ibid., pp. 753–54.

22. George, p. 173.

23. Appleman, p. 720; Chinese document "Primary Conclusions of Battle Experiences at Unsan," cited in note 20 above.

CHAPTER 42. *Attack into the Unknown*

1. Appleman, pp. 772–76; Schnabel and Watson, p. 321; Schnabel, pp. 257–63; Montross and Canzona, 3:121–24.

2. Appleman, p. 772.

3. Montross and Canzona, 3:134.

4. Appleman, pp. 732–38.

5. A fascinating study of this action was produced by 1st Lt Martin Blumenson, 3rd Historical Detachment, Eighth Army, "Task Force Kingston, 32d Infantry Regiment, 22–29 November 1950," National Archives.

6. Appleman, p. 756, cites X Corps PIR 58, 23 Nov 50.

7. Ibid., p. 754, cites EUSAK PIR 124, 13 Nov 50; PIR 129, Incl 2, 18 Nov 50, and PIR 131, 20 Nov 50.

8. *Korea 1950,* p. 234.

9. Appleman, p. 768.

10. *Korea 1950,* pp. 228, 233.

11. Appleman, p. 606, shows postwar tabulation of UN strength as of 30 Sep 50: 103,601 army (including 29,153 nondivisional combat troops); 21,525 First Marine Division; ROK army divisions 82,786, plus 18,787 ROKs attached to U.S. combat units; 27th British Brigade, 1,704; Philippine combat team, 1,369. Appleman, p. 668, gives strength of the Turkish Brigade on arrival in October, 1950 (5,190 soldiers). Appleman, p. 739, gives October, 1950, strength of 3rd Infantry Division (except 65th Regiment, estimated at 3,000 men): 7,494 men, plus 8,500 ROKs. U.S. Army ground service units, 28,507; ROK ground service units, 90,608. Strength of 29th British Brigade estimated at 2,800 men, and Australian Battalion at 900 men.

12. *Korea 1951–53,* p. 230.

13. Montross and Canzona, 3:92–93.

CHAPTER 43. *The "Home-by-Christmas" Offensive*

1. New York *Times,* 24 Nov 50, p. 1.

2. Schnabel and Watson, pp. 333–37.

3. The narrative on the Chinese counteroffensive against Eighth Army is based on Report in War Diary, "The 2d Infantry Division and the Korean Campaign," vol. 3 (part 1), 1 November 1950–30 November 1950, Historical Section, G-2, Hq 2d Infantry Division; War Diary, I U.S. Army Corps, 1 November 1950–30 November 1950; War Diary, Headquarters IX Corps, U.S. Army, 1 November 1950 to 30 November 1950; Joint Chiefs of Staff Highlights of the Korean Situation, 24–25 Nov 50, et seq., all in National Archives.

4. Schnabel and Watson, p. 336; *Korea 1950*, pp. 232–37; Montross and Canzona, 3:125–359.

5. After–action report, 1st Lt Martin Blumenson, 3rd Historical Detachment, Eighth Army, "Chosin Reservoir, 1st Battalion, 32d Infantry Regiment, 25 November–2 December 1950," in National Archives.

6. Second Infantry Division Command Report, 1 December 1950 through 31 December 1950, in National Archives.

7. Robert O. Holles, *Now Thrive the Armourers, A Story of Action with the Gloucesters in Korea* (November 1950–April 1951), (London: George G. Harrap and Co., 1952), p. 21; *Chronology*, 5 December 1950.

8. *Korea 1950*, p. 231.

CHAPTER 44. *The March to the Sea*
1. The narrative on the development of Hagaru-ri as a base, Chinese attacks on it, and on Task Force Drysdale is drawn from Montross and Canzona, 3:125-50, 197-243.

CHAPTER 45. *The Agony of the Three Battalions*
1. This chapter is based on Montross and Canzona, 3:243–45, and the remarkable afteraction report by 1st Lt Martin Blumenson on the ordeal of the 7th Division troops east of the Changjin reservoir cited in Chapter 43, n. 5.

2. Colonel Faith, who had distinguished himself in World War II as an aide to Maj Gen Matthew B. Ridgway, then commanding the 82nd Airborne Division, was awarded the Congressional Medal of Honor posthumously for his leadership and bravery at Changjin reservoir.

CHAPTER 46. *An Act of Defiance*
1. This chapter is drawn from Montross and Canzona, 3:151–95, 249–75.

2. Montross and Canzona, 3:192 cites Keyes Beech, *Tokyo and Points East*, (Garden City, N.Y.:Doubleday, 1954), p. 196.

CHAPTER 47. *The Breakout*
1. This chapter is drawn from Montross and Canzona, 3:277–359; Novem-

ber War Diary summaries, Headquarters X Corps, 1 November to 30 November 1950; Headquarters X Corps, Special Report on Hungnam Evacuation, 9–24 December 1950; Headquarters X Corps, Command Report for December 1950, in National Archives.

CHAPTER 48. *MacArthur Panics*

1. Schnabel and Watson, p.336, cites CINCFE C 69953 to JCS, 28 Nov 50.
2. Ibid., pp. 338–42, cites Memo of Conversation by Ambassador Jessup, 28 Nov 50, *Foreign Relations, 1950, Korea,* pp. 1242–49; Truman, *Memoirs,* 2:385–88; Acheson, pp. 469–71.
3. Schnabel and Watson, p.343, cites JCS 97592 to CINCFE, 29 Nov 50.
4. Ibid., p. 343, cites CINCUNC C 50021 to DA for JCS, 29 Nov 50, CM IN 15333.
5. Ibid., p. 344, cites JCS 97594 to CINCFE, 29 Nov 50; Truman, *Memoirs,* 2:384–85.
6. Schnabel, pp. 278–79.
7. Schnabel and Watson, p. 345, cites CINCUNC C 50095 to DA for JCS, 30 Nov 50, CM IN 15673.
8. Ibid., p. 345, cites Bradley marginal notes on CINCUNC C 50095 to DA for JCS, 30 Nov 50, CM IN 15673.
9. Ibid., p. 346, cites CINCUNC C 50107 to DA for JCS, 30 Nov 50, CM IN 15689.
10. Ibid., pp. 346–47, cites JCS 97772 to CINCFE, 30 Nov 50.
11. Ibid., p. 347, cites Dept. of State *Bulletin,* 4 Dec 50, p. 9–5; G-3 DA WAR 97819 to CINCFE, 1 Dec 50.
12. New York *Times,* 30 Nov 50, p. 1.
13. Schnabel and Watson, p. 348, cites G-3 DA WAR 97819 to CINCFE, 1 Dec 50.
14. Ibid., p. 349, cites *Public Papers, Truman, 1950,* pp. 724, 726–27; Margaret Truman, *Harry S. Truman* (New York: Morrow, 1973), pp. 495–98.
15. Ibid., p. 350, cites *Public Papers, Truman, 1950,* p. 727; Acheson, pp. 478–79; Truman *Memoirs,* 2:395–96.
16. Schnabel and Watson, p. 351, cites Memo of Conversation by Ambassador Jessup, 1 Dec 50, *Foreign Relations, 1950, Korea,* pp. 1276–82.
17. Ibid., p. 355, cites Sec State to UN General Assembly Delegation (GADEL 153), 2 Dec 50: memo by Lucius D. Battle, special assistant to secretary of state, of a meeting held on 2 Dec 50 (with annex by Ambassador Jessup), 3 Dec 50; *Foreign Relations, 1950, Korea,* pp. 1307-8, 1310-13; Acheson, pp. 473–74.
18. Schnabel and Watson, pp. 357–58, cites CINCUNC C 50332 to DA for JCS, 3 Dec 50, CM IN 16668.

19. Ibid., pp. 359–61, cites Memo of Conversation by Ambassador Jessup, 3 Dec 50, *Foreign Relations, 1950, Korea,* pp. 1323–34; two personal messages sent to General Collins on 3 Dec 50 by Gen Wade H. Haislip, vice chief of staff for the army, in CJCS outgoing message book, CINCFE, Jun 50–Jun 51 (one bears serial WAR 97929; the other, unnumbered, was sent in a one-time code).

20. Ibid., pp. 361–62, cites JCS 97917 to CINCFE, 3 Dec 50.

21. Ibid., pp. 365–66, cites Memo, D.O.H. (Maj Gen Doyle O. Hickey, chief of staff, FEC) to General Collins, 4 Dec 50, in National Archives JCS file CCS (Combined Chiefs of Staff) 383.21 Korea (3–19–45) sec. 40; CINCFE C 50371 to DA for JCS (Collins to Haislip), 4 Dec 50, CM IN 16815; Memo, CSA to JCS, "Report on Visit to FECOM and Korea, December 4-7, 1950," 8 Dec 50, in National Archives JCS file CCS 383.21 Korea (3-19-45) sec. 40.

22. Ibid., p. 368, cites CINCFE CX to CG 8th Army et al., 7 Dec 50, CM IN 18111, received in JCS Message Center 070402 Dec 50.

CHAPTER 49. *Back to the 38th Parallel*

1. New York *Times,* 3 Dec 50, p. 1.

2. Schnabel and Watson, p. 364; Acheson, pp. 471–72.

3. Schnabel and Watson, pp. 370–78, cites U.S. official record of conference, reprinted in *Foreign Relations, 1950, Korea,* as follows: US MIN (for Minutes-)-1, pp. 1361–74; US MIN-2, pp. 1392–1408; US MIN-5, pp. 1449–61, and US MIN-6, pp. 396-413; Acheson, pp. 480–85. The communique released after the meeting is printed in Department of State *Bulletin,* 18 Dec 50, pp. 959–61.

4. Schnabel and Watson, p. 376, cites Memo for Record by Ambassador Jessup, "Excerpts from Meeting between the President and Prime Minister in the Cabinet Room of the White House, Thursday, December 7, 1950," 7 Dec 50, which records Truman's oral summary of his private meeting with Attlee; Memo for Record, R. Gordon Arneson, special assistant to the Secretary of State, "Truman-Attlee Conversations of December 1950: Use of Atomic Weapons," 16 Jan 53 [sic, doubtless 1951]; *Foreign Relations, 1950 Korea,* pp. 1462–65; Acheson, p. 484.

5. Schnabel and Watson, p. 378; Collins, pp. 232–33.

6. New York *Times,* 6 Dec 50, p. 1. The countries joining India in this effort were Afghanistan, Burma, Egypt, Indonesia, Iran, Iraq, Lebanon, Pakistan, the Philippines, Saudi Arabia, Syria, and Yeman.

7. Schnabel and Watson, p. 380.

8. Ibid., pp. 383–84, cites Memo, JCS to SecDef, "United States Position Regarding the Terms of any United Nations General Assembly Cease-Fire Resolution for the Korean War," 12 Dec 50; Memo, SecDef to SecState,

12 Dec 50; Department of State *Bulletin,* 18 Dec 50, pp. 994-95, and 25 Dec 50, p. 1005.

9. Ibid., p. 384, cites New York *Times,* 13 Dec 50, p. 1 and 14 Dec 50, p. 1; Department of State *Bulletin* 18 Dec 50, pp. 994-95, and 25 Dec 50, p. 1005.

10. Ibid, p. 385, cites Department of State *Bulletin,* 25 Dec 50, p. 1033, and 15 Jan 51, pp. 113-14.

11. Ibid., p. 385, cites Department of State *Bulletin,* 15 Jan 51, pp. 115-16; Richard P. Stebbins, *United States in World Affairs, 1950* (New York: Harper & Bros., 1951), p. 424; New York *Times,* 23 Dec 50, p. 1.

12. Ridgway, p. 83.

13. Schnabel and Watson, pp. 397-99, cites JCS 99935 to CINCFE, 29 Dec 50, reproduced from a smooth typed copy of this message in National Archives JCS file CCS 381 Far East (11-28-50) sec. 1.

14. Ibid., pp. 399-402, cites CINCFE C 52391 to DA for JCS, 30 Dec 50, CM IN 5452.

15. Ibid., pp. 404-5, cites Memo, Chief of Naval Operations (Sherman) to JCS, "Courses of Action Relative to Communist China and Korea," no date (JCS 2118/5, 3 Jan 51), in National Archives JCS file CCS 381 Far East (11-28-50) sec. 1. The Sherman memo records that the admiral drafted it at his home on 1 Jan 51.

CHAPTER 50. *The New Year's Offensive*
1. The narrative on the New Year's Eve Offensive is drawn from *Korea 1951-53;* Command Report, I U.S. Army Corps, 1 January 1951-31 January 1951; Command Report, Headquarters IX Corps, 1 January 1951 to 31 January 1951; Command Report, Headquarters X Corps, 1-31 January 1951, including special reports on "The First Battle of Wonju" and "Battle of the Tunnels Area," in National Archives.

2. Ridgway, pp. 93-94.

3. Ibid., pp. 95-96.

4. Schnabel, p. 317.

5. Schnabel and Watson, pp. 408-10, cites JCS 80680 to CINCFE, 9 Jan 51.

6. Ibid., p. 410.

7. Ibid., pp. 410-11, cites CINCUNC C 53167 to DA, 10 Jan 51, DA IN 8796.

8. Ibid., p. 412; Truman, *Memoirs* 2: 434.

9. Schnabel and Watson, p. 412; Acheson, p. 515.

10. Schnabel and Watson, pp. 414-15.

11. Ibid., pp. 415-16 cites JCS 80902 to CINCFE, 12 Jan 51.

CHAPTER 51. *Acheson's Calculated Risk*
1. Schnabel and Watson, p. 428, cites State Circular 334, 3 Jan 51 (annex to

JCS 1776/184, 15 Jan 51), in National Archives JCS file CCS 383.21 Korea (3-19-45) sec. 4.

2. Ibid., pp. 428-29, cites Memo, A. C. Murdaugh to Major General Burns, "Cease Fire Resolution in the United Nations," 11 Jan 51, w/encl (text of report to be submitted by Cease Fire Committee), in National Archives JCS file CCS 383.21 Korea (3-19-45) sec. 43. The text of the report as submitted is also given in Department of State *Bulletin,* 29 Jan 51, p. 164.

3. Acheson, p. 513; New York *Times,* 12 Jan 51, p. 1; Schnabel and Watson, p. 429, cites Department of State *Bulletin,* 15 Jan 51, p. 117, and Ibid., 29 Jan 51, p. 163-65.

4. Acheson, p. 513; New York *Times,* 13 Jan 51, p. 9; 16 Jan 51, p. 9; 17 Jan 51, p. 1; Schnabel and Watson, p. 430, also cites Department of State *Bulletin,* 29 Jan 51, pp. 164-66.

5. Acheson, p. 513; Schnabel and Watson, pp. 431, 443, cites Department of State *Bulletin,* 29 Jan 51, pp. 166-69, 192-93; 5 Feb 51, pp. 235-36.

6. Schnabel and Watson, pp. 432-35, cites Memo, CSA to SecDef, "Morale and Capabilities of the Eighth Army and ROK Forces in Korea," 19 Jan 51, in National Archives JCS file CCS 381 Far East (11-28-50) sec. 2.

7. Ibid., p. 434; Schnabel, p. 327; *Military Situation in the Far East,* pt. 1, p. 329 (testimony of Secretary of Defense George Marshall).

8. Schnabel and Watson, p. 437, cites CINCFE C 53613 to DA for JCS. (Collins to Bradley) 17 Jan 51, DA IN 11108.

9. Schnabel and Watson, p. 438; Collins, p. 255; Memo by special assistant to secretary of state (Battle), 19 Jan 51, *Foreign Relations, 1951, Korea,* pp. 102-5, recording Secretary Acheson's summary of cabinet briefing by Generals Collins and Vandenberg.

10. Schnabel and Watson, p. 439-40.

11. The narrative on the January-February military action is drawn from *Korea 1951-53,* pp. 9-27; Ridgway, pp. 105-23; special report in X Corps Command Report for January, 1951, "Battle of the Tunnels Area, Inclosure No. 2"; Command Report, I U.S. Army Corps, 1 January 1951-31 January 1951, and Command Report, I U.S. Army Corps, 1 February 1951-28 February 1951; Command Report, Headquarters IX Corps, 1 January 1951 to 31 January 1951, and Command Report, Headquarters IX Corps, 1 February 1951 to 28 February 1951; Headquarters X Corps Command Report 1-31 January 1951 and Headquarters X Corps Command Report, 1-28 February 1951, in National Archives.

12. Ridgway, p. 109.

CHAPTER 52. *North to the Kansas Line*
1. The following account is drawn from Command Report, Headquarters

IX Corps, 1 March 1951 to 31 March 1951; Command Report, Headquar ters X Corps, 1 March 51 to 31 March 51; Command Report, I U.S. Army Corps, 1 March 1951–31 March 1951; Ridgway, pp. 112–23; *Korea 1951–53*.

2. Schnabel and Watson, pp. 466, cites National Archives, *Public Papers of the Presidents of the United States, Harry S. Truman, 1951* (Washington: U.S. Government Printing Office, 1965), p. 188. Schnabel and Watson, pp. 456–68, gives a full description of the thinking within the Joint Chiefs and the Truman administration over the question of crossing the 38th par allel again.

3. The remainder of this chapter is drawn from Command Report, Head quarters IX Corps, 1 April 1951 to 30 April 1951; Command Report, Head quarters X Corps, 1 April to 30 April 1951; Command Report, I U.S. Army Corps, 1 April 1951–30 April 1951; *Korea 1951–53*; Ridgway, pp. 116–23.

CHAPTER 53. *MacArthur Finally Does It*

1. Schnabel and Watson, p. 468.

2. Ibid., p. 469, cites Memo, JCS to SecDef, "United States Position Regard ing an Armistice in Korea," 27 Mar 51.

3. Schnabel, pp. 357–58, cites JSSC Report to the JCS, p. 131.

4. Schnabel and Watson, p. 525, cites JCS 86276 to CINCFE, 20 Mar 51. A draft of this message is in the National Archives JCS file CCS 383.21 Korea (3–19–45) sec. 44, and records SecDef approval.

5. Ibid., p. 526, cites CINCUNC C 58203 to DA for JCS, 21 Mar 51, CM IN 12977.

6. Text of MacArthur's message is reprinted in *Military Situation in the Far East*, pt. 5, pp. 3541–42, and in Truman, *Memoirs* 2:440–41.

7. Schnabel and Watson, p. 528.

8. MacArthur, pp. 387–89.

9. Truman, *Memoirs* 2:441–42.

10. Schnabel and Watson, p. 529, cites JCS 86736 to CINCFE (Personal to MacArthur), 24 Mar 51. The authors also refer to MacArthur's remarks in *Military Situation in the Far East*, pt. 1, p. 71, indicating he did not regard this message as a rebuke and did not connect it with his statement of March 24.

11. Text of MacArthur's letter to Representative Martin is reprinted in *Military Situation in the Far East*, pt. 5, pp. 3543–44, and in Truman, *Memoirs* 2:445–46. Schnabel and Watson, pp. 529–30, cites letter, Hon. Joseph W. Martin, Jr., to General MacArthur, 8 Mar 51.

12. Ridgway, p. 144.

13. These sources are the basis for the following narrative regarding the decision on MacArthur: Truman, *Memoirs* 2:445–48; Collins, pp. 271–87; Acheson, pp. 521–24; Schnabel, pp. 364–77; Schnabel and Watson, p. 536,

cites Cabell Phillips, *The Truman Presidency: The History of a Triumphant Succession*, 1966, pp. 340–47; Sherman Memo; Bradley Memo, no date, discussed and amended by JCS on 23 Apr 51, Encl to Memo for Record, Secy JCS, "Events in Connection with Change of Command in Far East," 24 Apr 51, in National Archives JCS file CCS 013.36 (4–20–51). Besides this version of the Bradley Memo there is another, attached to a memo for the record by "ofgm" (Lt. Olive F. G. Marsh), dated 25 Apr 51 (copy in files of JCS Historical Division; obtained from Bradley files, U.S. Army Military History Institute, Carlisle Barracks, Pennsylvania). The two do not entirely agree.

14. Collins, p. 283.

15. Ibid., p. 283.

16. Schnabel and Watson, p. 540, cites Sherman Memo.

17. Ibid., p. 545, cites JCS 88180 to CINCFE (Personal from Gen Bradley to Gen MacArthur), 11 Apr 51.

18. Ibid., pp. 545–46, cites JCS 88181 to CINCFE (Personal from Gen Bradley to Gen MacArthur), 11 Apr 51.

19. *Military Situation in the Far East,* pt. 1, p. 26; MacArthur, p. 395.

20. Ridgway, p. 157.

21. Matthew B. Ridgway as told to Harold H. Martin, *Soldier* (New York: Harper and Brothers, 1956), p. 223.

22. Ridgway, *Korean War*, p. 160.

23. Ibid, p. 161.

24. New York *Times*, 16–21 Apr 51. The text of the General's speech of 19 Apr 51 is in *Military Situation in the Far East*, pt. 5, pp. 3553–58, and MacArthur, pp. 400–5.

CHAPTER 54. *The MacArthur Hearings*

1. Schnabel and Watson, p. 547, cites the following sources on the aftermath of the MacArthur dismissal, including the congressional hearings: Cabell Phillips, *The History of a Triumphant Succession: The Truman Presidency*, pp. 347–50; Acheson, pp. 524–28; Collins, pp. 287–93; John W. Spanier, *The Truman-MacArthur Controversy and the Korean War* (Cambridge, Mass.: Harvard University Press, 1959), pp. 211–56; Trumbull Higgins, *Korea and the Fall of MacArthur* (New York: Oxford University Press, 1960), pp. 133–176.

2. *Military Situation in the Far East*, pt. 2, pp. 731–32.

3. McLellan, pp. 316–17.

4. Schnabel and Watson, pp. 549–50, mentions that a summary of the deleted passages, which now have been declassified, is given in John Edward Wiltz, "The MacArthur Hearings of 1951: The Secret Testimony," *Military Affairs*, December 1975, pp. 167–73.

5. *Military Situation in the Far East*, pt. 1, pp. 69–71; 26–28; pt. 5, pp. 3556–57; pt. 1, pp. 13–14. Before the committees, MacArthur used as evidence of JCS support of his position a JCS memorandum of January 12, 1951, which outlined a number of tentative actions in the event the United States became embroiled in an all-out war with China. A JCS committee study on this subject had been going on since November 28, shortly after the major Chinese intervention began, and General Bradley, in his testimony before the committees (pt. 2, pp. 735–36, 738) said the committee report had carried a preamble setting forth its contingent nature; this qualifier had been eliminated in the final JCS memo of January 12, which the JCS "tentatively agreed" to, and which MacArthur received from Generals Collins and Vandenberg on their visit to the Far East in January. Bradley told the committees, however, the memo was clear to him and his JCS colleagues that it was a study, and not a directive to MacArthur. This memo is in the National Archives as Memo, JCS to SecDef, "Courses of Action Relative to Communist China and Korea," 12 Jan 51, in JCS file CCS 381 Far East (11–28–50), sec. 2. Secretary Marshall, in his testimony before the Senate committees, emphasized the January 12 memo was written when the United States was "faced with the very real possibility of having to evacuate our forces from Korea," and the JCS recommendations were to be considered "if and when this possibility came closer to reality." The memo had been sent to the National Security Council for consideration, but the situation in Korea improved almost immediately thereafter and it became unnecessary to put into effect any of the tentative proposals advanced by the JCS. Marshall said the ultimate decision to implement them was rendered unnecessary and unwise (pt. 1, pp. 324, 329–41). General Collins testified before the Senate committees that, in his visit to MacArthur during which he delivered the memo, he had made it clear the courses of action in the memorandum were simply "under consideration" for execution under certain circumstances and had not been approved by the administration (pt. 2, pp. 1188, 1210–17, 1230–31, 1239–41). The January 12 memo's tentative provisions ranged over a large number of strategic matters relating to Far Eastern security, including the safety of Japan and measures to oppose communism in southeast Asia. The specific proposals relating to Red China and Korea would deny Taiwan to the communists; support South Korea as long as practicable, then maintain a Korean government in exile if forced to evacuate the peninsula; support a government in China friendly to the United States; prepare to impose a naval blockade of Red China "and place it into effect as soon as our position in Korea is stabilized, or when we have evacuated Korea, and depending upon circumstances then obtaining"; remove restrictions for air reconnaissance of the China coast and Manchuria; remove restrictions on

Chinese Nationalist forces and give them logistical support for operations against the communists; press for branding China an aggressor; send a military training mission and increase military aid to Taiwan; furnish covert aid to Nationalist guerilla forces in China, and "initiate damaging naval and air attacks on objectives in Communist China at such time as the Chinese Communists attack any of our forces outside Korea." Like many other tentative proposals drawn up by military strategists to provide for possible eventualities, this JCS memorandum recommended a set of actions in a "worst-case" crisis with Red China. The policy of the Joint Chiefs had consistently been against spreading the war to Red China, and these proposals were to be implemented only if the U.S. position in Korea became virtually untenable and the U.S. position in the Far East was threatened. MacArthur certainly knew the memo was tentative, but because the memo existed and in part supported his views, he decided to use it without explaining its provisional nature. The entire subject is covered thoroughly in Schnabel and Watson, and is referred to specifically in pages 552–54 in reference to the controversy.

6. *Military Situation in the Far East,* pt. 1, p. 126.

7. Ibid., pt. 1, p. 323.

8. Ibid., pt. 1, pp. 324, 329–41.

9. Ibid., pt. 1, pp. 324–25.

10. Ibid., pt. 1, p. 325.

11. Ibid., pt. 1, pp. 730–31.

12. Ibid., pt. 2, pp. 878–79.

13. Schnabel and Watson, pp. 556–57.

14. *Military Situation in the Far East,* pt. 4, pp. 3119–33; pt. 5, pp. 3135–64, 3561–3605.

15. Acheson, p. 524.

CHAPTER 55. *The Spring Offensive*

1. Schnabel, p. 379.

2. The narrative on the spring offensive is based on Command Report, Headquarters IX Corps, 1 April 1951 to 30 April 1951; Command Report, Headquarters X Corps, 1 April to 30 April 1951; Command Report, I U.S. Army Corps, 1 April 1951–30 April 1951; Command Report, Headquarters IX Corps, 1 May 1951 to 31 May 1951, and 1 June 1951 to 30 June 1951; Command Report, I U.S. Army Corps, 1 May 1951–31 May 1951, and 1 June 1951–30 June 1951; Command Report, Headquarters X Corps, 1 May to 31 May 1951 (plus special report on Battle of the Soyang River), and 1 June to 30 June 1951; *Korea 1951–53,* pp. 103–12; Ridgway, *Korean War,* pp. 163–83.

CHAPTER 56. *Talking Peace and Practicing War*

1. Schnabel and Watson, p. 563.

2. Acheson, pp. 531–34; McLellan, p. 318; Schnabel and Watson, pp. 564–65; Department of State, *Foreign Relations, 1951, Korea*, pp. 507–11.

3. Hermes, p. 17; Schnabel and Watson, p. 565, cites Department of State *Bulletin*, 9 Jul 51, p. 45.

4. Schnabel and Watson, p. 565 cites State 831 to Moscow, 25 Jun 51; Moscow 2181 to State, 27 Jun 51; copies of both in National Archives JCS file CCS 383.21 Korea (3–19–45) sec. 50.

5. Acheson, pp. 533–34; Schnabel and Watson, p. 566; Memo of Conversation by Director, office of NE Asian Affairs, Department of State (U. Alexis Johnson), 28 Jun 51; *Foreign Relations, 1951, Korea*, pp. 566–71.

6. Schnabel and Watson, p. 567, cites *Foreign Relations, 1951, Korea*, pp. 577–78, 583–87, 598–600, 607–9; JCS 95174 to CINCFE, 28 Jun 51; DA TT 4890, 29 Jun 51, (in CJCS book of outgoing messages to CINCFE, Jun 1950–Jun 1951; JCS 95258 to CINCFE, 29 Jun 51, giving text of message quoted in text); CINCFE C 66046 to JCS, 29 Jun 51, DA IN 9558.

7. Ibid., p. 568; Memo of Conversation, Department of State (Johnson), 29 Jun 51, *Foreign Relations, 1951, Korea*, pp. 597–600; Truman, p. 458. See also JCS 95354 to CINCUNC (Personal for Ridgway), 30 Jun 51.

8. CINCFE CX 66183 to DA for JCS, 1 Jul 51 (2 Jul 51 Washington time), DA IN 10130. This message is reprinted in *Foreign Relations, 1951, Korea*, p. 609.

9. CINCFE CX 66188 to DA for JCS, 1 Jul 51. This message is reprinted in *Foreign Relations, 1951, Korea*, pp. 610–11.

10. JCS 95438 to CINCUNC (Personal for Ridgway), 2 Jul 51 is in National Archives JCS file CCS 383.21 Korea (3–19–45) sec. 51. Schnabel and Watson, p. 576 n. says the original draft of this message bearing the notation "OK, H.S.T." is filed in this JCS section. In the copy of JCS 95438 I found in this file I could discern no such initials; however, I assume Schnabel and Watson are correct, and they must be referring to an earlier draft. The events bear out the assumption that President Truman approved the Chiefs' position. This message is reprinted in *Foreign Relations, 1951, Korea*, pp. 611–13.

11. CINCUNC CX 66160 to DA for JCS, 1 Jul 51; JCS 95438 to CINCUNC (Personal for Ridgway), 2 Jul 51.

12. General Ridgway chose Vice Admiral C. Turner Joy to head the peace talks, and together they selected the other team members. The selections were approved by the Joint Chiefs. Aside from one South Korean officer, they were all Americans. Ultimately, ten additional U.S. and four additional South Korean officers were to serve on the five-man UN team, and

three additional Chinese and six additional North Korean officers were to serve on the communist team. The original UN team members and the dates they served in parentheses were as follows: Admiral Joy (July 10, 1951–May 22, 1952); Major General Henry I. Hodes, deputy chief of staff, Eighth Army (July 10, 1951–December 17, 1951); Major General Laurence C. Craigie, vice commander, Far East Air Forces (July 10, 1951–November 27, 1951); Rear Admiral Arleigh A. Burke, deputy chief of staff, naval forces, Far East (July 10, 1951– December 11, 1951), and Major General Paik Sun Yup, commanding general of the ROK I Corps (July 10, 1951–October 24, 1951). Additional members of the UN team and their dates of service were Major General Lee Hyung Koon, ROK army (October 24, 1951–February 6, 1952); Major General Howard M. Turner, U.S. Air Force (November 27, 1951 – July 5, 1952); Major General Claude B. Ferenbaugh, U.S. Army (December 17, 1951–February 6, 1952); Rear Admiral Ruthven E. Libby, U.S. Navy (December 11, 1951–June 23, 1952); Lieutenant General William K. Harrison, Jr., U.S. Army (February 6, 1952–July 27, 1953); Major General Yu Chae Heung, ROK army (February 6, 1952–May 28, 1952); Brigadier General Frank C. McConnell, U.S. Army (May 22, 1952–April 26, 1953); Brigadier General Lee Han Lim, ROK army (May 28, 1952–April 26, 1953); Brigadier General Joseph T. Morris, U.S. Air Force (July 5, 1952–April 26, 1953); Rear Admiral John C. Daniel, U.S. Navy (June 23, 1952–July 27, 1953); Brigadier General Ralph M. Osborne, U.S. Army (April 26, 1953–July 27, 1953); Brigadier General Choi Duk Shin, ROK army (April 26, 1953–May 16, 1953); Brigadier General Edgar E. Glenn, U.S. Air Force (April 25, 1953–June 20, 1953); Brigadier General George M. Finch, U.S. Air Force (June 20, 1953–July 27, 1953). Upon Admiral Joy's departure on May 22, 1952, Major (later Lieutenant) General William K. Harrison, Jr., became chief delegate and remained so until the talks ended. The head of the original communist delegation was Lieutenant General Nam Il, chief of staff of the North Korean army and vice premier of North Korea. He served the entire length of the talks. Other original communist delegates (with their period of service in parentheses) were Major General Lee Sang Cho, chief of the Reconnaissance Bureau of the North Korean army and a former vice minister of commerce (July 10, 1951–July 27, 1953); Major General Chang Pyong San, chief of staff, I Corps, North Korean army (July 10, 1951–October 24, 1951); Lieutenant General Deng Hua, commander of the 15th CCF Army Group (July 10, 1951–October 24, 1951), and Major General Xie Fang, chief of propaganda of the Northeast Military District of China (July 10, 1951–April 26, 1953). Additional members of the communist team and their dates of service were General Bien Zhang-wu, Communist China (October 24, 1951–April 26, 1953); Major General Chung Tu Hwan, North

Korea (October 24, 1951–April 28, 1952); Rear Admiral Kim Won Mu, North Korea (April 28, 1952–August 11, 1952); Major General So Hui, North Korea (August 11, 1952–April 26, 1953); General Ding Guo-you, Communist China (April 26, 1953–July 27, 1953); Major General Chang Chun San, North Korea (April 26, 1953–May 25, 1953); Major General Cai Zheng-wen, Communist China (April 26, 1953–May 27, 1953); Admiral Kim Won Mu (second tour), North Korea (May 25, 1953–June 17, 1953); Major General Kim Dong Hak, North Korea (June 17, 1953–July 27, 1953). Sources: Hermes, pp. 17, 21, 23, 272, 422–23, 539; Schnabel and Watson, pp. 574, 582 cites CINCUNC CX 66160 to DA for JCS, 1 Jul 51, DA IN 10033.

13. Schnabel and Watson, p. 582 cites CINCUNC Advance HNC 048 to DA for JCS, 10 Jul 51, DA IN 13145; CINCUNC Advance HNC 096 to JCS, 15 Jul 51, DA IN 14877; CINCUNC Advance HNC 098 to DA for JCS, 15 Jul 51, DA IN 14955; CINCUNC Advance HNC 104 to DA for JCS, 16 Jul 51, DA IN 15086.

14. Ibid., p. 583.

15. Ibid., p. 583.

16. Hermes, p. 516.

17. Schnabel and Watson, p. 595, cites CINCFE C 68672 to DA for JCS, 10 Aug 51, DA IN 4466.

CHAPTER 57. *The Bloody Ridges*

1. Schnabel and Watson, p. 587 cites CINCFE HNC 142 to DA for JCS, 26 Jul 51, DA IN 18986; CINCFE C 67521 to DA for JCS, 23 Jul 51, DA IN 17623; JCS 9722 to CINCFE, 25 Jul 51; CINCFE HNC 142 to DA for JCS, 26 Jul 51, DA IN 18986.

2. Ibid., pp. 598–99 cites CINCFE C 68310 to DA for JCS, 4 Aug 51, DA IN 2213; DA TT 5018, 4 Aug 51, CJCS Message Book, CINCFE Incoming Jul-Oct 51 CINCFE C 68437 to DA for JCS, 6 Aug 51, DA IN 2821; JCS 98216 to CINCFE, 6 Aug 51; Hermes, pp. 40–51.

3. Schnabel and Watson, p. 600; Hermes, pp. 41–43.

4. Schnabel and Watson, p. 600; Hermes, p. 45.

5. Schnabel and Watson, p. 605; Hermes, p. 45.

6. Schnabel and Watson, p. 602 cites CINCFE C 68437 to DA for JCS, 6 Aug 51, DA IN 2821.

7. Ibid., pp. 607–10.

8. Ibid., p. 610. By August, 1951, the United Nations commitment to the war essentially reached the level it was to maintain for the remainder of the conflict. By this time, the Colombian Battalion had arrived to join forces from (in addition to the United States and South Korea) Australia, Belgium/Luxembourg, Canada, Ethiopia, France, Great Britain, Greece,

the Netherlands, New Zealand, the Philippines, Thailand, Turkey and the Union of South Africa (a squadron of Canberra bombers), in addition to small non-combatant units supplied by India, Norway, Sweden and (later) Italy. (See Chapter 19, note 3.) At this time, General Van Fleet had under his command 586,769 men, of whom 229, 339 were in Eighth Army proper and most of the remainder were in the South Korean army. As the war continued, the South Korean army grew in size and capability as a result of a strong U.S.-supported training program. At the end of the May counteroffensive, the Far East Command withdrew the U.S. 187th Airborne RCT to Japan. In July, 1951, all forces from the British Commonwealth of Nations were withdrawn from attachment to U.S. units and were consolidated into the 1st British Commonwealth Division, which thenceforth functioned as a full-fledged combat division under operational control of an American corps. The other UN units continued to be attached to American regiments. In late December, 1951, the U.S. National Guard 45th Division arrived in Korea and was replaced in the Japanese occupation force by the 1st Cavalry Division. In late January, 1952, another National Guard division called into federal service, the 40th, arrived in Korea and was replaced in the Japanese occupation by the 24th Division. Thus, the number of American combat divisions in Korea remained at seven: the two National Guard divisions, plus the 2nd, 3rd, 7th, 25th and 1st Marine. (Source *Korea 1951–53* pp. 116, 206, 208, 211.).

9. Sources for the narrative which follows on Eighth Army battles are Hermes, pp. 80–103; the detailed studies of the battles of Bloody and Heartbreak Ridges by commanders of four Historical detachments of Eighth Army, issued by the Military History Section of Eighth Army, "Bloody Ridge August-September 1951, 2d Division," and "Action on 'Heartbreak Ridge,'" by Maj Edward C. Williamson, Maj Pierce W. Briscoe, Capt Martin Blumenson, and 1st Lt John Mewha, in National Archives.

10. Hermes, p. 81 cites statement of Van Fleet, 30 Sep 51, in Department of State *Bulletin*, vol. 25, no. 641 (October 8, 1951), p. 589.

11. Second Division and attached units casualties for 18 Aug–5 Sep: killed in action, 326; wounded, 2,032; missing, 414; total, 2,772. Enemy casualties: counted killed, 1,389; estimated killed 4,288; estimated wounded 9,422; prisoners, 264; total, 15,363. See Williamson, et al., "Bloody Ridge," pp. 203, 211. Estimated casualties were educated guesses.

12. Schnabel and Watson, p. 610.

13. Second Division and attached units casualties for 13 Sep–15 Oct: killed in action, 593; wounded, 3,064; missing, 84; total, 3,741. See Williamson et al., "Heartbreak Ridge."

14. 1st Lt Bevin R. Alexander, 5th Historical Detachment, Eighth Army, "The Battle of Bloody Angle — September October 1951," in National Archives.

15. Schnabel and Watson, p. 625.

16. Appleman, p. 774.

17. Schnabel and Watson, p. 625.

18. Ibid., p. 626.

CHAPTER 58. *Another Try for Peace*

1. Schnabel and Watson, pp. 615–16.

2. Ibid., pp. 617–18.

3. Ibid., pp. 618–19.

4. Ibid., p. 619, cites "Memorandum on the Substance of Discussions at a Department of State-Joint Chiefs of Staff Meeting," unsigned, 12 Nov 51, *Foreign Relations, 1951, Korea,* pp. 1122–24; JCS 86804 to CINCFE, 13 Nov 51.

5. Ibid., p. 621; Hermes, p. 119.

6. Schnabel and Watson, pp. 649–50.

7. Ibid., pp. 651, 666–67.

8. Ibid., pp. 627–39.

9. Ibid., pp. 655–56.

10. Ibid., p. 657.

11. Ibid., p. 657.

12. Ibid., p. 659.

13. Ibid., pp. 659–60.

14. Ibid., pp. 660–66.

15. Ibid., p. 672.

16. Hermes, pp. 135–36.

17. Schnabel and Watson, p. 673, cites State 16 to Supreme Commander, Allied Powers (SCAP), Tokyo, 4 Jul 50, in National Archives JCS file CCS000.5 (5–12–49), Sec. 1.

18. Ibid., p. 673.

19. C. Turner Joy, *How Communists Negotiate* (New York: Macmillan, 1953), p. 152; see also Schnabel and Watson, p. 680 n.

20. Schnabel and Watson, pp. 675–76.

21. Ibid., p. 676.

22. Ibid., p. 677.

23. Ibid., p. 679.

24. Ibid., p. 681.

25. Ibid., p. 684.

26. Ibid., p. 688.

27. Ibid., p. 696.

28. Ibid., pp. 696–97.

29. Ibid., pp. 698–702.

CHAPTER 59. *The POWs Seize the Stage*

1. Hermes, pp. 230–231; Schnabel and Watson, pp. 809–17.
2. Ridgway, *Korean War*, pp. 205–9; Hermes, pp. 223–40; Schnabel and Watson, pp. 735–39.
3. Schnabel and Watson, pp. 783–39.
4. Truman, *Memoirs*, 2:460; Acheson, p. 653; Hermes, p. 150; Schnabel and Watson, p. 734.
5. Schnabel and Watson, p. 749.
6. Ibid., p. 767.
7. Ibid., p. 769.
8. The narrative on the Dodd incident is derived from Ridgway, *Korean War*, pp. 210–16; Hermes, pp. 243–54; Schnabel and Watson, pp. 768–74, and Gen Mark W. Clark, *From the Danube to the Yalu* (New York: Harper and Bros., 1954), pp. 35–49.
9. Schnabel and Watson, p. 771, cites CINCUNC C 68366 to DA for JCS, 12 May 52, DA IN 138016.
10. Hermes, p. 254.
11. Schnabel and Watson, pp. 821–22.
12. Ibid., p. 836; Hermes. pp. 255–61.

CHAPTER 60. *Rhee the Despot, Clark the Hawk*

1. Hermes, pp. 345–46; Schnabel and Watson, p. 785.
2. Hermes, p. 346; Schnabel and Watson, pp. 786–97; New York *Times*, 6 Aug 52, p. 2, and 7 Aug 52, p. 3; *Foreign Relations, 1952–54, Korea*, pp. 114–16, 187–88, 228–31, 242, 251–56, 264–95, 301–8, 323–43, 346–47, 349–55, 357–64, 368, 376–79, 397–98, 402–4, 414–15.
3. Schnabel and Watson, pp. 843–45.
4. Ibid., pp. 846–48.
5. Ibid., p. 848; Hermes, pp. 324-25.
6. Schnabel and Watson, pp.887–88 cites Department of State *Bulletin*, 3 Nov 52, p. 696; New York *Times*, 10 Sep 52, p. 3.
7. Ibid., pp. 899–905.
8. Ibid., p. 905, cites CINCUNC Z 23092 to DA for JCS, 28 Sep 52, DA IN 687567.
9. Ibid., pp. 906–7.
10. Ibid., p. 907, cites Department of State *Bulletin*, 20 Oct 52, pp. 600–601.
11. Ibid., pp. 920–21; Hermes, pp. 404–5.
12. Schnabel and Watson, pp. 926–27.
13. Ibid., pp. 927–28; Hermes, pp. 328–29.
14. Schnabel and Watson, pp. 932–33 cites CINCUNC OPLAN 8–52, 15 Oct 52, in National Archives JCS file CCS 383.21 Korea (3–19–45) BP pt. 4.

15. Ibid., p. 858, cites CINCFE C 69181 to DA for JCS 27 May 52, DA IN 143769.

16. Ibid., p. 933, cites Ltr, CINCUNC to CSA, 16 Oct 52, Encl to JCS 1776/330, 30 Oct 52, in National Archives JCS file CCS 383.21 Korea (3-19-45) sec. 116.

17. Ibid., pp. 933-34, cites Memo, SecArmy to SecDef, "Reduction of U.S. Manpower in Korea," 16 Oct 52, Encl to Memo, Office of the Secretary of Defense to JCS same subject, 29 Oct 52 (Encl and App to JCS 1776/331, 31 Oct 52), same file.

18. Ibid., p. 911.

19. Ibid., pp. 912-913; Stebbins, *The United States in World Affairs, 1952,* (New York: Harper & Bros., 1954), pp. 319-21.

20. Schnabel and Watson, p. 934, cites Letter, Gen Collins to Gen Clark, 7 Nov 52, in National Archives Department of the Army file G3 091 Korea (TS) Sec. I-C, Bk III, case 8.

CHAPTER 61. *Others Take a Hand*

1. Schnabel and Watson, pp. 914-15.

2. Ibid., pp. 918-20.

3. Ibid., pp. 934-36; Gen Mark W. Clark, *From the Danube to the Yalu* (New York: Harper and Bros., 1954), pp. 232-39; Dwight D. Eisenhower, *Mandate for Change, 1953-1956* (New York: Doubleday, 1963), pp. 130-34; New York *Times,* 6 Dec 52, p. 1.

4. Schnabel and Watson, p. 921; Hermes, pp. 405-406; Acheson, p. 705.

5. Schnabel and Watson, p. 962 cites JCS 931742 to CINCFE, 18 Feb 52, which summarizes the text of the resolution and gives voting results.

6. Ibid., pp. 962-63.

7. Ibid., pp. 963-64.

8. Ibid., pp. 964-66.

9. Ibid., pp. 964-67; Hermes, pp. 414-19, Appendix B-1; Clark, pp. 240-56.

10. Schnabel and Watson, pp. 971-76.

11. Ibid., pp. 775-84.

12. Hermes, p. 422.

13. Ibid., pp. 426-28; Schnabel and Watson, pp. 971-78.

14. Futrell, pp. 624-28; Hermes, p. 461; Schnabel and Watson, p. 980.

15. Schnabel and Watson, pp. 948-61, give a complete analysis of the development of the Far East contingency plans. The document containing the Chiefs' recommendations to the NSC on May 20 is contained in Memo, JCS to SecDef, "Courses of Action in Connection with the Situation in Korea (Analysis)," 19 May 53 in National Archives JCS file CCS 383.21 Korea (3-19-45), sec. 129. See also JCS 1776/374, 9 Jun 53.

16. Ibid., p. 987, cites CINCFE CX 62406 to DA for JCS, 13 May 53, DA IN 267117.

17. Ibid., p. 988, cites JCS 939673 to CINCFE, 23 May 53.

18. Ibid., pp. 988–89.

19. Ibid., pp. 995–96.

CHAPTER 62. *The Final Crisis*

1. Schnabel and Watson, pp. 999–1001; New York *Times*, 6 Jun 53, p. 1.

2. Schnabel and Watson, p. 1001.

3. Ibid., p. 1002. Clark's message, CINCUNC CX 62890 to DA for JCS, is printed in *Foreign Relations, 1952–54, Korea*, pp. 1149–51.

4. Schnabel and Watson, p. 1003.

5. Ibid., pp. 1040–41; Hermes, pp. 366–97, 465–68.

6. Schnabel and Watson, p. 1004.

7. Ibid., pp. 1005–7.

8. Ibid., p. 1007. *Foreign Relations, 1952–54, Korea*, pp. 1196–1200, discusses Rhee's action and reprints Rhee's letter to Gen Clark and Rhee's press release on the matter. The originals are in the Mark W. Clark Collection, Archives-Museum, The Citadel, Charleston, S.C.

9. Schnabel and Watson, p. 1005.

10. Ibid., p. 1013.

11. Ibid., p. 1013.

12. Ibid., p. 1015 cites CINCUNC CX 63325 to DA for State, Defense, and JCS, 25 Jun 53, DA IN 281220. Memo of discussion of the 24–25 Jun 50 Meeting in Tokyo is in *Foreign Relations, 1952–54, Korea*, pp. 1265–69. Ambassador Murphy was U.S. envoy to Japan, 9 May 52–28 Apr 53, and thereafter political advisor to the UN Command until 11 Jul 53 (*Foreign Relations, 1952–54, Korea*, p. xxi).

13. Schnabel and Watson, p. 1016, cites JCS 942368 to CINCFE, 25 Jun 53. Robertson's and Clark's 25 Jun 53 query to State, Defense and JCS (army message CX 63325) and the JCS reply (JCS 942368) are reprinted in *Foreign Relations, 1952–54, Korea*, pp. 1270–72.

14. Schnabel and Watson, p. 1017.

15. Ibid., p. 1023; *Foreign Relations, 1952–54, Korea*, pp. 1276–95, gives messages and responses between Robertson and Clark and Washington on the negotiations with Rhee and contains 1 Jul 53 letter from Rhee to Robertson (pp. 1292–95) from which the quote is drawn. See also Robertson's report on conversations with Rhee in *Historical Series*, vol. 5, 83rd Congress, 1st session, 1953, "Report by Asst Sec of State for Far Eastern Affairs, July 16, 1953" (Washington, D.C.: U.S. Government Printing Office).

16. Schnabel and Watson, p. 1024; *Foreign Relations, 1952–54, Korea*, pp. 1312–14, 1326–29.

17. Schnabel and Watson, p. 1025; *Foreign Relations, 1952–54, Korea,* p. 1328.

18. Schnabel and Watson, p. 1029; *Foreign Relations, 1952–54, Korea,* pp. 1357–59, reproduces Rhee's letter to Robertson.

19. Schnabel and Watson, pp. 1042–43; Hermes, pp. 474–77.

20. Schnabel and Watson, pp. 1044–52.

21. Ibid., pp. 1055–56.

22. Ibid., p. 1053, cites JCS 944462 to CINCFE, 23 Jul 53.

23. Ibid., p. 1059, cites Richard P. Stebbins, *The United States in World Affairs, 1954* (New York: Harper & Bros., 1956), pp. 117, 204–11, 215, 232–36.

24. Hermes, Appendixes B-2 and B-3.

25. Ibid., p. 477.

26. Joint Chiefs of Staff "Korean Highlights" of 27 Jul 53, in National Archives.

27. Sun Tzu, *The Art of War,* edited and with a foreword by James Clavell (New York: Delacorte Press, 1983), p. 13.

CHAPTER 63. *The Long Shadow of the Korean War*

1. U.S. Department of State, *Foreign Relations of the United States: China and Japan, 1952-54,* vol. 14, Washington: Government Printing Office, 1985, pp. 371-76, 386-88, 827-39.

2. Ibid., pp. 262-63, 270.

3. U.S. Department of State, *Foreign Relations of the United States, Indochina, 1952-54,* Washington: Government Printing Office, 1982, pp.1181-82.

4. U.S. Department of State, *Foreign Relations of the United States: 1952-54, Geneva Conference,* vol. xvi, Washington: Government Printing Office, 1981, sp. 734; Gabriel Kolko, *Anatomy of a War, Vietnam, the United States and the Modern Historical Experience,* New York: Pantheon Books, 1985, pp. 64-65.

5. "Communiqué on talks between Mr. Nehru and Mr. Chou en-Lai," June 28, 1954, Royal Institute of International Affairs, *Documents of International Affairs,* 1954, pp. 113-14.

6. *Foreign Relations, China and Japan, 1952-54,* vol. 2, Washington: Government Printing Office, 1986, pp. 83-85, 89-96, 115-119, 162-63, 167-72, 182-83, 204-208, 260.

9. Zbigniew K. Brzezinski, *The Soviet Bloc, Unity and Conflict,* Cambridge, Mass.: Harvard University Press, 1967, pp. 377-78, 397-409; Denis Twitchett and John K. Fairbank, eds., *Cambridge History of China,* vol. 14, Cambridge: Cambridge University Press, 1987, pp. 515-18.

10. Gordon H. Chang, "JFK, China and the Bomb," the *Journal of*

American History, vol. 74, no. 4, March, 1988, pp. 1287-1310.

11. Kolko, *Anatomy of a War*, p. 157.

12. Lyndon B. Johnson Presidential Library, Austin, Texas, China Memos, vol. II 9/64-2/65; Office files of Harry McPherson: Vietnam 1967, part II, "Statements by President Johnson and Secretary of State rusk on U.S. Policy toward the Republic of China and Communist China, 1964-67."

Afterword

I N JUNE 1996, forty-six years after the Korean War started, I was invited to speak at the Korean Army War College at Taejon; and, as a guest of the South Korean Army, I visited Panmunjom and the demilitarized zone still separating North and South Korea.

The trip was a pilgrimage for me, a return for the first time to Korea since I departed in the late summer of 1952. It was a remarkable experience both to see how South Korea has been transformed into a prosperous modern industrial state, and how the division which brought on the war still endures in all its venom.

When I first rode in my jeep through the streets of Seoul in 1951, the city was a shell; debris and ruined buildings were everywhere, devoid of human beings, and empty avenues seemingly lead nowhere. The National Capitol was scarred by shellfire and guarded by a single sentry, and the bridge over the Han River remained a makeshift device covering the spans that had been blown up in the first days of the war. A few miles south of the city, Kimpo, or K-14, was a dusty forward air base where I had watched a British Seafire fighter trying to land, flying round and round, unable to drop but one of its two wheels.

Kimpo in 1996 was a huge modern air terminal, indistinguishable from other great hubs like Dallas or O'Hare, and Seoul was a glittering world city of eleven million people—with traffic of Korean-made vehicles as thick and chaotic as rush hour in Washington, D.C., with immense, glass-encased international-class hotels, a skyscraper-packed downtown that looked like Atlanta, well-dressed pedestrians, numerous bridges spanning the Han, and no evidence whatsoever of the shattered, sad city I had remembered.

The visit to the DMZ was something else. Visitors to Panmunjom are rigidly controlled. There is a building a few miles south of the DMZ

549

where all visitors must be assembled, approved, and gathered into a small convoy. Our two-car convoy turned into a narrow roadway, where it was inspected at an American Army checkpoint. Then, we crossed a small railway bridge with planks laid on it to accommodate automobiles. The approach was hardly majestic. I looked questioningly at my host, a Korean Army general. He read my expression perfectly.

"Yes, " he said, "everything is like it was in 1951 when the peace talks started."

"Even the approach over the same broken railway bridge?" I asked.

"Even that," he replied.

When we arrived at a Korean-American base just south of Panmunjom, we received a lecture on the dangers we might face once we reached the joint contact point of Pamunjom. A young American sergeant pointed out that the Korean War was only in remission. The two sides were merely observing an armistice; the war had not ended. "Incidents," meaning violence, might occur at any time, he warned, and they had occurred in the past. Visitors entered at their own peril. Panmunjom, then, was not an ordinary tourist site with crowds led around by talkative guides—with gift shops, blaring music, and smiling North Korean soldiers arm-in-arm with smiling South Korean soldiers.

Sobered, we climbed aboard a bus and rode up to Panmunjom, which despite the sergeant's warnings, appeared quiet and peaceful. But when we walked into the little wooden building and stood at the very table where the negotiations between the Communists and the United Nations had dragged on from 1951 into 1953, we saw two South Korean soldiers standing fiercely on guard, ready at an instant to rush forward and confront any North Korean who might disturb in the slightest the delicately maintained status quo.

Outside, I asked my host, the general: "Is this all a show, or are the two sides actually within a hair of collision?"

"It could happen at any time," he answered simply. Then, he launched into a discussion of the agreement the South Korean government had reached shortly beforehand to provide grain and other food for the people of North Korea, whose own crops had failed and who were in danger of starving. He demonstrated the depth of the antagonism that sill exists on the Korean peninsula.

"Did you know," he asked me in tones of horror, "that the North Koreans are giving some of our food to the North Korean army?"

I realized that my host perceived a distinction that I did not: to him, it was acceptable to feed the North Korean people, but it was not acceptable to feed the army of the North Korean people. Baffled and saddened, I turned away. Here, forty-three years after the war had ended, the bitternesss of division still remained. Elsewhere, the Cold War had ended long before. Germany had reunited, the Soviet Union had vanished, all the satellite states had turned to the West (except anachronistic Cuba), and Washington and Hanoi had come to an understanding, laying the Vietnam War to rest at last; with China, the United States was more concerned with trade than with confrontation. But here, still roughly along the 38th parallel, one of the original flashpoints between East and West, between Communism and freedom, the old hostility remained. Nothing had changed.

It was even more poignant when my host led me up to a vantage point near Panmunjom where we could look out at the mountains and into North Korea. As I stood there, a strange sensation came over me; it was as if the forty-four years since I had left Korea had vanished, as if I once more was standing along the Main Line of Resistance (MLR) looking over at the enemy lines. I was seized with an intense feeling of déja vu, and realized with a start that I was listening, despite the passage of time and despite that morning quiet, for the sounds of incoming artillery and mortar fire.

My host had been a soldier in the war, just as I, and he at once caught the stricken look in my eyes.

"It looks the same, doesn't it?" he said.

"Yes!" I answered, my heart pounding. "Only, the hills have vegetation on them now. Before, you know, they were bare and burned out."

"Yes," the general replied. "The hills at least have recovered from the war."

My hosts took me on a tour of the DMZ. Except for the fact that all the soldiers I saw were Korean, and except for the absence of the sounds and evidence of battle, the feel was markedly like it had been four decades before when this had been the MLR. I had passed along this line numbers of times in 1952, and the tension then was pronounced. Now, the tension remained as palpable in the summer of 1996. The constant, if unspoken, orientation of everyone toward the enemy ahead could be discerned in numerous subtle ways: the roads cut below the crests of the hills to shield vehicles from view, the gun positions and bunkers masked to avoid being picked up by the other side, and the blank face presented to the enemy.

But the greatest sign that this remained a battleline was evident to any soldier who had ever spent time on an MLR; it was manifestly an entity unto itself, forming its own interconnected space, with its own purpose, separate, distinct, the uttermost frontier, the point of the spear protecting the society and the nation to the rear.

The sense of incipient war became even more intense when my hosts took me to one of the twenty deep tunnels—three to four-hundred feet below the surface of the earth—which the North Koreans are believed to have dug over the decades to infiltrate spies, and, in case of war, soldiers, under the DMZ into South Korea.

The South Koreans have discovered four of these tunnels, cut with high-grade Swedish ore-mining machines, and started so deeply on the North Korean side that underground water drains backward into the North, concealing the locations. A lieutenant led me down the steep access tunnel—at a 30-degree angle, less than 6 feet wide and 6 feet high—which the South Koreans had dug to intersect the enemy passage. At the bottom, the enemy tunnel, about the same height and width as the access shaft, leads directly back into North Korea.

The South Koreans are outraged by talk about the tunnels, convinced that the passageways are evidence of the dishonesty and evil-intentions of those men who rule North Korea, and their refusal to come to terms.

This concept of division was emphasized in the numerous ceremonies marking the war that took place while I was in Korea. There is a huge national war memorial in Seoul, where all the names of the South Korean dead are enshrined. There, I joined hundreds of Koreans my age who had fought in the war and were being honored for their service. Yet, the sense of an unwillingly divided nation was evident everywhere I went in South Korea. The question most often asked of me was: How did I think North and South could come together again as a single, united nation? As a foreigner, I declined to answer—not only because this is the single most controversial subject on both sides of the DMZ right now (and an outsider should keep his mouth shut about it)— but also because the reunion of the Korean people must come on the basis of a settlement agreed to by the people on both sides, taking into account their half-century of separate, mutually hostile existences.

I had scarcely left for home when a series of demonstrations by university students calling for unification erupted in Korea. And, on the heels of this evidence of the deep desire of the Korean people for reunion, a North Korean submarine washed up on a South Korean shore. The story came out that the sub had delivered dozens of North Korean saboteurs who had spread out through the country, and had been hunted down by South Korean troops.

But, on December 29, 1996, North Korea apologized for sending the submarine. Suspicious observers in South Korea said the gesture came only to start food flowing north again. But, a North Korean apology on any subject was unprecedented, and gave hope to many that the days of separation were nearing an end.

As a former soldier who has a deep affection for the Korean people, it saddens me that this beautiful land remains divided. The people of Korea have suffered deeply as pawns in a great power struggle that consumed most of the last half of this century. But, the contest between East and West is over, and I hope the animosities that still stir the people on both sides of the DMZ will abate soon, and that the Land of the Morning Calm will once again become a single, united, happy land.

I believe this will happen. I am not presumptuous enough to predict when and how. I trust to the good judgment of the Korean people to find a way. But now, the pressures to reunite are far greater than the pressures to remain separate. And the benefits of reunion are immense.

When Korea becomes one state again, it will have the most splendid opportunity in its history to become as great a nation economically as it has been a great nation socially and culturally.

Historically, Korea has been a buffer state between China and Japan. In this century, Korea's troubles commenced when it lost its buffer status after Japan occupied it in the years follwing the Sino-Japanese War of 1894-95, and used it as a staging area to invade Manchuria and China.

Who would have imagined that a temporary line drawn in 1945 to ease the surrender of Japanese forces to Soviet troops to the north and American troops to the south would harden into a political and ideological frontier that has persisted into 1996 and beyond?

It is no longer sensible for Korea to think of itself as a buffer between East and West, since the two sides no longer are at odds. Even Korea's historical role as a buffer between China and Japan has faded, since the military rivalry between China and Japan also has vanished. Some observers might say that Korea still serves as a buffer, but between China and the United States. However, the U.S. has no need to confront China, and most intelligent leaders recognize this.

Once reunited, Korea possesses the capacity to develop into one of the world's great powers. It has the potential for increasing its production and world trade to a level scarcely different than that attained by Japan. The principal reason for Korea's latent greatness is the courage, industry, and capability of its people. These attributes have been proved in war and in peace. Presently, many of these assets are being directed inward by the conflict between North and South. Once it becomes a single nation again, Korea can turn these wasted energies outward into productive enterprises.

Korea has never walked upon the modern world stage as a great power. Throughout most of its modern history, it has been inhibited by larger neighbors who have pursued their own interests, not those of Korea. A buffer state by definition is a pawn in a larger game.

I believe Korea must renounce its role as a buffer. This does not imply giving up its allies, especially its connection with the United States, but it does imply a more independent foreign policy. Such a policy should be easier to apply in the coming century because the world no longer is divided into two hostile camps. However, other great powers will be eager to keep Korea in a subordinate role.

Can Korea exist without being tied to another nation's apron strings? I think it can and must. The conditions existing in the Korean War have now vanished. In 1950, the American alliance with Chian Kai-shek's Nationalists in Taiwan forced Communist China to side with North Korea to avoid seeing an American army, and perhaps Chinese Nationalist troops, on the Yalu River threatening China. In that situation, North Korea served as a buffer for Red China. The danger of Nationalist troops invading mainland China ended long ago. China no longer has a need to treat Korea as a buffer, and will be more willing to enter into mutual economic relations, with great benefits to each power.

The same applies to Japan. Japan would be anxious if Korea allied itself with China, as was the case for centuries when Korea was a tributary state to Imperial China. To prevent this, Japan will inevitably be more accommodating to Korea. Indeed, looking down the long corridor of history into the next century, Korea can benefit greatly by the competition between China and Japan. These nations will remain the major economic machines of East Asia. China is certain to mature into the greatest economic power on earth in the coming century. Nevertheless, because of its inherent capacity to become a great power in its own right, Korea no longer needs to subordinate itself to either China or Japan—or, for that matter, to the United States.

An independent Korea working as an equal with other countries to ensure security and prosperity of East Asia seems a viable possibility.

We have shown in the past half century that we can solve our major international conflicts peacefully. The horrible disputes that have erupted since the end of the Cold War have been essentially local arguments, some of long standing, but have little danger of setting off major international collisions.

I hope in the coming century that countries will continue to sit down and work out their difficulties together and as equals. In any system of world alliances, like the East and West blocs of this century, the goals of the larger nations inevitably take precedence over those of smaller nations. Smaller nations are forced to renounce some of their interests to ensure their protection by the larger powers. It would be a great tragedy to freeze the world again into the rigidities of such competing alliances.

—Bevin Alexander

Index

Acheson, Dean, secy of state, 18, 24, 32, 49, 149, 163, 231, 246, 296, 414, 415, 417, 456, 465, 469; White Paper on China, 19-20; intervention in Korea, 33-34; regarding Taiwan, 34-35, 38, 40, 164, 166, 177, 178; plan to conquer North Korea, 167, 233, 234, 235, 238, 242-43; Chinese intervention, 288-89; 291-92; 295, 369, 373; bombing Yalu bridges, 289; on use of A-bomb, 371; cease-fire proposals, 372, 426-28; 434, 467; limiting war aims, 384; POW issue, 454; isolating Red China, 387-88; relief of MacArthur, 405, 409, 411

Adams, James Y., Col., 444-45

Airborne units. *See* United States Army

Air Force. *See* United States Air Force

Air War College, 239

Aleman, Miguel, 466, 471

Aleutians, 18

Allan, Halle C., Capt., 198

Allen, Frank A., Brig. Gen., 253

Allenby, Edmund Henry H., Field Marshal, 151

Almond, Edward M., Maj. Gen., 53, 120, 157, 170, 171, 186, 197, 203, 204, 206, 207, 211, 212, 214, 218, 307, 309, 321, 356, 357, 380, 382

Amyotte, George A.J., Cpl., 365, 366

Anderson, Clarence R., Capt., 282

Anderson, Orvil A., Maj. Gen., 239

Anderson, Vernice, 247

Andong, 74, 116, 117, 383

Anju, 254, 255, 270, 274, 283, 313, 314, 316, 318

Anshan, China, 260

Ansong, 56, 62, 63, 381

An-tung (Dandong), China, 254

Anui, 106, 114, 226

Appleman, Roy E., 31, 73, 107, 123, 248

Argyll and Sutherland Highlanders Regiment. *See* British Commonwealth forces

Armored units. *See* United States Army

Army, Department of , U.S., 242, 243. *See also* Defense, Department of, U.S. Joint Chiefs of Staff, U.S.

Army units. *See* United States Army

Artillery units. *See* United States Army

Ashiya air base, Japan, 266

Associated Press, 235

Atomic bomb: on Hiroshima, 9; American reliance on, 47-48; the Soviet Union's, 239; possible use against China, 258, 371, 468, 475; British-American statement, 374

Atrocities: against U.S. troops, 72, 143-44, 192-93, 226, 253, 254-

555

India, 42, 44, 242-44, 370, 375, 471, 473-74, 476-77, 480
Indian 60th Field Ambulance and Surgical Unit. *See* British Commonwealth forces
Infantry units. *See* United States Army and United States Marine Corps
Inje, 230, 240-41, 400, 402, 419, 422-25
Ipsok, 261, 269, 272, 274, 276-77, 279
Iron Triangle, 230, 240-41, 399, 402, 404, 418, 424, 467
Itami air base, Japan, 358
Itazuke air base, Japan, 55, 197
Iwon, 250, 308

Jackson, Thomas J. (Stonewall), 151
Jamestown line, 447
Japan, 259, 383-84; in World War II, 7-10; strategic importance, 18, 20; peace treaty, 39; U.S. occupation, 46-47; air strikes from, 69, 96, 143, 266; R&R leaves in, 396-98
Japanese Navy, 8
Jensen, Carl C., Lt. Col., 72
Jessup, Philip C., amb.-at-large, 246, 247
Johnson, Harold K., Lt. Col., 280
Johnson, Louis, secy of defense, 34, 37, 164-65, 169, 175, 178-79
Johnson, U. Alexis, 243
Joint Chiefs of Staff, U.S., 18, 22, 32, 36, 45, 77, 148-50, 153-57, 159-60, 163-66, 169-71, 175, 177, 180-81, 188-90, 195, 216, 218, 229-31, 235-37, 241, 244-46, 251, 255-56, 258, 287-96, 368-69, 372-73, 375-77, 383, 385, 387, 389, 405-07, 409, 413-16, 426-30, 432-34, 439, 449-51, 453-54, 458, 462, 465, 468-69, 475, 477, 479-80
Jones, Glen C., Lt., 264
Jones, Jack R., Capt., 347
Jones, Robert E., Maj., 337
Joy, C. Turner, Vice Adm., 159, 171, 175, 186, 434, 452, 458-59, 465
Judd, Roland D., Capt., 318

Kadong-ni, Map 4, 82, 84, 86
Kaesong, 26, 249, 250, 319, 429, 431-33, 436, 438-39, 449
Kang, Younghill, 15
Kanggye, 254, 321
Kansas line, 402, Map 12, 404, 418, 424
Kansong, 424-25, 439
Kapaun, Emil J., Chaplain, 281
Kapchon river, Map 5, 93, 96-98, 100
Kapsan, 308-09
Kapyong, 419-22, 424
Ka-san. *See* Hill 902
Kean, Task Force, 127
Kean, William B., Maj. Gen., 120, 127
Keiser, Lawrence B., Maj. Gen., 184, 313, 315
Kennan, George, 426-27
Khrushchev, Nikita, 21, 22
Kim Il Sung, Premier, 13-14, 16, 21-22, 249, 429, 430, 433, 482
Kim Koo, 12
Kim Paik Il, Maj. Gen., 30
Kim Tai Sun, 226
Kimchi, 15
Kimpo airfield, 29, 33, 171, 204-06, 213, 217, 381, 392
Kimpo peninsula, 421-22
Kingston, Robert C., Lt., 309
Kirk, Alan G., Amb., 427
Knowland, William F., Sen., 19, 233
Kobe, Japan, 196-97
Kochang, 111, 114
Koesan, 74
Kogan-ni, 127-28
Kojang, 263, 266-67
Koje-do (island), 457-59, 462-63
Kojo, 463
Koksan, 430
Komam-ni, 183
Kongju, 68, 73, 78-79, 81, 93, 96, 226
Konyang, 112
Korangpo-ri, 26
Korea: under Japanese rule, 10; partition, 11; UN election, 11-13; reliance on big power, 13; strategic position, 18
Korea, People's Republic of (North Korea), 9, 14, 21-22, 38, 40, 43, 149, 158, 167, 229-36, 241-46, 249, 251, 254, 259, 288, 370, 377, 424, 427, 429-30, 434-35, 438-39, 450-51, 456-57, 465, 471, 473; Soviet weapons shipments, 22